Kerala

Teresa Cannon
Peter Davis

LONELY PLANET PUBLICATIONS
Melbourne • Oakland • London • Paris

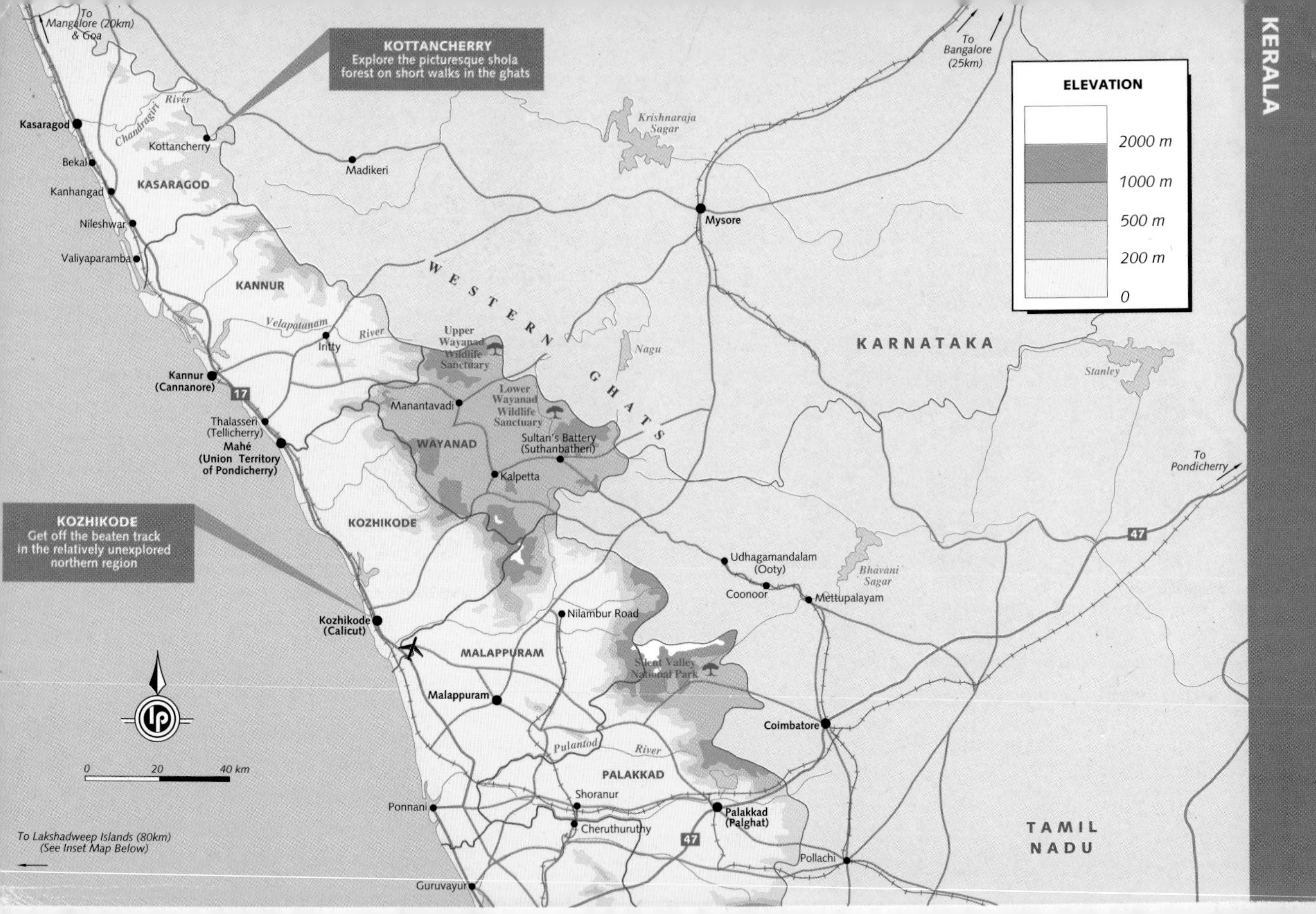
KOTTANCHERRY
Explore the picturesque shola forest on short walks in the ghats
To Mangalore (20km) & Goa
To Bangalore (25km)
ELEVATION
2000 m
1000 m
500 m
200 m
0
Chandragiri River
Kasaragod
Kottancherry
Bekal
Kanhangad
KASARAGOD
Madikeri
Krishnaraja Sagar
Mysore
Nileshwar
Valiyaparamba
KANNUR
WESTERN GHATS
Velapatanam River
Iritty
Upper Wayanad Wildlife Sanctuary
Nagu
KARNATAKA
Stanley
Kannur (Cannanore)
17
Manantavadi
Lower Wayanad Wildlife Sanctuary
Thalasseri (Tellicherry)
Mahé (Union Territory of Pondicherry)
WAYANAD
Sultan's Battery (Suthanbatheri)
Kalpetta
To Pondicherry
KOZHIKODE
Get off the beaten track in the relatively unexplored northern region
KOZHIKODE
47
Udhagamandalam (Ooty)
Bhavani Sagar
Coonoor
Mettupalayam
Nilambur Road
Kozhikode (Calicut)
MALAPPURAM
Silent Valley National Park
Malappuram
Coimbatore
Pulantod River
0
20
40 km
PALAKKAD
Shoranur
Ponnani
Palakkad (Palghat)
Cheruthuruthy
To Lakshadweep Islands (80km) (See Inset Map Below)
47
TAMIL NADU
Pollachi
Guruvayur

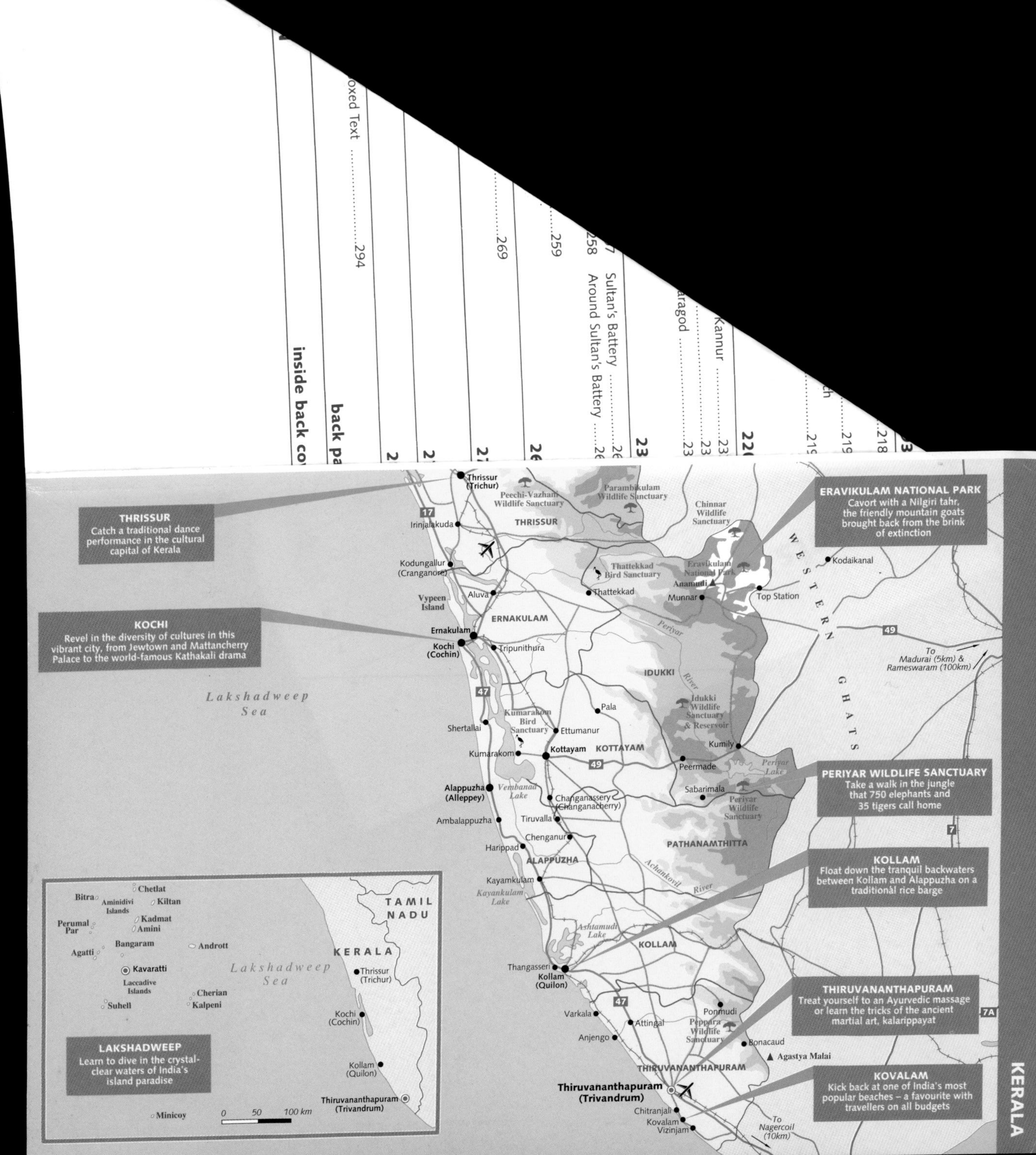

KERALA
ERAVIKULAM NATIONAL PARK
Cavort with a Nilgiri tahr, the friendly mountain goats brought back from the brink of extinction
THRISSUR
Catch a traditional dance performance in the cultural capital of Kerala
KOCHI
Revel in the diversity of cultures in this vibrant city, from Jewtown and Mattancherry Palace to the world-famous Kathakali drama
PERIYAR WILDLIFE SANCTUARY
Take a walk in the jungle that 750 elephants and 35 tigers call home
KOLLAM
Float down the tranquil backwaters between Kollam and Alappuzha on a traditional rice barge
THIRUVANANTHAPURAM
Treat yourself to an Ayurvedic massage or learn the tricks of the ancient martial art, kalarippayat
KOVALAM
Kick back at one of India's most popular beaches – a favourite with travellers on all budgets
LAKSHADWEEP
Learn to dive in the crystal-clear waters of India's island paradise
WESTERN GHATS
Lakshadweep Sea
Thrissur (Trichur)
Peechi-Vazhani Wildlife Sanctuary
Parambikulam Wildlife Sanctuary
Chinnar Wildlife Sanctuary
Eravikulam National Park
Anamudi
Kodaikanal
Top Station
Munnar
Thattekkad Bird Sanctuary
Thattekkad
Irinjalakuda
Kodungallur (Cranganore)
Aluva
Vypeen Island
Ernakulam
Kochi (Cochin)
Tripunithura
THRISSUR
ERNAKULAM
IDUKKI
Periyar River
Idukki Wildlife Sanctuary & Reservoir
To Madurai (5km) & Rameswaram (100km)
Pala
Kumarakom Bird Sanctuary
Ettumanur
Shertallai
Kumarakom
Kottayam
KOTTAYAM
Kumily
Peermade
Periyar Lake
Periyar Wildlife Sanctuary
Sabarimala
Alappuzha (Alleppey)
Vembanad Lake
Changanassery (Changanacherry)
Ambalappuzha
Tiruvalla
Chenganur
Harippad
ALAPPUZHA
PATHANAMTHITTA
Achankovil River
Kayamkulam
Kayankulam Lake
Ashtamudi Lake
KOLLAM
Thangasseri
Kollam (Quilon)
Varkala
Attingal
Anjengo
Ponmudi
Peppara Wildlife Sanctuary
Bonacaud
Agastya Malai
THIRUVANANTHAPURAM
Thiruvananthapuram (Trivandrum)
Chitranjali
Kovalam
Vizinjam
To Nagercoil (10km)
17
47
49
7
7A
TAMIL NADU
KERALA
Bitra
Chetlat
Aminidivi Islands
Kiltan
Perumal Par
Kadmat
Amini
Bangaram
Andrott
Agatti
Kavaratti
Laccadive Islands
Cherian
Suhell
Kalpeni
Minicoy
0 50 100 km

Kerala
1st edition – January 2000

Published by
Lonely Planet Publications Pty Ltd A.C.N. 005 607 983
192 Burwood Rd, Hawthorn, Victoria 3122, Australia

Lonely Planet Offices
Australia PO Box 617, Hawthorn, Victoria 3122
USA 150 Linden St, Oakland, CA 94607
UK 10a Spring Place, London NW5 3BH
France 1 rue du Dahomey, 75011 Paris

Photographs
All of the images in this guide are available for licensing from Lonely Planet Images.
email: lpi@lonelyplanet.com.au

Front cover photograph
A fisherman floats towards the end of the day on Kerala's backwat
(Eddie Gerald)

ISBN 0 86442 696 8

Printed by Colorcraft Ltd, Hong Kong

Although the au... and Lonely Planet try to make the information as accurate as possible, we accept no responsibility for any loss, injury or inconvenience sustained by anyone using this book.

Contents – Maps

SOUTHERN KERALA

CENTRAL KERALA

NORTHERN KERALA

THE WESTERN GHATS

LAKSHADWEEP

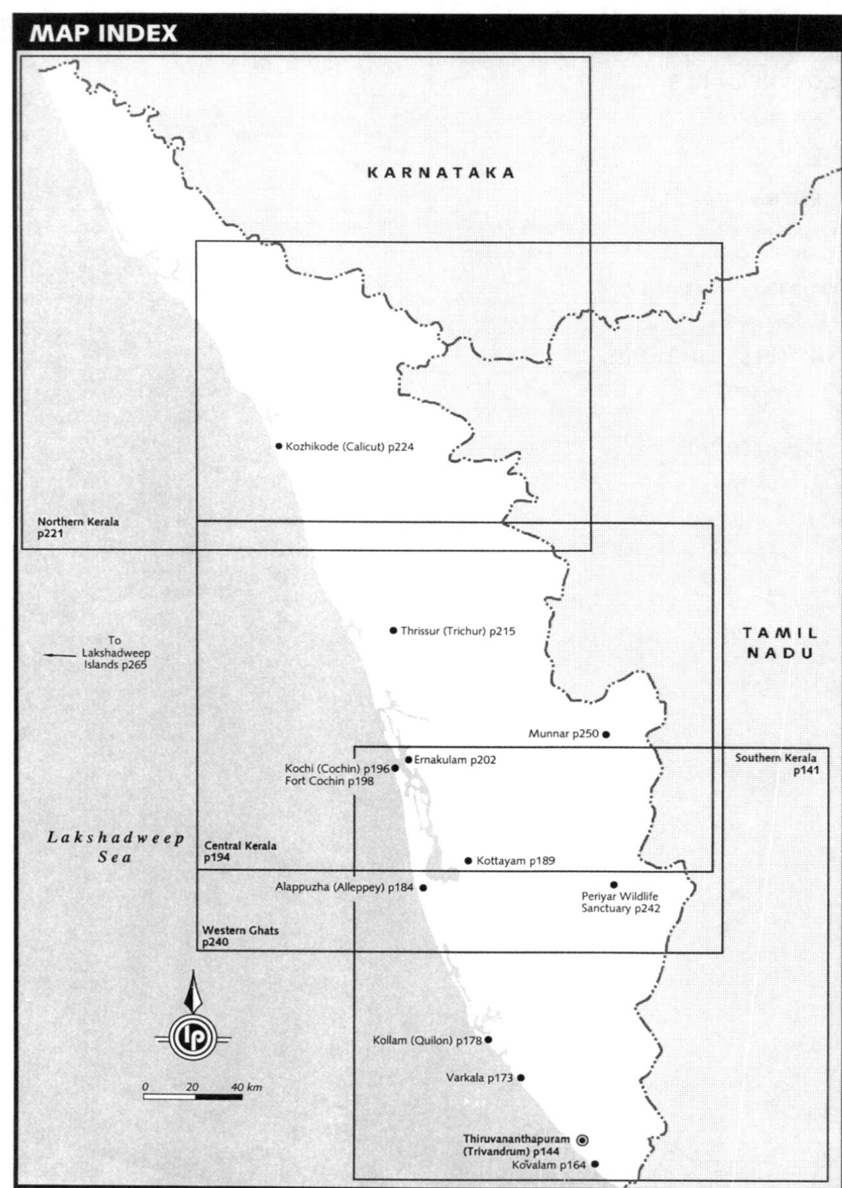
MAP INDEX
KARNATAKA
Kozhikode (Calicut) p224
Northern Kerala
p221
Thrissur (Trichur) p215
TAMIL
NADU
To
Lakshadweep
Islands p265
Munnar p250
Ernakulam p202
Southern Kerala
p141
Kochi (Cochin) p196
Fort Cochin p198
Lakshadweep
Sea
Central Kerala
p194
Kottayam p189
Alappuzha (Alleppey) p184
Periyar Wildlife
Sanctuary p242
Western Ghats
p240
Kollam (Quilon) p178
0
20
40 km
Varkala p173
Thiruvananthapuram
(Trivandrum) p144
Kovalam p164

The Authors

Teresa Cannon

After too many years in a suffocating bureaucracy Teresa Cannon felt compelled to escape to the rarefied environment of the Himalaya. There she trekked through century-old rhododendron forests and traversed the peaks and passes of the western moonscape region. She succumbed to the continuing welcome *namaste*, which flowed like a mantra throughout the landscape. She wanted to stay. But visas run out and bank balances diminish.

Her love of travel led her to Asia several times where she gathered material and co-authored a book on Asian elephants which was published in 1995. A children's version was published by Cambridge University Press in 1998. This is her fourth project for Lonely Planet.

Peter Davis

Following a brief stint as a cadet photographer on the Melbourne Herald, Peter lost himself at university to study economics and politics followed by graduate studies in Media. His first real job was selling fire extinguishers. He regards this as the beginning of his extinguished career. He drifted into freelance journalism and photography and has published hundreds of features and photographs from numerous locations around the world. Elephants play a big part in Peter's life. He is co-author and photographer of the book Aliya – Stories of the Elephants of Sri Lanka. Peter is also a contributor to Lonely Planet's India guide, the regional guide to South India, and the pictorial book Sacred India. When he's not chasing a story or an elephant he lectures in professional writing at Deakin University and in photojournalism at Photography Studies College in Melbourne.

FROM TERESA & PETER

This book would not have been possible without the generosity of many people who gave their time and knowledge and who made the seemingly impossible become possible. To name everyone individually would require almost another book. You know who you are and we thank you for your support. However, we do wish to say a particular thank you to the following individuals:

Mr D Venkatesan for his quiet persistence; Mr Shankaran who could turn his skills to almost anything – driver, interpreter, guide and tailor; Nalini Chettur for her ability to unearth yet another relevant tome; Mr MR Hari and Mr KV Ravisankar for their invaluable time and cooperation; Mr PJ Varghese whose knowledge of and passion for his country is infectious and Mr MS

Venugopal who offered many good contacts and never shied away from our constant questions. In Kollam, Ms Usha Tytus made sure we sustained a frenetic schedule. At the Malayala Manorama Mr & Mrs KM Matthew and Lt Col Jose Vallikappan were generous with their advice and hospitality. For opportunities to meet elephants and understand more about these majestic creatures, we remain indebted to Dr KC Panicker and Ms Nibha Namboodhiri, as well as to the mahouts at Guruvayur who gave so generously of their time. Mr B Girirajan and Mr GB Kiran enlightened us on the significance of gold and jewellery and Dr MP Parameswaran keenly shared his knowledge of matters scientific and environmental. Mr Vasudevan and his friends at Beypore made New Year's Eve an unforgettable experience and opened our eyes to yet another layer of Keralan culture. We are grateful to Mr Harikumar who generously provided us with information on Krishnapuram Palace. We also issue a very special thanks to Mr D Karunanidhi, Dr Venu, Mr Mani Madhavan, Mr Vikram, Mr Joseph Iype and to all those people who helped further our appreciation of Indian food, culture and hospitality.

We are particularly grateful to Douglas Streatfeild-James who wrote the text on Lakshadweep and who responded quickly and generously to our requests for information.

At home in Australia we wish to thank Christine Niven for her ideas and supportive emails; Dr Robin Jeffrey for his guidance and contacts; Mrs Tara Rajkumar and her Natya Sudha Company for their guidance into the intricacies of Malayali theatre and dance; Adam, Sharan, Lindsay, Joyce, Michelle, Mark, Maree, Quentin et al at LP HQ, with special congratulations to Monique for her coordinating skills and staying power; Isobel for minding our home and feeding the possums, cockatoos and kookaburras, and our friends and family who never complained when we rejected invitations with the excuse 'sorry, we're still working on the book'.

This Book

From the Publisher

This first edition of Kerala was designed and mapped by Mark Germanchis, a guy who knows how to clip a moustache. Monique Choy was the coordinating editor. Michelle Coxall, Joyce Connolly, Brigitte Ellemor and Thalia Kalkipsakis contributed their considerable editing and proofing skills, while Maree Styles and Shahara Ahmed assisted ably with mapping. Sharan Kaur and Adriana Mammarella double checked everything and answered the tricky questions. The cover was designed by Indra Kilfoyle. Quentin Frayne and Vicki Webb edited the language chapter. Ann Jeffree and Kerrie Williams tagged the index.

Special thanks to the Nilgiri tahr for sticking around and to Teresa and Peter for their research and testing of Indian products beyond the call of duty.

Foreword

ABOUT LONELY PLANET GUIDEBOOKS

The story begins with a classic travel adventure: Tony and Maureen Wheeler's 1972 journey across Europe and Asia to Australia. Useful information about the overland trail did not exist at that time, so Tony and Maureen published the first Lonely Planet guidebook to meet a growing need.

From a kitchen table, then from a tiny office in Melbourne (Australia), Lonely Planet has become the largest independent travel publisher in the world, an international company with offices in Melbourne, Oakland (USA), London (UK) and Paris (France).

Today Lonely Planet guidebooks cover the globe. There is an ever-growing list of books and there's information in a variety of forms and media. Some things haven't changed. The main aim is still to help make it possible for adventurous travellers to get out there – to explore and better understand the world.

At Lonely Planet we believe travellers can make a positive contribution to the countries they visit – if they respect their host communities and spend their money wisely. Since 1986 a percentage of the income from each book has been donated to aid projects and human rights campaigns.

Updates Lonely Planet thoroughly updates each guidebook as often as possible. This usually means there are around two years between editions, although for more unusual or more stable destinations the gap can be longer. Check the imprint page (following the colour map at the beginning of the book) for publication dates.

Between editions up-to-date information is available in two free newsletters – the paper *Planet Talk* and email *Comet* (to subscribe, contact any Lonely Planet office) – and on our Web site at www.lonelyplanet.com. The *Upgrades* section of the Web site covers a number of important and volatile destinations and is regularly updated by Lonely Planet authors. *Scoop* covers news and current affairs relevant to travellers. And, lastly, the *Thorn Tree* bulletin board and *Postcards* section of the site carry unverified, but fascinating, reports from travellers.

Correspondence The process of creating new editions begins with the letters, postcards and emails received from travellers. This correspondence often includes suggestions, criticisms and comments about the current editions. Interesting excerpts are immediately passed on via newsletters and the Web site, and everything goes to our authors to be verified when they're researching on the road. We're keen to get more feedback from organisations or individuals who represent communities visited by travellers.

Lonely Planet gathers information for everyone who's curious about the planet – and especially for those who explore it first-hand. Through guidebooks, phrasebooks, activity guides, maps, literature, newsletters, image library, TV series and Web site we act as an information exchange for a worldwide community of travellers.

Research Authors aim to gather sufficient practical information to enable travellers to make informed choices and to make the mechanics of a journey run smoothly. They also research historical and cultural background to help enrich the travel experience and allow travellers to understand and respond appropriately to cultural and environmental issues.

Authors don't stay in every hotel because that would mean spending a couple of months in each medium-sized city and, no, they don't eat at every restaurant because that would mean stretching belts beyond capacity. They do visit hotels and restaurants to check standards and prices, but feedback based on readers' direct experiences can be very helpful.

Many of our authors work undercover, others aren't so secretive. None of them accept freebies in exchange for positive write-ups. And none of our guidebooks contain any advertising.

Production Authors submit their raw manuscripts and maps to offices in Australia, USA, UK or France. Editors and cartographers – all experienced travellers themselves – then begin the process of assembling the pieces. When the book finally hits the shops, some things are already out of date, we start getting feedback from readers and the process begins again ...

WARNING & REQUEST

Things change – prices go up, schedules change, good places go bad and bad places go bankrupt – nothing stays the same. So, if you find things better or worse, recently opened or long since closed, please tell us and help make the next edition even more accurate and useful. We genuinely value all the feedback we receive. Julie Young coordinates a well travelled team that reads and acknowledges every letter, postcard and email and ensures that every morsel of information finds its way to the appropriate authors, editors and cartographers for verification.

Everyone who writes to us will find their name in the next edition of the appropriate guidebook. They will also receive the latest issue of *Planet Talk*, our quarterly printed newsletter, or *Comet*, our monthly email newsletter. Subscriptions to both newsletters are free. The very best contributions will be rewarded with a free guidebook.

Excerpts from your correspondence may appear in new editions of Lonely Planet guidebooks, the Lonely Planet Web site, *Planet Talk* or *Comet*, so please let us know if you *don't* want your letter published or your name acknowledged.

Send all correspondence to the Lonely Planet office closest to you:

Australia: PO Box 617, Hawthorn, Victoria 3122
USA: 150 Linden St, Oakland, CA 94607
UK: 10A Spring Place, London NW5 3BH
France: 1 rue du Dahomey, 75011 Paris

Or email us at: talk2us@lonelyplanet.com.au

For news, views and updates see our Web site: www.lonelyplanet.com

HOW TO USE A LONELY PLANET GUIDEBOOK

The best way to use a Lonely Planet guidebook is any way you choose. At Lonely Planet we believe the most memorable travel experiences are often those that are unexpected, and the finest discoveries are those you make yourself. Guidebooks are not intended to be used as if they provide a detailed set of infallible instructions!

Contents All Lonely Planet guidebooks follow roughly the same format. The Facts about the Destination chapters or sections give background information ranging from history to weather. Facts for the Visitor gives practical information on issues like visas and health. Getting There & Away gives a brief starting point for researching travel to and from the destination. Getting Around gives an overview of the transport options when you arrive.

The peculiar demands of each destination determine how subsequent chapters are broken up, but some things remain constant. We always start with background, then proceed to sights, places to stay, places to eat, entertainment, getting there and away, and getting around information – in that order.

Heading Hierarchy Lonely Planet headings are used in a strict hierarchical structure that can be visualised as a set of Russian dolls. Each heading (and its following text) is encompassed by any preceding heading that is higher on the hierarchical ladder.

Entry Points We do not assume guidebooks will be read from beginning to end, but that people will dip into them. The traditional entry points are the list of contents and the index. In addition, however, some books have a complete list of maps and an index map illustrating map coverage.

There may also be a colour map that shows highlights. These highlights are dealt with in greater detail in the Facts for the Visitor chapter, along with planning questions and suggested itineraries. Each chapter covering a geographical region usually begins with a locator map and another list of highlights. Once you find something of interest in a list of highlights, turn to the index.

Maps Maps play a crucial role in Lonely Planet guidebooks and include a huge amount of information. A legend is printed on the back page. We seek to have complete consistency between maps and text, and to have every important place in the text captured on a map. Map key numbers usually start in the top left corner.

Although inclusion in a guidebook usually implies a recommendation we cannot list every good place. Exclusion does not necessarily imply criticism. In fact there are a number of reasons why we might exclude a place – sometimes it is simply inappropriate to encourage an influx of travellers.

Introduction

Kerala is a microcosm of India. Renowned for its lush vegetation, tranquil beaches and stunning mountains, Kerala offers a rich and beguiling culture that embraces Hinduism, Christianity, Islam, Jainism and Judaism. The temples, churches, mosques and synagogues echo a long history of global connections. These edifices exist for devotees but are very much part of the travellers' experience.

Kerala's creation myth tells of how the sea god, Varuna, raised land from beneath the ocean to create the region now known as Kerala (see the boxed text 'Kerala's Creation Myth' in the Facts about Kerala chapter).

Geologically and politically, Kerala is relatively new. Its geological origins support the popular creation myth. The Western Ghats, the mountains which run down the east of the state, once formed the coastline of the Arabian Sea. The land rose above the sea, rendering Kerala a later addition to the main Indian landmass. Politically, the state was formed by a merging of three regions – Travancore, Cochin and Malabar (Southern, Central and Northern Kerala) – in 1956, almost a decade after Indian Independence.

The name Kerala has several possible meanings. It may derive from the Sanskrit *keralam* meaning 'land added on', an obvious association with its mythical and geological origins. Some claim the state is named after the coconut (*kera*), Kerala being known as the land of coconuts. Another

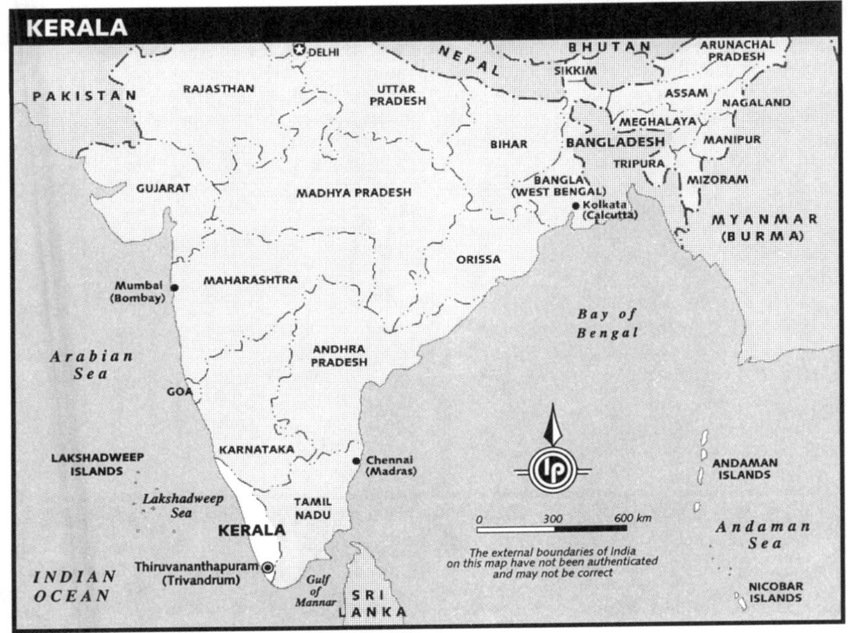

version suggests the state is named after the early Chera dynasty. Like its name, Kerala embraces many narratives. The language of Kerala is Malayalam and its people are known as Malayalis – after *malai* – the mountains.

Throughout Kerala it is possible to see mysterious temple rituals where ancient traditions are encapsulated in the sustained rhythmic trance of the dancer. The region is also the home of the famous Kathakali – a complex and ritualised theatre based on the ancient epics.

The state is the birthplace of the highly stylised martial art of *kalarippayat*, said to be the precursor to martial arts around the world. And of course Kerala is renowned for Ayurvedic medicine. At beach resorts or hill stations the traveller can indulge in massage or in an intensive course of Ayurvedic treatments.

Serious beach junkies can relax on the deserted northern sands or at the developed beaches of Kovalam and Varkala in the south where every possible budget is catered for. Despite the development, fishermen still work these beaches using centuries' old techniques.

The labyrinthine backwaters allow for an altogether different experience. Here the traveller can drift in almost perfect silence from one village to the next and simply watch life gently unfold.

Within the ruggedness of the Western Ghats, spice gardens indicate the wondrous fertility of the soil. Beyond these gardens are expansive tea plantations, while close by, on craggy rocks, the gentle Nilgiri tahr – a wild mountain goat – has been rescued from the brink of extinction. Also in the Ghats is the Periyar Wildlife Sanctuary, one of the most popular and well organised in India.

Festivals are a regular part of life in Kerala. Some showcase arts, crafts, theatre and dance. Others are sacred festivals where richly caparisoned elephants flanked by musicians and torch bearers encircle a temple to honour a deity.

Kerala enjoys the highest level of literacy in all of India. It also receives enormous income repatriated from its citizens who live and work in the Middle East countries. The hospitality of Kerala, its customs and culture, coupled with its exquisite cuisine and unique architecture, provide delights for a short holiday or a lengthy exploration.

Facts about Kerala

HISTORY

Early History – From Megaliths to Megakings

Huge stone monuments commemorating death are the earliest indicators of human life in Kerala. The early settlers, who probably arrived somewhere between the 10th and 5th centuries BCE (before common era), created megalithic structures similar to those found in Europe and southern England. Some of these monuments are human-like statues encircled by stones. Others take the form of caves and dolmens, associated with funeral rites. Remnants of these monuments remain along the ridges and valleys of the Western Ghats.

Early inhabitants hunted animals and cultivated grain using implements which included axes, swords and grinding stones. They created pots, vessels, terracotta images, and beads. Their monuments and ceremonial artefacts provide evidence of a sophisticated society.

Besides the huge stone monuments there are other indicators that give clues to the early history of Kerala – trade and literature. There is evidence of trade links with the Middle East and a thriving commercial exchange that developed with nations such as the Phoenicians, the Romans and the Greeks.

The land now delineating Kerala is mentioned in the literature of the east and the west. It was described in the *Periplus* (a first century geographical text, possibly Greek). Pliny and Ptolemy also made reference to it.

The early Tamil literature of the Sangam period, generally considered to extend from the 1st to the 5th centuries CE (common era), describes the land of Tamilakam, an area identified as the land of the Tamils. This area was in the very south of India. Its northern border was roughly aligned to the current northern border of Tamil Nadu and it extended to both coasts and south to Kanyakumari (Cape Comorin), the southernmost tip of India. Kerala formed the western part of this land. Like the remainder of Tamilakam, Kerala received Dravidian migrants from the north.

The early Tamil literature describes three dynasties – the Cholas of the eastern Coramandel Coast, the Pandyas of the central peninsula and the Cheras of the western Malabar Coast. These dynasties came into existence in the later centuries BCE. Although the dynasties engaged in conflict, South India prospered during the Sangam period. The arts – literature, dance and music – all flourished.

The Chera dynasty in conjunction with chieftains ruled the Kerala area. The Chera capital was Vanchi. Its exact location is still a matter of conjecture. Possibilities range from Karur, near Coimbatore in Tamil Nadu, to areas closer to Kochi (Cochin). Twenty-five Cheran kings, with details of their reigns and accomplishments, are recorded. They secured and maintained large armies. They fought neighbouring fiefdoms to acquire or expand their domain. They confronted and crushed piracy on the high seas. In an attempt to restore harmony they sometimes married women of warring neighbours. In appreciation of their victories, they established festivals to honour deities.

Throughout the reign of the Cheras, trade continued to bring prosperity to Kerala with spices, ivory, timber and gems being exported to the Middle East and southern Europe.

Belief systems as well as products were exchanged. Early beliefs and religious practices generally had a naturist or animist basis – people honoured the elements of the cosmos as well as the trees and animals, believing that such entities embodied the spirits of deities. It seems that ancestor worship was also practised – the early stone monuments being indicative of this custom. Chera kings prayed to a goddess whom they honoured with chanting, drumming and rice offerings.

Around the 3rd to 2nd centuries BCE, both Buddhism and Jainism came to Kerala. Trade with the Middle East may have established early contact with Judaism. In fact some accounts relate Solomon's court as receiving spices, ivory and peacocks from Kerala. Fleeing the ravages of Jerusalem, Jewish settlers may have arrived as early as 70 CE. Christianity may also have made an inroad, with some accounts suggesting that Thomas the Apostle arrived in 52 CE.

Little is known of Kerala's history from approximately the 6th to 8th centuries CE. Some sources postulate that during this time Kerala was under the influence of the Kalabhras, a regime that plunged Kerala (and much of South India) into a long period of social turbulence. In the early part of the 9th century a new Chera dynasty, often referred to as the Second Chera empire, procured power and retained it until the turn of the millennium. Its first ruler was Kulasekhara Alwar. Subsequent rulers retained the name Kulasekhara with the designation of Perumal, meaning emperor.

Although their second reign was to be infringed upon by Chola invasions and their intermittent control, the Cheras managed to implement many beneficial changes. They divided up their empire into provinces where regional concerns were administered through local authorities. The Perumal had ultimate power but through representation of the populace, people's rights were acknowledged. Once again cultural activity flourished. Tamil as well as Sanskrit literature was supported. Grand temples were built and reflected the developing devotion to several Hindu deities. Trade continued to expand with many areas, including the Middle East, the Mediterranean, Sumatra and China.

At the turn of the 10th century, the Second Chera empire succumbed to a 35-year Chola offensive. The region disintegrated but maintained a semblance of its former provinces albeit in a weakened form. Local chieftains enforced a feudal-type system exploiting land labourers and bringing about forms of inequity previously unknown.

Kerala's Creation Myth

In mythology Kerala was created by Parusurama, an incarnation of Vishnu.

Parusurama was a warrior, renowned for his physical strength, who acquired his name from his weapon – a *parasu* (axe). He engaged in a 21-year battle, killing many people. Finally he retired to the Western Ghats where he undertook a long penance. Distraught at his murderous behaviour, he beseeched the gods for help. The sea god Varuna responded, pledging to give Parusurama land which equalled the distance that he could throw his axe. Parusurama mustered all his mighty physical strength and swung his axe which soared through the air to Kanyakumari, India's southern tip. With that the seas receded, exposing the strip of land that forms Kerala.

Parusurama's act was a repudiation of war and therefore, for many, Kerala was created as a land of peace and harmony.

Gradually three separate states developed: Travancore in the south; Cochin in the central area and Kozhikode in the north. Kozhikode came under the auspices of a Hindu royal line, headed by rulers known as Zamorins. The history of these states is one of gradual advance from quarrelling provinces to statehood under strong leaders.

The Period of the Portuguese

The arrival of the Portuguese navigator Vasco da Gama in 1498 seriously affected the economic and social customs of Kerala. The Portuguese had two aims: to secure sea trade routes and to curtail the commercial monopoly of the Ottoman empire. With its wealth of resources and strong Arab trade links, Kerala became an obvious target. Portuguese involvement was to result in massive internal and external conflict for Kerala.

Vasco da Gama's efforts to form a trade pact with the Zamorin rulers upset long-established trade links between the Zamorin and Arab merchants. He then turned his focus to neighbouring rulers. Hostilities developed between states, and with the Portuguese. The Portuguese remained determined in their desire to attain trade supremacy in Kerala. They introduced agricultural methods and new crops including cashews, papaya, potatoes and tomatoes. Their promotion of the coconut industry expanded trade. But gradually, under their command, Kerala experienced severe economic decline.

With strong resistance from the Zamorins' army, Portuguese power in Kerala began to weaken. In Europe, Spanish annexation of Portugal, and the subsequent defeat of the Spanish by the British, impeded further Portuguese objectives for trade expansion.

Domination by the Dutch

Having accomplished a treaty with the Zamorins in 1604, the Dutch entered into various skirmishes with the Portuguese and by 1663 they succeeded in displacing them. The Dutch wished to expand their power in Kerala to capture the market for pepper and cardamom. They became involved in convoluted relations playing rulers off against each other. This created chaos and confusion, but ironically it also had advantages.

The monarchs of Travancore (Marthanda Varma) and Cochin (Saktan Tampuran) sought Dutch support to attack feudal landlords and overthrow a cruel and inequitable system. Dutch influence also saw increased trade, new farming methods and an expanded coconut industry. And they organised a multicultural feat – the compilation of *Hortus Malabaricus*, a 12 volume work that describes the medicinal properties of Indian plants. This work was undertaken by local medical and botanical experts, Brahmin priests and Carmelite monks.

Kerala & the Sultans

In the late 18th century, the region came under attack from the Muslim sultan of Mysore, Hyder Ali and later his son, Tipu Sultan. The Dutch, eager to protect their trade interests, failed to support Kerala and sought the favour of Mysore. But they found themselves isolated and much of northern Kerala eventually came under the jurisdiction of Tipu Sultan. Unimpressed by the Hindu social order, based on caste and the remnants of feudalism, he implemented changes that saw the exodus of many high-caste people and the promotion of former lower-caste people to influential positions. He also improved systems of finance and transportation.

But all this was achieved at a high social cost and animosity developed between the Muslim and Hindu populations, resulting in rebellion. Local rulers enlisted British support to remove the sultan, and in 1792 Tipu Sultan relinquished his claim on Kerala to the British. In 1800 Kerala became part of the Madras Presidency (administered from modern-day Chennai), the southern region of India under British control.

Kerala & the British

Although the British did not take official control of Kerala until 1800, their interests dated from the early 17th century when they established a base at Kozhikode (Calicut). Like other foreign powers, their relations with the local people were ambiguous. Having attained control, however, the British entered into treaties with the Cochin and Travancore rulers, assigning the local rulers limited power with the British retaining ultimate authority. In effect this enabled the maharajas in both Travancore and Cochin to continue their cultural influence, especially in their support for education and the arts.

Under the Madras Presidency, the northern area of Kerala (which was under direct British control) was known as the Malabar district. The British implemented new legal, economic and transportation systems, established new schools and improved the roads and waterways. They also introduced coffee into the Wayanad district and built some of the earliest weaving factories in India. However, their policies tended to sanction the reversion to the former feudal order. Tensions started to increase between the predominantly

Hindu landlords and the Muslim tenants. A series of terrorist attacks were the result, and during the unrest landlords were murdered and Hindu temples were ransacked. Known as the Mappila Riots, these uprisings lasted from 1836 to 1856. Initially the riots were forcefully subdued, and in 1900 legal efforts in the form of the Tenants Improvement Act attempted to create a more equitable situation.

The Path to Independence

Many aspects of British rule created animosity: the British history of equivocal dealings with the rajas, their similar liaisons with the sultans, their assumed right to govern and their action to reinstate the former landlords. Those who complied with British dictates often faced conflict within their communities. Revolts were successfully crushed by the British, but the passion against injustice was not quashed and this served to later fuel the activities aimed at independence.

In 1885 the Indian National Congress was born to instigate discussions with the British about their rule. Many people from Kerala were involved in the political activity that ensued and which resulted in India becoming an independent nation on 15 August 1947.

Post-Independence

In 1956, the Malayalam speaking areas – Malabar, Cochin and Travancore – as well as Kasaragod and Hosdurg (formerly part of South Karnataka) were united to form the state of Kerala. The first election was held early in the next year with the Communist Party procuring power under Chief Minister EMS Namboodiripad (see the boxed text 'EMS: From Ancient Vedas to Historical Materialism', later in this chapter). Since then, Kerala has had a series of coalition governments of various persuasions, generally alternating between the Congress and communist parties. At the time of writing the government constituted the Left Democratic Front (LDF) headed by Chief Minister, EK Nayanar.

GEOGRAPHY & GEOLOGY

The state of Kerala is in the south-west of India and covers an area of 38,863 sq km. This represents just over 1% of the total area of India. A narrow strip, bordered by the Lakshadweep Sea on the west and the Western Ghats, or mountains, on the east, Kerala is 550km long. Its width never exceeds 100km and in some parts is as narrow as 12km.

In geological terms, the area now known as Kerala is relatively new, having been formed later than the main landmass of India. Two major developments have contributed to its existence – volcanic action and a peculiar coalition between the rivers and the sea. The volcanic action resulted in a rising of the sea bed and produced the area from the ghats to the sea. Once formed, the land became the stage for a dramatic performance by the rivers and seas. This activity served to extend the original area, as well as carve it into an interesting mosaic. Rivers, laden with silt, carried their deposits to the sea. Coastal ports were transformed to inland cities. Simultaneously the huge tides of the Lakshadweep Sea surged back into the river courses, creating islands of silt, deep backwaters and huge lakes. Such processes continually reshape the character of the land today.

Geographically, Kerala can be viewed in three main sections: the western coastal lowlands, the central undulating hills and the mountain ranges and peaks of the Western Ghats (named because of their western position relative to the Indian landmass, but they actually form the eastern border to Kerala).

The coastal lowlands extend for some 550km, and comprise highly fertile plains with wide deltas, deep backwaters, lakes and shifting mud flats. Coconut groves and rice fields dominate the landscape here. The backwaters are linked by canals to form a 1920km water network easily traversed by small crafts. Of the inland lakes, Vembanad, at 205 sq km, is the largest. It extends some 65km from Alappuzha (Alleppey) to Kochi. An interesting phenomenon of the river-tide interaction is the formation of *chakara*, the coastal mud flats. Another feature of the landscape are islands, with several occurring in the Ernakulam area, ranging in size from 3 sq km to 25 sq km.

In the central area, small hills act as intermediaries with the mountains farther east. The mountains rise to an average height of 900m with Anamudi, the highest in India south of the Himalaya, at 2694m. The highlands comprise a continuous hilly range except for passes, which for centuries have enabled access to the east. Once they were thickly forested with rosewood, ebony and teak. Now much forest has been replaced by rice, tea and coffee plantations, huge dams and eucalyptus trees.

Forty-four rivers, with their myriad tributaries, cut through the landscape. All, except three, flow west. The average length of the rivers is 64km, with only four longer than 160km. The Periyar (in the south) and Bharatapuzha (central) are the longest – both over 200km. The rivers of Kerala are fed by the monsoons and although their capacity may vary greatly between wet and dry seasons, they provide plentiful resources all year round.

To the west of Kerala is Lakshadweep consisting of some two dozen islands, with a total land area of around 32 sq km.

CLIMATE

Kerala's position, approximately halfway between the equator and the Tropic of Cancer, endows it with a tropical marine to tropical rainforest climate. Its proximity to the Lakshadweep Sea has a moderating effect on its temperatures, which are relatively stable, from 18° to 35°C. The months from April to October are the hottest and December and January are the coolest. The mountains, with their higher altitude, have lower temperatures ranging from 0° to 25°C.

While there is little variation in temperatures, rainfall is a different matter. Being a monsoonal region, Kerala experiences either dry or wet seasons. The abundant rainfall of the two annual monsoons means that droughts are rare. Kerala is the first place in India to receive the south-west monsoon, with the onset traditionally regarded as 1 June. It drenches the state as it sweeps in eastward from the Lakshadweep Sea, rising over the Western Ghats and soaking the windward slopes.

During the monsoon Kerala can receive over 2500mm of rainfall. Powerful winds blast across sea and land. Huge tidal waves lash the coast. Trees and buildings may be flattened. The wind and rains rejuvenate the environment. Waterways are replenished and the land is nourished.

A second soaking occurs in November and early December when the retreating monsoon (commonly referred to as the north-east or winter monsoon) blows in from the Bay of Bengal. Obstructed by the Western Ghats its fall is much less than its earlier counterpart.

FLORA

Kerala has over 25% of India's 15,000 plant species. Most grow in the Western Ghats and include over 150 ferns, 4000 flowering plants, 600 fungi, 800 lichens and 200 mosses. Of these 1500 (63% of the nation's plant species) are endemic to this region.

Kerala's forest types include tropical wet evergreen, semi-evergreen and tropical moist deciduous. Teak, mahogany, rosewood and sandalwood are common in (and smuggled from) the Western Ghats. The area is also abundant in orchids, anthirium, balsam and medicinal plants. There are banyan figs and bamboo as well as 40,000-year-old grasslands. Along the coasts there are pockets of mangroves.

In the valleys and steep, protected slopes of the Ghats, moist evergreen forests known as *sholas* provide essential shelter and food for animals.

FAUNA

Kerala's abundant and diverse habitat supports a wildlife population of 100 species of mammals, 550 species of birds and 169 species of reptiles.

Antelopes, Gazelles & Deer

You'll see plenty of these browsers and grazers in the national parks. The common sambar *(Cervus unicolour)* is the largest of the Indian deer, reaching up to 1.5m tall. It sheds its impressive horns around the end of April, new ones start growing a month later. The attractive chital (cheetal) or spotted deer *(Axis axis)* is common throughout India and can be seen in most of Kerala's reserves, particularly those with wet evergreen forests. This deer is never seen far from water. The barking deer *(Muntiacus muntjak)* is a small deer that bears tushes (elongated canines) as well as small antlers. Its bark is said to sound much like that of a dog but it is a difficult animal to spot in its thick forest habitat.

Not so lucky is the blackbuck *(Antilope cervicapra),* whose distinctive spiral horns and attractive dark coat make it a prime target for poachers. The blackbuck is one of the few antelopes where males and females differ in coat colour. As the name suggests, dominant males develop dark, almost black, coats (usually dark brown in South India), while the 20 or so females and subordinate males in their herd are fawn. The little mouse deer *(Tragulus meminna)* grows to no more than 30cm. Delicate and shy, its speckled olive-brown/grey coat provides excellent camouflage in the forest understorey.

Tigers

The tiger *(Panthera tigris)* is a shy and solitary creature, preferring to live and hunt under the cover of tall grass or forest. It has poor eyesight and smell, but excellent hearing. Tigers prefer to eat deer, although they will settle for frogs, rodents and fish. They do not normally attack humans. Tigers live for about 20 years, and can grow to nearly 3m long. While claims abound about tigers, you'll be very lucky to see one.

Other Cats

The leopard *(Panthera pardus)* has been sighted at Wayanad and Eravikulam. Usually golden brown, in the Western Ghats it may be almost entirely black.

Leopard-like markings grace the forest-dwelling leopard cat *(Felis bengalensis)*, which is only slightly bigger than an ordinary house cat. It is strictly nocturnal and very rarely seen. Slightly larger than the leopard cat is the widely distributed jungle cat *(F. chaus)*, which can be seen hunting in villages even in broad daylight. Its distinguishing features are a relatively short, thick tail and a fairly uniform grey coat.

Dog Family

The wild dog or dhole *(Cuon alpinus)* can weigh up to 20kg and is found throughout India. This tawny predator hunts during the day in packs that have been known to bring down animals as large as a buffalo. They are relentless pursuers with an energy-efficient gait, exhausting their prey before the pack attacks.

The Indian fox *(Vulpes bengalensis)* has a black-tipped tail and a greyish coat, and, because of its appetite for rodents, can coexist more comfortably with farming communities than can other carnivores.

Elephants

There are some 27,000 elephants *(Elephas maximus)* in the wild in India and an estimated 4000 in Kerala. But although these figures may seem healthy, tuskers, perennial targets for poachers, are as endangered as tigers. In Periyar Wildlife Sanctuary there are now 122 females for every male, 20 years ago there were around six females per male. At Periyar, which comes under Project Elephant, wildlife experts are testing the breeding of tuskless elephants, known as *makhnas*. (See the boxed text 'Elephants in Kerala', later in this chapter.)

Primates

You'll see these creatures all over Kerala. Whether you're passing through monkey-lined roads as you traverse the Western Ghats or fending off over-friendly macaques as you board a boat at Periyar, you can't miss them.

The little pale-faced bonnet macaque *(Macaca radiata)* is named after the 'bonnet' of dark hair that covers its head. These macaques live in highly structured troops where claims on hierarchy are very noisily contested. They are opportunistic feeders: barely a grub, berry or leaf escapes their alert eyes and nimble fingers. The lion-tailed macaque *(M. silenus)* has a thick mane of greyish hair that grows from its temples and cheeks. This endangered macaque is more likely to be seen in promotional material than in its own habitat. Silent Valley National Park is an important refuge for this primate (see the Western Ghats chapter).

Less shy is the common langur *(Presbytis entellus),* or Hanuman monkey, recognisable by its long limbs and black face. India's most hunted primate is the Nilgiri langur *(P. johni)*, which inhabits the dense forests of the Western Ghats including the shola areas. This vegetarian monkey is pursued by poachers for its supposed medicinal qualities.

The peculiar-looking slender loris *(Loris tardigradus)* has a soft, woolly brown/grey coat and huge, bush-baby eyes. It's nocturnal, and comes down from the trees only to feed, which it does on virtually anything it can find: insects, leaves, berries and lizards. At home in dense or open rainforest, from the coastal plains to the steep mountain valleys, it's rarer than it once was. There's still a trade in South India for live lorises – their eyes are believed to be a powerful medicine for human eye diseases as well as a vital ingredient for love potions.

Other Mammals

The Nilgiri tahr *(Hemitragus hylocrius)* is gradually increasing in numbers after a close shave with extinction. A shy goat-like animal, it is endemic to the Western Ghats, preferring grassy, rocky habitats. It is easily sighted in the Eravikulam National Park (see the Western Ghats chapter).

The sloth bear *(Melursus ursinus)* is about 80cm high, and weighs up to 150kg. It has short legs and shaggy black or brown hair, with a touch of white on its chest. It lives in forested areas, is nocturnal and feeds on termites, honey and fruit, and the occasional carrion.

The gaur *(Bos gaurus)*, a wild ox (sometimes referred to as the Indian bison), can be seen in the parks. Up to 2m high, it is born with light-coloured hair, which darkens with age. With its immense bulk and white-stockinged legs, the gaur is easily recognised. This gentle giant prefers the wet sholas and bamboo thickets in its prime territory, the Western Ghats. The large herds of the past are no longer a common sight.

Other furred creatures include: Jerdon's Palm Civet *(Paradoxurus jerdoni)*, endemic to the Western Ghats; the forest rat *(Rattus rattus)*, found in the Nilgiri Hills; common shrew *(Suncus murinus)*; giant flying squirrel *(Petaurista petaurista)*, Malabar giant squirrel *(Ratufa indica)* and porcupine *(Hystrix indica)*.

The common dolphin *(Dolphinus delhis)* and dugongs *(Dugong dugong)* are found off the coastline.

Reptiles & Amphibians

For centuries Kerala was known as the land of *nagas* (snakes), with the Western Ghats being referred to as Sahyadri – the mountains abundant with snakes. Kerala's 169 reptile species represent almost 40% of India's total and comprise crocodiles, tortoises, lizards and snakes, some of which are endemic to Kerala.

Fish

Along the Malabar Coast, mackerels and sardines are prevalent. Other marine life includes moray eels, crabs and sea cucumbers. Migratory visitors include the sperm whale *(Physeter catodon)*.

In some rivers in the south, you'll see huge mahseer (once the preferred quarry of the British Raj angler), carp and mully fish. The coral reefs around the islands of Lakshadweep support a myriad of tropical fish including the butterfly fish, the parrot fish, the porcupine fish, and the light-blue surgeon fish.

Insects

Kerala has spectacular butterflies and moths, including the Malabar banded swallowtail *(Papilio liomedon)* and the peacock hairstreak *(Thelca pavi)*. The most magnificent

Elephants in Kerala

To watch an elephant, whether it is shackled or wild, is to witness an integral part of the history and culture of India, especially Kerala. Today Kerala has an estimated wild elephant population of 4000. And it has the second-highest domestic elephant population (600) in India after Bihar, which has 2000.

The elephant, the largest of all land mammals, was once highly revered but in these days of material values, the elephant is struggling. Domestic elephants suffer from shortages of food, water and trained mahouts (elephant keepers). Appropriate employment is another issue. Elephant labour, once crucial in the logging and construction industries, has been replaced by machinery, and elephants no longer provide a viable economic return to their owners. Temple festivals and tourist enterprises are now the main but inadequate source of income.

The once popular Elephant March has now ceased due to declining patronage and protests over animal maltreatment. Plans to stage similar, smaller events are distressing elephant lovers, concerned about further elephant exploitation.

Elephants require large quantities of food and water. Inadequate mahout training has led to their neglect and consequent decline in health. However, in an effort to redress the situation, a comprehensive training program has begun to rekindle some of the knowledge and skills that were once passed down through generations. The program was initiated by Nibha Namboodiri, who trained as a mahout in order to teach others. She is one of only two women in India with such elephant expertise.

In spite of all the challenges, experts insist that the population of native domestic Keralan elephants must be increased to ensure 'quality stock' and to provide elephants for temple festivities. Some argue that as the wild population decreases, maintenance of domestic numbers is one method to ensure elephant survival. Given that wild elephant capture is illegal and that domestic breeding has been unsuccessful, it remains to be seen just how the population can be sustained, let alone increased.

For more information contact Elephant SOS (☎ 0487-382819), SPCA Ayyanthole, Elephant Wing, Kousthubham, PO Elthuruth, Thrissur.

butterflies can be seen in the Silent Valley area, an area little affected by pollution and pesticides.

Birds

There are over 500 species of birds in Kerala. However, less than 5% of these are endemic. Species include large birds of prey, such as the cinerous vulture *(Aegypius monachus)* and the osprey *(Pandion haliaetus)*, nocturnal birds such as the long-eared owl *(Asio otus)* and the brown fish owl *(Bubo zeylonensis)* and numerous waterbirds such as the little cormorant *(Phalacrocorax niger)*.

Some of the more unusual bird species include the paradise flycatcher *(Terpsiphone paradisi)*, which has a distinct blue neck and two long ribbon-like tails and can be seen in mixed bamboo areas or on the forest fringe; the greater racket-tailed drongo *(Dicrurus paradiseus)*, which has a long fork-like tail and a bright blue crest and is an excellent mimic of other birds; and the Nilgiri laughing thrush *(Garrulax cachinnans)*, which is prone to loud outbursts of laughter-like screeching.

The three main places for bird enthusiasts are Periyar Wildlife Sanctuary, Kumarakom

Elephants in Kerala

Some Facts about Indian Elephants

- An adult elephant weighs between 2.5 and 5 tonnes.
- Elephants are vegetarian.
- A full-grown elephant consumes about 300kg of fodder and 250L of water daily.
- Elephants eat for 18 hours a day and defecate 15 to 20 times a day.
- Elephants are highly sensitive to sound, smell and touch. They love water and are good swimmers.
- The elephant trunk is an extension of the upper lip. It has no bones and approximately 80,000 muscles. It can pluck a single blade of grass or uproot an entire tree.
- In the wild elephants live in matriarchal herds, led by the oldest female. It is she who makes the decisions about where to roam, where to rest and when to flee.
- Elephant gestation is 22 months and a newborn calf can weigh 80 to 100kg.
- Only the male elephant develops tusks but not all males have them. Males without tusks are known as *makhnas*.
- Every year mature male elephants experience a time of musth. They produce a discharge from the temporal gland and their behaviour may become aggressive.
- The only enemies of elephants are people.
- A trained male elephant can be purchased for around US$25,000. The upkeep is a further US$2500 a year.

Elephants & Tourists

Elephant experts in Kerala have compiled a publication called *Elephant SOS* in which they offer the following useful hints:

- Do not accept rides offered by any random mahout or owner.
- Do not allow a mahout to force an elephant to show acrobatics or tricks.
- Do not accept ivory or elephant tail hair sold by mahouts or anyone else. This is illegal.
- Do not pay the mahout to buy food for the elephant. Instead you should buy the food yourself (bananas, other fruits or vegetables such as spinach).
- Do not offer alcohol or any drugs to a mahout on duty.

Bird Sanctuary on Vembanad Lake and the Thattekkad Bird Sanctuary.

NATIONAL PARKS & WILDLIFE SANCTUARIES

Kerala has national parks, wildlife sanctuaries and reserves, which vary in size, type and facilities. The main ones are listed in the 'National Parks & Wildlife Sanctuaries' table, further details are in the relevant sections.

Visiting Parks & Sanctuaries

Travellers often bring memories of elsewhere to their experiences of Indian parks and sanctuaries. As such they find themselves frustrated and disappointed. If you hope to visit a national park or wildlife sanctuary you may need to adjust your expectations. Here are some guidelines, which may help to place things in context.

- There is no clear definition between federal and state responsibilities for national parks and wildlife sanctuaries, and park administrations must survive on minuscule budgets. As a result, information and services for visitors are often barely adequate. (See the boxed text 'Misinformation Centres' in the Facts for the Visitor chapter.)

National Parks & Wildlife Sanctuaries

national park/ wildlife sanctuary	features	location & best time to visit
Aralam Wildlife Sanctuary	sambar, sloth bears, elephants, mouse-deer, birdlife, reptiles, butterflies	55km east of Kannur; difficult to visit
Chinnar Wildlife Sanctuary	endangered giant grizzled squirrel, elephants, common langur, deer, dry scrub, deciduous forest	58km north-east of Munnar; Jan-Feb
Eravikulam National Park	Nilgiri tahr, grassland, shola forest, walks	16km north-east of Munnar; Nov-Mar
Idukki Wildlife Sanctuary	bisons, bears, elephants, wild boar, jackals, wild dogs, sambar	20km north-east of Kottayam; Nov-Mar
Kumarakom Bird Sanctuary	winter home of Siberian stork, snake birds, night herons, egrets	16km west of Kottayam; Nov-Mar
Neyyar Wildlife Sanctuary	Agastya Peak, breeding crocodiles, boating, walking, safari park	30km north-east of Thiruvananthapuram; Nov-Mar
Parambikulam Wildlife Sanctuary	gaur, wild boar, elephants, langur, macaques, otters, crocodiles, tahr, boating, jeep trips	135km from Palakkad; Sep-May
Peechi-Vazhani Wildlife Sanctuary	jungle fowl, peacocks, boating	15km east of Thrissur; Dec-Mar
Peppara Wildlife Sanctuary	closed to visitors at the time of writing	30km north east of Thiruvananthapuram; closed
Periyar Wildlife Sanctuary	tiger reserve, elephants, wild boar, sambar, watchtowers, birds, boat trips, jungle walks, treks	120km east of Kottayam; Sep-May
Silent Valley National Park	tropical evergreen forest, butterflies, birds, Nilgiri tahr, leopards, tigers, Nilgiri leaf monkeys, elephants	80km north of Palakkad; Dec-Feb
Thattekkad Bird Sanctuary	300 species of birds such as Ceylon frog-mouths, Malabar grey hornbills, parakeets, jungle fowl, herons, egrets, jungle mynas, woodpeckers, rose-billed rollers	78km east of Kochi; Oct-Mar
Wayanad Wildlife Sanctuary (Muthanga Wildlife Sanctuary)	elephants, chital, gaur, sambal, barking deer, swamps, grassland, bamboo	100km north-east of Kozhikode; Nov-Mar

- Training of park and forestry personnel is often inadequate. Advice provided to visitors therefore may be deficient, even inaccurate. Don't rely on the 'experts'. Use common sense and your own judgement.
- Tourist agencies promote parks as places for adventure and leisure, while forestry personnel, concerned to protect wildlife, often discourage tourists. For the visitor, this can result in confusing information, no information and/or critical delays in entry permits.
- Usually, but not always, entry to parks for a day visit (from 6 am to 6 pm) requires no permits.
- It is on the whole *not* permissible to walk/trek in the parks, or any forested area, without a guide. However, finding the right guide may be difficult. Many have little or no training, little knowledge and take no responsibility. Maps generally don't exist. If they do, they are usually inadequate and incorrect. Find the right guide and you are assured of an experience that is educational and rewarding.
- Movement in the parks is often confined to very small areas (apparently leaving the bulk of the park as sanctuary for animals). This can result in hordes of people gathering at one site, shattering the peace and leaving unsightly litter.
- Many parks are not easily accessible by public transport. However, private travel within the confines of most parks is not allowed and you may find you've gone to considerable expense to hire transport only to be advised that you must use an organised tour bus or boat. Such tours are of limited time and generally not conducive to viewing wildlife activity except for the raucous behaviour of your companions. So you'll be lucky to see anything.
- Most parks have some accommodation, but this is often reserved for officials. Length of stay (if permitted) is also limited, usually to one or two nights. Most parks will not allow you to stay unless you have booked your accommodation *in advance*. Some may waive this rule, but rarely.
- The booking office is always some distance (30 to 50km) away and is often not easily accessible, particularly by public transport. And it's invariably not the office advertised in brochures, nor the one you've been advised with such certainty to approach.
- Some travellers prefer to stay in accommodation outside but close to the parks and make day visits. This is possible at some, but not all, parks; quite a few of them are too isolated to have accommodation nearby.
- Except for the more organised sanctuaries and parks (such as Periyar or Eravikulam), your request for entry may simply be denied. The reasons (sometimes real, sometimes fictitious) may be due to circumstances completely outside forestry personnel control – there may be fires or insufficient water, or the place may have been booked by VIPs. In the latter event, you have no chance. The more likely event is that you'll be given long, convoluted directions as to the procedures you must follow for park entry. The more you adhere to the directions and persist in following them, the more convoluted they'll become. After several days of dealing unsuccessfully with the intricacies of bureaucratic processes, you'll wish you were denied entry at the outset.
- In some situations, inadequate forestry personnel have been supplanted by private operators, eager for the tourist dollar but less eager to consider environmental issues and visitor safety.
- Understandably many travellers, fed up with government red tape, go with the private operators. This is not to say that many private operators do not offer adequate services. However, there are cases where the companies, themselves frustrated by the bureaucracy, break the rules, bribe the officials and trespass into highly sensitive areas.
- The words 'wildlife', 'national park', 'sanctuary' 'jungle', 'trekking' and 'safari' conjure up exciting ideas in many travellers' minds, especially for those who have travelled in Nepal, Africa, Australia or North America. In Kerala (and other parts of India) it can be quite different.
- A safari may mean a one hour trip in a jeep through urban areas and a little picnic by a river.
- A trek may mean a short walk through developed areas. It could also mean the 'real thing'. Take care to ascertain exactly what the tour involves, and ensure that safety standards and environmental issues are respected.
- Understand too that no matter how careful you are in your endeavours to find accurate information, your actual experience may differ markedly from promises made.
- Many of the parks have several names that are used interchangeably depending on the politics, ethnicity, geographical origin and whim of the user. Initially this may be confusing, but it can usually be clarified.
- It's probably wise to avoid bribery, no matter how strong the temptation. There are protocols about how to do this. Unless, and even if, you're aware of them, bribery could get you into some serious trouble.

Remember there are several issues at stake:

Your safety in the natural environment There are wild animals out there (or at least the hope is that there are some left). Do you or your guide have the knowledge and skills to deal with wild animal behaviour? Where will you sleep? Will the lodgings/tents and equipment protect you from the elements and from night wandering animals?

Your safety with others Travellers are on the whole very safe most of the time. Unfortunately, however, there have been some recent tragic accounts from South India that, once in the isolation of nature, the hired 'guides' became the very antithesis of guides and incidents of sexual assault have been reported. It must be stressed that such situations are rare, but healthy caution is always recommended.

Environmental damage The forests of India are screaming for a break. They have been plundered too much and little habitat remains. It may be great for you to enter into a pristine environment, but what about the environment itself and the animals that inhabit it? It's crucial therefore to observe environmental codes, even if they are not locally enforced. Respect areas cordoned off for regeneration. Is your satisfaction at entering a pristine environment worth even more environmental damage?

Finally, in spite of environmental damage, Kerala's parks provide unique and diverse natural locales. Most parks and the areas around them are beautiful, secluded and peaceful – a welcome break from the dust and excitement of the towns. Once you've survived the discombobulating bureaucratic processes, the parks will provide space and time for solitude, reflection and restoration.

ECOLOGY & ENVIRONMENT

Kerala has a rich and distinct environment featuring a long coastal region, an elaborate system of waterways, and biodivese mountains. It is their intricate ecology that makes Kerala a site of major environmental significance. For further reading on the environment, see the Books section in the Facts for the Visitor chapter.

Mountain Ecology

Almost half (42%) the area of the Western Ghats lies in Kerala. These mountains play an important role in the state's abundant rainfall and consequent fertility. On the eastern border of Kerala, they are ideally located to receive the south-eastern monsoon. Their height forces the air to rise, causing atmospheric activity that increases precipitation. The abundant rain and fertile soils, formed from ancient rock, have been the critical factors in determining the richness of the area's vegetation and wildlife. (See the Flora and Fauna sections, earlier in this chapter.) It is not only home to bountiful flora and fauna; it is also the source of some of India's major river systems, including the Godavari, Krishna, Kaveri and the Periyar. As such, it is an important life source for areas way beyond its domain.

The ecological importance of the Western Ghats has elicited the attention of major environmental organisations. The World Wide Fund for Nature (WWF) and the International Union for the Conservation of Nature (IUCN) classify the Ghats as deserving the highest priority for conservation. The Zoological Survey of India predicts that in 50 years the Western Ghats will be irretrievably changed unless urgent conservation measures are undertaken to arrest and reverse current destructive trends.

Problems began for the mountains during the Dutch period with the development of plantations, removal of timber and poaching of animals. Concern expressed by conservation organisations is based on several factors.

Deforestation Development, plantations, human encroachment, dam construction, hunting and poaching have all served to create serious deforestation in the Ghats. It is estimated that forest is cleared at the rate of 60 to 100 sq km per year. Seven hundred species of trees, herbs and climbers are either endangered or vulnerable to extinction. With forest losses there is inevitable reduction in rainfall. Attempts to rectify forest loss by reforestation have been ineffective because of the introduction of inappropriate species such as eucalyptus and acacia, which hinder rather than restore ecological balance.

Erosion & Soil Degradation Large cash crop plantations of cardamom, coffee and tea have led to erosion and deficient soils. Agricultural organisations predict that the viability for further production in some degraded areas will cease early in the new millennium.

Relocation of Adivasi Communities Development in the Ghats has forced the relocation of Adivasi (tribal) communities. They have lost their homes, habitats and the source of their livelihood. Relocation of these communities has placed burdens on already existing communities. It also creates another serious problem – in new locations tribal societies lose their indigenous knowledge, which is crucial to understanding and maintaining the environment.

Reduction in Wildlife Loss of forest cover means that much of Kerala's flora and fauna is now vulnerable or endangered. Some of these include the elephant, tiger and Nilgiri tahr, the blackbuck, gaur, sloth bear, palm civet, lion-tailed macaque, the olive ridley and Cochin forest cane turtle and the Travancore tortoise. The estuarine crocodile, once endemic to Kerala, is now extinct.

Four species endemic to the Ghats and considered to be of primary conservation significance are the lion-tailed macaque, the Nilgiri leaf monkey (also known as Nilgiri langur), the brown palm civet and the goat-like Nilgiri tahr. Now protected by Indian law, Nilgiri tahr numbers are increasing (see the Other Mammals section, earlier). The Ghats are also home to the Indian elephant, which lives in small isolated pockets threatened by further development. Isolated and under threat, elephants may raid crops and even injure and kill humans.

Waterways Ecology

Renowned for its tranquil backwaters, Kerala is sometimes called the 'Venice of Asia'. However, environmental damage is taking its toll here too.

The degradation in the mountains has resulted in rivers which are polluted by silt. Industrial effluent, the major polluter, is believed to deliver 800,000 cubic metres of toxic substances daily into the waterways, killing fish and presenting significant health risks. Many wells, one of the traditional sources of water, have become waste tips, creating serious ground water pollution. It's ironic that, due to pollution, a state with abundant rainfall now has an inadequate supply of drinking water.

The wetland habitats of frogs and worms have been severely affected by chemicals, used for pest reduction. In another irony, the use of chemicals has depleted the very creatures that would naturally inhibit insects that attack crops.

Rivers and inland waterways are exhibiting notable losses of fish species. In some rivers, particularly in the Kochi and Kollam (Quilon) areas, dredging has resulted in the loss of fish breeding areas. In Akkulam-Veli Lake, just 10km from Thiruvananthapuram (Trivandrum), only 8% of the original 300 species remain.

Sewage, noxious weeds and irrigation projects preventing the free flow of rivers are all additional hazards for wetland environments.

Marine Ecology

Coastal Erosion During the monsoons, high seas lash the coast, placing coastal populations at risk and altering the seashore landscape. Government attempts to impede the erosion by erecting sea walls have had little effect. Coastal sand mining has reduced the area between the coast and the backwaters, thereby exacerbating the monsoonal effects.

Overfishing The small catches harvested by traditional fishing methods did not interfere with the ocean ecology. However, with the introduction of trawler fishing in the early 1950s, many species disappeared and by the 1980s yields had declined by over 50%. This overexploitation effected the economy and health of the local fishing community who lost an important component of their diet.

Salinity

In some areas, salinity is a threat. In the Thalasseri (Tellicherry) area, locks were installed to prevent salt water penetrating crop and residential areas. However, government changes here have resulted in less support for the lock completion and maintenance, and damaging salt water has led to crop reduction and pollution of ground water resources.

Energy

Once a state with surplus power, Kerala now depends on its neighbours. Even so, there are frequent power shortages. Given Kerala's low oil and gas resources and its difficulties in importing coal, hydropower is its main energy source. More recently, however, environmental considerations have precluded some dam constructions (including the massive Silent Valley project) and consequently extension of the hydrosystem has been impeded.

In an effort to balance ecological need with energy demand, alternative sources of energy, such as wave, wind, solar and small hydel (hydro) units, are being researched.

The Future

Traditional customs respected the natural environment. Water was viewed as sacred – the fountainhead of life. Sacred groves served to safeguard the ecology by guaranteeing protection to nature within certain tracts of land. Domestic gardens, with their plant varieties, emulated forest diversity. However, recent practices, such as plantation development with its monoculture bias, prohibit diversity and the consequent benefits of ecological interaction. Experts warn that the loss of biodiversity is resulting in an ineffectual ecology – one that can no longer sustain itself.

Authorities are often helpless to intervene. Short-term governments mitigate against long-term solutions. Some environmentalists claim that parts of Kerala, the Western Ghats in particular, are among the most seriously damaged ecosystems in the world. Others argue that there are still sufficient (albeit dwindling) areas, still thriving, from which to base positive measures for recovery. And there are stories of environmental triumph over some destructive developments. At least two hydroelectric projects, dams, a new rail system and tourist developments threatening the environment have all been cancelled.

In 1987-88, in an attempt to raise awareness about the plight of the ghats, 6000 people supported by over 160 environmental groups undertook a 2250km, 100 day *padayatra* (foot-march) along the Western Ghats.

Ten years later, a US$39 million World Bank loan enabled forestry programs to examine the negative effects of human development on biodiversity. Emphasis is on empowering Adivasi and farming communities, with tribal knowledge forming the basis of strategies to develop forest products and at the same time maintain forest integrity.

Another strategy, developed by the Keralan Departments of Biotechnology and Space, employs satellite monitoring to record the state of the environment, in particular the remaining wildlife and vegetation. The aim is to develop strategies for regeneration and future minimal impact.

GOVERNMENT & POLITICS

National Government

India, the world's largest democracy, has a parliamentary system. There are two houses within the parliament: a lower house known as the Lok Sabha (House of the People), and an upper house known as the Rajya Sabha (Council of States).

The lower house has 544 members (excluding the speaker), with all but two elected on a population basis (proportional representation). Elections for the Lok Sabha are held every five years, unless the government calls an earlier election. All Indians over the age of 18 have the right to vote. Of the 544 seats, 125 are reserved for the Scheduled Castes (also known as Untouchables or Dalits) and Tribes. This is a positive discrimination effort favouring the disadvantaged communities.

The upper house has 245 members. Police, education, agriculture and industry are reserved for the state governments. Other areas are jointly administered by both levels of government.

The federal government has the controversial right to assume power in any state if the situation in that state is deemed to be unmanageable. Known as President's Rule, this right has been exercised in Kerala on several occasions for short periods, due to political unrest or insoluble parliamentary situations.

The 1998 elections saw an end to the long-standing Congress government with Bharatya Janata Party (BJP) leader Atal Bihari Vajpayee attaining office with a coalition of numerous disparate parties.

Almost instantly, the BJP followed through on its pledge to make India a formidable world power by detonating a series of nuclear explosions. The immediate response to the tests, nationally and internationally, was one of condemnation and outrage. The Indian government, however, remained defiant and in spite of repeated difficulties and constant threats to his party, Vajpayee managed to hold together an odd combination of parties in coalition until it disintegrated in April 1999.

A national election was held in September 1999. At the time of going to press another BJP-led coalition was widely tipped to win.

State Government

As with the other Indian states, Kerala has a governor who is appointed by the president of India for five years, a legislature (elected for five years) and a Council of Ministers under the leadership of a chief minister.

The state government is comprised of one house – the Legislative Assembly, with 141 seats. Of these, 11 are reserved for Scheduled Castes and one for Tribes.

The Union Territories in Lakshadweep are administered by lieutenant-governors who are appointed by the president of India.

At the time of writing, the Communist-led Left Democratic Front formed the government of Kerala.

Politics of Kerala

Politics in Kerala is a lively, participatory process. Malayalis have a high political awareness. Voter turnout for elections is high, generally 75% to 86% of the electorate. But political involvement is not limited to the ballot box. People exert a political voice through membership of political parties and community organisations such as trade unions, social groups and churches. Malayalis are not averse to protest and street marches are common. As well as an assertion of protest, such rallies often act as a platform for informative comment and increased awareness.

Historical Background Political activity in Kerala has a historical base. In the late 19th century people of the southern states – Cochin and Travancore – petitioned their monarchs for greater political access. Legislative councils were then established and monarchs were continually responsive to communal pressure for increased democratic practices. British-controlled Malabar instituted an electoral system in 1939. With the development of the National Congress, political organisation and activity developed.

Political parties have often developed from social groups formed to represent the aims of their members. The Nair Service Society (NSS) formed to promote the aims of the Nair (former warrior caste) community. Generally comprised of land owners, it has alternated between support for Congress and the communist parties. The Sri Narayana Dharma Paripalana Yogam (SNDP) has furthered the aspirations of the Ezhavas (a former low-caste community) and has generally supported the communist parties. Its wealthier members support Congress. Initially the Christian churches were behind Congress, which led to it being called the 'Christian Congress'. The more liberal church elements, however, back the Kerala Congress and the communists.

Political Parties The practice of furthering political goals through group pressure has resulted in the formation of numerous political parties. In fact over 50 political parties have been formed since Independence and up to 38 may contest elections. Some of the major parties include:

Communist Parties The fledgling Communist Party formed mainly in the Malabar area (at Kozhikode in 1937). Its numbers were expanded when Congress split and the Congress socialists joined their communist comrades, affiliating with them in 1940. After WWII, communist aggressive activity transformed into involvement in the parliamentary process, and this served to legitimise the communists as a valid prospect for government. While support for the communists comes from the poorer and previously lower-caste members of society, its leadership is generally from the upper echelons. The major communist parties are the Communist Party of India (Marxist) – CPI(M), which split from its parent, the Communist Party of India (CPI) in 1964. The CPI(M) has been a major political force in Kerala and is well known for its celebrated leader, EMS Namboodiripad, who led the split and headed the party to power in the first democratically elected communist government in the world in 1957. See the boxed text 'EMS: From Ancient Vedas to Historical Materialism'.

Indian National Congress (I) – INC(I) Although the Congress in Kerala originated from the Indian National Congress, which was initially concerned with independence, it had little in common with it. In the early stages of the party, all major groups were represented. Over time, however, varying ideologies resulted in several splits. The INC(I) remains a major party and usually attains about 30% of the vote.

Indian Union Muslim League – IUML Although not officially formed until 1933, the Muslim League had its dawn in the activities of the Mappilas (Muslims of Kerala) who, in the mid-19th century, rioted against their landlords and British authority. Through coalition with other parties IUML has maintained an almost constant presence in government, enabling it to achieve favourable results for the Muslim community.

Kerala Congress This party came into being in 1964 as a result of disputes within its parent party, the Indian National Congress. Its support is mainly from Christian and Nair groups. Since its inception it has split, resulting in five Kerala Congress parties. Together they usually gain about 10% of the vote. Through coalition these parties have enjoyed a position similar to the IUML.

The Political Landscape Today The political history of Kerala since Independence is a complex saga of splits, mergers and often hastily formed coalitions. A clear majority is rare and many a government has resulted in power being shared by either Congress or the communists with some unlikely partners. At times, coalitions have faltered and confusion has reigned resulting in federal intervention and the imposition of President's rule. But while coalition governments have caused instability and confusion, there have also been positive outcomes. Small parties have been able to participate in government, attaining benefits for their communities. The need to debate and compromise has furthered the participatory process and this in turn has meant that comparatively little violence has occurred.

ECONOMY

India has enjoyed strong economic growth since the reforms that began in 1991. These included lowering market entry barriers, relaxing import licensing for some goods and liberalising the foreign investment policy. Throughout the 1990s there was a sustained growth in Gross Domestic Product, which primarily came from activity in the industrial sector.

Kerala

While current economic rhetoric espouses the advantages, indeed the necessity, of global trade and global relations, interaction with the world market is not a new phenomenon in Kerala. Indeed such associations, based on trade in spices, especially pepper and cardamom, have existed for over 2000 years. Much later with British colonisation, coffee and tea became important export crops. Today these crops are still major earners with Kerala producing 75% of India's spices (see the Food & Spice section in the Facts for the Visitor chapter).

The Keralan economy relies heavily on cash crops. The state produces almost all of India's lemongrass oil, 92% of its rubber, 70% of its coconut, 60% of its tapioca and 36% of its seafood exports. This predomi-

EMS: From Ancient Vedas to Historical Materialism

EMS – first leader of a democratically elected communist government

On 20 March 1998 business in Kerala ceased. Tens of thousands of people moved slowly through the streets. Large street marches are a way of life in Kerala, but this was no ordinary street march. This was a farewell to a long loved leader whose body, now clothed in the red flag, with its hammer and sickle emblem, asserted in death the ideals he had espoused throughout life.

Elamkulam Manackal Shankaran Namboodiripad, known affectionately as EMS, was the first leader of a democratically elected communist government in the world – a government that stood for democracy and secularism.

Born into the superior Brahmin caste and steeped in its rites and scriptures, EMS might have been considered an unlikely leader of the underprivileged. But he assumed their cause with a vigilance that never waned. He relinquished the property and privilege of his caste, but retained its scholarship, producing a myriad of commentaries, verbal and written, which strongly influenced political discourse, often setting the agenda. As a Brahmin scholar interprets the scriptures of the *Vedas*, EMS interpreted the scriptures of the Marxist dialectic.

He began his political career with Congress but later became an ardent critic of its policies. He joined the Communist Party in 1940. During the Indian/Chinese border dispute in 1962, the communist party split, with EMS leading the breakaway group and forming the CPI(M) (Communist Party of India – Marxist). As general secretary until 1992, he led the party that became one of the major forces in Keralan politics. He was twice chief minister of Kerala, from 1957 for two years and again in 1967 for another two years.

EMS was a mass of contradictions. It is said that of all his statements, there was not one that he did not later repudiate. By accepting the parliamentary process he gained a certain legitimacy for the Communist Party. Challenged about this apparent contradiction, he displayed his usual wit for his detractors – communist involvement in parliament would reveal the deficiencies of bourgeois tactics. He is also credited with developing the process of coalition, crucial to Keralan politics, where, on the whole, no one party receives an absolute majority in elections.

As the thousands stood in silence at the funeral, party chiefs with clenched and raised fists uttered 'Comrade EMS, Lal Salaam, Lal Salaam'.

nance of cash crops has resulted in a shortage of locally grown food – Kerala produces only one-third of its rice requirements. To meet its needs for meat, vegetables and rice, Kerala imports from other Indian states.

In comparison to the neighbouring state of Karnataka, Kerala is relatively unindustrialised and its workforce is highly unionised. These two factors are often cited as reasons for Kerala's relatively high unemployment, which has fuelled an exodus of skilled labour abroad, mainly to the Gulf states in the Middle East. In 1996 Gulf remittances amounted to 25% of the state's total domestic income. Some sources put the current figure at a staggering 40%.

Lakshadweep

Fishing is important in the island territory of Lakshadweep, where in 1993-94 8000 tonnes of fish were netted. There is a tuna canning factory at Minicoy Island. Lakshadweep also produces the coconut by-products copra and coir as well as *jaggery* (palm sugar) and vinegar.

POPULATION & PEOPLE

The second most populous country in the world after China, India's population rose to 1 billion in August 1999, according to UN estimates. In all states, men outnumber women (927 females to 1000 males), except in Kerala, which has some 1036 females to every 1000 males. Kerala's population at the last census (1991) was 29 million and the estimated population for 1999 was 32 million. With a growth rate of 1.34%, this is lower than most states. Most of Kerala's people (21.5 million) live in rural areas.

Lakshadweep has almost 52,000 people with a population density of about 1616 people per sq km (the national average is 273). Kerala, the most densely populated mainland state after Bangla (West Bengal), has some 750 people per sq km, but in some areas this increases to 1800.

Kerala also has a small population of Adivasis (tribal people), some of whom have managed to preserve their cultural traditions. They live in the remote, hilly, forested regions of the Western Ghats. Nationally the highest proportion of Adivasis to the total state population is in Lakshadweep (94%), the lowest is in Kerala (about 1%).

Dress

Traditional dress varied depending on community, caste and gender. In some caste groups both men and women were naked from the waist up. Many people wore a white *mundu* (sarong-like garment) with women using a *neryathu* (cloth draped over the shoulder). Muslim women wore scarves, with some being in full purdah – this custom continues in some Muslim communities to this day.

Today most women wear saris although the neryathu is still common. The *salwar kameez* (loose shirt and trousers) is popular with younger women. Working men wear a coloured mundu while professional men usually wear the western-style suit, but in their homes they're more likely to dress in the more comfortable mundu, and at the temple they wear a white *dhoti* (cloth worn around the waist that falls to the ankles).

EDUCATION

India's literacy rate has increased from 18% in 1951 to 52% in 1991. Kerala, with over 90% literacy (almost 100% for younger adults), holds the top spot as India's most literate state. Kerala boasts the largest expenditure of any Indian state, and for that matter many other countries, on education. Certainly on many measures – duration at school, number of educational institutions, enrolments in higher education and results, Kerala attains impressive standards. But for Kerala this is no new phenomenon. Education has always been considered important as a means of imparting cultural traits, dignified behaviour and respect. The gaining of independence and democracy has been attributed to education, and once acquired, education has helped maintain them.

Unfortunately high levels of education have not meant an improved economic situation for many Malayalis. At 84% of the national average per capita income, Kerala remains one of the poorest states in India.

SCIENCE & TECHNOLOGY

Kerala may lack a sizeable manufacturing base but when it comes to scientific research and development the state is at the cutting edge. Space research is significant with the state hosting three key organisations that contribute to the Indian Space Research Organisation (ISRO). These are the Vikram Sarabhai Space Centre (VSSC), the Liquid Propulsion Systems Centre (LPSC) and the ISRO Inertial System Unit, all in Thiruvananthapuram.

The Educated State

Sangam literature, from the first centuries CE (common era), describes education in Kerala as significant for all sectors of society. Buddhists and Jains developed educational institutions known as *salais* and these continued with the conversion from these faiths to Hinduism. However, as the caste system developed, only the more advantaged sections of society were educated.

In the mid to late 19th century, with the requirement for a well-trained government workforce, dramatic changes occurred. Christian missionaries, often supported by local rulers, established schools for lower-caste people. While these moves were not without their problems, the blending of the castes in the educative process tended to broaden understanding and curtail the inequitable effects of the caste system.

During the 19th century, with increased state involvement, education became free and compulsory for children up to the age of 10. Private educational organisations continued and today play a major role with 66% of schooling and 80% of tertiary education under private administration. The establishment of a university in Travancore in 1937 facilitated scholarship in the Malayalam language and culture. Translations of books from other countries enabled Malayalis to become learned in their own culture as well as developing an understanding of others. With the formation of the new state of Kerala in 1956, this institution became the University of Kerala. Since then six more universities have been established, many of which are affiliated with Kerala's 186 colleges.

On the software front things are moving fast. Government and private funding has been pumped into Technopark, a state-of-the-art venture near Thiruvananthapuram adjacent to the University of Kerala. The aim is to provide increased opportunities for local talent in the hope that Kerala may eventually rival Bangalore as a software development centre. Bangalore, the capital of Karnataka state, is considered to be India's 'Silicon Valley'.

ARTS

Kerala has a long and proud tradition of support for all the major art forms. Each region has been influenced by its varying landforms, distinct cultures and religions. The arts, therefore, with access to different materials and inspiration, frequently express regional differences and unique styles.

Performing Arts

The literature of the Sangam era describes intricate performances created to please and appease the gods, see the Performing Arts special section for more details.

Music

South India's own brand of classical music, called Carnatic (Hindustani is North India's classic form), originated in Vedic times, some 3000 years ago. Essentially, there are two basic elements in Indian music: the *tala* and the *raga*. Tala is the rhythm and is characterised by the number of beats. The raga provides the melody. In Carnatic music both are used for composition and improvisation.

While it has many things in common with its northern counterpart, Carnatic music differs as it has been less influenced by Islam. Song, for example, is more important in Carnatic music, and this influences even purely instrumental performances.

The ancient text *Chilappatikaram* (the Epic of the Anklets) of the 7th century describes a musical culture of song and instruments that was sophisticated and advanced. Several later texts detail the talas and ragas of compositions and performance. Fourteenth century poems described the magnificence of temple chanting.

continued on page 38

PERFORMING ARTS

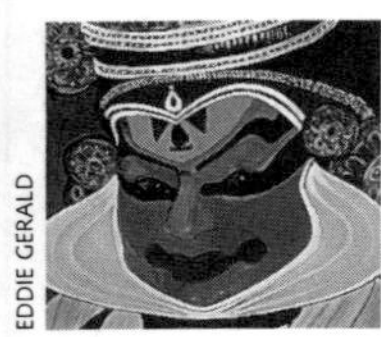
EDDIE GERALD

From the earliest times of human settlement in Kerala, people danced for their gods – to the village goddess for protection, to the sea god for successful trade, to the land gods for fertility and good harvests. With Aryan migrations to the south, a new language, Sanskrit, was introduced and dramatic plays conveyed the stories of the land and messages to and from the gods. Later art forms combined elements of the ancient with contemporary themes.

The performing arts seek to communicate a message. Usually the message is derived from classical texts and the communication is achieved through narration, song, and the intricate movements of gesture and dance.

Kathakali

Possibly the most renowned drama of Kerala, Kathakali may have had its beginnings in ancient performance methods of the 2nd century CE. However, the contemporary form dates from the 17th century.

Kathakali literally means 'story play' and the Kathakali performance is actually the dramatised presentation of a play. Originally there were over 100 plays but now only 30 are performed. They are based on the Hindu epics the *Ramayana* and the *Mahabharata* as well as the *Puranas*. The themes explored are all those canvassed in the great stories – righteousness and evil, frailty and courage, poverty and prosperity, war and peace. The landscapes are also broad – the terrestrial and the cosmic.

The script *attakatha* or poetic text of the Kathakali performance is Manipravalam, a Sanskritised form of Malayalam. While the script is vocalised by singers, the performers actually 'narrate' the drama through precise movements and gestures. Traditionally performances took place in temple grounds and while this is still a common venue, other open-air locales as well as indoor halls are also popular.

Preparation for the performance is lengthy and disciplined. Each performer is reconstructed; his/her own being becomes subjugated to the essence of the character. Paint, a fantastic costume and a highly decorated headpiece aid in the reconstruction. Seeds, placed on the eyelids, redden the whites of the eyes – soft pink for a beautiful woman or kindly character, blood red for ferocious demons. The final part of the preparation is a short meditation.

Performers play the various characters, which can be generally divided into the following:

Pacca – the royal and divine creatures, such as Vishnu or Rama. The make-up consists of green faces (green symbolising heroism and righteousness) with large crown headgear – the *kesabhara kiritam*.

Katti – these are the demons and villains such as Ravana, the evil king who abducted Sita in the *Ramayana*. (Katti refers to the knife-shape on

Right: Kathakali performers spend hours perfecting their intricate make-up before the show. Visitors can often come early to see the preparations.

ALL PHOTOGRAPHS BY EDDIE GERALD

BOTH PHOTOGRAPHS BY EDDIE GERALD

Top: *Mukhabhinaya*, or facial gestures, play a crucial role in narrating the Kathakali drama. **Bottom:** Women's roles are often played by men, although increasingly women are becoming performers themselves. **Facing page:** Green facial make-up is reserved for royal and divine characters. Sometimes they are righteous; sometimes, like this one, they are evil.

The Educated State

Sangam literature, from the first centuries CE (common era), describes education in Kerala as significant for all sectors of society. Buddhists and Jains developed educational institutions known as *salais* and these continued with the conversion from these faiths to Hinduism. However, as the caste system developed, only the more advantaged sections of society were educated.

In the mid to late 19th century, with the requirement for a well-trained government workforce, dramatic changes occurred. Christian missionaries, often supported by local rulers, established schools for lower-caste people. While these moves were not without their problems, the blending of the castes in the educative process tended to broaden understanding and curtail the inequitable effects of the caste system.

During the 19th century, with increased state involvement, education became free and compulsory for children up to the age of 10. Private educational organisations continued and today play a major role with 66% of schooling and 80% of tertiary education under private administration. The establishment of a university in Travancore in 1937 facilitated scholarship in the Malayalam language and culture. Translations of books from other countries enabled Malayalis to become learned in their own culture as well as developing an understanding of others. With the formation of the new state of Kerala in 1956, this institution became the University of Kerala. Since then six more universities have been established, many of which are affiliated with Kerala's 186 colleges.

On the software front things are moving fast. Government and private funding has been pumped into Technopark, a state-of-the-art venture near Thiruvananthapuram adjacent to the University of Kerala. The aim is to provide increased opportunities for local talent in the hope that Kerala may eventually rival Bangalore as a software development centre. Bangalore, the capital of Karnataka state, is considered to be India's 'Silicon Valley'.

ARTS

Kerala has a long and proud tradition of support for all the major art forms. Each region has been influenced by its varying landforms, distinct cultures and religions. The arts, therefore, with access to different materials and inspiration, frequently express regional differences and unique styles.

Performing Arts

The literature of the Sangam era describes intricate performances created to please and appease the gods, see the Performing Arts special section for more details.

Music

South India's own brand of classical music, called Carnatic (Hindustani is North India's classic form), originated in Vedic times, some 3000 years ago. Essentially, there are two basic elements in Indian music: the *tala* and the *raga*. Tala is the rhythm and is characterised by the number of beats. The raga provides the melody. In Carnatic music both are used for composition and improvisation.

While it has many things in common with its northern counterpart, Carnatic music differs as it has been less influenced by Islam. Song, for example, is more important in Carnatic music, and this influences even purely instrumental performances.

The ancient text *Chilappatikaram* (the Epic of the Anklets) of the 7th century describes a musical culture of song and instruments that was sophisticated and advanced. Several later texts detail the talas and ragas of compositions and performance. Fourteenth century poems described the magnificence of temple chanting.

continued on page 38

PERFORMING ARTS

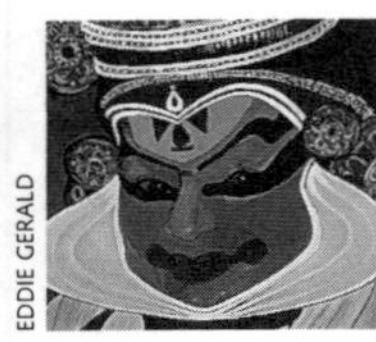
EDDIE GERALD

From the earliest times of human settlement in Kerala, people danced for their gods – to the village goddess for protection, to the sea god for successful trade, to the land gods for fertility and good harvests. With Aryan migrations to the south, a new language, Sanskrit, was introduced and dramatic plays conveyed the stories of the land and messages to and from the gods. Later art forms combined elements of the ancient with contemporary themes.

The performing arts seek to communicate a message. Usually the message is derived from classical texts and the communication is achieved through narration, song, and the intricate movements of gesture and dance.

Kathakali

Possibly the most renowned drama of Kerala, Kathakali may have had its beginnings in ancient performance methods of the 2nd century CE. However, the contemporary form dates from the 17th century.

Kathakali literally means 'story play' and the Kathakali performance is actually the dramatised presentation of a play. Originally there were over 100 plays but now only 30 are performed. They are based on the Hindu epics the *Ramayana* and the *Mahabharata* as well as the *Puranas*. The themes explored are all those canvassed in the great stories – righteousness and evil, frailty and courage, poverty and prosperity, war and peace. The landscapes are also broad – the terrestrial and the cosmic.

The script *attakatha* or poetic text of the Kathakali performance is Manipravalam, a Sanskritised form of Malayalam. While the script is vocalised by singers, the performers actually 'narrate' the drama through precise movements and gestures. Traditionally performances took place in temple grounds and while this is still a common venue, other open-air locales as well as indoor halls are also popular.

Preparation for the performance is lengthy and disciplined. Each performer is reconstructed; his/her own being becomes subjugated to the essence of the character. Paint, a fantastic costume and a highly decorated headpiece aid in the reconstruction. Seeds, placed on the eyelids, redden the whites of the eyes – soft pink for a beautiful woman or kindly character, blood red for ferocious demons. The final part of the preparation is a short meditation.

Performers play the various characters, which can be generally divided into the following:

Pacca – the royal and divine creatures, such as Vishnu or Rama. The make-up consists of green faces (green symbolising heroism and righteousness) with large crown headgear – the *kesabhara kiritam*.

Katti – these are the demons and villains such as Ravana, the evil king who abducted Sita in the *Ramayana*. (Katti refers to the knife-shape on

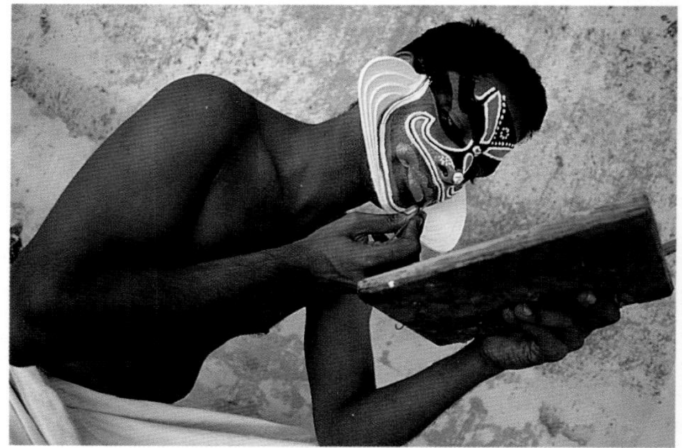

Right: Kathakali performers spend hours perfecting their intricate make-up before the show. Visitors can often come early to see the preparations.

ALL PHOTOGRAPHS BY EDDIE GERALD

BOTH PHOTOGRAPHS BY EDDIE GERALD

Top: *Mukhabhinaya*, or facial gestures, play a crucial role in narrating the Kathakali drama. **Bottom:** Women's roles are often played by men, although increasingly women are becoming performers themselves. **Facing page:** Green facial make-up is reserved for royal and divine characters. Sometimes they are righteous; sometimes, like this one, they are evil.

EDDIE GERALD

BOTH PHOTOGRAPHS BY PAUL BEINSSEN

Left: Teyyam dancers glitter in their elaborate make-up and head-dresses.

their foreheads.) Coming from the same noble grouping as pacca, they are similarly attired. But they are opposite in temperament and character.

Tati – the red, black and white beards (tati meaning beards). The Hindu monkey god, Hanuman, instrumental in assisting Rama in the search for his abducted wife Sita, is a white beard.

Kari – the demoness, including the likes of Shurpanakha, Ravana's sister. This creature with her wide black beard, menacing fangs and huge breasts is all in black. Her male counterpart, Kattalan, is similarly dressed and disposed.

Teppu – represents many different and unique performers. Such characters may represent human beings or may give expression to animals or even weapons.

Minukku – the servant class. These are gentle souls. Usually make-up is of subtle tones and costumes are simple and unadorned.

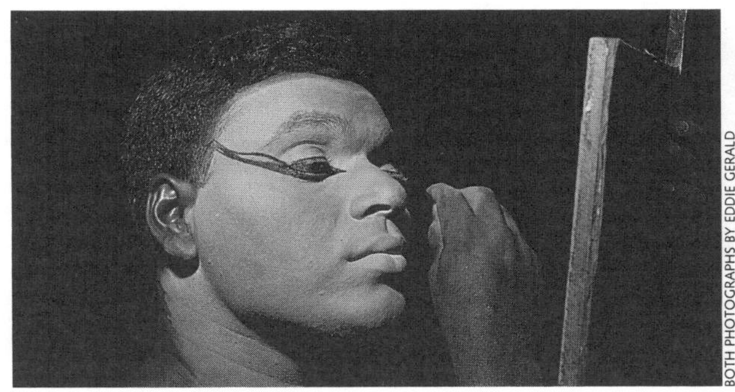

BOTH PHOTOGRAPHS BY EDDIE GERALD

Right: During the lengthy preparations, the Kathakali performer's own being is subjugated to that of the character.

The first sound of the Kathakali is made on the *sudda mandalam*, the long barrel-shaped drum that is struck at both ends to achieve a resonant rhythm. The initial drumming performance may take up to two hours.

The rhythms of the drums and style of the singers suggest the temperament of the characters and create the mood of the drama.

Kathakali is not a static art. Although it is the result of ancient codes, precise training, and disciplined practices it is an art form, or synthesis of art forms, that is always fresh and alive. It is ancient yet, at once, new. And this freshness is the result of the interpretation and improvisation brought to the work by the actors. Through gestures – both facial *(mukhabhinaya)* and hand *(mudra)* – the actor brings the narrative to life. Rather than voice, it is hands and face that tell the story.

The characters with their extravagant costumes and their excessive gestures may appear unreal, yet they portray a reality all too evident in human nature, its frailties as well as its morality.

In recent times, several changes have been made to prevent the decline of Kathakali. Performances are shorter; women and lower castes (once denied participation) now perform and a wider audience has been accessed, nationally and internationally. With its transition to the larger stage, its appeal has widened, but its supporters hope it will retain its traditional base, steeped in culture and aesthetic.

Mohinyattam

Mohinyattam, the Dance of the Enchantress, embodies the traditional feminine aesthetic. Based on *lasya*, the form that gives homage to the god, it is a dance that expresses worship.

The origin of Mohinyattam is unclear. Certainly dancing by women in Kerala dates back maybe to the 3rd century CE. Some suggest it dates from the practice of goddess worship. It was the custom for each village to have a sacred grove, which the villagers believed was the home of their protector – the village mother or goddess. Artists began to depict the goddess in drawings known as *kolams*. In time choreographers developed dance movements from these depictions.

The dance derives its name from the female form, Mohini, portrayed throughout the *Purana* legends. Such legends tell of Vishnu who assumed the female form of Mohini in order to quell the destructive rage of demons. These stories imply that when the universe is under the threat of male power, it is the feminine form that will redeem it by luring it away from destruction.

While on the one hand bewitching and captivating, the qualities expressed in the Mohinyattam are also noble and dignified. It is a dance of the enchantress who creates chaos and devastation for evil doers and pleasure and ecstasy for the righteous. It is a solo performance where the woman stands alone in grace, dignity and pure aesthetic pleasure. The *rasa* (sentiment) evoked by the dance is said to be one of love. The dancer moves with soft, flowing fluidity. She wears a white sari edged in gold. From her neck hangs the serpent figure; jasmine flowers bedeck her hair and from her ankles brass bells tinkle. On her forehead she wears the vermilion *tilaka*, representative of the radiance of the deity.

Mohinyattam became threatened by the popularity of Kathakali.

However, its artistry was rekindled in the early 19th century, during the reign of Maharaja Swati Tirunal. In the 1930s the poet Vallathol employed experts to teach the art form, thereby ensuring its survival.

Dances for Temples Deities

Many of Kerala's dances are rituals for the deities, seeking their powers as custodians of land and people.

Teyyam A temple ritual dance of northern Kerala and southern Karnataka, Teyyam is usually performed in honour of the temple deity to seek protection from disease and other harmful events. Dancers are attired in elaborate paint and costumes as they take on a trance-like presence, which many believe encapsulates aspects of the deity.

Mutiyettu This temple dance depicts the story of Bhagavati, a manifestation of the fierce goddess Kali, who is widely worshipped in Kerala, and her triumph over the destructive demon, Darika. The dance is named after *muti* which refers to the head. This symbolises the decapitated head of the demon as well as the head/crown of the goddess. Once the performer dons the headgear he is said to assume aspects of the goddess.

Patayani This dance, performed mainly in central Keralan temples, honours Bhagavati, but rather than celebrating her victory over the demon Darika, it seeks to deal with her all-consuming rage. Dancers present kolam drawings to an idol of the goddess, in an attempt to distract her from her fury. It is the kolam of her own wrathful image that finally brings about a more cheerful goddess.

Kummattikali Performed in the Palakkad (Palghat) and Thrissur (Trichur) districts, this dance is a localised version of Patayani, and includes songs, dances and kolam drawings – all attempts to appease the goddess.

Right: Traditional dances often involve difficult hand gestures.

PETER DAVIS

Kootiattam

This Sanskrit drama performed in a *kootampalam* (temple theatre) may be some 1800 years old. It is known as Koothu when performed by an individual; as Kootiattam when performed by several artists. Based on the epics and *Puranas*, this form of drama is the precursor of Kathakali.

Krishnanattam Based on the life of Krishna, the Krishnanattam (Dance of Krishna) was patronised by the Zamorin rulers of Kozhikode (Calicut) and became associated with the Guruvayur Temple near Thrissur. In Sanskrit the performance incorporates singing, dance and drama and, along with Kootiattam, it has provided a significant foundation from which the Kathakali drama evolved.

Thullal Seen as a most accessible art form, Thullal (meaning to jump) places emphasis on the physical, but the literary significance of the art form is not insubstantial. Although the form of the Thullal had existed for centuries, it is the poet Kunchan Nambiar, of the 18th century, who is credited with advancing the art form by integrating the sophistication of the classical tradition with the simplicity of folk. Using ancient myths and legends, Nambiar conveyed contemporary scenes with satire and humour. Usually with one performer and two musicians, the Thullal is quick (two hours), engaging and penetrating.

PETER DAVIS

EDDIE GERALD

Top: A new generation learns to dance at Malayala Kalagramam. **Bottom:** The Bharata Natyam, originating in neighbouring Tamil Nadu, is India's oldest form of classical dance.

Puppetry

Pavakathakali In the Palakkad district is the little village of Paruthippully, home to the Andi Pandaram families who came originally from Andhra Pradesh. For centuries they practised the art of Pavakathakali, or glove puppetry, with stories based on the *Mahabharata* and *Ramayana*.

The puppets, at 30cm to 60cm high, are carved in wood with their limbs joined by cloth. They are painted and decorated with peacock feathers, pieces of tin and coral. Pavakathakali was in existence prior to Kathakali, but it is clear that it has been influenced by it. Nowadays the popularity of the art form has waned.

Tolpava Koothu Tolpava Koothu, or Shadow Puppet Play (after *tol* – leather, *pava* – puppet, *koothu* – play), is presented at Kali temples mainly in the Palakkad area. Plays based on the *Ramayana* are depicted by projecting shadows of leather puppets onto a white screen. The performances derive from the legend about Kali's annihilation of a demonic monster during the battle between Rama and Ravana. Her action saved the universe, but she was absent at Rama's victory. She expressed her indignation and each year to appease her disappointment, her devotees perform the shadow puppet play of the *Ramayana*.

The stage, with coconut leaves, flowers and oil lamps, faces the deity. Over 100 puppets, which may be up to 80cm high, are required for a performance. They are made from deer hide, which is considered to have sacred qualities. The operator has small anklet bells on his hand. As he moves the puppet, the bells quiver in accordance with the actions of the puppet. To intensify the action, during scenes of conflict, red liquid is tossed onto the curtain.

Now widely recognised, Tolpava Koothu is performed both nationally and internationally. .

Yakshagana Bombeyata This form of puppetry is based on Yakshagana, a folk art from Karnataka, employing song, elaborate costume and movement to relate classic stories of the *Ramayana* and the *Mahabharata*. Performances involve rod as well as string puppets and can be seen in Kasaragod.

Below: Puppets on display in Kasaragod.

PETER DAVIS

continued from page 31

The 18th century poems of Kunchan Nambiar, expressed through the literary style *Thullal* (a style noted for its satirical tone) inspired a matching musical form. Rare compositions resulted, where the raga and tala developed in unique ways giving voice to the humour of the poems.

One of the most prolific periods in Kerala's musical history occurred during the reign of the maharaja of Travancore, Swathi Thirunal, whose 18 year leadership began in 1829. A fervent supporter of the arts, he was committed to a vibrant musical society. He commissioned the country's most acclaimed musicians to develop musical expertise in Kerala. A composer himself, many of his 500 works demonstrate a rare ability that extended the prevailing musical aesthetic.

The development of Kathakali presented further opportunities for musical composition. See the Performing Arts section for more on Kathakali. Kuttikunja Thankachi (1820-1904) was noted for her Kathakali librettos and Thullal compositions. Her *kirtana* (song of praise) in honour of the goddess Katyayani (another name for Durga), with its challenges for singers to achieve exceptional dexterity, is a classic.

The Contemporary Scene In the new shopping centres of Thiruvananthapuram and in the lobbies of upmarket hotels you're

Kalarippayat

Kalarippayat is an ancient tradition of martial training and discipline. Still taught throughout Kerala, some believe it is the forerunner of all martial arts. Its roots can be traced back to the 12th century CE (common era), when skirmishes among the many feudal principalities in the region were common.

Masters of kalarippayat, called *Gurukkal*, teach their craft inside a special arena called a *kalari*. The kalari is part gymnasium, part school and part temple. Its construction follows traditional principles: its rectangular design is always aligned east-west and Hindu deities are represented in each corner.

Training begins at a very young age for both girls and boys. The regime involves ritual stretching and flexing to achieve concentration and balance. Body massage increases the suppleness of limbs. As the trainee develops, various weapons are introduced including the sword and shield of the medieval warrior.

A traditional system of medical treatment has evolved in partnership with this training. Based on Ayurvedic principles, the treatment is for bone and soft tissue injuries resulting from the practice of kalarippayat.

Kalarippayat can be observed or studied in Thiruvananthapuram and Kozhikode.

JENNY BOWMAN

more likely to hear reggae than raga. The ubiquitous strains of Hindi pop can also be heard throughout the cities and villages. Although Kerala may not be contributing much by the way of local talent to contemporary pop music, it is contributing scenery. Several bands from Delhi have shot their video clips against the tranquillity of the Keralan backwaters.

At festivals the music remains traditional, but with the customary improvisation musicians seem to create a more contemporary sound. You might catch them playing in a temple festival or hotel lobby. The result will no doubt be an exciting blend of the old and the new.

Literature

In a region delineated on linguistic lines, with almost 100% literacy, and where children are initiated into the alphabet at the shrine of the goddess of learning, it comes as no surprise that literature in Kerala is a significant cultural feature. Malayali writers have excelled as playwrights, novelists, poets, translators and critics. Their writing, both fiction and nonfiction, has contributed substantially to discourse and debate on significant issues, including science, health, education, history, politics, social justice and philosophy.

The Origins of Malayalam Script & Language Different opinions exist as to the derivation of the Malayalam script. General belief is that it was based on the Brahmi script, the structure from which most Indian writing developed and the one that the Tamil languages adopted. Similar to the Brahmi script, Vattezhuthu, the first script of Kerala, had been in use for some time prior to the 9th century and continued until the 18th century when the script of the Brahmins, Grandha, became prevalent. Although it originally consisted of over 900 characters, the Malayalam script has been transformed into 90 characters, rendering it compatible with modern-day technologies.

The Malayalam language includes aspects of many other languages, no doubt a consequence of the numerous influences on Kerala over the centuries. Words and expressions from Tamil and Sanskrit, as well as those from the Middle East and Europe, are evident. Writing from Kerala's Muslim community is particularly indicative of this tendency, with literature written in Arabic, Malayalam and sometimes a blend of the two. Topics, too, are diverse, encompassing everything from sacred texts about the Sufis to themes of the erotic.

Early Texts & Translations Sonnets and folk songs comprise the earliest writing in Malayalam, with themes from the epics popular subjects. The *Ramacharitam* of the 12th century, with over 1800 verses, is one of the earliest poems and is considered a classic. Important translations of Sanskrit texts were also undertaken, that of the *Bhagavad Gita* by Madhava Panniker thought to be the first into a colloquial language.

The earliest existing Malayalam work of prose is the *Bhashakautaliyam*. Written in the 12th century it is an elucidation of the *Artha Sastra*, the renowned Hindu text that outlines the moral codes for human existence. Some sources claim the first Malayalam classic as the 15th century *Krishna Geetha*, by Cherusseri. In the 16th century, Thunchath Ramanujan Ezhuthachan, who is considered to be the father of Malayalam literature, translated the major epics, the *Ramayana* and the *Mahabharata,* into Malayalam. Although translations, scholars proclaim that his versions, written in the style of the devotional Bhakti tradition, demonstrate a creativity characteristic of originality. His rendering of the *Ramayana* is still recited in Hindu family homes throughout Kerala.

Anticipating Contemporary Literature When Kottayam Raja composed the *Ramanattam* in the 17th century a new literature form was born. This new poetic text, known as the *Attakatha*, formed the narrative plays of the Kathakali, and as the Kathakali artform developed, so too did the *Attakatha*.

The 18th century witnessed a marked change in the focus of literature from the legendary to the contemporary. Poets such as Kunchan Nambiar negotiated these transformations in the style known as the Thullal. While retaining the ancient Puranic motifs, Kunchan Nambiar used them as a basis for skilful analysis of society and state. His satiric repartee quickly developed a broad following. For many, Kunchan Nambiar's work was instrumental in shaping an independent future literature.

European colonisation also had its impact, with the literature of the newcomers, including dictionaries, *Bibles* and grammatical texts, being translated into Malayalam.

Paremmakal Thoma Kattanar's work *Varthamana Pusthakam* (1786), about his trip to Rome, is celebrated as the first travelogue in an Indian language. The first Malayalam book on the history of Kerala, *Kerala Pazhama,* was written by a German missionary, Dr Herman Gundert, who also wrote several other titles on geography and language. In 1860, Pachu Moothathu also completed a history of Kerala, *Tiruvitamkoor Charitam*, and followed this in 1871 with the first autobiography. In 1887, the first novel in Malayalam, *Kundalatha*, by TM Appu, was published and two years later O Chandu Menon received immense acclaim for *Indulekka*, a novel that depicted the established order of caste and feudalism as unwarranted. He is hailed as the primary force in modern Malayalam literature.

At the turn of the 18th century, Thiruvananthapuram was home to a vibrant and productive community of poets and songwriters. This period ushered in the 'Golden Age of Malayalam Poetry' and its 'big three' poets – Ullur S Parameswara Iyer, Kumaran Asan and Vallathol Narayana Mennon. All three emphasised social justice and in his later years Vallathol became ardently committed to the rekindling of the Kathakali.

Writers also engaged in literary criticism of local, as well as foreign, works. The acclaimed reviewer, Swadesabhimani Ramakrishna Pillai, devised a code of journalistic ethics and his biography of Karl Marx may be the first in an Indian language.

The Literary Landscape Today All through the 20th century the writers of Kerala have continued in the strong tradition of their forebears. The Kottayam Writers' Cooperative, formed in 1945, provided Malayalam writers not only the opportunity for publication, but also respectable royalties. In 1944, P Kesava Dev wrote *From the Gutter*. Inspired by *Les Miserables*, it was hailed as one of Malayalam's favourite stories of recent history. In addition to local novels, works of other Indian fiction writers have been translated for Malayalam readers. Playwrights have transformed the work of novelists to dramas for the stage. In the 1960s, the Malayali poet – Mahakavi G Sankara Kurup received the Gynanpith award (presented for the best Indian literary achievement) for his work *Odakuzhal* (The Flute). In 1984 Kamala Das, Kerala's best-known poet, was nominated for the Nobel prize for literature.

Like the other literary styles, the short story has been employed to explore and elucidate many of Kerala's important social and political issues. The stories by Lalitambika Antatjanam (winner of the 1977 Kerala Sahitya Akademi award for her novel *Agnisakshi*) speak of her strong regard for the dispossessed.

Booker prize winner Arundhati Roy also continued in the custom of her forebears with her work, *The God of Small Things*, which explores the monstrous injustices of the caste system. Her offer to support Dalit writing with royalties from Malayalam translations of her book will no doubt further the long tradition of literature in Kerala.

The writing of Vaikom Muhammad Basheer provides an insight into the Muslim community of Kerala. One of his most recent translated works *Poovan Banana and Other Stories* is a fine selection of his work.

Lalitambika Antatjanam's *Cast Me Out If You Will* gives in-depth insights into the isolation and difficulties once experienced by Namboodri women.

Keralan author Arundhati Roy donated her Booker prize money for *The God of Small Things* to the anti Narmada dam campaign

One of India's best-known writers, RK Narayan, hails from Mysore and many of his stories centre on the fictitious South Indian town of Malgudi. His most well known works include: *Swami & His Friends*, *The Financial Expert*, *The Guide*, *Waiting for the Mahatma* and *Malgudi Days*.

The Revised Kama Sutra by Richard Crasta takes an irreverent look at growing up in Mangalore in the 1960s and 1970s. It's a book that leaves you with a lasting insight into the local life of Mangalore and similar South Indian cities. More importantly it gives a first hand account of the tensions of growing up as an intelligent and well-educated youngster with frustratingly few opportunities.

Architecture

Kerala's architecture has incorporated internal as well as international influences. However, in spite of this fusion, Keralan traditional architecture has distinctive features, including a pagoda-style shape, a predilection for simplicity rather then ostentation and a form that encapsulates the private rather than the public sphere.

The traditional architecture of Kerala follows the principles of *Vastu Shastra* (The Treatise on Architecture). This ancient body of knowledge sought to derive maximum advantage from natural sources to ensure the comfort and wellbeing of the inhabitants of a dwelling. Construction sites were carefully chosen, usually near a river and on solid fertile soil. Buildings had to capture light but protect from heat, create air flow but safeguard from the ravages of monsoons, capture water but shelter from storms.

Modern constructions of steel and concrete do not embody such principles and all too frequently they sacrifice aesthetics for a false notion of function. Invariably they are environmentally inappropriate. One architectural visionary who has resisted the tide to cement is the Englishman Laurie Baker, who made India his home over 40 years ago. His designs incorporate traditional styles and materials as well as the ancient principles. His work can be seen at the Centre for Development Studies, Thiruvananthapuram and St John's Cathedral near Tiruvalla.

Hindu Temples Generally lower than the surrounding vegetation, the temples of Kerala, are not conspicuous – unlike those of neighbouring states with their huge towering *gopurams* (gateways). Possibly the feature that most readily identifies the temples of Kerala is the roof, with its generous slopes and broad sweeping eaves. It tends to emphasise width rather than height thereby giving the impression of small stature and modest nature. Some speculate that the purpose of this style of roof is protection from the elements, but others suggest that the roof resembles a crown and therefore denotes the regal nature of the structure.

Most of Kerala's remaining temples date from the 13th century, but many of the art forms on which they are based date from a much earlier time. While many Keralan temples are Dravidian in style and therefore square or rectangular, others are round, elliptical or semicircular. Round temples replicate the earliest temple constructions in Kerala in the 6th century CE.

Most temples face east, but some face west or south. They are usually located near streams or lakes because of the picturesque and functional value, enabling bathing for devotees. They are usually enclosed by a wall with entrances (or recesses) at the cardinal points. A gopuram graces each entrance.

A wide pathway generally surrounds each temple and nearby is the *namaskara mandapam* (hall of prostration). This is somewhat akin to an entrance area and the place where offerings are made. Beyond this is the *srikovil*, or inner sanctum, guarded at its entrance by ferocious images of *dvarapalas*, protectors of the deity. The srikovil may be of one or more storeys, and its roof may be domed or sloping. Much of its upper section is highly decorated denoting its significance as the *garbhagraha*, the receptacle for the symbol or image of the deity.

Like other temples in India, the Keralan temple often forms a complex comprising one area for worship and one for food storage, cooking and eating. Several other shrines to deities such as Parvati and Ganesh may be included as well as a large hall, the *kootampalam*, used at festival times for the recitation of prayers and sacred stories, such as the *Puranas*.

Religious structures elsewhere in India are often positioned high on mountain tops, and are meant to incite a sense of exaltation. However, the Keralan temple with its horizontal form is meant to emanate a sense of goodness and harmony.

Many of Kerala's temples have undergone extensive renovations, restoring them to their former grace. Some of the more impressive examples of Keralan temple architecture are at Thiruvananthapuram, Ettumanur, Kollam and Guruvayur.

Mosques The first mosque in Kerala was reputedly built at Kodungallur by Malik Ibn Dinar, the follower of Mohammed, who came to Kerala in 643 CE to disseminate the teachings of Islam. Later he built several mosques down the coast from Kasaragod to Kollam.

Unlike mosques elsewhere, the Keralan mosque initially followed the distinctly Keralan style with the wide sloping roof. Early Keralan mosques had no minaret, the tower from which Muslims are called to prayer. However, during the later Mughal period minarets appeared.

Mosques face Mecca and in Kerala this means they must be positioned from 20° to 30° north of west. Mosques are usually expansive structures where people pray facing the *qibla,* the direction of Mecca. This is indicated by the *mihrab*, the elaborate niche within the mosque.

In order to cope with the climatic conditions many Keralan mosques were raised on a high foundation with a large inner hall, a small outer hall and verandas. An outside well provided water for washing. In many mosques the water was channelled from the well to an underground tank within the mosque.

Mosques became centres for education and the architecture adapted accordingly. The verandas were used for instruction leaving the main prayer hall free from noise and distraction. Sometimes a second storey was added where pupils from outlying areas could be accommodated.

Sadly many Keralan mosques have deteriorated or been destroyed. But the Kuttichira Mosque, Kozhikode, provides an excellent example of the traditional Keralan mosque.

Synagogues Kochi, being the area of Jewish settlement, is also the region of synagogues, the most notable being the one in Mattancherry, which was built in 1568. After its partial destruction by the Portuguese in 1662 it was rebuilt in 1664. In 1761 Ezekial Rahabi undertook further extensive construction during which he added a clock tower and laid the floor with impressive blue willow-pattern tiles imported from China. The synagogue is unique in that it has two (instead of one) pulpits – one in the usual position on the lower level and an additional one upstairs. Its entrance is graced by two columns in honour of the Temple of Solomon in Jerusalem.

Churches Unlike most Keralan temples, many churches are positioned on mountain tops. Generally constructed in European style, churches are often rectangular or cruciform, with a long hall for the congregation and the sanctuary comprising the altar from where the priest conducts the ceremonies. The area behind the altar is often elaborately decorated depicting scenes from the crucifixion.

The walls are set with regular windows. Some windows contain coloured glass, which filters natural light and generates an internal atmosphere conducive to prayer.

A recent construction near Tiruvalla in southern Kerala provides a fascinating example of a modern church in traditional style. St John's Cathedral, designed by Laurie Baker, is a circular structure with a huge roof that slopes from a high centre to its low outer walls.

Domestic Architecture Like Hindu temples, domestic architecture was based on the principles of Vastu. The code outlined the requisites for a happy, prosperous home. East-facing was preferred, since it was believed that other directional aspects would result in misfortune such as poverty or misery.

Initially stone, seen as befitting only the gods because of its permanent qualities, was reserved for temples. All other buildings used a less permanent material – mud. From the 16th century, however, building practices changed and palaces and homes began to use other materials.

In principle, the *nalukettu*, or traditional family home of royalty and the wealthy classes, very much resembled the temple. The site of the inner sanctum of the temple was analogous to the space for an inner courtyard. Slightly lower than the base level of the house, it was open to light and fresh air and connected to the outside world by corridors. Surrounding the central courtyard the house had four two-storey blocks.

The layout of the home was functional and able to accommodate large, extended, communal families. Interior shrines catered for the spiritual needs of the family, the surrounding paddy fields (usually owned by the family) supplied their material needs.

Grand halls enabled gatherings for meetings or entertainment. And comfort was not overlooked. Louvre-type wooden slats served as air ducts, directing the flow to moderate temperatures. Through ingenious design, some rooms were fitted with adjustable roofs that captured, not only light, but water as well. A sealed floor beneath secured the water for household use.

The 20th century saw dramatic changes to family life and consequent changes to Keralan architectural style. However examples of the former styles may be seen in Thiruvananthapuram, as well as the former palaces of Cochin (Kochi) and Padmanabhapuram (now in Tamil Nadu). And today the mansions of the wealthy and some five star resorts are harking back to traditional styles.

Sculpture

Sculpture in Kerala has almost always been for religious purposes so most images represent deities or scenes from the major epics.

Stone Of all the Hindu deities, Vishnu has been the most popular subject with stonemasons. The earliest remaining sculptures, however, are not of Vishnu but of Buddhas and guardians. Eighth century dvarapalas, or guardians, can be seen in a cave temple at Kaviyoor and Buddhist sculptures from the 9th century have been found in southern Kerala near Kayamkulam. One such statue, discovered in 1936 near Mavelikkara, is believed to be at least 1000 years old. Local people have erected a shrine around the statue, which is now a place of worship. Another statue of the same period is in the gardens of the Krishnapuram Palace.

Later sculpture of the 12th century digresses from the gods to show dancers and elephants. A good place to see stone sculpture is the Sri Padmanabhaswamy Temple in Thiruvananthapuram (Hindus only).

Wood Keralan artists are renowned for their wooden sculpture. Woodcarvings were an aspect of both temple and home decoration. Images of deities, statues and pillars were ornately carved. In Hindu temples, wooden panels depicted stories of Rama and Krishna. The churches chose scenes from the Old and New testaments. Doors and window frames, ceilings and awnings frequently displayed a fine wooden aesthetic. This work often had a functional purpose, facilitating air flow and light.

The impermanent nature of wood has meant that many of the earlier works have not survived.

Ivory Ivory carving, once a highly valued art form in Kerala, is believed to have been practised as far back as 1000 years. A famous ivory work of Kerala was the throne presented to Queen Victoria in 1851 by the then maharaja of Travancore.

In 1873 a government department for the encouragement of ivory carving was established. Today the ivory trade is outlawed in Kerala. However, you can still see 18th century items at the Napier Museum in Thiruvananthapuram.

Metalwork Traditional cast metalwork in Kerala used *panchaloha,* a combination of five metals – silver, gold, copper, tin and iron. The process involved several stages. A cast of the subject was made from a mixture of beeswax and resin. This was then coated with fine clay on which the image became perfectly delineated. A hole was left in the clay mould. When the clay dried the whole object was heated. The wax-resin solution melted and was emptied from the mould via the hole. Molten metal was then poured into the mould. When this solidified the clay mould was removed exposing the metal image.

Deities, mythical creatures and temple lamps were the favoured subjects for metal artisans. As in other parts of India, the bronze image of the deity became extremely important in Kerala, because of its lasting qualities. When devotees honour their deity, they do so in the knowledge that the idol has been held in veneration by their ancestors for centuries.

A favoured metal of Kerala is bell metal. Consisting of copper (four parts) and tin (one part) it is named after its bell-like sounds. Lamps, bells and deities are created from this metal. Thrissur (Trichur) is one of the best places to view and purchase this art and in Thiruvananthapuram at the art gallery and museum you can see 14th century images of the Hindu goddess and god, Parvati and Shiva.

Cement Contemporary sculptor Canai Kunuram, has departed from the traditions developing controversial works and placing them in new landscapes. His work can be seen at the Veli Tourist Park in Thiruvananthapuram. (See the Veli Tourist Park section in the Southern Kerala chapter.)

Painting

Until recent times the visual arts of Kerala have been closely associated with spiritual themes, mainly in the Hindu and Christian communities.

Hindu Keralan Hindu paintings depict deities and chivalrous characters from the Kathakali in a style distinct from other classical Indian paintings, where deities are represented within a background illustrative of their mythical narratives. Like the Kathakali images they often portray, Keralan paintings suggest potency and vitality, the totality of their presence encourages the devotee to focus all attention on the deity, without the potential for distraction that a background might provide.

When and where Keralan painting began is unknown. Because of the priestly belief that expressions of the soul belong to the gods, paintings were not a feature of secular life. Rather, they were placed in temples to honour and please the gods. Given the simplicity of Keralan temples, painting was not a major feature there either. The only early paintings to endure are those created on rock, but today they are scarcely recognisable.

The murals in the Mattancherry Palace in Kochi are believed to date from the late 17th to 19th centuries, with those depicting Krishna and the epic of the *Ramayana* being the earliest. The former palace of Travancore at Padmanabhapuram (now in Tamil Nadu) contains over 40 murals depicting scenes from the epics.

In the 19th century the maharaja of Travancore, Swathi Thirunal (1829-47), concerned at the decline in the visual arts, commissioned several painters from Tamil Nadu to revive an artistic culture. This had a profound impact on his successor, Ravi Raja Varma (1848-1906), whose Hindu images became the subject of mass appeal. While this created controversy, because some considered the work popularised the sacred images, the artist provided an impetus for the development of art in Kerala. In particular, members of his own family produced works of academic and aesthetic significance.

Christian Church walls display many examples of Christian art. Images of Christ, the Madonna, and the life of Christ (as portrayed in the Stations of the Cross) are characteristic of most churches. Some of the rituals around the images replicate those of Hinduism. Some images are seen only once a year – when they are taken in procession for the feast honouring the saint.

Contemporary Art In the last decade, concern about the situation of art, its denigration under colonial powers and its importance as a force in society, has resulted in a contemporary scene. Lectures, seminars and exhibitions are increasingly popular, especially in the Kochi area. Although much of the work is derivative of traditional styles, the use of photography and multimedia forms is leading to some radical departures.

Cinema

The makers of Malayalam cinema are proud of the depth and strong narrative in their films. Unlike their Tamil neighbours, who have been governed by film idols strutting awkwardly across the political stage, Malayalis are not easily seduced by the cult of the screen. It is often said that no Malayali actor would dare enter politics because a highly literate people cannot easily be deceived.

Shallow melodrama is certainly present in Malayalam cinema (you might witness it in the making on Kovalam Beach – a popular shooting location) but there is also a focus on quality drama.

Malayalam cinema began with silent movies back in 1928. The industry has experienced peaks and troughs in the decades since with many film buffs claiming that quality was highest in the late 1970s. In 1981, the film *Elippathayam* (Rat Trap), which portrayed an authoritarian man unable to adjust to societal change, struck a national and international chord. Its director, Gopalakrishnan, received the British Film Institute award for the 'maker of the most original and imaginative film'.

Malayalam cinema is not averse to tackling political and social issues. In 1989 Shaji Karun scooped international awards with his first feature *Pivari* (The Birth), based on a famous murder case during the Emergency of the 1970s. The film explored the search of an old man for his lost son. More recently *Mangamaa* (1997), directed by TV Chandran, tells the story of Kerala under President's Rule in 1960 and later during the political witch-hunting of the Emergency in 1976.

In an attempt to reclaim quality of product, there has been a deliberate reduction in the output of Malayalam movies from an astonishing 300 per year in the late 1980s to a more manageable average of 75 per year.

Through a program of financial incentives the Kerala State Film Development Corporation is working to secure a greater proportion of production in the state of Kerala. Some of the finance comes from the lucrative export market of Malayalam movies to the expat communities in the Middle East.

According to one veteran director, Malayalam cinema is poised on the brink of a new wave. 'The traditional formulas will always be there. But there is a lot of experimentation happening. Our budgets are a fraction of what you'll find in Hindi or Tamil cinema but our creative people are more willing to go out on a limb to tell a good story'.

SOCIETY & CONDUCT

Life Transitions

While modern life may have impacted on many traditional practices, most Malayalis observe the significant stages of life with long-honoured customs.

Birth The arrival of a child in Kerala is an occasion for much celebration. About 28 days after the birth of a Hindu child the *namakaranam* or naming ceremony is celebrated. After the lighting of a lamp, the child is positioned on the father's lap. He whispers the child's name into the right ear.

At six months the child is taken to the temple for the *chorunu* ceremony. Before a statue of Ganesh, the child receives solid food for the first time. Each family member takes turn in feeding rice and curry to the child. Many parents visit the Sri Krishna Temple at Guruvayur for this ceremony, since the aspect of Krishna here is in the form of a small child enjoying the delights of infancy, especially sweet foods.

The next important ceremony occurs between the child's third and fifth birthdays. Usually occurring at the temple of Sarasvati, the goddess of speech and learning, the child is inducted into the letters with the ceremony of *vidyarambham*. Seated before the Ganesh statue, the child's finger is placed in rice and, after a written salutation to the deity, the child's finger is carefully guided through the rice as it traces out each letter of the alphabet. A popular place for such ceremonies is Tirur (in northern Malappuram district) the birthplace of Tunchat Ezhuthachan, the acclaimed 'Father of Malayalam'.

Another important ceremony is that of head shaving, and some parents travel to the famous Vishnu temple in Tirupathi for this ritual. In a gesture of submission to the deity, the child's head is shaved after which the family make *puja* (an act of worship) to the deity.

Muslim families celebrate the birth of a child with the call to prayer, which is repeated gently into the baby's ear. The arrival of puberty is usually a cause for celebration. A girl may have a ceremonial bath while her guests enjoy a banquet. For most boys there are celebrations with gifts.

Christians celebrate the birth of a child with the christening or baptism. Reminiscent of the bathing of John the Baptist, blessed water, symbolic of purification, is poured over the forehead of the child. The ritual has two purposes, to cleanse the child symbolically so it may be included in the church community and to give the child a name, usually identified with Christianity, such as the name of a Christian saint. In Kerala such names might include Miriam or Chacko (Jacob). Some Christians whisper the child's name and the name of Jesus into the child's ear. Sometimes a sacred thread, maybe with a relic attached, is placed around the child's neck. Ceremonies common to the other faiths are also performed, including initiation to solid food and writing.

Traditionally, the new mother had 90 days rest after a birth during which she received considerable support from relatives and was treated with herbal baths and massage.

Marriage Marriage is important socially, emotionally and economically. Parents often go to great lengths to procure a suitable partner for a son or daughter. Desirable attributes in the potential partner include a good job, a good position in society, upstanding character and reasonable looks. Discreet inquiries are made within the community and sometimes the family deity is consulted.

Marriage has travelled through a long and varied evolutionary path in Kerala. Each section of society has its own rituals and practices but there are two practices common to all – *tali*-tying and celebration. Tali-tying is an old custom that, although altered over time, involves the tying of a thread by the groom around the neck of the bride. In Christian weddings the thread contains a cross. In the Adivasi communities it is often adorned with beads.

For the Hindu marriage *jatakam koda*, the exchange of horoscopes, takes place to determine the compatibility of the couple. Astrologers ordain the auspicious time for the marriage. Most marriages take place in a temple or the *kalyanamandapam*, marriage hall. Of all the Hindu groups, it is probably the Brahmins who have the most intricate ceremonies, involving not only the tali-tying but also an exchange of gifts and ritualistic circling of fire by the bride and groom. Other Hindu ceremonies are usually of a less formal nature. The bridegroom is presented with *ashtamangalyam*, eight items of good fortune that include rice, coconut flowers, a lamp, and cloth – reminiscent of the days when men indicated their desire for marriage by placing cloth on a woman.

The Muslim marriage begins with the *nikar,* a ceremony involving the men of the family. With hands joined the father-of-the-bride and the groom listen to the reading of the marriage speech and the contract. When the groom agrees, the amount that he will pay is publicly announced and agreed to by both men. The wedding feast follows, during which the groom is surrounded by guests who celebrate by singing. The groom and his sister tie the tali around the bride's neck.

Christian marriages are performed in a church where the priest outlines the importance of the marital relationship, particularly in respect to children. Relatives and friends witness the bride and groom pronouncing their marital vows, after which the priest proclaims that the marriage may never be terminated, except through death. The priest and guests pray for the couple's future and often a mass is celebrated.

The dowry system was abolished in 1961, but it persists in some quarters creating financial pressures on the bride's family.

Divorce & Remarriage Although divorce is more common today, it is still strongly resisted within the Christian and Hindu communities, where religious authorities and families will actively work to help the parties to stay together. Hindus in particular consider divorce acceptable only in cases where there is no other option – where one of the partners is insane, has an infectious disease or if the wife is infertile. Although the constitution allows for divorcees (and widows) to remarry, few women can avail themselves of this option because of the stigma attached to divorce and the resources required to amass another dowry. In some cases a divorced woman's own family will reject her, and there is no social security net to provide for her. On the whole, however, a woman can expect family support, especially if she is widowed. To neglect such support attracts strong social disapproval.

The departure of so many people to the Middle East (albeit temporarily) has created new pressures sometimes resulting in the breakdown of marriage, family and social life.

Death As with other life transitions in Kerala, death is commemorated by each group with its own particular rituals.

For Hindus, death is a time of transition and detachment from physical and earthly realms. The rituals surrounding death are based on this belief and may last 15 days. Cremation, the chosen method for disposal of the body, is founded on the premise that burning the body is the quickest way to release the spirit from its physical state and from any remaining links to its life on earth. On death the body is washed and anointed with sandal paste and blessed ashes. It is then dressed and placed on a base of leaves. The body of a saint is placed in a meditation position. With the initial preparations completed the body is taken to the cremation ground. The eldest son lights the pyre, and circumambulates it three times. On the fifth day after cremation, *sanchayanam* takes place, where relatives return to collect any remains from the pyre. These are placed in a pot and positioned in the relatives' garden. Here people come to pay their respects to the dead person. Following further rituals the remains may be buried in the garden. But they will not stay there. The ashes of every Hindu will be eventually released to the waters of a sacred river.

At the end of each Keralan year (July/August), the ritual for *moksha* (liberation from rebirth) is performed for the deceased. This ritual, particularly common in south Kerala, is especially important at the Tiruvallum Temple near Thiruvananthapuram.

For Christians the time before death is a time for reconciliation with relatives and friends as well as their God. With the person facing east, the priest anoints each of the senses with oil. Prayers are recited giving thanks and requesting forgiveness for any transgressions of the senses. After death the body is laid in a coffin and taken in procession to the church. At the burial service prayers are offered giving thanks for the person's life and requesting a contented life after death. The body is then buried and the mourners return with the priest to the home where vegetarian food is eaten.

On the death of a Muslim the body is dressed in fresh white clothes and is sprinkled with rose-water. The *mullah* (religious leader or teacher) visits the home to recite the *Qur'an* (Koran). The body is then taken to the mosque where relatives and friends file past to offer prayers and pay their last respects. As the burial occurs people chant verses from the *Qur'an*. The body is placed facing Mecca and following the burial the mullahs usually continue to recite the *Qur'an* at the grave and within the mosque. In the days following the funeral it is customary for friends and relatives to donate to charity.

Caste System

Caste systems, even social stratification in general, were relatively unknown in ancient Kerala. However, with the arrival of the Aryans and particularly the Brahmin tenets, a rigid caste system developed. Society became divided into Savarnas, the upper castes and Avarnas, the lower castes. And within these two categories numerous other classifications (some sources quote as many as 650) existed. This system held Brahmins, the Namboodris, as superior, with the ruling Kulasekharas and the warrior Nairs in close station to the Brahmins. Labourers and artisans were assigned to several lower-caste ranks including the Kammala artisans, the Mukkuvan fisherfolk and the Ezhava *toddy* tappers. But the system was far more complex than simple ranking. Within the castes, subcastes existed and the oppression metered out down the ranks was often practised within the ranks. The system therefore produced grave inequities causing profound hardship, especially for those in the lower castes.

The legal system that was executed by the Brahmins was prejudicial and unjust. It accorded privilege and immunity to the upper castes while imposing harsh punishment on the lower castes even for minor misdemeanours. Customs pertaining to dress, transportation, house construction and even the use of domestic utensils were all ordained and enforced according to caste law. It was not only the legal system that the high castes controlled. Their ownership of the land gave them economic control. While the Avarnas cultivated the land, the landowners prospered from its produce. And the high castes had the 'rights' over spirituality – Avarnas were forbidden to enter and worship in temples.

The caste system, although predominantly a Hindu mandate, affected non-Hindus, who were generally ranked according to profession or wealth. So obsessive was the system that precise distances specified how far lower-caste people should remain from Savarnas. Distances ranged from 7.5m for Kammalas (artisans) to 22m for those farther down the hierarchy. Should the prescribed distance be encroached upon, the higher-caste person would be contaminated and could only reclaim their status by purification through bathing. To forgo this purging process could result in exile or slavery. To preclude such a fate, Savarnas issued loud orders as they walked the streets, for all Avarnas to observe the designated distances. Such commands were usually heeded – failure to do so could result in death for the recalcitrant.

Many in the lower castes, accustomed to their station, apparently accepted the hardship with little or no resistance. However,

Marumakkathayam – Kerala's Matrilineal System

Marumakkathayam is Kerala's traditional matrilineal system. During its time, this system resulted in large extended families being organised through the female line. Property and inheritance were attained through relationship to the mother, not the father as in most other societies.

The origin of the Marumakkathayam is unknown and is very much the subject of debate. It may have resulted from the requirement for Nair men (the warriors of the society) to be away from home at battle. Another theory speculates that the Marumakkathayam served the practices of polyandry and polygamy. Namboodri Brahmins, in attempting to consolidate their power, allowed only their eldest sons to marry Namboodri women. Their remaining sons developed relationships with Nair women and their children remained with the mothers and were raised as Nairs.

In this social environment, paternity was often difficult to establish. Consequently, traditions vested in male ancestry became inappropriate. Family structure, ownership of property and inheritance were transferred from the male to the female line. Whatever the origin of the system, it existed for at least 500 years before its abolition through several legislative procedures from the 1930s to 1970s.

The units of the Marumakkathayam were the large extended families known as Tarawad, where women lived together with their children, their sisters and brothers. All members of the family had equal shares to and equal rights in the property of the household. The affairs of the household were managed by the *karanavar,* usually a brother of one of the older women.

Families sometimes extended to 80 members. They lived in a large house *(nalukettu)* with verandas and courtyards and shared kitchen and dining facilities. The well provided drinking water, a granary supplied rice and the garden produced fruits, vegetables and herbs. Many houses contained a shrine or temple for worship. Outside cows, those treasured creatures and suppliers of milk, ghee and cheese, roamed the wood stacks that fuelled the stoves. The households were independent and self-sufficient units, providing for the cultural, spiritual and material needs of their members. In addition to the Nairs, many other castes lived in the Marumakkathayam system.

Several factors combined to end the Marumakkathayam. Religious opposition from Christian and Hindu groups outside Kerala were critical of what they considered to be immoral practices. With fewer battles, Nair men stayed at home and began to contest the established order. Conflict within families arose over rights to property and inheritance, as well as over opportunities for education and training. Young people left home to engage in employment and political activity or to marry and set up their own homes. From 1933 several parliamentary acts altered the practices of polyandry and polygamy and the procedures of inheritance. In 1956 the Hindu Succession Act instituted monogamy as the practice for all Hindus and gave equal rights to inheritance for men and women. Even so, many Christian women were denied rights until Mary Roy (mother of the celebrated novelist Arundhati Roy) succeeded in her 1984 case for Christian women to have property rights. With the Joint Hindu Family System (Abolition) Act, the matrilineal system in Kerala was abolished in 1976.

Because of its matrilineal system, Kerala was sometimes referred to as Penn Makayalam, or the Malaya of Women. Although not granting equality to women, Keralan women attained an influence beyond that of their other Indian sisters. Many believe the communal nature of the Marumakkathayam system produced a societal awareness and cooperativeness that translated into political action, support for the independence movement, as well as an impetus for beneficial social conditions such as education, literacy and an adequate health system.

for some the anguish was too much. To escape their wretched fate they converted to Islam or Christianity.

It was not only the injustices of the caste system, evil as they were, which caused social distress and misery. The excessive complexity of the system, with its numerous castes and subcastes, gave rise to myriad restrictions on almost all behaviours. Marriages across caste, and even across subcastes, were forbidden. Consuming food could only be done in the company of one's caste. Such severe obstacles to social relationships resulted in segregation and placed societal harmony and integration in grave jeopardy.

By the mid-19th century many people from the lower as well as the upper castes formed organisations to work towards ending the caste system. Schools were opened to lower-caste children. Government positions were earmarked for their parents. Political representation was secured for all sectors of society. But for many it was recognition by the religious authorities that actually gave substance to the endeavours to end the caste system. From 1936 to 1947 the princely states of Kerala declared temples open to all Hindus. This action had profound consequences symbolically as well as in reality and it served to a large extent to heal the huge rifts that had developed over centuries. As Mahatma Gandhi upheld, it was 'a miracle of modern times'.

Ideas and customs, inculcated over centuries, die hard and remnants of the caste system persist in pockets of Keralan society today, but such behaviour is unusual and not condoned. Given the ingrained nature of the caste system, it is remarkable that a society can change so dramatically in such a relatively short time.

Women in Society

The popular view holds that women in South India, especially in Kerala, have traditionally enjoyed rather more freedom than their northern sisters. Kerala is unique in many ways: it is the most literate state in India; it's the only state where women outnumber men; and it is also famous for its tradition of matrilineal kinship. Women and men have similar educational opportunities and women are widely represented within the labour market. The matrilineal system is frequently cited as the basis of Kerala's more equitable society. But even a cursory look at the position of women in Keralan society suggests that the situation is a complex one. While social systems accord women a certain justice and equity, various attitudes mitigate against women. They may be segregated, excluded or condemned as contaminants.

One of the most obvious prejudicial practices is that meted out at the popular Sabarimala Temple (see the boxed text 'The Tale of Two Temples' in the Western Ghats chapter). A reading of statements supporting women's prohibition would curdle anyone's blood.

In mixed company, Malayali women defer to men. Rarely do they express an opinion. Rarely do they include themselves in the social circle and rarely are they included.

At night women remain in their homes. Streets, cinemas, beaches and restaurants, and now even the mushrooming Internet cafes, are devoid of women. The night is the province of men.

Many women claim that by observing the social attitudes that require segregation, prohibition and closeted evenings, they actually gain respect. But such assertions are dubious. Surely association, discussion and debate, concern for another's viewpoint and delight in the freedom of sisters, wives, mothers and grandmothers, is a worthy basis for respect.

The segregation assertion is dubious for other reasons. In recent years there has been a significant increase in reported rapes – what respect is accorded here? Kerala has the highest suicide rate in India and many of the victims are young women ashamed and unable to raise their marriage dowry.

In temples male dancers emulate women as they beseech a wrathful goddess to cast out all evil and harm. Will the goddess, in all her wrath, desert her terrestrial sisters forever?

Dos & Don'ts

On the whole common sense is your best guide to sensitive and courteous behaviour. If you approach encounters with goodwill, any mistake you may make will generally be overlooked. Understanding something of the local etiquette, however, always helps.

Religious Etiquette Take particular care when attending a religious place (temple,

Hindu Temples & Non-Hindu Visitors

Unlike some other states, the temples of Kerala have seen few non-Hindu visitors. Being centres for worship and prayer they retain a high degree of peace and serenity. Some temples forbid admittance to non-Hindus. However if you're a non-Hindu with a genuine interest in Hinduism, you may find that you are granted entry to many temples. The following guidelines will help if you're unfamiliar with temple customs, and ensure that your presence does not disturb devotees.

- Always remain quiet within a temple – refrain from talking and walk slowly and respectfully in a clockwise direction.
- Always heed restrictions on photography – sometimes it's acceptable to photograph within the first wall. However photographing images of deities is not acceptable.
- Wear appropriate dress – different temples have different requirements. Many require that women wear a sari (not a *salwar kameez*, or traditional loose shirt and trousers). Appropriate western dress (loose fitting clothes from neck to ankle, with sleeves to elbow) is also acceptable. Men may be asked to remove their shirts and/or wear a *dhoti* (sarong). These can often be hired near the temple. And in all sacred places shoes must be removed. You'll see the shoe deposit place just before the entrance.
- Most temples have a similar layout – a walled complex containing several shrines to various deities. The shrine of the main deity, the sanctum, is in the centre of the complex and is also usually surrounded by a wall. Paths lead from one shrine to the next. Once inside the entrance you will see a tall flag post. Usually you follow the path to the left and walk in a clockwise direction, always keeping the sanctum to your right. This may be reversed in some Shiva temples.
- Keep to the above principal as you approach and pass each shrine. It's best to remain on the paths – refrain from taking short cuts.
- You will rarely be approached to make a contribution, but donation boxes are there should you wish to do so.
- Some temples have special procedures for *pujas* (offerings or blessings) and as a visitor you may be able to participate. You buy a ticket (either within or outside the temple) and present this to the priest at the shrine. Different procedures apply to different pujas, but if you are unsure, the temple staff will advise as to the appropriate behaviour.
- If you are permitted into the inner sanctum, you will no doubt see the idol of the deity and possibly a puja will be performed. When this is complete, it's usual to move away slowly, while still facing the idol of the deity for a few steps at least. If not permitted into the sanctum, you may still get a glimpse of it (and even sometimes the idol) through the windows on either of the four walls.
- Some temples are now under the jurisdiction of the Archaeological Department and may appear to have ceased their former function. However they often retain their significance to the local people and should be accorded respect similar to that shown in functioning temples. Remove shoes and approach such places tentatively, especially if you see shrines with lighted lamps.

shrine, church, mosque) or event. Dress and behave appropriately; don't wear shorts or sleeveless tops (this applies to men and women) and don't smoke or display affection. Remove your shoes before entering a holy place and never touch a carving or statue of a deity. In some places such as mosques and synagogues, if you're a man, you will be required to cover your head.

For religious reasons, do not touch local people on the head and similarly never direct the soles of your feet at a person, religious shrine, or image of a deity, as this may cause offence. Never touch another person with your feet. (For more information on behaviour in holy places see the boxed text 'Hindu Temples & Non-Hindu Visitors'.)

Eating & Visiting Don't touch food or cooking utensils that local people will use. You should use your right hand for all social interactions, whether passing money, food or any other item. Eat with your right hand only.

If you are invited to dine with a family, take off your shoes before entering the home and wash your hands before taking your meal. The hearth is the sacred centre of the home, so never approach it unless you have been invited to do so.

Never enter the kitchen without an invitation and never enter the area where drinking water is stored unless you have removed your shoes. Do not touch terracotta vessels in which water is kept. At a meal, unless invited, don't help yourself; wait until you are served.

Dress It's a good idea to wear clothes that blend in with local standards. Loose fitting shirts with sleeves and long skirts or trousers are best. Not only do they avoid offence, but they're most appropriate for the climate. If you're a foreigner, it's best not to get into local gear unless you know exactly what you're doing. Some foreign women purchase light cotton 'skirts', which are actually sari petticoats. Wearing them in the street is similar to going out in your underwear. Likewise some foreigners wear sarongs, which are actually the dress for particular events, such as festivals or pilgrimages. Unless you're part of the event, it's inappropriate to don the dress.

Foreigners who 'try to emulate the masses' by wearing dirty, torn clothes do not exactly earn much local respect.

Photographic Etiquette Kerala is often regarded as a photographer's paradise. Every step reveals a new picture. However, you should be sensitive about taking photos of people and temples. For more information see the Photography & Video section in the Facts for the Visitor chapter.

Swimming & Bathing Nudity is completely unacceptable and a swimsuit must be worn even when bathing in a remote location. In public, at the seaside, or under waterfalls, Indian women generally take a dip fully clothed.

Treatment of Animals

While religious teaching and tradition gives animals a privileged position of protection in Kerala, you may encounter instances of cruelty to animals during your visit.

The major welfare issue in Kerala relates to elephants and the World Society for the Protection of Animals (WSPA) has expressed concern in regard to their exploitation. They claim many animals have welts from constant shackling and some have sores where sharp goads are placed to control them. The large annual elephant festival, which many believed was cruel to elephants, no longer occurs – some people say due to international pressure.

For further information on animal welfare issues contact WSPA (☎ 020-7793 0540, fax 7793 0208, email wspa@wspa.org.uk Internet www.way.net/wspa), 2 Langley Lane, London SW8 1TJ, UK.

RELIGION

All the major religions have existed in Kerala, each one almost since its inception. For the most part Kerala and its people welcomed newcomers and their beliefs, so each religion found acceptance and, if necessary, refuge.

In Kerala today 60% of the population is Hindu, 20% is Muslim and the remaining 20% is Christian. While people of differing faiths live throughout the state the Muslim population is generally located in the north, with Christians more centrally situated.

Local customs and Hinduism have often influenced each of the other religions, and it's not uncommon to see people of different faiths worshipping together, especially at the major festivals or feast days.

Local and tribal deities have been absorbed into Hinduism over the millennia, although some local deities retain a strong individual presence at village level. For further reading on religion, see the Books section of the Facts for the Visitor chapter.

Hinduism

Hinduism, the belief system of more than half the population of Kerala, is one of the oldest extant religions. Hinduism in Kerala has evolved from the combined religious practices of the Dravidians and the Aryan Brahmins.

Hinduism is based on the Vedic scriptures, which were documented in approximately 1000 BCE. It also has a number of holy books, the most important being the four *Vedas* (divine knowledge), which are the foundation of Hindu philosophy. The *Upanishads* are contained within the *Vedas* and delve into the metaphysical nature of the universe and soul. The *Mahabharata* (Great Story of the Bharatas) is an epic poem of good and evil, which describes the battles between members of the Bharata dynasty – the Kauravas and Pandavas. The other famous Hindu epic, the *Ramayana*, is the story of Rama and Sita and their battle with the demon king Ravana, who abducted Sita. Rama is assisted by Hanuman, the monkey god. Since much of the *Ramayana* occurred in southern India, it has particular relevance for Kerala.

Hinduism postulates that we will all experience a series of rebirths or reincarnations that eventually lead to *moksha*, the spiritual salvation that frees us from the cycle of rebirths. With each rebirth we can move closer to or farther from moksha; the deciding factor is our *karma*, which is literally a law of cause and effect. Bad actions during our lives result in bad karma, which ends in a lower reincarnation. Conversely, if our actions have been righteous, we will reincarnate on a higher level and be a step closer to eventual freedom from rebirth.

Hinduism has a vast pantheon of deities – according to the scriptures there are 330 million gods, goddesses and demons. All these different deities are manifestations of Brahman or the godhead. Brahman is seen as the absolute – creation in stasis, yet to unfold and materialise. The force that gives impetus to the unfolding is known as Shakti. Brahman has three main physical representations, which comprise the Hindu triad – Brahma the creator, Vishnu the preserver and Shiva the destroyer. Shakti is represented by goddess power in the forms of Sarasvati, Lakshmi and Parvati, who are associated with the male deities as wives or consorts.

Bhakti The teachings of the Bhakti movement, which became popular in Kerala in the 8th century, placed emphasis on devotion rather than on a particular deity. This had two strong repercussions – it consolidated Hinduism as the predominant religion; and it tended to reconcile differences between Vaishnavites (followers of Vishnu) and Shaivites (followers of Shiva), so that today in Kerala (unlike other areas) Vishnu and Shiva are both worshipped with no apparent preference. Sometimes both deities are accommodated within the same temple.

In Kerala some of the favoured deities are Vishnu, Shiva, Krishna, Bhagavati, Sarasvati, Parvati and Ayyappan.

Vishnu Vishnu, the preserver or sustainer, protects and supports all that is good in the world. He is often depicted reclining on a couch constructed from the coils of a serpent whose many heads cradle his own head. His symbols include the conch shell, symbolising clarity and purity and the discus, symbolising the wheel of time.

Vishnu's vehicle is the half-man half-eagle known as the Garuda. Vishnu is known by at least 1000 names and he has had nine incarnations including Matsya (the fish), Rama, Krishna and Gautama Buddha. It is said that he will come again.

In Kerala, it is Vishnu in his form as Sri Padmanabha that is most often revered. Padmanabha (*padma* – lotus, *nabha* – navel) refers to Vishnu as the one with the lotus emanating from his navel. The lotus is understood to be the source of all creation; in the form of Padmanabha, therefore, Vishnu gives birth to creation. The serpent on which he reclines represents infinity. And the serpent's five heads represent the five elements – earth, water, air, fire and ether.

The Hindus of Kerala believe that this powerful master of creation, cushioned by infinity, has continually blessed and protected their land and its inhabitants.

Shiva Shiva, the destroyer, is the agent of death and destruction, without which growth and rebirth could not take place. He is represented with either one or five faces, and four arms that may hold fire (symbolising destruction) and a drum (the symbol of creative energy). Sometimes he gestures with reassurance, indicative that as he destroys, so too he protects. Shiva's creative role is phallically symbolised by the lingam, representative of male energy. He is seen as the faithful husband to his wife Parvati. One of Shiva's many incarnations is as Nataraja, the cosmic dancer, whose graceful movements transformed the cosmos and created the world. Shiva's vehicle is the bull known as Nandi.

Krishna Krishna, one of Vishnu's incarnations, is a popular deity in Kerala, where large temples are dedicated to him. He is well known for his mischievous nature, his peasant background and his legendary exploits with the *gopis* (milkmaids). Krishna is often blue and plays a flute.

In the *Mahabharata* it is Krishna who utters the *Bhagavad Gita*, the celestial poem, acclaimed for its literary beauty as well as its profound philosophical propositions. The author is unknown, but for Hindus, the words of the *Bhagavad Gita* in their universality and their invocation to devotion and duty are the words of the divine. And the speaker, Krishna, is seen in that light.

Krishna is often revered as an infant – a reminder of the significance of the divine, expressed through the child.

Bhagavati Also known as Bhadrakali, Bhagavati is the manifestation of Kali, the fierce and powerful goddess. The importance of the goddess Bhagavati in Kerala cannot be underestimated. Her shrine graces almost every town and village. Bhagavati means fortunate and it's believed that fortune is what the goddess bestows on her followers.

As the powerful goddess of war, she is the patron of kalarippayat, Kerala's martial arts (see the boxed text kalarippayat, earlier in this chapter). She is ferocious and destructive, obliterating all signs of evil and harm. People turn to her to end their distress and pain, to cure their ills and to protect them from future tragedy. When the dancers in the temples accomplish their frenzied and crazed state, it is the spirit of Bhagavati they are invoking.

As the powerful destroyer of ill, she is the bestower of good – protection sustenance and life. And as such she is the embodiment of the divine mother.

Sarasvati The goddess of learning, Sarasvati represents wisdom and knowledge. Being associated with Brahma, the creator, she encompasses the intelligence of all creation. She is depicted with the symbols of creation and knowledge – the lotus, swan, *veena* (a stringed instrument), beads and book. While the book signifies the importance of learning, the veena indicates that such learning cannot be divorced from emotion. The beads, raised in her right hand, remind her devotees of the significance of spiritual learning.

Parvati Known also as the universal or divine mother, Devi has many forms, but usually under the name of Parvati, she is viewed as the compassionate one. With her husband, Shiva, she has two sons, Ganesh and Subramanya. She is seen as the perfect wife and mother and in return receives Shiva's constant devotion and loyalty.

Ganesh The elephant-headed god is one of the most popular deities throughout Hinduism. Since he is understood to be the god of obstacles, no endeavour is begun without his blessings. He is the first deity approached at the temple, the one to whom offerings are made before marriage, business ventures and journeys. His elephant-human form embodies a myriad of profound concepts. At the same time it encompasses a whimsical nature that accords him possibly the greatest affection of any of the Hindu deities.

Subramanya The second son of Parvati and Shiva, Subramanya is known as the god of war, and is also referred to as Murugan and Kartikkaya. His weapon is the *vel*, spear and his vehicle is the peacock. He is young and virile, and has six heads. Five are symbolic of the senses and the sixth, the mind, disciplines the senses. So with this achievement the young, virile man becomes a potent, superior force.

Ayyappan Once a village deity, Ayyappan has risen in importance and is now popular in Kerala as well as throughout India, with millions of people visiting his shrine in Sabarimala. Legend relates that he was born of the union of Shiva and Vishnu, when Vishnu had adopted his female form, known as Mohini. Ayyappan was found abandoned by the Pandyan king, Rajasekhara, who named him Manikanda and raised him as his own. Later the queen gave birth to a boy and both children grew up in the palace as brothers. The inevitable dispute arose about which son should assume the throne. But it became evident to all that Manikanda was an avatar – a reincarnation of a deity. (See also the boxed text 'The Tale of Two Temples' in the Southern Kerala chapter.)

Nagaraja Nagaraja is the serpent deity. Although considered a minor deity in Kerala, Nagaraja is significant in that he denotes the ancient practice of serpent worship in Kerala. One of the most famous Naga temples is at Mannarsala – see that section in the Southern Kerala chapter.

Islam

The long-established connections between Kerala and the Middle East predestined Kerala for the coming of Islam. Just 30 years after the religion's founder, the Prophet Mohammed, documented his revelations from Allah (God) one of his followers Malik Ibn Dinar, in 643 CE, brought the new belief to Kerala.

The revelations received by Mohammed are contained in the holy book of Islam, the *Qur'an*, which emphasises the conviction that there is one God who is all-powerful, all-knowing and compassionate. To be Muslim (or of Islam) is to submit to the will of God as portrayed in the *Qur'an*. Muslim teachings correspond closely with the *Old Testament* of the *Bible*, and Moses and Jesus are both accepted as Muslim prophets, although Jesus is not believed to be the son of God.

Converts to Islam have only to announce that 'There is no god but Allah and Mohammed is his prophet' to become Muslim. This act of faith is known as *shahada*. In addition to this declaration, Muslims are expected to observe daily prayers, to support the poor, to observe the annual Ramadan fast and to make the pilgrimage *(haj)* to Mecca. Friday is the Muslim holy day and the main mosque in each town is known as the Jama Masjid or Friday Mosque.

As with other belief systems in Kerala, Islam found a tolerant and accepting society as well as royal patronage. The legend of the Chera king, Cheraman, and his conversion after a visit to Mecca, is generally dismissed by most historians. However, royal patronage for Islam, especially from the

Zamorins of Kozhikode, is well documented. Most of Kerala's Muslims are often referred to as Mappilas and they belong to the Sunni community.

The people of Lakshadweep were early converts to Islam and are now almost entirely Muslim.

Christianity

According to legend it was the apostle St Thomas who introduced Christianity to Kerala in 52 CE. He is said to have converted many people and built seven churches along the coast, each identified with a miracle he performed.

In 345 CE Thomas Cana (Knaithomman), a Syrian merchant, arrived at Cranganore. The king of Malabar granted him land and other privileges such as a title, status and property. Inscriptions on copper plates and palm leaves record the title and gifts bestowed on Thomas. He expressed his wish to preach Christianity and immediately set about his task, converting many families. Rites and practices exercised by these Christians were in compliance with the Syrian Church and Syriac was the language adopted for their services. They preserved these practices by continual association with their patriarchate (although this was not always located in Syria). In the 9th century the local Christian community was augmented by the arrival of large numbers of Christians from Syria. This served to bolster the established practices.

Francis Xavier arrived in 1542 and administered to coastal Christians, many of whom had been converted earlier by the Portuguese. These mainly lower-caste people were hopeful that their inclusion in a Christian community might liberate them from the hardships of their caste status as well as afford them some protection from their new masters, the Portuguese. Francis Xavier is reputed to have worked assiduously to support and assist them.

The Portuguese instigated harsh policies to eradicate what they perceived to be heathen customs. They were determined to exercise complete authority over the local Christian community and they endeavoured to implement Latin services in place of the former Syriac ones. Such impositions were strongly opposed by the Syrian Christians. With Latinisation, their cherished services, such as weddings, funerals and christenings, were conducted in an unfamiliar language and became distant and without meaning.

When, in 1653, the Portuguese detained the Christians' chosen bishop from Antioch, public demonstrations resulted. Christians took the Oath of the Koonan Kurisu (Leaning Cross), where they declared that the Portuguese priests were not their spiritual leaders. They then rebuffed the Portuguese action by consecrating their chosen clergyman as their bishop. This created a schism in the Christian community and the Christian Syrian Church became an autonomous organisation with no links to Rome. But the schism did not simply operate between the two groups. At times, members of one group sympathetic to the other and seeking reconciliation were ostracised by their own group. Such misunderstandings created deep divisions within the Christian community.

In 1662, after a papal delegation visited Malabar, many of the Syrian Christians reunited under Rome supremacy. Others, however, joined the Syrian Jacobite Church and some of this community later became members of the Anglican community. Others, wishing to conduct their services in Malayalam, broke away to form the Marthoma Syrian Church.

From the late 18th century requests were made to Rome for the appointment of a local bishop in the hope that this might heal the rift. But Rome was undecided. In 1930 the matter was settled to some extent with the formation of the Syro-Malankara Church, which enabled Syrian Christians and Latin Christians to follow their own practices under the jurisdiction of Rome.

With the arrival of the British, the Anglican Church was established.

Judaism

Jewish history in Kerala goes back a long way, but its exact origin is still a matter for debate. Varying accounts tell of trade between Kerala and the court of King Solomon, of Jewish settlers arriving in the 8th century BCE having escaped injustice in Assyria, of Jews coming to Kerala in the 6th century BCE as they fled slavery under the Babylonians and of Jewish migration to Kerala when Jerusalem was destroyed in 70 CE.

By the 10th century CE, Jews had become influential merchants and had developed associations to protect and advance their artisans and industries. Such activities were acknowledged by the ruler, Bhaskara Ravi Varma, when he granted a series of privileges to the Jewish community via the merchant, Joseph Rabban. The privileges included a grant of land comprising the village of Anjuvannam (near Kodungallur) and the revenues derived from it. The award is recorded on copper plates engraved in ancient Tamil and is now held in the synagogue at Fort Cochin, Mattancherry. The inscriptions clearly indicate that the gratuity was for the Jews and was to remain in their possession for perpetuity.

In addition to land, Rabban was honoured with a palanquin and parasol, attributes which distinguished royalty. This meant in fact that a small kingdom and title had been conferred upon him. The kingdom remained the domain of the Jews until Rabban's ancestral line ceased. Neighbouring princes fought for the sovereignty of the kingdom and the Jews were finally stripped of their entitlements.

In the early 16th century the Jewish community was all but destroyed by Arab traders envious of their successful enterprises. In 1565 the remaining Jews fled from Portuguese oppression to Cochin, where they survived under the protection of the raja of Cochin. They were joined there by European Jews fleeing the Spanish Inquisition. The raja granted them land on which they built their synagogue in 1568. Like his predecessor, the raja also granted privileges of title, thereby once again establishing a place and status for the Jewish community. So protective was he that the Portuguese titled him 'king of the Jews'. In 1662 the Portuguese completely destroyed the synagogue, but it was rebuilt two years later.

In 1954 many Jews migrated to the newly established state of Israel. Now only a few Jewish families remain in Kerala.

Jainism & Buddhism

Both these faiths came to Kerala in approximately the 3rd century BCE. It was drought and famine in North India that possibly forced many Jains south. Originally arriving in Mysore they eventually spread throughout South India. In Kerala, Jainism was well patronised, with several locales, particularly in the south near Kanyakumari in Tamil Nadu, becoming major Jain centres. Jainism prospered in Kerala until well into the 8th century when it was subsumed by Hinduism and many former Jain temples became Hindu sites. There are still Jain sites at Palakkad (Palghat), Sultan's Battery and Alappuzha.

Buddhism arrived with missionaries sent by the Emperor Ashoka, and it had a similar history to Jainism. The area, which is now Kollam and north to Alappuzha, was an important Buddhist centre. Like Jainism, many of the former Buddhist temples became Hindu. Even the shrine at Sabarimala, now dedicated to the popular deity, Ayyappan, is said to have originally been Buddhist. Buddhism had a profound influence on literature, art, architecture and the Ayurvedic medical system. Although Buddhism was finally subsumed by Hinduism, some Buddhist ceremonies, including *utsavam* (festive) processions, persist within the Hindu framework.

Facts for the Visitor

HIGHLIGHTS

Bazaars

Almost every town has a bazaar. For the traveller, bazaars are more about looking than shopping. It is here that you'll see hectares of plastic kitsch and mountains of cooking utensils alongside the finest silks and cottons.

The food stalls present an olfactory as well as a visual delight. Some bazaars specialise in jewellery, tailoring or ready-made clothing. Others seem to have everything including live chickens, goats, vegetables and spices, flowers, human hair and even dental equipment. The antique shops around Jew St in Fort Cochin offer endless hours of hunting and bartering.

place	bazaar	page
Fort Cochin	Antiques	208
Munnar	Mixed goods	253
Thiruvananthapuram	Connemara market	155
Thrissur	Underpants, herbs & Hungarian literature	216
Statewide	Temple festival bazaars	

Backwaters

The myriad canals, rivers and lakes that make up Kerala's famed backwaters are more than just aquatic thoroughfares. They provide a window into village life with its labour intensive cottage industries and agricultural practices. Fishing, prawn farming, sand mining, lime burning, boat building, coir (coconut fibre) making, coconut collecting, rice cultivation and duck farming are just some of the activities you'll witness as the boat meanders through these palm-lined waterways. Sometimes you can even catch a Kathakali performance or visit an ashram. And if you'd like to live on the waters for a few days you can hire a *kettuvallam* (traditional rice barge converted to a houseboat). Some of the most popular routes are:

route	page
Alappuzha (Alleppey) – Kottayam	176
Kochi (Cochin) area	200
Kollam (Quilon) – Alappuzha	176
Kovalam area	165
Valiyaparamba, near Kasaragod	234

Beaches

Whether you want resorts with all your needs indulged (including Ayurvedic treatment) or isolated stretches of sand far removed from creature comforts, the beaches of Kerala have something to offer.

Name Changes

A number of towns and districts have had name changes but these are far from universally used. New names are used throughout this book, with the exception of Sultan's Battery, as this is the most commonly used name. The major places affected include:

old name	new name
Alleppey	Alappuzha
Calicut	Kozhikode
Cannanore	Kannur
Changanacherry	Changanassery
Cochin	Kochi[1]
Palghat	Palakkad
Quilon	Kollam
Sultan's Battery	Suthanbatheri
Tellicherry	Thalasseri
Trichur	Thrissur
Trivandrum	Thiruvananthapuram

[1]Refers to the area of Ernakulam, Mattancherry and Fort Cochin.

Developed beaches may not be everybody's mug of sand but they offer creature comforts and abundant excellent seafood. Watching the fishermen haul in the daily catch is another highlight.

In southern Kerala you can choose between luxurious resorts or basic budget hotels, between the lively crowds of Kovalam or the more laid-back scene at Varkala. A world away from the touristy beaches are those of northern Kerala. Some of these may be mooted for development but others remain relatively untouched.

The beaches of Lakshadweep are still pristine and deserted. Here you can be left alone to string a hammock between trees, star gaze at night and snorkel or dive during the day.

place	page
Bekal Fort	233
Kovalam	162
Lakshadweep	264
Varkala	171

Hill Stations

If you've had too many bus rides, if your temper is becoming dangerously frayed, your patience has expired and your sense of humour is conspicuously absent, maybe it's time to head for the hills. Hill stations are relatively cool in summer and almost cold (especially at night) in winter. If you can visit in the low season, you'll be able to get bargain accommodation.

Walking, boating and fireside chats are all popular pastimes in hill stations. And in Munnar it's just a short distance to Rajamala, where the Nilgiri tahr (mountain goat) has re-emerged from the brink of extinction.

Residents of the plains think that hill residents are a little crazy. Perhaps they are, but there's nothing like a dash of altitude to save you from complete insanity.

place	page
Around Periyar	246
Kuttikkanam	248
Munnar	248

Music, Dance & Performance

Music, dance and performance are everywhere in Kerala. There are also many places where the serious student can learn these arts. The state is of course famous for Kathakali, one of the most ritualised and colourful performances in India. The mesmerising Teyyam dance is unique to northern Kerala while other forms of dance are staged across the state, sometimes in formal public venues and at other times in temples as rituals to the deities.

Where there is dance there is also music. Temples, churches, community halls, palaces and tourist hotels are all venues for music. Often you'll hear it long before you see it. Follow the sound and you'll happen upon a cluster of musicians doing what they do best – creating traditional, evocative and haunting sounds.

Festivals

Elaborately caparisoned elephants, cacophonous fireworks, ancient temple rituals and classical music and dance are just some of the features of Kerala's numerous festivals. Many festivals are local, pivoting on a particular temple or church. Other festivals embrace many communities and last for days and nights. Some festivals are sacred and rooted in ancient traditions. Others are secular and are staged by tourist authorities to showcase the culture. (For more information on Kerala's rich diversity of festivals, see the Public Holidays & Special Events section later in this chapter.)

SUGGESTED ITINERARIES

Spices, Synagogues & Jungle Walks

Kochi – Kottayam – Kumily – Munnar – Thrissur – Guruvayur (7 to 10 days)

This route, which weaves in and out of the Western Ghats, highlights the spice-growing areas with an opportunity to view wildlife, spectacular mountain scenery, picturesque tea estates and a stable of temple elephants. After arriving in Kochi (Cochin) and exploring the bazaars of Fort Cochin catch a bus to the Cardamom Hills via the rubber-producing centre of Kottayam. A relaxing day could be spent around Kottayam at the Kumarakom Bird Sanctuary on the shores of Vembanad Lake. From Kottayam head to the spice-growing centre of Kumily and the Periyar Wildlife Sanctuary. While you probably won't see a tiger, an early-morning jungle walk will give you a taste of forested India, and a chance to see monkeys, squirrels and birds.

A scenic road connects Kumily with the tea-growing centre of Munnar. You may wish to spend several days in Munnar exploring the groomed hills and Eravikulam National Park or just enjoying the cool climate. The bus ride from Munnar down the Western Ghats escarpment to the cultural centre of Thrissur (Trichur) is spectacular. Near Thrissur is the important temple town of Guruvayur and the temple elephant stable at Punnathur Kota. In the grounds of an old palace more than 40 elephants are cleaned, preened and fed by their mahouts (elephant caretakers).

Beaches, Backwaters & Bustling Cities

Thiruvananthapuram (Trivandrum) – Kovalam – Varkala – Kollam – Alappuzha – Kottayam – Kochi (7 to 10 days)

Tropical beaches and idyllic backwaters fringed with swaying coconut palms are the attractions of southern Kerala. You can head directly for Kovalam, and avoid Thiruvananthapuram (Trivandrum), the busy and dusty capital, but if you do you'll miss its subtle delights, the ease and gentleness of the city and the pleasures of a culture mostly free from tourists and hawkers. At Kovalam, as well as the sun, salt and sand, you can take day trips to an old wooden palace or along quiet backwaters. Varkala is a little more relaxed than Kovalam and a good place to unwind. A short train ride from Varkala is Kollam (Quilon), from this ancient port you can explore the labyrinthine system of backwaters. You can mingle with other tourists on the scheduled cruises or hire your own kettuvallam (traditional Keralan rice barge) for the memorable trip to Alappuzha (Alleppey). From Alappuzha there are further backwater experiences on the way to Kochi, either directly along Vembanad Lake or via the rubber-producing centre of Kottayam.

Rites, Rocks & Remote Locations

Kozhikode (Calicut) – Mahé – Kasaragod (7 to 10 days)

The infrastructure of northern Kerala is nowhere near as developed as that in the south. However, the north does have the attraction of being relatively unexplored by travellers. The bustling city of Kozhikode (Calicut) is a good base from which to start a northern venture. From here you can travel inland to the Edakkal Caves with their ancient scripts and images. On the way you can witness the industrious workers at the Patchilakkad arecanut (betel nut) factory or relax beside the Pookote Lake (see the Western Ghats chapter for details of these attractions).

At Beypore just out of Kozhikode you can see ships being built according to ancient traditions (not a nail or drawing in sight). In the small community of Mahé, the Malayala Kalagramam Centre encourages many traditional as well as contemporary forms of artistic expression, including dance, music, sculpture and painting, and visitors are welcome to watch classes, with permission.

Farther north at the Parasinikadavu Temple, Kannur (Cannanore), early-morning Teyyam ritual dance seeks to placate the gods. In Kasaragod you can witness puppetry based on the ancient art form, Yakshagana.

PLANNING

When to Go

October to March is the best time to visit Kerala. At this time it is relatively dry and cool, although in November and the beginning of December parts of Kerala come in for a drenching as the monsoon retreats across them. In the popular beach resorts many facilities (such as beach shacks) don't open until November and, in the weeks immediately after the monsoon (ie October), there can be strong rips that make swimming hazardous. The Western Ghats can get misty in winter (late December/January) and the nights are often cold regardless of the time of year.

Temperatures start to rise in most places in March and by April it's warm and humid, but the sea breeze tends to have a moderating effect. The mountains, where it's not nearly as hot and the atmosphere isn't as dusty, can be pleasant in April and May, just before the monsoons. The cooling monsoon rains arrive in June and last until the end of September or early October.

Maps

Maps are a scarce resource in Kerala. Those available are usually inaccurate.

Lonely Planet's *India Travel Atlas* breaks down the country into over 100 pages of maps, with Kerala covered by two of them. It's fully indexed and is easily accessed, especially on buses and trains. The text is in English, French, German, Spanish and Japanese. Nelles Verlag publishes a good series that covers the whole of India with Part 4 of the series covering *Southern India* (1:1,500,000).

The Survey of India has maps covering all of India, but to obtain them you need special permission from the District Commissioner, something that is difficult if not impossible to obtain. Maps in the area within 150km of India's coastline (which includes all of Kerala) are virtually impossible to obtain. However, pressure is on to change things and tourist officials keep making optimistic promises that accurate maps will be available in 2000 – so it's worth checking. At the Survey of India's office (☎ 0471-320874) in Thiruvananthapuram you can pick up an out-dated map of Kerala – so out of date, in fact, that most printed place names don't correlate with actual ones.

What to Bring

What you bring depends on your length of stay and whether your visit is to Kerala only. For any visit, heavy luggage presents problems, even if you're intending to travel only by plane and car.

If you are undertaking a longer trip, the usual budget traveller's rule applies – bring as little as possible. In Kerala that's easy to do since you will seldom need more than light clothing. In the hills, especially during the cool season, you will need a reasonably warm jacket for chilly nights.

If you are visiting temples or other sacred places, be sensitive to dress requirements. Sleeveless tops and short skirts or shorts are unacceptable in such situations, often a sari for women or a *dhoti* (similar to a sarong) for men are required. A reasonable clothes list would include:

- cotton underwear
- swimming gear
- one pair of cotton trousers
- one long (ankle-length) cotton skirt (women)
- a few lightweight shirts
- sweater for cool nights in the hills
- one pair of runners (sneakers) or shoes
- socks
- flip-flops (thongs) – handy to wear when showering
- lightweight jacket or raincoat
- set of 'dress up' clothes
- hat or umbrella – hats can be sweaty and uncomfortable, and are sometimes unacceptable in temple grounds. Umbrellas can be bought cheaply everywhere, and they protect from both sun and rain
- sunglasses

If you are going camping or trekking you will need to take:

- walking boots, broken in beforehand
- warm jacket
- wool shirt or sweater
- breeches or shorts – shorts are ideal but should not be worn in places where they may cause offence to locals
- shirts – those with collars and sleeves will give added protection against the sun
- socks – bring a sufficient supply of thick and thin pairs
- sun hat

Bedding A sleeping bag, although a hassle to carry, can come in handy. You can use it to spread over unsavoury-looking hotel bedding, as a cushion on hard train seats, and as a seat for long waits on railway platforms. If you are planning to camp or spending time in the hills (especially during the cool season) a sleeping bag is essential.

Generally guesthouses and hotels provide a sheet to cover the bed, an extra sheet and a pillowcase. Not all places provide a sheet to put over you – this is when you'll be pleased you brought a sleeping sheet (or sleeping bag liner). This is sufficient for most places because of the heat. In the hill country blankets are usually provided.

If you find a sleeping bag too cumbersome, a space blanket (for cool, even damp nights in the hills) may be adequate.

For visitors on a package tour or those staying in mid-range hotels (more than Rs 350 a night) in places where there is a good tourist infrastructure, bedding will definitely be available in your hotel room.

Toilet Paper Indian sewerage systems are generally overloaded enough without having to cope with toilet paper as well. However, if you can't adapt to the Indian method of a jug of water and your left hand, toilet paper is widely available. A basket is sometimes provided in toilets for used toilet paper. Use it. Do not put sanitary napkins or tampons in toilets.

Toiletries Soap, toothpaste, shampoo and other toiletries are readily available. Conditioner can be hard to find. A sink plug is worth having since few cheaper hotels have plugs. A nail brush or scourer is very useful for scrubbing the dirt off your feet at the end of the day. For women, sanitary pads are widely available but tampons are difficult to obtain. Bring condoms with you, although these too are fairly easy to procure.

Men can safely leave their shaving gear at home. One of the pleasures of Indian travel is a shave in a barber shop. With AIDS becoming more widespread in India, however, make sure that a fresh blade is used. For just a few rupees you'll get the full treatment – lathering, shave, a repeat of the process, and finally there's the hot, damp towel and sometimes talcum powder, or even a scalp massage.

Miscellaneous Items Some handy items to stow away in your pack could include the following. See the Health section later in this chapter for details about medical supplies.

- padlock – especially for budget travellers. Most cheap hotels and some mid-range places have flimsy door locks. You'll find your own sturdy lock does wonders for your peace of mind.
- a knife – preferably Swiss Army; it has a whole range of uses, such as peeling fruit, opening bottles etc.
- a miniature electric element – to boil water in a cup.
- a sarong – it can be used as a bed sheet, an item of clothing, an emergency towel, a pillow on trains, and as head covering.
- insect repellent, mosquito coils or an electric mosquito zapper – you can buy them in most places but remember that Kerala is subject to power cuts. Insect repellent is available locally but comes in tubes and is messy to apply. A mosquito net can be useful, although setting it up might be a problem. Whatever you do make sure you're well protected – mosquito-borne diseases are becoming more prevalent.
- a torch (flashlight) and/or candles – power cuts ('load shedding' as it is euphemistically known) are not uncommon and there's little street lighting at night.
- a voltage stabiliser – for travellers bringing sensitive electronic equipment.
- moisture-impregnated disposable tissues.
- a spare set of glasses and your spectacle prescription.
- ear plugs – many travellers find these indispensable for protection from noisy hotels and early-morning loud speakers. Some like a sleeping mask as well.
- a water bottle – it should always be by your side. If you're not drinking bottled water, use water purification tablets (and choose not to add to India's growing problem with plastic trash). Throughout Kerala boiled water is generally safe. (See the Health section for more information on drinking water.)
- high-factor sunscreen – it's becoming more widely available in India, but it's *expensive*!
- lip balm – it might come in handy if you are planning to spend a lot of time outside.
- a bit of string – very useful as a makeshift clothes line. Elasticised double-strand nylon is

good to secure your clothes if you have no pegs.

- plastic bags – they have a variety of uses, and will protect your clothes inside your pack from the numerous liquids emitted on public transport. It's not nice to arrive at your hotel smelling of fish or urine!
- a pair of binoculars – for birdwatching and wildlife spotting.
- a high-pitched whistle – as a possible deterrent to would-be assailants.
- extra passport photos – there are places in Kerala where you can obtain these, but carrying your own can avoid inconvenience when they're suddenly demanded by institutions.
- photocopies of documents – keep these separately from your documents in case you and your documents somehow become detached.

How to Carry It For visitors who intend travelling by taxi from the airport to their hotel, a suitcase is a good option. It's lockable, keeps your clothes flat and is less likely to get damaged. Don't make the mistake of thinking you can wander around with a suitcase on wheels. With pavements far less prevalent than potholes, you'll come a cropper in no time. A suitcase with backpack straps can be a good choice.

For others, the backpack is still the best option and it's worth paying the money for a strong, good quality one that's much more likely to withstand the rigours of Indian travel.

RESPONSIBLE TOURISM

Every traveller experiences the contradictions of tourism. On the one hand governments and tourist authorities bend over backwards to accumulate revenue by promoting pristine beaches, accessible parks and cultural experiences. Regrettably such promotion frequently results in over-development where natural resources are threatened and so-called cultural experiences are actually thinly veiled traps for the tourist dollar.

Responsible tourism is about separating the hype from the reality. It may mean forsaking 'exciting' ventures, in an attempt to safeguard the environment. It may mean refusing to bribe. It certainly means respecting dress codes and obeying public signs.

Misinformation Offices

You'll soon learn not to expect information from information offices and booths. Such an expectation clearly defies logic. Many information offices are like archaeological sites, perfectly preserved and no longer performing their former functions. Indeed it seems most never had any former functions. As one forest officer so aptly put it 'they're for the namesake'.

But the fact that information centres do not provide information should not deter you. You'll find the tourist offices in Thiruvananthapuram very helpful and people everywhere are always happy to assist. If you can't speak Malayalam, just name the place you want and make sure you understand the responses *walla totta* (right), *yerra totto* (left) and *narra* (straight ahead). If people run away when you approach them and speak in a foreign language, just wait. No doubt they'll return with someone who understands your language.

For more specific details see the boxed text 'Hindu Temples & Non-Hindu Visitors' and the boxed text 'Visiting Parks & Sanctuaries', in the Facts about Kerala chapter.

TOURIST OFFICES

Local Tourist Offices

Making sense of the myriad tourist organisations in Kerala is a major feat in itself. The Government of India Department of Tourism has an office in Kochi. The State Government operates the Kerala Tourism Development Corporation (KTDC) and the District Tourist Promotion Council (DTPC). In addition, some districts have offices – the Idukki District Tourist Information Office (IDTIO), the Thekkady Tourism Development Council (TTDC). Sometimes they elevate themselves to corporations – Bekal Resort Development Corporation (BRDC) and at other times they are cooperatives – Alleppey Tourism Development Co-op Society. Some offices are linked;

others may compete with each other, but this is rarely a problem except in the lethargy stakes. Then there are the private operators. The following chapters will provide you with details on the best sources of information for each town.

Offices vary widely in their usefulness. They are rarely good places for picking up brochures and maps. Some seem to do little more than sell tours, promote their own businesses or those of their friends. Some, such as the KTDC, run their own accommodation networks.

For those visitors coming to Kerala via the international gateways, the Government of India has the following tourist offices:

Chennai (Madras)
(☎ 044-852 4295) 154 Anna Salai
Mumbai (Bombay)
(☎ 022-203 2932)
123 Maharishi Karve Rd, Churchgate

Tourist Offices Abroad

The Government of India Department of Tourism maintains a string of tourist offices in other countries where you can get information about Kerala. There are also smaller 'promotion offices' in Osaka (Japan), Dallas, Miami, San Francisco and Washington DC (USA).

Australia
(☎ 61-2-9264 4855, fax 9264 4860)
Level 2, Piccadilly, 210 Pitt St, Sydney, NSW 2000
Canada
(☎ 1-416-962 3788, fax 962 6279)
60 Bloor St West, Suite No 1003, Toronto, Ontario M4W 3B8
France (☎ 33-1-4523 3045, fax 4523 3345)
11-13 Bis Blvd Hausmann, 75008, Paris
Germany
(☎ 49-69-2429 9490, fax 2429 4977)
Baseler Strasse 48, 60329, Frankfurt, AM-Main-10
Israel
(☎ 972-3-510 1431, fax 510 1434)
c/o Indian Embassy, 4 Kolfman St, Tel Aviv
Italy
(☎ 39-2-804952, fax 720 21689)
Via Albricci 9, 20122 Milan
Netherlands
(☎ 31-20-620 8991, fax 638 3059)
Rokin 9-15, 1012 KK Amsterdam
Singapore
(☎ 65-235 3800, fax 235 8677)
United House, 20 Kramat Lane, Singapore 0922
Sweden
(☎ 46-8-215081, fax 210186)
Sveavagen 9-11, S-II 157, Stockholm 11157
UK
(☎ 020-7437 3677, fax 494 1048, 24 hour brochure line ☎ 01233-211999)
7 Cork St, London W1X 2LN
USA
(☎ 1-212-751 6840, fax 582 3274)
Suite 1808, 1270 Ave of Americas, New York, NY 10020

VISAS & DOCUMENTS

Passport

Keep your passport with you at all times; it's your most important travel document. Make sure your passport is valid for the entire period you intend to be overseas. If your passport is lost or stolen, immediately contact your country's embassy or consulate. It's also a good idea to keep your health certificate with your passport, in case you suddenly have to prove your immunisation status.

Visas & Extensions

Virtually everybody needs a visa to visit India. The application is (in theory) straightforward and the visas are usually issued with a minimum of fuss.

Tourist visas are issued for six months, are multiple entry, and are valid from the date of issue of the visa, not the date you enter India. This means that if you enter India five months after the visa was issued, it will be valid for one month only. One year visas are only available to businesspeople or students. Tourist visas are not extendable. If you want to stay longer than six months you will have to go to a neighbouring country, eg Sri Lanka (but not Nepal, see following), and get a new six month visa.

Six month multiple entry tourist visas cost A$55 for Australians, UK£19 for Britons, US$50 for Americans, and 200FF for French passport holders.

Nepal According to recent reports, it's no longer possible to get a new Indian visa in

Kathmandu if you already have a six month visa in your passport. Some travellers have managed to get a short extension, when their current visa has been validated from date of entry instead of from date of issue, but such processes are rare.

Pakistan The high commission in Islamabad usually issues visas within a few days. If there's an Indian embassy in your home country, they may fax there to check your legal status – that you're not a thief, wanted by the police or in some other way undesirable.

Sri Lanka Here you can obtain visas at the Indian embassy in Colombo (see the Embassies & Consulates section, later in this chapter), as well as in Kandy at 47 Rajapilla Mawatha. It takes approximately seven working days.

Thailand It takes four working days for non-Thai nationals to obtain an Indian visa.

Visas to Other Countries If you are travelling to several different countries where visas are required organise this at home before you set out. Some travellers have experienced considerable difficulties obtaining their required visas – not because of the Indian system, but because of the requirements of the countries of their future destination.

Travel Permits

Even with a valid visa you are not allowed to go everywhere.

Lakshadweep No special permits are required for Lakshadweep, but you must book with a recognised operator or resort. See the Lakshadweep chapter for more details.

Trekking Permits Foreigners require permits for trekking in areas in or around national parks. The permits are obtainable from forest departments (details are given in the regional chapters). In theory these permits aren't difficult to get, but as the wheels of bureaucracy tend to grind slowly and sometimes halt altogether, it's wise to allow several days per permit. Alternatively you can join an organised trek where the company arranges everything including your permit.

Onward Tickets

Many Indian embassies and consulates will not issue a visa to enter India unless you are holding an onward or return ticket, which is taken as sufficient evidence that you intend to leave the country.

Travel Insurance

A travel insurance policy to cover theft, loss and medical problems is very important. There are many to choose from. The international student travel policies handled by STA Travel and Council Travel are usually good value. Some policies offer a range of medical expense options, including adventure activities such as scuba diving and trekking. Always check the small print:

- Some policies specifically exclude 'dangerous activities', which can include motorcycling and even trekking. If such activities are on your agenda you don't want that sort of policy. A locally acquired motorcycle licence may not be valid under your policy.
- You may prefer a policy that ensures immediate payment to doctors or hospitals rather than one where you pay on the spot and claim later. If you have the latter, make sure you keep all documentation. Some policies ask you to call back (reverse charges) to a centre in your home country where an immediate assessment of your problem is made. Keep a photocopy of your policy, with this phone number, separate from the original, for reference in the event of loss.
- Check if the policy covers ambulances, an emergency helicopter airlift out of a remote region, or an emergency flight home with a medical escort. If you're injured and need to stretch out on the home journey, you'll need two seats and somebody has to pay for them!

Driving Licence & Permits

If you're planning to drive in Kerala, get an international driving permit from your local national motoring organisation. However, if you're travelling by car, it's preferable to hire a car and driver. In some places in Kerala it's possible to hire a motorcycle; see the Kovalam and Varkala sections in the Southern Kerala chapter for more information. An international permit can also be used for other identification purposes, such as plain old bicycle hire.

Certificates & Concession Cards

A health certificate, while not necessary in India, may be required for onward travel. It's useful to have in case evidence of immunisation is required. These days student cards don't attract much in the way of concessions, but always ask. A youth hostel (Hostelling International – HI) card is not generally required for youth hostels, but you do pay slightly less at official youth hostels if you have one. All Indian nationals over the age of 65 receive concessions on all forms of travel within India. Students and senior citizens (including foreigners) will find that some venues and tours give concessions. Proof, of course, is mandatory.

Other Documents

Tax Clearance Certificates If you stay in India for more than 120 days you need a tax clearance certificate to leave the country. This supposedly proves that your time in India was financed with your own money, not by working in India or by playing the black market. The Tourist Facilitation Centre (☎ 0471-321132), Museum Rd, Thiruvananthapuram, will set you on the right track to sort all this out.

Photocopies

It's a good idea to carry photocopies of your important travel documents, which obviously should be kept separate from the originals in the event that these are lost or stolen.

Take a photocopy of your passport details and photograph, your Indian visa, travel insurance policy, airline ticket and credit card. Keep a record of cashed travellers cheques – place, amount and serial number. Encashment receipts should also be kept. You may be required to provide them on departure, as evidence of exchange and in-country expenditure. It's not a bad idea to leave photocopies of your important travel documents with a relative or friend at home. Carry a copy of your health certificate too. It may save you extra jabs (with maybe a used needle) if there's an epidemic.

There is another option for storing details of your vital travel documents before you leave – Lonely Planet's online Travel Vault. Storing details of your important documents in the vault is safer than carrying photocopies. It's the best option if you travel in an area with easy Internet access. Your password-protected travel vault is accessible online at any time. You can create your own travel vault for free at www.ekno.lonelyplanet.com.

EMBASSIES & CONSULATES

Indian Embassies & Consulates

India's embassies, consulates and high commissions abroad include:

Australia
- Canberra
  (☎ 61-2-6273 3999, fax 6273 3328)
  3-5 Moonah Place, Yarralumla, ACT 2600
- Sydney
  (☎ 61-2-9223 9500, fax 9223 9246)
  Level 27, 25 Bligh St, Sydney, NSW 2000
- Melbourne
  (☎ 61-3-9384 0141, fax 9386 7399)
  13 Munro St, Coburg, Melbourne, Vic 3058
- Perth
  (☎ 61-9-221 1207, fax 221 1206)
  195 Adelaide Tce, East Perth, WA 6004

Canada
  (☎ 1-613-744 3751, fax 744 0913)
  10 Springfield Rd, Ottawa K1M 1C9

China
  (☎ 8621-6275 8881, fax 6275 8885)
  1008, Shanghai International Trade Centre, 2200 Yan An Xi Lu, Shanghai

France
  (☎ 01 40 50 70 70, fax 01 40 50 09 96)
  15 rue Alfred Dehodencq, 75016 Paris

Germany
  (☎ 49-228-540 5161, fax 538 245)
  Baunscheidtstrasse 7, 53113 Bonn

Nepal
  (☎ 71-410900, fax 413132)
  PB No 292 Lazimpat, Kathmandu

The Netherlands
(☎ 70-346 9771, fax 361 7072)
Buitenrustweg 2, 2517 KD Den Haag, The Hague
New Zealand
(☎ 4-473 6390, fax 499 0665)
180 Molesworth St, Wellington
Pakistan
Islamabad
(☎ 51-814371, fax 820742)
G5 Diplomatic Enclave, Islamabad
Karachi
(☎ 21-522275, fax 568 0929)
India House, 3 Fatima Jinnah Rd, Karachi
Singapore
(☎/fax 732 6909) 31 Grange Rd
Sri Lanka
(☎ 1-421 605, fax 446 403)
36-38 Galle Rd, Colombo 3
Thailand
(☎ 2-258-0300, fax 258-4627)
46 Soi 23 (Prasarnmitr) Sukhumvit Rd, Bangkok
UK
London
(☎ 020-7836 8484, fax 7836 4331)
India House, Aldwych, London WC2B 4NA
Birmingham
(☎ 0121-212 2782, fax 212 2786)
8219 Augusta St, Birmingham B18 6DS
USA
Washington
(☎ 202-939 7000, fax 939 7027)
2107 Massachusetts Ave NW, Washington DC 20008
New York
(☎ 212-879 7800, fax 988 6423)
3 East 64th St, Manhattan, New York NY 10021-7097
San Francisco
(☎ 415-668 0662, fax 668 2073)
540 Arguello Blvd, San Francisco CA 94118

Embassies & Consulates in India

Most foreign diplomatic missions are in the nation's capital, Delhi, but there are also quite a few consulates in the major cities of Mumbai and Chennai, which are closer to Kerala.

Mumbai (Bombay) Consulates in Mumbai, Maharashtra, include the following (the telephone area code is 022):

Australia
(☎ 2181071, fax 2188228)
16th floor, Maker Towers, E Block, Cuffe Parade, Colaba
Canada
(☎ 2876028, fax 2875514)
4th floor, Maker Chambers VI, J Bajaj Marg, Nariman Point
France
(☎ 4950918)
2nd floor, Datta Prasad Bldg, 10 NG Cross Rd, off N Gamadia Marg, Cumballa Hill
Germany
(☎ 2832422, fax 2025493)
10th floor, Hoechst House, Vinayak K Shah Rd, Nariman Point
Ireland
(☎ 2024607, fax 2871087)
2nd floor, Royal Bombay Yacht Club, Shivaji Marg, Colaba
The Netherlands
(☎ 2016750, fax 2069436)
International Bldg, Marine Lines Cross Rd 1, Churchgate
Singapore
(☎ 2043209, fax 2855812)
9th floor, 94 Sakhar Bhavan, Nariman Point
Sri Lanka
(☎ 2045861, fax 2876132)
Ground floor, Sri Lanka House, 34 Homi Modi St, Fort
UK
(☎ 2830517, fax 2027940)
2nd floor, Maker Chambers IV, J Bajaj Marg, Nariman Point
USA
(☎ 3633611, fax 3630350)
Lincoln House, 78 Bhulabhai Desai Marg, Cumballa Hill

Chennai (Madras) Consulates in Chennai, Tamil Nadu, include the following (the telephone area code is 044):

France
(☎ 827 0469) 16 Haddows Rd
Germany
(☎ 827 1747) 22 C-in-C Rd
Sri Lanka
(☎ 827 2270)
9-D Nawab Habibullah Rd, off Anderson Rd
UK
(☎ 827 3136) 24 Anderson Rd
USA
(☎ 827 3040) Gemini Circle, 220 Anna Salai

CUSTOMS

The usual duty-free regulations apply for India; that is, one bottle of whiskey (or

Your Own Embassy

It's important to realise what your own embassy – the embassy of the country of which you are a citizen – can and can't do to help you if you get into trouble overseas.

Generally speaking, your embassy or consulate won't be much help in emergencies, especially if the trouble you're in is remotely your own fault.

Remember that you are bound by the laws of the country you are in. Your embassy will not be sympathetic if you end up in jail after committing a crime locally, even if such actions are legal in your own country.

In genuine emergencies you might be able to get some assistance, but only if all the other channels have been exhausted. For example, if you need to get home urgently, a free air ticket home is exceedingly unlikely – the embassy would expect you to have adequate travel insurance. If you are a victim of theft and you have all your money and documents stolen, it might be able to assist you with getting a new passport, but a loan for onward travel is out of the question.

Some embassies used to keep letters for travellers or have a small reading room with home newspapers, but these days the mail holding service has usually been stopped and even newspapers tend to be out of date.

other spirits) and 200 cigarettes. You're allowed to bring in all sorts of western technological wonders, but big items, such as video cameras, are likely to be entered on a 'Tourist Baggage Re-Export' form to ensure you take them out with you again when you go. This used to be the case with notebook computers, but it seems that this restriction has been waived. It's not necessary to declare still cameras, even if you have more than one.

Note that if you are entering India from Nepal you are not entitled to import anything free of duty.

MONEY

Currency

The rupee (Rs) is divided into 100 paise (p). There are coins of five, 10, 20, 25 and 50 paise, Rs one, two and five, and notes of Rs one, two, five, 10, 20, 50, 100 and 500.

You are not allowed to bring Indian currency into the country and you can't take it out either. You are allowed to bring in an unlimited amount of foreign currency or travellers cheques, but you are supposed to declare anything over US$10,000 when you arrive.

Exchange Rates

country	unit		rupee
Australia	A$1	=	Rs 28
Canada	C$1	=	Rs 30
euro	€1	=	Rs 45
France	10FF	=	Rs 69
Germany	DM1	=	Rs 23
Japan	¥100	=	Rs 40
Nepal	Nep Rs100	=	Rs 63
New Zealand	NZ$1	=	Rs 23
Sri Lanka	SL Rs100	=	Rs 61
UK	UK£1	=	Rs 71
US	US$1	=	Rs 44

Exchanging Money

In the gateway cities (Chennai and Mumbai) and Thiruvananthapuram you can change most foreign currencies or travellers cheques – but generally it's best to stick to US dollars or pounds sterling.

In the main tourist areas you'll find foreign exchange centres. Because banks can be slow, it can be easier to deal with agencies. They keep longer hours, and commissions (if any) are low. The top-end hotels will also change money, with commissions usually higher than banks and exchange centres.

Outside the main areas, the State Bank of India is usually the place to change money, although occasionally you'll be directed to another bank, such as the local state bank. In the more remote regions, few banks offer exchange facilities, so be prepared. Also take note of public holidays. You don't want to be caught with no money in a remote area with the sole bank closed.

For more details refer to the Money sections in the regional chapters. Some banks charge an encashment fee, which may be levied for the entire transaction or on each cheque.

Cash US dollars or pounds sterling are useful to carry. They can get you out of difficulties when money-changing facilities don't exist.

Travellers Cheques Although it's usually not a problem to change travellers cheques, it's best to stick to the well-known brands – American Express or Thomas Cook – as more obscure ones may cause problems.

Thomas Cook and American Express can be exchanged readily in most major tourist centres. Thomas Cook has offices in Thiruvananthapuram, Ernakulam and Chennai and changes all major currencies and travellers cheques.

Beyond these, facilities can be limited. For more details see the relevant section in the regional chapters.

A few simple measures should be taken to facilitate the replacement of travellers cheques, should they be stolen (see Stolen Travellers Cheques in the Dangers & Annoyances section, later in this chapter).

ATMs There are ATMs in Thiruvananthapuram and Ernakulam.

Credit Cards Credit cards are widely accepted at mid-range and top-end hotels, for buying rail and air tickets and in many shops. In more remote places, however, credit card facilities just don't exist. You can get cash advances in Thiruvananthapuram on many credit cards.

International Transfers Don't run out of money in India unless you have a credit card against which you can draw travellers cheques or cash. Having money transferred through the banking system can be time consuming – it may take a fortnight and will be a hassle.

Black Market The rupee is a fully convertible currency; that is, the rate is set by the market not the government. For this reason there's not much of a black market, although you can get a couple of rupees more for your dollars or pounds in cash. In the major tourist centres you'll get offers to change money. There's little risk involved although it's officially illegal.

Encashment Certificates All money is supposed to be changed at official banks or moneychangers, and you should receive an encashment certificate for each transaction. You'll usually get one, but if you don't, ask for one. It's worth getting them for several reasons. You may want to re-exchange excess rupees for foreign currency when you

Change

A perennial problem in Kerala is the lack of small change. There just never seems to be enough small denomination notes or coins, which can lead to all sorts of hassles when it comes to settling bills. Always have several Rs 10 notes and better still, a selection of Rs 2 and Rs 5. Handing over a Rs 50 note to a rickshaw driver will invariably elicit the response: 'no change'. Some supermarkets will issue sweets as a substitute for small change.

Banks will invariably give you bundles of Rs 100 or Rs 50 notes when you change money. Rs 500 do exist but banks have always run out of them. This means if you are changing even a small amount of money expect to emerge from the bank with a wad of rupees that you can barely squeeze into your moneybelt.

depart India and you'll have problems if you can't prove an exchange. If your stay has been more than four months, you may be requested to show a tax clearance certificate at the airport. See Tax Clearance Certificates earlier in this chapter for details. And finally, some shipping agents may insist on encashment certificates to prove you've actually changed money to purchase your goods.

Security & Carrying Money

A moneybelt worn around your waist beneath your clothes is probably one of the safest ways to carry important documents such as your passport and travellers cheques. Some travellers prefer a pouch attached to a string that is worn around the neck, with the pouch against the chest concealed beneath a shirt. Leather pouches worn over the clothing are inadvisable; they are too conspicuous (as are 'bum bags'). Many temples insist that all leather be removed anyway.

Costs

From top to bottom: if you stay in luxury hotels, use car-and-driver combinations for sightseeing and fly from Kerala to other destinations in India, you can spend a lot of money. Kerala has plenty of hotels which cost US$100 or more a day and some where a room can cost US$200 or more. Lakshadweep is an especially pricey destination. The high taxes levied against luxury (even mid-range) accommodation also need to be taken into account. At the other extreme, if you scrimp and save, stay in the cheapest hotels (or hostels and dormitories), always travel 2nd class on trains, and learn to exist on *thalis* (vegetable and rice meals), you can see Kerala on less than US$8 a day.

Most travellers will probably be looking for something between these extremes. Prices are not necessarily lower in off-the-beaten-track places, but for those visiting the usual travellers' haunts and prepared to splash out on occasional tours (eg a backwater cruise), expect to average about US$20 to US$25 a day. Organised trekking and diving trips can be very expensive, but remember prices are almost always negotiable.

Tipping & Bargaining

In tourist restaurants or hotels, where service is usually tacked on, 10% tipping usually applies. In smaller places, where tipping is optional, you only need to tip a few rupees, not a percentage of the bill. Hotel porters expect Rs 5 to Rs 10; other possible tipping levels are Rs 2 for bike-watching, Rs 10 to Rs 15 for train conductors or station porters who perform miracles for you, and Rs 5 to Rs 15 for extra services from hotel staff. Remember many staff are paid very low salaries and it is expected they will be compensated by way of commissions and tips. Some establishments have the view that you, the visitor, should pay two bills – one to the establishment (the accommodation bill) and the other to the employees (the tips). To ensure that employees receive their tip, it's better to pay them personally.

How much you pay for a wide range of goods and services from souvenirs to accommodation is very often subject to negotiation. Government emporiums and larger shops invariably have fixed prices (often rather higher than similar goods would fetch in the bazaars) as do small, general purpose shops. But in other places, bazaars for example, you will generally have to bargain. If you have no idea how much something should cost, a rough guide is about 10% to 20% less than that charged in the fixed price outlets. When you're quoted a price in the bazaar, begin by offering about half the noted fixed price. This will invariably elicit an incredulous response from the vendor, but it's a point from which to begin the bargaining process. Some shopkeepers will lower their 'final price' if you move towards the door saying that you'll 'think about it'.

Negotiating is an art. The four most important ingredients for success are respect, time, patience and humour. Once mastered, negotiating can be enjoyable and satisfying. Given that it's so much a part of the Indian way, it's an important skill to acquire. But if you find it all too much, shop at the fixed-price stores.

POST & COMMUNICATIONS

Postal Rates

It costs Rs 6 to airmail a postcard and Rs 6.50 to send an aerogramme anywhere in the world from India. A standard airmail letter (up to 20g) costs Rs 11. Post office-issued envelopes cost Rs 1 within India. The larger post offices have a speed post service. International rates are Rs 200 for the first 200g and Rs 60 for every additional 200g. Internal rates are Rs 20 for places within 500km and Rs 30 for places beyond 500km.

Sending Mail

You can buy stamps at larger hotels, saving a lot of queuing in crowded post offices. The Indian postal service is generally excellent. Letters you send invariably arrive.

Posting Parcels

Most people discover how to do this the hard way, in which case it will take half a day – but even when you know the ropes, it can take half a day. Go about it as described below:

- Approach the post office and ask if they have a professional parcel packer. If not take the parcel to a tailor and ask that it be stitched up in cheap linen. The tailor will stitch it according to the contents – books will have an 'open packet' parcel, which allows for easy customs inspection and much reduced postal rates (see later in this section). Discuss the possibilities with the tailor then negotiate your price, which is usually minimal (although not as minimal at Thiruvananthapuram post office as at other places).
- Obtain the necessary customs declaration forms from the post office. Fill them in and glue one to the parcel. The other will be stitched on to it. To avoid excise duty at the delivery end it's best to specify that the contents are a 'gift'.
- Be careful how much you declare the contents to be worth. If you specify over Rs 1000, your parcel will not be accepted without a bank clearance certificate, which is a hassle to get. State the value as less than Rs 1000.
- Have the parcel weighed and franked at the parcel counter.

Ordinary air parcel rates are Rs 678 for the first 250g and Rs 88 for each additional 250g. The maximum weight is 20kg. For ordinary seamail the first 10kg is Rs 660, plus Rs 80 for each additional kilo. Registration of air or sea parcels is an additional Rs 35.

Be cautious of places that offer to mail things to your home address after you have bought them. Government emporiums can usually be trusted. If you are seduced into shopping at one of the ubiquitous Kashmiri emporiums you'll be presented with numerous ways of having your goods sent. Many emporiums use international air couriers such as United Parcel Service. These are reliable but very expensive – often they cost more than the value of your purchases and sometimes the price quoted on purchase is far less than the price expected on delivery.

Bookpost

Books or printed matter can go by bookpost, which is considerably cheaper than parcel post. The maximum weight for a bookpost parcel is 5kg, which costs about Rs 1000 airmail and Rs 175 seamail. Parcels must be sent by 'open packet' mode, meaning they must be able to be easily opened and inspected. The packaging technique is best left to the professionals (the tailors) either at the post office or through major bookshops. Not only will they stitch the packets appropriately for inspection, they ensure that your books are packaged for protection and the lowest postal rates. Rates for airmail bookpost are:

weight (g)	cost (Rs)
200g	Rs 45
250g	Rs 54
500g	Rs 102
760g	Rs 159
1000g	Rs 195
1260g	Rs 252
1500g	Rs 288
2000g	Rs 363

If you are not in a hurry to receive your books you can send them by sea bookpost. This will cost Rs 75 for the first 2kg and Rs 33 for each additional kilogram.

Receiving Mail

The poste restante service is generally very good. Expected letters are almost always there.

Have letters addressed to you with your surname in capitals and underlined, followed by 'poste restante', the post office, and the city or town in question. Many 'lost' letters are simply misfiled under given (first) names, so always check under both your names. Letters sent via poste restante are held for one month only, after which, if unclaimed, they are returned to the sender.

Having parcels sent to you in India is an extremely hit-and-miss affair. Don't count on anything bigger than a letter getting to you. And don't count on a letter getting to you if there's anything of market value inside it.

American Express, in its major city locations, offers an alternative to the poste restante system.

Telephone

Throughout Kerala you'll find private STD/ISD call booths with direct local, interstate and international dialling. These phones are usually found in shops or other businesses and are well signposted. A digital meter lets you keep an eye on costs, and gives you a printout at the end. Then you just pay the shop owner – quick, painless and a far cry from the not so distant past when a night spent at a telegraph office waiting for a line was not unusual. Direct international calls from these phones cost around Rs 70 per minute, depending on the country you are calling. To make an international call, you will need to dial the following:

00 (international access code from India) + country code (of the country you are calling) + area code + local number.

In some centres, STD/ISD booths may offer a 'call back' service – you ring your folks, give them the phone number of the booth and wait for them to call you back. The booth operator will charge about Rs 2 to Rs 3 per minute for this service, in addition to the cost of the preliminary call. Advise your caller how long you intend to wait at the booth in the event that they have trouble getting back to you. The number your caller dials will be as follows:

(caller's country international access code) + 91 (international country code for India) + area code + local number (booth number).

The Central Telegraph/Telecom offices in major towns are usually efficient and very helpful. Some are open 24 hours.

Also available is the Home Country Direct service, which gives you access to the international operator in your home country. You can then make reverse charge (collect) or credit card calls, although this is not always easy. If you are calling from a hotel beware of exorbitant connection charges on these sorts of calls (or any calls for that matter). You may also have trouble convincing the owner of the telephone that they are not going to get charged for the call. The countries and numbers to dial are listed in the 'Home Country Direct Numbers' table.

Fax

Fax rates at telegraph offices (usually found at or near the central post office) are Rs 60

Home Country Direct Numbers

country	number
Australia	☎ 0006117
Canada	☎ 000167
Germany	☎ 0004917
Italy	☎ 0003917
Japan	☎ 0008117
The Netherlands	☎ 0003117
New Zealand	☎ 0006417
Singapore	☎ 0006517
Spain	☎ 0003417
Taiwan	☎ 00088617
Thailand	☎ 0006617
UK	☎ 0004417
USA	☎ 000117

per page for neighbouring countries, Rs 95 per page to other Asian destinations, Africa and Europe, and Rs 125 to Australia, New Zealand, USA and Canada. Main telegraph offices are open 24 hours. Rates within India are Rs 30 per page for A4 size transmissions. In Kerala, telegraph offices provide the most reliable and helpful service but you will have to fill out forms, sometimes pay before the fax is transmitted and then wait a considerable time for a refund if transmission is unsuccessful. Apart from that, staff usually go to extraordinary lengths to ensure your fax is despatched successfully.

Many STD/ISD booths also have fax machines but they're not reliable and if your fax doesn't go through you are usually liable for a fee, which can be quite hefty if there's a charge levied for each unsuccessful attempt. In northern Kerala, there are few fax centres and fewer still that transmit overseas. Hotels may have a fax service but because many turn off their machines when they're not sending faxes, incoming messages may not arrive. Both hotel and private operators have been known to insist that a fax has been transmitted when in fact it hasn't. Always get a transmission receipt. Sometimes the form filling and long waits at the telegraph offices are worth the hassle – you get a successful transmission or at the very least an accurate statement.

Telegram
You can send telegrams from telegraph offices. The cost is around Rs 2.50 per word.

Email & Internet Access
You can send and receive email at major centres such as Thiruvananthapuram, Kollam, Kottayam, Kochi, Thrissur and Kozhikode but at the time of writing facilities elsewhere were nonexistent or not operational. Take care with less than efficient places – they may charge large fees to link you up to a service that doesn't work. The Information sections in the regional chapters provide details of reliable email bureaus.

The easiest way to send and receive email at cybercafes is to make use of a free Web-based email account, such as HotMaiL (www.hotmail.com), Yahoo! (mail.yahoo.çom) or try Lonely Planet's eKno service (www.ekno.com). It's easiest to register with one of these email services before you leave home.

Tell your family and friends to avoid sending long attached documents. They take an eternity to download and usually cause the system to drop out.

INTERNET RESOURCES
There are numerous online services relevant to India, but services come and go with some frequency. The Lonely Planet Web site (www.lonelyplanet.com) has up-to-date advice, photographs, travel tales and general information on travelling throughout the region, with many links to other relevant sites.

For information on Kerala you can try www.kerala.org and for up-to-date travel information check out the well-maintained www.keralatourism.org. At this site you'll also receive a weekly update on attractions and current events.

For general news it's worth checking out the Web sites run by India's best-known newspapers and magazines. They include:

Asian Age
www.asianage.com
Hindu
www.hinduonline.com or www.the-hindu.com
India Today
www.india-today.com

BOOKS
In Kerala, you'll find numerous books on India by Indian publishers, which are generally not available in the west. Thiruvananthapuram, Kochi and Kumily have well-stocked stores offering plenty of choice in several Indian languages as well as English and in some cases, French.

India is one of the world's largest publishers of books in English. Recently producers British and American books also reach Indian bookshops very quickly with very low mark-ups.

Several Indian publishers publish Indian authors whose work has been translated, catalogues are available for those interested. Macmillan India recently launched a project specifically aimed at publishing 55 English translations from 11 Indian languages. You'll be able to obtain many translations of Malayalam works.

Most books are published in different editions by different publishers in different countries. As a result, a book might be a hardcover rarity in one country while it's readily available in paperback in another. It's best to ask for books by their title and author. For information on literature by Keralan authors, see the Literature section in the Facts about Kerala chapter.

Lonely Planet

It's pleasing to be able to say that for more information on India and its neighbours, and for travel beyond India, most of the best guides come from Lonely Planet!

Lonely Planet's *India* has comprehensive information on the whole of the country. The Himalaya is well covered, with a trekking guide and a regular travel guide (*Indian Himalaya*). Lonely Planet's *South India* gives more detailed information than any other guide on the southern states. There are also Lonely Planet guides to *Delhi*, *Mumbai (Bombay)*, *Rajasthan* and *Goa*, for travellers spending more time in these places.

Lonely Planet guides to the South Asian region include: *Nepal*, *Trekking in the Nepal Himalaya*, *Bhutan*, *Tibet*, *Karakoram Highway*, *Pakistan*, *Bangladesh*, *Myanmar*, *Sri Lanka*, *Maldives*, and *South-East Asia*.

Lonely Planet also produces a *Healthy Travel Asia & India* guide, a *Read This First: Asia* guide for first time travellers, a *Hindi/Urdu phrasebook* and *Sacred India*, a pictorial book on the spiritual side of India.

Guidebooks

Blue Guide's *Southern India* by George Michell provides excellent information on the region's architecture, art, archaeology and history. The author has written numerous other books on the history and art of India.

South India – Travel Information Guide by PS Kurian & PJ Varghese is a handy guide with transport listings and information on attractions.

Travel

Dervla Murphy's classic on South India *On a Shoestring to Coorg* is still one of the most comprehensive accounts of travelling in this region although much has changed in recent decades.

Chasing the Monsoon by Alexander Frater is an Englishman's account of a journey north from Kovalam, all the while following the onset of the monsoon. It's a fascinating insight into the significance of the monsoon, and its effect on people.

Three-Quarters of a Footprint by Joe Roberts is another Englishman's experiences of his travels through South India, including Kerala. Sometimes he stays with his Indian friends, sometimes he travels independently. His impressions are informative and discerning.

History & Culture

For a thorough account of Kerala's early history see the four volumes *History of Kerala* written in letter form by KP Padmanabha Menon. Another authority in the area is the *Malabar Manual* in two volumes by William Logan.

Social and Cultural History of Kerala by A Sreedhara Menon gives an accessible reading on all aspects of Keralan life including geography, social systems and custom, religion and the arts. The author's more recent text *Kerala and Freedom Struggle* is interesting, not only for its documentation but also for the controversy it provoked about the interpretation of Kerala's history.

In *Kerala – A Portrait of the Malabar Coast*, George Woodcock provides another useful and interesting historical overview of Kerala.

Kerala Gazetteer produced by the Government of Kerala provides a history of Kerala as well as information on the development of Malayalam language.

The most established work on the history of the South Indian region is *A History of South India From Prehistoric Times to the Fall of Vijayanagar* by Nilakanta Sastri. Heavy going at times, it nevertheless provides comprehensive and detailed coverage.

If you want a thorough introduction to Indian history then look for the two-volume Pelican *A History of India*. In the first volume Romila Thapar follows Indian history from 1000 BCE (before common era) to the coming of the Mughals in the 16th century. Volume two by Percival Spear follows the rise and fall of the Mughals through to India since Independence.

The Wonder That Was India by AL Basham gives good descriptions of the Indian civilisations, origins of the caste system and social customs, and detailed information on Hinduism, Buddhism and other religions in India. It is also very informative about art and architecture.

The Career and Legend of Vasco da Gama by Sanjay Subrahmanyam is one of the best recent investigations of the person who is credited with 'discovering' the sea route to India. For more background on the Indian Ocean trade Kenneth McPherson's *The Indian Ocean – A History of People and the Sea* provides a comprehensive overview.

India – A Celebration of Independence 1947 to 1997 is a photographic record of the first 50 years of Indian Independence. It begins with an image of Mahatma Gandhi and ends more than 200 images later with a picture of chaos at a Mumbai port. Some of the world's leading photographers including Henry Cartier-Bresson, Mary Ellen Mark and Sebastiao Salgado are represented in this evocative photographic study.

South Indian Customs by PV Jagadisa Ayyar seeks to explain a range of practices including the formation of snake images beneath the banyan tree.

Sree Padmanabha Temple by Aswathi Thirunal Gouri Lakshmi Bayi (from the royal family of the former Travancore state in Southern Kerala) is an account of the history, legends and architecture of her family's temple.

Festivals of Kerala by PJ Varghese et al, details numerous Keralan festivals as well as giving information about many of Kerala's art forms.

Kalarippayattu by P Balakrishan provides an account of Kerala's ancient martial art through text, diagram and photos.

Sree Narayana Guru by K Sreenivasan considers the life and philosophy of this acclaimed social reformer while giving an insight into the huge problems created by the caste system.

Inner Spaces: New Writing by Women from Kerala by KM George et al affords a glimpse into the lives of women in Kerala.

Ayurveda – The Science of Self Healing by Vasant Lad details in text and diagrams the fundamentals of the art as well as providing practical advice for self health care. *Ayurveda* by Robert E Svoboda speaks to a western audience about this ancient craft.

The Arts

The Archaeological Survey of India publishes a series of booklets on major sites and works, which are available at museums and various sites throughout Kerala.

The Arts and Crafts of Kerala by Stella Kramrisch is a large, authoritative and well illustrated volume that describes Keralan architecture as well as the various arts and crafts of the state.

Performing Arts of Kerala edited by Mallika Sarabhai is a large beautifully illustrated volume describing many of the rituals, dance and drama of Kerala. The text is well complemented with photographs by Pankaj Shah.

The History of Architecture in India: From the Dawn of Civilisation to the End of the Raj by Christopher Tadgell provides a good overview, including important sites in South India, and has plenty of illustrations.

Architecture and Art of Southern India by George Michell provides details on the Vijayanagar empire and its successors, encompassing a period of some 400 years. Michell's *The Hindu Temple* is an excellent introduction to the symbolism and evolution of temple architecture.

A Guide to Kathakali by David Bolland provides a detailed insight into the performance and includes 35 plays on which the art form is based.

Appreciating Carnatic Music (Ganesh & Co) by Chitravina Ravi Kiran is available in India for Rs 125 and is aimed at helping those more familiar with western music get to grips with this South Indian art form. It's a compact little book with masses of useful information including a question-and-answer section.

Arts and Crafts of India by Ilay Cooper and John Gillow covers the entire country, including information on folk arts in South India.

Cuisine

Kerala Cookery and *The Family Cook Book* by Mrs KM Mathew have traditional as well as contemporary recipes, focusing on the food of the Syrian Christians.

101 Kerala Delicacies by G Padma Vijay provides a range of recipes from Kerala's different ethnic groups.

Religion

A Handbook of Living Religions edited by John R Hinnewls provides a succinct and readable summary of all the various religions you will find in India, including Christianity and Judaism.

The English series of Penguin paperbacks are among the best and are generally available in India. In particular, *Hinduism* by KM Sen is brief and to the point. If you want to read the Hindu holy books these are available in translations: *The Upanishads* and *The Bhagavad Gita*. *Hindu Mythology*, edited by Wendy O'Flaherty, is an interesting annotated collection of extracts from the Hindu holy books.

A Classical Dictionary of Hindu Mythology & Religion by John Dowson (Rupa, Delhi, 1987) is an Indian paperback reprint of an old English hardback. As the name suggests, it is in dictionary form and is one of the best sources for unravelling who's who in Hinduism.

Travels Through Sacred India by Roger Housden is a very readable account of popular and classical traditions and contains a gazetteer of sacred places plus a roundup of ashrams and retreats.

Am I a Hindu? is a Hinduism primer edited by Viswanathan that attempts to explore and explain the fundamental tenets of Hinduism through a discourse of questions and answers.

Hinduism, an Introduction by Shakunthala Jagannathan is a popular, well-illustrated book that seeks to explain what Hinduism is all about. If you have no prior knowledge of the subject matter, this book is a good starting point.

The Marriage of East and West by Bede Griffiths is the famous book by the equally famous monk who lived for many decades in Tamil Nadu. The author examines the essence of eastern and western thought in an attempt to forge a fresh approach to spirituality.

Temples of South India by NS Ramaswami gives a rare and detailed account of the structure, history and mythology of many of Kerala's better-known temples.

Ramayana in Palm Leaf Pictures from the University of Kerala has fine drawings of palm leaves that depict the story of Rama. Each leaf has an English translation.

For an account of the St Thomas Christians see *The Indian Christians of St Thomas* by Leslie Brown.

The seven essays in *Studies of Indian Jewish Identity* edited by Nathan Katz examine Indian Jewish identity from a historical, cultural and ethnographic perspective.

Indian Mythology by Veronica Ions is a comprehensive and well-illustrated book that covers all of the major religions in India.

Environment & Wildlife

The Book of Indian Animals by SH Prater was first written in 1948 but remains one of the best overviews of Indian wildlife and includes colour illustrations. The Insight Guide *Indian Wildlife* provides interesting background and plenty of colour illustrations.

The National Book Trust of India publishes a series of books on ecological topics, including *Endangered Animals of India* by

SM Nair, *Flowering Trees* by MS Randhawa, and *Our Environment* by Laeeq Futehally. Though mainly aimed at children the books are informative, illustrated, cheap (Rs 35) and easy to find in India.

The National Council for Science and Technology and the Bombay Natural History Society have jointly published a series of small books, all with black covers and priced at Rs 125. For a brief, readable overview, titles such as *Indian Elephants*, *Moths of India* and *Extinction is Forever* are worth picking up.

Cheetal Walk: Living in the Wilderness by ERC Davidar describes the author's life among the elephants of the Nilgiri Hills and looks at how they can be saved from extinction.

This Fissured Land: An Ecological History of India by Madhav Gadgil & Ramachandra Guha provides an excellent overview of ecological issues.

Birds of Kerala by S Ali gives a thorough documentation with illustrations of the birds of the region.

The Natural Resources of Kerala produced by the World Wide Fund for Nature in Thiruvananthapuram contains numerous papers on all aspects of Kerala's ecology.

General

The annual *Manorama Yearbook* is published in Kerala and gives information and statistics on international as well as Indian issues.

The magazine *Tourism India* gives a broad coverage of travel possibilities with frequent articles and information on Kerala.

CD ROMS

Kerala: The Green Symphony (Invis Media) has plenty of cultural, geographical and historical information, and lots of graphics. It's available from bookshops and tourist offices. *India: A Multimedia Journey* includes videos, slides, maps and travelling tips. *India Mystique* highlights Indian philosophy, history and religion. *Indian Wildlife* has more than 650 pictures and slides as well as information about more than 30 national parks, including some in South India.

NEWSPAPERS & MAGAZINES

Of the English-language dailies the *Asian Age* is arguably the best in South India. Its foreign coverage is excellent. National newspapers include the *Times of India*, the *Hindu*, and the *Indian Express*. They are printed in Bangalore and carry a section dedicated to the particular areas of Kerala where they are distributed.

The *Hindu* is one of the more comprehensive papers and has an excellent literary supplement on Sunday that examines books published both inside and outside India. The *Deccan Herald,* available throughout South India, appears to have little critical comment and virtually no world news. The *Economic Times* is a serious publication for those interested in business and economic analysis.

There's a very wide range of general interest magazines published in English in India. *India Today* is a national magazine, which after 21 years of publishing fortnightly, became weekly from June 1997. It purports to give important information on happenings in India, but it's pretty light on. *Frontline* is a fortnightly magazine published by the *Hindu* newspaper group. It has comprehensive coverage of national, political and social events as well as a reasonable foreign news section. It costs Rs 15.

Gentleman is a glossy magazine for male yuppies. *Sportstar*, published by the *Hindu* group, is a weekly national magazine, containing reams of information on cricket. *Better Photography* is a high-quality, national monthly magazine published in Mumbai. *Biznet*, a self-described 'cyber mag' dedicated to Web surfers, is published in Mumbai. In addition to feature articles and cyber news it contains reviews and addresses of Indian and foreign Web sites. It costs Rs 30 and is a 'sister' publication to *Gentleman*.

Time and *Newsweek* are only available in the main cities, and anyway, once you've become used to Indian prices they seem very expensive.

You may also find newspapers like the *Herald Tribune* and *Guardian* and magazines like *Der Spiegel* and its English, French and Italian clones in the major cities and at expensive hotels.

Manushi is a monthly magazine, with analysis on issues pertaining to women. Their Web site is at www.freespeech.org/manushi.

RADIO & TV

Radio programs can be heard on All India Radio (AIR), which provides the usual interviews, music and news features. There is also an FM band with programs in different languages. Details on programs are found in the major dailies.

Satellite TV runs 24 hours and includes up to 30 channels including BBC, CNN, Discovery and Asianet. Various local channels broadcast in the local languages. The national broadcaster is Doordarshan.

PHOTOGRAPHY & VIDEO

Film & Equipment

Colour print film processing facilities are readily available in larger cities. Film is about the same price as anywhere and the quality is usually (but not always) good. Always check the use-by date on local film stock. Heat and humidity can play havoc with film, even if the use-by date hasn't been exceeded. Developing costs for prints are around Rs 50, plus Rs 5 per photo for printing.

Colour slide film is available in Thiruvananthapuram and Kochi. For guaranteed quality, slide processing is best done in Bangalore – or take your film home. Kodachrome and other 'includes developing' film will have to be sent overseas.

Remember, if you buy film from street hawkers you do so at your own risk. Some travellers report that old, useless film is loaded into new-looking canisters. The hapless tourist only discovers the trick when the film is developed back home.

A UV filter permanently fitted to your lens will not only cut down ultraviolet light, but will protect your lens. Spare batteries should be carried at all times. Serious photographers will consider bringing a tripod and fast film (400 ASA) for interior shots. It's a good idea not to carry your gear around in a flashy bag. Either get an old battered-looking one or put your expensive bag inside a less salubrious carrier.

Technical Tips

In general, photography is best done in the early morning and late afternoon. The stark midday sun eliminates shadows, rendering less depth to your photographs.

Film manufacturers warn that, once exposed, film should be developed as quickly as possible; in practice the film seems to last, even in Kerala's summer heat, without deterioration for a few months. Try to keep your film cool, and protect it in water and airproof containers if you're travelling during the monsoon. Silica gel sachets distributed around your gear will help to absorb any moisture. As places on the coast can be very humid throughout the year, silica is useful any season.

It's worthwhile investing in a lead-lined (x-ray proof) bag, as repeated exposure to x-ray (even so-called 'film proof' x-ray) can damage film. *Never* put your film in baggage that will be placed in the cargo holds of aeroplanes. It will probably be subjected to large doses of x-ray that will spoil or completely ruin it.

Restrictions

Be careful what you photograph. Authorities are touchy about places of military importance – this can include train stations, bridges, airports and military installations. Always take heed of signs prohibiting photography.

Some temples prohibit photography especially of deities or in the *mandapam* (outer hall of a temple) and inner sanctum. Don't photograph religious ceremonies. Taking photos of a death ceremony or of people bathing (in baths or rivers) will almost certainly cause offence. If in doubt, ask.

Most places levy a fee to bring a still camera or video camera onto the premises. See the individual entries in the regional chapters for more information.

Photographing People

Although most people are very happy to be photographed, don't assume this. Ask first and be prepared to invest time to engage them and seek their cooperation. People who make their living by entertaining may expect you to pay them for the photos you take. Always seek permission before using a flash at night, especially at cultural shows. If people request copies of your pictures, make sure you get their address and honour your promise.

Video

It's usually worth buying a few cassettes duty-free to start off your trip. It's possible to obtain them in Thiruvananthapuram and Ernakulam.

Remember to follow the same rules regarding people's sensitivities as for still photography – having a video camera shoved in one's face is probably even more annoying than a still camera. Always ask permission first.

TIME

India is 5½ hours ahead of GMT/UTC, 4½ hours behind Australian EST and 10½ hours ahead of American EST. It is officially known as IST – Indian Standard Time.

When it is noon in Kerala:

	late March-late Oct	late Oct-late March
London	6.30 am	7.30 am
New York	1.30 am	2.30 am
San Francisco (the previous day)	10.30 pm	11.30 pm
Sydney	4.30 pm	5.30 pm
Auckland	6.30 pm	7.30 pm

ELECTRICITY

The electric current is 230-240V AC, 50 cycles. Electricity is widely available in the main towns and tourist destinations. Sockets are of a three round-pin variety, similar (but not identical) to European sockets. European round-pin plugs will go into the sockets, but as the pins on Indian plugs are somewhat thicker, the fit is loose and connection is not always guaranteed. Tape may be required to hold the plug in place.

Power cuts ('load shedding') and 'brown outs' (partial power cuts, ie when the power drops below normal levels, dimming lights and slowing fans, etc) are common in Kerala. If you are bringing sensitive electronic equipment, eg a notebook computer, a voltage stabiliser is essential.

WEIGHTS & MEASURES

Although India is officially metricated, imperial weights and measures are still used in some areas of commerce. Some of the measures you will frequently come across in the media are: one *lakh* (100 thousand); one *crore* (10 million). Your requests for directions may be met with replies in furlongs (200m). A conversion chart is included on the inside back cover of this book.

LAUNDRY

All of the top-end hotels and most mid-range and budget hotels offer a laundry service. Costs are minimal and service is usually very good.

TOILETS

Most accommodation (even budget) has rooms with attached bath and toilet. Toilets may be squat (often referred to as Indian style) or seated (western style).

HEALTH

Travel health depends on your predeparture preparations, your daily health care while travelling and the way you handle any medical problem that may develop. While the potential dangers can seem quite frightening, in reality few travellers experience anything more than upset stomachs. The information given here is for travellers to Kerala as well as those who may be visiting other places in India.

Predeparture Planning

Immunisations Plan your vaccinations carefully and seek medical advice at least six weeks before travel. Some vaccinations require more than one injection, while others cannot be given together. Note that some vaccinations are not advisable during pregnancy or for people with allergies – discuss this with your doctor.

Record all vaccinations on an International Certificate of Vaccination, available from your doctor or government health department. There's no risk of acquiring yellow fever in Kerala, but you'll need proof of vaccination against it if you are arriving from a yellow-fever infected country (parts of South America and sub-Saharan Africa).

Discuss your requirements with your doctor. A combined hepatitis/typhoid vaccine has recently been developed, although its availability is limited – again, check with your doctor to find out its status in your country. Other vaccinations you should consider for this trip include the following (for more details about the diseases themselves, see the individual disease entries later in this section).

Diphtheria & Tetanus Vaccinations for these two diseases are usually combined and are recommended for everyone. After an initial course of three injections (usually given in childhood), boosters are necessary every 10 years.

Polio Everyone should keep up to date with this vaccination, which is normally given in childhood. A booster every 10 years maintains immunity.

Hepatitis A Hepatitis A vaccine (eg Avaxim, Havrix 1440 or VAQTA) provides long-term immunity (possibly more than 10 years) after an initial injection and a booster at six to 12 months. Hepatitis A vaccine is also available in a combined form, Twinrix, with hepatitis B vaccine. Three injections over a six month period are required, the first two providing substantial protection against hepatitis A.

Alternatively, an injection of gamma globulin can provide short-term protection against hepatitis A – two to six months, depending on the dose given. It is not a vaccine, but is a ready-made antibody collected from blood donations. It is reasonably effective and, unlike the vaccine, it gives immediate protection, but because it is a blood product, there are current concerns about its long-term safety.

Hepatitis B If you're intending to stay for a long time you should consider vaccination against hepatitis B. This involves three injections, with a booster at 12 months. More rapid courses are available if necessary.

Typhoid Vaccination against typhoid may be required if you intend to stay in Kerala for more than a couple of weeks. It is now available either as an injection or as capsules taken orally.

Cholera The current vaccine against cholera has low protection and many side effects, so it's generally not recommended.

Rabies Vaccination should be considered if you're intending to spend a month or longer in Kerala, especially if you may be handling animals, caving or travelling to remote areas. It's also important to consider for children who may not report a bite. Pre-travel rabies vaccination involves three injections over 21 to 28 days. If someone who has been vaccinated is bitten or scratched by an animal, they'll require two booster injections, those not vaccinated require more.

Japanese B Encephalitis Consider vaccination against this disease if spending a month or longer in Kerala. It involves three injections over 30 days.

Tuberculosis (TB) The risk of TB to travellers is usually very low, unless you'll be living or closely associated with local people. Vaccination against TB (BCG) is recommended for children and young adults whose stay is for more than three months.

Malaria Medication Antimalarial drugs do not prevent you from being infected, they kill the malaria parasites during a stage in their development and significantly reduce the risk of illness or even death. Expert advice on medication should be sought, as there are many factors to consider, including the area to be visited, the risk of exposure to malaria-carrying mosquitoes, the side effects of medication, medical history, age and pregnancy.

Health Insurance Make sure that you have adequate health insurance. See Travel Insurance under Visas & Documents, earlier in this chapter.

Travel Health Guides If you are planning to be away or in remote areas for a long period of time, you may like to consider taking a more detailed health guide.

CDC's Complete Guide to Healthy Travel, Open Road Publishing, 1997, gives the US Centers for Disease Control & Prevention recommendations for international travel.
Healthy Travel Asia & India, Dr Isabelle Young, Lonely Planet Publications, 2000. Covers it all from how to treat a nose bleed in Delhi to finding a doctor in Mumbai.
Staying Healthy in Asia, Africa & Latin America, Dirk Schroeder, Moon Publications, 1994, is probably the best all-round guide; it's detailed and well organised.
Travel with Children, Maureen Wheeler, Lonely Planet Publications, 1995, includes advice on travel health for children.
Where There Is No Doctor, David Werner, Macmillan, 1994, is a detailed guide intended for workers in underdeveloped countries.

There are also a number of excellent travel health sites on the Internet. From Lonely Planet there are links at www.lonelyplanet.com/weblinks/wlprep.htm#heal to the World Health Organization and the US Centers for Disease Control & Prevention.

Other Preparations Make sure you're healthy before you start travelling. An awareness of general health indicators may assist. Normal body temperature is up to 37°C (98.6°F); more than 2°C (4°F) higher indicates a high fever. The normal adult pulse rate is 60 to 100 per minute (children 80 to 100, babies 100 to 140). As a general rule the pulse increases about 20 beats per minute for each 1°C (2°F) rise in fever.

Respiration (breathing) rate is also an indicator of health. Count the number of breaths per minute: between 12 and 20 is normal for adults and older children (up to 30 for younger children, 40 for babies). People with a high fever or serious respiratory illness breathe more quickly than normal. More than 40 shallow breaths a minute may indicate pneumonia.

If you are going on a long trip make sure your teeth are OK. If you wear glasses take a spare pair and your prescription. If you require a particular medication take an adequate supply, as it may not be available locally. To facilitate replacements, take part of the packaging showing the generic name rather than the brand. To avoid problems, it's a good idea to have a legible statement from your doctor indicating that you require medication for legal use.

Basic Rules

Food Good food is obviously an important component of good health. With an exciting cuisine waiting to be sampled, you don't want to spoil your experience with senseless hang-ups about health. Of course it's wise to be cautious, but it's pointless to be so cautious you miss out on new and exciting experiences. Since stomach upsets are high on the list of health problems (mostly minor), care in what you eat and drink is obviously important. There's an old colonial adage: 'If you can cook it, boil it or peel it, you can eat it'. It's probably a wise base from which to work. If an eating place is busy, it should be fine. Locals are proud of their cuisine and choose only the best places to enjoy it.

When choosing vegetables and fruits select those that you can peel. Bananas, pineapples, papaya and coconuts are all safe. Avoid fresh salads or wash them with purified water. Beware of ice cream, cold milk, and undercooked meats or fish. It's unlikely you'll encounter the latter since many Keralan meat dishes are cooked slowly – more like a stew. If you have any

Medical Kit Check List

Following is a list of items you should consider including in your medical kit – consult your pharmacist for brands available in your country.

- ☐ **Aspirin** or **paracetamol** (acetaminophen in the USA) – for pain or fever
- ☐ **Antihistamine** – for allergies, eg hay fever; to ease the itch from insect bites or stings; and to prevent motion sickness
- ☐ **Antibiotics** – consider including these if you're travelling well off the beaten track; see your doctor, as they must be prescribed, and carry the prescription with you
- ☐ **Loperamide** or **diphenoxylate** –'blockers' for diarrhoea; **prochlorperazine** or **metaclopramide** for nausea and vomiting
- ☐ **Rehydration mixture** – to prevent dehydration, eg due to severe diarrhoea; particularly important when travelling with children
- ☐ **Insect repellent**, **sunscreen**, **lip balm** and **eye drops**
- ☐ **Calamine lotion**, **sting relief spray** or **aloe vera** – to ease irritation from sunburn and insect bites or stings
- ☐ **Antifungal cream** or **powder** – for fungal skin infections and thrush
- ☐ **Antiseptic** (such as povidone-iodine) – for cuts and grazes
- ☐ **Bandages**, **Band-Aids (plasters)** and other wound dressings
- ☐ **Water purification tablets** or **iodine**
- ☐ **Scissors**, **tweezers** and a **thermometer** (note that mercury thermometers are prohibited by airlines)
- ☐ **Syringes** and **needles** – in case you need injections in a country with medical hygiene problems. Ask your doctor for a note explaining why you have them.
- ☐ **Cold** and **flu tablets**, **throat lozenges** and **nasal decongestant**
- ☐ **Multivitamins** – consider for long trips, when dietary vitamin intake may be inadequate

concerns, eat vegetarian dishes, which are delicious and always available.

Although the Keralan cuisine is tasty and healthy, a change from the norm can sometimes get you down physically or psychologically. If you're travelling hard and fast and missing meals or if you simply lose your appetite, you can soon start to lose weight and place your health at risk. You may feel lethargic and drained of energy. The answer is to increase your protein intake – eat more eggs, fruit and nuts – bananas, mandarins, oranges or peanuts. Try to eat plenty of grains, including rice and bread. All of these are easily found in the markets and restaurants. Many travellers carry multivitamins with them.

You will no doubt be quickly enticed by the variety and tastes of Keralan food and weight gain, rather than loss, will more likely be the problem.

Make sure you drink enough – don't rely on feeling thirsty to indicate when you should drink. Not needing to urinate or small amounts of dark yellow urine is a danger sign. *Always* carry a water bottle with you. Excessive sweating can lead to a loss of salt and muscle cramping. Salt tablets are not a good idea as a preventative; adding salt to food can help.

Water Generally in India, the No 1 rule is *be careful of the water* and especially ice. If you don't know for certain that the water is safe, avoid it. In Kerala, however, as long as you boil the water, it should be safe.

Some travellers drink the water everywhere and never get sick, others are more careful and still get a bug. Basically, you should not drink the water in small towns unless you know it has been boiled. Although top-class hotels would never serve anything other than safe water, in some mid-range places the water is only filtered and not boiled. The local water filters remove solids, but usually don't remove bacteria. Things are changing though and some places now have very effective filters. Water is generally safer in the dry season than during the monsoon when it really can be dangerous.

Throughout Kerala you should have no problems if you stick to boiled water – just ask at each place you stay for your water container to be filled with boiled water.

Bottled Water Most visitors to Kerala stick to bottled water, available just about everywhere. If you prefer this solution, stock up before you hit the road or embark on a long train trip. The price for a 1L bottle ranges from about Rs 15 to Rs 25. Expect to pay a little more in restaurants (anything up to Rs 70). Virtually all so-called mineral water is actually treated tap water.

Generally, if you stick to bottled water, any gut problems you might have will be from other sources – food, dirty utensils, dirty hands and so on. One of the best (real) mineral waters is Pondicherry from Tamil Nadu, and is distributed throughout Kerala.

Reputable brands of bottled water or soft drinks are generally fine, although in some places bottles may be refilled with tap water. Only use water from containers with a serrated seal – not tops or corks. However, you can go easy on your pocket, as well as the environment, if you follow the advice above about boiled water.

Water Purification The simplest way of purifying water is to boil it thoroughly for five minutes. In Kerala, this is sufficient to make it safe. Accommodation places will do this for you. Just carry a container and fill it as necessary.

In other states you can buy 5L containers of mineral water for Rs 80. The containers can be recycled so each time you return with an empty container it will be replaced with a full one for a Rs 20 reduction. At the time of writing, this product was not available in Kerala, but keep an eye out for it.

For a long trip, consider purchasing a water filter. There are two main kinds of filter. Total filters take out all parasites, bacteria and viruses, and make water safe to drink. They are often expensive, but they can be more cost effective than buying bottled water. Simple filters (which can even be a nylon mesh bag) take out dirt and larger foreign bodies so that chemical solutions work more effectively; if water is dirty, chemical solutions may not work at all.

It's very important when buying a filter to read the specifications, so that you know exactly what it removes and what it doesn't. Simple filtering will not remove all dangerous organisms, so if you cannot boil water it should be treated chemically. Chlorine tablets (Puritabs, Steritabs or other brand names) will kill many pathogens, but not parasites such as giardia and amoebic cysts. Iodine is more effective in purifying water and is available in tablet form (such as Potable Aqua). Follow the directions carefully and remember that too much iodine can be harmful.

Medical Problems & Treatment

Self-diagnosis and treatment can be risky, so you should always seek medical help. Although drug dosages are given in this section, they are for emergency use only. Correct diagnosis is vital.

An embassy, consulate or hotel can usually recommend a local doctor or clinic. Antibiotics should ideally be administered only under medical supervision. Take only the recommended dose at the prescribed intervals and use the whole course, even if the illness seems to be cured earlier. Stop immediately if there are any serious reactions and don't use the antibiotic at all if you are unsure that you have the correct one. Some people are allergic to commonly prescribed antibiotics such as penicillin or sulpha drugs; carry this information (eg on a bracelet) when travelling.

Hospitals Kerala has several hospitals and private clinics where you can go in an emergency. The usual fee for a clinic visit is about Rs 100, Rs 250 for a specialist. Home calls usually cost about Rs 150.

Environmental Hazards

Heat Exhaustion Dehydration and salt deficiency can cause heat exhaustion. Take time to acclimatise to high temperatures, drink sufficient liquids and don't do anything too physically demanding.

Salt deficiency is characterised by fatigue, lethargy, headaches, giddiness and muscle cramps; salt tablets may help, but adding extra salt to your food is better.

Anhidrotic heat exhaustion is a rare form of heat exhaustion that is caused by an inability to sweat. It tends to affect people who have been in a hot climate for some time, rather than newcomers. It can progress to heatstroke. Treatment involves removal to a cooler climate.

Heatstroke This serious, occasionally fatal, condition can occur if the body's heat-regulating mechanism breaks down and the body temperature rises to dangerous levels. Long, continuous periods of exposure to high temperatures and insufficient fluids can leave you vulnerable to heatstroke.

The symptoms are feeling unwell, not sweating very much (or at all) and a high body temperature (39° to 41°C or 102° to 106°F). Where sweating has ceased, the skin becomes flushed and red. Severe, throbbing headaches and lack of coordination will also occur, and the sufferer may be confused or aggressive. Eventually the victim will become delirious or convulse. Hospitalisation is essential, but in the interim get victims out of the sun, remove their clothing, cover them with a wet sheet or towel and then fan continually. Give fluids if they are conscious.

Jet Lag Jet lag is experienced when a person travels by air across more than three time zones (each time zone usually represents a one hour time difference). Jet lag occurs because many of the functions of the human body (such as temperature, pulse rate and emptying of the bladder and bowels) are regulated by internal 24 hour cycles. When we travel long distances rapidly, our bodies take time to adjust to the 'new time' of our destination, and we may experience fatigue, disorientation, insomnia, anxiety, impaired concentration and loss of appetite. These effects will usually be gone within three days of arrival, but there are ways to minimise the impact of jet lag.

- rest for a couple of days prior to departure.
- select flight schedules that minimise sleep deprivation; arriving late in the day means you can sleep soon after you arrive. For very long flights, organise a stopover.
- avoid excessive eating (which bloats the stomach) and alcohol (which causes dehydration) during the flight. Instead, drink plenty of non-carbonated, nonalcoholic drinks such as water.
- avoid smoking.
- make yourself comfortable by wearing loose-fitting clothes and perhaps bringing an eye mask and ear plugs to help you sleep.
- try to operate on Kerala time as soon as you arrive.

Motion Sickness Eating lightly before and during a trip will reduce the chance of motion sickness. If you are prone to motion sickness try to find a place that minimises movement – near the wing on aircraft, close to midship on boats, near the centre on buses. Fresh air usually helps; reading and cigarette smoke don't. Commercial motion-sickness preparations, which can cause drowsiness, have to be taken before the trip commences. Ginger (available in capsule form) and peppermint (including mint-flavoured sweets) are natural preventatives.

Prickly Heat Prickly heat is an itchy rash caused by excessive perspiration trapped under the skin. It usually strikes people who have just arrived in a hot climate. Keep cool, bathe often, dry your skin and use a mild talcum or prickly heat powder. Resorting to air-conditioning may help.

Sunburn In Kerala's hot climate you can get sunburnt surprisingly quickly, even through cloud. Use a sunscreen with a high sun protection factor (SPF), a hat (or use an umbrella), and a barrier cream for your nose and lips. Calamine lotion or Stingose are good for mild sunburn. Aloe vera is a natural alternative. Protect your eyes with good quality sunglasses, particularly if you will be near water or sand.

Infectious Diseases

Diarrhoea Simple things like a change of water, food or climate can all cause a mild bout of diarrhoea, but a few rushed toilet trips with no other symptoms is not indicative of a major problem.

Dehydration is the main danger with diarrhoea, particularly in children or the elderly. Under all circumstances *fluid replacement* is most important. Weak black tea with a little sugar, soda water, or soft drinks allowed to go flat and diluted 50% with clean water are all good. With severe diarrhoea a rehydrating solution is preferable to replace minerals and salts lost. Commercially available oral rehydration salts (ORS) are very useful, add them to boiled or bottled water. In an emergency you can make up a solution of six teaspoons of sugar and a half teaspoon of salt to a litre of boiled or bottled water. You need to drink at least the same volume of fluid that you are losing in bowel movements and vomiting. Urine is the best guide to the adequacy of replacement – if you have small amounts of dark yellow urine, you need to drink more. Keep drinking small amounts often. Stick to a bland diet as you recover.

Gut-paralysing drugs such as loperamide or diphenoxylate can be used to bring relief from the symptoms, although they do not actually cure the problem. Only use these drugs if you do not have access to toilets, eg if you *must* travel. These drugs are not recommended for children under 12 years or for people with a high fever or who are severely dehydrated.

In certain situations antibiotics may be required: diarrhoea with blood or mucus (dysentery), any diarrhoea with fever, profuse watery diarrhoea, persistent diarrhoea not improving after 48 hours and severe diarrhoea. These suggest a more serious cause of diarrhoea and in these situations gut-paralysing drugs should be avoided.

In these situations, a stool test may be necessary to diagnose what bug is causing your diarrhoea, so you should seek medical help urgently. Where this is not possible the recommended drugs for bacterial diarrhoea (the most likely cause of severe diarrhoea in travellers) are norfloxacin 400mg twice daily for three days or ciprofloxacin 500mg twice daily for five days. These are not recommended for children or pregnant women. The drug of choice for children would be co-trimoxazole (Bactrim, Septrin or Resprim) with dosage dependent on weight. A five day course is given. Ampicillin or amoxycillin may be given in pregnancy, but medical care is necessary.

Two other causes of persistent diarrhoea are giardiasis and amoebic dysentery.

Giardiasis This is caused by a common parasite, Giardia lamblia. Symptoms include stomach cramps, nausea, a bloated stomach, watery, foul-smelling diarrhoea and frequent gas. Giardiasis can appear several weeks after you have been exposed to the parasite. The symptoms may disappear for a few days and then return; this can go on for several weeks.

Amoebic Dysentery This is caused by the protozoan *Entamoeba histolytica* and is characterised by a gradual onset of low-grade diarrhoea, often with blood and mucus. Cramping abdominal pain and vomiting are less likely than in other types of diarrhoea, and fever may not be present. It will persist until treated and can recur and cause other health problems.

You should seek medical advice if you think you have giardiasis or amoebic dysentery, but where this is not possible, tinidazole or metronidazole are the recommended drugs. Treatment is a 2g single dose of tinidazole or 250mg of metronidazole three times daily for five to 10 days.

Fungal Infections Fungal infections can occur in Kerala's hot, humid weather. They are usually found on the scalp, between the toes (athlete's foot) or fingers, in the groin and on the body (ringworm). You get ringworm (which is a fungal infection, not a worm) from infected animals or other people. Moisture encourages these infections.

To prevent fungal infections wear loose, comfortable clothes, avoid artificial fibres, wash frequently and dry yourself carefully. If you do get an infection, wash the infected area at least daily with a disinfectant or medicated soap and water, and rinse and dry well. Apply an antifungal cream or powder like tolnaftate. Try to expose the infected area to air or sunlight as much as possible and wash all towels and underwear in hot water, change them often and let them dry in the sun.

Hepatitis Hepatitis is a general term for inflammation of the liver. It is a common disease worldwide. There are several different viruses that cause hepatitis, and they differ in the way that they are transmitted. The symptoms are similar in all forms of the illness, and include fever, chills, headache, fatigue, feelings of weakness and aches and pains, followed by loss of appetite, nausea, vomiting, abdominal pain, dark urine, light-coloured faeces, jaundiced (yellow) skin and yellowing of the whites of the eyes. People who have had hepatitis should avoid alcohol for some time after the illness, as the liver needs time to recover.

Hepatitis A is transmitted by contaminated food and drinking water. You should seek medical advice, but there is not much you can do apart from resting, drinking lots of fluids, eating lightly and avoiding fatty foods. **Hepatitis E** is transmitted in the same way as hepatitis A; it can be particularly serious in pregnant women.

There are almost 300 million chronic carriers of **Hepatitis B** in the world. It is spread through contact with infected blood, blood products or body fluids, for example through sexual contact, unsterilised needles and blood transfusions, or contact with blood via small breaks in the skin. Other risk situations include having a shave, tattoo or body piercing with contaminated equipment. The symptoms of hepatitis B may be more severe than type A and the disease can lead to long-term problems such as chronic liver damage, liver cancer or a long-term carrier state. **Hepatitis C** and **D** are spread in the same way as hepatitis B and can also lead to long-term complications.

There are vaccines against hepatitis A and B, but there are currently no vaccines against the other types of hepatitis. Following the basic rules about food and water (hepatitis A and E) and avoiding risk situations (hepatitis B, C and D) are important preventative measures.

HIV & AIDS Infection with the human immunodeficiency virus (HIV) may lead to acquired immune deficiency syndrome (AIDS), which is a fatal disease. Just north of Kerala, Goa has up to three times the national average of HIV cases. Thirty-five per cent of Goa's prostitutes are HIV positive.

Any exposure to blood, blood products or body fluids may put an individual at risk. The disease is often transmitted through sexual contact or through contact with dirty needles – vaccinations, acupuncture, tattooing and body piercing can all be potentially as dangerous as intravenous drug use. HIV/AIDS can also be spread through infected blood transfusions.

In case you need an injection, it's best to take a needle and syringe pack with you. If you don't have one, ask to see the syringe unwrapped in front of you.

Fear of HIV infection should never preclude treatment for any serious medical conditions.

Sexually Transmitted Infections (STIs) HIV/AIDS and hepatitis B can be transmitted through sexual contact – see the previous entries for more details. Gonorrhoea, herpes and syphilis are sexually transmitted infections; sores, blisters or rashes around the genitals and discharges or pain when urinating are common symptoms. In some STIs, such as wart virus or chlamydia, symptoms may be less marked or not observed at all, especially in women. Syphilis symptoms eventually disappear completely but the disease continues and can cause severe problems in later years. While abstinence from sexual contact is the only 100% effective prevention, using condoms is also effective. The treatment of gonorrhoea and syphilis is with antibiotics. The different sexually transmitted infections each require specific antibiotics. There is no cure for herpes or AIDS.

Intestinal Worms These parasites are most common in rural, tropical areas. The different worms have different ways of infecting people. Some may be ingested with food such as undercooked meat (eg tapeworms) and some enter through your skin (eg hookworms). Infestations may not show up for some time, and although they are generally not serious, if left untreated some can cause severe health problems later. Consider having a stool test when you return home to check for these and determine the appropriate treatment.

Typhoid Typhoid fever is a dangerous gut infection caused by contaminated water and food. Medical help must be sought.

In its early stages sufferers may feel they have a bad cold or flu, as early symptoms are a headache, body aches and a fever that rises a little each day until it is around 40°C (104°F) or more. The victim's pulse is often slow relative to the degree of fever present – unlike a normal fever where the pulse increases. There may also be vomiting, abdominal pain, diarrhoea or constipation.

In the second week the high fever and slow pulse continue and a few pink spots may appear on the body; trembling, delirium, weakness, weight loss and dehydration may occur. Complications such as pneumonia, perforated bowel or meningitis may occur.

Insect-Borne Diseases

Filariasis, leishmaniasis, Lyme disease and typhus are all insect-borne diseases, but they do not pose a great risk to travellers. For more information on them see Less Common Diseases at the end of the Health section.

Malaria This serious and potentially fatal disease is spread by mosquito bites. It's extremely important to avoid mosquito bites and to take tablets to prevent this disease. Symptoms range from fever, chills and sweating, headache, diarrhoea and abdominal pains to a vague feeling of ill-health. Seek medical help immediately if malaria is suspected. Without treatment malaria can rapidly become more serious and can be fatal.

If medical care is not available, malaria tablets can be used for treatment. You need to use a malaria tablet that is different from the one you were taking when you contracted malaria. The standard treatment dose of mefloquine is two 250mg tablets and a further two six hours later. For Fansidar, it's a single dose of three tablets. If you were previously taking mefloquine and cannot obtain Fansidar, then other alternatives are Malarone (atovaquone-proguanil; four tablets once daily for three days), halofantrine (three doses of two 250mg tablets every six hours) or quinine sulphate (600mg every six hours). There is a greater risk of side effects with these dosages than in normal use if used with mefloquine, so medical advice is preferable. Be aware also that halofantrine is no longer recommended by the World Health Organization as emergency stand-by treatment, because of side effects, and should only be used if no other drugs are available.

Travellers are advised to prevent mosquito bites at all times. The main points to remember are:

- wear light-coloured clothing
- wear long skirts/trousers and long-sleeved shirts
- use mosquito repellents containing the compound DEET on exposed areas (prolonged overuse of DEET may be harmful, especially to children, but its use is considered preferable to being bitten by disease-transmitting mosquitoes)
- avoid perfumes or aftershave
- use a mosquito net impregnated with mosquito repellent (permethrin) – it may be worth taking your own
- impregnating clothes with permethrin effectively deters mosquitoes and other insects

Dengue Fever This viral disease is transmitted by mosquitoes and occurs mainly in tropical and subtropical areas of the world. Generally, there is only a small risk to travellers except during epidemics, which are usually seasonal (during and just after the rainy season).

The *Aedes aegypti* mosquito, which transmits the dengue virus, is most active during the day, unlike the malaria mosquito, and is found mainly in urban areas, in and around human dwellings.

Signs and symptoms of dengue fever include a sudden onset of high fever, headache, joint and muscle pains (hence its old name, 'breakbone fever') and nausea and vomiting. A rash of small red spots appears three to four days after the onset of fever. Dengue is commonly mistaken for other infectious diseases, including influenza.

You should seek medical attention if you think you may be infected. Infection can be diagnosed by a blood test. There is no specific treatment for dengue. Aspirin should be avoided, as it increases the risk of haemorrhaging. Recovery may be prolonged, with tiredness lasting for several weeks. Severe complications are rare in travellers but include dengue haemorrhagic fever (DHF), which can be fatal without prompt medical treatment. DHF is thought to be a result of secondary infection due to a different strain (there are four major strains). It's important to know that if you have had dengue fever you become more susceptible to contracting another strain.

There is no vaccine against dengue fever. The best prevention is to avoid mosquito bites at all times – see the malaria section earlier for more details.

Japanese B Encephalitis This viral infection of the brain is transmitted by mosquitoes. Most cases occur in rural areas as the virus exists in pigs and wading birds. Symptoms include fever, headache and alteration in consciousness. Hospitalisation is needed for correct diagnosis and treatment. There is a high mortality rate among those who have symptoms; of those who survive many are intellectually disabled.

Cuts, Bites & Stings

See Less Common Diseases for details of rabies, a disease which is passed through animal bites.

Bedbugs & Lice Bedbugs live in various places, but particularly in dirty mattresses and bedding, evidenced by spots of blood on bedclothes or on the wall. Bedbugs leave itchy bites in neat rows. Calamine lotion or Stingose spray may help.

All lice cause itching and discomfort. They make themselves at home in your hair (head lice), your clothing (body lice) or in your pubic hair (crabs). You catch lice through direct contact with infected people or by sharing combs, clothing and the like. Powder or shampoo treatment will kill the lice and infected clothing should then be washed in very hot, soapy water and left in the sun to dry.

Bites & Stings Bee and wasp stings are usually painful rather than dangerous. However, people who are allergic to them require urgent medical care. Calamine lotion or Stingose spray will give relief and ice packs will reduce the pain and swelling. There are some spiders with dangerous bites but antivenins are usually available. Scorpion stings are notoriously painful.

Cuts & Scratches Cuts and scratches, usually a minor problem in cooler climes, can present challenges in the tropics. If treated immediately, however, there is usually little to worry about. Wash well and treat any cut with an antiseptic such as povidone-iodine. Where possible avoid bandages and Band-Aids (plasters), which can keep wounds wet. Coral cuts are notoriously slow to heal and if they are not adequately cleaned, small pieces of coral can become embedded in the wound.

Jellyfish Avoid contact with these sea creatures, which have stinging tentacles – seek local advice. Dousing in vinegar will deactivate any stingers that have not 'fired'. Calamine lotion, antihistamines and analgesics may reduce the reaction and relieve the pain.

Leeches & Ticks Leeches are present in damp rainforests; they attach themselves to your skin to suck your blood. They're often small and difficult to detect. Salt or a lighted cigarette end will make them fall off. Don't pull them off, as the bite is then more likely to become infected. Clean and apply pressure if the point of attachment is bleeding. Insect repellent usually deters leeches.

You should always check all over your body if you have been walking through a potentially tick-infested area as ticks can cause skin infections and other more serious diseases. If a tick is found attached, press down around the tick's head with tweezers, grab the head and gently pull upwards. Avoid pulling the rear of the body as this may squeeze the tick's gut contents through the attached mouth parts into the skin, increasing the risk of infection and disease. Smearing chemicals on the tick will not make it let go and is not recommended.

Snakes There are a few poisonous snakes in Kerala, including the deadly king cobra. To minimise your chances of being bitten always wear boots, socks and long trousers when walking through undergrowth where snakes may be present. Don't put your hands into holes and crevices, and be careful when collecting firewood.

Snake bites do not cause instantaneous death and antivenins are usually available. Immediately wrap the bitten limb tightly, as you would for a sprained ankle, and then attach a splint to immobilise it. Keep the victim still and seek medical help, if possible bring the dead snake for identification. Don't attempt to catch the snake if there is a possibility of being bitten again. Tourniquets and sucking out the poison are now comprehensively discredited.

Less Common Diseases

The following diseases pose a small risk to travellers, and so are only mentioned in passing. Seek medical advice if you think you may have any of these diseases.

Cholera This is the worst of the watery diarrhoeas and medical help should be sought. Outbreaks of cholera are generally widely reported, so you can avoid such problem areas. *Fluid replacement is the most vital treatment* – the risk of dehydration is severe as you may lose up to 20L a day. If there is a delay in getting to hospital, then begin taking tetracycline. The adult dose is 250mg four times daily. It is not recommended for children under nine years nor for pregnant women. Tetracycline may help shorten the illness, but adequate fluids are required to save lives.

Filariasis This is a mosquito-transmitted parasitic infection found in many parts of India. Possible symptoms include fever, pain and swelling of the lymph glands; inflammation of lymph drainage areas; swelling of a limb or the scrotum; skin rashes; and blindness. Treatment is available to eliminate the parasites from the body, but some of the damage already caused may not be reversible. Medical advice should be obtained promptly if the infection is suspected.

Leishmaniasis This is a group of parasitic diseases transmitted by sandflies, which are found in many parts of India. Cutaneous leishmaniasis affects the skin tissue causing ulceration and disfigurement, and visceral leishmaniasis affects the internal organs. Seek medical advice, as laboratory testing is required for diagnosis and correct treatment. Avoiding sandfly bites is the best precaution. Bites are usually painless, itchy and yet another reason to cover up and apply repellent.

Lyme Disease This is a tick-transmitted infection that may be acquired throughout North America, Europe and Asia. The illness usually begins with a spreading rash at the site of the tick bite and is accompanied by fever, headache, extreme fatigue, aching joints and muscles and mild neck stiffness. If untreated, these symptoms usually resolve over several weeks but over subsequent weeks or months disorders of the nervous system, heart and joints may develop. Treatment works best early in the illness. Medical help should be sought.

Rabies This potentially fatal viral infection is found in many countries. Animals (such as dogs, cats, bats and monkeys) can be infected and it is their saliva that is infectious. Any bite, scratch or even lick from an animal should be cleaned immediately and thoroughly. Scrub with soap and running water, and then apply alcohol or iodine solution. Medical help should be sought promptly to receive a course of injections to prevent the onset of symptoms and death.

Tetanus This disease is caused by a germ that lives in soil and in the faeces of horses and other animals. It enters the body via breaks in the skin. The first symptom may be discomfort in swallowing, or stiffening of the jaw and neck; this is followed by painful convulsions of the jaw and whole body. The disease can be fatal. It can be prevented by vaccination.

Tuberculosis (TB) This is a bacterial infection usually transmitted from person to person by coughing. It may also be transmitted through consumption of unpasteurised milk. Milk that has been boiled is safe to drink, and the souring of milk to make yoghurt or cheese also kills the bacilli. Travellers are usually not at great risk as close household contact with the infected person is usually required before the disease is passed on. You may need to have a TB test before you travel as this can help diagnose the disease later if you become ill.

Typhus This disease is spread by ticks, mites or lice. It begins with fever, chills, headache and muscle pains followed a few days later by a body rash. There is often a large painful sore at the site of the bite and nearby lymph nodes are swollen and painful. Typhus can be medically treated. Seek local advice on areas where ticks pose a danger and always check your skin carefully for ticks after walking in a danger area such as a tropical forest. An insect repellent can help, and walkers in tick-infested areas should consider having their boots and trousers impregnated with benzyl benzoate and dibutylphthalate.

Women's Health

Gynaecological Problems Antibiotic use, synthetic underwear, sweating and contraceptive pills can lead to fungal vaginal infections, especially when travelling in hot climates. Thrush, or vaginal candidiasis, is characterised by itching, discharge and a rash. Nystatin, miconazole or clotrimazole pessaries or vaginal cream are the usual treatment, but some people use a more traditional remedy involving vinegar or lemon-juice douches, or yoghurt. Maintaining good personal hygiene and wearing loose-fitting clothes and cotton underwear may help prevent these infections.

Sexually transmitted infections are a major cause of vaginal problems. Symptoms include a smelly discharge, painful intercourse and sometimes a burning sensation when urinating. Medical attention should be sought and male sexual partners must also be treated. For more details see the Sexually Transmitted Infections section, earlier. Besides abstinence, the best thing is to practise safer sex using condoms.

Pregnancy If you're pregnant and you want to visit Kerala, check first with a medical travel service. Some vaccinations are not advisable during pregnancy. In addition, some diseases (eg malaria) are much more serious for the mother and may increase the risk of a stillborn child.

While there are good medical facilities for pregnant women in Kerala, some travellers reported that their pregnancies were not diagnosed and miscarriages did not receive appropriate treatment. Obtain all necessary advice before departure and/or seek appropriate referral in Kerala. Your embassy will assist you to locate relevant doctors.

WOMEN TRAVELLERS

Most women travellers in India are local and almost always travel with their families. The practice of foreign women travelling alone or with a female companion is still uncommon in India. While many foreign women travel without problems, others have been hassled, stared at, spied on in hotel rooms, and even groped, although the situation is rarely threatening.

Kerala is generally perfectly safe for women travellers, even for those travelling alone. But like elsewhere, you are advised not to walk in isolated spots (down lonely alleys, along the beach) on your own – after dark especially. If you are in doubt about safety, ask hotel personnel, police or older people.

Although you are unlikely to be at any physical risk, one of the wearying aspects of travelling in parts of Kerala, especially if you are alone, is the unwanted attention you will attract from young local men. If you don't want to be the constant object of what is euphemistically called 'Eve teasing' (harassment in various forms) then pay attention to the local norms of dress and behaviour. While it won't eradicate the problem totally, dressing modestly helps. This means no sleeveless tops, shorts or even jeans. Loose clothing that covers your legs and shoulders is best. The *salwar kameez* or traditional Punjabi suit is becoming increasingly popular among both local and foreign women, because it's practical and considered respectable. A cotton salwar kameez is also surprisingly cool in Kerala's steamy heat and keeps the burning sun off your skin. But some temples prohibit entry in such dress.

Other irksome behaviours include assumptions about your intelligence and stamina. Don't let such notions discourage you from participating in activities, especially if you're experienced or have a particular interest. When in mixed company, you'll often be ignored, especially in the 'better class' establishments. No doubt you've experienced such behaviour often enough in your life to have developed effective strategies to deal with it – you'll get plenty of opportunities to hone your skills. Don't assume you're included when the word 'everyone' is used – it may mean 'men only'.

Communication by way of physical touch may be second nature to you, but avoid such gestures with men. Generally it's not acceptable and can create misunderstanding. If you enjoy going out at night you may find you're the sole woman in the theatre or restaurant. In Kerala, evenings seem to be the province of men.

As in other states, many eating places have separate areas for women and families – often referred to as the 'family room'. If you are on your own and you feel uncomfortable in the main eating area, head for the family room. The food is the same as 'outside', the service usually very good but sometimes you may be charged a little more.

On buses, front seats are often reserved for women, but if you get on at the 'male' end, that's usually OK. Long-distance trains generally have special carriages reserved for women and children, but you may find them noisy with small children and you may wish you'd opted for an ordinary carriage.

Lone women travellers in Kerala may evoke seemingly strange behaviour. However, such behaviour is more likely to be an expression of concern for your safety and welfare; you'll find that most people will go out of their way to assist you.

Organisations

If you wish to learn more about the situation of women in India try the Web site at www.umiacs.umd.edu/users/sawweb/sawet/. This excellent site is hosted by SAWNET, the South Asian Women's NETwork, and provides information on a range of issues affecting South Asian women.

GAY & LESBIAN TRAVELLERS

While overt displays of affection between members of the opposite sex, such as cuddling and hand-holding, are frowned upon in India, it is not unusual to see Indians of the same sex holding hands with each other or engaged in other close affectionate behaviour. This does not necessarily suggest that they are gay. The gay movement in India is confined almost exclusively to larger cities and Mumbai is really the only place where there's a gay 'scene'. Since marriage is seen as very important, to be gay is a particular stigma – most gays stay in the closet or risk being disowned by their families.

As with relations between heterosexual western couples travelling in India – both married and unmarried – gay and lesbian travellers should exercise discretion and refrain from displaying overt affection towards each other in public.

Legal Status

Homosexual relations for men are illegal in India. Section 377 of the national legislation forbids 'carnal intercourse against the order of nature' (that is, anal intercourse). The penalties for transgression can be up to life imprisonment. Because of this gay travellers could be the subject of blackmail – take care. There is no law against lesbian relations.

Publications & Groups

There are no organisations for lesbians and gays in Kerala. The following are given as points of contact for further information and advice. *Bombay Dost* is a gay and lesbian publication available from 105 Veena Beena Shopping Centre, Bandra (W) Mumbai; The People Tree, 8 Parliament St, New Delhi; and Classic Books, 10 Middleton St, Kolkata (Calcutta). Support groups include Bombay Dost (address above); Pravartak, Post Bag 10237, Kolkata, Bangla (West Bengal) 700019; Sakhi (a lesbian group), PO Box 3526, Lajpat Nagar, New Delhi 110024; and Sneha Sangama, PO Box 3250, RT Nagar, Bangalore 560032.

DISABLED TRAVELLERS

Travelling in Kerala can entail some fairly rigorous challenges, even for the able-bodied traveller – long bus trips in crowded vehicles between remote villages and endless queues in the scorching heat at bus and train stations can test even the hardiest traveller. If you can't walk, these challenges are increased many-fold. Few buildings have wheelchair access; toilets have certainly not been designed to accommodate wheelchairs; footpaths, where they exist (only in larger towns), are generally riddled with holes, littered with obstacles and packed with throngs of people, severely restricting mobility.

If your mobility is restricted you will require a strong, able-bodied companion to accompany you. Hiring a private vehicle and driver would certainly ease the journey.

Publications & Groups

Disability Express Travel & Disability Resource Directory
(☎ 417-836 4773, fax 836 5371)
South-west Missouri State University, USA

Royal Association for Disability & Rehabilitation
(☎ 020-7250 3222, fax 7250 0212)
12 City Forum, 250 City Rd, London, England ECIV 8AF

SENIOR TRAVELLERS

Senior travellers will enjoy the respect accorded to older citizens in India. If you're in good health, there's no reason why you shouldn't consider India as a potential holiday destination. It may be helpful to discuss your proposed trip with staff from a travellers' medical service.

TRAVEL WITH CHILDREN

Children can enhance your encounters with local people, as they often possess little of the self-consciousness and awareness of the cultural differences that can inhibit interaction between adults. Kerala is a very family-oriented society.

Children are welcome in places to eat and stay; most hotels provide family rooms or will happily provide extra beds. You would certainly not be discouraged from bringing children on visits to most places – if it's OK for adults, it's OK for children. There are few facilities dedicated solely to children's entertainment so it would be wise to bring books, favourite toys, games and so forth with you. Disposable nappies (diapers) are not available.

Any good hotel will locate reliable babysitters for you.

Travelling with children can be hard work, and ideally the burden needs to be shared between two adults. For more information, see the Health section earlier in this chapter, and get hold of a copy of Lonely Planet's *Travel with Children* by Maureen Wheeler.

DANGERS & ANNOYANCES

Ocean Swimming

Be aware that many of Kerala's beaches can be dangerous places to swim if you are not used to the conditions. Undertows (or 'rips') are the main problem, especially around Varkala.

Don't swim too far from the beach, and never swim after drinking alcohol. If you find yourself being carried out by a rip, the main thing to do is just keep afloat; don't panic or try to swim against the rip. In most cases the current stops within a couple of hundred metres of the shore, and you can then swim parallel to the shore for a short way to get out of the rip and then make your way back to the shore.

Theft

Common sense is your best safeguard when it comes to protecting your valuables. There's no need to be paranoid about the risk of theft; most people are scrupulously honest. Just make sure you don't set yourself up as an easy target. Never walk around with valuables casually slung over your shoulder. The less you look like a tourist, the less of a target you'll be.

Never leave important valuables (passport, tickets, health certificates, money, travellers cheques) in your room; they should be with you or secured in a hotel safe. Wear your passport pouch or moneybelt under your shirt.

When travelling on trains at night keep your gear near you; padlocking a bag to a luggage rack can be useful. Take extra care on crowded public transport and in places most frequented by tourists. These include beach resorts and popular town destinations such as Kochi.

Be aware that in India there are occasional instances where travellers are drugged and their belongings stolen. Be careful, but don't let this stop you from accepting drinks or food from people you meet, or you'll miss one of the best experiences – generous Indian hospitality.

Beware also of your fellow travellers. There are more than a few backpackers who make their money go farther by helping themselves to other people's. Remember also that something of little value to a thief may have great importance to you – film, for example.

Although you may not be able to replace stolen goods, a good travel insurance policy helps to alleviate the economic loss. If you do have something stolen, report it to the police and obtain a statement as evidence of the report, for insurance. Insurance companies, despite their rosy promises of full protection and speedy settlements, will often attempt every trick in the book to avoid paying out on a baggage claim. Some policies specify that, for a claim to be successful, you must report a theft to the police within a specified time after the loss.

Stolen Travellers Cheques If you're unlucky enough to have things stolen, some precautions can ease the pain. All travellers cheques are replaceable, although this does you little immediate good if you have to go home and apply to your bank. What you want is instant replacement. Furthermore, what do you do if you lose your cheques and money and have a day or more to travel to the replacement office? The answer is to keep an emergency cash-stash in a totally separate place. In that same place you should keep a record of the cheque serial numbers, proof of purchase slips, encashment vouchers and your passport number.

American Express makes considerable noise about 'instant replacement' of their cheques but a lot of people find out, to their cost, that without a number of precautions 'instant' can take longer than you think, especially if you don't have the purchase receipt. Chances are you'll be able to get a limited amount of funds on the spot, and the rest will be available when the bank has verified your initial purchase of the cheques. American Express has a 24 hour number in Delhi (☎ 011-6875050), which you must ring within 24 hours of the theft. Note that thieves have been known to remove one or two cheques from the back of a wad of travellers' cheques – by the time the traveller is aware of the loss, the cheques have long been cashed.

Discrimination

Some travellers find their ethnicity or skin colour can result in discrimination. This is illegal in Kerala, and while most people respect this law, prejudicial behaviour does occur. Indian people, considered 'low caste' can be treated in a discriminatory way by their compatriots. If you are the subject of such unjust behaviour, like women, you will no doubt already have adopted strategies to deal with it. Blatant discrimination is rare, as is intolerance towards foreigners. Challenge or ignore the bad behaviour and spend most of your time enjoying the sincere hospitality offered by most Malayalis.

LEGAL MATTERS

In the Indian justice system it seems the burden of proof is on the accused, and proving one's innocence is virtually impossible. The police forces are often corrupt and will pay 'witnesses' to give evidence. For serious problems don't deal with the local police station; contact your embassy and try to get a good lawyer – your hotel or the Tourist Facilitation Centre (☎ 321132) on Museum Rd, Thiruvananthapuram, will help you.

Drugs

Penalties for possession, use and trafficking in illegal drugs are strictly enforced. If convicted on a drugs-related charge, sentences are long (a *minimum* of 10 years) and accompanied by a hefty fine, even for minor offences, and there is no remission or parole. In some cases it has taken three years just to get a court hearing.

Child Prostitution

As problems with sex crimes against children become more alarmingly evident, there is now greater vigilance by police and locals and the legal procedure is in place to deal with paedophiles. Offenders face life imprisonment in an Indian jail if convicted.

The Indian Penal Code and India's Immoral Traffic Act impose penalties for kidnapping and prostitution. In addition, the international community has responded to what is essentially a global problem with laws that allow their nationals (including those from Australia, New Zealand, Germany, Sweden, Norway, France, USA) to be prosecuted for child sex offences upon their return home.

If you know of anyone engaged in these activities, you should report it to police in Kerala and again to the police when you get home.

BUSINESS HOURS

Officially, business hours are Monday to Friday, 9.30 am to 5.30 pm. Unofficially they tend to be 10 am to 5 pm. Government offices have lengthy lunch hours that are sacrosanct and can last from noon to 3 pm. Many public institutions such as museums, galleries and so on close at least one day during the week. Banks are open Monday to Friday, 10 am to 2 pm, and 10 am to noon every second Saturday.

Travellers cheque transactions usually cease 30 minutes before the official bank closing time. In tourist centres there are foreign exchange offices that keep longer hours. Post offices are open Monday to Friday 9.30 am to 5.30 pm and Saturday to 2 pm. In Thiruvananthapuram the general post office (GPO) is open to 8 pm every day.

PUBLIC HOLIDAYS & SPECIAL EVENTS

At any time of the year, there will be a festival somewhere in Kerala. Most festivals follow the lunar calendar or the Islamic calendar and therefore change from year to year according to the Gregorian calendar. See the boxed text 'Calendars', earlier in this chapter for details. If you'd like to find out the exact date of a festival, check with the Tourist Facilitation Centre (☎ 0471-321132) in Museum Rd, Thiruvananthapuram (Trivandrum) or with your hotel.

The following is just a selection of the numerous festivals and public holidays celebrated throughout Kerala (months are given as a guide only).

January

Cultural Festivals

Secular; Kochi, Alappuzha (Alleppey), Kollam, Kovalam & Thiruvananthapuram

These festivals take place throughout January in major centres. Theatre and dance, such as Kathakali and Moyhinyattam, as well as kalarippayat (traditional martial arts) and boat races comprise these festivals.

Drama Festival

17-22 Jan; secular; Kottayam

A Malayalam festival of drama at the Municipal Ground & Stage, dedicated to the memory of the Keralan actor Achan Kunju.

Feast of St Sebastian

Jan; Christian; St Thomas Church, Irinjalakuda & statewide

This feast day celebrates the patron saint of health who is believed to have performed miracles to cure fatal diseases.

Festival of Women's Theatre

Jan; secular; Thrissur

Annual festival organised by the Sangeetha Nataka Academy in which leading actors gather in Thrissur to discuss, debate and perform.

Ernakulathappan Temple Festival

Jan; Hindu; Kochi

The legend of Nagarshi is celebrated with colourful rituals each January at the Ernakulathappan Temple in Ernakulam, Kochi.

Gramam-Kovalam Fair

14-23 Jan; secular; Gramam & Kovalam

This fair exhibits traditional arts and crafts.

Musical Festival

27 Jan-3 Feb; secular; Thiruvananthapuram

Hosted by the Puthe Maliga Palace, this festival features some of Kerala's finest musicians.

New Year's Day

1 Jan; secular; statewide

The new year is heralded with low key celebrations throughout the state.

Pongal

Jan/Feb; Hindu; statewide

The festival of Pongal during the Hindu month of Makaram (Jan/Feb) celebrates rural life. The initial ceremonies occur in temples and homes. Following this cows are honoured. After bathing, they are fed special foods and decorated.

Republic Day

26 Jan; secular; statewide

The anniversary of India's establishment as a republic in 1950 is celebrated on this day. There are activities in all the state capitals as well as throughout the rural areas.

Sabarimala Festival

Jan/Feb; Hindu; Sabarimala

This is one of the largest festivals in Kerala, held during Makaram. Honouring the deity Ayyappan, pilgrims travel from all over India, many having fasted (except for light vegetarian food) for over a month.

Thaipooram (Thai Pussam)

Jan/Feb; Hindu; statewide

This festival honours Subramanya, the youngest son of Shiva and Parvati. Devotees may travel for many kilometres to honour the deity during Makaram. Often they carry kavadi (arches) decorated with peacock feathers – the plumage of the deity's vehicle.

February

Bakrid (Id-ul-Azha – Valia Perunnal)

16 Mar 2000, 6 Mar 2001, 23 Feb 2002; Muslim; statewide

This festival commemorates Ibrahim and his obedience to God in offering his son in sacrifice. As well as prayers, it is celebrated with a huge feast. Some Muslims undertake the pilgrimage to Mecca (haj) at this time.

Feast of Our Lady of Lourdes

11 Feb; Christian; statewide

This feast day celebrates the apparitions of Our Lady to the small girl, Bernadette, at Lourdes.

Holi

Feb/Mar; Hindu; statewide

Whilst more a north Indian festival, Holi is still celebrated in Kerala during the Hindu month of Kumbham (Feb/Mar), where large fires symbolising the destruction off the evil demon, Holika, are lit. As part of the revelry, coloured water is thrown at anyone and everyone.

Krishna's Festival

Feb/Mar; Hindu; Guruvayur

Krishna is honoured at the Sri Krishna temple during Kumbham. Elephant processions occur on each day of the 10 day festival. On the final day the image of Krishna is paraded atop an elephant and then bathed. Devotees also bathe, believing the sharing of the waters with the deity to be auspicious. The Krishnanattam dance is usually performed.

Mannanam Convention

Feb; Christian; Mannanam

First held in 1894, this convention has grown to be one of the largest Christian conferences in Asia. Tens of thousands of people attend to listen to scholarly discourse on Christian issues. In addition to the debates, several festivities and a large fair are held.

Nishagandhi Dance Festival
21-27 Feb; secular; Thiruvananthapuram
Each night of this festival, at the Nishagandhi Stadium, Kanakakunna Palace, classical dance is performed free of charge.

Purim
9 Mar 2000, 26 Feb 2001, 18 Mar 2002; Jewish; Kochi area
Purim commemorates the escape of Jews from persecution under the Persian empire in the 5th century BCE (before common era). Regarded as the first victory of Jews over the forces of oppression, it is celebrated with gifts and feasts.

Shivaratri
Feb/Mar; Hindu; Aluva, Attappady & Kovalam
All of India celebrates Shivaratri, the festival of the night of Shiva, during Kumbham. At the time of the full moon, special chants and prayers are recited in honour of Shiva. There are three sites in Kerala where this festival is particularly significant – Aluva and Attappady, where on completion of the rituals both places have month-long colourful fairs, and Kovalam where, in the evening, a special celebration completes the festival.

March

Passover
8-9 Apr 2000, 28-29 Mar 2001, 17-18 Apr 2002; Jewish; Kochi
Passover commemorates the Jewish exodus from Egypt led by Moses in 1000 BCE. During this eight day period, homes are cleared of all leavened bread and unleavened bread is consumed as a symbol of the haste in which the Jews had to flee.

Thiruvananthapuram Arat Festival
Mar/Apr; Hindu; Thiruvananthapuram
This festival, held at the Sri Padmanabhaswamy Temple, lasts for 10 nights during the Hindu month of Meenam (Mar/Apr). It concludes with a procession in which the idol of the deity, accompanied by decorated elephants, is taken to the sea for a ritual bath.

April

Easter
21 Apr 2000, 13 Apr 2001, 29 Mar 2002 (Good Friday); Christian; statewide
Easter, incorporating Good Friday, commemorates the death and resurrection of Christ, following a 40 day Lenten period during which many Christians fast.

Food Festival
5-11 Apr; secular; Thiruvananthapuram
This annual festival at Kanakakunna Palace showcases Indian cuisine. Food is also available for sampling.

Calendars

Keralan

Like the Hindu calendar, the Keralan calendar is divided into 12 lunar-solar months. The year begins with the month of Chingam, which roughly equates to the Gregorian August/September period. The calendar is reputed to have begun in Kollam in the year equating to 825 CE (common era), see the History section in the Southern Kerala chapter for further details. In August 2000 the year in Kerala will be 1176 KE (Kollam era).

Hindu

The Hindu calendar is also divided into 12 lunar-solar months and remains constant with the Gregorian calendar. Each month has 30 or 31 days. The year begins with 1 Chaitra, corresponding with 22 March (21 March during a Gregorian leap year). The calendar was introduced as the all-India calendar by the central government in 1957 and is based on the calendar used by the Saka kings of Ujjain around the time of Christ. Thus 2000 CE is Saka 1921-22.

Muslim

The Muslim (Hijra) calendar is also lunar and starts from 622 CE, the date of the Prophet Mohammed's flight *(hijra)* from the city of Medina. It has 12 lunar months totalling 354 days, which means events fall 11 days earlier each year according to the Gregorian calendar. The Gregorian year 2000 corresponds with 1420-1421 AH *(anno hejirae)*. The Hijra New Year's Day (1 Muharram) is 6 April.

Other Calendars

The Jain calendar starts at 527 BCE, when Lord Mahavira, the founder of the religion, attained nirvana, which makes 2000 CE the year 2526 in Jain terms.

The Buddhist calendar starts at a similar time, on the 'triple blessed' day in 560 BCE, making 2000 the year 2544 according to Buddhist tradition.

Keralan Calendar

Keralan month	Gregorian
Chingam	Aug-Sep
Kanni	Sep-Oct
Thulam	Oct-Nov
Virchikam	Nov-Dec
Dhanu	Dec-Jan
Makaram	Jan-Feb
Kumbham	Feb-Mar
Meenam	Mar-Apr
Medam	Apr-May
Idavam	May-Jun
Mithunam	Jun-Jul
Karkatakam	Jul-Aug

Hindu Calendar

Saka month	days	Gregorian
Chaitra	30 (31)	22 Mar-20 Apr
Vaishaka	31	21 Apr-21 May
Jyaistha	31	22 May-21 Jun
Asadha	31	22 Jun-22 Jul
Sravana	31	23 Jul-22 Aug
Bhadra	31	23 Aug-22 Sep
Asvina	30	23 Sep-22 Oct
Kartika	30	23 Oct-21 Nov
Aghan	30	22 Nov-21 Dec
Pausa	30	22 Dec-20 Jan
Magha	30	21 Jan-19 Feb
Phalguna	30	20 Feb-21 Mar

Muslim Calendar

Hijra month	2000 Gregorian
Muharram	Apr-May
Safar	May-Jun
Rabi' al-Awal	Jun-Jul
Rabei ath-Thani	Jul-Aug
Jumada al-Awal	Aug-Sep
Jumada ath-Thani	Sep-Oct
Rajab	Oct-Nov
Shaaban	Nov-Dec
Ramadan	Dec-Jan
Shawwal	Jan-Feb
Thul qi'dah	Feb-Mar
Thul hijjah	Mar-Apr

Pooram Festival

Apr/May; Hindu; Thrissur (Trichur)

The Hindu month of Medam (Apr/May) is the time for the Pooram Festival, the most notable celebration being in Thrissur, outside the Vadakkunathan Kshetram temple. Processions of elephants, musicians and drummers create an elaborate spectacle, culminating with a massive fireworks display.

Vishnu Festival

Apr/May; Hindu; statewide

This important festival is celebrated on the first day of Medam, which represents the first day of the astrological New Year. Several rituals are associated with this festival, the most significant being the Kani Kanal, the 'first seeing'. The first thing a person sees in the New Year must be auspicious or else, according to the belief, the observer will suffer a bad year. Every attempt is made therefore to gather the most auspicious objects and to ensure that every member of the household is awakened at dawn and led to view them. Such objects include lighted candles, a cadjan leaf book, rice, gold, a mirror, coconuts and jackfruit.

May

May Day (International Workers' Day)

1 May; secular; statewide

This day is celebrated with street marches and rallies.

Muharram

27 Jun 2000, 28 May 2001, 17 May 2002; Muslim; statewide

This 10 day festival honours the martyrdom of Imam Hussain, the Prophet Mohammed's grandson.

Vanakka Masam

May; Christian; statewide

May is the month of Mary, known as Vanakka Masam. Special devotions take place in churches and homes while shrines to Mary are decorated with fresh flowers.

June

Milad-un-Nabi

16 Jun 2000, 5 Jun 2001, 24 May 2002; Muslim; statewide

This festival celebrates the birth of Mohammed.

July

Feast of St Thomas the Apostle

Jul; Christian; statewide

The feast day of St Thomas the Apostle, considered the father of Christianity in Kerala, is celebrated on this day.

August

Ashtami Rohini (Sri Krishna Jayanthi)

Aug/Sep; Hindu; Kollam

Krishna's birthday is celebrated during the month of Chingam (Aug/Sep) in all Krishna temples, but particularly in Kollam. During the day people pray and fast and at night they celebrate with a feast.

Independence Day

15 Aug; Secular; statewide

This public holiday celebrates the anniversary of Independence from Britain in 1947 and the formation of the nation of India.

Onam

Aug/Sep; secular; statewide

The most important festival in Kerala – Onam, the harvest festival – occurs at the time of Chingam, the first month of the Kerala calendar (Aug/Sept). All Malayalis take part in this 10 day festival, which celebrates the return of the mythical king, Mahabala (see the boxed text 'Honouring Benevolence – The Festival of Onam' in the Northern Kerala chapter), who is believed to have ruled in a halcyon time of prosperity when all members of society lived in equality. Women make floral carpets and the celebrations include numerous events throughout the state. Garlanded elephants parade at Thrissur, while exciting boat races take place at Alappuzha.

Snake Boat Races

2nd Saturday in Aug; secular; Alappuzha

The famous Nehru Trophy Boat Race takes place at Alappuzha.

September

Rosh Hashana

11-12 Sep 2000, 30 Sep-1 Oct 2001, 18-19 Sep 2002; Jewish; Kochi

This marks the beginning of the Jewish year and of the 10 day period known as High Holidays, which culminates in Yom Kippur – the day of atonement – which is the holiest day in the Jewish calendar.

Sarasvati Festival

Sep/Oct; Hindu; statewide

Synonymous with Dussehra, Durga Puja and Navaratri, this 10 day festival is celebrated in the Hindu month of Kanni (Sept/Oct). It honours the goddess in her various manifestations. In Kerala this festival honours Sarasvati, the goddess of learning and inventor of Sanskrit, and is the time when many children are initiated into the letters of the alphabet. (See the Society & Conduct section of the Facts about Kerala chapter.)

October

Chandanakkudham Mahotsavam

Oct; Muslim; near Thiruvananthapuram

This 10 day festival commemorates the anniversary of the death of Bheema Beevi, a pilgrim who travelled to Kerala from Mecca, who is now honoured as a saint. Thousands of pilgrims visit her tomb at Bheemapally, where they leave offerings of money and flowers. The festival is held at the Bheemapally Mosque, about 5km south-west of Thiruvananthapuram.

Diwali (Deepavali)

Oct/Nov; Hindu; statewide

The festival of lights, is celebrated throughout India in the Hindu month of Thulam (Oct/Nov). In Kerala it does not involve the same extensive festivities as in other parts of India.

Festival of the Nagaraja Temple

Oct/Nov; Hindu; Mannarsala

Annual temple festival during Thulam when offerings are made to the Serpent king.

Gandhi Jayanthi

2 Oct; secular; statewide

On this day the birth of Mahatma Gandhi is celebrated.

Sarasvati Festival

Oct/Nov; Hindu; Thiruvananthapuram

At the Padmanabhaswamy Temple, the Sarasvati Festival is celebrated during Thulam when members of the Travancore royal family escort a procession elaborately decorated idols of the Gods Krishna, Padmanabha and Narasimha to the sea.

November

Karthika Festival

Nov/Dec; Hindu; statewide

This festival during the Hindu month of Virchikam (Nov/Dec) is particularly significant in South India with its focal point at Tiruvannamalai in Tamil Nadu where a huge beacon blazes for several days. Many people travel from Kerala for the festival at Tiruvannamalai. Those who remain in Kerala light fires or illuminate their homes.

Mandalam

Nov/Dec; Hindu; statewide

The month of Virchikam holds particular significance for Hindus, many of whom fast and attend special prayers in temples.

December

Ashtamudi Craft & Art Festival of India

26 Dec-10 Jan; secular; Kollam (Quilon)

Artists from around the country come to Asramam Maidan to perform, teach and sell their artwork.

Christmas Day
25 Dec; Christian; statewide
Christmas day is celebrated with masses (especially at midnight) in honour of Christ's birth.

Hanukkah (Festival of Lights)
22-29 Dec 2000, 10-17 Dec 2001, 30 Nov-7 Dec 2002; Jewish; Kochi
This is a time of re-dedication of the temple involving the lighting of candles. It dates back to 175 BCE when the temple at Jerusalem was rededicated, following its desecration a decade earlier.

Kochi Carnival
25-31 Dec; secular; Kochi
This carnival celebrates Kerala's many art forms with performances, exhibitions and demonstrations.

Ramadan (Ramzan, Id-ul-Fitr)
7 Jan 2000, 26 Dec 2001, 15 Dec 2002; Muslim; statewide
Known locally as Cheria Perunnal, Ramadan is the 10th month of the Islamic calendar and marks the time of fasting when Muslims take no food or drink until after sun down. Id-ul-Fitr celebrates the end of the fast.

Thiruvathira Festival
Dec/Jan; Hindu; statewide
For some this festival honours the birth of Shiva. For others, it honours Kamadeva, a deity associated with love and desire. This festival is celebrated in the Hindu month of Dhanu (Dec/Jan) and has traditionally been celebrated by Nair women who go to the temple for early-morning rituals. Young girls often perform the Thiruvathirakali, a ring dance with singing and clapping.

ACTIVITIES

Walking, Hiking & Trekking

Within easy reach of the coastal chaos are peaceful, rural spots that provide a good antidote to big-city life – a chance to stretch your legs and breathe some fresh air.

The Western Ghats are full of potential for hikers and other outdoor enthusiasts. Trekking in sanctuaries and national parks is only possible with a guide and a special permit from the forestry department unless you take an organised trek with a travel agency.

Swimming & Surfing

Kerala has many beaches and Kovalam and Varkala are the most popular with visitors. Just after the monsoons there can be dangerous rips in the sea – take care. There are few lifeguards and even strong swimmers have lost their lives to the tidal forces.

Away from the beach, many four and five star hotels have pools, which they may even allow nonguests to use for a fee, but ring first. Many people swim in the lakes and rivers but, due to pollution, this is not advised.

Fishing

In most places along the coast in Kerala you'll see the fisherfolk pursuing their daily tasks. Sometimes you'll be invited to join in. If you are particularly interested in a fishing holiday you can organise this at the Tharayil Tourist Home in Alappuzha, see the Southern Kerala chapter for more details.

Boating & River Rafting

You can drift around the backwaters and on the numerous lakes throughout Kerala. All manner of boats are available for hire from canoes and row boats to motorboats and ferries. For longer trips you can hire luxurious houseboats. (See the boxed text 'The Backwaters' section in the Southern Kerala chapter for more details.)

Beach Volleyball

On some beaches, particularly at Kovalam and Varkala, you'll see volleyball nets strung casually between poles or trees. Local youths have a passion for the game and delight in inviting visitors to join their teams.

Diving & Snorkelling

You can dive and snorkel in Lakshadweep. See the Lakshadweep chapter for more details on courses and diving conditions there.

Golf

India's golf clubs were once affiliated with the Royal Calcutta (Kolkata) Golf Club (established 1829), which followed rules laid down by St Andrews in Scotland. Golf today is under the aegis of the Indian Golf Union, which is affiliated with the World Amateur Golf Council. Some golf clubs allow visitors to use their course – usually you'll need to supply your own equipment.

Horse Riding

If you're looking for something to keep the kids amused this might be a good option. You'll sometimes find, at picnic sites, a tiny, solitary horse awaiting the opportunity to take you on a short (20 minute) ride led by its owner. It's all pretty tame – much more suitable for young children.

COURSES

Language

The Vijnana Kala Vedi Cultural Centre at Aranmula, a village 12km from Changanassery (Changanacherry), offers courses in many subjects including Malayalam, Hindi and Sanskrit. For further details see the Southern Kerala chapter.

Drama, Dance & Music

There are many places where Kerala's performing arts are taught. Most places accept only genuine students who are in it for the long haul (several years).

In Thiruvananthapuram, the Margi Kathakali School runs courses in Kathakali and Kootiattam – see the Southern Kerala chapter.

Near Thrissur, there's Kerala Kalamandalam, which conducts both long and short courses in Kathakali, Mohinyattam, Kootiattam and Thullal. Courses are also available in percussion, voice and violin. Also near Thrissur, at Irinjalakuda, the Natana Kairali Research & Performing Centre for Traditional Arts runs courses in dance as well as lesser-known art forms, such as puppetry. For more information on both these institutions, see the Central Kerala chapter.

The Vijnana Kala Vedi Cultural Centre (see earlier under Language) offers courses including Kathakali, Mohinyattam and Bharata Natyam (a dance which originated in Tamil Nadu). Carnatic vocal and percussion music. For details see the Southern Kerala chapter.

Cooking

For courses in cooking try the Vijnana Kala Vedi Cultural Centre (see previously under Language).

Arts & Crafts

The Vijnana Kala Vedi Cultural Centre at Aranmula (see under Language, earlier), offers courses in woodcarving, painting and *kolams* (auspicious decorations). The International Centre for Cultural Development (ICCD), Thiruvananthapuram, provides opportunities for foreign artists to learn new skills from local artists, while the Indian Council for Cultural Relations (ICCR, ☎ 326712) grants scholarships to foreign students for study and research into issues on culture and society. See the Southern Kerala chapter for more details.

Tasara Creative Weaving Centre, near Kozhikode, provides an environment for artists to learn and develop skills with textiles. See the Kozhikode section in the Northern Kerala chapter for details.

Martial Arts

You can study the ancient martial art of *kalarippayat* at the CVN Kalari Sangham in Thiruvananthapuram. See the Southern Kerala chapter for details.

Yoga & Ayurveda

Just 32km from Thiruvananthapuram the Sivananda Yoga Vedanta Dhanwantari Ashram conducts short and long-term yoga courses. Details are in the Around Thiruvananthapuram section in the Southern Kerala chapter. At Varkala Beach and Kovalam, among other places, you can learn yoga, meditation and Ayurvedic massage. At Thrissur, Universal Yoga Consciousness runs courses from three days to a year.

VOLUNTEER WORK

Charities & International Aid

Numerous charities and international aid agencies have branches in Kerala and sometimes there are volunteer opportunities for visitors. Though it may be possible to find temporary volunteer work after you arrive, you'll probably be of more use to an organisation if you write in advance.

For long-term posts, there are a number of organisations which may be able to help or offer advice and further contacts.

Australian Volunteers International
(☎ 03-9279 1788, fax 9419 4280, email ozvol@ozvol.org.au)
PO Box 350, Fitzroy Vic 3065, Australia
Web site: www.ozvol.org.au

Co-ordinating Committee for International Voluntary Service (CCIVS)
(☎ 01-45 68 27 31)
c/o UNESCO House, 1 rue Miollis, 75732 Paris Cedex 15, France.
Web site: www.unesco.org/ccivs

Council of International Programs (CIP)
(☎ 703-527 1160)
1101 Wilson Blvd Ste 1708, Arlington VA 22209, USA

Peace Corps of the USA
(☎ 1-800 424 8580, fax 202 692 2201, email webmaster@peacecorps.gov)
1111 20th St NW, Washington, DC, 20526.
Web site: www.peacecorps.gov

Voluntary Service Overseas (VSO)
(☎ 020-8780 7200, fax 8780 7300, email enquiry@vso.org.uk)
317 Putney Bridge Rd, London SW15 2PN, UK.
Web site: www.vso.org.uk

Conservation & the Environment

For voluntary work in the environmental area, contact Mitraniketan, 20km north-east of Thiruvananthapuram. See the Southern Kerala chapter for more details.

ACCOMMODATION

Kerala has a huge range and variety of accommodation, from the most basic hostels to upmarket forest lodges and former aristocratic homes. The best value for money is usually in the middle price range – Rs 250 to Rs 600 per night for a double. In a city like Thiruvananthapuram, this range will buy you a clean room, a private bathroom (with hot water most of the time), colour satellite TV, room service (a 10% surcharge usually applies), a telephone and a fan (sometimes air-con). However, in places where there is little tourist infrastructure, especially in the north, don't expect anywhere near the same standard, although you may still pay high prices. Price doesn't necessarily equate with cleanliness. A higher rate may simply buy you a piece of carpet (dirty) or a TV (which may not work).

At the budget end of the market it's important to distinguish between services for pilgrims and cheap accommodation. While it may appear there is an abundance of accommodation, it may be primarily for pilgrims and provided by temples at no, or very low, cost. In such situations it's unfair for foreign visitors to expect tourist facilities.

Many hotels claim to provide hot water, but in reality don't. Very often hot water only comes on for a few hours per day. A hotel claim of '24 hour running water' may simply mean that a room boy will be running up to your room with a bucket of hot water. This is usually a much better option than waiting for hot water to appear via the shower. Buckets and jugs will be provided so you can have a decent wash.

Don't be afraid to inspect the room first. Even in the most basic establishments, hotel staff are usually more than happy to show you around so your needs can be met.

Accommodation is known by many names – resort, hotel, lodging, tourist home, and so on. Such terms, however, may have varied meanings and may differ greatly from what is understood in other countries. All over Kerala you will come across the word 'hotel'. This doesn't automatically signal a place to stay. A hotel may be a place to eat. And as for 'resort', this may simply be a hyped-up name for a very run-down hotel – but it's usually by the beach.

Having arrived at the hotel of your choice, you may be told that it's full. It's sometimes worth persevering in these cases, especially if you're travelling off the beaten track. If you're a foreign visitor it may be assumed that you want air-conditioning and a western-style (sit-down) toilet. If you're happy with a ceiling fan and a squat toilet, say so. (After being ricocheted off one too many toilet seats, you may be happy to squat.) It's amazing how often a room, exactly to your requirements, suddenly appears.

Hotels very often want at least two nights' payment in advance. If you only stay one night the balance is happily refunded. You will usually be offered a receipt, but if you aren't, ask for one. Many places operate on a 24 hour basis, ie your 24 hours starts when you check in. Generally you can't pay by the hour if you go over the limit; you will be asked for another 24 hours payment even though you may only want the room for three or so hours extra. In the more touristy areas, hotels generally have a noon (or earlier) checkout rule. See also the earlier comments in the Bedding section under What to Bring.

Due to the paperwork involved for foreigner check-in, some establishments have an 'Indian only' policy, but this is rarely explicit. If you're foreign and experiencing difficulty securing accommodation, this may be the reason.

Hostels

Indian youth hostels (HI – Hostelling International) are generally very cheap. You are not usually required to be a YHA (HI) member (as in other countries) to use the hostels, although your YHA/HI card may get you a lower rate. The charge is typically Rs 15 for members, Rs 30 for nonmembers.

Private Jungle Lodges

To cater for upmarket Indian and foreign tourists visiting the major national parks, increasing numbers of private resorts and lodges are being constructed close to the parks. The settings, standards, prices and facilities vary considerably. Prices can range from about Rs 500 a double (singles are rarely available) to an impressive US$250. At the cheaper places, rates are usually for room only; meals, jeep hire and guides are all extra. As you would hope, at the expensive places, everything is usually included: meals, guides, jeep and boat tours, park entrance fees and so on.

These places are often hard to reach by public transport so you will probably have to charter a vehicle some of the way or organise something with the lodge (but you will pay heavily for any transfers). You must always prebook, often months ahead for peak times. Never just turn up expecting an empty room and a meal.

Some lodges have the best possible settings, and the best equipment, vehicles and facilities for viewing wildlife – usually far better than that offered by the forest departments (and better than you could hope to organise yourself). So if you *really* want to see some wildlife, you may have to dig deep into your wallet.

Forest Department Bungalows

Several government departments – notably the Public Works Department (PWD), as well as the various forest departments – have inspection or holiday bungalows. They are ostensibly for staff, but if rooms are available, travellers can sometimes use them. You are far less likely to be successful with the bungalows run by the forest departments.

Bungalows are often excellent value. Prices range from Rs 40 to Rs 150 a double, and while facilities are rustic, the rooms are usually clean. Food is available and alcohol and smoking are usually not allowed.

The bungalows should usually be prebooked; however, there are PWD managers who will find you a room if they have a vacancy. The difficulty in finding out how and where to book the bungalows is often a disincentive, but the information provided in the regional chapters should steer you in the right direction.

Tourist Bungalows

Usually run by the state government, tourist bungalows often serve as replacements for the older government-run accommodation units. Tourist bungalows are generally excellent value, although they vary enormously in facilities and the level of service offered.

They usually have dorm beds as well as private rooms – typical prices are around Rs 40 for a dorm bed, and Rs 120 to Rs 350 for a double room. The rooms have a fan, two beds and bathroom; air-con rooms are often also available at around Rs 500. Generally there's a restaurant or 'dining hall' and often a bar.

Railway Retiring Rooms

These are just like regular hotels or dormitories except they are at train stations. To stay here you are generally supposed to have a train ticket or Indrail Pass. The rooms are, of course, extremely convenient if you have an early train departure, although at busy stations, they can be noisy. In most places they are also excellent value. Railway retiring rooms are let on a 24 hour basis. The main problem is getting a bed, as they are very popular and often full. The staff at retiring rooms are often very helpful, a great advantage in places lacking tourist information.

Railway Waiting Rooms

When all else fails or when you just need a few hours rest before your train departs at 2 am, train station waiting rooms are a free place to rest your weary head. The trick is to rest in the (usually empty) 1st class waiting room and not the crowded 2nd class one.

Officially you need a 1st class ticket to be allowed into the 1st class room and its superior facilities. In practice, luck, a 2nd class Indrail Pass or simply a foreign appearance will work.

Many stations have separate waiting rooms for women.

Tea Plantations & Coffee Estates

An interesting accommodation option is to stay at a tea or coffee estate. These can be quiet places to relax, hike and watch crop picking and processing (in season). Prices and facilities vary – there are upmarket resorts, plain rooms in the back of family homes and just about everything in between. Tourist offices and travel agencies may be able to assist with lists of new places offering this sort of accommodation.

Budget Hotels & Guesthouses

There are cheap hotels all over Kerala, ranging from filthy, uninhabitable dives to ones that are clean and comfortable. Ceiling fans, mosquito nets on the beds, private toilets and bathrooms are all possibilities, even in rooms that cost Rs 120 or less per night for a double.

Although prices are generally quoted in this book for singles and doubles, most hotels will put an extra bed in a room to make a triple for about an extra 25%. In many hotels it's possible to bargain a little. On the other hand these places will usually put their prices up if there's a shortage of accommodation in the area.

Top End Hotels

Kerala's big, air-con, swimming pool places are for the most part confined to the major tourist centres such as Kovalam, Thiruvananthapuram and Kochi. All the hotels in Lakshadweep are top-end places. The Taj Group has some of India's flashiest hotels including the Malabar Hotel in Kochi (Cochin). The Oberoi and Casino chains also operate within India. Unlike their cheaper cousins, expensive hotels usually have a noon checkout time. Often there's a different price scale for locals and foreigners – prices for foreigners are quoted in US dollars, are much higher and taxes can also be very high.

Home Stays

Sometimes referred to as paying guest accommodation, staying with a family can be a most rewarding experience. It's a change from dealing strictly with tourist-oriented people, and it can give an intimate insight into everyday Indian life. Places are listed throughout this guide. Word of mouth, however, is one of the best ways to find out about this type of accommodation; places come and go all the time. The Tourist Facilitation Centre (☎ 0471-321132) on Museum Rd, Thiruvananthapuram, will also give you the latest details.

Rental Accommodation

For long-term stays, rental accommodation may be the best alternative. Some hotels will accept long-term residents at much cheaper rates. There are many possibilities. If you plan to stay a long time and you fancy a particular place, you can often negotiate a reasonable deal. Other rental alternatives come and go. Check with the Tourist Facilitation Centre (☎ 0471-321132) on Museum Rd, Thiruvananthapuram, for the latest on the scene.

Other Possibilities

There are a few YMCAs and YWCAs in the larger centres. They're usually well run, well equipped and good value. This makes them popular and they're often booked out.

Taxes & Service Charges

Accommodation taxes can add substantially to your costs, especially if you are using top-end accommodation. Always check at hotels and restaurants which taxes apply.

In Kerala luxury tax on accommodation is up to 7.5% on a standard room in a budget hotel (10% on an air-con room); 7.5 to 10% on a standard room in a mid-range hotel (10 to 15% for air-con); and 25% on a top-end hotel (usually made up of 15% luxury tax plus 10% luxury expenditure tax). Tax is often applied, even though you may feel it's unwarranted. As hotel staff sometimes say, 'no luxury, just a luxury tax'.

Seasonal Variations

In the popular tourist places, hoteliers crank up their prices in the high season by a factor of two to three times the low-season price. The high season tends to coincide with the cooler, non-monsoon months of November to February. Prices in this book are high-season rates. Always check around and bargain hard. In places like Kovalam you may find excellent accommodation for Rs 300 while next door inferior accommodation can be Rs 1000!

Touts

Touristy areas attract hordes of touts all vying for your money. Touts often work for arts and crafts places, tour operators and hoteliers. They are generally employed on a commission basis and can be most persuasive, very skilful and extremely annoying. Often they are the rickshaw drivers who meet you at the bus or train station. They earn a commission for taking you to a particular hotel, which may not be the hotel of your choice but you'll hear lots of stories about your preferred hotel being full or closed or whatever. Stand your ground and insist on your preference. Some very good hotels simply refuse to pay the touts, which means your rates will be much cheaper.

Touts do have a use though – if you arrive in a town during the high season finding a place to stay can be very difficult. Hop in a rickshaw, tell the driver how much you're prepared to pay for a room, and off you go. The driver will know which places have rooms available and unless the search is a long one you shouldn't have to pay the driver too much. Remember that he'll be getting a commission from the hotel, too, which will be added to your bill; but what's that, when it's hot, you're tired and he's helpful and has a great sense of humour?

FOOD

Eating Out in Kerala

The food of Kerala is diverse and delectable. For the traveller, food is a focal point, not merely as a commodity for consumption but as an entree into the culture and customs of the state. Given the majority Hindu population, much food is vegetarian, although many Hindus now eat meat. Muslims and Christians have always eaten meat, and more recently meat intake is increasing. Even beef and pork, especially for Christian communities, is prevalent.

If you're travelling during the Muslim fast period of Ramadan, you'll find Muslim eating places usually close during the day. If you're staying in a Muslim hotel the staff will usually arrange for food to be brought to your room during the day – in the evening the dining room will be open.

Meals served on trains are usually palatable and cheap (Rs 15 to Rs 25). The conductor will take your order and the food will be served sometime later. At most stops you'll be besieged by food and drink sellers. Even in the middle of the night that raucous cry of 'ah, omlee, omlee' (omelette) will inevitably break into your sleep.

While some dishes may be hot (spiced with chilli), many are mild, and flavoured with tempting spices. If you do find yourself unprepared with a hot curry, water may help, but some people find rice, curd or fruit relieves the fire more effectively.

Food is eaten with fingers of the *right hand only* – using the left hand is definitely impolite. All eating establishments have washing facilities where you can wash your hands before and after the meal. Scooping up food with the fingers takes a little practice but you'll soon become quite adept at it. It is said that eating this way allows you to experience the food in the fullest sense – touch, as well as aroma and taste. But don't worry if you find this too difficult. Cutlery is supplied in most places and it is not impolite to request and use it.

In the most basic restaurants and eating places, often referred to as hotels or *bhavans*, where turnover is great, food is prepared and served quickly. It's good, it's fresh and it's cheap.

At the other end of the price scale, there are many restaurants in five star hotels that border on the luxurious and yet by western standards are absurdly cheap. Many of the international-standard hotels offer all-you-can-eat buffet deals and these often involve showcasing special cuisines. Don't be fooled, though. The quality of the food does not necessarily correspond to the price – the best food (the tastiest and cheapest) is invariably found in the small eating houses, packed with locals.

Sometimes the word *thali* (vegetarian plate meal) is used interchangeably with 'meal'. When eating houses claim they only serve 'meals', it usually means that *only* thalis will be served. (See The Cuisine of Kerala section for more details.)

Western Food

For people seeking western food, there's plenty of it. For breakfast, eggs – fried, boiled, scrambled, poached or an omelette – are all are widely available. But take care if you don't like hot food, since egg dishes, particularly omelettes, may be prepared with onions and chillies. Toast and jam may be tempting, but the toast will often be disappointingly unpalatable – made of thin, tough bread loaded with sugar. Delicious soups of all descriptions, even if not on the menu, are usually prepared for the asking.

Chips or french fries (or finger chips as they are known in Kerala) are a common western dish. But it can be a hit and miss affair – sometimes they're excellent, at other times truly dreadful.

Most mid-range hotels serve good western food.

Other Cuisines

There is a wide variety of cuisines available in Kerala from other parts of India as well as many other Asian countries. Other Indian dishes, not necessarily of Keralan origin, include the spicy vegetarian meals that may be ordered with or without a gravy. These include *muttar*, *gobi*, *aloo* and *paneer* (peas, cauliflower, potato and cheese). These make delicious lunches or evening meals and may be combined with rice or bread. Chinese food is widely available and generally quite good, but it's more likely to be an Indianised version than genuine Chinese cuisine.

Fruit

Fresh fruit is widely available throughout Kerala. Bananas, pineapples, mangoes, jackfruit, custard apples, watermelons and papaya are all locally grown.

Watermelons are fine thirst quenchers when you're unsure about the water and are fed up with soft drinks. Green coconuts are even better, but they're few and far between, reserved mostly for tourist areas. When you've drunk the juice the stallholder will split the coconut open and cut you a 'spoon' from the outer shell. Use this to scoop out the flesh.

After the Meal

After a meal a small container of sugar, aniseeds and spices is often served. A small amount gives the mouth a refreshing taste.

A meal may also be finished with *murukan* (also known as *paan*) – the name given to the collection of spices and condiments chewed with betel nut. Betel is a mildly intoxicating and addictive nut, but by itself it is quite inedible. After a meal you chew paan as a mild digestive. Restaurants may provide them on a tray.

Vendors have a whole collection of little trays, boxes and containers in which they mix the paans. The ingredients may include, apart from the betel nut itself, lime paste (the ash not the fruit), the powder known as *catachu*, various spices and even a dash of opium in a pricey paan. The whole concoction is folded up in a piece of edible leaf that you pop in your mouth and chew. When finished you spit the leftovers out and add another red blotch to the ground. Over a long period of time, indulgence in paan will turn your teeth red-black and even addict you to the betel nut. Trying one occasionally won't do you any harm. Nowadays you can buy prepacked paan with a warning that chewing tobacco (a common ingredient) is injurious to health.

DRINKS

Nonalcoholic Drinks

Tea & Coffee In Kerala, you can get both tea and coffee. Tea may be served with spices or herbs, milk and/or sugar. Whatever the combination, it's generally very good. Usually tea houses will prepare your preference. In many hotels tea also comes in thermos containers with the milk and sugar combined or served separately.

If you're a coffee addict you may well be disappointed with the beverage in Kerala. Some of the mid-range hotels have coffee lounges, where for about a hundred times the street price, you can drink coffee, but it won't necessarily be a savoured experience.

Water It's generally best to avoid local water straight from the tap. In Thiruvananthapuram and Kochi it's safe to drink but if you've just arrived, the change from what you're used to and the amount you need to drink may cause slight diarrhoea. For more information on drinking water, see Water in the Health section earlier in this chapter.

Soft Drinks Soft drinks are a safe but not healthy alternative to water. Coca-Cola and Pepsi are widely available, especially in cities. There are also many indigenous brands with names like Campa Cola, Thums Up, Limca, Gold Spot or Double Seven. They are reasonably priced at around Rs 10 for a 250ml bottle (more in restaurants). They're usually refreshingly cold, but they're so sickly sweet they rarely appease the thirst.

Juices & Other Drinks Coconut water, straight from the young green coconut, is a popular drink. It's refreshing and safe, but not so readily available. One drinking coconut costs about Rs 8 – more in some places. Another alternative to soft drinks is soda water – several brands are widely available. With soda water you can make excellent, and safe, lemon and lime sodas.

Small cardboard boxes of various fruit juices are generally available. However, they too can be very sweet and are scarcely thirst quenchers. In the cities particularly you'll come across sugarcane and fresh fruit juice vendors. Be cautious if you decide to try fresh fruit juice; it may have been mixed with ordinary (dodgy) water.

Milk should be treated with suspicion as it is often unpasteurised, though boiled milk is fine if it is kept hygienically.

Finally there's *lassi*, a refreshing and delicious curd (yoghurt) drink. But again, be careful of the water (and ice) used in its making.

Alcoholic Drinks

Alcohol is relatively expensive – a bottle of Indian beer can cost anything up to Rs 180 in a flash hotel; Rs 50 to Rs 70 is the usual price range. At Mahé, in the Union Territory of Pondicherry, beer is much cheaper. Some Indian beers available are Golden Eagle, Kingfisher, Kingfisher Diet, Royal Challenge, United Breweries (UB), Eagle, King's, Arlem, London Pilsener, Kalyani Black Label, and Sandpiper. They're good if you can find them cold, which you will about 50% of the time.

Strictly speaking alcohol is not to be consumed in public places – or at least in places not specifically designated for such consumption (eg bars). Having a beer with your meal can therefore be an interesting experience. At Kovalam Beach alcohol is easily purchased, but at Varkala Beach, due to drownings after excessive alcohol intake, alcohol is officially banned. Alcohol is generally prohibited in Muslim establishments.

Indian interpretations of western alcoholic drinks are known as IMFL (Indian Made Foreign Liquor). They include imitations of whiskey and brandy under a plethora of different brand names. The taste varies from hospital disinfectant to passable imitation whiskey. Always buy the best brand, or just go without.

Indian white wines range from sweet to sherry-like. The best of the bunch is Riviera, a dry white wine that is OK, but far from cheap. It's difficult to describe Indian red wines – maybe best to have a beer!

Toddy is the local brew made from the sap of the coconut tree. After a second distillation the alcoholic strength can be as high as 35% proof. Although usually drunk straight, it can be quite good mixed with Coke or Pepsi.

Arak is what the peasants drink to get blotto. It's a clear, distilled rice liquor and it creeps up on you without warning. Treat it with caution and only ever drink it from a bottle produced in a government-controlled distillery. *Never, ever* drink it otherwise – hundreds of people die or are blinded every year in India as a result of drinking arak produced in illicit stills. You can assume it contains methyl alcohol (wood alcohol).

Cashew nut liquor is distilled in some homes illegally. People swear by its health-giving properties.

ENTERTAINMENT

Depending on your understanding of entertainment, Kerala may be lacking or it may be packed with fascinating and attractive activities. Much entertainment is self-made and opportunities are limited only by your imagination.

Temple Festivals

It would be just about impossible to travel through Kerala and not happen upon a festival. Although the origins and rituals of each festival may be different, they are generally a spectacle of passion and colour. They can involve massive temple cars (chariots) as well as music, dance, and colourfully garlanded deities. For entertainment value they are hard to beat. See the Public Holidays & Special Events section earlier and the regional chapters for details.

Wedding Watching

December to February is the wedding season in Kerala. The colourful ceremonies take place in hotels, wedding halls, temples, city streets and village homes. Some of the more elaborate weddings involve elephants, horses and bands of roaming musicians. As an outsider you may be invited to partake in the ritual blessing of the couple.

Bringing the Boats In

Throughout the day along the Keralan coast, fishermen bring in their catch. Watching them land their sturdy vessels is a great way to spend time. Helping them bring the boats in will generate much laughter and camaraderie. You may even score some fish or an offer of a ride on the next boat.

Cinemas

This is a must. To experience the movie culture is to experience India. It doesn't matter if you don't speak the language. In Malayalam, Hindi or Tamil cinema, the plot can usually be figured out. Besides, it's the visual rather than the verbal narrative that counts. Malayalam and Tamil cinema in particular lend a whole new meaning to that often quoted phrase from Federico Fellini that 'Going to the movies is like dreaming with your eyes open'. Enjoying the audience reaction is usually as entertaining as the film itself.

Performing Arts

Performances of classical dance, music and drama are held at numerous venues including temples, municipal halls, star hotels, beach venues, and harbour fronts. Consult tourist offices for details of specific performances.

In major centres, local cultural bodies as well as international ones such as Alliance

Française and the British Council sponsor performing arts including stage plays, concerts and films. Consult the newspapers for details.

SPECTATOR SPORTS

Throughout Kerala various sporting organisations promote and foster a myriad of different activities.

Martial Arts

Kerala is renowned for its ancient martial arts form *kalarippayat*. Finely tuned bodies dexterously achieve remarkable movements, postures and rhythms. You can also visit the training school and watch the students go through their paces. Some of the best places to do this are in Thiruvananthapuram at CVN Kalari Sangham (☎ 0471-474182) and Nair Kalari, Cotton Hill (☎ 0471-65140) and in Ernakulam in Kochi at Arjuna Kalari Centre (☎ 0484-365440) and ENS Kalari, Nettoor (☎ 0484-700810). Performances are held at many of the hotels.

Soccer

Soccer is very popular, with Kerala fielding some of the strongest Indian teams. Kerala has hosted international events. Important events are the GV Raja Memorial Football Tournament in Thiruvananthapuram, the Chackola Gold Trophy in Thrissur and the Sait Nagjee Football Tournament in Kozhikode. The soccer season is from October to April and local newspapers carry details of important matches.

Cricket

India's No 1 spectator sport is not so popular in Kerala even though Kerala was one of the first places in India to establish a cricket club, the Tellicherry (Thalasseri) Cricket Club.

If you are from a cricketing country yourself, no doubt as you travel around you will meet people able to rattle off the names of your top players and discuss the successes or otherwise of your country's international performances to date.

If you are interested in attending a game, check the local dailies for details. Your hotel will be able to assist with information.

Boat Racing

The annual boat races are spectacular events. Crews of over 150 oarsmen race boats over 100m long. You can see these in August in Alappuzha and in January in Thiruvananthapuram and Kochi.

SHOPPING

Kerala has everything from high-quality and high-priced crafts to inexpensive kitsch. A mere US$10,000 will secure you an exquisite hand-carved traditional Keralan-style bedroom suite fit for a maharaja or maharani. Shipping is extra! If your rupees don't extend to this, try a packet of spices. They make excellent gifts.

Popular purchases such as Kashmiri papier mâché and carpets, Tibetan rugs, Rajasthani and Tibetan jewellery, Rajasthani miniature painting and other products from the north are also available, mainly in tourist centres.

Government emporiums can be found in major centres and usually stock a large range of local crafts. Prices are fixed and are a little higher than one would pay in the bazaar, but for novices who don't know the going rates or quality, the emporiums are a reasonably safe bet. Shipping can be arranged at these places.

Some small handicraft shops exist as outlets for particular cultural groups and are sometimes operated by NGOs.

Kairali, the showroom of the Handicrafts Development Corporation of Kerala, is at PB No 171, Thiruvananthapuram (☎ 331358/9). It also has stores in Kollam, Kozhikode, Kochi, Kottayam, Kannur and Thekkady.

Antiques & Collectibles

Whether you are a collector or a browser the antique market at Fort Cochin is one of India's finest. Especially popular are quaint spice chests and boxes, dowry boxes and bronze statues. But also on show are discarded figurines from Keralan churches, clocks, Dutch and Chinese crockery, glassware of various vintages and faded prints. Dealers regularly come from London and New York to buy container-loads of collectibles. Ferreting through the cobwebbed, dusty warehouses for something special to take home is one of the pleasures of a visit to Fort Cochin. Shops here are well used to shipping purchases all over the world; even huge articles, such as traditional wooden boats bound by ropes.

Articles more than 100 years old may not be exported from India without an export clearance certificate. If you have doubts about any item and think it could be defined as an antique, you can check with branches of the Archaeological Survey of India. Contact a Government of India tourist office (see the Tourist Offices section earlier in this chapter) for details.

If you want something radically different head out to the boat-building area of Beypore near Kozhikode, where you can purchase every type of ship's anchor that you'll ever need. For something uniquely Keralan why not purchase a working model of a Chinese fishing net, complete with small stones as counterweights. These are available in Thiruvananthapuram.

Textiles

South India produces one of India's most famous silks at Kanchipuram, not far from Chennai in Tamil Nadu. Saris are handloomed, with gold and silver woven into the more expensive ones. Kozhikode is a good place to shop for silk saris but they're available in all centres throughout Kerala.

Khadi emporiums (known as Khadi Gramodyog) can be found in major centres. These are good places to buy handmade items of homespun cloth, such as the popular Nehru jackets and the *kurta pyjama*. Bedspreads, tablecloths, cushion covers or material for clothes are other popular khadi purchases.

Clothes

The trendy fashions of Mumbai and Delhi are not yet visible in Kerala but with the superb fabrics and excellent tailors you can do what travellers in India have been doing since before the time of Vasco da Gama – have your gear made to measure. If you're interested in this, take designs with you. You'll find the tailors only too happy to meet your requirements. At the popular tourist destinations of Kovalam, Varkala and Thekkady, you can purchase the usual New Age and hippie fare. The quality is good and the prices get better with a little negotiation.

Spices, Tea & Coffee

Spices have lured travellers to these parts for thousands of years. And the lure still works. After you've savoured the spices why not purchase them? With almost every other shop selling spices, Kumily has become spice town. Here you can purchase conveniently packaged spices, as well as oils, tea, coffee and nuts. In Munnar you can buy packets of the high altitude tea grown in the surrounding hills.

And if you miss out in these towns, try Thiruvananthapuram, where you'll pick up all manner of goodies.

Woodwork

Throughout Kerala you can buy sandalwood and rosewood carvings of deities, animals, and many other objects. Rosewood is used for making furniture and carving animals; elephants are a speciality of Kerala. Kerala has centres for marquetry (inlaid work), which uses woods of various hues (including rosewood). Carved wooden furniture and other household items, either in natural finish or lacquered, are also available. Dowry boxes are usually made from the wood of the jackfruit tree (sometimes rosewood) and are reinforced with brass hinges and brackets. You may find them in the antique shops of Fort Cochin. Brightly coloured wooden toys are also available in many parts of Kerala.

In Thiruvananthapuram you can purchase classical Keralan-style furniture. You can also have it made to your specifications.

Metal Craft

Carvings and bronzes are readily available in the ubiquitous Kashmiri emporiums or in the Kairali handicraft stores. The quality in these places can vary so it pays to shop around.

Kerala's famed bell metal products can be purchased around the state and particularly in Thrissur.

Jewellery

Gold rivals coconuts and bananas for popularity in Kerala. Opulent jewellery shops abound, especially in the cities of Kochi and Kozhikode. From cradle to grave gold plays a crucial role in the life of people in Kerala (see the boxed text 'Going for Gold' in the Western Ghats chapter). Skilled goldsmiths and creative designers turn out exquisite traditional as well as contemporary pieces. Even if you don't buy, it's fascinating to watch families make their purchase.

A wide range of jewellery from northern India and Tibet is generally available in the Kashmiri emporiums.

Contemporary Art

Although most contemporary painting and sculpture is clearly derivative of the classical styles there are a number of artists who are breaking away with radical new concepts and styles. The best place to see and purchase cutting edge work is in Fort Cochin and Kozhikode.

Leatherwork

Indian leatherwork is not made from cowhide but from buffalo-hide, camel, goat or some other substitute. People selling *chappals*, those basic sandals found all over India, will hound you in many centres. There isn't a lot of variety in leatherwork, but prices are relatively low.

Paintings & Drawings

In the more touristy areas you'll come across vibrant miniature paintings depicting domestic and rural scenes as well as gods and goddesses. These are carefully portrayed on leaf skeletons and enclosed on a printed card.

Other Items

Books, music CDs and tapes, masks and musical instruments are available in Thiruvananthapuram as well as some of the larger cities such as Kozhikode and Kochi.

THE CUISINE OF KERALA

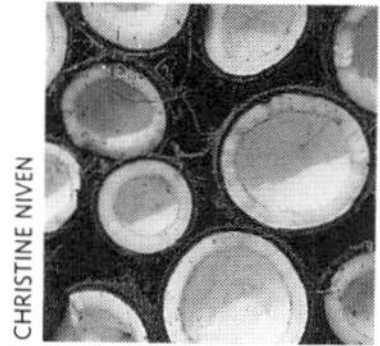
CHRISTINE NIVEN

As with many aspects of Keralan culture, the cuisine has been influenced by numerous traditions. It is a creative and delectable combination of vegetables, meats and seafood flavoured with a variety of spices and almost always cooked in coconut milk. The result is delicately prepared dishes, which are healthy and exciting.

Some believe the cuisine of Kerala has been influenced by Ayurvedic philosophies, which prescribe combinations of ingredients with the particular purpose of promoting health and vitality.

Breakfast

Aappam is a Keralan favourite and there are many varieties. For breakfast this pancake is usually made from a rice flour and *toddy* (fermented palm juice) batter. It has a thick, spongy centre and very fine lacy outer section. It's usually eaten with spiced sauces, sometimes with fruit.

Idlis and *dosas* are popular breakfast dishes in Kerala. Both originate in neighbouring Tamil Nadu. An idli is a small steamed cake made of rice flour and black lentil (blackgram) flour. Dosa is the famous pancake, large and very fine.

Puri is also popular. It's made of a batter that is quickly deep-fried causing it to puff up. All these dishes are usually served with small pots of spiced sauces.

Puttu is another popular breakfast dish. It is made from rice flour dough combined with shredded coconut and steamed in a bamboo tube. It is served with banana or plain with sugar. *Idi-appam* is rice noodles usually served with coconut milk but they may also accompany meat dishes.

Uthappam (also considered to be a dosa) is a thick pancake-like dish. It may be plain or combined with vegetables such as onion or tomatoes. It's gently fried and has a consistency somewhat like an omelette.

EDDIE GERALD

Breakfasts in Kerala are a special occasion with *vadais*, fluffy *idlis* **(left)** and puffy *puris* **(right)**.

Main Dishes

For lunch there's the *thali* – named after the plate on which it's served, although banana leaves are still popular serving dishes in Kerala. A thali includes rice and a number of different side dishes. These are placed directly on the banana leaf, in small pots or in the indentations in the thali plate. Rice is heaped in the centre and sometimes a pappadam or *chapati* (flat bread) is served. The side dishes may include such delicacies as:

avial – combination of vegetables and coconut sauce, it is a very popular Keralan accompaniment. Sometimes avial also includes fruits such as mango and jackfruit and even cashew nuts.
thoren – vegetables with coconut and mustard seed, which may be fried or steamed. Sometimes green papaya is used.
sambhar – vegetables like onions and eggplant in a sauce with lentils.
olen – beans and gourds in a coconut sauce.
kaalen – yoghurt and banana mixed with several spices including chilli.
rasam – similar to a clear broth, rasam may be flavoured with tamarind, lemon, tomato, lentils and/or pepper.
pachadi – curd with coconut and a curry leaf, a pleasing finish to the meal.
paayasam – sugared rice or noodles, served as a sweet.

In a nonvegetarian restaurant, spiced meats may also be served.

The thali is basically a banquet where you eat as much as you like for a set amount (usually minuscule, from Rs 10 to Rs 20). Unless you indicate otherwise, the portions you eat will quickly be replaced by diligent waiters who carry multibucket servers from which they ladle out replacements. The thali is eaten by adding small quantities of the side dishes to the rice. This is then mixed into a ball and popped into the mouth.

Varieties of *dhal* (cooked and spiced lentils) are also available.

Malayalis speak of *kappa* (tapioca) with respect. Certainly the plant has served them well since it became an important staple about one hundred years ago. The maharaja of Travancore sought to avert famines after witnessing the death and disease they caused. He researched several plants to find one that might be easily grown as well as providing a staple for the population. The chosen plant was tapioca.

Stews form a substantial part of the Keralan cuisine, usually served with aappams. Kottayam stew, popular with Syrian Christians, combines

BOTH PHOTOGRAPHS BY EDDIE GERALD

Naan tastes great soake[d] in a spicy curry **(left)** while the delicate *dosa* **(right)** often comes wrapped in its own curried vegetables, to make *masala dosa*.

EDDIE GERALD

GREG ELMS

GREG ELMS

LINDSAY BROWN

Top: According to one theory, Kerala is named after the coconut, which appears n so much of its cuisine.
Middle left: Packaged spices make a nice souvenir.
iddle right: A tempting fruit display.
ottom: Dried chillies are n essential item in every Keralan kitchen.

LINDSAY BROWN

KAREN TRIST

TERESA CANNON

GREG ELMS

KAREN TRIST

Top & middle: Bananas are used both green and ripe in Keralan cooking. **Bottom:** The *thali* meal is one of the cheapest and tastiest ways to fill your belly in Kerala. It is served on a banana leaf or metal tray with small compartments for each dish. These are constantly refilled by waiters.

chicken and vegetables in a coconut sauce with cinnamon and cloves, pepper, chillies and a dash of lime. *Erachi olarthiathu* is a beef or lamb dish cooked slowly and gently in a mixture of ginger, garlic, chilli and other spices. Just before serving it is fried quickly in aromatic herbs.

Fish is a very important part of the Malayali diet and there are numerous seafood dishes. *Meen pathichadhu* combines small fish or prawns with shredded coconut. *Meen vevichathu* is fish in a hot chilli sauce. *Kodampuli* is a fish meal cooked with sour fruit and chillies. Sometimes mangoes are used; or the rind of the *kokum* fruit is added.

Rice While rice is served with most dishes, in others it's the basic ingredient. *Biryanis*, meals of the Arabic tradition, are popular in Kerala, as they are throughout India. The Malabar (northern) area, with the largest Muslim population, is especially noted for its biryanis. The dish consists of rice that is layered with meat, seafood, vegetables, spices, nuts and sometimes fruits, then baked in an oven.

Breads Breads make an addition to many meals. The menu may list the flat-style breads such as *chapati* (dry-fried bread) or *naan* (baked bread), or the favourite fluffy *paratha* (fried bread).

Snacks Popular snacks include banana chips (sliced and deep-fried banana) and yam crisps.

Sweets There's no shortage of sweets in Kerala. *Jaggery* (palm syrup) is often used as a sweetener. It can be boiled and reduced to a thick liquid, then used as a sweet sauce with curd (yoghurt) or fruit.

Milk rice, coconut rice, or vermicelli sweetened with jaggery are all common desserts. *Inji thayir* (ginger in curd) is very popular. *Kaalen-an* are bananas coated in jaggery and cooked in a sauce of thick yoghurt spiced with turmeric, cumin and chilli. *Malayali pachadi* is sweet yoghurt with grated coconut, chillies, mustard seeds and spices.

Avalose is a rice-based sweet rolled into a ball with jaggery. *Unni-appam* is pulped jackfruit, mixed with rice flour and jaggery, wrapped in a leaf and steamed.

Prathaman is lentils boiled with coconut, cardamom and ginger. Jaggery and cashew nuts are also added. *Halwa* is made from bananas. Ice cream, often flavoured with cardamom, is available everywhere.

GREG ELMS

Right: Indulge yourself with the wide variety of olourful sweets on offer.

Spices

Spices have been integral to Kerala's history. For centuries they have lured people from all parts of the globe. As natural preservatives of food, they have helped prevent starvation and disease. As a trade commodity, they have generated prosperity and conflict. They have imbued cultural customs, provided cures for the sick and offerings to the deities.

Popular spices include turmeric, chilli, ginger and coriander (said to cool the body). Many other spices and flavourings, including nutmeg, poppy seeds, caraway seeds, basil, fenugreek, mace, garlic, cloves, bay leaves and curry leaves are freshly ground and may be blended in certain combinations to produce masalas (mixes), thus creating some distinctly Keralan cuisine. If you wish to visit spice gardens see the Periyar Wildlife Sanctuary and Munnar sections, and if you have an academic interest see the Indian Cardamom Research Institute entry – all of which appear in the Western Ghats chapter.

The spices below are listed with their common, botanical and Malayalam names.

Basil (*Ocimum sanctum*; Pudina) In Kerala basil comes in three varieties – wild; Krishna, with a purplish colour; and Rama, which is green and the most pungent. Basil is considered to be the plant of Vishnu and is often presented to the deity in temples.

Cardamom (*Elettaria cardamomum*; Elathari) Kerala is home to the small cardamom, considered to be superior in flavour, oil content and aroma. Known as the queen of spices, the native stands in the Western Ghats were supplemented by plantations by the British. Cardamom, with its tall strap-like leaves, produces its bounty from 10 to 200 panicles at its base. Each panicle may produce 100 to 300 pods. Kerala produces 40 to 45% of India's total cardamom harvest. Aromatic cardamom is used in desserts and in rich meat dishes and is employed medicinally to treat stomach ailments. You can visit a cardamom factory near Kumily, see the Indian Cardamom Research Institute section in the Western Ghats chapter for details.

Chilli (*Capsicum frutescens/Capsicum annuum*; Mulaka) Chillies are ground, dried or added whole to supply the heat in the cuisine. They come in red and green varieties but the red ones are the hottest. Chilli is almost indispensable to Keralan cooking; dishes that include it sometimes render a fiery result, at other times the outcome is more subtle. Whatever the mix, chilli enhances the flavours of the other ingredients.

Cloves (*Syzygium aromaticum, Eugenia caryophyllus*; Karambu) Cloves are latecomers to Kerala, being introduced by the British East India Company in the early 19th century. From within the tall, glossy foliage, small flower buds form, but are picked before they develop, and are dried in the sun to produce the tiny woody florets. Often used in meat dishes and dhal, they are also used to subdue toothache.

Above: Cardamom is used in both sweet and savoury dishes. Chillies were introduced by Portuguese traders.

Curry Leaves (*Murraya koenigii;* Karivepilla) Curry leaves add a subtle yet tangible zest to a dish, but are generally discarded before serving. Mostly they are used at the start of the cooking process by being tossed into hot oil; sometimes they flavour a sauce that is added to the meal towards the end of the cooking. Almost every home has a curry leaf tree. Fresh leaves are plucked, just as they are required.

Ginger (*Zinger officianale*; Inji) The tuberous ginger, believed to be good for the digestion, is used to flavour almost every dish. Pounded, grated, chopped or ground, it is one of the first ingredients added and sometimes one of the last, when sprinkled on food. In Kerala, ginger is combined with basil, pepper and sugar, to make a cough mixture. Kerala produces one third of India's total ginger yield.

Nutmeg (*Myristica fragrans*; Jathikka) (also Mace – Jathipatri) The nutmeg tree grows from 4m to 20m high. Its leaves resemble lemon leaves. In April the small rounded fruit ripens. Within is the nut, encased by a hard kernel, which in turn is enclosed in a mesh-like sheath. When dried the sheath becomes mace and the nut is released from its shell as nutmeg. The spice adds flavour to sweet dishes or, as an oil, is added to soap, toothpaste and ointments. Kerala produces 90% of India's nutmeg, and each tree produces an average 2500 fruits annually.

Pepper (*Piper nigrum, Piper longum*; Kurumalagu) Known as 'black gold' to Europeans who sought its preservative qualities, pepper is actually a vine. If it doesn't create its own attachments, it's supported by coir (rope). A plant may produce berries – picked green from December to February – for 20 years. Those high on the vine are gathered with the aid of a bamboo ladder. They are dried in the sun for one to two months, after which they turn into the famous black pepper. For white pepper, the black peppercorns are left for another two months, then soaked in water and the skin is removed to reveal the white peppercorn within. Kerala produces almost 98% of India's pepper.

Tamarind (*Tamarindus indica*; Puli) Tamarind provides the tangy, fruity flavour in a dish. Keralans are proud of their black tamarind which is usually reserved for fish dishes. The black variety common around Kottayam is believed to be superior, providing the rich sour flavours that form the basis of many dishes. Medicinally it's useful for digestion.

Turmeric (*Curcuma longa*; Manjal) Turmeric has a yellow colouring and acts as a preservative. It is highly regarded for its cleansing and curative properties. Similar to the ginger plant, it is believed to kill bacteria and is therefore an important ingredient in most dishes. It's used as an antiseptic and applied to the skin to counteract allergies and acne. People are sometimes anointed with turmeric – a symbol of purification. Kerala produces just under 2% of India's total production.

Above: Curry leaves add a subtle flavour; while ginger is often used in Ayurvedic medicine. All illustrations by Trudi Canavan

Vanilla (*Vanilla planifolia)* In April the Vanilla plant (which belongs to the orchid family) is pollinated manually. Flowers only open for one day so work is done quickly and with precision; one person might pollinate over 2500 flowers in a day. When the beans mature eight months later they are processed by alternate curing and sun drying.

Getting There & Away

Warning

The information in this chapter is particularly vulnerable to change: prices for international travel are volatile, routes are introduced and routes are cancelled, schedules change, special deals come and go, and rules and visa requirements are amended.

Please use the information in this chapter as a guide only.

At present, there are direct flights to Kerala and Lakshadweep from the Middle East and Singapore, as well as some countries in the region. Charter flights from the UK are also available. However, the most common route for travellers is via one of the gateway cities of Mumbai (Bombay) or Chennai (Madras).

Your journey is therefore likely to be in two parts, flying into one of the gateway cities and making your way to Kerala or Lakshadweep from there. This chapter has been organised into three sections. The India section gives general information on travelling to India. The second section is devoted to the gateway cities of Mumbai and Chennai, and includes information on the respective airport terminals, and a selection of accommodation in case you have to stop over. The Kerala section gives information on domestic services, such as how to travel from Mumbai and Chennai to Kerala.

India

AIR

Airports & Airlines

It is possible to fly directly to Kerala. Both Kerala and Lakshadweep are serviced by major international airports. In Kerala they are at Thiruvananthapuram, Kochi (Cochin), Kozhikode (Calicut) and in Lakshadweep at Agatti.

Most of the international flights for Kerala are to/from the Middle East with Air India, Gulf Air and Kuwait Airways. Air India also flies to Thiruvananthapuram from Singapore on Wednesday and Sunday.

Buying Tickets

The plane ticket will probably be the single most expensive item in your budget, and buying it can be an intimidating business. It's always worth putting aside a few hours to research the current state of the market. Start early: cheap tickets have to be bought months in advance. Talk to other recent travellers – they may be able to stop you making some of the same old mistakes. Look at the ads in newspapers and magazines, consult reference books and watch for special offers. Then phone around travel agencies for bargains. (Airlines can supply information on routes and timetables; however, except at times of inter-airline war, they do not supply the cheapest tickets.) Find out the fare, the route, the duration of the journey and any restrictions on the ticket. Then sit back and decide which is best for you.

You may discover that those cheap flights are 'fully booked, but we have another one that costs a bit more...'. Or the cheap flight may be on an airline that's notorious for its poor safety standards and you may have to wait for long hours in the world's least favourite airport. Don't be swayed by the claim that there are only two seats available for the whole month in which you want to travel. And don't panic – it always pays to keep ringing around.

Use the fares quoted in this book as a guide only. They are approximate and based on the rates advertised by travel agencies at the time of going to press. Quoted airfares do not necessarily constitute a recommendation for the carrier.

If you are travelling from the UK or the USA, you will probably find that the cheapest flights are being advertised by obscure

International Flights to/from Thiruvananthapuram (Trivandrum)

For domestic flights to/from Thiruvananthapuram, Kochi and Kozhikode, see the air fare tables in the regional chapters.

destination	airline	frequency (to Thiruv.)	frequency (from Thiruv.)	fare (US$)
Colombo	IC	Mon, Wed, Fri	Mon, Wed, Fri	150
	UL	Daily except Sun	Mon, Wed, Thur, Fri, Sat	150
Male'	IC	Tue, Thur, Sat, Sun	Tue, Thur, Sat, Sun	75
	L6	Wed, Thur, Fri, Sat, Sun	Wed, Thur, Fri, Sat, Sun	75
Singapore	AI	Wed, Sun	Tue, Sat	1094

Several airlines operate from Thiruvananthapuram to the Middle East. Each week flights go to Abu Dhabi (6), Bahrain (6), Doha (4), Dhahran (4), Dubai (4), Kuwait (2), Muscat (5) and Riyadh (2). Flights also operate between Kochi (Cochin) and Kozhikode (Calicut) and the Middle East.

Abbreviations: IC = Indian Airlines, UL = SriLankan (Air Lanka), L6 = Air Maldives, AI = Air India

bucket shops whose names haven't yet reached the telephone directory. Many such firms are honest and solvent, but there are a few rogues. If you feel suspicious about a firm, don't give them all the money at once – leave a deposit of 20% or so and pay the balance when you get the ticket. If they insist on cash in advance, go somewhere else. Once you have the ticket, ring the airline to confirm that you are actually booked on the flight.

You may decide to pay more than the rock-bottom fare by opting for the reputation of a better-known organisation. Firms such as STA Travel, who have offices worldwide, and Council Travel in the USA have a good track record and they offer good prices to most destinations.

Once you have your ticket, write down its details and keep the information somewhere separate, see also the Photocopies section in the Facts for the Visitor chapter. If the ticket is lost, this will help you get a replacement. It's sensible to buy travel insurance as early as possible. If you buy it the week before you fly, you may find, for example, that you're not covered for delays to your flight.

Round-the-World Tickets & Circle Pacific Fares

Round-the-World (RTW) tickets have become very popular and are often real bargains. The official airline RTW tickets are usually put together by a combination of two airlines and permit you to fly anywhere on their route systems so long as you do not backtrack. Other restrictions usually require that you book the first sector in advance and cancellation penalties then apply. There may be restrictions on the number of stopovers and the validity of the ticket – usually 90 days to a year.

Circle Pacific tickets use a combination of airlines to circle the Pacific – Australia, New Zealand, North America and Asia. As with RTW tickets there are advance purchase restrictions and limits to how many stopovers you can take. These fares are likely to be around 15% cheaper than RTW tickets.

Travellers with Special Needs

If you have special needs of any sort – you've broken a leg, you're vegetarian, travelling in a wheelchair, taking the baby,

Air Travel Glossary

Baggage Allowance This will be written on your ticket and usually includes one 20kg item which can go in the hold, plus one item of hand luggage.

Bucket Shops These are unbonded travel agencies specialising in discounted airline tickets.

Bumped Just because you have a confirmed seat doesn't mean you're going to get on the plane (see Overbooking).

Cancellation Penalties If you have to cancel or change a discounted ticket, there are often heavy penalties involved; insurance can sometimes be taken out against these penalties. Some airlines impose penalties on regular tickets as well, particularly against 'no-show' passengers.

Check-In Airlines ask you to check in a certain time ahead of the flight departure (usually one to two hours on international flights). If you fail to check in on time and the flight is overbooked, the airline can cancel your booking and give your seat to somebody else.

Confirmation Having a ticket written out with the flight and date you want doesn't mean you have a seat until the agent has checked with the airline that your status is 'OK' or confirmed. Meanwhile you could just be 'on request'.

Courier Fares Businesses often need to send urgent documents or freight securely and quickly. Courier companies hire people to accompany the package through customs and, in return, offer a discount ticket which is sometimes a phenomenal bargain. In effect, what the companies do is ship their freight as your luggage on regular commercial flights. This is a legitimate operation, but there are two shortcomings – the short turnaround time of the ticket (usually not longer than a month) and the limitation on your luggage allowance. You may have to surrender all your allowance and take only carry-on luggage.

Full Fares Airlines traditionally offer 1st class (coded F), business class (coded J) and economy class (coded Y) tickets. These days there are so many promotional and discounted fares available that few passengers pay full economy fare.

ITX An ITX, or 'independent inclusive tour excursion', is often available on tickets to popular holiday destinations. Officially it's a package deal combined with hotel accommodation, but many agents will sell you one of these for the flight only and give you phoney hotel vouchers in the unlikely event that you're challenged at the airport.

Lost Tickets If you lose your airline ticket an airline will usually treat it like a travellers cheque and, after inquiries, issue you with another one. Legally, however, an airline is entitled to treat it like cash and if you lose it then it's gone forever. Take good care of your tickets.

MCO An MCO, or 'miscellaneous charge order', is a voucher that looks like an airline ticket but carries no destination or date. It can be exchanged through any International Association of Travel Agents (IATA) airline for a ticket on a specific flight. It's a useful alternative to an onward ticket in those countries that demand one, and is more flexible than an ordinary ticket if you're unsure of your route.

No-Shows No-shows are passengers who fail to show up for their flight. Full-fare passengers who fail to turn up are sometimes entitled to travel on a later flight. The rest are penalised (see Cancellation Penalties).

Air Travel Glossary

On Request This is an unconfirmed booking for a flight.

Onward Tickets An entry requirement for many countries is that you have a ticket out of the country. If you're unsure of your next move, the easiest solution is to buy the cheapest onward ticket to a neighbouring country or a ticket from a reliable airline which can later be refunded if you do not use it.

Open Jaw Tickets These are return tickets where you fly out to one place but return from another. If available, this can save you backtracking to your arrival point.

Overbooking Airlines hate to fly empty seats and since every flight has some passengers who fail to show up, airlines often book more passengers than they have seats. Usually excess passengers make up for the no-shows, but occasionally somebody gets 'bumped' onto the next available flight. Guess who it is most likely to be? The passengers who check in late.

Point-to-Point Tickets These are discount tickets that can be bought on some routes in return for passengers waiving their rights to a stopover.

Promotional Fares These are officially discounted fares, available from travel agencies or direct from the airline.

Reconfirmation If you don't reconfirm your flight at least 72 hours prior to departure, the airline may delete your name from the passenger list. Ring to find out if your airline requires reconfirmation.

Restrictions Discounted tickets often have various restrictions on them – such as needing to be paid for in advance and incurring a penalty to be altered. Others are restrictions on the minimum and maximum period you must be away, such as a minimum of 14 days or a maximum of one year.

Round-the-World Tickets RTW tickets give you a limited period (usually a year) in which to circumnavigate the globe. You can go anywhere the carrying airlines go, as long as you don't backtrack. The number of stopovers or total number of separate flights is decided before you set off and they usually cost a bit more than a basic return flight.

Stand-by This is a discounted ticket where you only fly if there is a seat free at the last moment. Stand-by fares are usually available only on domestic routes.

Transferred Tickets Airline tickets cannot be transferred from one person to another. Travellers sometimes try to sell the return half of their ticket, but officials can ask you to prove that you are the person named on the ticket. This is less likely to happen on domestic flights, but on an international flight tickets are compared with passports.

Travel Agencies Travel agencies vary widely and you should choose one that suits your needs. Some simply handle tours, while full-service agencies handle everything from tours and tickets to car rental and hotel bookings. If all you want is a ticket at the lowest possible price, then go to an agency specialising in discounted fares.

Travel Periods Ticket prices vary with the time of year. There is a low (off-peak) season and a high (peak) season, and often a low-shoulder season and a high-shoulder season as well. Usually the fare depends on your outward flight – if you depart in the high season and return in the low season, you pay the high-season fare.

terrified of flying – you should let the airline know as soon as possible so that they can make arrangements accordingly. You should remind them when you reconfirm your booking (at least 72 hours before departure) and again when you check in at the airport. It may also be worth ringing around the airlines before you make your booking to find out how each one of them can handle your particular needs.

Airports and airlines can be very helpful, but they do need advance warning. Most international airports will provide escorts from check-in desk to plane where needed, and there should be ramps, lifts, and accessible toilets and telephones for wheelchair-bound travellers. Aircraft toilets, on the other hand, are likely to present a problem; travellers should discuss this with the airline at an early stage and, if necessary, with their doctor.

Guide dogs for the blind will often have to travel in a specially pressurised baggage compartment with other animals away from their owner, smaller guide dogs will be subject to the same quarantine laws (six months in isolation, etc) as any other animal when entering or returning to countries currently free of rabies, such as Australia.

Deaf travellers can ask for airport and inflight announcements to be written down for them.

Children under two travel for 10% of the standard fare (or free on some airlines), as long as they don't occupy a seat. They don't get a baggage allowance either. 'Skycots' should be provided by the airline if requested in advance; these will take a child weighing up to about 10kg. Children between two and 12 can usually occupy a seat for half to two-thirds of the full fare and do get a baggage allowance. Push chairs can often be taken as hand luggage.

Charter Flights

Charter flights are the cheapest way to get to Kerala from the UK. The most common scheduled route is Air India via Mumbai, SriLankan (formerly Air Lanka) via Colombo or with several airlines direct to Kochi. The Charter Flight Centre (☎ 020-7565 6788/6777) has special deals. The best source for information on charter flight details is the *Evening Standard* newspaper. Check also the travel page ads in the *Times, Business Traveller* and the weekly what's-on magazine *Time Out*. Some travel agencies you could try include the following:

Bridge the World
(☎ 020-7911 0900)
1-3 Ferdinand St, Camden Town, London NW1
STA Travel
(☎ 020-7937 9962)
74 Old Brompton Rd, London SW7
(☎ 020-7465 0484)
117 Euston Rd, London NW1

Departure Tax

For flights departing from India for neighbouring countries (such as Pakistan, Sri Lanka, Bangladesh, Nepal) the departure tax is Rs 150, but to other countries it's Rs 500. The airport tax applies to everybody, even to babies who do not occupy a seat. The method of collecting the tax varies, generally you have to pay it when you buy your ticket, but check in case you are required to do so at the check-in .

Africa

Due to the large Indian population living in Nairobi there are plenty of flights between East Africa and Mumbai. Typical fares from Nairobi to Mumbai are about US$565 return with Ethiopian Airlines, Kenya Airways, Air India or Pakistan International Airlines (PIA), via Karachi.

Australia & New Zealand

Advance purchase return fares from the east coast of Australia to Chennai range from A$1349 to A$1699 depending on the season. Fares are slightly more expensive to Mumbai and fares are cheaper from Western Australia. The low travel period is from March to October, peak is from November to February.

Return advance purchase fares from New Zealand to India range from NZ$1995 to NZ$2395 depending on the season.

Continental Europe

Fares from continental Europe are mostly far more expensive than from London. Amsterdam, however, can be a good place for a cheap fare. In Amsterdam, NBBS is a popular travel agency. You can get Paris to Mumbai fares for 3600FF, 3850FF to Chennai.

Hong Kong

Hong Kong has a reputation for being the discount ticket capital of the region. However, its bucket shops are about as pricey as those of other cities. Ask other travellers for advice before buying a ticket. One-way tickets to Mumbai can be picked up for US$620 or to Chennai for US$595.

Malaysia

Not many travellers fly between Malaysia and India because it is cheaper from Thailand, but there are flights between Penang or Kuala Lumpur and Chennai. You can generally pick up a one-way ticket for the Malaysia Airlines flight from Kuala Lumpur to Chennai for RM796 one way and between Penang and Chennai for RM905. A ticket from Kuala Lumpur to Mumbai is RM1250 one way.

The Maldives

From Thiruvananthapuram (Trivandrum) to Male' in the Maldives costs US$75 one way. See the 'International Flights to/from Thiruvananthapuram (Trivandrum)' table in the Kerala section, later in this chapter, for more information.

Nepal

Royal Nepal Airlines Corporation (RNAC) and Indian Airlines share routes between India and Kathmandu. Both airlines give a 25% discount to people under 30 years of age on flights between Kathmandu and India; no student card is needed. Between Kathmandu and Mumbai it's US$277 one way.

Singapore

Singapore is a great cheap ticket centre and you can pick up Singapore-Chennai tickets for about S$445.

Sri Lanka

There are flights to and from Colombo and Mumbai, Chennai or Thiruvananthapuram, see the 'International Flights to/from Thiruvananthapuram (Trivandrum)' table for more information on the last of these. Flights are most frequent on the Chennai-Colombo route (US$95).

Thailand

Bangkok is a popular departure point from South-East Asia into Asia proper. It will cost about US$300 to fly from Bangkok to Chennai.

The UK

Charter flights are probably the least expensive way to get from the UK to Kerala. See Charter Flights in the Kerala section, later in this chapter, for more information.

From London to Mumbai, fares range from around UK£199/339 one way/return in the low season or about UK£279/479 one way/return in the high season. The cheapest fares are usually with KLM-Royal Dutch Airlines or Alitalia. You'll also find very competitive airfares to the subcontinent with Biman Bangladesh Airlines or SriLankan (formerly Air Lanka). Lufthansa Airlines has good deals but on these special offers there are restrictions, once you've bought the ticket no changes to dates of travel are allowed.

If you want to stop in India en route to Australia expect to pay between UK£369 and UK£599 for a one-way fare through to Australia.

Most British travel agencies are registered with ABTA (Association of British Travel Agents). If you have paid for your flight with an ABTA-registered agency that then goes out of business, ABTA will guarantee a refund or an alternative. Unregistered bucket shops are riskier but also sometimes cheaper.

The USA & Canada

The cheapest return airfares from the US west coast to India are about US$1350. Another way of getting there is to fly to Hong

Kong and get a ticket from there. Tickets to Hong Kong cost about US$695 one way and around US$750 return from San Francisco or Los Angeles. In Hong Kong you can find one-way tickets to Mumbai for US$620 or Chennai for US$595. Alternatively, you can fly to Singapore for about US$799/920 one way/return, or to Bangkok for US$785/875 one way/return, and pick up a cheap onward ticket from there.

From the east coast you can get return flights to Mumbai for around US$1099/2025 in the low/high season, and to Chennai for US$1177/2585. Another way of getting to India from New York is to fly to London and then buy a cheap fare from there.

The *New York Times*, the *San Francisco Examiner*, the *Chicago Tribune* and the *LA Times* all produce weekly travel sections in which you'll find any number of travel agencies' adverts. Council Travel and STA Travel have offices in major cities nationwide. The magazine *Travel Unlimited* (PO Box 1058, Allston, Mass 02134) publishes details of the cheapest airfares and courier possibilities for destinations all over the world from the USA.

Fares from Canada are similar to the US fares. From Vancouver the route is like that from the US west coast, with the option of going via Hong Kong. From Toronto it is easier to travel via London.

Travel CUTS has offices in all major Canadian cities. The *Toronto Globe & Mail* and the *Vancouver Sun* carry travel agencies' ads. The magazine *Great Expeditions* (PO Box 8000-411, Abbotsford BC V2S 6H1) is useful.

Cheap Tickets in India

You can get cheap tickets in Chennai and Mumbai but it's in Delhi that the real wheeling and dealing goes on. There are a number of bucket shops around Connaught Place, but inquire with other travellers about their current trustworthiness. And if you use a bucket shop, double-check with the airline itself that the booking has been made.

SEA

You can't get to Kerala by sea. Services from Sri Lanka to Tamil Nadu across the Palk Strait and between Penang and Chennai are no longer operating, and shipping services between Africa and India carry freight (including vehicles), but they don't carry passengers.

ORGANISED TOURS

There are numerous companies offering standard, eco-travel and adventure travel organised tours. You'll find them listed in newspapers and travel magazines such as *Earth Journal* (USA). Companies that organise tours to various parts of India include the following:

Australia & New Zealand

Ferris Wheels Classic Enfield Motorcycle Safaris
(☎ 02-9904 7419)
61 Elizabeth St, Artarmon 2064, Australia
Peregrine Adventures
(☎ 03-9663 8611)
258 Lonsdale St, Melbourne 3000, Australia. Also offices in Sydney, Brisbane, Adelaide, Perth and Hobart
Venturetreks
(☎ 09-379 9855, fax 377 0320)
164 Parnell Rd (PO Box 37610), Parnell, Auckland, New Zealand
Window to the World
(☎ 91-452-745 711, fax 452-747 784)
Hotel Chentoor, 106 West Perumal Maistry, Madurai, Tamil Nadu
Australian Office
(☎/fax 02-6493 8595)
36 Fieldbuckets Road, Quamma 2550
World Expeditions
Sydney
(☎ 02-9264 3366, fax 9261 1974)
3rd floor, 441 Kent St, Sydney 2000, Australia
Melbourne
(☎ 03-9670 8400, fax 03-9670 7474)
1st floor, 393 Little Bourke St, Melbourne 3000, Australia

The UK

Encounter Overland
(☎ 020-7370 6845)
267 Old Brompton Rd, London SW5 9JA, UK
Exodus Expeditions
(☎ 020-8673 0859)
9 Weir Rd, London SW12 OLT, UK

The USA

Adventure Center
(☎ 800-227 8747)
1311 63rd St, Suite 200, Emeryville, CA 94608, USA
All Adventure Travel, Inc
(☎ 303-440 7924)
PO Box 4307, Boulder, CO 80306, USA
Asian Pacific Adventures
(☎ 800-825 1680)
826 S Sierra Bonita Ave, Los Angeles, CA 90036, USA
Inner Asia Expeditions
(☎ 415-922 0448, fax 346 5535)
2627 Lombard St, San Francisco, CA 94123, USA

Gateway Cities

This section includes information on the two gateway cities of Mumbai and Chennai, including international airline offices, accommodation and airport-city transfers.

MUMBAI (Bombay)

☎ 022 • pop 15 million

Mumbai, the main international gateway to India, is a convenient entry point for Kerala. The international terminal (Sahar) is 30km north of central Mumbai, the domestic terminal (Santa Cruz) is close by. Officially, the two have been renamed Chhatrapati Shivaji airport. There are regular shuttle buses between the two terminals. Facilities at Sahar include Government of India and MTDC tourist counters, 24 hour moneychanging facilities and a prepaid taxi booth.

International Airlines

Most international airline offices in Mumbai are in, or close to, Nariman Point. Addresses of international carriers include:

Air Canada
(☎ 202 1111, fax 285 5694)
Amarchand Mansion, Madame Cama Rd
Air France
(☎ 202 5021, fax 202 9264)
1st floor, Maker Chambers VI, J Bajaj Marg, Nariman Point
Air India
(☎ 202 4142, fax 285 6846)
Air India Bldg, Nariman Point
Alitalia
(☎ 204 5023, fax 204 0167)
Industrial Assurance Bldg, Veer Nariman Rd, Churchgate
British Airways
(☎ 282 0888, fax 283 3221)
Valcan Insurance Bldg, 202B Veer Nariman Rd, Churchgate
Japan Airlines
(☎ 287 4936, fax 287 0610)
Ground floor, Raheja Centre, Free Press Journal Marg, Nariman Point
KLM-Royal Dutch Airlines
(☎ 283 3338, fax 838 0488)
Khaitan Bhavan, 198 J Tata Rd, Churchgate
Lufthansa Airlines
(☎ 202 3430, fax 283 3936)
Ground floor, Express Towers, Nariman Point
Malaysia Airlines
(☎ 218 1431, fax 218 5699)
GSA Stic Travels & Tours, 6 Maker Arcade, Cuffe Parade
Qantas Airways
(☎ 202 9297, fax 282 8795)
4th floor, Sakhar Bhavan, Nariman Point
Singapore Airlines (SIA)
(☎ 202 2747, fax 285 6345)
Taj Mahal Hotel, Apollo Bunder, Colaba
SriLankan (formerly Air Lanka)
(☎ 282 2388, fax 283 3864)
Ground floor, 12D Raheja Centre, Free Press Journal Marg, Nariman Point
Swissair
(☎ 287 2210, fax 204 0692)
Ground floor, Maker Chambers VI, J Bajaj Marg, Nariman Point
Thai Airways International (THAI)
(☎ 215 5301, fax 215 4597)
15 World Trade Centre Arcade, Cuffe Parade

Places to Stay

In Mumbai, it's a good idea to book at least your first night's accommodation. Bear in mind that luxury hotels levy taxes as high as 30%; prices listed here don't include tax.

Around the Airport There are a few mid-range and top-end places near the airport.

The ***Hotel Aircraft International*** *(☎ 612 1419, 179 Dayaldas Rd)* is one of the cheapest places near the airports, with air-con singles/doubles from Rs 850/950.

Avion Hotel *(☎ 611 3220, Nehru Rd)* has some single rooms for Rs 1175, but the majority of the rooms are in the Rs 1525 to Rs 1825 bracket.

The ***Centaur Hotel*** *(☎ 611 6660, fax 611 3535)*, right outside the domestic terminal, has all the usual five star amenities. Rooms cost US$185.

Leela Kempinski *(☎ 836 3636, fax 836 0606)*, 1km from the international terminal, is an award-winning five star establishment charging US$315/335 for singles/doubles.

Colaba Colaba has plenty of budget and mid-range hotels.

The Salvation Army Red Shield Hostel *(☎ 284 1824, 30 Mereweather Rd, Colaba)* is the cheapest place to stay. A bed in a separate-sex dorm costs Rs 100 (including breakfast) or Rs 150 (full board).

Bentley's Hotel *(☎ 288 2890, 17 Oliver Rd, Colaba)* offers enormous and ordinary-sized doubles for between Rs 700 and Rs 970, including breakfast. It's popular and reservations are recommended.

Hotel Suba Palace *(☎ 202 0636, Battery St, Colaba)* is a comfortable, efficiently run, modern establishment with air-conditioned singles/doubles with TV and fridge for Rs 1195/1800. The hotel gets consistently favourable reviews from travellers.

Taj Mahal Hotel *(☎ 202 3366, fax 287 2711, Apollo Bunder, Colaba)* has all the facilities you'd expect in one of the best hotels in the country. Rooms cost from US$295/325 in the atmospheric old wing.

Fort Directly to the north of Colaba is the area known as Fort.

Hotel Lawrence *(☎ 284 3618, 3rd floor, Rope Walk Lane, Fort)* is one of the best budget options in Mumbai. Don't expect anything more than a clean, plain room in a central location, but it's a bargain at Rs 300/400/600 for singles/doubles/triples with common bath. It has only a handful of rooms and is very popular so book at least 21 days in advance.

Hotel Residency *(☎ 262 5525, fax 261 9164, 26 Rustom Sidhwa Marg, Fort)* is one of the few really comfortable budget options in the heart of the Fort. It's quiet, well located and great value. Spotless air-conditioned singles/doubles with bath and TV start at Rs 990/1090, and rise to Rs 1150/1250 in the deluxe annexe next door. There's a 4% tax on all rooms. The hotel has a small restaurant. Bookings are recommended, credit cards are accepted.

Churchgate & Marine Drive Churchgate is to the west of Fort, while just to the south is Marine Drive, which has the advantage of a seafront location.

Chateau Windsor Hotel *(☎ 204 3376, fax 202 6459, 5th floor, 86 Veer Nariman Rd, Churchgate)* is a friendly, spic and span establishment offering rooms with TV and common bath for Rs 750/970 and with bath for Rs 970/1190.

Sea Green Hotel *(☎ 282 2294, 45 Marine Drive)*, and its adjacent twin ***Sea Green South Hotel*** *(☎ 282 1613)* are good-value hotels charging Rs 1100/1500 for decent-sized air-con singles/doubles with TV, fridge and bath.

The Oberoi *(☎ 202 5757, fax 204 1505, Nariman Point)* overlooks Marine Drive and the Arabian Sea. It competes with the Taj Mahal Hotel in a bid to be Mumbai's most opulent hostelry. Singles/doubles cost from US$325/355.

Getting There & Away

For information on getting to Kerala from Mumbai, see the Kerala section later in this chapter.

Getting Around

To/From the Airports An airport bus service operates between Sahar (international) and Santa Cruz (domestic) terminals and the Air India Building at Nariman Point in central Mumbai. The journey from Sahar takes about 1¼ hours and costs Rs 60; from Santa Cruz it takes about an hour and costs Rs 50. During peak hours the trip can take well over two hours, so don't cut things too fine if you're catching a flight. Baggage costs Rs 5 per piece.

From Sahar, departures are at 2.30, 6.30, 8.30, 9.30 and 11.30 am, and at 2, 3.30, 5,

7.30, 9.30 and 10.30 pm; the buses leave from Santa Cruz half an hour later. From Nariman Point, departures are at 12.30, 4.15, 8.15, 10.15 and 11.30 am, and 1.15, 2.15, 3.45, 5.30, 7.15, 9.15 and 11.15 pm. Tickets can be bought on the bus or at the booth outside the Air India Building in Nariman Point.

There's a prepaid taxi booth at the international airport, with set fares to various city destinations. It costs Rs 275 to Colaba during the day and Rs 350 at night; you pay Rs 5 per item of luggage. A prepaid fare is higher than the meter rate but it saves haggling. Don't try to catch an auto-rickshaw from the airport to the city as they're prohibited from entering central Mumbai.

CHENNAI (Madras)

☎ 044 • pop 5.9 million

The Anna international airport is 16km from the city. It's efficient and not too busy, making Chennai a good entry or exit point.

International Airlines

Contact details of international airlines with offices in Chennai include:

Air Canada
(☎ 826 2409/825 0882)
GSA: Jetair, G 1/A Apex Plaza, 3 Nungambakkam High Rd
Air France
(☎ 855 4899)
Thapa House, 43/44 Montieth Rd, Egmore
Air India
(☎ 855 4477) 19 Marshalls Rd, Egmore
Alitalia
(☎ 434 9822)
GSA: Ajanta Travel, 548 Anna Salai
American Airlines
(☎ 826 2409)
GSA: Jetair, G 1/A Apex Plaza, 3 Nungambakkam High Rd
British Airways
(☎ 855 4680)
Alsamall, Khaleeli Centre, Montieth Rd, Egmore
Japan Airlines
(☎ 852 4832)
GSA: Global Travels, 733 Anna Salai
KLM-Royal Dutch Airlines
(☎ 852 0123) Hotel Connemara, Binney Rd
Lufthansa Airlines
(☎ 852 5095) 167 Anna Salai
Malaysia Airlines
(☎ 434 9291) Karumuthu Centre, 498 Anna Salai
Qantas Airways
(☎ 827 8680)
G3, Eldorado Bldg, 112 Nungambakkam High Rd
Singapore Airlines (SIA)
(☎ 852 1871)
West Minster, 108 Dr Radhakrishnan Salai
SriLankan (formerly Air Lanka)
(☎ 852 4232)
Mount Chambers, 758 Anna Salai
Swissair
(☎ 852 2541) 191 Anna Salai
Thai Airways International (THAI)
(☎ 822 6149)
GSA: Inter Globe Air Transports, Malavikas Centre, 144 Kodambakkam High Rd, Nungambakkam
United Airlines
(☎ 822 6149)
GSA: Inter Globe Air Transports, Malavikas Centre, 144 Kodambakkam High Rd, Nungambakkam

Places to Stay

Many budget travellers gravitate towards Egmore, in the heart of the city. Taxes range from 20% to 30% and are not included in prices listed. Chennai has no shortage of top-end hotels. A room in the five star hotels listed here will cost from US$130 to US$150.

Around the Airport The ***Hotel Mars*** *(☎ 840 2586, Pallavaram)* is well priced. Singles start at Rs 300 and doubles are Rs 395. It's clean and tidy, and has hot water. Lone women travellers find the prevalence of female staff here reassuring.

Hotel Mount Heera *(☎ 234 9563, fax 233 1236, 287 MKN Rd, Alandur)* has very pleasant staff, and similar services to Hotel Mars. Both hotels are about 20 minutes by taxi from the airport.

The Trident *(☎ 234 4747, fax 234 6699, 1/24 GS T Rd),* is a five star place, 5km from the airport.

Egmore In the city, Egmore, on and around Kennet Lane, is the main budget and mid-range accommodation hub, but competition for rooms can be fierce.

Salvation Army Red Shield Guest House *(☎ 532 1821, 15 Ritherdon Rd)* is about a 20 minute walk from Egmore station and welcomes both men and women. It's a clean, quiet place in leafy surroundings. A dorm bed costs Rs 40 and doubles/triples are Rs 175/200. Bathroom facilities are communal. Checkout is 9 am.

Retiring rooms at Central and Egmore train stations have doubles from Rs 145, or Rs 260 with air-con. At Rs 80 for 12 hours, air-con dorm beds (men only) are quiet, and clean. There's a small sitting area. Washing and toilet facilities are next door. Smoking, eating and alcohol are not permitted.

The YWCA International Guest House *(☎ 532 4234, fax 532 4263, 1086 Periyar EVR High Rd – formerly Poonamallee High Rd)* accepts both men and women and is so popular you'll need to book well in advance. The rooms are bright and spacious. In the low season (April to July; September to October) singles/doubles/triples with clean bathrooms cost Rs 360/430/580, or Rs 520/580 for single/double with air-con. Add around Rs 50 per room for the high season. There's a transient membership fee of Rs 20 – valid for one month. Checkout is usually by noon, visitors are forbidden in the rooms, lunch and dinner in the restaurant must be ordered in advance, alcohol is not served and meals finish by 9 pm.

Hotel Pandian *(☎ 825 2901, fax 825 8459, 9 Kennet Lane)* is a popular place. It's clean and comfortable but the cheaper rooms aren't great value as the plumbing is temperamental. Ordinary singles/doubles are Rs 450/550, air-con rooms start at Rs 700/800.

Hotel Connemara *(☎ 852 0123, fax 852 3361, Binny Rd)*, just off Anna Salai, is an institution. Renovated recently, rooms cost from Rs 3850/4330 for standard singles/doubles, Rs 5000/5500 for 'superior' and Rs 6500/7000 for 'old world'.

Grand Orient *(☎ 852 4111, fax 852 3412, 693 Anna Salai)* has rooms starting from Rs 1195/1800.

The ***Hotel Taj Coromandel*** *(☎ 827 2827, fax 825 7104, 17 Nungambakkam High Rd)* is a five star hotel as luxurious as all the Taj Group hotels.

Also in the five star range, the ***Welcomgroup Chola Sheraton*** *(☎ 828 0101, fax 827 8779, 10 Cathedral Rd)*, is closer to the centre than the Park Sheraton.

Getting There & Away

For information on getting to Kerala from Chennai, see the Kerala section following.

Getting Around

To/From the Airport The cheapest way to the city is by suburban train from Tirusulam to Egmore. The trains run from 4.30 am until 11 pm, the journey takes about 40 minutes, and the fare is Rs 6/80 in 2nd/1st class. These trains are not overly crowded, except during peak hours.

Public buses are not such a good bet, particularly if you've got a lot of luggage. Nos 18J, 52, 52A/B/C/D and 55A will take you along Anna Salai (the main street) to the central Parry's Corner. There's an airport bus that runs every 30 to 45 minutes to the Egmore station area. It's purple and easy to spot. And there's a minibus for Rs 80 (Rs 50 during the day) but it's a slow way to get into town because of the number of stops.

An auto-rickshaw to the city should cost Rs 70, but you'll need to haggle hard to pay anywhere near this. About Rs 100/150 for a day/night trip is what they'll normally charge.

A yellow-and-black taxi costs Rs 200. You can buy a ticket for a taxi into the city for Rs 200 to Rs 250 (depending on the distance) at the prepaid taxi kiosk inside the international terminal. There's also a prepaid kiosk in the baggage collection area inside the domestic terminal – it's about 10% cheaper.

Kerala

This section gives details on how to get to Kerala from other parts of India.

AIR

Air India, Indian Airlines and other domestic airlines operate many flights to each of

Kerala's airports at Thiruvananthapuram, Kochi and Kozhikode from major Indian cities. For details see the tables in the regional chapters.

Special Fares

Indian Airlines has 14/21 day 'Discover India' passes that cost US$550/800. These allow unlimited travel on its domestic routes, but you aren't allowed to backtrack. There's also a 25% youth discount if you're under 30 on both Indian Airlines and Jet Airways.

Buying Tickets

Computerised booking is the norm when buying air tickets, so getting flight information and reservations is relatively simple – it's just getting to the head of the queue that takes all the time. In some Indian Airlines offices you are required to enter your name in a book at the counter and then wait your turn. All flights are heavily booked and you need to plan as far in advance as possible.

Air tickets must be paid for with foreign currency or by credit card, or rupees backed by encashment certificates. Change, where appropriate, is given in rupees. Infants up to two years old travel at 10% of the adult fare, for children aged from two to 12 the reduction is 50%. There is no student reduction for overseas visitors but there is a youth fare (25% discount) for people 12 to 29 years old.

Refunds on adult tickets attract a charge (usually Rs 150) and can be obtained at any office. If a flight is delayed or cancelled, you cannot refund the ticket, although you can change it. Failing to show up 30 minutes before the flight is regarded as a 'no-show' and you forfeit the full value of the ticket.

Indian Airlines accepts no responsibility if you lose your ticket. They absolutely will not refund lost tickets, but at their discretion they may issue replacements.

Check-In

Check in at least one hour before departure. Sometimes earlier check-in is required, and as a security measure, you may be requested to identify your checked-in baggage on the tarmac immediately prior to boarding.

Domestic Airlines

Mumbai All carriers have ticketing counters at Santa Cruz domestic airport. The larger ones also have offices in the city centre.

Indian Airlines
(☎ 022-202 3031, fax 283 0832)
Air India Bldg, Nariman Point
Jet Airways
(☎ 022-838 6111, fax 837 0134)
Amarchand Mansion, Madame Cama Rd

Chennai Addresses of domestic carriers that fly into Chennai include:

Indian Airlines
(☎ 044-855 3039, fax 855 5208)
19 Marshalls Rd, Egmore
Jet Airways
(☎ 044-855 5353)
43 Montieth Rd, Egmore

BUS

Because of the long distances involved between major cities and Kerala, you may find the train preferable to the long, dusty and bumpy bus rides. If, however, you decide buses are your thing, here's the lowdown on getting from the major cities.

Mumbai

Private operators and state governments run long-distance buses to and from Mumbai. Private operators provide faster service, more comfort and simpler booking procedures. It's usually possible to secure a seat on a privately run bus departing the same day that you purchase a ticket. Private long-distance buses depart from Dr Anadrao Nair Rd, near Mumbai Central train station. If you want to call a booth before you journey out here, try NTC (☎ 022-307 0780).

Long-distance state-run buses depart from the State Road Transport terminal close to Mumbai Central train station. The booking office (☎ 022-307 4272, inquiries only) is on the 1st floor, and is open 8 am to 8 pm daily.

Chennai

The Tamil Nadu state bus company (SETC) terminal is on Esplanade Rd in George Town, behind the High Court building. Both intrastate and interstate buses leave from here.

The bus reservation offices there are computerised and open 4 am to 11 pm daily. There's a Rs 2 reservation fee, and you have to pay Rs 0.25 for the form! Six buses daily leave for Thiruvananthapuram (Bus No 794 takes 17 hours and costs Rs 165).

There are also private bus companies with offices opposite Egmore station that run superdeluxe video buses daily to cities such as Thiruvananthapuram. Prices are similar to the state buses, although the private buses tend to be more comfortable.

TRAIN

Buses are generally faster than trains, but Indian buses make no concessions to comfort and drivers can be reckless. If you prefer to keep your adrenaline levels down, the train is a relaxing alternative. See also the Train section in the Getting Around chapter.

Mumbai

Two systems operate out of Mumbai. The one you need for Kerala is Central Railways, which operates from Victoria Terminus (VT), also known as Chhatrapati Shivaji Terminus (CST). The reservation centre behind VT is open Monday to Saturday, 9 am to 1 pm, and 1.30 to 4 pm. Tourist-quota tickets and Indrail passes can be bought at counter No 8.

Note that a few useful expresses heading southwards depart from Kurla, which is inconveniently located 16km to the north of VT. Some Central Railways trains also depart from Dadar, several stops north of VT on the suburban line.

Trains operating on the new Konkan Railway also leave from VT. The 1081 *Mumbai-Kanyakumari Express* leaves every day for Thiruvananthapuram at 3.35 pm from VT and takes almost 42 hours to travel the 1540km for Rs 311/1156 in 2nd/1st class. Along the way it stops at Thrissur (Trichur), Ernakulam Junction, Kottayam and Kollam (Quilon). The *Kurla-Trivandrum* is a similar service leaving at 12.15 pm (also from VT, in spite of its name). The daily 6635 *Netravati Express* leaves for Ernakulam Junction at 4.40 pm from Kurla and takes 28 hours to travel the 1300km and costs Rs 289/1049.

Chennai

The 6041 *Alleppey Express* to Ernakulam in Kochi and Alappuzha (Alleppey) leaves Madras Central at 7.35 pm and takes 14½ hours for Rs 211/737 in 2nd/1st class. For Thiruvananthapuram, catch the 6319 *Trivandrum Mail*, which also departs from Madras Central at 6.55 pm and takes almost 17 hours. It costs Rs 235/805 (2nd/1st).

CAR & MOTORCYCLE

Few people bring their own vehicles to India. If you decide to bring a car or motorcycle to India it must be brought in under a carnet (a customs document guaranteeing its removal at the end of your stay). Failing to do so will be very expensive. For more information on driving in India, see the Car section of the Getting Around chapter.

Rental

Renting a self-drive car in any of the main cities in India and driving to Kerala is possible but not recommended. India holds the unenviable record of having the most dangerous roads in the world. Hertz has offices in Mumbai (☎ 022-492 1429) and Chennai (☎ 044-433 0684). Costs are about Rs 1000 a day, for up to 250km. Drivers must be 25 years old or over and a deposit of Rs 5000 is required.

If you want to travel by car to Kerala, it's best to hire a car and driver. Check prices with various car-hire companies and the tourist office, then negotiate a rate with the company of your choice – your driver may have been recommended by word of mouth (other travellers) or by your hotel. In Chennai (☎ 044-852 0908, fax 858 6655) you could try Welcome Tourrs (sic) and Travels, 150 Mount Rd.

Getting Around

AIR

Although there are three airports in Kerala, there are no intrastate flights. However, given the beauty and small size of Kerala, you'll no doubt be happy to travel by land and inland waterways.

At the time of writing the only air services within the region are the daily Indian Airlines services from Kochi (Cochin) to Agatti in Lakshadweep. See the Lakshadweep chapter for more information.

BUS

Generally you will find there are two main types of bus: private and state. The state buses are operated by the Kerala State Road Transport Corporation (KSRTC). Both private and state services ply the same routes, although private buses offer more comfort and tend to be a bit more expensive.

In Kerala, bus signs are usually in the local script, but if you don't understand Malayalam, someone will invariably set you on to the right bus.

One of the hair-raising aspects of bus travel in Kerala (which applies throughout India) is the speed at which the buses travel.

Beware of touts. At many bus stands they will sell tickets to any destination of your choice. While some tickets may be valid, many travellers have been caught forking out rupees for services that simply did not exist. Every bus stand has an office where staff are generally quite helpful – better to locate it than to trust the touts.

Classes

Generally bus travel is crowded, cramped, slow and uncomfortable. Sometimes there is a choice of buses on the main (or long-haul) routes: ordinary, superfast (this category simply means the bus stops more often than does the express or superexpress), express, superexpress, semi-luxe, deluxe and deluxe air-con. Ordinary buses generally have five seats across (two seats by three seats) they tend to be frustratingly slow and are usually in an advanced state of dilapidation. They're certainly colourful – for short journeys; on longer trips you'll probably wish you hadn't come. Express buses are also overcrowded but they stop less often.

Semi-luxe and deluxe have luxuries such as slightly padded seats and tinted windows. The big difference between deluxe and semi-luxe is that deluxe buses have only four seats across (instead of five) and these might even recline.

Reservations

State buses and some private operators have computer booking. This means you can book ahead, you'll be allocated a seat, and you won't have to join a scrum to get a seat.

Baggage

Baggage is generally carried free on the roof. Make sure it's secure. You won't be able to avoid having things dumped on it – like cases of smelly fish. Having your gear in a strong plastic bag inside your bag or pack might prevent it from being impregnated with unwanted smells.

Theft is unlikely but keep an eye on your bags if you stop for any length of time. If someone carries your bag onto the roof, expect to pay a few rupees for the service.

Toilet Stops

On long-distance bus trips, tea stops can be far too frequent or, conversely, agonisingly infrequent. Long-distance trips can be a real hassle for women travellers – toilet facilities are often hopelessly inadequate.

TRAIN

The first step in coming to grips with India's rail network is to get a timetable. *Trains at a Glance* or *Southern Central Railway* (Rs 15, from major stations) are handy guides covering the main routes, services and prices.

Train travel is popular, so bookings are usually required. Life on board is a communal experience. You not only share a compartment, but *chapatis* (bread), water, newspapers and conversation (even if you don't have a language in common). Meals on board are generally pretty good.

Trains are reliable and punctual but during monsoons services may be reduced or delayed.

Classes

There are generally two classes – 1st and 2nd – but there are a number of subtle variations on this basic distinction. For a start there is air-con, in both classes. The fare for air-con is more expensive whether it's 1st or 2nd class. Then there's air-con two-tier and three-tier sleeper and air-con chair. Air-con carriages are only found on the major routes.

Sleepers There are 2nd class and 1st class sleepers, although by western standards even 1st class is not very luxurious. Bedding is available but only on certain 1st class, air-con services. First class sleepers are generally private compartments with two or four berths and sometimes a toilet. It's generally a good idea to get as far as possible away from the toilet. Sleeping berths fold up to make a sitting compartment during the day.

Second class sleepers are arranged in doorless sections of six berths each. During the day, the middle berth is lowered to make seats for six or eight. At night they are folded into position, everybody has to bed down at the same time and a Travelling Ticket Examiner (TTE) ensures that nobody without a reservation gets into the carriage – most of the time. If someone has taken your spot, you may need to assert your rights. Time, patience and persistence usually resolves the situation.

Train Types

What you want is a mail or express train – not a passenger train. No Indian train travels very fast, but at least the mail and express trains keep moving more of the time. Air-con 'superfast' express services operate on certain main routes, and are usually faster.

Reservations

The cost of reservations is nominal and computerisation quickens the process.

class	reservation (Rs)
2nd class sitting	10
2nd class three-tier sleeper	15
1st class & air-con chair class	20
air-con 1st class	30

There are rarely any 2nd class sitting compartments with reservations. There are also some superfast express trains that require a supplementary charge (from Rs 5 to Rs 25 depending on the class).

For any sleeper reservation you should try to book at least several days ahead. If the train is fully booked, it's often possible to get a Reservation Against Cancellation (RAC) ticket. This entitles you to board the train and get a seat. Once the trip is under way, the TTE will find a berth for you, but it may take an hour or more. This is different from a wait-listed ticket, as the latter does not give you the right to actually board the train.

For women there are often separate 'Ladies Queues' for purchasing a ticket, 'Ladies Lounges' at train stations and also a 'Ladies Compartment' for travel. This can sometimes provide easier and more pleasant train travel.

Costs

Fares operate on a distance (and time) basis. Timetables indicate distance and cost between any two stations.

Refunds

Booked tickets are refundable, but cancellation fees apply – from Rs 10 to Rs 50 depending on the class, and up to 25% to 50% of the ticket value depending on the distance and time of cancellation. Tickets for unreserved travel can be refunded up to three hours after the departure of the train, and the only penalty is Rs 10 per passenger.

Indrail Passes
Indrail passes permit unlimited travel on Indian trains for the period of their validity, but they are generally not worth the expense, especially in a small state like Kerala. Costs range from US$80/150 (2nd/1st class) for a seven day pass to US$235/530 for a 90 day pass. In purely dollar terms, to get the full value out of any of the passes you need to travel around 300km per day; with the speed of Indian trains that's at least six hours travel, day in and day out.

Getting a Space Despite Everything
If you want a sleeper and there are none left then it's time to try to break into the quotas. Ask the stationmaster if there's a tourist quota, station quota or a VIP quota. The last of these is often a good bet because VIPs rarely turn up to use their quotas. These options rarely fail; every stationmaster has quotas and if this one can't help he can usually contact someone who can.

But if all fails then you're going to be travelling unreserved and that can be no fun at all. To ease the pain get yourself some expert help. For, say, Rs 10 (a small consideration) you can get a porter who will absolutely ensure you get a seat if it's humanly possible. If it's a train starting from your station, the key to success is to be on the train before it arrives at the departure platform. Your porter will do just that, so when it rolls up you simply stroll on board and take the seat he has warmed for you. If it's a through train then it can be a real free-for-all, and you can be certain he'll be better at it than you are – he'll also not be encumbered with baggage.

Women can ask about the Ladies Compartments, which are often a refuge from the crowd in other compartments.

Left Luggage
Most stations have a luggage facility (cloak room) where baggage can be left for Rs 2 per day. This is very useful if you're visiting (but not staying in) a town, or if you want to find a place to stay, unencumbered by gear. The regulations state that any luggage left in a cloak room must be locked, although this is not strictly enforced.

Don't Get Lost, Get Help!

If you're a foreigner you may be unfamiliar with, or reluctant to, avail yourself of the most helpful assistance in getting around. Indians are often most bemused at how far foreigners will travel (in all the wrong directions) before they ask for help. Foreigners, reluctant to be intrusive or to create inconvenience, often seek out official information. But people on the street are often the best source of information and are usually more than happy to assist. Save time and the hassles of long-winded dealings with bureaucracies – simply ask.

CAR
Few people bring their own vehicle to India. If you do decide to bring a car or motorcycle to India, it must be brought in under a carnet, a customs document guaranteeing the vehicle's removal at the end of your stay. Failure to do so will be very expensive.

Road Rules & Conditions
Driving in India is legally (but often only theoretically) on the left side of the road, in right-hand drive vehicles, as in Britain and Australia.

Roads are not highways for transport but rather pathways for life. Narrow and bumpy, they provide the place for all manner of activities: children play, people cycle, grains are spread to dry, carts deliver produce to market, and chickens, ducks, goats and geese amble along while aristocratic cows parade with impunity as their birthright. This means that car transport is a stop-start process – hard on you, the car and fuel economy – but it's interesting. Parts and tyres are not always easy to obtain, but this is easily compensated for by skilful mechanics who can create brilliant improvisations and there are always plenty of puncture-repair places.

Rental

Due to regulations that place the responsibility for vehicle operation on the owner, rather than the driver, car rental in Kerala is unusual, although it does occur in the major tourist areas such as Kovalam and Varkala. If you want to travel by car, it's much safer to hire a car with driver. (For more information, see the Taxi section later in this chapter.)

Purchase

Buying a car is expensive and not worth the effort unless you intend to stay long-term. If you do, try the showroom (☎ 0471-333666, fax 332251) at Kulathunkal Building, MG Rd, Thiruvananthapuram (Trivandrum).

Fuel

Petrol is around Rs 27 per litre (Rs 29 with oil). Diesel is much cheaper at Rs 9 per litre. Petrol is readily available in all larger towns and along main roads.

MOTORCYCLE

Biking gives you the freedom to go where you like when you like, and it is becoming increasingly popular. To get a taste of what long-distance motorcycling is like in India on an Enfield get hold of a copy of *Bullet up the Grand Trunk Road* by Jonathan Gregson.

This section is based largely on information originally contributed by intrepid Britons, Ken Twyford and Gerald Smewing, with updates from Mike Ferris, Jim and Lucy Amos and Bill Keightley.

What to Bring

An International Driving Permit is technically not mandatory, but you'd be foolish not to bring one. The first thing a policeman will want to see if he stops you is your licence, and an international permit is incontrovertible.

If you know you will be biking, bring quality riding gear with you. Helmets, boots, gloves and jackets are available in India but the quality can be suspect. If you are planning to be in Kerala during the monsoon, bring a good set of wet-weather gear. A few small bags will be a lot easier to carry than one large rucksack.

Rental

Local regulations mean that renting is not really an option in Kerala, except in the tourist areas of Kovalam and Varkala.

Purchase

Second-Hand India has few used-vehicle dealers, motorcycle magazines or weekend newspapers with pages of motorcycle classified advertisements. To purchase a second-hand machine you simply need to inquire. Whether buying or selling, it's best to go to a reputable dealer who has a good track record. In Thiruvananthapuram try the showroom (☎ 0471-333666, fax 332251) at Kulathunkal Building, MG Rd, next door to Higginbothams bookshop.

New When buying second-hand, all you need to give is an address, but if you're buying a new bike, you'll need to have a local address and be a resident foreign national. However, unless the dealer you are buying from is totally devoid of imagination and contacts, this presents few problems. New bikes are generally purchased through a showroom. There is an Enfield showroom at Marikar Motors (☎ 0484-341083), Lissie Junction, Ernakulam, Kerala (Marikar Motors also sells second-hand Enfields). Enfield motorcycles are manufactured at Eicher Motors (☎ 044-543066, fax 544249), Tiruvottiyur, 17km north of Chennai (Madras). Their Web site is www.royalenfield.com.

Documents A needless hint perhaps, but do not part with your money until you have the ownership papers, receipt and affidavit signed by a magistrate authorising the owner (as recorded in the ownership papers) to sell the machine. Not to mention the keys to the bike and the bike itself!

Get assistance from the agent from whom you're buying the machine, or from one of the many 'attorneys' hanging around under tin roofs near Motor Vehicles Department offices. They will charge you a fee of up to Rs 300, which will consist largely of a bribe to expedite matters.

Alternatively, you could go to one of the many typing clerk services and request them to type out the necessary forms, handling the matter cheaply yourself – but with no guarantee of a quick result.

Check that your name has been recorded in the ownership book and stamped and signed by the department head. If you intend to sell your motorcycle in another state then you will need a 'No Objections Certificate'. This confirms your ownership and is issued by the Motor Vehicles Department in the state of purchase, so get it immediately when transferring ownership papers to your name. The standard form can be typed up for a few rupees, or more speedily and expensively through one of the many attorneys.

Insurance & Tax As in most countries, it is compulsory to have third party insurance. The New India Assurance Company or the National Insurance Company are just two of a number of companies who can provide it. The cost for fully comprehensive insurance is around Rs 1000 for 12 months, and this also covers you in Nepal.

Road tax is paid when the bike is bought new. This is valid for the life of the machine and is transferred to the new owner when the bike changes hands.

Which Bike?

The big decision to make is whether to buy new or second-hand. Obviously cost is the main factor, but remember that with a new bike you are less likely to get ripped off as the price is fixed, the cost will include free servicing and you know it will be reliable. Old bikes are obviously cheaper, and you don't have to be a registered resident foreign national, but you are far more open to getting ripped off, either by paying too much or by getting a dud bike.

Everyone is likely to have their own preferences and there is no one bike that suits everybody. The following is a rundown of what's readily available.

Mopeds These come with or without gears. As they are only 50cc capacity, they are really only useful around towns or for short distances.

Scooters There are the older design Bajaj and Vespa scooters, or the more modern Japanese designs by Honda-Kinetic and others. The older ones are 150cc while the Honda is 100cc and has no gears.

Scooters are economical to buy and run, are easy to ride, have a good resale value, and most have built-in lockable storage. The 150cc Bajaj Cheetak costs around Rs 30,000 and has plenty of power and acceleration for Indian road conditions. It's reliable as long as the plug is kept clean, newer models have electronic ignition so there's no need to adjust the points. Many riders rate these bikes well.

100cc Motorcycles The four main Japanese companies – Honda, Suzuki, Kawasaki and Yamaha – all have 100cc, two-stroke machines, while Honda and Kawasaki also have four-stroke models. There's little to differentiate these bikes; all are lightweight, easy to ride, economical and reliable, with good resale value. They are suitable for intercity travel on reasonable roads, but they should not be laden down with too much gear. Spares and servicing are readily available. The cost of a new bike of this type is about Rs 38,000 to Rs 45,000.

If you're buying second-hand avoid the Rajdoot 175 XLT, based on a very old Polish model, and the Enfield Fury, which has a poor gearbox, spares that are hard to come by and low resale value.

Bigger Bikes The Enfield Bullet is the classic machine and is the one most favoured by foreigners. Attractions are the traditional design, thumping engine sound, and the price, which is not much more than the new 100cc Japanese bikes. It's a wonderfully durable bike, easy to maintain and economical to run, but mechanically they're a bit hit and miss, largely because of poorly engineered parts and inferior materials – valves and tappets are the main problem areas. Another drawback is the lack of an effective front brake – the small drum brake is a joke, totally inadequate for a heavy machine.

In addition to the 350cc, the Bullet is available in a 500cc single cylinder version. It has a functional front brake and 12V electrics that are superior to the 350's 6V. If you opt for a 350cc, consider paying the Rs 5000 extra to have the 500cc front wheel fitted.

If you are buying a new Enfield with the intention of shipping it back home, it's definitely worth opting for the 500cc as it has features – such as folding rear footrest and longer exhaust pipe – which most other countries require. The emission control regulations in some places, such as California and Australia, are so strict that there is no way these bikes would be legal. You may be able to get around this by buying an older bike, as the regulations often apply to new machines only. Make sure you check all this out before you go lashing out on a new Enfield, only to find you can't register it at home. The price is around Rs 60,000, or Rs 65,000 for the 500cc model. There's a hopelessly underpowered diesel version for Rs 68,000.

The Yezdi 250 Classic (or Monarch, or Deluxe) is a cheap, basic, rugged machine, and one that you often see in rural areas.

The Rajdoot 350 is an imported Yamaha 350cc. It's well engineered, fast and has good brakes. Disadvantages are that it's relatively uneconomical to run, and spares are hard to come by. These bikes are also showing their age badly as they haven't been made for some years now. They cost around Rs 12,000.

If you have Rs 530,000 to spare, the BMW F650 is now available in India.

On the Road

It must be said that, given the general road conditions, motorcycling is a reasonably hazardous endeavour, and one best undertaken by experienced riders only.

In the event of an accident, call the police straight away (if you're able), and don't move anything until the police have seen exactly where and how everything ended up. One foreigner reported spending three days in jail on suspicion of being involved in an accident, when all he'd done was take a child to hospital from the scene of an accident.

Don't try to cover too much territory in one day. A high level of concentration is needed to survive and long days are tiring and dangerous. On the busy national highways expect to average 50km/h without stops; on smaller roads, where driving conditions are worse, 10km/h is not an unrealistic average. On the whole you can expect to cover around 100km a day on good roads. Night driving should be avoided at all costs.

Putting the bike on a train for really long hauls can be a convenient option. You'll pay about as much as a 2nd class passenger fare for the bike. It can be wrapped in straw for protection if you like, and this is done at the parcels office at the station, which is also where you pay for the bike. The petrol tank must be empty, and there should be a tag in an obvious place detailing name, destination, passport number and train details.

Repairs & Maintenance

In India anyone who can handle a screwdriver and spanner can be called a mechanic, so be careful. If you have any mechanical knowledge, it may be better to buy your own tools and learn how to do your own repairs. This will save a lot of arguments over prices. If you are getting repairs done by someone, don't leave the premises while the work is being done or you may find that good parts have been ripped off your bike and replaced with old ones.

Original spare parts bought from an 'authorised dealer' can be rather expensive compared to the copies available from your spare-parts dealer.

If you buy an older machine you would do well to check and tighten all nuts and bolts every few days. Indian roads and engine vibration tend to work things loose, and constant checking could save you rupees and trouble. Check the engine and gearbox oil level regularly. As the quality of oil available is poor, it is advisable to change it and clean the oil filter every 2000km.

Punctures Chances are you'll get punctures fairly often but places to change tyres are everywhere, often in the most surprising places. However, it's advisable to at least have tools sufficient to remove your own wheel and take it for changing. Given the annoyance of frequent punctures, it's worth lashing out on new tyres if you buy a second-hand bike with worn tyres. A new rear tyre for an Enfield costs around Rs 650.

Fuel Should you run out, try flagging down a passing car (not a truck or bus since they use diesel) and beg for some. Most Indians are willing to let you have fuel if you have a hose or siphon and a container.

Organised Motorcycle Tours

Classic Bike Adventure (☎ 0832-273351, fax 277624, 277343), Casa Tres Amigo, Socol Vado No 425, Assagao, Bardez, Goa, is a German-based company that organises tours on well-maintained Enfields, with full insurance. Costs are from DM2450 to DM 3680. Ferris Wheels (☎/fax 02-9904 7419), 61 Elizabeth St, Artarmon, 2064, Australia, also organises tours in South India on Enfields.

BICYCLE

Kerala offers plenty of variety for the cyclist. There are (relatively) smooth-surfaced highways, rocky dirt tracks, coastal routes through coconut palms, winding country roads through spice plantations and more demanding routes in the Western Ghats. The following information comes from Ann Sorrel, with updates from various travellers.

Information

Before you set out, read some books on bicycle touring such as the Sierra Club's *The Bike Touring Manual* by Rob van de Plas (Bicycle Books, 1993). Cycling magazines provide useful information, including listings for bicycle tour operators and the addresses of spare-parts suppliers. They're also good places to look for a riding companion.

For a real feel of the adventure of bike touring in strange places, read Dervla Murphy's classic *Full Tilt*, Lloyd Sumner's *The Long Ride* or Bettina Selby's *Riding the Mountains Down* (subtitled 'A Journey by Bicycle to Kathmandu').

Your local cycling club may be able to help with information and advice. In the UK, the Cyclists Touring Club (☎ 01483-417217), 69 Meadrow, Godalming, Surrey GU7 3HS, has country touring sheets that are free to members. The International Bicycle Fund (IBF, ☎ 206-628 9314), 4887 Columbia Drive South, Seattle, Washington 98108-1919, USA, publishes two handy guides: *Selecting and Preparing a Bike for Travel in Remote Areas* and *Flying with Your Bike.*

If you're a serious cyclist or amateur racer and want to contact counterparts while in India, there's the Cycle Federation of India; contact the Secretary, Yamun Velodrome, New Delhi.

Using Your Own Bike

If you are going to keep to sealed roads and already have a touring bike, by all means consider bringing it. Mountain bikes, however, are especially suited to countries such as India. Their smaller, sturdier construction makes them more manoeuvrable and less prone to damage, and allows you to tackle rocky, muddy roads unsuitable for lighter machines. An imported multi-geared machine is generally considered essential for the serious cyclist in Kerala.

Your machine is likely to be a real curiosity and subject to much pushing, pulling and probing. If you can't tolerate people touching your bicycle, don't bring it to Kerala.

Spare Parts If you bring a bicycle to India, prepare for the contingencies of part replacement or repair. Bring spare tyres, tubes, patch kits, chassis, cables, freewheels and spokes. Ensure you have a working knowledge of your machine. Bring all necessary tools with you as well as a compact bike manual with diagrams in case the worst happens and you need to fix a rear derailleur or some other strategic part. Indian mechanics can work wonders and illustrations help overcome the language barrier. Roads don't have paved shoulders and are very dusty, so keep your chain lubricated. Most of all, be ready to make do and improvise.

Although India is officially metricated, tools and bike parts follow 'standard' or 'imperial' measurements. Don't expect to find tyres for 700cm rims, although 27 x 1¼ tyres are produced in India by Dunlop and Sawney. Some mountain-bike tyres are available but the quality is dubious. Indian bicycle pumps cater to a tube valve different from the Presta and Schraeder valves commonly used in the west. If you're travelling with Presta valves (most high-pressure 27 x 1¼ tubes), bring a Schraeder (car-type) adaptor. In India you can buy a local pump adaptor for the Schraeder, which means you'll have an adaptor on your adaptor. Bring your own pump as well, most Indian pumps require two or three people to get air down the leaky cable.

In major cities Japanese tyres and parts are available but pricey – although so is postage, and transit time can be considerable. If you receive bike parts from abroad, beware of exorbitant customs charges. Say you want the goods as 'in transit' to avoid these charges. They may list the parts in your passport!

For foreign parts try Metre Cycle, in Thiruvananthapuram, or Popular Cycle Importing Company on Popham's Broadway, Chennai. Alternatively, take your bicycle to a cycle market and ask around – someone will know which shop is likely to have things for your 'special' cycle. Beware of Taiwanese imitations and watch out for tyres that may have been sitting collecting dust for years.

Luggage Your cycle luggage should be as strong, durable and waterproof as possible. Don't get a set with lots of zippers, as this makes pilfering easier. As you'll be frequently detaching luggage when taking your bike to your room, a set designed for easy removal from the racks is a must; the fewer items, the better. *Never* leave your bike in the lobby or outside your hotel – take it to bed with you!

Bike luggage that can easily be reassembled into a backpack is also available and is just the thing when you want to park your bike and go by train or foot.

Theft If you're using an imported bike, try to avoid losing your pump (and the water bottle from your frame), their novelty makes them particularly attractive to thieves. Don't leave anything on your bike that can easily be removed when it's unattended.

Don't be paranoid about theft – outside the major cities it would be well-nigh impossible for a thief to resell your bike as it would stand out too much. Your bike is probably safer in Kerala than in western countries.

Rental

If you want to rent a bicycle, you'll find that prices vary markedly throughout the state. In touristy areas (such as Kovalam) expect to pay Rs 40 per day. In other areas prices start from Rs 1.50 per hour. About Rs 25 would be average.

Purchase

Finding an Indian bike is no problem: every town will have at least a couple of cycle shops. Shop around for prices and remember to bargain. Try to get a few extras – bell, stand, spare tube – thrown in. There are many brands of Indian clunkers – Hero, Atlas, BSA, Raleigh, Bajaj, Avon – but they all follow the same basic, sturdy design. A few mountain-bike lookalikes have recently come on the market, but most have no gears. Raleigh is considered to produce bikes of the finest quality, followed by BSA, which has a big line of models, including some sporty jobs. Hero and Atlas both claim to be the biggest seller. Look for the cheapest or the one with the snazziest plate label.

Once you've decided on a bike, you have a choice of luggage carriers – mostly the rat-trap type varying only in size, price and strength. There's a wide range of saddles available but all are equally bum-breaking. A stand is certainly a useful addition and a bell or air-horn is a necessity. An advantage of buying a new bike is that the brakes actually work. Centre-pull and side-pull brakes are also available but at extra cost and may actually make the bike more difficult to sell. The average Indian will prefer the standard model.

Sportier 'mountain bike' styles with straight handlebars are popular in urban areas. In big cities and touristy areas it's also possible to find used touring bikes left by travellers. Also check with diplomatic community members for bikes.

Reselling is no problem. Count on getting about 70% of what you originally paid if it was a new bike. A local cycle-hire shop will probably be interested or you could ask the proprietor of your hotel if they know any prospective purchasers.

Spare Parts As there are so many repair 'shops' (some consist of a pump, a box of tools, a tube of rubber solution and a water pan under a tree), there is no need to carry spare parts, especially as you'll only own the bike for a few weeks or months. Just take a roll of tube-patch rubber, a tube of Dunlop patch glue, two tyre irons and the wonderful 'universal' Indian bike spanner, which fits all the nuts. There are plenty of people in all towns and villages who will patch tubes for a couple of rupees, so chances are you won't have to fix a puncture yourself anyway. Besides, Indian tyres are pretty heavy duty, so with luck you won't get too many flats.

On the Road

The 'people factor' makes cycling in Kerala both rewarding and frustrating. Those with Indian bikes are less likely to be mobbed by curious onlookers.

At times the crowd may be unruly – schoolboys especially. If the mob is too big, call over a *lathi*-wielding policeman. The boys will scatter pronto! Sometimes the hostile boys throw rocks. The best advice is to keep pedalling; don't turn around or stop, and don't leave your bike and chase them as this will only incite them further. Appeal to adults to discipline them.

Routes

You can go anywhere on a bike that you would on trains and buses, with the added pleasure of seeing all the places in between. If mountain biking is your goal, consider the hill stations of the Western Ghats.

The downside of leaving the congested highways is the deterioration in the quality of the road surfaces. Some stretches, especially away from the coast, have become so potholed that village tracks become a much more attractive option. The Western Ghats provide excellent opportunities for cycling as far as the scenery goes, but the roads, with their huge potholes and rough surfaces, make cycling somewhat challenging. Travelling on major highways for any length of time is frustrating. Highway 17 between Goa and Kochi is a case in point. The melee continues all the way down this highway and on through Highway 47 all the way to Kanyakumari. One solution is to plan your trip so that you get regular breaks at reserves, the verdant lushness of these areas is a welcome respite from the hot, dusty roads outside them.

Steven Ireland (Australia)

Distances

If you've never cycled long distances, start with 20km to 40km a day and increase this as you gain stamina. Cycling long distances is 80% determination and 20% perspiration. Don't be ashamed to get off and push your bike up hills. For an eight hour pedal, a serious cyclist and interested tourist will average 90km to 130km a day on undulating plains, or 70km to 100km in mountainous areas.

Accommodation

There's no need to bring a tent. Inexpensive places to stay are widely available, and a tent pitched by the road would merely draw crowds. Bring a sleeping bag, especially if you intend exploring the Ghats. Consider buying a mosquito net if you're heading off the beaten track; they are inexpensive in Kerala and widely available. There's no need to bring a stove and cooking kit, as there are plenty of tea stalls and restaurants (called hotels). When you want to eat, ask for a hotel. On major highways you can stop at *dhabas*, the Indian version of a truck stop.

Transporting Your Bike

Sometimes you may want to quit pedalling. For sports bikes, air travel is easy. With luck, airline staff may not be familiar with procedures, so use this to your advantage. Tell them the bike doesn't need to be dismantled and that you've never had to pay for it. Remove all luggage and accessories and let the tyres down a bit.

Bus travel with a bike varies. Generally it goes for free, or for a minimal charge, on the roof. If it's a sports bike stress that it's lightweight. Secure it well to the roof rack, check it's in a place where it won't get damaged and take all your luggage inside.

Train travel is more complex – pedal up to the train station, buy a ticket and explain you want to book a cycle in for the journey. You'll be directed to the luggage offices (or officer) where a triplicate form is prepared. Note down your bike's serial number and provide a good description of it. Again leave only the bike, not luggage or accessories. Your bike gets decorated with one copy of the form, usually pasted on the seat, you get another, and God only knows what happens to the third. Produce your copy of the form to claim the bicycle from the luggage van at your destination. If you change trains en route, *personally* ensure the cycle changes too!

As part of a small group chartering a boat to ply the backwaters from Alappuzha (Alleppey) to Kollam (Quilon) my bike proved little problem lashed to the stern of the cabin. This was the case on other river crossings where in some situations the only means of crossing was a simple outboard-motor canoe. Aboard buses the bike is loaded on the roof and luggage is stowed inside the bus. Check for yourself that your bike is properly secured. Toe clip straps are an ideal method of restraint. A small charge will apply for the bike. If you are transporting your bike on a domestic flight, international rules apply (handlebars straightened, tyres deflated). There is no requirement that your bike be packed in a box.

Steven Ireland (Australia)

HITCHING

Hitching is never entirely safe in any country in the world, and it's therefore not recommended. Travellers who decide to hitch should understand that they are taking a small but potentially serious risk. If you do choose to hitch, travel in pairs and let someone know where you are planning to go.

That said, hitching is not a realistic option in Kerala anyway. There are few private cars so you are likely to be on board trucks.

It is a very bad idea for a woman on her own to hitch. India is a country far less sympathetic to rape victims than the west, and that's saying something. A woman in the cabin with a truck driver on a lonely road has, needless to say, only her own strengths and resources to call upon if things turn nasty.

For those few sites that are inaccessible by public transport, hitching or a taxi are the only options. Indian families are often very happy to give you a lift in these areas.

BOAT

There are several river and sea crossings as well as the trips through the backwaters. Local people will always help with information. See also 'The Backwaters' boxed text in the Southern Kerala chapter.

LOCAL TRANSPORT

Taxi

Taxis are generally Ambassador cars. Rates differ depending on whether you are simply travelling within a city or whether you're going farther afield (out-station). There are two ways to pay: per hour or per kilometre. Generally the rate per kilometre is Rs 4.40 (non air-con) and Rs 8.10 (air-con) plus the driver's expenses (around Rs 125 per day). If you are travelling interstate you will also be liable for road toll fees, which are minimal. You will always have to pay the return fare (eg Thiruvananthapuram-Kochi-Thiruvananthapuram) whether or not you are returning. Very often your hotel or travel agency will be able to arrange a 'car and driver' (as taxis are often known). Shop around – different agencies have different services and prices so be prepared to bargain. If you're contemplating a long trip consider meeting the driver and checking the vehicle before signing a deal.

Within a city a non air-con Ambassador car, including driver and fuel, costs either Rs 400 (five hours, 50 km) or Rs 800 (10 hours, 100 km). For air-con expect to pay Rs 560 and Rs 1120 respectively. Outstation trips are calculated for 24 hours from midnight and cost Rs 1300 for non air-con (200km, Rs 4.40 for every extra kilometre) and Rs 1800 for air-con (200km, Rs 7 for every extra kilometre). Non air-con cars are usually fine, unless you find the heat oppressive. Take care if you choose air-con – you may not travel in a cool, pleasant environment, but rather in a hot car with air-con that doesn't work and windows that won't open because it's 'air-con'.

In Kerala, especially in the hilly areas, taxis are actually jeeps, which will get you to the most inaccessible areas for similar prices to non air-con cars.

It is customary at the end of a lengthy trip to give the driver a generous tip. Skilled drivers are worth their weight in sandalwood – but many drivers are also smooth operators who are in cahoots with various hotels and shop owners. Although this is vehemently denied, they receive commissions and will do everything in their power to ensure you use their preferred services, you can't blame them, their salary is generally very low and needs to be topped up with commissions. However, if their agenda doesn't suit your requirements, be assertive. But remember, if they yield to your requests, they may suffer a loss in income.

If you're travelling out-station, with overnight stops, it is usually expected that the driver will sleep in the car. This makes many travellers feel awkward but, even if offered a room, many drivers will choose the car, and save the money. Some hotels offer services to drivers that include meals, bathing facilities, sheets and blankets (in the hill areas). If you indicate to the hotel reception that you care about your driver, they may offer driver facilities. Sometimes it's not the commission that is motivating the driver to take you to a certain hotel – it may be his need for a wash, some warmth or dignity. Again, can you blame him?

Auto-Rickshaw

An auto-rickshaw (or 'auto' or 'three-wheeler') is a noisy three-wheel device powered by a two-stroke engine with a driver up front and seats for two (or sometimes more) passengers behind. Because of their size auto-rickshaws can manoeuvre through heavy traffic more adeptly than taxis, but they don't offer nearly as much protection in the event of a collision.

Auto-rickshaws have meters that invariably don't work (or so the driver will claim). However, if you do find an auto-rickshaw with a working meter, which you will in Kozhikode (Calicut), the flag fall is Rs 7 and it's generally about Rs 3 per kilometre after that. Sometimes meters are tampered with and tick over at an alarming speed. Keep an eye on the meter just in case. If you can't find a metered vehicle, or your requests to have the meter turned on are laughed at, be sure to settle on a price before you get in. Expect to pay more at night and during holidays. Avoid taking a rickshaw from the rank outside your hotel, especially if it is an up-market hotel. Prices will be higher. Walk a few hundred metres and hail a rickshaw in the street.

Drivers will very often wait if you are making a return journey (as opposed to a 'drop only'). Generally the 'waiting' fee will be about Rs 50 for one hour, Rs 10 to Rs 15 for a quick stop.

Drivers vary widely in their knowledge of their cities. It helps, if you are going to a fairly obscure destination, to have it written down in Malayalam to show the driver.

ORGANISED TOURS

If you have little time and want to see as much as possible, consider an organised tour. Tours to the backwater villages are particularly good. Both government tourist offices and private operators organise tours. Some travellers prefer to use private agencies, which can put together an individualised package with a car and driver – or in some cases team you up with others in order to fill a minibus. For more details, see the entries in the regional chapters.

Southern Kerala

Beaches and backwaters are what lure most travellers to this part of Kerala. The beaches are some of the best in India while the backwaters flow like arteries through the many layers of Keralan life. These waterways give an altogether different experience of Kerala. Southern Kerala is also home to the capital, Thiruvananthapuram (Trivandrum), fascinating for its political and cultural complexities.

HISTORY

According to Sangam texts, southern Kerala was part of the ancient Chera kingdom. Conflict with neighbouring dynasties such as the Pandyas and Cholas, altered the regional influence of the Cheras and led to a continuing shift in the political boundaries. Subsequently, the southern region was known as Tiruvarumcode – Abode of Prosperity – from which it acquired the name Travancore.

In 825 CE (common era), at Kollam (Quilon), in central Travancore, the then king of Travancore, Udaya Marthanda Varma, is reputed to have gathered an assembly of learned people to investigate zodiac patterns, on which a new calendar and era was established. Details surrounding this event are very much a matter of contention. However, it's generally accepted that a new era, referred to as the Kollam era (KE), began on 15 August 825 CE.

As with neighbouring states, the fortunes of the region waxed and waned. Under the 18th century king Marthanda Varma, substantial irrigation works took place enabling an expansion of the domestic economy and an increase in prosperity. Salt became a prized commodity. As colonial powers fought for the rights to export it, the state coffers swelled with the revenue.

In 1750 King Marthanda Varma devised a brilliant strategy to secure his power base. With pomp and ceremony, he declared himself the *dasa* or servant of the deity,

Highlights

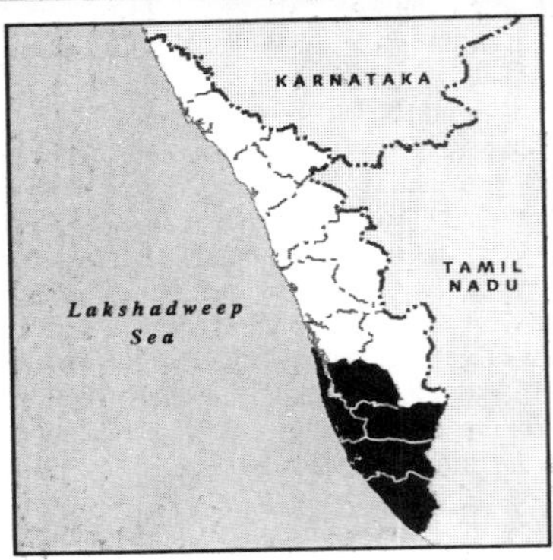

- Explore Kerala's famed backwaters on a *kettuvallam*, or traditional rice barge
- View *kalarippayat*, the traditional martial art of Kerala, at the CVN Kalari Sangham academy in Thiruvananthapuram
- Soak up the sun, swim in the surf and sample the seafood at Kerala's renowned beaches at Kovalam and Varkala
- Visit the 400-year-old Padmanabhapuram Palace in Tamil Nadu, home of the former princely rulers of the state of Travancore
- Get totally rejuvenated with an Ayurvedic treatment at one of the many centres in Kovalam or elsewhere in Southern Kerala
- Watch the remarkable Snakeboat Races, held here in Alappuzha in August and January
- View an all-night performance of Kerala's renowned Kathakali dance drama at the Sri Vallabha Temple in Tiruvalla
- Stay at the ashram of Sri Matha Amrithanandamayi Devi at Amrithapuri, and receive an embrace from India's celebrated 'Hugging Mother'

Padmanabha, enshrined at the Padmanabhaswamy Temple in Thiruvananthapuram and he dedicated his entire kingdom of Travancore to the deity. With this action, he secured the support of the military, the clergy and civilians and ensured succeeding generations would respect the royal family. He died seven years later to be succeeded by his nephew – Rama Varma – under whose reign public works and prosperity increased.

During this period stronger ties were forged with the British East India Company, but there was also conflict with Tipu Sultan, the ruler of Mysore, who sought to gain control over Travancore. Eventually, with British help, Tipu Sultan was defeated.

Internal conflict during the 19th century resulted in military action and increased British control. Under succeeding rulers, the maharanis Lakshmi and Parvati, the British sought to strengthen their authority. Lakshmi Rani took the radical step of appointing a British officer, Colonel Munro, as chief minister. He instigated massive public works

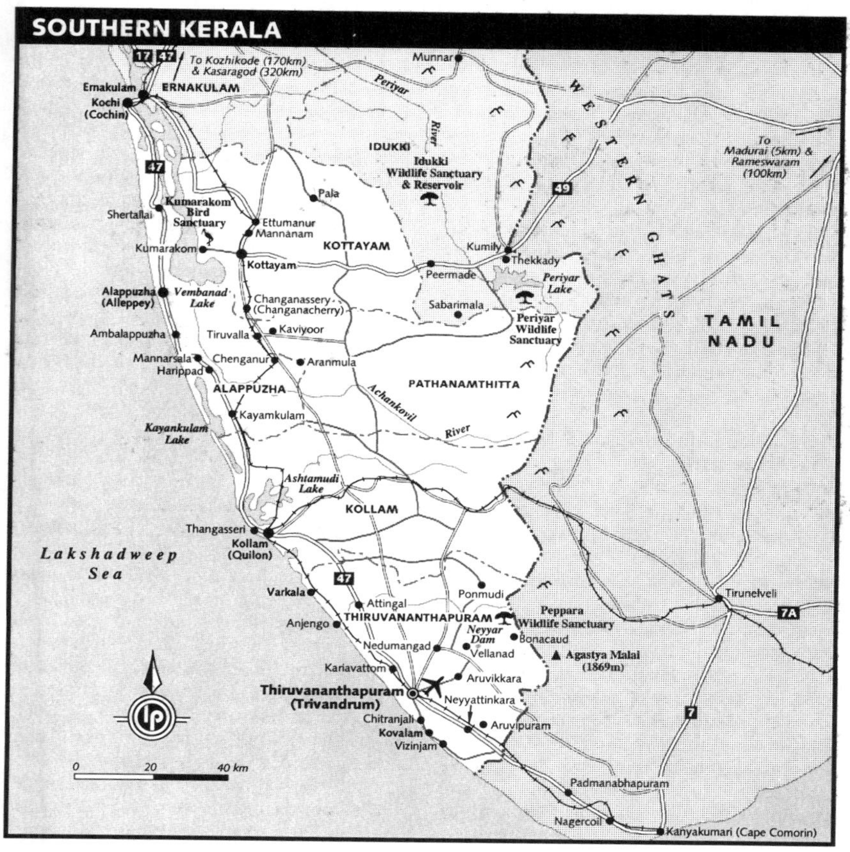

including the building of the canals and irrigation schemes. Educational institutions were also established and there were significant improvements in public health, including the introduction of vaccines. However, in spite of British authority, the rulers of Travancore (like their northern relatives in Cochin) retained a certain autonomy.

From 1829, under the exceptional rule of Swathi Tirunal Rama Varma, son of Rani Lakshmi, significant developments took place, including the establishment of printing presses, hospitals and schools. The public humiliation and banishment of female criminals was abolished. With representatives from all states of India residing at the maharaja's court, a sophisticated level of diplomacy was instituted. Swathi Tirunal, an accomplished scholar, musician and linguist, reinvigorated the arts scene. His successors continued a program of development and reform, perhaps the most significant being the abolition of slavery by 1885.

By 1920 Gandhi's civil disobedience movement had struck a strong chord in Travancore. Citizens worked hard to secure national independence, which was finally achieved in 1947. In 1956, Travancore became part of the newly created state of Kerala and its capital, Trivandrum, became the new state capital.

THIRUVANANTHAPURAM (Trivandrum)

☎ 0471 • pop 854,000

Built over seven hills, Thiruvananthapuram is a noisy, polluted and bustling city, but as Indian cities go, it's easy-going and relaxed. Many travellers find it a hot, noisy shock after a few days of relative peace and quiet at Kovalam or Varkala. But away from the transport hubs and busy Mahatma Gandhi (MG) Rd, Thiruvananthapuram has managed to retain some of the ambience characteristic of old Kerala: red-tiled roofs and narrow winding lanes.

Political slogans, emblems and flags – especially those of the Communist and Muslim parties – are a notable feature of the urban landscape. So too are the flags promoting all manner of interesting events and festivals.

You may prefer to base yourself at Kovalam Beach, just 16km south, where you can enjoy the sea breeze. From there you can make short visits to the capital to take in its few sites, but if you do this you'll miss the subtle charms of Thiruvananthapuram.

History

The area known as Thiruvananthapuram has, since ancient times, linked its name to the local deity. During the colonial era a diminutive aspect of the name – Trivandrum – was used. However more recently Thiruvananthapuram has reclaimed its ancient appellation. Known as the City of the Sacred Serpent, Thiruvananthapuram derives its name from *anantha*, the serpent upon which the deity of the city, Padmanabha, reclines. Padmanabha is a manifestation of Vishnu, the deity who preserves and restores order. Indeed Thiruvananthapuram, which has witnessed dynasties and colonisers come and go, stands testament to preservation and a continual return to order.

By the time the maharajas moved from their Padmanabhapuram Palace (in present-day Tamil Nadu) in 1750 to make their capital at Thiruvananthapuram, it already had an illustrious history. Although it had not been the chosen headquarters of successive sovereignties it had witnessed many of their activities. From the earliest times it had been an important spiritual centre, the ancient Cheras honouring its deity, Padmanabha, with colourful rituals, fasts, bathing and processions.

It was near here that 8th century stonemasons sculpted a small Shiva temple, similar to those in Mamallapuram. As part of the early southern principalities, Thiruvananthapuram's rulers played a major role in developing the arts, particularly literature.

It was at Thiruvananthapuram, in 1070, that the Cheran armies struggled to hold their own against the Cholas and some 600 years later, the British, wishing to seize the pepper trade from the Dutch, became interested in the area. They sought approval of the rani of

Attingal, within whose jurisdiction Thiruvananthapuram lay, to build a fort at Anjengo, just a few kilometres north. So began an association that was to result in a treaty in 1723 between the Travancore rajas and the British, which established the British as the foremost traders in the area. The treaty was signed on behalf of the heir to the throne, the future Marthanda Varma. Six years later, on attaining the sovereignty, he proved to be a resolute monarch, intent on extending his realm. Partly assisted by his new friends, their military accoutrements, and what he called their 'good fellowship and honourable company' he set out to achieve his aims and extended his territory from Padmanabhapuram far beyond Thiruvananthapuram to Cochin (Central Kerala). He also struck an accord of sorts with the northern rulers and averted conflict by achieving the compliance of the Dutch.

In 1798, under the reign of Bala Rama Varma, treasury officials engaged in corruption and bribery. Alarmed by this behaviour, a member of the warrior Nair community, Velu Thampi, assembled an army and marched on Thiruvananthapuram. There his numbers were expanded by the citizens of the city. Their action forced Bala Rama Varma to replace the officials with Nair administrators. Velu Thampi was appointed *diwan* (chief minister), a post he undertook with diligent alacrity.

His tactics to reorganise the treasury and reduce the pay of military personnel were not received favourably. An uprising ensued and Velu Thampi sought British help to subdue it. With that action and the subsequent treaty of 1805, Travancore partly forfeited its autonomy to the British.

As the loss of autonomy became more evident Velu Thampi relinquished his alliance with the British and began to plot against them. Once again armies marched through Thiruvananthapuram – this time on their way north to confront the British. This they did at Kollam, where they suffered defeat. The British stormed both Padmanabhapuram and Thiruvananthapuram in an attempt to capture Velu Thampi. Rather than suffer the shame of British capture, he killed himself before they reached him. The British returned his body to Thiruvananthapuram where they hung it on the gallows, with the bodies of many of his troops, already executed by the British.

From 1829 Swathi Thirunal, the maharaja of Travancore, assumed power in Thiruvananthapuram. Under his jurisdiction Travancore advanced in the areas of the arts and education, as well as in its social and economic systems. He also instigated new administrative and legal processes, and his reforms continued well after his reign.

The first legislative council was formed in Thiruvananthapuram in 1888. This was the result of the then maharaja's (Rama Varma) response to a groundswell of discontent and calls for a more democratic system. It was the first of its kind in any Indian state. Almost fifty years later it proclaimed the historic and revolutionary Temple Entry Act, enabling Hindus of all castes access to their spiritual edifices.

In August 1938 a huge crowd, inspired by Gandhian principles, gathered at Thiruvananthapuram to embark upon a campaign of civil disobedience. These early stirrings would later translate into communist activity. When, in 1957, Malayalis elected a communist government, it was at Thiruvananthapuram in their thousands that they heard the ardent address of their leader EMS Namboodiripad pledging a new life of equity and justice for all Malayalis.

In 1956, with the forming of the new state of Kerala, Thiruvananthapuram (then called Trivandrum) assumed the status of state capital. As capital of the first state to freely elect a communist government, Thiruvananthapuram became a focus of international interest. Today the buildings and monuments are reminders of its history; the meetings and marches, indicators of its future.

Orientation

Most of Thiruvananthapuram's services and places of interest are on or very close to MG Rd, which runs north-south, from the museums and zoo to the Sri Padmanabhaswamy Temple – a distance of about 4km.

THIRUVANANTHAPURAM (Trivandrum)

PLACES TO STAY
15 KTDC Mascot Hotel
36 The Heritage Point
40 South Park
46 YWCA Guesthouse
54 YMCA
57 Hotel Pankaj
58 Wild Palms Guest House
61 Hotel Navaratna
62 Hotel Residency Tower
71 Sivada Tourist Home
73 Sundar Tourist Home
74 Hotel Regency
76 Manacaud Tourist Paradise & Hotel; Hotel Sukhvas
77 Pravin Tourist Home
78 Vijai Tourist Home
84 Hotel Highland; City Queen Restaurant
85 Hotel Ammu
87 Gokulum; Bank of India; Tourist Reception Centre
92 Nalanda Tourist Home
98 Hotel Luciya Continental

PLACES TO EAT
43 Indian Coffee House; Spencer's Store
47 Ananda Bhavan
56 Sree Arul Jyothi; New Arul Jyothi
63 Snoozzer Ice Cream
72 Asok Veg Restaurant
75 Manacaud Restaurant
83 Hotel City Tower
86 Ambika Cafe; Prime Square
88 Maveli Cafe
90 Azad Restaurant
91 Rangoli

OTHER
1 Kerala State Archives
2 Kerala Travels Interserve (trekking)
3 Niranjan Towers
4 Bishop's House
5 British Bank (ATM)
6 Air India
7 Kerala Gazeteer
8 Kanakakunna Palace
9 Natural History Museum
10 Sri Chitra Art Gallery
11 Napier Museum
12 State Bank of India; Kerala Travels Interserve (ticketing)
13 Mateer Memorial Church
14 Indian Airlines
16 Science & Technology Museum; Planetarium
17 Kerala Legislative Assembly
18 Stadium
19 Airtravel Enterprises (Jet Airways, Gulf Air, Kuwait Airways)
20 Tourist Facilitation Centre; Kairali
21 C Kesavan Statue
22 Academy of Fine Arts
23 Police Headquarters
24 Victoria Diamond Jubilee Library
25 Christ Church
26 Stadium
27 Multidata (Internet)
28 St Joseph's Cathedral
29 Mosque
30 Kerala Book Marketing Society
31 Connemara Market
32 SriLanka Airlines
33 District Forest Office; Chief Conservator of Forests
34 WWF
35 Survey of India
37 Victoria Jubilee Town Hall
38 Government Sanskrit College
39 Pattom A Thanu Pillai Statue
41 St George's Orthodox Syrian Church
42 Canara Bank
44 General Hospital
45 Air Maldives
48 DC Books; Current Books
49 Central Telegraph Office
50 Secretariat Building; Sreedhari Ayurveda Kendrum
51 Commissioner of Police
52 SMSM Institute
53 British Library
55 State Bank of Travancore
59 GPO
60 Modern Book Centre
64 CLS Books
65 Priya Books
66 Hastkali Indian Arts & Crafts
67 Sankar's Tea & Coffee
68 Ayurveda College
69 Natesan's Antiqarts
70 Khadi Gramodyog Bhavan
79 Higginbothams
80 Kulathunkal Building
81 Continental Book Company
82 Tourindia
89 KSRTC Long-Distance Bus Terminal
93 Sri Padmanabhaswamy Temple
94 Puthe Maliga Palace Museum
95 Ganapathy Temple
96 Municipal Bus Stand
97 Bus Stand No 19 (Buses & Taxis to Kovalam)
99 CVN Kalari Sangham

To Tennis & Golf Clubs (500m) & Government Hospital (2km)
To Alliance Française (500m), WWO (PTP Nagar) (2km) & Ponmudi (58km)
To Centre for Development Studies (2.5km), Kariyam (7km) & Kochi (222km)
Zoo
Museum Road
Vellayambalam Junction
Palayam
Vazhuthacaud Road
Vazhuthacaud
Thycaud Hospital Road
The Academy of Magical Sciences (4km)
Statue Road
To Pettah Junction & ICCD (2km)
Press Rd
Manjalikulam Rd
MG Road
Dharmalayam Road
Central Station Road
o Airport (6km), Veli Tourist Park (8km) & Shanghumugham Beach (8km)
To Train Station (100m)
Thakaraparambu Road
Power House Road
Padmavilasam Road
East Fort
Chalai Bazaar Road
Fort
South Road
To Chitranjali Studio Complex (7km) & Kovalam (15km)
To Kanyakumari (88km)
0 250 500 m

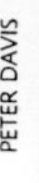

PETER DAVIS

LINDSAY BROWN

EDDIE GERALD

PAUL BEINSSEN

op: Street performers come from all walks of life. **Middle left:** Fisherman at Vizhinjam. **Middle right & bottom:** The *salwar kameez* is popular with young Keralan women, while tourists often stand out in nore skimpy attire.

PAUL BEINSSEN

PETER DAVIS

EDDIE GERALD

PAUL BEINSSEN

You can experience the splendour of Keralan festivals at almost any time of year. **Top:** Drummers at the Pooram Festival in Thrissur. **Middle left & middle right:** At a tourist festival, performers take on the attributes of animals such as peacocks or tigers. **Bottom:** Gilded elephants join the celebrations.

The Kerala State Road Transport Corporation (KSRTC) long-distance bus terminal, train station, Tourist Reception Centre and many of the budget hotels are all close together, while the municipal bus stand is close to the temple. The large Secretariat building, halfway along MG Rd, is a handy landmark.

Information

Tourist Offices The Tourist Facilitation Centre (☎ 321132), Museum Rd, has literature and maps, organises tours and provides a range of information. Whether your interest is general or specific, they'll accommodate all inquiries. The Tourist Reception Centre (☎ 330031), in front of the KTDC Hotel Chaithram, arranges Kerala Tourism Development Corporation (KTDC) guided tours (see Organised Tours later in this section). There's a helpful tourist information desk at the airport.

General Information Alliance Française (☎ 327776, fax 327772) is at Mani Bhavan, Sasthamangalam. It has a library and is about to set up a Web page with information on French-Kerala connections. It organises a range of regular events, including film festivals, art exhibitions, book fairs and concerts. It's open daily except Sunday, 9 am to 2.30 pm.

For information and permits for entry to parks and sanctuaries see the Chief Conservator of Forests (☎ 325385), Vazhuthacaud.

The World Wide Fund for Nature (WWF) (☎/fax 325183, Rupa A-10 Tagore Nagar, Vazhuthacaud) sells a comprehensive publication, *The Natural Resources of Kerala,* for Rs 750. The office is open every day 8.30 am to 5.30 pm. For further information on environmental issues try the Centre for Earth Science Studies (CESS, ☎ 442187), near Veli Lake, which has an extensive library of over 10,000 publications.

The Centre for Development Studies (☎ 448881, fax 447137), at Prasanth Nagar, Ulloor, has a library and produces a wide range of publications on issues pertaining to economics and development.

For out-of-date maps you can visit the Survey of India Office (☎ 320874). For more information on maps, see the Maps section of the Facts for the Visitor chapter.

Detailed publications on Kerala are available from the Kerala Gazeteer.

Money Travellers cheques can be cashed and credit card cash advances for all major cards can be arranged at the Canara Bank near the South Park Hotel and at the Bank of India counter in the lobby of the Hotel Chaithram. Hours are Monday to Friday 10 am to 2 pm and 10 am to noon Saturday. The State Bank of India near the Secretariat keeps the same hours but will only accept American Express travellers cheques and the process can take nearly an hour.

A super-efficient money exchange service is TT Travels Foreign Exchange. The branch (☎ 500335) at Thiruvananthapuram airport opens for all incoming and outgoing flights. The other branch (☎ 500335), at Vellayambalam, is in Niranjan Towers on KP Elankath Rd (north-east of the zoo). It's open daily 9.30 am to 7.30 pm. ATMs are at the State Bank of Travancore near the Secretariat and at the British Bank, at the junction of Vathuthacaud and Museum Rds.

Post & Communications The general post office (GPO) is on MG Rd. Most of the counters are open Monday to Saturday 8 am to 8 pm. Poste restante is open every day, 8 am to 4 pm. A packing service for books and other items operates from a rather grotty desk under the stairwell in the building adjacent to the post office (where private post boxes are located). The packing man is supposed to be there every weekday at 10 am. If you can't locate him ask the watchman in the driveway. The service is quick and efficient. Your items will be tied, stitched in a white cloth and sealed with wax. Expect to pay around Rs 1000 for a 5kg book parcel if you send it airmail, Rs 175 for seamail.

The Central Telegraph Office, on MG Rd opposite the Secretariat, is 20 minutes walk from either Museum Rd or Central Station

Rd. The office is open 24 hours. There are numerous STD/ISD counters and kiosks around town.

Email in Thiruvananthapuram is beginning to take off but at the time of writing it was still a hit and miss affair, with most places having only one or two terminals where lines frequently drop out. The Central Telegraph Office charges Rs 35 to Rs 125 for 15 to 120 minutes – you can book your session in advance. Hotel Chaithram has a reliable 24 hour cybercafe with three terminals. Another good place is Multidata (☎ 321082), a computer training college on the 3rd floor of the Kottaathil Building behind the Bank of Baroda. These places have email as well as Internet facilities but the demand outweighs the supply, so surfing the net when people are waiting to receive email is not usually possible.

Visa Extensions The office of the Commissioner of Police (☎ 320486) on Residency Rd issues visa extensions, but the process takes four days to a week, and approval is not guaranteed. You don't have to leave your passport, and it speeds things up if you give a Thiruvananthapuram address rather than somewhere in Kovalam. The office is open daily, except Sunday, 10 am to 5 pm.

Bookshops & Libraries The state public library – the Victoria Diamond Jubilee Library – housed in a classic Victorian building is on MG Rd and is open daily 8 am to 8 pm.

The British Library (☎ 328716), in the YMCA grounds near the Secretariat building, is officially only open to members, but visitors are welcome. It has British newspapers and a variety of magazines. The library is open Tuesday to Saturday 11 am to 7 pm.

Along or just off MG Rd you'll find many bookshops, including the Continental Book Company, Current Books, Higginbothams, Modern Book Centre, DC Books, CLS Books and Priya Books.

In a little shed near the mosque, the Kerala Book Marketing Society (no phone), in VJT Hall, has a large selection of books in Malayalam and English on Keralan history and society. Discounts of up to 30% are available. Though tiny, the handy bookshop in the lobby of the Hotel Chaithram (☎ 330977) has a good range of books on Kerala and also sells a basic map.

Medical Services The General Hospital (☎ 443870) is west of MG Rd, about 1km along Statue Rd.

Emergency

Police	☎ 100
Ambulance	☎ 101

Sri Padmanabhaswamy Temple

Facing east, the Sri Padmanabhaswamy Temple covers an area of 2400 sq m. Its main entrance, the eastern *gopuram* (gateway), towers to over 30m and is devised, like those in Tamil Nadu, in the Dravidian style. An 8m-wide colonnade makes its way 130m to the inner sanctum of the deity, Padmanabha (an aspect of Vishnu), who reclines there on the sacred serpent. The 6m image is viewed in three sections through three doors. The first section shows Vishnu's head cradled by the cobra's multi-headed apex. The central section displays a lotus growing from Padmanabha's navel. A small idol of Brahma resides in the lotus symbolising creation. A symbol of Shiva completes the Hindu triad, representing creation (Brahma), preservation (Vishnu) and destruction (Shiva).

Legends tell of a shrine in Thiruvananthapuram as far back as 3000 years but the current temple dates from the reign of Marthanda Varma (1729-58), who pledged to have it rebuilt even before he came to office. On attaining the sovereignty he set about the task, with the construction reputedly taking only seven months in 1733. The mammoth project was allegedly achieved in such a short time through the employment of 100 elephants along with 10 times as many artisans and building workers. The main hall, the Kulashekhara Mandapa, containing sculptures and murals, is supported by more than 360 granite pillars.

The temple is the focus for several festivals, see the Special Events section, later.

Although the temple is open to Hindus only, visitors are occasionally permitted entry if wearing a sari, for women, or a *dhoti* (similar to a sarong) for men. If you're a non-Hindu, you'll be greeted by a priest at the entrance who will explain the reason for your nonadmittance – the temple is owned by the royal family and is therefore their private place of worship. He'll then direct you to the best places to photograph the gopuram, take you to a sandalwood outlet for shopping and demand a handsome tip.

Puthe Maliga Palace Museum

The Puthe Maliga Palace Museum, adjacent to the temple, is housed in several wings of the 200-year-old palace of the maharajas of Travancore, their headquarters after leaving their former palace in Padmanabhapuram (in present-day Tamil Nadu). Notable mostly for its wonderful Keralan architecture, the museum also offers a rare glimpse into the formal and private lives of one of India's most celebrated royal families.

It took 5000 workers four years to complete the palace. Statues of Kathakali characters stand beneath carved wooden ceilings. Many of the exhibits reflect the spice trade with China and Europe. There are two ornate thrones, one made entirely of Bohemian crystal, the other carved from 50 elephant tusks. Lining the walls beneath the eaves are 122 finely carved horses, hence the popular name for the palace – horse palace.

The maharaja's reading room has hexagonal walls with bookcase inserts and a magnificent lotus ceiling. To the side of the music room, a room shaped like a howdah (elephant saddle-seat) is said to be the place where Maharaja Swathi Thirunal (1829-46) derived inspiration for many of his musical compositions.

Of the 80 rooms, 20 are open for inspection. A 20 year plan is in progress to restore and open the remaining areas. Currently the walls bear the reminders of earlier lighting – oil lamps – which have often not been replaced by contemporary lighting, meaning you'll walk around the palace mostly in the dark. Even so it's worth a visit.

The palace hosts a classical music festival, see the Special Events section, later.

The museum is open every day except Monday 8.30 am to 12.30 pm and from 3 to 5.30 pm; entry is Rs 20. Use of a camera in the palace grounds is Rs 15, but note that photography is strictly prohibited within the building.

Other Museums, Gallery & Zoo

The zoo and a collection of museums are in a park to the north of the city. The museums are open Tuesday to Sunday 10 am to 4.45 pm (closed till 1 pm on Wednesday for cleaning). A single Rs 5 entry ticket covers all the museums and can be purchased from the Natural History Museum.

Housed in a whimsical, decaying, Keralan-style building dating from 1880, the **Napier Museum** has an eclectic display of bronzes, historical and contemporary ornaments, temple carts, ivory carvings and life-size figures of Kathakali performers in full costume.

The **Natural History Museum** has a rudimentary ethnographic collection, including whale and elephant skeletons, displays of hill tribes and dolls representing various regions. There's also an interesting replica of a *Tarawad* – the traditional wooden residence of the Nair warrior family/caste – complete with model elephant procession and Kathakali performance.

The **Sri Chitra Art Gallery** has paintings of the Rajput, Mughal and Tanjore schools, together with works from China, Tibet, Japan and Bali. There are also many modern Indian paintings, including works by Ravi Varma, and Svetoslav and Nicholas Roerich.

The **Zoological Gardens** are among the best designed in Asia – set among woodland, lakes and well-maintained lawns – but some of the animal enclosures (and their inhabitants) are miserable. The zoo is open Tuesday to Saturday 9 am to 5.15 pm. Entry is Rs 4 and there's an additional Rs 5 charge for a camera or Rs 250 for a video camera.

South-east of the zoo is the **Kanakakunna Palace**, which was once a royal residency, built early in the 20th century. The vast rooms and manicured grounds are now used for public exhibitions and trade shows.

The **Science & Technology Museum** and **Planetarium**, about 100m west of the Mascot Hotel, cater mostly to high-school students. The museum has numerous interactive displays and is open 10 am to 5 pm daily (except Monday) with a Rs 2 entry fee. The planetarium (☎ 446976) has 35 minute shows in Malayalam (10.30 am, 3 and 5 pm) and in English at noon (Rs 5/10 child/adult). It's also closed Monday.

Kerala Legislative Assembly

Opened in January 1999, it seems that no expense has been spared with this new building. Set in spacious landscaped grounds complete with fountains and sculptures, the structure is an expression of confidence in the political future of the state.

Churches

There are many churches in Thiruvananthapuram. Some are small and almost hidden. Others are large and surrounded by generous grounds. The **Mateer Memorial Church** near Indian Airlines was built in 1906 in memory of the Anglican missionary, Samuel Mateer. The stone edifice with green wooden slatted windows has a decidedly English appearance. The entire structure including the roof and the stained glass windows is original. Like most of the churches, visitors are welcome. Sunday services are in Tamil (7 am), Malayalam (8 am and 4.15 pm) and English (9.45 am). There is also a midweek service on Thursday at 6.15 pm in Malayalam.

CVN Kalari Sangham

The CVN Kalari Sangham (☎ 474182) in East Fort, near the Sri Padmanabhaswamy Temple, is a small but remarkable building – part training centre, part temple and part hospital. Built in 1956, its founders played a significant role in the revival of *kalarippayat*, the traditional martial art of Kerala, believed to be the forerunner of all eastern martial arts and integral to the technical development of all other performing arts in Kerala, including Kathakali. (See the boxed text 'Kalarippayat' in the Facts about Kerala chapter.)

Each morning the pit has an expectant air. Its walls bear imprints of oily, sweaty hands. Tiny shrines to Ganesh, Sarasvati and Lakshmi share the pit surrounds with sticks, swords and spears. No student begins without respectful *pujas* (worship) to the deities.

The pujas are followed by a thorough oiling of the body. Men wear a loincloth; women remain fully clothed. Then the action begins, slowly at first, gradually increasing to the swift, skilful movements that are the hallmark of kalarippayat.

Individuals and small groups can view the training sessions for free between 6.30 and 8.30 am every morning except Sunday, when the centre is closed. Ayurvedic treatments (especially for soft tissue injuries) are available Monday to Saturday 10 am to 1 pm and 5 to 7.30 pm, 10 am to 1 pm on Sunday. You can purchase books on kalarippayat here.

It is also possible to learn the art of kalarippayat. See the Courses section, later.

Ganapathy Temple

Also in East Fort is the Ganapathy Temple, dedicated to Ganesh. It's worth a visit during morning puja, when the sound of temple bells, the ritual smashing of coconuts and the smell of incense are magical, but all too fleeting as the chaos on MG Rd soon gets into full swing.

Academy of Magical Sciences

Tourist brochures promote Kerala as a land of magical experiences. At the Academy of Magical Sciences (☎ 345910, fax 345920, 17/1643 Poojapura), 5km east of the town centre, the magic is taken to new heights. Established in 1996 the academy aims to rekindle some of the traditional magical arts of India. Under the directorship of Gopinath Muthukad, a renowned escapologist and master of illusions and prestidigitation (sleight of hand), the academy has successfully lobbied the government of Kerala to recognise magic as an art. This means that along with classical dancers and musicians, magicians can now be part of the prestigious Sangeeta Nadaka Academy, which supports professional artists. Each year the academy takes in a new batch of aspirants for the two-year course. Graduates carve lucrative careers on the wedding and festival circuits around India as well as in the tourist hotels. Members of the academy have also trodden on sacred toes, by exposing the 'tricks' used by swamis such as Sai Baba.

Magic shows are often held at the academy and visitors are welcome. Telephone first for timings. Keep an eye out for the ancient Indian mango tree trick. The magician places a mango seed into the ground, covers the area with an empty cane basket, mutters some incantations and then lifts the basket to reveal a mango tree complete with fruit. Amazed spectators are invited to share the fruit!

Kerala State Archives

The Kerala State Archives, Nalanda (☎ 313759), boasts one of the largest collections of palm leaf manuscripts in Asia, with over three million leaves. The leaves contain significant records such as historical background on the Padmanabhaswamy Temple, as well as notable proclamations issued by past rulers. The archives are available for study by Indians for a Rs 100 fee. Foreigners with a serious interest in the manuscripts may apply in writing for permission to view and use the leaves. Such applications are rarely rejected. However, the process for approval is usually arduous and long – so long, in fact, that your letter of application could become classified as an ancient manuscript! Applications, with passport details and three photographs, should be addressed to the Director, Kerala State Archives, Nalanda, Thiruvananthapuram.

Shanghumugham Beach

At Shanghumugham Beach, 8km west of the city, criminals were allegedly once tossed to caged tigers and crowds gathered on surrounding balconies to watch the gruesome sight. The beach today gives no indication of its hideous history. It's a pleasant place to walk or watch the fishermen securing their catch. A large sculpture of a mermaid graces the roadside, an example of the work of the local artist Canai Kunuram. At dusk, during temple festivals, the beach is the site of the ritual bathing of the temple idols.

Veli Tourist Park

Positioned within frangipani and hibiscus gardens, this well-designed park, 8km west of the city, contains finely crafted **sculptures** by local artist Canai Kunuram. The sculptures portray a distinctive sense of balance and harmony sometimes combined with erotic elements. The artist's work, particularly his statue of the *yakshi* (maiden) near Palakkad (Palghat), has attracted much acclaim as well as controversy. Kunuram has played a significant role in the development of Keralan sculpture, by removing it from its traditional architectural environment and placing it in natural landscapes. Kunuram's less controversial works include the statue of the early 20th century political agitator Netaji at Pottom Thanu Pillai in Thiruvananthapuram. He's currently working on a statue of EMS Namboodiripad, Kerala's noted communist and first chief minister. The park is well worth a visit, and is open daily 10 am to 5.30 pm. Admission is free. Boats can be hired; costs for 30-minute sessions are: motorboat safari Rs 10 per person (maximum 20 people), two/four-seater pedal boat Rs 40/50.

Activities

Visitors to Thiruvananthapuram can enjoy a game of **tennis** at the Trivandrum Tennis Club (☎ 322737), Kowdiar. Courts are available 9 am to 3 pm and club members boast that the Rs 200 fee is the cheapest in the country. You'll need to supply your own balls and racquet. If it's too hot outside you can play **billiards** indoors. There's a canteen and even air-con accommodation for visitors sponsored by a member. It's friendly, welcoming and in a pleasant environment.

Book by phone at least one day ahead with the secretary.

Similar facilities exist at the nine hole **golf course** (☎ 315834), just 1km away. For details and bookings contact the secretary.

Alliance Française (☎ 327776, fax 327772) has facilities for **table tennis** and also organises **trekking**.

Ayurveda

Numerous places offer various Ayurvedic treatments from a one hour massage for Rs 300 to longer term treatments (10 to 21 days) ranging from US$300.

CVN Kalari Sangham
(☎ 474128) East Fort (see entry on this institute, earlier in this section)

Shiva Ayurvedic Centre
(☎ 331695) Udarasiromani Rd, Vazhuthacaud (near the Police Headquarters)

Sreedhari Ayurveda Kendrum
(☎/fax 331138) Narasimhavilasam Bldgs, south gate of the Secretariat

Courses

If you wish to learn the art of kalarippayat and join the combatants in the pit at the CVN Kalari Sangham (see earlier in this section) you need to sign up for a course (three month minimum) at Rs 500 per month. You'll need to arrange your own accommodation, meals and transport. For details, write to the Director, CVN Kalari Sangham, East Fort, Thiruvananthapuram.

The International Centre for Cultural Development (ICCD, ☎ 465368) at 31/1719 Anayara Rd, Pettah Junction, was established by an Indian/Dutch couple to provide opportunities for foreign artists to learn from local artists, as well as develop and exhibit their work. Some of the possibilities include woodcarving, blacksmithing and bronze casting. Costs for accommodation and work space are US$425/625 single/double for a month. For rules and booking details, interested artists should contact the centre or the Netherlands office at ☎ 31-20-665 3890, fax 665 6710.

Nadabrahama Academy of Fine Arts (☎ 321057) offers tuition in a range of Indian and western musical instruments as well as Carnatic vocal tuition. It's open every day except Sunday. Tuition is Rs 150 for eight lessons spread over one month.

Courses in Kathakali and Kootiattam drama are conducted for genuine students at the Margi Kathakali School (☎ 434066), West Fort. No experience is necessary, tuition is for beginners or advanced students. Fees are organised with the teachers, and accommodation is supplied for male students. Female students may board outside the school. If you are interested write to or phone the treasurer, Mr Ramaiyer.

The Indian Council for Cultural Relations (ICCR, ☎ 326712, fax 332479), Vazhuthacaud, organises cultural exchange programs and scholarships for foreign students. For full details write to the ICCR, Vazhuthacaud, Thiruvananthapuram.

Organised Tours

The KTDC operates a variety of tours in the city and farther afield. They all depart from the Tourist Reception Centre opposite the train station.

The daily Thiruvananthapuram city tour departs at 8 am, returns at 7 pm, and costs Rs 50/95 for a child/adult. The tour visits the Sri Padmanabhaswamy Temple (non-Hindus not admitted), the Napier Museum, art gallery, zoo, Veli Lagoon, an aquarium, and Kovalam Beach. On Monday, when the museums and zoo are closed, the tour includes Neyyar Dam (see Neyyar Dam & Wildlife Sanctuary, later in this chapter).

There's a half-day tour of Thiruvananthapuram (Rs 60), which leaves daily except Wednesday at 1 pm to Veli Lagoon and Kovalam Beach.

The daily Kanyakumari (Cape Comorin) tour to Tamil Nadu departs at 7.30 am, returns at 9 pm, and costs Rs 50/180. It includes Padmanabhapuram Palace (except on Monday), Suchindram Temple and Kanyakumari, and is good value if you want to avoid public buses or don't want to stay overnight in Kanyakumari. There's also a daily tour to the Ponmudi hill resort (see Ponmudi & the Cardamom Hills, later in

Ayurveda

With its roots in Sanskrit, the word Ayurveda is derived from *ayu* (life), and *veda* (knowledge). It is therefore the knowledge or science of life. For the layperson it is a set of principles for a happy and healthy life. For the practitioner Ayurveda is a rich and complex body of knowledge from which to understand, diagnose and treat disease.

The principals of Ayurvedic medicine were first documented in the *Vedas* some two thousand years ago, but it is reputed to have been practised for centuries prior to its documentation. Ayurvedic practice is based on the insights understood by the *rishis* – the ancient people who through meditative practice developed understandings and knowledge about life and wellbeing.

Ayurveda sees the world as having an intrinsic order. Illness is a departure from the established order, a loss of balance or equilibrium. Ayurveda attempts to instruct its adherents with the means by which order may be achieved and maintained.

According to the Ayurvedic system, human beings have four basic needs: spiritual sustenance, material satisfaction, reproduction and liberty. Ayurveda maintains that any impediment to the satisfaction of these needs inhibits health. It encourages health through a balanced realisation of these basic needs. In addition to the balancing of human drives, Ayurveda considers internal and external balance important. Human beings are intimately connected to the environment in which they live. Health or ill health result from the individual's active impression on and response to the environment. Ayurveda sees the elements in the natural environment – air, fire and water – as not only essential to the human body but also mirrored in it. Three body types are described, each one corresponding to a different element. These types, known as *doshas*, are *vatu* (air), *pitta* (fire) and *kapha* (water/earth). In the Ayurvedic system, each individual may express various aspects of each type, but usually one type predominates. If there is deficiency or excess of any dosha, disease can result. More specifically, an excess of vatu (air) may result in dizziness and debility. An increase in pitta (fire) may lead to fever, inflammation and infection. Kapha (water) is essential for hydration and lubrication. A deficiency here could produce painful limbs and influenza-type illness.

The practise of Ayurveda develops these principles further to include emotional states. Excessive body heat is aligned to anger and jealousy; excess water and earth (the products of the environment) is equated to greed. These are, however, simple examples and Ayurveda, while based on common sense, is not a simple system. It is a complex framework that carefully details the source of, and remedy for, disease, whether it be physical, mental or emotional.

Ayurvedic diagnosis and treatment is based on individual body type categories with their particular physical, emotional and psychological attributes. Diagnosis involves several processes including palpation (touch), pulse reading and examination of bodily excretions.

Treatment may involve several stages, and begins with a thorough cleansing of the body to eliminate toxins. This is achieved by administering enemas, laxatives and nasal purgatives. Diet is also a crucial aspect to treatment. Exercise, usually in the form of yoga, meditation and massage, is also a technique employed by Ayurveda.

After centuries of practise throughout India, Ayurveda suffered severe setbacks during British colonisation. Education in Ayurveda was banned and all schools were closed. Ayurvedic medicine lost not only status, but without its continued practise much scholarship and experience were lost. However, among those excluded from 'official' western medicine due to location or cost, Ayurvedic methods persisted. Now, 50 years after Independence, Ayurvedic medicine has reclaimed its prestige and significance as an important preventative and treatment model. Ironically, once banned by the west, it is now the subject of much interest in western countries.

this chapter), which departs at 7.45 am, returns at 7 pm, and costs Rs 50/160.

There are other, longer, tours including destinations such as Munnar (three days, Rs 475), Thekkady (two days, Rs 375) and Rameswaram, in Tamil Nadu (four days Rs 525). These tours include basic accommodation and meals.

The Tourist Facilitation Centre (☎ 321132), on Museum Rd, also organises tours. Its popular one day tour to Ponmudi, which includes a visit to a tea plantation and spice garden as well as an elephant ride, costs Rs 3000.

Kerala Travels Interserve (☎ 324158, fax 323154), opposite the Gulf Air building near Vellayambalam Junction, is highly regarded and offers a wide range of specialised tours including trekking and camping in the Periyar Wildlife Sanctuary (see the Western Ghats chapter for more information on Periyar). It has a second office for general ticketing and hotel reservations at LMS Junction above the State Bank of India (☎ 314712, fax 323154). Both offices can be contacted via email at keralt@md2.vsnl.net.in.

Tourindia (☎ 330437, fax 331407), MG Rd, can organise treehouse stays near the Wayanad Wildlife Sanctuary – see the Western Ghats chapter for information on Wayanad.

Special Events

An annual **craft exhibition** takes place from 8 to 15 December at the Kanakakunna Palace. Craft associations from around Kerala display their work and give demonstrations. Displays include woodcarving, batik, caneware, brass metal and embroidery. Many of the items are available for sale.

The principal festivals celebrated at the Padmanabhaswamy Temple are in the months of Meenam (March/April) and Thulam (October/November). The latter, the 10 day **Sarasvati Festival**, honours the goddess of learning, and is particularly significant, given the importance placed on education in Kerala. Celebrations include a special initiation for children into the letters of the alphabet. At the end of both festivals, the idols of Krishna, Narasimha and Padmanabha are ceremoniously escorted to Shanghumugham Beach for ritual bathing. The elaborate dusk procession to the Lakshadweep Sea is escorted by members of the Travancore royal family. As darkness descends, the idols are returned to the temple by lighted cortege.

In keeping with royal Travancore tradition, the Puthe Maliga Palace hosts an annual **Classical Music Festival** from 27 January to 3 February, tickets can be purchased at the palace museum. The musicians perform under the glow of oil lamps on the veranda – don't forget the mosquito repellent.

The **International Film Festival of Kerala**, with its screening, lectures and discussions, is now an annual event. Like the International Film Festival of India, it showcases products from around the world and often includes a retrospective of a select director. Dates and venues vary – either January or April, in either Thiruvananthapuram or Kochi (Cochin). For details, contact the Chitranjali Studio Complex (☎ 461450).

Places to Stay – Budget

There are many cheap places around Central Station Rd, near the train station and KSRTC long-distance bus terminal, but most of them are very basic and the road is busy and noisy. The best hunting ground is Manjalikulam Rd, which runs parallel to MG Rd. Despite its central location, it's quiet and has a collection of cheap to mid-range hotels.

Pravin Tourist Home *(☎ 330753)* is a cheerful if not spotless place with large singles/doubles/triples for Rs 90/160/225; tea and coffee are available.

Sundar Tourist Home *(☎ 330532)* has simpler rooms for Rs 40/75 with common bath, Rs 45/85 with bath.

Vijai Tourist Home *(☎ 331727)* is friendly but the double rooms for Rs 125 have rather dingy bathrooms.

Sivada Tourist Home *(☎ 330320)* has non air-con singles/doubles with bath for Rs 85/135 and air-con rooms for Rs 230/350.

Manacaud Tourist Paradise & Hotel *(☎ 327578)*, at the Central Station Rd end of

Manjalikulam Rd, has large, clean rooms with bathroom for Rs 110/220.

Hotel Sukhvas *(☎ 331967)*, next door, is OK with standard rooms for Rs 120/250 or air-con rooms for Rs 500 but some of the staff are happy to point out better deals elsewhere!

Hotel Ammu *(☎ 331937)*, nearby, is small and popular and has singles/doubles with bath from Rs 160/230, more expensive rooms with TV (Rs 250/285) or TV and air-con (Rs 450). There is a small air-con restaurant.

Nalanda Tourist Home *(☎ 471864)*, south of the train line, is on busy MG Rd, but the rooms at the back are not too noisy and it's cheap at Rs 70/100 (all with bath).

YWCA Guesthouse *(☎ 446518, MG Rd)* is clean with single/double/family rooms with bath for only Rs 150/250/300. There are not many rooms and it is often full.

YMCA *(☎ 330059)* is open to members only and charges Rs 40/75 or Rs 85 for a double with bath.

Retiring rooms at the train station are Rs 25 for a dorm bed (men only).

Places to Stay – Mid-Range

KTDC Hotel Chaithram *(☎ 330977, fax 331446, Central Station Rd)*, next to the KSRTC long-distance bus terminal, is efficient, modern and often full. Rooms cost Rs 475/575, or Rs 750/900 with air-con. The tariff includes a buffet breakfast. Facilities include a bookshop, a Bank of India branch office, a bright and friendly bar, a good air-con veg restaurant and an average nonveg restaurant. Checkout is 24 hours.

Hotel Highland *(☎ 333200, fax 332645, Manjalikulam Rd)* is welcoming and has a good choice of rooms from Rs 230/295, or from Rs 450/550 with air-con. There's also an air-conditioned multicuisine restaurant called City Queen.

Hotel Regency *(☎ 331541, fax 331696, Manjalikulam Cross Rd)* has comfortable rooms for Rs 250/400, or Rs 750/950 with air-con, all with TV and phone. There are two restaurants, but at the time of writing the one on the rooftop was closed. Checkout is 24 hours.

Hotel Residency Tower *(☎ 331661, fax 331311, Press Rd)*, just off Manjalikulam Rd, is clean and comfortable with friendly staff. Singles/doubles cost Rs 390/590, or Rs 790/990 with air-con. It has a bar, nonveg restaurant, direct dial phones and TV.

Hotel Navaratna *(☎ 331784, YMCA Rd)*, just around the corner, is a favourite of Indian business travellers. It has rooms for Rs 220/250, or Rs 600 for an air-con suite. The modern rooms have satellite TV and direct dial STD, and there's a reasonable restaurant and coffee shop.

Wild Palms Guest House *(☎/fax 454071, Puthen Rd)*, off Convent Rd, offers a welcome break from the hotel environment. Situated in a quiet back street, this clean and cosy guesthouse has seven large, well-furnished and spotless rooms. Non air-con is Rs 845 and air-con starts at Rs 1145 and finishes at Rs 1595 for a huge deluxe suite complete with private balcony. Tariffs include breakfast, and dinner can be arranged.

If you want to get away from the bustle of the city and experience village life, you can try a homestay arrangement in Kariyam at ***Mele Panichal House*** *(☎ 695587)*, just 7km north of Thiruvananthapuram and 2km off the main Thiruvananthapuram-Kollam Highway from Sreekaryam Junction. A two bedroom apartment with kitchen, lounge and dining room costs Rs 500 per night (discounts for stays of over three days). Transport from the train station or airport can be arranged. If you need to get to the city, buses (Rs 2.50) leave every 20 minutes from Kariyam or even more regularly from the junction, to which it's a Rs 10 rickshaw ride. If you want to take it easy, meals (Rs 100 per person per day) and a car (Rs 800 per day) can be arranged. Prior bookings are necessary.

Places to Stay – Top End

Top-end accommodation in the city is tight so make sure you have a booking.

Hotel Luciya Continental *(☎ 463443, fax 463347, East Fort)* is close to the Sri Padmanabhaswamy Temple. It's centrally air-conditioned and has rooms from Rs 1775/2250, as well as more expensive suites, all with satellite TV and direct dial STD/ISD. There's also a bar, restaurant, coffee shop, bookshop, business centre and pool.

South Park *(☎ 333333, fax 331861, MG Rd)*, a swanky, centrally air-conditioned hotel farther north, has rooms for US$55/65 to US$100/110. It has one of the city's best restaurants, a coffee shop, a terrific cake shop and a bar.

KTDC Mascot Hotel *(☎ 318990, fax 317745, Museum Rd)*, north of the centre, is a pleasant hotel with a gloomy design. Rooms all have air-con and start from Rs 1195/1395. There's an air-con restaurant, a coffee shop, and an open-air bar and ice cream parlour near the pool.

Hotel Pankaj *(☎ 464645, fax 465020, MG Rd)*, opposite the Secretariat, has central air-con and rooms from Rs 1050/1405 up to Rs 2200 for a suite. There's a bar and two restaurants, one offering fine views from the top floor and a daily buffet lunch. Rooms have direct dial STD and satellite TV, and there are foreign exchange and travel desks.

The Heritage Point *(Tagor Nagar)* is a 1920s mansion that once belonged to the royal family of Travancore. The three double rooms (two downstairs and one up) are vast, airy and authentically renovated. Meals can be arranged in the large kitchen. Cultural shows are staged in the front garden and an elephant is sometimes on call to greet guests. The entire house can be yours for US$120 per night. If you want only one room it is Rs 2000. Book through Kerala Travels Interserve (☎ 324158, fax 323154).

Places to Eat

Maveli Cafe *(Central Station Rd)* is a bizarre, circular Indian Coffee House, next to the KSRTC long-distance bus stand. The food is good and cheap. Watch your knees on the tables.

Manacaud Restaurant *(Aristo Junction)* is a favourite for its authentic Keralan breakfasts from 7 to 9 am.

Ambika Cafe *(cnr Central Station and Manjalikulam Rds)* is a good spot for a cheap breakfast.

Prime Square, next door, has good-value veg and nonveg restaurants, as well as an ice cream parlour. It's a deservedly popular lunch spot.

Asok Veg Restaurant *(Manjalikulum Rd)*, farther north, is a typically inconspicuous but good-value 'meals' restaurant.

Hotel City Tower *(MG Rd)*, near the railway bridge, is another popular lunch spot; *thalis* (vegetarian plate meals) are Rs 15.

Central Station Rd has a number of vegetarian restaurants serving the usual thalis, and there are several good, cheap vegetarian places opposite the Secretariat on MG Rd, including ***Sree Arul Jyothi***, ***New Arul Jyothi*** and ***Ananda Bhavan***.

Rangoli *(MG Rd)* is south of the railway line, and has a small entrance leading to a neat and tidy air-con 'family restaurant' upstairs.

Azad Restaurant, a few doors north, is also clean, air-conditioned and good value.

Indian Coffee House is just off MG Rd, tucked away behind Spencer's Store.

There are restaurants in many of the hotels. ***City Queen Restaurant*** *(Manjalikulam Rd)*, in the Hotel Highland, serves very good Indian dishes and also does Chinese and western food. ***Gokulum*** in the Hotel Chaithram is a good air-con restaurant with tasty vegetarian meals at very reasonable prices.

Mascot Hotel, ***Hotel Pankaj*** and in particular ***South Park*** all have popular lunchtime buffets as well as being pleasant places for dinner. At the Mascot you can also eat outside – the menu's somewhat limited but the atmosphere's pleasant and service is very good.

The ***Mascot*** and the ***Chaithram***, both KTDC hotels, have outdoor ice cream parlours. Alternatively, try the engagingly named ***Snoozzer*** *(Press Rd)*, it has air-con and is a great escape from the midday heat.

Shopping

The SMSM Institute (☎ 330298, fax 331582), YMCA Rd, is a government-sponsored handicrafts outlet with the usual sandalwood carvings, textiles and bronzes. Visit here before paying big money in one of the private antique shops. Kairalai, also government sponsored, has an outlet at the Tourist Facilitation Centre on Museum Rd.

Natesan's Antiqarts (☎ 331594, fax 330689), opposite the Ayurveda College on MG Rd, has a collection of exquisite bronzes and some fine Keralan furniture. They even make items to order including carved swings for US$5000. Shipping can be arranged. Next door is Khadi Gramodyog Bhavan, with its full range of interesting handicrafts.

Hastkala Indian Arts & Crafts off MG Rd is a Kashmiri shop with all the usual artefacts, such as jewellery, trays, wooden boxes and cushion covers. For nuts, tea and coffee try Sankar's Tea & Coffee, on MG Rd. You'll also see many shopping complexes from where you can purchase basic items such as toiletries and stationery.

Chalai Bazaar, along Chalai Bazaar Rd, is a labyrinth of tiny streets with bustling stalls that sell everything from clothes and kitchenware to magazines and recorded music. For more bustle and trinkets try the Connemara Market.

General and personal items are readily available around town and at the conveniently located Spencer's Store, MG Rd.

Entertainment

Keep an eye out for the flags along the Secretariat fence. They'll inform you of many interesting events around town to which visitors are 'co-ordially invited'. See also Special Events, earlier.

Cultural Evenings The tourist offices as well as many of the hotels organise special cultural evenings that include Kathakali, kalarippayat and other demonstrations. You'll see details on the Secretariat fence or ask at tourist offices.

Film Several cinemas show films in Malayalam, Tamil, Hindi and English. For details of what's on and where, check the daily papers. ***Alliance Française*** *(☎ 327776)* also organises regular film festivals.

Dance Venues There are no actual nightclubs or discos as such, but the larger hotels such as ***Hotel Luciya Continental*** or ***South Park*** have bands where you might enjoy a dance.

Spectator Sports

Sporting events tend to be somewhat irregular. For details check at the Tourist Facilitation Centre (☎ 321132) or the local papers.

You can see students of kalarippayat sparring at their schools at CVN Kalari Sangham (☎ 474182) and Nair Kalari, Cotton Hill (☎ 65140).

Getting There & Away

See the Kovalam section for transport information on getting from Thiruvananthapuram to the beach.

Air Indian Airlines (☎ 438288) is on Museum Rd, next to the KTDC Mascot Hotel; the office is open 10 am to 5.35 pm daily, with a lunch break from 1 to 1.45 pm. Other airlines include:

Air India	☎ 328767
Air Maldives	☎ 461315
Gulf Air	☎ 322156
Jet Airways	☎ 325267
Kuwait Airways	☎ 328651
SriLankan (formerly Air Lanka)	☎ 328767

Most flights to Thiruvananthapuram are from other major Indian cities or from the Middle East (the result of the huge number of Malayalis who work overseas). Thiruvananthapuram is a popular place from which to fly to Colombo (Sri Lanka) and Male' (Maldives).

Bookings for all airlines can be made at the friendly and efficient Airtravel Enterprises (☎ 327627, fax 331704, email atetrv@md2.vsnl.net.in), New Corporation Building, Palayam. For details on flights from Thiruvananthapuram, see the table following.

Bus The KSRTC bus terminal (☎ 323886), opposite the train station, is total chaos.

Domestic Flights to/from Thiruvananthapuram (Trivandrum)

For international flight details, see the Getting There & Away chapter.

destination	airline	frequency (to Thiruv.)	frequency (from Thiruv.)	fare (US$)
Bangalore	IC	Tue, Thur, Sat	Mon, Thur	105
Chennai (Madras)	IC	Mon, Wed, Fri, Sun	daily	105
	9W	daily	daily	105
Delhi	IC	daily	daily	345
Mumbai (Bombay)	IC	daily	daily	175
	9W	daily	daily	175
	AI	Mon, Wed, Thur, Fri	Tue, Wed, Thur, Fri, Sun	175

Abbreviations: IC = Indian Airlines, 9W = Jet Airways, AI = Air India

The law of the jungle applies each time a battered old bus comes to a screeching halt in a cloud of dust.

Buses operate regularly to destinations north along the coast, including Kollam (Rs 17, 1½ hours), Alappuzha (formerly Alleppey, Rs 49, 3¼ hours), Ernakulam (Rs 57, five hours) and Thrissur (formerly Trichur, Rs 72, 6¾ hours). Buses depart hourly for the two hour trip to Kanyakumari (Cape Comorin). There are two morning buses daily for the eight hour trip to Thekkady (Rs 85) for Periyar Wildlife Sanctuary.

Most of the bus services to destinations in Tamil Nadu are operated by the Tamil Nadu state bus service (SETC). Its office is at the eastern end of the long-distance bus stand. It has services to Chennai (formerly Madras, eight daily, 17 hours), Madurai (10 daily, seven hours), Pondicherry (one daily, 16 hours), Coimbatore (one daily), as well as Nagercoil and Erode. KSRTC also operates several services daily to Coimbatore (Rs 68). Long-distance buses operate to Bangalore (Rs 198), but it's better to catch a train if you're going that far.

Buses to towns close to Thiruvananthapuram also operate from the municipal bus stand, near the Hotel Luciya Continental in the south of the town.

Train Although buses are generally faster, trains are a relaxing alternative.

The reservation office, on the 1st floor of the station building, is efficient and computerised but you should reserve as far in advance as possible because long-distance trains out of Thiruvananthapuram are heavily booked. The office is open Monday to Saturday 8 am to 2 pm and 2.15 to 8 pm; Sunday 8 am to 2 pm. If you're just making your way up the coast in short hops or to Kochi, there's no need to reserve a seat. The 'booking office' for buying tickets just prior to departure is open 24 hours.

Helpful telephone information lines are in Malayalam (☎ 1363), Hindi (☎ 1362) and English (☎ 1361).

Numerous trains run up the coast via Kollam and Ernakulam to Thrissur. Some trains branch off east and north-east at Kollam and head for Shencottah. Beyond Thrissur, many others branch off east via Palakkad to Tamil Nadu. To get to Udhagamandalam (Ooty) in Tamil Nadu, take a train to Coimbatore from where you can get connections to Mettupalayam and Ooty.

For long-haulers, there's the Friday-only *Himsagar Express* to Jammu Tawi, which goes via Delhi.

For more details on trains, see the table following.

Major Train Services from Thiruvananthapuram

destination	train No & name	departure time	distance (km)	duration (hrs/mins)	fare (Rs) (2nd/1st)
Alappuzha	6306 *Nagercoil-Guruvayur Exp*	8.15 pm	160	4.30	24/224
Bangalore	6525 *Kanyakumari-Bangalore Exp*	9.20 am	851	19.00	224/767
Chennai (Madras)	6320 *Trivandrum-Chennai Mail*	1.30 pm	920	18.30	235/805
Coimbatore	2625 *Kerala Exp*	11.00 am	390	9.30	89/447
Delhi	2625 *Kerala Exp*	11.00 am	3010	52.00	472/1213
	6317 *Himsagar Exp*	12.45 pm	3010	60.00	452/1983
Ernakulam	6349 *Parasum Exp*	6.00 am	224	5.00	61/286
(Kochi)	6329 *Malabar Exp*	5.40 pm	224	5.00	61/286
	6336 *Nagercoil-Gandidham Exp*	2.10 pm	224	5.00	61/286
Kannur	6329 *Malabar Exp*	5.40 pm	504	12.30	152/531
	6349 *Parasum Exp*	6.00 am	504	12.30	107/531
Kanyakumari	6526 *Kanyakumari-Bangalore Exp*	3.10 pm	80	2.30	29/150
Kasaragod	6329 *Malabar Exp*	5.40 pm	589	14.00	174/604
	6349 *Parasum Exp*	6.00 am	589	14.00	122/604
Kollam	1082 *Kanyakumari Exp*	7.15 am	65	1.40	26/129
	6525 *Kanyakumari-Bangalore Exp*	9.20 am	65	1.40	26/129
	6329 *Malabar Exp*	5.40 pm	65	1.40	26/129
	6302 *Venad Exp*	5.00 am	65	1.40	26/129
	6349 *Parasum Exp*	6.00 am	65	1.40	26/129
Kottayam	1082 *Kanyakumari Exp*	7.15 am	161	4.00	47/224
	6525 *Kanyakumari-Bangalore Exp*	9.20 am	161	4.00	47/224
	6329 *Malabar Exp*	5.40 pm	161	4.00	47/224
	6302 *Venad Exp*	5.00 am	161	4.00	47/224
	6349 *Parasum Exp*	6.00 am	161	4.00	47/224
Kozhikode	6329 *Malabar Exp*	5.40 pm	414	9.50	132/460
	6349 *Parasum Exp*	6.00 am	414	9.30	132/460
	2431 *Trivandrum-Rajdhani Exp* [1]	7.30 pm	414	7.30	655/1635
Mumbai (Bombay)	1082 *Kanyakumari Exp*	7.15 am	1540	42.00	311/1540
	6332 *Trivandrum-Kurla Exp*	4.20 am	1540	42.00	311/1540
	2431 *Trivandrum-Rajdhani Exp* [1]	7.30 pm	1540	25.00	2080/6070
Thrissur	1082 *Kanyakumari Exp*	7.15 am	382	6.30	88/434
	6525 *Kanyakumari-Bangalore Exp*	9.20 am	382	6.30	88/434
	6329 *Malabar Exp*	5.40 pm	382	6.30	88/434
	6302 *Venad Exp*	5.00 am	382	6.30	88/434

[1] Air-con only; includes catering

Getting Around

To/From the Airport The small, relaxed airport is 6km from the city, or 15km from Kovalam Beach. A No 14 bus from the municipal bus stand will take you there for Rs 2. Prepaid vouchers for taxis cost Rs 90 to stops in the city; Rs 190 to Rs 225 to Kovalam.

Local Transport Auto-rickshaws are your best bet for transport around the city. Flagfall is Rs 6, then around Rs 3 per kilometre. The drivers may not use meters but you can usually negotiate a fair deal. From the train station to the Napier Museum costs about Rs 15.

Local buses also operate around the city.

Car Hire Cars, with driver, may be hired from any number of travel agencies including Kerala Travels Interserve (☎ 324158, fax 323154), near Vellayambalam Junction. Prices average Rs 4 per kilometre for a non air-con Ambassador or Rs 7 with air-con. To travel outstation (beyond city limits) it's around Rs 1100 per day for up to 250km.

Motorcycle & Bicycle Hire Due to laws that proscribe that the owner of a vehicle must ride it, bike and cycle hire is not possible in Thiruvananthapuram (although this does occur in the more touristy centres such as Kovalam and Varkala).

If you're in the market to purchase a new or used scooter you might try the showroom at Kulathunkal Building, MG Rd (☎ 33366, fax 33251), next door to Higginbothams.

AROUND THIRUVANANTHAPURAM

Thiruvananthapuram can be used as a base from which to take a range of interesting day trips and excursions.

Chitranjali Studio Complex

Seven kilometres south of Thiruvananthapuram, along the old Kovalam road, the Chitranjali Studio Complex was established in 1980. The studios are set in 40 magnificently landscaped hectares that once formed a rubber plantation. Of the 75 Malayalam movies produced each year, around 20% are made in Kerala, most of the rest are produced in Chennai. In an attempt to lure the industry back to its home state the Kerala State Film Development Corporation provides generous incentives to local producers, including subsidised use of the studio complex. By 2001, the corporation aims to have 50% of Malayalam films produced locally.

The elevation allows spectacular views across the coconut trees, the airport and the Lakshadweep Sea. The studio grounds are dotted with various film sets as well as all the necessary infrastructure including editing, sound recording, indoor studios and a processing lab. If you have a genuine interest in film production you can organise a studio tour by contacting the studio manager (☎ 461450, fax 460946). The friendly staff may work to hectic schedules, but they are always willing to debate with fellow film buffs on the age-old topic of aesthetics and commercial viability.

Buses between Kovalam and Thiruvananthapuram bypass the old Kovalam road so you'll need to ask the driver to stop at the turn-off and then walk the remaining 2km. An easier way is to take an auto-rickshaw.

Padmanabhapuram Palace (TN)

Padmanabhapuram Palace, in Tamil Nadu, is 65km south-east of Thiruvananthapuram. It was once the seat of the rulers of Travancore, a princely state for more than 400 years, which included a large part of present-day southern Kerala and the western coast of Tamil Nadu.

The palace is an excellent example of Keralan architecture, superbly constructed of local teak and granite, standing within massive stone town walls. Dating from the 16th century, it is reputedly the largest wooden palace in India, with 127 rooms, many intricately carved in teak and the wood of the jackfruit tree. It consists of private dwelling areas, administrative sections, public spaces and a small temple. Narrow verandas surround many of the structures. Stairs from the small massage room lead to a large tank, once the bathhouse of the royals. There are closeted quarters, with small shafts in the walls from which royal women watched events in the world outside. A huge dining hall, 80m by 8m, once entertained up to two thousand people. As a gesture of patronage, the royals hosted Brahmin priests here.

The oldest parts of the palace date from 1550. The architecture is exquisite, with rosewood ceilings carved with floral patterns, windows with jewel-coloured mica, and floors finished to a high polish with a special compound of crushed shells, coconuts, egg white and the juices of local plants.

The 18th century murals in the puja (prayer) room on the upper floors have been beautifully preserved, and surpass even those at the Mattancherry Palace in Kochi. Ask your guide or at the curator's office for special access. You will have to wait around until any tour groups have left the vicinity and you will probably have to help the guide open the heavy trap door entrance.

The palace was occupied from 1550 to 1750 at which time the raja moved to Thiruvananthapuram. Of the 14 rajas that occupied this palace, the 13th, Marthanda Varma (1729-58), was the most powerful. He dedicated the palace to Vishnu and changed its former name, Kalkulam, to the present mouthful.

Chinese traders sold tea and bought spices here for centuries and their legacy is evident throughout the palace. There are intricately carved rosewood chairs, screens and ceilings as well as large Chinese pickle jars.

If you are visiting this part of the country, the palace is a must. Entry is Rs 2/4 and Rs 5 for a camera. Visitors are guided through in small groups, so you may have to wait a short time until enough people of the same language arrive to constitute a group. The tour is interesting if you ignore the petty sexist and racist comments. The palace is open 9 am to 5 pm (closed Monday).

Getting There & Away Padmanabhapuram is 5km over the border in Tamil Nadu. To get there, catch a local bus from Thiruvananthapuram or Kovalam Beach to Kanyakumari (Cape Comorin) and get off at Thuckalay (Thakalai). If approaching from the east take a bus from Kanyakumari to Thuckalay. From Thuckalay you have a few options for the remaining 2km to the palace – catch a bus (somewhat irregular), take a rickshaw or walk for about 15 minutes.

Alternatively, take one of the tours organised by the KTDC, see Organised Tours in the Thiruvananthapuram section for details. Another option is to organise your own taxi (about Rs 800 return) or arrange one through a private travel agency.

Aruvikkara

Aruvikkara, 16km north-east of the capital, can be visited en route to Ponmudi (see later in this chapter). Aruvikkara is the source of the city's water supply. There is a small temple here dedicated to Parvati (Bhagavati). From her inner shrine, via several open doors, she surveys the Karamana River as its waters surge across massive rocks. Just down from the temple, in a calmer section of the river, people feed rice and other delicacies to fish, believed to be sacred and protected by the goddess. This is a pleasant place to relax on the rocks, picnic and feed the fish. There are numerous small boys, who, for a few rupees, will supply you with edibles for the fish so you can contribute to the feeding frenzy. Bus 382 will bring you here from Thiruvananthapuram's municipal bus stand at 8 am or 10.55 am.

Mitraniketan

About 20km north-east of Thiruvananthapuram, Mitraniketan (Abode of Friends) is a development project based on the premise that education enables self-determination. Established in 1956 the centre now has 500 members, 300 of whom are students (most from Adivasi, or tribal, and scheduled caste communities), who are educated in the arts, technology, agriculture, sports and many crafts. The centre focuses on an awareness of cultural, social and ecological issues. It also undertakes research projects.

Currently the centre is investigating the possibility of new cattle breeds from wild species. The aim is to achieve a pedigree breed, more disease resistant than their domestic cousins. Visitors, with particular interests in these issues, are welcome to volunteer their services. Currently the centre is seeking the assistance of nurses, doctors, medical technicians, librarians and teachers. Accommodation (spartan) is provided from Rs 150 per day and includes all meals. If you are interested write to the Directors, Mitraniketan, Vellanad, Thiruvananthapuram, 695543. Enclose your resume and give full details of how you believe you may be able to contribute to the work of the centre.

Neyyar Dam & Wildlife Sanctuary

On the road to Ponmudi, 25km north-east of Thiruvananthapuram, you will pass the turn-off to Neyyar Dam and the surrounding sanctuary. These are popular picnic and day trip locations on weekends. The small **Crocodile Park**, breeds *Crocodylus palustris*, the marsh freshwater crocodile, which, due to hunting, was almost extinct. Information boards advise that mating occurs from December to February and that the female may lay from 15 to 60 eggs, which take 60 days to hatch. In spite of their protected status, the crocs don't seem too happy. Entry is free.

The **Lion Safari Park**, established to preserve the Indian lion, accommodates nine lions including two cubs, almost as big as their parents. A regular bus leaves from the Wildlife Information Centre for a 20 minute visit to the park. The bus hoons and hoots its way along the narrow road, shattering the peace of the Sivananda Ashram and scaring every duck, chook and child on the road. Once within the confines of the sanctuary you'll no doubt see the healthy and contented lions basking in the sun. The ranger will point out the 'lioness' – the one with the balls! Bus tickets cost Rs 10 (Rs 5 for children). There's a minimum payment of Rs 50 if the bus runs with one or two people.

To see the remaining wildlife, you must hire a boat, which will take you to an island reputedly teeming with elephants, bisons, tigers, deer and bears. Most travellers see some deer. Boat prices range from Rs 10 to Rs 40 depending on the size of the vessel and duration of the trip. Boats leave from the Wildlife Information Centre.

There are two **waterfalls**, Kombaikani and Meenmutti, which can be visited by a 2km walk to each.

Agastya House *(☎ 0471-290660)*, operated by the KTDC, has quite good rooms from Rs 200/250 for a single/double to Rs 300/350 with air-con. They have balconies with a fine view of the dam. Make sure you get a room away from the noise and smell of the bar on the 2nd floor. It's best to book, to ensure you get a room. The attached restaurant manages to serve huge numbers of people very tasty meals in a most efficient manner. Veg meals range from Rs 15, nonveg from Rs 20 with great thalis for Rs 20. And they serve cold beer.

Photography is permitted in the sanctuaries but strictly prohibited in the dam embankment area. Buses leave hourly for Neyyar Dam from the KSRTC long-distance bus stand in Thiruvananthapuram.

Sivananda Yoga Vedanta Dhanwantari Ashram

This ashram (☎ 0471-290493), about 25km north-east of Thiruvananthapuram, was established in 1978. It overlooks the Neyyar Dam and surrounding forested hills. Peaceful and welcoming, the ashram conducts two week yoga courses, starting on the 1st and 15th of each month. Beginners and advanced students may attend, and there are one-month courses for yoga teachers. Costs (donations) for the two week course range from Rs 150 to Rs 300 depending on whether you stay in a tent, dormitory or double room with bathroom. Prices include tuition and all meals, and prior bookings (up to 15 days) are recommended. Write to the ashram at PO Neyyar Dam, Thiruvananthapuram 695576.

Ponmudi & the Cardamom Hills

Ponmudi, a small hill resort just 61km from Thiruvananthapuram, makes for a pleasant day trip or overnight excursion. That said, there is not a lot to do here other than walk in the lightly wooded hills and valleys, frequent the beer parlour or just enjoy the slight relief from the humid coastal climate. The sad-looking deer park is hardly an attraction. The journey to Ponmudi, through banana, rice, rubber, teak, and finally tea and pepper plantations, provides glimpses of village life in the hills and along the picturesque banks of the Kalar River.

There *are* good views here, though perhaps not as spectacular as those farther north in the Ghats. Accommodation in the ***Government Guesthouse*** is arranged by ringing the manager (☎ 0471-890320). Basic doubles are Rs 45. The KTDC runs a vegetarian dining room as well as the ***Sabala Restaurant*** (veg and nonveg) and a beer parlour. Close to the guest rooms there's a post office and small snack bar that sells essentials as well as tea and spices.

The mix of lightly populated hills, carloads of young men and a bar suggests that women travellers should exercise due care, especially on weekends.

Getting There & Away Three or four KSRTC buses leave each day for Ponmudi from the long-distance bus stand at Thiruvananthapuram. At Nedumangad you will change to a smaller bus capable of negotiating the hairpin corners. A taxi booked through a tour agent will cost about Rs 900 for a half-day trip. The KTDC organises tours that include Ponmudi and Neyyar Dam, see Organised Tours in the Thiruvananthapuram section for details.

Peppara Wildlife Sanctuary

This small (53 sq km) reserve is about 50km from Thiruvananthapuram. While promoted in some tourist literature, it is actually off-limits to visitors, but plans are afoot to develop amenities here. Check first with the District Forest Office, Vazhuthacaud, Thiruvananthapuram (☎ 0471-325385).

Agastya Malai (Tamil Nadu)

At 1869m, Agastya Malai, about 60km north-east of Thiruvananthapuram, is the highest peak in the vicinity of southern Kerala but is actually situated just over the border in Tamil Nadu. In January and February you can take a 28km trek (one way) up the mountain. In your attempts to get there you may receive inconsistent advice. Ignore any advice that directs you to Agastya Malai via Neyyar Dam, or by boat from numerous other locations. All these routes may be possible but are reserved for forestry personnel. Take the authorised route only – the one described here. It's also an important pilgrimage path, especially at the festival of Shivaratri when thousands of pilgrims make the journey to the top. After the festival the track is closed until the following January.

The forest staff (see under The Trek, following) are particularly helpful. The watchers have a keen knowledge of the area and are well equipped to understand your safety needs. You'll learn much from them, particularly if you understand Malayalam. There are no resthouses; you just sleep somewhere out in the open along the way, so you'll need to be appropriately equipped. The guides receive a small payment from the Forest Department, but it's customary to leave a tip.

Permits You must obtain a permit by going in person to the Wildlife Warden's Office (WWO), PTP Nagar, Thiruvananthapuram. Permits cost Rs 50 per person, may take two days to process and are valid for two days only. Don't turn up at the starting point without a permit; the forest personnel here are very helpful but they have no authority to let you in without a permit, so you'll be politely referred back to Thiruvananthapuram.

The Trek The trek begins 59km north-east of Thiruvananthapuram at the Bonacaud Forest Station. It's open 9 am to 9 pm, but there's always someone there available for assistance. Make sure you arrive before 1 pm; you will not be permitted to begin the walk after this time. The walk takes two days. Guides/watchers, who are assigned at the Bonacaud Forest Station, are compulsory for all trekkers except experienced pilgrims.

At all times you must stay on the track and observe the guide's directions. You must bring all provisions including those for your guide. To ensure that food preferences are provided for, it's probably best that you purchase your needs in Thiruvananthapuram, and pay your guide (Rs 100) when you meet him. He will either have the food on hand, or make a quick trip to the nearby village to obtain it.

For the first 10km it's easy walking along a well-maintained path through forests of fig trees, palms and ferns, passing almost pristine waterfalls. The next 16km are steep as you make the final ascent taking in views of the Peppara and Neyyar dams. At the top there's a statue of the saint, Agastya.

Getting There & Away To get to the beginning of the trek, catch a bus to Bonacaud leaving daily at 5.50 am from the municipal bus stand in Thiruvananthapuram. The 2½ hour journey takes the Ponmudi road to Vithura (Vythira), then turns right for the remaining 19km. The bus will set you down at the Bonacaud Tea Estate. From here it's a 2km walk to the Forest Station. For the return journey the bus leaves the Bonacaud estate at 3.20 pm. Or if you prefer you can hire a jeep in Vithura which will cost about Rs 150 one way, or Rs 200 drop-off and pick-up. The jeep is permitted to take you directly to the Forest Station and the beginning of the trek proper. If you happen to stop at Vithura, ***Hotel Ganga*** serves a fiery chicken curry.

Oriental Research Institute & Manuscripts Library

At Kariavattom, just 15km to the north of Thiruvananthapuram, the library at the University of Kerala is reputed to hold over 65,000 palm leaf manuscripts. Eighty percent are in Sanskrit, with the remainder in numerous languages including Malayalam, Assamese, Bengali and Kannada. Copper plates, birch-bark and paper manuscripts are also held. The collection boasts a wide range of subjects including medicine, astronomy, astrology and philosophy with the writings of almost every notable ancient Malayali and Sanskrit writer held here.

The library is a result of efforts initiated by the Travancore rajas, over a century ago, to collect and store valuable manuscripts. It moved to its present building in 1982. As well as the Kerala palm leaves (some of which are 600 years old) the library holds leaves from other parts of India, and other countries including Nepal, Burma and Indonesia. The library has provided an important base for research and scholarship as well as producing over 100 publications.

It's open daily 10.30 am to 4 pm except Sunday, holidays and every second and fourth Saturday. There's no lunch break but if you can't find the man with the key, then you can't get in – even the director will not encroach upon the key man's functions. Regular buses come here from the municipal bus stand in Thiruvananthapuram.

Technopark

Also in Kariavattom, 5km north of Thiruvananthapuram and next door to the University of Kerala, Technopark is a state of the art international business and computing centre that presents a side of India that many locals are keen to promote. With links to the university as well as the Vikram Sarabhai Space Centre of the Indian Space Research Organisation, Technopark is attracting significant international investment. Travellers with a particular interest in computing technology are welcome to visit. Contact the public relations department (☎ 0471-417222, fax 417971) during business hours to arrange a time.

KOVALAM

☎ 0471

Thirty years ago Kovalam was a hippie idyll: a picture-perfect tropical beach; a traditional Keralan fishing village providing fresh fish, fruit and *toddy* (coconut beer); and about as far from decadent western civilisation as you could get and still hear Jim, Janis and Jimi. It is no longer the mellow backpackers' hang-out catering to budget travellers that it once was. Today this tiny beach is the focus of a multimillion dollar business, ferrying thousands of tourists from Britain and Europe on chartered jumbos for a two week dose of ozone, UV and a sanitised Indian 'experience'.

The result has been an influx of some get-rich-quick merchants, chaotic beachfront development, an uncontrollable avalanche of garbage, exorbitant prices, and desperate souvenir sellers. All of which threatens to destroy the ambience that made Kovalam so attractive in the first place.

But while it's far from paradise, Kovalam retains a certain charm and is still popular with backpacking travellers craving rest from the long haul across the subcontinent as well as families wishing to introduce their young children to Indian culture. With the downturn in tourism, it's not as busy as it used to be. The beaches are generally safe and clean (but see the notes under Dangers & Annoyances, later in this section), and the powerful Lakshadweep Sea swells are inviting and invigorating. There's little local colour left in the village behind the beach, though local fishermen still row their boats to sea each night.

Keep in mind that bold displays of flesh are offensive to local sensibilities, even on the beach.

Orientation

Kovalam consists of two palm-fringed coves (Lighthouse Beach and Hawah Beach) separated from less-populated beaches north and south by rocky headlands. The southern headland is marked by a prominent red-and-white striped lighthouse; the northern headland is topped by the Ashok Beach Resort. It's a 15 minute walk from one headland to the other. A maze of poorly lit paths runs through the coconut palms behind the beach, leading to a multitude of guesthouses and restaurants.

Information

There's a helpful tourist office just inside the entrance to the Ashok Beach Resort. Tourism Promotion & Information Centre – TOPIC (☎/fax 480431), just behind the Hawah Beach Restaurant, has a range of brochures and can offer advice on organised tours. It's open until around 10 pm.

The Central Bank of India has a counter at the Ashok Resort that changes travellers cheques quickly and without fuss. It's open Monday to Friday 10.30 am to 2 pm and on Saturday 10.30 am to noon. Up the road towards Kovalam village, Pournami Handicrafts is an authorised moneychanger, and is open 9 am to 6.30 pm daily. Wilson Tourist Home also has an official moneychanging counter.

There's a post office and a telephone centre (open Monday to Friday 9 am to 5 pm) in Kovalam Village.

Visit India (☎ /fax 481069), at the foot of Lighthouse Rd, is a friendly travel agency that can arrange ticketing, tours, and car hire. It's also an official moneychanger and has a fax and phone service.

Dangers & Annoyances Don't drink the local well water at Kovalam. There are so many pit toilets adjacent to wells that you're guaranteed to get very sick if you do. Stick to bottled water or bring a purifying kit.

Theft from hotel rooms, particularly cheap hotels, does occur. Ensure your room has a decent bolt and windows that lock, and stash your gear out of sight in a cupboard or under the bed. Keep an eye on any possessions you take to the beach.

It's safest to swim between the flags, in the area patrolled by lifeguards. Strong rips at both ends of Lighthouse Beach carry away several swimmers every year.

Kovalam is subject to electrical supply 'load-shedding' for 30 minutes every evening. Carry a torch (flashlight) after dark.

Activities

Surfboards and **boogie boards** can be rented from young men on the beach for around Rs 50 per hour.

Ayurveda

There are a number of Ayurvedic centres in Kovalam. Some just offer an oily massage others offer up to 21-day treatments including a special diet and daily massage. Medicus Ayurvedic Centre (☎/fax 480596), on Lighthouse Rd, offers a one hour body massage for Rs 300, plus several intensive treatments from two to 21 days. The 10 day treatment costs US$300 or US$600 including meals, massage and room. Twenty-one days is the minimum recommended duration to achieve a noticeable effect. At the Ayurveda & Naturopathy Massage Centre at the Hotel Samudra Tara, a one hour body massage costs Rs 250. The Arsha Ayurvedic Hospital treats people with pre-existing ailments. Contact Visit India (☎/fax 481069), Lighthouse Rd, for details. See the Around Kovalam section later in this chapter for more information on Ayurvedic centres.

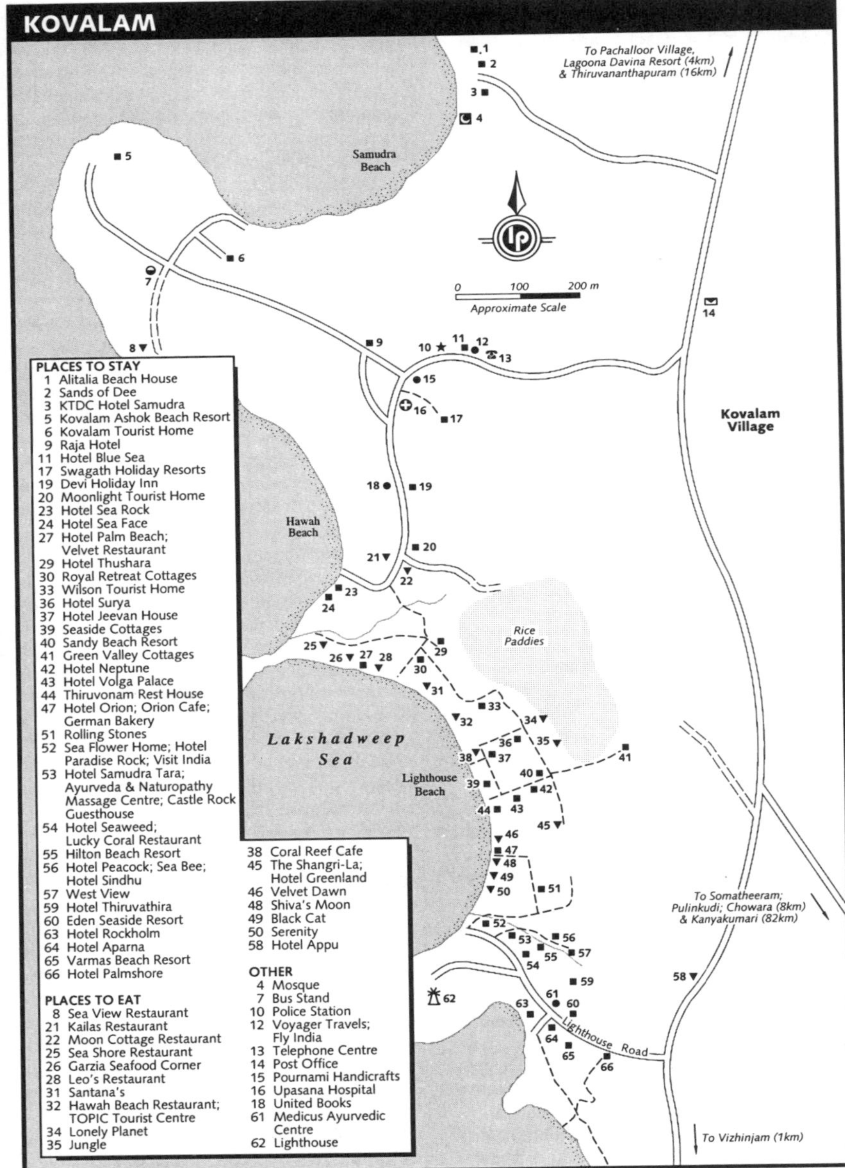
KOVALAM
To Pachalloor Village, Lagoona Davina Resort (4km) & Thiruvananthapuram (16km)
Samudra Beach
0 100 200 m
Approximate Scale
Kovalam Village
Hawah Beach
Rice Paddies
Lakshadweep Sea
Lighthouse Beach
To Somatheeram; Pulinkudi; Chowara (8km) & Kanyakumari (82km)
Lighthouse Road
To Vizhinjam (1km)
PLACES TO STAY
1 Alitalia Beach House
2 Sands of Dee
3 KTDC Hotel Samudra
5 Kovalam Ashok Beach Resort
6 Kovalam Tourist Home
9 Raja Hotel
11 Hotel Blue Sea
17 Swagath Holiday Resorts
19 Devi Holiday Inn
20 Moonlight Tourist Home
23 Hotel Sea Rock
24 Hotel Sea Face
27 Hotel Palm Beach; Velvet Restaurant
29 Hotel Thushara
30 Royal Retreat Cottages
33 Wilson Tourist Home
36 Hotel Surya
37 Hotel Jeevan House
39 Seaside Cottages
40 Sandy Beach Resort
41 Green Valley Cottages
42 Hotel Neptune
43 Hotel Volga Palace
44 Thiruvonam Rest House
47 Hotel Orion; Orion Cafe; German Bakery
51 Rolling Stones
52 Sea Flower Home; Hotel Paradise Rock; Visit India
53 Hotel Samudra Tara; Ayurveda & Naturopathy Massage Centre; Castle Rock Guesthouse
54 Hotel Seaweed; Lucky Coral Restaurant
55 Hilton Beach Resort
56 Hotel Peacock; Sea Bee; Hotel Sindhu
57 West View
59 Hotel Thiruvathira
60 Eden Seaside Resort
63 Hotel Rockholm
64 Hotel Aparna
65 Varmas Beach Resort
66 Hotel Palmshore
PLACES TO EAT
8 Sea View Restaurant
21 Kailas Restaurant
22 Moon Cottage Restaurant
25 Sea Shore Restaurant
26 Garzia Seafood Corner
28 Leo's Restaurant
31 Santana's
32 Hawah Beach Restaurant; TOPIC Tourist Centre
34 Lonely Planet
35 Jungle
38 Coral Reef Cafe
45 The Shangri-La; Hotel Greenland
46 Velvet Dawn
48 Shiva's Moon
49 Black Cat
50 Serenity
58 Hotel Appu
OTHER
4 Mosque
7 Bus Stand
10 Police Station
12 Voyager Travels; Fly India
13 Telephone Centre
14 Post Office
15 Pournami Handicrafts
16 Upasana Hospital
18 United Books
61 Medicus Ayurvedic Centre
62 Lighthouse

Organised Tours

Several travel agencies organise tours, which include three-hour jaunts in the backwaters, elephant rides in the hills, eight-day tours of South India or trips to the Maldives. If you like boating, walking or just sightseeing with minimal hassle then negotiate a deal with one of these agencies. The short backwater cruises on a traditional rice barge are a good counterbalance to the beach scene and the air of Thiruvananthapuram. As with other backwater tours in Kerala, you may get to go ashore and witness toddy tapping, coir (coconut fibre) making and boat building/repairing. A three hour boat trip costs about Rs 250 per person. If given the choice, elect to have a boat with proper sunshade – it's hot out there. And choose your boat operator carefully. The brochures promise much but some operators fail to deliver.

Places to Stay

There are dozens of places to stay at the budget end of the market – the coconut groves behind the beach are littered with small lodges, houses for rent and blocks of recently constructed rooms. Shop around – with the downturn in tourists you should be able to get a reduced rate especially if you are staying longer than a few days.

Prices climb the closer you get to the beach, and a few minutes walk can often mean lower prices or much better rooms for the same price. Some travellers regret paying the extra to be near the beach, which they find too noisy for sleep or relaxation. Prices climb even more dramatically when the package tourists begin to arrive, November to February is the high season but most places have a peak high season over the Christmas/New Year period when prices go even higher and rooms become scarce. From about 15 December to 7 January it is best to book ahead. Outside the high season it's a buyer's market, most places drop their prices by half. With the downturn in tourism, you should be able to get a bargain at any time. The prices quoted here are typical high-season prices excluding tax, unless otherwise stated. In the low season, prices drop to half, even a third of those stated here.

Places to Stay – Budget

Most, though not all, of the cheapest places are along or just back from the beach. There are others along the road from Thiruvananthapuram and along Lighthouse Rd.

Eden Seaside Resort *(☎ 481749, Lighthouse Rd)*, opposite the Varmas Beach Resort, is basic but all rooms have bathrooms; doubles cost Rs 550.

Hotel Thiruvathira *(☎ 480787)*, almost next door, has downstairs doubles for Rs 355 and upstairs doubles with balcony and bay views for Rs 500.

Hotel Samudra Tara *(☎ 481608)*, farther down Lighthouse Rd towards the beach, has clean and comfortable non air-con rooms for Rs 330 (Rs 450 with a balcony) and air-con rooms for Rs 800. There's an Ayurvedic massage and naturopathy clinic here as well (see Ayurveda, earlier).

Hotel Palm Beach *(☎ 481500)*, tucked behind the excellent Velvet Restaurant, has spotless and airy double rooms for Rs 400.

Castle Rock Guesthouse *(☎/fax 481995)*, next door and sharing the same entrance off Lighthouse Rd, has clean, non air-con singles/doubles for Rs 550/850, and air-con doubles are Rs 1100 (including breakfast).

Green Valley Cottages *(☎ 480636)*, in a wonderfully peaceful location next to the paddy fields, has clean, neat and colourful rooms with bathroom for Rs 500.

Hotel Greenland, also well back from the beach, is attached to the well-known Shangri-La restaurant. Simple but clean rooms cost Rs 330 for single or double occupancy.

Kovalam Tourist Home *(☎ 480441)*, a long walk back from the beach, has simple rooms with bathroom and air-con for Rs 400/450.

Sandy Beach Resort *(☎ 480012)* has refurbished rooms for Rs 560 and a restaurant.

Hotel Jeevan House *(☎ 480662)*, right behind the Coral Reef Cafe, has a range of accommodation from Rs 230 to Rs 1400.

Devi Holiday Inn is a clean and cosy place up the hill from the beach opposite

United Books. There's no phone (they've been waiting nearly three years) but at Rs 350/450 for singles doubles it's good value.

Other places worth considering include the no-frills ***Hotel Surya*** *(☎ 481012)*, just back from the beach, with rooms from Rs 240; and the beachfront ***Sea Flower Home*** *(☎ 480554)*, a touch too close to the drain, but friendly and clean with rooms for Rs 220 downstairs and Rs 440 for a balcony.

Hotel Paradise Rock *(☎ 480658)*, nearby, offers clean, small rooms for Rs 120/160.

Seaside Cottages *(☎ 481937)* has basic rooms for Rs 260 (single and double).

Thiruvonam Rest House *(☎ 480661)* is perhaps a tad overpriced at Rs 420, up to Rs 550 (with a balcony), but will rent an interesting looking air-cooler for Rs 130.

Rolling Stones has basic rooms for Rs 220 (single and double).

West View, a few minutes stroll from the beach, has standard rooms from Rs 160 to Rs 260.

Places to Stay – Mid-Range

The best hunting ground for mid-range hotels is Lighthouse Rd. Many of the newer hotels in this category may be booked out by charter tourism groups from December to April, but there are usually rooms available in November. The charter companies have demanded higher standards than backpackers and certain luxuries such as fridges, telephones and hot water are often found in each room.

Hotel Seaweed *(☎ 480391)* is an excellent, friendly and secure place with sea breezes and bay views. There's a wide variety of rooms from Rs 550 to Rs 1350, and Rs 1050 to Rs 1400 with air-con.

Hilton Beach Resort *(☎ 481476)*, nearby, has air-con singles/doubles costing Rs 1000/1400.

Hotel Peacock *(☎ 481395)* has non air-con rooms for Rs 550 and air-con rooms with fridge for Rs 900. Prices are inclusive of tax and there is a restaurant, the Sea Bee.

Hotel Rockholm *(☎ 480306)*, farther up Lighthouse Rd (ie away from the beach), is also an excellent choice. It has great views over the small cove beyond the lighthouse. Rooms cost Rs 1000/1100.

Hotel Aparna *(☎ 480950)* has doubles for Rs 1150 (inclusive of tax).

Varmas Beach Resort *(☎ 480478)* has balconies overlooking a small cove. Doubles are Rs 1390/1850 without/with air-con.

Hotel Palmshore *(☎ 481481, fax 480495)* fronts onto the private sandy cove south of the lighthouse headland, which is a pleasant escape from the frenetic activity on Lighthouse Beach. The rooms are pleasantly designed, all with bathroom and a balcony facing the sea. Doubles cost US$60 (US$65 with air-con).

Hotel Neptune *(☎ 480222)* is set back from Lighthouse Beach and has standard rooms for Rs 550, balcony rooms for Rs 600 and air-con rooms for Rs 800.

Hotel Volga Palace *(☎ 481663)* is similar with rooms ranging from Rs 450 for the ground floor to Rs 850 for the gloomy palace suite on the top floor.

Wilson Tourist Home *(☎ 480051)* is a few steps closer to the beach and slightly cheaper. It's large and friendly, with a range of non air-con rooms from Rs 450 and air-con courtyard rooms for Rs 1000. It also has moneychanging facilities.

Hotel Sea Rock *(☎ 480422, fax 480722)* on Hawah Beach is as close to the beach as you can get. In fact some guests complain that the ocean is too noisy from here. It's a good place from which to watch the fishermen haul in their catch, but it's way overpriced at Rs 1250 for a double, non air-con room. Maybe its prices match its planned upgrade.

Hotel Thushara *(☎/fax 481693)*, back in the coconut palms, has superbly built and beautifully furnished self-contained cottages and rooms for Rs 850.

Royal Retreat, next door, is a cluster of brand new air-conditioned cottages from Rs 850 to Rs 1000 a double. There are also non air-con singles from Rs 350 to Rs 800.

Moonlight Tourist Home *(☎ 480375, fax 481078)*, 300m south of Upasana Hospital, is popular and squeaky clean. The spacious rooms have poster beds and mosquito nets.

Doubles, some with small balconies, cost Rs 900, or Rs 1400 with air-con.

Hotel Orion *(☎ 480999)* is a friendly place overlooking Lighthouse Beach just 20m from the high-tide mark, and its prime position is reflected in its tariff. Doubles are Rs 1290 in the high season and suites (with air-con and fridge) are Rs 2250.

Hotel Blue Sea *(☎ 48140, fax 480401)* is away from the frenzy of beach life. It was once the family home of Sanji and Sabu, the brothers who have run it as a hotel for more than 20 years. Keralan-style three-storey cottages are located behind the house, in an attractive garden with a pool. It's well priced from Rs 700 for a ground floor room to Rs 1500 for a penthouse, but you may have to ask for clean linen. Prices include breakfast and tax. The hotel also has a very good restaurant.

Raja Hotel *(☎ 480355)*, well back from the beach, has sea-facing rooms with bathroom from Rs 1000 to Rs 2000 depending on the quality of the furniture. Non air-con rooms are Rs 800. It also has a bar and a veg/nonveg restaurant.

Places to Stay – Top End

Kovalam Ashok Beach Resort *(☎ 480101, fax 481522)* is superbly located on the headland at the northern end of the second cove. The hotel is centrally air-conditioned and has a bar, restaurants, swimming pool, sports and massage facilities, bank and bookshop. Room prices are Rs 4500/5000. Uninspiring cottages are Rs 500 cheaper, while the Castle suite costs Rs 16,000.

Hotel Sea Face *(☎ 481835, fax 481320)* is right on Hawah Beach. Standard rooms are Rs 2250 (Rs 2640 with air-con), deluxe rooms are Rs 3500, and suites are Rs 5000. All rooms have TV and direct dial facilities, and the pool overlooks the beach.

Swagath Holiday Resorts *(☎ 481148, fax 330990)* is set in well-tended gardens high above the beach looking over the coconut palms to the lighthouse. It has a range of comfortable rooms with TV and phone that cost from Rs 1000 to Rs 3500 (Rs 900 to Rs 1800 for non air-con). There's an excellent multicuisine restaurant (lawn-service available). Be warned: rooms with a view of the lighthouse are strafed with brilliant light all night long.

Places to Eat

Open-air restaurants line Lighthouse Beach and are scattered among the coconut palms behind it. Almost all the restaurants offer the standard menu: porridge, muesli, eggs, toast, jam and pancakes for breakfast, and curries or seafood with chips and salad for dinner.

At night, you stroll along the beachfront and select your fish from the enticing displays. The range of fresh seafood includes seer fish, barracuda, sea bass, catfish, king and tiger prawns, lobster and crabs. You can also select your preferred method of preparation. Fish in the tandoor is delicious but on the dry side. A sizzler is fish on a hot plate with a variety of spices. If you enjoy spicy food, be sure to ask for it – the default setting for the spices has been toned down for western palates. Always check the prices before ordering. Fish and chips with salad typically costs between Rs 90 and Rs 110, depending on variety and portion size; tiger prawns or lobster will push the price beyond Rs 400.

There's plenty of competition so don't be afraid to negotiate if the asking price is too high. The quality can vary widely from place to place and from month to month; ask other travellers or diners for their recommendations. Beer is available in most restaurants, but is expensive, even by Keralan standards – expect to pay at least Rs 70.

Santana's, ***Hawah Beach Restaurant***, ***Coral Reef Cafe***, ***Velvet Dawn***, ***Garzia Seafood Corner***, ***Velvet Restaurant*** (at Hotel Palm Beach), ***Leo's Restaurant*** and the ***Orion Cafe*** (at the Hotel Orion) all have a reputation for quality and value. Be patient when waiting for your meal: the best ones are marinated in a range of spices and can take up to 30 minutes.

Serenity, at the south end of the beach, turns out good travellers' breakfasts and recognisable 'spegatty'; nearby ***Black Cat*** and ***Shiva's Moon*** are similar. The ***Sea View***

Restaurant is popular all day long, and just beyond the headland the ***Sea Shore Restaurant*** is a wonderful spot to sip a beer while the sun sets. For cappuccino, apple strudel and croissants try the rooftop cafe at the ***German Bakery***.

There are quite a few places back from the beach, although seafood is not the number one concern.

Lonely Planet vegetarian restaurant is nicely situated by a water lily pond with two proud geese, plenty of fish and a rich birdlife including the occasional bright blue kingfisher. Excellent meals range from typical South Indian cuisine to a more westernised fare such as capsicums stuffed with potato and rice. Please note, Lonely Planet Publications has absolutely no connection with this restaurant and we are not planning to open a franchised chain!

Kailas Restaurant near Moonlight Tourist Home is run by the Lonely Planet restaurant. It's friendly with good music and excellent veg and nonveg meals.

Jungle is run by a couple of Italian guys; yes, there's pasta as well as other western, Indian and Chinese dishes. ***The Shangri-La***, ***Hotel Sindhu***, and ***Moon Cottage Restaurant*** are also worth a look.

If you get tired of the interminable wait for meals at the beachside places, consider the mid-range hotels back from the beach. These places have better equipped kitchens than the beach shacks and can turn out more consistent food with much greater speed.

Lucky Coral rooftop restaurant at the Hotel Seaweed is ever-popular.

The ***Rockholm***'s celebrated restaurant includes a terrace overlooking the sea.

At the ***Palmshore,*** you can eat indoors or on the open balcony. The ***Sea Rock*** has a balcony overlooking the beach. For a splurge, head off to the ***Ashok Beach Resort*** or the ***Swagath Holiday Resorts***, but don't expect a warm welcome if you haven't scrubbed up first.

Hotel Appu, well away from the beach, has the best cheap Indian food in Kovalam, and is packed with lunching locals from 1 to 1.30 pm.

On the beach, a number of local women sell fruit to sun worshippers. The ring of 'Hello. Mango? Papaya? Banana? Coconut? Pineapple?' will soon become a familiar part of your day. You'll soon establish what the going rate is and, after that, they'll remember your face and you won't have to repeat the performance. The women rarely have any change, but they're reliable about bringing it to you later. Toddy (coconut beer) is available from shops in Kovalam village.

Entertainment

During the holiday season, a shortened version of traditional ***Kathakali drama*** is performed every night except Sunday in Kovalam: every Monday, Wednesday and Saturday at the Hotel Neptune, and Tuesday and Friday at the Ashok Beach Resort. You can watch make-up and dressing from 5 to 6.45 pm and the program from 6.45 to 8.15 pm. Cost is Rs 100.

On some weekends, ***cultural programs*** of music and dance are held on the beach. Keep an eye out for the promotional banners. For a less cultural pursuit, western ***videos*** are shown twice a night in a number of restaurants.

Shopping

Kovalam Beach has numerous craft and carpet shops (usually of Tibetan, Kashmiri and Rajasthani origin), clothing stores (ready to wear and made to order), book exchanges, general stores selling everything from cornflakes to sunscreen, travel agencies, and even yoga schools. Beach vendors sell batik *lungis* (sarongs), beach mats, sunglasses and leaf paintings, while others offer cheap (and illegal) Keralan grass and other substances.

Getting There & Away

Bus The local No 111 bus between Thiruvananthapuram and Kovalam Beach runs every 30 minutes between about 5.30 am and 9.30 pm and costs Rs 4. The bus leaves Thiruvananthapuram (East Fort) from stand 19 on MG Rd, 100m south of the municipal bus stand, opposite the Hotel Luciya Continental. Although the bus starts out ridiculously overcrowded, it rapidly empties. At Kovalam, the buses start and finish at the entrance to the Ashok Beach Resort.

There are also direct services to Ernakulam (Rs 63, 5½ hours) and Kanyakumari, or Cape Comorin, in Tamil Nadu (Rs 22, 1½ hours, four daily) – good ways of avoiding the crush at Thiruvananthapuram. Kanyakumari is two hours away and there are four departures daily. One bus leaves each morning for Thekkady in the Periyar Wildlife Sanctuary (Rs 95, 8½ hours). Direct buses go to Kollam (Rs 20, two hours).

Taxi & Auto-Rickshaw A taxi between Thiruvananthapuram and Kovalam Beach will cost around Rs 250 depending on pick-up and set-down point. Auto-rickshaws make the trip for around Rs 100. It's best to arrive at the lighthouse (Vizhinjam) end of the beach because this is much closer to the hotels and there usually aren't as many touts around. Prepaid taxis from Thiruvananthapuram airport to the beach cost around Rs 190 to Rs 225. Don't assume a rickshaw will be cheaper than a taxi – shop around.

Getting Around

Kovalam is an easy place to walk around. For trips farther afield you can take a bus from the Ashok Beach Resort, or you can hire your own two-wheeler transport from Voyager Travels (☎ 481993) or the next door Fly India (☎ 481763). Both have well-maintained machines. Prices per day (including helmet and insurance) are Rs 500 for an Enfield Bullet, Rs 350 for a Honda (100cc) and Rs 300 for a scooter. Discounts are available after five days. You'll need a current driver's licence and you'll be asked to surrender a passport or an air ticket as security. Try to negotiate something less valuable.

AROUND KOVALAM

Vizhinjam

Vizhinjam (formerly Vilinjam – pronounced *Virinyam*) was a capital of the 7th to 11th century Ay kingdom. Rock-cut temples have been found around the village – reminders of the period when the kingdom was under Tamil influence.

This small fishing village, just 1km south of Kovalam Beach, is a sobering reminder of your geographic and cultural situation after the resort atmosphere of Kovalam. Its big artificial harbour is dominated by a pink and green mosque on the northern end and a huge Catholic church to the south; from Kovalam you can sometimes hear them trading amplified calls to prayer and mass in the early hours. Christian/Muslim relations have been tense during resettlement programs following the harbour project, erupting in periodic violence in recent years in which several villagers have died. The peace is now maintained by a permanent police presence and a 'no mans land' between the two harbourside settlements.

The beach is packed with boats that set out to fish at sunset. From the beach at night, you can see their lights strung like a necklace along the horizon.

The church of St Mary's, newly painted in pinks, yellows and mauves, towers above the village. A statue of Mary, in her guise as Star of the Sea, stands appropriately above the main altar. Tiny alleyways, covered in discarded betel, old fish and oil, lead from the mosque to the church.

It would be easy to offend locals and court danger by wandering into Vizhinjam in the same manner as going down to Kovalam Beach from your hotel. Take care in 'no mans land' – its edges, and several other areas, are well-used public toilets. The narrow paths and economic divide make a visit to Vizhinjam somewhat intrusive, so it's possibly best visited only by those who have religious or similar specific duties.

Pulinkudi & Chowara

☎ 0471

Eight kilometres south of Kovalam there are interesting alternatives to Kovalam's crowded beaches. To reach these establishments, organise transport through the resort, or take a taxi.

Dr Franklyn's Panchakarma Institute (☎ 481632, fax 222043), promoted as 'no

Ayurvedic tourist resort' is in Chowara. It offers treatments from a one hour massage for US$10, to a 51 day program for US$1650. You can also study courses on yoga (one hour US$5) massage (15 days US$750), Ayurvedic principles (one month US$750) and Ayurvedic treatment (one month US$1500).

The Surya Samudra Beach Garden *(☎ 480413, fax 481124)* is a small and very select hotel with individual cottages, many of them constructed from transplanted traditional Keralan houses. There are private beaches, a fantastic natural rock swimming pool and music, and martial arts or dance performances at night. The food is superb. Room rates range from US$100 to US$360. Ayurvedic treatments are available from US$10 to US$20 for one-off treatments, US$500 to US$1000 for two to three week treatments.

Somatheeram Ayurvedic Beach Resort *(☎ 481600, fax 480600)*, a little farther south at Chowara, combines beach life with Ayurvedic medical treatment. Room prices start at US$45 and stop at US$170. Various treatment packages are available, which cost extra, as do meals. There is a sister resort, ***Manaltheeram***, nearby.

Ideal Ayurvedic Resort *(☎/fax 481632, Chowara Beach)* offers luxury accommodation and a wide range of Ayurvedic treatments and courses. Room rates are from US$40 to US$50, with treatments from US$49 (seven days) to US$1100 (28 days).

Samudra Beach & Pozhikkara Beach
☎ 0471

At Samudra Beach, about 4km by road north of Kovalam, there are a number of resorts competing for space with the local fishing villages. Some of the ostentatious newer resorts are closed to all but charter tourists, and the steep and rough beach, often crowded with fishermen, is not as amenable for swimming as the beaches farther south. The pace is more relaxed than Kovalam, but this may change with the influx of charter tourists. Also, local resentment to tourism is discernible.

KTDC Hotel Samudra *(☎ 480089, fax 480242)*, a pleasant retreat from hectic Kovalam, has been recently renovated. It offers top-quality service with all rooms facing the sea. Air-con doubles range from Rs 1800 to Rs 3990.

Sands of Dee *(☎ 480887)* would appear to be vulnerable to a king tide and certainly offers beach frontage. Pleasant rooms go for Rs 800 and there's a restaurant.

Alitalia Beach House *(☎ 480042)*, run by the amiable Shah Jahan, has singles/doubles for Rs 550/1100. There is also a rooftop restaurant.

As well as the restaurants associated with the hotels, there are several seafood/tandoori restaurants set up on the beach, such as the ***Fat Fish***, producing the usual offerings found at Kovalam's beachfront restaurants.

Lagoona Davina *(☎ 480049, fax 450041)*, at Pachalloor village, behind Pozhikkara Beach, 5km north of Kovalam, is a small, exclusive resort with several tiny cabins, which cost from Rs 3750 for room and breakfast. Lunch and dinner (and you are a long hike from other restaurants) costs Rs 950 per person. It's quiet, peaceful and isolated. There is a boat that shuttles across the narrow lagoon to the beach, and backwater trips are available.

Neyyattinkara & Aruvipuram

Just 20km south-east of Thiruvananthapuram, on National Highway 47, the town of Neyyattinkara is historically significant. It's alleged that during conflict with his attackers, Marthanda Varma hid in an *ammachi plavu* (jackfruit tree) at the Sri Krishna Swamy Temple (Hindus only), which dates from 1757. There are no trees there now.

Four kilometres farther east, Aruvipuram (Village of Flowing Water), on the Neyyar River, attracts many pilgrims, who believe the energy of the torrential waters has healing qualities. Steps lead to the waters, enabling pilgrims to dip in a foot or fill a container – the force of the waters prohibits bathing.

A few metres before the steps, there's a branch of the ***Sree Narayana Dharma Sangham Trust*** and a small shrine devoted to Sri

Narayana Guru (1855-1928), who preached 'one caste, one religion, one god for humanity'. It was here at Aruvipuram in 1888 that the guru began his teaching that formed the basis for social reform and spiritual practice. Non-Malayalam speakers may have difficulty with translation here so it's best to obtain information from the headquarters at Varkala (see the Varkala section, later in this chapter).

The small Shiva temple nearby is the site of festivities particularly at the time of Shivaratri (February/March) when Shiva is honoured with chanting and the anointing of the lingam.

This is a peaceful area, but unless you're a devotee or pilgrim seeking healing you may not find it of interest. There's no accommodation and the eating houses are basic.

You can get a bus to Neyyattinkara from the municipal bus stand in Thiruvananthapuram. To get to Aruvipuram catch another bus from Neyyattinkara. It's Rs 2 for the 4km journey, but you'll probably find it easier to hire transport.

VARKALA

☎ 0472 • pop 41,400

Varkala is a developing beach resort 42km north of Thiruvananthapuram. One look and it's apparent that authorities have not learned from the mistakes made at Kovalam. Several inappropriate developments already mar the beach, and the garbage is piling up fast. Cultures mix – sometimes easily, other times not so easily. Fat white swimmers, reddened by the sun, lie almost naked watched by slender locals on their way to prayers at the nearby mosque. The narrow divide, a small stream, is used as a toilet.

Nevertheless, the Lakshadweep Sea sunsets, volleyball with the locals, religious discussions with devotees and good food are unlikely to be forgotten in a hurry.

Orientation & Information

The town and the train station are 2km from the beach, which lies beneath towering cliffs and boasts a mineral water spring.

Varkala's beach can disappear almost entirely during the monsoon, gradually reappearing in time for the tourist onslaught from November to February.

> **Coastal Dangers**
>
> Like much of the Keralan coast, Varkala experiences strong coastal rips. Sadly, each year lives – even those of experienced swimmers – are lost to the turbulence of the tides. Take great care, and don't swim too far from the beach. See the Dangers & Annoyances section in the Facts for the Visitor chapter for what to do if you find yourself caught in a rip.

The post office is south of most of the restaurants, just before the helipad. There's a police aid post nearby.

An email facility exists in theory but at the time of writing the server had been down for three months.

The very friendly Bureau de Change (☎ 602749) at Temple Junction cashes travellers cheques, has an STD/ISD phone service, cold drinks and film, and can arrange taxis at fair rates. It's open daily 9 am to 10 pm. Efficient money exchange is also available at JK Tours & Travels (☎ 600713), opposite the Sree Padman Restaurant.

The Tourist Helping Centre, at the beach end of Beach Rd, is a friendly travel agency that organises elephant rides (full day, Rs 800 including Keralan lunch) and backwater trips (full day, Rs 600 including lunch). It also arranges longer, overnight trips to the tea plantations, rubber factories and forests near the Tamil Nadu border (Rs 1000 including food and accommodation). There's a privately run Tourist Information Centre just near the post office, which is primarily for ticketing and tour bookings. There are a number of other travel agencies that can organise sightseeing trips, taxis, air tickets and hotel reservations (but see the boxed warning 'Beware Varkala's Middlemen' in this section).

Several shops stock basic supplies, for more exotic shopping try the Little Tibet Refugee Market on the clifftop. Along

Beware Varkala's Middlemen

Middlemen posing as travel agents and promoting bogus adventures proliferate in Varkala. Some travellers pay what they believe to be a full fee for a tour or activity, only to learn that payment at the other end has not been passed on to the operator. They then have to cough up again.

Another trick is for the boat guide to ply passengers with plenty of 'complimentary' drinks and to present a massive drinks bill at the journey's end.

If you are planning a backwater trip or any other journey, book wisely. Ask many questions, shop around, take notes and don't pay a single rupee until you have clarified that all bookings have been confirmed and will be paid for. As usual, seek the opinions of other travellers. Obtain advice and recommendations from the KTDC in Thiruvananthapuram before setting out.

Beach Rd, Maria Spices sells a range of oils, spices, coffee and incense.

Many small stores offer a limited range of food items plus a few handy essentials such as soap, batteries, razors and condoms.

Janardhana Temple

Despite initial perceptions, Varkala is first and foremost a temple town with a sacred beach. The Janardhana Temple is at Temple Junction at the beginning of Beach Rd. Janardhana refers to Krishna and means 'the revered of humankind'. A shrine at this site may have existed for over 800 years – certainly temple chronicles date from this time – although some authorities place its origins as far back as 2000 years. Non-Hindus are not permitted to enter the inner sanctum but may be invited to wander around the temple grounds with its huge banyan tree and shrines to deities such as Ayyappan, Hanuman and others.

Sivagiri Mutt

This is the headquarters of the Sree Narayana Dharma Sangham Trust (☎ 602221, fax 550651). The ashram is devoted to Sree Narayana Guru (1855-1928) who preached 'one caste, one religion, one god for humanity' and attracted a large following among the lower castes. Inquiries are welcome.

Yoga, Massage & Ayurveda

There are numerous centres for yoga and massage. Some of these places are seasonal and the quality of offerings varies. At the **Progressive Yoga Centre** (no phone) a one week yoga course is Rs 450, lessons in Ayurvedic massage cost Rs 1750 for one week, and a massage costs Rs 180 for just over an hour. Meditation is taught by Swami Sukshmaanda from Sivagiri Mutt. At the **Scientific School of Yoga & Massage** (no phone) you can enjoy a 1½ hour massage combining Ayurvedic and Swedish techniques (Rs 200), attend a meditation course (Rs 500), learn yoga over five days (Rs 500) or learn Ayurvedic and Swedish massage techniques over 10 days (Rs 3000, Rs 5000 per couple).

Places to Stay

Most places to stay are at the beach, either at Temple Junction, on Beach Rd, or 500m north along the clifftops. As at Kovalam, prices vary considerably depending on the season, and it pays to shop around. At the

Reclamation at Janardhana

Many legends surround the temple at Varkala. One tells of the original temple being engulfed and destroyed by tidal waves. Years later, a Pandyan king came to the site to do penance to Brahma. Brahma pardoned him and in return the king built another temple. In a dream he was informed of the location of the original temple idol, now deep beneath the sea. With the help of local fisherfolk he reclaimed the idol and reinstalled it in the temple. As the ceremony for consecration was taking place, devotees were struck with awe, as Brahma appeared and duly completed the rituals.

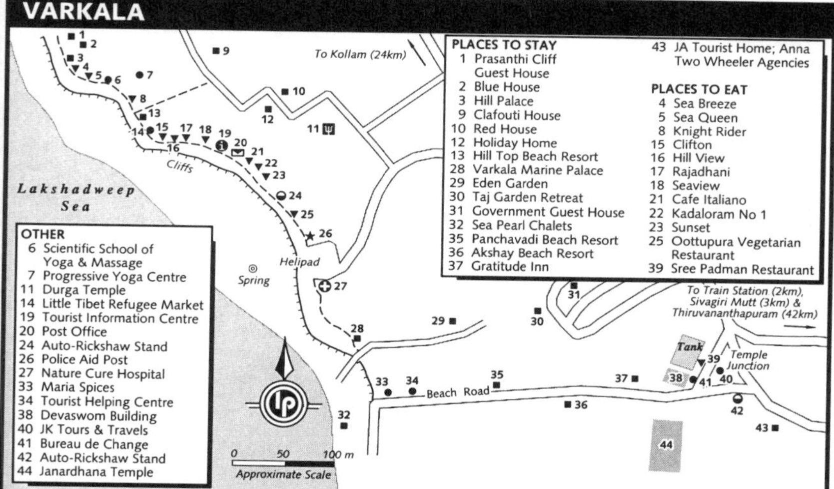

budget and mid-range end, rooms are generally clean and good value for money. All prices quoted here are for the high season (December to January) and do not include tax unless otherwise stated.

Places to Stay – Budget

Anandan Tourist Home *(☎ 602135)*, opposite the train station, is neat and orderly and has rooms for Rs 150, or Rs 300 with air-con and TV.

Government Guest House *(☎ 402227)*, north of the Janardhana Temple, near the Taj Garden Retreat, has cavernous rooms in a former palace belonging to the raja of Travancore. It's a bit spooky, but at Rs 55 these rooms, with bath, are a bargain. However, it's a long haul to the beach and cheap restaurants.

JA Tourist Home *(☎ 602453)*, close to the Janardhana Temple, has basic accommodation ranging from Rs 75 to Rs 150.

Gratitude Inn *(Beach Rd)* has small, clean singles/doubles for Rs 100/150. You may also be asked to purchase handicrafts from the owner's Cottage Emporium.

Akshay Beach Resort *(☎ 602668)* has single rooms with shared facilities for Rs 100 and singles/doubles with bath for Rs 150/200. Air-con doubles cost Rs 500.

Varkala Marine Palace *(☎ 603204)* has rooms from Rs 200 to Rs 500 (cold water only). It also has an open-air tandoor restaurant overlooking the beach.

On the cliffs, 10 minutes walk north (follow the indistinct path beside the Varkala Marine Palace), accommodation is provided by small hotels and local families who offer rooms from around Rs 300. Some places to stay haven't yet acquired names, so just look for the ***Blue House*** or ***Red House***.

Prasanthi Cliff Guest House is run by the folks at Cafe Italiano (make inquiries there) and has three small, charmingly decorated but low-ceilinged rooms with common bath for Rs 250.

Hill Palace has very basic though acceptable rooms for Rs 75 with shared facilities or Rs 125 with bath.

Holiday Home *(☎ 601054)* is new, quiet and very good value at Rs 200 for a double.

Places to Stay – Mid-Range & Top End

Eden Garden *(☎ 603910, fax 481004)*, overlooking the paddy fields, is delightfully situated. The 10 rather small, low-ceilinged rooms are Rs 350 for doubles. There is an in-house masseur.

Hill Top Beach Resort has simple rooms with bathroom for Rs 700 downstairs and Rs 800 upstairs. There's a restaurant.

Panchavadi Beach Resort *(☎ 600200)*, almost opposite Akshay Beach Resort, has six small rooms for Rs 400 and two family rooms (each with two double beds) for Rs 700. There's hot water but no air-con.

Clafouti House *(☎ 601414)* offers an intimate home-like atmosphere with clean double rooms for Rs 300. The daily display of French pastries is totally seductive. One bite and your yoga or Ayurvedic treatment will be immediately negated.

Sea Pearl Chalets *(☎ 605875)* consists of 10 concrete wigwams on the headland south of Beach Rd. The four rooms overlooking the sea cost Rs 500 a double, the others are Rs 400. The wigwams are self-contained and the beds have mosquito nets.

Taj Garden Retreat *(☎ 603000, fax 602296)*, a resort set among terraced gardens and coconut palms overlooking the beach, eclipses every other building in this tiny hamlet and is certainly a harbinger of future developments. Standard air-con rooms are US$80/90 to US$110/120. There's a restaurant, bar, pool, tennis courts and a health club.

Places to Eat

Since a drunken tourist allegedly fell over the clifftop, Varkala has been declared a dry area (no alcohol available). If you are desperate, however, ask for the special coffee!

Anandan Tourist Home, opposite the train station, has a restaurant downstairs.

Sree Padman Restaurant, perched right at the edge of the tank at Temple Junction, is popular with locals and travellers alike. The restaurant is divided into an Indian and a tourist section. The Indian section generally serves tastier and more authentic food.

Clafouti House & Bakery has delicious French pastries and coffee.

Many of the clifftop eating places are seasonal, opening up at the northern part of Varkala Beach from November to February. The clifftop restaurants are: ***Sea Breeze***, ***Sea Queen***, ***Knight Rider***, ***Hill Top***, ***Clifton***, ***Hill View***, ***Seaview***, ***Rajadhani***, ***Cafe Italiano***, ***Kadaloram No 1*** and ***Sunset***. All these restaurants offer similar standards (shaky tables and a diverse collection of rickety chairs), similar food (fresh fish on display out the front at night) and similar service (usually incredibly slow). A small tuna cooked in the tandoor served with rice or chips and salad costs about Rs 100.

For vegetarians, ***Oottupura*** serves a range of dishes.

Entertainment

Kathakali performance can be experienced in the atmospheric, though stiflingly hot, surroundings of the old ***Devaswom Building*** beside the tank at Temple Junction. Facial make-up and costume dressing is from 5 to 6.45 pm and the program with English commentary is from 6.45 to 8.15 pm. Performances are every Sunday, Wednesday and Friday during December and January and cost Rs 75.

Getting There & Away

Varkala is 42km north of Thiruvananthapuram (by train, Rs 21/112 in 2nd/1st class, 55 minutes) and just 24km (by train) south of Kollam (Rs 18/100, 45 minutes). There are regular buses to/from Thiruvananthapuram and Kollam that stop at Temple Junction. Look for the timetables in the Bureau de Change. From Varkala, it's easy to get to Kollam in time for the morning backwater boat to Alappuzha. A taxi from Thiruvananthapuram direct to Varkala Beach costs about Rs 550 (Rs 650 from Kovalam).

Getting Around

Auto-rickshaws shuttle back and forth between the train station and Varkala's Temple Junction for Rs 20. A taxi to the beach costs about Rs 60. You can hire a 350cc Enfield

Bullet (Rs 350 per day), a small Yamaha (Rs 300 per day), a Kinetic Honda (Rs 250 per day) or a Hero bicycle (Rs 40 per day) from Anna Two Wheeler Agencies, on the ground floor of JA Tourist Home on Beach Rd.

ANJENGO FORT

Having acquired the permission of the rani of Attingal, the British East India Company established its first factory in Kerala at nearby Anjengo (also known as Anchuthengu) in 1684. The outer wall, all that remains of the fort, is now protected as an archaeological site, and is almost eclipsed by coconut trees. While the ruins aren't much to look at, the solid fortifications make it not too difficult to appreciate the courage and determination that was needed to do a little trading on the spice coast.

From the south Anjengo can be reached along the National Highway 47. The turn-off to the fort is 2km north of Anjengo town, then it's another 11km to the fort. Regular buses make the journey.

Explosive Devotions

In Keralan temples you'll often find the peace shattered by massive bangs. Fear not! This is not a military crackdown. It's a unique devotion to the gods, known as *vedi vashipadu* (explosive devotion). Such explosions may once have served a practical purpose – warding off wild animals. Today, however, they are purely symbolic.

It's worth watching the man prepare the big bang, usually just outside the temple, but if you're sensitive to loud, sudden noises, maintain a good distance. The vedi man scoops gunpowder into a cast iron shell, rams broken masonry on top, places the shell on the ground and puts a flame to it. He has about two seconds to get clear before the air is ripped apart by the thunderous noise.

Multiple explosions are known as double or triple vedis and depend on the rupees contributed by the devotee.

From Varkala, Anjengo is about 15km – around Rs 100 for the return trip by autorickshaw – and the trip alone is time well spent. You travel alongside the beach through thatched fishing villages, first Muslim then Christian/Hindu, always accompanied by the smell of fish drying in the sun.

KOLLAM (Quilon)

☎ 0474 • pop 374,400

Surrounded by coconut palms and cashew plantations, on the edge of Ashtamudi Lake, Kollam is a typical market town, where the red-tiled roofs of the few remaining old wooden houses, overhang winding streets.

Kollam is also the southern gateway to the backwaters of Kerala, and is most well known as the starting or finishing point for Kollam-Alappuzha backwater cruises (see the boxed text 'The Backwaters', following, for more information).

It was here in 825 CE that the then king of Travancore, Udaya Marthanda Varma, is reputed to have established a new calendar and therefore a new era. The town's later history is interwoven with the Portuguese, Dutch and English rivalry for control of the Indian Ocean trade routes and the commodities grown in this part of the subcontinent.

Thirteen kilometres south of Kollam, Paravur, now a bustling market town, is the birthplace of two of Kerala's leading literary figures – KC Kesava Pillai and Kesava Asan, both of whom lived from the mid-19th to early 20th centuries.

Information

There's a very helpful DTPC tourist information centre (☎ 745625, fax 742558) near the KSRTC bus stand (open daily 9 am to 5.30 pm) and another at the train station.

At the Bank of Baroda, opposite the Hotel Sudarsan, you can cash travellers cheques slowly, or you can go to the DTPC tourist information centre, where you'll get government rates, more quickly, 10 am to 2 pm.

Email and Internet browsing are available at the DTPC Automation Centre (part of the DTPC tourist information centre) and also at the highly efficient Net 4 You (☎ 741266) at

The Backwaters

Fringing the coast of Kerala and winding far inland is a vast network of lagoons, lakes, rivers and canals. These backwaters represent a unique geological formation and are the basis of a distinct lifestyle. Travelling the backwaters is one of the highlights of a visit to Kerala. The larger boats are motorised but there are numerous smaller boats propelled by human muscle and a long bamboo pole. The boats cross shallow, palm-fringed lakes studded with cantilevered Chinese fishing nets, and travel along narrow, shady canals where coir (coconut fibre), copra (dried coconut meat) and cashews are loaded onto boats.

Along the way are small settlements where people live on narrow spits of reclaimed land only a few metres wide. Although surrounded by water, they still manage to keep cows, pigs, chickens and ducks and small vegetable gardens. Prawns and fish, including the prized *karimeen*, are also farmed, and shellfish are dredged by hand to be later burnt with coal dust to produce lime. On the open stretches, traditional boats with huge sails and prominent prows drift by.

Tourist Cruises The most popular backwater cruise is the eight hour trip between Kollam and Alappuzha. You can also explore the backwaters near Valiyaparamba, see the boxed text 'Northern Backwaters' in the Northern Kerala chapter.

There are virtually identical daily cruises operated between Kollam and Alappuzha on alternate days by the Alleppey Tourism Development Co-op Society (ATDC) and the state government District Tourism Promotions Council (DTPC). The ATDC office is in Komala Rd, Alappuzha, while the Alappuzha DTPC can be found at the Tourist Reception Centre. In Kollam, the DTPC is near the KSRTC bus terminal.

Many hotels in Kollam and Alappuzha take bookings for these services. The cost is Rs 150 one way. Direct bookings with DTPC in Kollam attract significant discounts for all, students and pensioners discounts are greater. There are many new arrivals on the scene, some of which are competitively priced. Cruises depart at 10.30 am and arrive at their destination at 6.30 pm.

Generally only two major stops are made along the way: a midday lunch stop and a brief afternoon *chai* (tea) stop. **Ayiramthengu** or the coir village of **Thrikkunnappuha**, and the island of **Lekshmithuruthu** are popular stopping places. Lekshmithuruthu is the lunch stop. Here you can witness a 15 minute demonstration of Kathakali expressions and gestures. While this provides a good basis for understanding a performance, at Rs 250 per person, it is somewhat overpriced. A better option is to stay overnight and witness a performance that begins at 5.30 pm. Basic accommodation can be arranged for Rs 200 per double. You can then pick up the boat the following afternoon. To book ring ☎ 0476-826449.

The crew have an ice box full of fruit, soft drinks and beer to sell, although you might want to bring along additional refreshments and snacks. Bring sunscreen and a hat as well.

Boats also stop at the **Matha Amrithanandamayi Mission** (☎ 0476-897578, fax 897678) at Amrithapuri. This is the headquarters of Sri Matha Amrithanandamayi Devi, one of India's very few (but in this case very much revered) female gurus, popularly known as 'The Hugging Mother' (see 'The Mother of all Hugs' boxed text, later). Visitors should dress conservatively and observe the strict code of behaviour. You can stay at the ashram for Rs 100 per day (includes meals), and you can pick up an onward or return cruise a day or two later. The trip also passes the **Kumarakody Temple**, where the noted Malayalam poet Kumaran Asan drowned. Close to Alappuzha, is the 11th century **Karumadi Kuttan Buddha image** near the canal bank.

The cruise between Alappuzha and Kottayam is shorter – about 4½ hours (it follows a longer route than the ferry, see later in this section) – and stops are made to sample toddy, to have a

EDDIE GERALD

LINDSAY BROWN

PAUL BEINSSEN

he many faces of the backwaters: a moored fishing boat is enveloped by water hyacinth; stillness at
nset; the turbulent excitement of the snakeboat races.

ALL PHOTOGRAPHS BY LINDSAY BROWN

The backwaters at work: ferrying passengers near Alappuzha (**top**); washing saris on Monroe Island (**middle left**); a *kettuvallam* houseboat in Kollam (**right**); sand for construction is dredged by hand from beneath the backwaters (**bottom**).

The Backwaters

quick look at a snakeboat, and to visit an old church in **Pulincunnu** – note the umbrella on the statue of Jesus. The operator is a new cooperative, the Bharath Tourist Service Society (BTSS, ☎ 0477-262262), based in Alappuzha at the Raiban Shopping Complex on Boat Jetty Rd, and the cost is Rs 100 one way. Boats depart Alappuzha at 9.30 am, and Kottayam at 2.30 pm.

The DTPC also runs a popular four hour cruise that departs Alappuzha at 10 am and returns at 2 pm. This cruise is daily during December and January, and on weekends during the rest of the year. The cost is Rs 100, or Rs 60 concession (students and children). Many people prefer this shorter trip to a full day on a boat, and it also navigates some of the narrower waterways, offering a more intimate glimpse of backwater life.

Houseboats & Charters A very popular, but at times overpriced, option is to hire a houseboat, converted from a *kettuvallam*, or traditional rice barge. There are many companies in Alappuzha providing these houseboats, all following in the footsteps of the ATDC, which has several new boats coming on stream. Boats can be chartered through the DTPC in Kollam and Alappuzha. Houseboats cater for groups (up to eight bunks) or couples (one or two double bedrooms). They can be hired either on a day basis (Rs 3500 per boat) or overnight (Rs 5000), allowing you to make the Kollam-Alappuzha trip over two days, mooring in the backwaters overnight. Delicious Keralan food can be provided for an extra Rs 400 per person.

The DTPC also hires four-seat speedboats for Rs 300 per hour, and slower six-seaters for Rs 200 per hour. Between a group of people, this can be quite an economical proposition and allows you to make stops and plan your own itinerary – an option not available on the public ferries or tourist cruises. In Alappuzha, the baby blue tourist boats are moored across the North Canal from the boat jetty. Go directly to the boats if you don't want to deal through an intermediary tout. A one-way trip to Kottayam costs about Rs 500. Alternatively, there are boat operators like the efficient Penguin Tourist Boat Service (☎ 0477-261522) on Boat Jetty Rd. It has a long list of suggested backwater trips from Alappuzha. Vembanad Tourist Services (☎ 0477-251395) and Blue Lagoon (☎ 0477-260103), both in Alappuzha, also have boats for hire.

Backwater Village Tours An increasingly popular way to explore the backwaters is on a village tour. Usually this involves small groups of less than 10 people, a knowledgeable guide and an open work boat or covered kettuvallam. The tours last from 2½ to six hours. You are taken to villages to watch coir making, boat building, toddy tapping and fish farming, and on the longer trips a traditional Keralan lunch is provided. These tours are more rewarding to the tourist and the villagers, and they are very accessible – some of the best village tours operate out of Kochi and Kollam (see Organised Tours in the relevant sections).

Public Ferries Most passengers on the eight hour Kollam-Alappuzha cruise will be western travellers. If you want the local experience, or you simply want a shorter trip, there are still State Water Transport boats from Alappuzha to Kottayam (six boats daily, Rs 6, 2½ hours) and Changanassery (two boats daily, Rs 9, three hours). The trip to Kottayam crosses Vembanad Lake and then runs along a fascinating canal. Changanassery is on the road and railway line, 18km south of Kottayam and 78km north of Kollam.

For a comprehensive listing of backwater tours, see the brochure *The Backwaters of Kerala Tourist Guide*, available at tourist offices. It includes prices and telephone booking contacts. See also their Web site at www.keralatourism.org. Make sure when booking that boats actually go as per advertised – some services only operate when there are enough passengers.

Bishop Jerome Nagar. They're even equipped with a digital camera so you can send your mugshot into cyberspace and show your friends how much India has changed you. The rates are Rs 100 per hour.

Things to See

If you have the time, wander along Main Rd, an old thoroughfare (almost peaceful compared with Alappuzha Rd) where **jewellery** and **sari shops** with polished marble and brass entrances incongruously abut dusty, dirty footpath/sewers. The potholed road is full of well-polished chauffer-driven cars. If you want to see some local action the **fruit market** offers some colourful street theatre. And if you're interested in classic Keralan architecture, check out the **Opthamology Hospital** along Jetty Rd.

The rather bizarre-looking **Shrine of Our Lady of Velamkanni**, near the KSRTC bus stand, attracts many devotees. Somehow they manage to sustain their focus in spite of the constant cacophony of buses, motorbikes and auto-rickshaws. There are Chinese fishing nets on **Ashtamudi Lake** and also some 18th century churches at **Thangasseri**, 5km from Kollam's centre.

Activities

In its efforts to promote Kollam as more than a mere stopping place for a backwater cruise, the DTPC has pulled out all stops to develop a wide range of tours and activities to suit all budgets. An example of their entrepreneurial acumen is the new monsoon packages for Arabs who have never seen serious rain!

Backwater Tours Most people come to Kollam to enjoy the backwaters. For details of the many possibilities, see the boxed text 'The Backwaters' earlier.

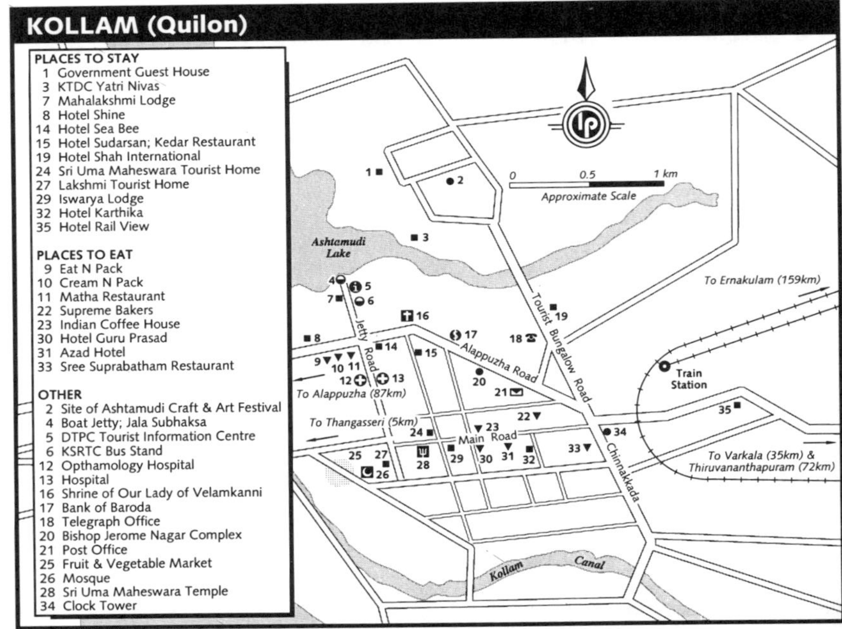

Houseboat Trips As well as short trips along the backwaters, many visitors are taking advantage of the numerous house boat possibilities, which range from a few hours for Rs 600 to several days with full accommodation and food for Rs 15,000. The DTPC can provide all details and arrange bookings.

Ayurveda

A wide range of treatments including massage and steam bath is available from Prince Health Club & Ayurvedic Resort (☎ 749009, fax 745551) at Kollam Beach. There is also a fully equipped gym with trained instructors.

Organised Tours

Guided tours on foot and in traditional country boats through the myriad paths and canals of **Monroe Island** in Ashtamudi Lake are organised by the DTPC (inquire at the information centre). The first part of the journey is by road through the outskirts of Kollam, passing cashew nut processing factories. The boat trip starts at a quiet backwater village, and the next few hours are spent observing village life – prawn and fish farming, coir making, copra (coconut kernels) drying, even matchstick making. Also, there are wonderful opportunities for birdwatching, with scores of kingfishers, bee-eaters, egrets, Brahminy kites and others. The tour lasts from 9 am to 1 pm and costs Rs 250 per person.

The Kairali Darshan tour focuses on 'traditional Kerala' and includes demonstrations of kalarippayat and yoga, visits to a traditional weaving centre, a coir village, a cashew nut processing factory and an Ayurvedic medicine preparation plant. Lunch at a traditional Kerala house and a Kathakali performance are also part of the busy agenda. The daily tour in a luxury coach from 8 am to 7 pm, costs Rs 750 and you can book at the DTPC.

Special Events

A major event is the newly established **Ashtamudi Craft & Art Festival of India** (also known as Paramparya – 'threading the traditions'). The festival draws artists from across the nation to create, demonstrate and, in some cases, teach. There is also a film festival (with a focus on art and craft) and a wide range of performing arts. The work produced during the festival is available for sale. The festival is held annually from 26 December to 10 January at Asramam Maidan and entry is free.

Plans are well in place for centres that provide yoga and Ayurvedic treatments, water sports and performing arts. Check with the DTPC for details.

Places to Stay – Budget

The ***Government Guest House*** *(☎ 70356)*, 3km north of the centre by the water's edge on Ashtamudi Lake, is a large, forgotten relic of the Raj. The immense rooms are sparsely furnished and decorated with old willow pattern plates, large Chinese pickle jars and old lithographs depicting British victories during the 1857 Uprising. Rooms with bath are a bargain at Rs 55 per person but getting into town can be difficult because of the scarcity of auto-rickshaws.

Lakshmi Tourist Home *(☎ 741067)*, in an alley off Main Rd, is a clean no-frills lodge with singles/doubles Rs 60/100 with bath.

Hotel Karthika *(☎ 76241)* is a large, popular place built around a central courtyard. Decent rooms are Rs 125/220 with bathroom or Rs 350 with air-con.

Iswarya Lodge *(☎ 77801, Main Rd)*, nearby, is slightly cheaper at Rs 70/129.

The Sri Uma Maheswara Tourist Home *(☎ 743712)* has basic doubles with bath for Rs 140. The staff are friendly and the premises clean. The view onto the street offers a unique insight into Indian electrical wiring.

Mahalakshmi Lodge *(☎ 79440)*, opposite the KSRTC bus stand, is cheap but very basic with rooms with common bathroom for just Rs 50/75.

Hotel Shine is nearby and offers better rooms for Rs 110/125 with bath.

Hotel Rail View *(☎ 76918)*, opposite the train station, has rooms for Rs 70/100 and a bar and restaurant.

There are ***retiring rooms*** at the train station.

Places to Stay – Mid-Range & Top End

Hotel Sudarsan *(☎ 744322, fax 740480)* is good value at Rs 210/260 or from Rs 420/500 with air-con, although rooms at the front can be noisy because of the traffic. There is an executive suite for Rs 795/895. All rooms have TV and there are restaurants and a bar. This hotel is particularly welcoming and apart from the traffic noise, it's probably the best place in town.

Hotel Sea Bee *(☎ 75371, Jetty Rd)* is conveniently located, but the plush foyer gives no indication of the unkempt and grotty rooms. Singles/doubles cost Rs 165/220, or Rs 520 for an air-con double.

Hotel Shah International *(☎ 742362, fax 719435)* is in a quieter location but the rooms are clearly on the decline. Rates are Rs 200/250, or Rs 300/350 for air-con. There's also an executive suite for Rs 695/995, and a restaurant.

KTDC Yatri Nivas *(☎ 745538)*, just across the inlet from the boat jetty, is large and rather lost looking. The grubby rooms are from Rs 120/175 to Rs 180/250, or Rs 400 for an air-con double. The riverside location is terrific: there's a pleasant waterfront lawn and the staff will run you across the river to the boat jetty in the hotel's speedboat if you ask nicely. Alternatively you can arrange for the DTPC to send an auto-rickshaw to you at the hotel for about Rs 20.

Hotel Palm Lagoon *(☎/fax 523974)* is a resort 18km from Kollam on the shores of Ashtamudi Lake. In an attempt to increase patronage it has reduced its prices. Self-contained thatched cottages cost Rs 750, Rs 820 with breakfast or Rs 1900 for full board (10% discount if you book through the DTPC). Backwater tours and Ayurvedic rejuvenation programs are available. A taxi from Kollam will cost about Rs 200 or you can take the KTDC speedboat for Rs 250.

Places to Eat

Matha Restaurant, near the jetty, serves up a wickedly spicy fried chicken and is a firm favourite with the rickshaw-drivers.

Eat N Pack and ***Cream N Pack*** flank Hollow Footwear. Eat N Pack is an excellent choice for inexpensive Keralan cuisine. A thali is Rs 10, with fish it's Rs 15. At Cream N Pack you can select your ice cream or a wide range of fresh seasonal juices.

Hotel Guru Prasad *(Main Rd)* is a fairly ordinary vegetarian place where a thali costs just Rs 10.

Azad Hotel, on the same side of the road, is a rather brighter restaurant with both vegetarian and non-vegetarian meals. Main Rd also has a decent branch of the ***Indian Coffee House***.

Sree Suprabatham Restaurant is another typical South Indian 'meals' restaurant. It's particularly good for breakfast with all you can eat for around Rs 10.

The restaurants in the ***Iswarya Lodge*** and the ***Mahalakshmi Lodge*** both have good vegetarian food.

Kedar Restaurant, in the Hotel Sudarsan, is an air-con haven with white tablecloths and relatively cheap meals. It has acquired a reputation for good seafood. Indian mains are about Rs 40, although the vegetable curry is somewhat bland. Western and Chinese cuisine is also available. It's a good spot to have breakfast before taking a backwater cruise.

Hotel Shah International has a good veg and nonveg restaurant. This is where the cool dudes of Kollam come dressed in Reeboks to sample noodles and tomato sauce after surfing the Internet.

Jala Subhaksa, a converted Keralan rice barge moored at the boat jetty, is Kollam's floating restaurant, which serves multicuisine food.

Supreme Bakers, opposite the post office, is great for a treat. Select a cake and enjoy the air-con with a coffee.

Kollam is a cashew-growing centre and the nuts are on sale in shops and hotels and from street vendors. Small packets can be bought for Rs 10 to Rs 20. As with other Keralan towns a beguiling array of food vendors ply the streets. For as little as Rs 15 you can satiate a significant appetite with bananas in batter.

Getting There & Away

Bus Kollam is on the well-serviced Thiruvananthapuram-Kollam-Alappuzha-Ernakulam bus route. Superexpress services (which can be reserved) take 1½ hours to Thiruvananthapuram (Rs 30); 1¾ hours to Alappuzha (Rs 30); and 3½ hours to Ernakulam (Rs 65). You can also take the KSRTC service which costs Rs 17 to Thiruvananthapuram and Rs 55 to Ernakulam, and takes the same time as the superexpress.

Train Kollam is 159km south of Ernakulam and the three to four hour trip costs Rs 47/224 in 2nd/1st class. The 2625 *Kerala Express* to Delhi and the 6320 *Trivandrum Mail* to Chennai (Madras) go through Kollam, as do the 1082 *Kanyakumari Express* to Mumbai (Bombay) and the Thiruvananthapuram-Mangalore coastal services.

Boat See the boxed text 'The Backwaters' earlier in this chapter for information on the popular backwaters cruise to Alappuzha. There are public services across Ashtamudi Lake to the villages of Guhanandapuram (one hour), Muthiraparam (2½ hours) or Perumon (2½ hours), fares are around Rs 6 return. The daily ATDC (Alleppey Tourism Development Co-op) and DTPC tourist boats to Alappuzha can be booked at various hotels around town, but direct bookings attract substantial discounts for everyone with further discounts for students and pensioners.

Getting Around

The KSRTC bus stand and the boat jetty are side by side, but the train station is on the opposite side of town. Auto-rickshaw drivers are reasonably willing to use their meters, expect to pay around Rs 10 from the train station to the boat jetty. The *Yatri Nivas* speedboat can be hired to explore the waterways around Kollam for Rs 300 an hour.

AROUND KOLLAM

Krishnapuram Palace Museum

Two kilometres south of Kayamkulam (almost half way between Kollam and Alappuzha), the Krishnapuram Palace, fully restored in March 1999, is a fine example of Keralan architecture. Now a museum, the two-storey palace houses paintings, antique furniture and sculptures. A small, cushion-lined chariot, in which the married women of the royal household were once transported, sits on the outside veranda. Concealed within, they were carried by four bearers, whose shoulders held the poles that extend from the carriage. Within the palace complex is the tank where the monarch, Varma Rama, bathed.

The palace's prized mural, some three metres high, depicts the *Gajendra Moksha* – the story of Vishnu's deliverance of the elephant chief, as related in the Hindu text, the *Bhagavata Purana*.

The palace is set in ornamental gardens, which house an ancient Buddha statue carved out of a single rock piece – a relic of the nearby Krishnapuram Temple.

The palace is well worth a visit. Buses (Rs 12) leave Kollam every three minutes for Kayamkulam. Get off the bus at the bus stand near the temple gate, 2km before Kayamkulam (all the drivers will know where to set you down). From the bus stand it's a 600m very obvious walk to the palace. The palace is open 10 am to 5 pm (lunch 1 to 2 pm) every day except Monday. Entry is Rs 2.

Alumkadavu

Just near the Krishnapuram Palace, on the outskirts of Kayamkulam, Alumkadavu has long been a boat building centre. The traditional *kettuvallams* (rice barges) are still constructed here – no longer for rice transportation, but as luxury houseboats for tourists. You can also see these constructions in Alappuzha, near the ATDC office.

Mannarsala

Fifteen kilometres north of the Krishnapuram Palace, and 32km before Alappuzha, Mannarsala, on National Highway 47, is the site of the Nagaraja (serpent king) Temple, and the most significant site for snake worship in Kerala. According to the *Mahabharata*, snakes fled from a fire started by

Arjuna in the Khandava forest (believed to be an area near Alappuzha). They prayed for protection and the area around Mannarsala cooled down providing them a refuge.

Local legend relates that subsequently a Namboodri woman developed sacred groves for the snakes and dedicated the land to the snake deities, Nagaraja and Sarpayakshi. Today the tradition continues and the oldest female member (known as *valiama*) of the *illam* (women's section of the Namboodri household), has the role of priestess and conducts the rituals at the temple. On accepting the role she relinquishes her earthly marital status and assumes a spiritual one – that of wife of the serpent king deity. She lives alone in premises within the temple complex.

The temple is in typical Keralan architectural style, with the larger central shrine surrounded by many smaller ones. Infinite numbers of cobra idols encompass the complex, it's said that many of their earthly cousins are there as well. The two main idols are those of the serpent king and queen.

The annual festival is in the month of Thulam (October/November). At this time the main idols are taken in procession by the priestess and offerings of milk, turmeric and rice are made.

As with Keralan temples generally, this is a peaceful place, apart from the *vedis* (explosive devotional sounds – see the boxed text, 'Explosive Devotions' earlier in this chapter). Visitors who respect the rituals and serenity of the temple are welcome. Men must remove their shirts, women must wear saris or similar clothing. There are frequent buses from both Kollam and Alappuzha (Rs 10 to Rs 15).

ALAPPUZHA (Alleppey)

☎ 0477 • pop 274,000

Like Kollam, this is a pleasant, easy-going market town surrounded by coconut plantations and built on the canals that service the coir industry of the backwaters. It is a walking town and a stroll through the streets reveals many examples of Keralan architecture. If you arrive in mid-December you can enjoy the festivities at the Mullakal Devi Temple.

Alappuzha is also 'houseboat city' (see 'The Backwaters' boxed text). The options are numerous and confounding as is the competition for your custom – there are infinite numbers of touts to sway your decision. If you'd like to see a houseboat (kettuvallam, or traditional rice barge) under construction check at the ATDC office (see under Orientation & Information).

If you happen to need an umbrella, Alappuzha is the place to buy it. The town is a centre for umbrella manufacture and umbrella shops with comical displays proliferate. The annual Nehru Cup Snakeboat Race is an event not to be missed.

Orientation & Information

The bus stand and boat jetty are conveniently close to each other, and within easy walking distance of most of the cheap hotels. The train station is 4km south-west of the town centre. The DTPC Tourist Reception Centre (☎ 253308) at the boat jetty and the ATDC (☎ 243462) across the canal, are both very helpful. The Bank of India on Mullakal Rd will cash travellers cheques.

Alappuzha's water is notoriously unhealthy – take the colour and pollution as a warning. Even if you drink tap water elsewhere, it's advisable to give it a miss here.

Backwater Tours

There is an amazing choice of backwater tours to select from in Alappuzha. Both the DTPC and ATDC offer a wide range, and there are also many private operators. See the boxed text 'The Backwaters' for further information. Houseboat tours, where you live, eat and relax for days on a luxurious boat while you travel the calm backwaters, are also a favourite here.

Nehru Cup Snakeboat Race

This famous regatta takes place on the second Saturday of August each year. It's held on Vembanad Lake to the east of the town. Scores of long, low-slung *chundan vallams*

The Mother of all Hugs

She travels the globe to hug people. And hug her they do – in their thousands. She'll hold audience throughout the night as people queue patiently for their brief embrace. 'To be hugged by her is to feel the true power of unconditional love' claim her millions of devotees. And that is how they regard Matha Amrithanandamayi – the hugging mother – as the embodiment of pure love. For them, she is the divine.

Born as Sudhamanin to a poor family in Kerala in 1953, she developed a strong affinity with poor people, treating them all as members of her own family. She went without food so that others could eat. From the age of five she became obsessed with composing and singing devotional songs of love for Krishna. At 14 she was forced to leave school and care for her family. Believing her to be eccentric, they eventually totally ostracised her.

Away from her family, Sudhamanin began a life of asceticism, sleeping under the stars and eating whatever became available. Some people scorned her but others were inspired by her selfless devotion. When her followers demanded a miracle as evidence of her claim that she was 'at one with the divine' she replied 'The greatest miracle of all is for one to realise the true self'.

Eventually, however, she conceded to requests for a miracle, reputedly producing two. Her first transformed a small amount of milk into a large amount of jam – enough to feed a crowd. She performed her second miracle after her brother (one of her antagonists) smashed an oil lamp. She organised replacement lamps, which burned brightly throughout the night, and which were fuelled not by oil, but by water. People responded with the call, Holy Mother.

Today Matha Amrithanandamayi, or Amma as she is known, has followers and ashrams around the globe and the Matha Amrithanandamayi Mission Trust supports a wide range of projects including orphanages, hospitals and training centres throughout India, especially in Kerala.

Literature on Matha Amrithanandamayi is readily available at the ashram in Amrithapuri (☎ 0476-897578, fax 897678). Information is also available on the official Web site at www.ammachi.org/contact_us.

JENNY BOWMAN

Devotees from around the world flock to be hugged by Matha Amrithanandamayi

(snakeboats) with highly decorated sterns compete for the cup. Each boat is crewed by up to a hundred rowers shaded by gleaming silk umbrellas, all watched avidly from the banks by thousands of spectators. The annual event celebrates the seafaring and martial traditions of ancient Kerala.

Tickets are available on the day from numerous ticket stands on the way to the lake where the race is held. Tickets entitle you to a seat on the bamboo terraces, which are erected for the occasion and which give an excellent view of the lake. Ticket prices range from Rs 10 for standing room to Rs 250 for the tourist pavilion, offering the best view at the finishing point.

Take food and drink to the race because there's little available on the lakeshore. An

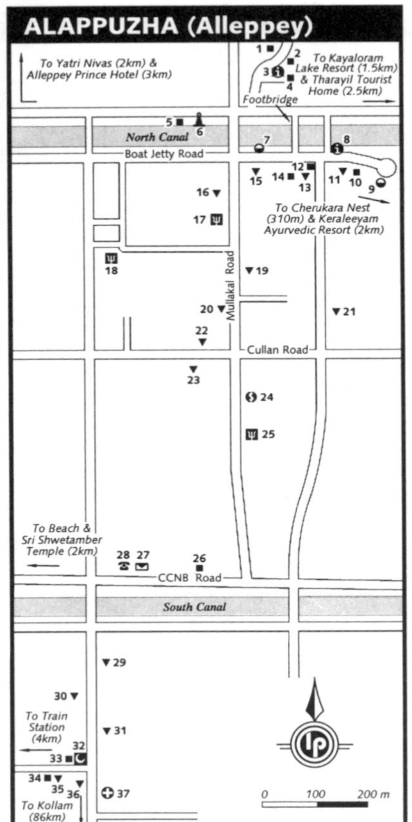

ALAPPUZHA (Alleppey)

PLACES TO STAY

1 Hotel Karthika
2 Sheeba Lodge
4 Komala Hotel
5 YMCA
10 Hotel Arcadia
12 Hotel Raiban Annexe
14 Krishna Bhavan Lodge
26 St George's Lodging
33 Hotel Brothers
34 Hotel Raiban

PLACES TO EAT

11 Zion Restaurant & Bakers
13 Annapoorna
15 Vijaya Restaurant
16 Sree Ganapath Restaurant
19 Hotel Aryas
20 Indian Coffee House
21 Hotel Sowrashtra
22 Hotel Rajas
23 Sree Durga Bhavan
29 Babus
30 Vegetarian Town Restaurant
31 Thaff Hotel
35 Annapoorna
36 Indian Coffee House

OTHER

3 Alappuzha Tourism Development Corporation (ATDC)
6 Mermaid Statue
7 Boat Jetty
8 DTPC Tourist Reception Centre & Restaurant
9 Bus Stand
17 Kidangamparambu Devi Temple
18 Temple
24 Bank of India
25 Mullakal Devi Temple
27 Post Office
28 Telegraph Office
32 Mosque
37 Hospital

umbrella is another necessity because the race takes place during the monsoon and the weather can alternate between driving rain and blistering sunshine.

The race is now repeated during the January tourist season as the ingeniously named **Tourism Snakeboat Race**.

Temples

The **Mullakal Devi Temple**, in the centre of town, is linked to legends of the goddess who is believed to have appeared at the site many times to care for a jasmine plant. Each year there is a 12 day festival, around the time of the December full moon. Some of India's best musicians create an energetic program of music and dance during the temple rituals and lavish elephant processions. The nearby **Kidangamparambu Devi Temple** also participates, with devotees alternating between the temples.

The small Jain community in Alappuzha constructed a new temple in 1990, which now stands next to their ancient shrine. **Sree Jain Shwetamber Temple** in Gujarathi St is open daily 6 to 8 am and 4.30 to 8 pm. You can walk there or take a rickshaw – about Rs 10 from the town centre.

Places to Stay – Budget

The price of accommodation can rise during the races if the crowds are large. But, as always, prices are negotiable.

YMCA *(☎ 245313)* has clean basic rooms that are mostly reserved for students. However, two double rooms with bathrooms are available to travellers for Rs 200 or Rs 300 with air-con. There is a good restaurant on the premises.

Komala Hotel *(☎ 243631)*, just north of the North Canal, has a range of rooms. Singles/doubles/triples/quads are Rs 100/140/200/230 and air-con singles/doubles are Rs 400/530 (taxes included). There are reports that it is on the decline.

Sheeba Lodge *(☎ 244871)*, behind the Komala, is cheap and habitable at Rs 80/90, with some more expensive doubles upstairs (Rs 140).

Hotel Karthika, nearby, is probably the poorest choice of the three hotels in this area. Seriously neglected doubles cost Rs 100.

Hotel Arcadia *(☎ 251354)*, opposite the boat jetty, has been renovated, and has clean bright rooms. Non air-con singles/doubles with bath are Rs 125/200. A deluxe room is Rs 300. There's also a restaurant and bar downstairs.

Krishna Bhavan Lodge *(☎ 250453)*, nearby, has small, rock-bottom rooms built around a courtyard/rubbish pile. It's cheap at Rs 30/50 with common bath and Rs 45/65 with bath, but barely habitable.

St George's Lodging *(☎ 251620, CCNB Rd)*, opposite South Canal, is the best of the cheapies. Clean rooms cost Rs 33/58 with common bath or Rs 45/83 with bath.

Hotel Brothers *(☎ 251653)*, has OK rooms for Rs 70/140/210 and musty air-con doubles for Rs 295. There is a veg/nonveg restaurant.

Hotel Raiban *(☎ 251930)* is south of the South Canal, en route to the train station. Rooms are Rs 100/180, or Rs 350 for an air-con double. There's a restaurant and an ice cream parlour offering some intriguing flavours like 'Apricot Quark' and 'Bunny'.

Hotel Raiban Annexe *(☎ 261017)*, with the same management and prices, is at the other end of town near the boat jetty.

Yatri Nivas *(☎ 244460)* is 2km north of town and offers clean basic rooms with bathrooms, though the room size is not generous. A double is Rs 150 and a double deluxe (with air-con) is Rs 300.

Places to Stay – Mid-Range & Top End

Alleppey Prince Hotel *(☎ 243752, fax 243758, AS Rd)*, 3km north of the centre, is centrally air-conditioned and a good choice if you don't mind the distance. It has a bar, an excellent restaurant (opens at 7 pm) and an inviting swimming pool. Rooms are Rs 780/880 and Rs 1250 for a suite. It's popular, so reservations are recommended. An auto-rickshaw from the jetty or town centre should cost about Rs 30, a taxi is Rs 80.

Kayaloram Lake Resort *(☎ 260573, fax 252918)* is a plush and relaxed place 1.5km north of town. Rates for double rooms (including all taxes and boat transfer from Alappuzha) range from US$60 for room only to US$86 for full board. Prices fall by around 20% in the low season (April to October). The resort offers all mod cons as well as a range of backwater trips and Ayurvedic treatments. The booking office for the resort is down a small lane directly across the road from the DTPC.

The Keraleeyam Ayurvedic Resort *(☎ 241468, fax 251068)*, 15 minutes by boat from the Alappuzha boat jetty, is a heritage home with a backwater frontage. Prices are US$20/25/30 for singles/doubles/triples. Breakfast, lunch and dinner (traditional Keralan, Chinese or European) are available for US$15 per person per day. Ayurvedic treatments are available. Prices start at around US$14 for a single day to US$78 for seven days with longer stays attracting discounts.

Backwater Ecology

The backwaters are severely threatened by population growth, tourism, industry and agriculture. Kerala has 29 major lakes on the backwater system, seven of which drain to the sea. Land reclamation projects, legal and illegal, have reduced the area of these lakes from 440 sq km in 1968 to less than 350 sq km today. The vast Vembanad Lake has dropped from 230 sq km to 179 sq km. The backwaters are only one-third of their mid-19th century levels.

Pollution and destructive fishing (using dynamite, poison and very fine nets) has resulted in the extinction of mangroves, crocodiles and migratory fish. Many migratory birds no longer visit the backwaters. To the casual eye, the most visible danger is the unhindered spread of water hyacinth (African moss or Nile cabbage), which clogs many stretches of canal and causes great difficulties for the boat operators. For more information, see the Waterways Ecology section in the Facts about Kerala chapter.

Guesthouses in the form of converted private homes are becoming a popular alternative to hotel accommodation. They are more personal and often quieter than hotels and while families and young children are welcome throughout India, this style of accommodation is particularly suitable.

Cherukara Nest *(☎ 252509, fax 243164, 1X/774 Cherukara Buildings),* near the KSRTC, is a large heritage home built in classic Keralan style. The heavily timbered cavernous rooms range from Rs 400/550 for a standard non air-con room to Rs 800/950 for a heritage deluxe with air-con. Good meals are available if ordered in advance.

Tharayil Tourist Home *(☎/fax 243543, Lake Punnamada Rd, Thathampaly)* is 2.5km north-east of town near the finishing point for the snakeboat race. It's set in a private garden with clean, bright rooms without air-con for Rs 200/350, or Rs 750 with air-con. Prices are reduced out of season. It is possible to go fishing on the lake (basic equipment is available) and the friendly staff will willingly cook your catch.

Places to Eat

The restaurant attached to the ***DTPC Tourist Reception Centre*** on the North Canal is cheap, clean and airy and serves a wide variety of breakfasts, snacks and meals.

There's an ***Indian Coffee House*** on Mullakal Rd in the town centre and another south of the South Canal, opposite the hospital. They're open 7 am to 9 pm and a range of drinks and meals are served by Raj style waiters.

Hotel Aryas *(Mullakal Rd)* serves good, cheap vegetarian meals.

The Hotel Rajas is a basic veg/nonveg restaurant.

Sree Durga Bhavan is a cheerful place where a good *masala dosa* will only set you back Rs 8.

Komala Hotel and ***Hotel Raiban*** both have OK restaurants, and there are two ***Annapoorna*** vegetarian restaurants, one is next door to the Hotel Raiban and the other is on Boat Jetty Rd.

Vembanad Restaurant at the Alleppey Prince Hotel is the best restaurant in town. It's comfortable and air-conditioned (or you can elect to eat by the pool) and serves excellent veg/nonveg food.

Sree Ganapath Restaurant serves good vegetarian meals.

Zion Restaurant & Bakers is good for cool drinks including fresh juices, as well as snacks. There's a small shoppe (sic) selling biscuits and chocolate.

Vijaya Restaurant and ***Hotel Sowrashtra*** are both good for vegetarian meals.

Babus, ***Vegetarian Town Restaurant*** and ***Thaff Hotel***, at the southern end of town, are all good for drinks and inexpensive vegetarian meals.

Getting There & Away

Bus On the Thiruvananthapuram-Kollam-Alappuzha-Ernakulam route, buses operate frequently. To Thiruvananthapuram, it's about 3¼ hours and Rs 45/60 by superfast/express bus. It takes 1¾ hours and costs Rs 20/27 to reach Ernakulam from Alappuzha. To Kottayam a superfast is Rs 18 and to Changanassery (Changanacherry) it's Rs 9.50. Buses for destinations farther afield go to Bangalore (2 pm, 16 hours) and Coimbatore (6.15 am, 7½ hours).

Train The train station is about 4km southwest of the town centre, close to the seafront. An auto-rickshaw from town costs about Rs 25. Nine trains daily make the 57km journey to Ernakulam, which takes one hour and costs Rs 23/125 in 2nd/1st class. There are also plenty of trains to Kayamkulam (Rs 18/105). To Thiruvananthapuram, trains leave at 12.47 am and 2.40 pm. To Chennai they leave at 3 pm and to Guruvayur they leave at 12.48 am.

Boat Alappuzha is the best starting point to explore the backwaters. See 'The Backwaters' boxed text, earlier, for general information on this fascinating means of travel. Regular ferries make the three hour trip to Kottayam.

AROUND ALAPPUZHA

Ambalappuzha

Ambalappuzha, 14km south of Alappuzha, is the site of the Krishna Ananda Temple, dedicated to the infant aspect of the deity. Of the seven temples in the former Travancore state of Southern Kerala, this is considered to be of most importance. Several legends are associated with the temple. It's believed that the idol of the deity was self created. The temple is noted for its fine *palpayasam*, the daily offering of milk rice, the legendary gift of a former Brahmin to the poor. The 18th century poet, Kunchan Nambiar, credited with developing the literary style of Thullal, is said to have staged his influential performances here. The temple is on the Kollam-Alappuzha Rd. It's open daily 3 to 8.30 am and 4.30 to 8.30 pm and buses from Alappuzha come here regularly.

Arthungal

The old St Sebastian Church cuts a poignant image, standing next to its more recent neighbour, St Andrew's (which is also affectionately, and confusingly, referred to as St Sebastian's), built in 1925. The original church was built by the Portuguese in 1591 and some claim it housed a small statue of St Sebastian, brought by the Portuguese. Each year in late January, St Sebastian is honoured as a procession bearing his statue makes its way to the beach and the landing point of the Portuguese. If you have an interest in Christian history, you will no doubt wish to visit the church. Buses come here but it's easier to hire your own transport. Arthungal is 25km north of Alappuzha. Take the coast road for 15km to Mararikulam, turn left and it's a farther 10km to the church. A rickshaw will cost Rs 200 to Rs 300 depending on time.

KOTTAYAM

☎ 0481 • pop 172,000

Once a focus for the Syrian Christians of Kerala, Kottayam is now a place of churches and seminaries, and an important centre for rubber production. Through political agitation and civil disobedience the citizens of Kottayam played an important role in the struggle to end caste injustice.

Kottayam is the headquarters of the *Malayala Manorama*. Published in Malayalam, it has a circulation of 1.2 million, an estimated readership of eight million – second only to the English-language daily the *Times of India* – and a staff of 2000. The *Malayala Manorama* is much more than a newspaper: it's a giant state-of-the-art publishing house. Its stable includes *Vanita*, India's largest-selling women's magazine and the popular English-language *Manorama Yearbook*, which is packed with statistical information on India and the world, and is a good source for researchers and teachers.

Several literary figures hail from Kottayam district (including the Booker prize winner, Arundhati Roy). In 1945, Kottayam saw the establishment of the Sahitya Pravarthaka Sahakarana Sangham Writers Cooperative, which seeks to ensure a fair royalty to its member authors.

Orientation & Information

The train station, boat jetty and KSRTC bus stand are 2km to 3km from the city centre.

The tourist information centre in the centre of town has been demolished. At the time of writing, inquiries were being 'handled' by the District Tourism Office at the Collectorate – but don't waste your time, unless you like the prospect of looking at posters of Ladakh and empty whiskey bottles. There's a very helpful tourist information office at the KSRTC bus stand. The Tourist Police are also here.

The telegraph office is open 24 hours daily for STD/ISD, local calls and fax. It is quiet and helpful. There are a number of email facilities in town. However, most are not fully operational. Base Station Internet Club (☎ 583463, fax 562837, KPB Complex, Sastri Rd) offers a good service for Rs 79 per hour. It's open Monday to Saturday 9 am to 7.30 pm and on the first and third Sunday of each month from 11.30 am to 5 pm.

You can cash travellers cheques and get Visa cash advances at the Canara Bank on KK Rd.

Kottayam has a number of large shopping centres with supermarkets, electrical stores, stationers and services such as photocopying. Should you need a private detective you can try International Private Detectives on the top floor of Adam Tower near Hotel Aida.

For books and cassettes, visit Bookmart and Paico, both in the Padinjarekara Chambers, opposite Civil Station and just 500m east of the *Malayala Manorama*.

Things to See & Do

The **Thirunakkara Shiva Temple** in the centre of town is built in typical Keralan style. It is noted for its Kootiattam, traditional Sanskrit drama. Visitors may sometimes be admitted.

About 3km north-west of the centre are two interesting Syrian Christian churches. **Cheriapally**, St Mary's Orthodox Church, has an elegant façade spoilt by tacked-on entrance porches. The interior is notable for the 400-year-old vegetable dye paintings on the walls and ceiling.

Valiyapally, also St Mary's Church or the 'big' church, is 100m away. The church was built in 1550. The altar is flanked by stone crosses, one with a Pahlavi Persian inscription. The cross on the left is probably original, but the one on the right is a copy. The guestbook goes back to 1899, and was signed by Haile Selassie of Ethiopia in 1956, among others. The extraordinary disembodied arms projecting from the wall relate to a story in the book of Daniel, which will be happily given to you to read. A donation towards restoration and upkeep will be expected.

Backwater trips from Kottayam are also popular (see Boat under Getting There & Away, later in this section).

Special Events

Every year from 17 to 22 January the Municipal Ground & Stage, at the junction of TB Rd and KK Rd, hosts a **drama festival** in memory of the famous Keralan actor Achan Kunju who died in the early 1990s. Even if you don't understand Malayalam, the music and the visuals are entertaining and not difficult to fathom.

Places to Stay

***Kaycees Lodge** (☎ 563440, YMCA Rd)* is central, and has OK rooms with bathroom for Rs 80/135. Women will find better options.

***KTDC Hotel Aiswarya** (☎ 581254)* is also close to the centre, just off Temple Rd. Singles/doubles are Rs 150/200, Rs 400/500 (deluxe) or Rs 600/750 (air-con). It has a multicuisine restaurant and a beer parlour, and the lift goes all the way to the roof from where you can get a good view of the grounds of the Thirunakkara Shiva Temple.

***Ambassador Hotel** (☎ 563293, KK Rd)* is less conveniently located. Keep a sharp lookout because it's set back from the road

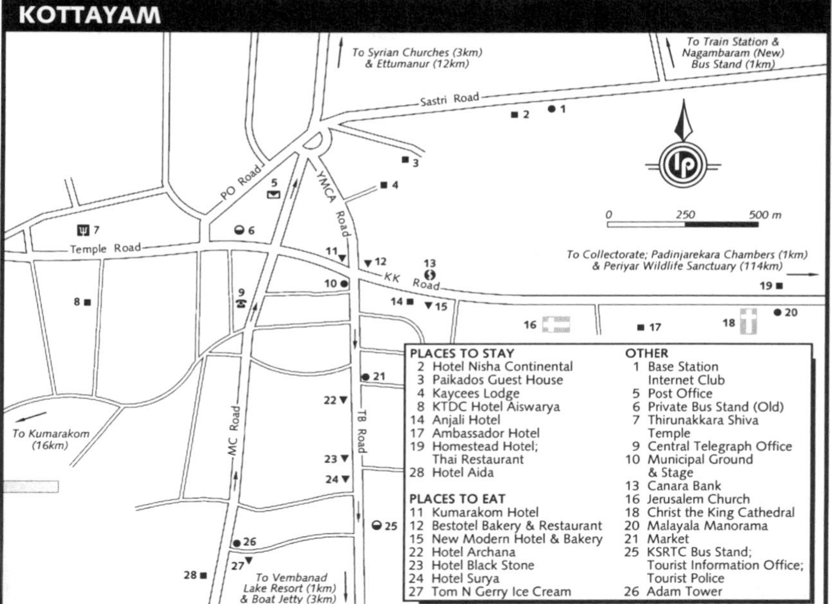

and it's easy to miss the driveway. Singles/doubles are Rs 110/137 and there's a small bakery in the lobby and a good veg/nonveg restaurant.

Homestead Hotel *(☎ 560467, KK Rd)*, farther east, has pleasant rooms from Rs 130/280, or Rs 600 for an air-con double. There's a vegetarian restaurant.

Hotel Nisha Continental *(☎ 563984, Sastri Rd)* has ordinary rooms for Rs 195/270, and has a fairly ordinary restaurant as well.

Paikados Guest House *(☎ 584340)* is very clean, very quiet and good value with rooms for Rs 100/160.

Hotel Aida *(☎ 568391, fax 568399, MC Rd)* is more expensive and much more comfortable with rooms for Rs 300/500, or Rs 400/600 with air-con. It has a bar, restaurant, currency exchange for guests and cable TV. Backwater cruises and expeditions into the hills to visit rubber and tea plantations can be arranged here.

Anjali Hotel *(☎ 563661, fax 563669, KK Rd)*, near the town centre, is part of the excellent local Casino hotel chain, which makes it sound a lot better that it actually is. It's centrally air-conditioned, gloomy and tatty with rooms from Rs 675/975 to Rs 1150/1500. It has a bar, coffee shop and restaurant.

Vembanad Lake Resort *(☎ 564866)*, 2km south of the town centre, has cottages in a pleasant lakeside setting for Rs 450, or Rs 690 with air-con.

Places to Eat

Hotel Black Stone has basic but good vegetarian food.

Bestotel Bakery & Restaurant is another fairly typical South Indian restaurant fronted by a decent bakery where you can stock up on cakes, biscuits and chocolates for the long bus ride to Kumily or a backwater trip.

There are a number of good cheap eating places on TB Rd and KK Rd including the ***Kumarakom Hotel***, which is similar to an Indian Coffee House. The ***New Modern Hotel & Bakery***, ***Hotel Archana*** and ***Hotel Surya*** all offer good vegetarian cuisine.

The excellent, partly air-con ***Thali Restaurant*** *(KK Rd)*, at the Homestead Hotel, does good thalis for Rs 20.

The restaurant at the ***Anjali Hotel*** has superb food, and at the ***Ambassador Hotel*** there's a buffet lunch of Keralan delights for Rs 100.

At ***Hotel Aida*** the food is also very good. The restaurant is clean and spacious but you'll have to share it with two giant TV screens pumping out Malayalam and Hindi songs at full volume.

The tranquil ambience of the ***Vembanad Lake Resort*** is a welcome relief from the usual noises that permeate dining places in India. There's an outdoor dining area as well as a floating restaurant built in a converted kettuvallam (traditional rice barge). Both places share the same kitchen but if you dine in the boat don't expect it to travel – it remains moored throughout your meal. The food here is mediocre, the portions are small and the service is, at best, reluctant.

Ice cream parlours are everywhere including a ***Tom N Gerry*** opposite Adam Tower.

Entertainment

If you want to witness some free entertainment head for the ***Municipal Ground & Stage*** (see earlier under Special Events). In the evenings large crowds (mostly men) gather on the dusty ground to watch various dramas and colourful shows that begin at 7.30 pm.

Getting There & Away

Bus Kottayam has three bus stands. The KSRTC bus stand is south of the centre on TB Rd. Bus destinations are signed in Malayalam and English. There are numerous buses to Thiruvananthapuram via Kollam and to Kochi. It takes about four hours and costs Rs 36 to reach Thekkady in the Periyar Wildlife Sanctuary. Seven express buses daily come through from Ernakulam and either terminate at Thekkady, in the sanctuary, or continue to Madurai, a farther three hours away.

The two other bus stands are private and are known as Old and Nagambaram (new). Buses from these stands mainly operate locally to destinations within 10km to 30km. However, you can get to Munnar and Kumily from the Nagambaram bus stand.

Train Kottayam is well served by express trains running between Thiruvananthapuram (165km, Rs 47/224, three hours) and Ernakulam (65km, Rs 26/129, 1½ hours. To Kollam it's 1½ hours (100km, Rs 32/173 in 2nd/1st class).

Boat The boat jetty is about 3km from the town centre. Six ferries daily make the 2½ hour trip to Alappuzha for Rs 6 or you can take the BTSS 4½ hour cruise for Rs 100 (see the boxed text 'The Backwaters' earlier in this chapter). This interesting trip is worthwhile if you don't have the time or the inclination for the day-long cruise between Kollam and Alappuzha. You can also charter your own boat for Rs 400 to Rs 500, although it's easier to do this from Alappuzha.

Getting Around

An auto-rickshaw from the train station is Rs 35 to the ferry (ask for 'jetty') and Rs 20 to the KSRTC bus stand.

AROUND KOTTAYAM

Mannanam

Just 8km north of Kottayam, Mannanam is an important pilgrimage centre for Christians from around India and the world, and the site for the largest Christian Convention in Asia, held each January. It's the burial site of the 19th century priest, Father Kuriakose Elias Chavara, who is regarded as a saintly figure by Syrian Christians because of his dedication to lower caste people, for whom he established schools. Ten years before his death in 1871, he also established a

Catholic press and became vicar general of the Syro-Malabar church.

Ettumanur

The Shiva temple at Ettumanur, 12km north of Kottayam, is noted for its superb woodcarvings and murals. The murals, just within the entrance, are similar in style to those at Mattancherry Palace in Kochi. The one on the right shows Padmanabha (Vishnu) reclining happily on the multiheaded serpent. The left mural depicts Shiva, surrounded by heavenly beings and crushing evil. To get here, catch the Ernakulam bus from Kottayam. It'll take about 30 minutes and cost Rs 6. Or you can hire an auto-rickshaw for around Rs 50 to Rs 100 depending on how long you stay and how well you negotiate.

Pala

Among the many churches in this area there are two at Pala, about 25km north-east of Kottayam, dedicated to St Thomas. Local sources date one of the churches from 1002, but others claim the original church was destroyed and the current one is actually no more than 200 years old. Whatever the age, the churches are impressive. The churches hold their annual celebration at Epiphany (6 January). Regular buses travel from Kottayam to Pala from where it's 2km to the churches. From the Pala bus stand you can take a rickshaw or walk along the road east (left), and turn right over the bridge. After 100m you'll see the signpost to the right from where it's another 100m.

In the centre of Pala there's an interesting clock tower cum **shrine** dedicated to Mary, the Immaculate Conception.

St John's Cathedral

By road and rail between Kottayam and Thiruvananthapuram there are several places worth exploring. On the way to Sri Vallabha Temple (see under Tiruvalla, following), at the Kayamkulam 30km post, you'll see this Syrian Christian cathedral. Designed by the renowned architect, Laurie Baker, this round structure pays homage to traditional Keralan design, and features red brick walls with slits that facilitate ventilation, and a tiled roof that slopes from a 40m central peak. The circular interior, with a 40m diameter, has no central support. Its timber ceiling follows the roof shape to its high central peak. A plaque inside the church indicates that it was consecrated on 28 December 1972 by Zacharius Mar Athanasios on the 19th century anniversary of the martyrdom of St Thomas.

Tiruvalla

Traditional, all-night **Kathakali** performances are staged almost every night at the Sri Vallabha Temple, 2km from Tiruvalla on the Kayamkulam road. Non-Hindus may watch. Tiruvalla, 35km south of Kottayam, is on the rail route between Ernakulam and Thiruvananthapuram. The ***DTPC complex*** (no phone), 100m before the temple, has very basic double rooms for Rs 60. To get there you can take a Kayamkulam bus from Tiruvalla centre or a rickshaw.

Kaviyoor

At Kaviyoor you can see the ancient rock-cut **Thrikakudy Temple**. Now under the jurisdiction of the Archaeological Department, the sculptures in the temple are believed to date from the 8th century and constitute some of the earliest of Kerala's stone sculptures. The small temple, enclosed within massive black rock, has a tiny outer *mandapam* with Ganesh on the left and a sagacious figure to the right. The interior shrine with a central lingam is guarded by two sculptured watchmen.

Kaviyoor is on the road to Sabarimala, 5km east of Tiruvalla. To get there take the Sabarimala bus and alight at the 5km bus stand. From here you can walk the remaining 3km to the temple or take a rickshaw. If you walk, follow the road directly opposite the bus stand. After about 2km you'll pass a large Shiva temple. Turn right here (your only option) and about 500m farther on, the road will fork at a large fig tree near the NSS Training Institute. Take the right path and after another 500m you'll see some large black rocks on the left. Follow the path at the side of the rocks for about 100m to the temple.

Chenganur

Thirty kilometres south of Kottayam, Chenganur is home to the **Kunnathumalai Mahadeva Temple**. The temple is 1km east of the Thiruvananthapuram-Kottayam Rd, and is dedicated to Shiva and Parvati, although it's Parvati who is the main attraction here. See the boxed text 'The Tale of Two Temples' in the Western Ghats chapter for more information.

Kumarakom Bird Sanctuary

☎ 0481

This bird sanctuary, on an island in Vembanad Lake, is 16km west of Kottayam in a former rubber plantation. Local waterfowl can be seen in abundance, as well as overwintering migratory species. There are two seasons for birds here. Between October and February, it's the time for cormorants, teals and other ducks. From February to July snake birds, night herons, egrets and Siberian storks take their turn. The best time to see the most birds is around 6.30 am. The 1.5km walking track that enables you to view the island sanctuary is an easy and pleasant way to enjoy the place. You can also view the birds by boat available from the KTDC Kumarakom Tourist Village. A motorboat is Rs 300 per hour (maximum 10 people). A row boat is Rs 10 per half hour and a paddle boat Rs 15 per half hour. Boats also go to the island but it's highly unlikely that they, or the humans they bring there, would have a positive impact on the delicate ecosystem.

Places to Stay & Eat Inexpensive as well as luxury accommodation is available at Kumarakom, making early-morning birdwatching more viable. ***KTDC Kumarakom Tourist Village*** *(☎ 524258)* has houseboats for Rs 1200 (one double bedroom) and for Rs 2000 (two double bedrooms). To cruise the lake costs an extra Rs 600 per hour. At the time of writing 40 KTDC cottages were nearing completion. Aesthetically designed and connected by waterways they will be priced in the mid-range category.

Coconut Lagoon Resort *(☎ 524491, Kochi ☎ 0484-668221)*, part of the luxury Casino Group, has bungalow rooms for US$95/105 and mansion rooms for US$105/115. The setting is beautiful and there's a swimming pool. To get to this place from Kumarakom, telephone the hotel reception from the gatekeeper's cottage at the roadside and a boat will collect you and your luggage.

Taj Garden Retreat *(☎ 524371, Kochi 0484-668377)* is small but luxurious and is similarly priced. All of these resorts have expensive house restaurants.

Getting There & Away Buses run regularly from Kottayam to Kumarakom and the resorts will organise private transport.

Vijnana Kala Vedi Centre

The Vijnana Kala Vedi Cultural Centre at Aranmula, a village 38km from Kottayam and about 12km from Changanassery, offers courses in Indian arts under expert supervision. Subjects include Kathakali, Mohinyattam and Bharata Natyam (from Tamil Nadu) dancing, Carnatic vocal and percussion music, woodcarving, painting, cooking, languages (Hindi, Malayalam, Sanskrit), *kolams* (auspicious decorations), kalarippayat (Keralan martial art), Ayurvedic medicine, mythology, astrology and religion.

You can put your own course together and stay as long as you like, though a minimum commitment of one month is preferred. Fees, which include full board and lodging and two subjects of study, start at around US$200 a week – less for longer stays. For further details, write to The Director, Vijnana Kala Vedi Cultural Centre, Tarayil Mukku Junction, Aranmula 689533, Kerala. Changanassery is around 18km south of Kottayam and makes an interesting backwater trip from Alappuzha.

Central Kerala

Central Kerala, is a veritable masala of cultures, faiths, cuisines and architecture and (roughly) matches the area of the former princely state of Cochin. The main city of Central Kerala is Kochi, which was also called Cochin during the British Raj. It encompasses a large harbour with numerous islands and the ancient areas of Fort Cochin and Mattancherry, as well as the bustling metropolis of Ernakulam. North of Cochin, the bustling yet relaxed city of Thrissur (Trichur) is the state's cultural capital, renowned for its arts training centres and numerous festivals and performances.

Highlights

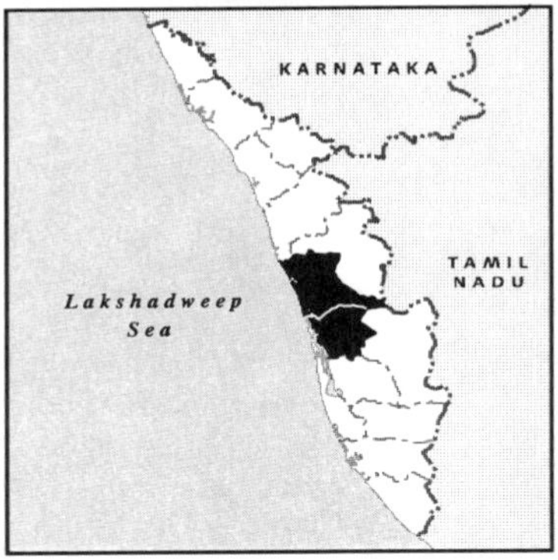

- Hunt for bargains in the antique shops of Fort Cochin
- Discover Kerala's Jewish heritage at Fort Cochin's synagogue
- Catch an evening performance of Kathakali
- Join the revelry of the many animated temple festivals

HISTORY

Throughout its history, Cochin has drawn people from all parts of the globe. They came primarily to trade, some were seeking refuge, others brought new belief systems; and later they came to plunder and colonise. Local influence helping to shape the region in the early centuries came from invasions by the Cholas, Pandyas and Chalukyas. However Kerala generally managed to remain immune from the 14th century invasions by Malik Kafur that swept much of the rest of South India.

The area has always been a trading centre first and foremost. Arab and Jewish spice traders had settled here in the 1st century CE and trade with the Middle East and eastern Mediterranean countries prospered under the patronage of the local rajas. The area's capital, now the city of Kochi, received a boost in the 14th century when the nearby ancient port of Cranganore (Kodungallur) silted up, the increase in business would eventually see Kochi become the most important port on the Malabar Coast.

For centuries the rajas of Cochin competed with their northern neighbours, the Zamorins of Calicut (modern-day Kozhikode), for territory and the spice trade. When the Portuguese arrived in the early 1500s, they were welcomed by both sides. However, the relationship began to sour as the Portuguese forged a treaty with the Zamorin royals and later transferred their regional headquarters from Cochin to Goa. By 1663, the Portuguese had lost their domination of the spice trade and their control of Kochi to the Dutch.

The Dutch negotiated a series of treaties in order to placate other competing powers – especially the Zamorins. During the 18th century, the rule of Cochin passed from one ineffective leader to another until 26-year-old Dharma Raja (also known as Rama Varma V and Saktan Tampuran) assumed power in 1769. A generous and tolerant

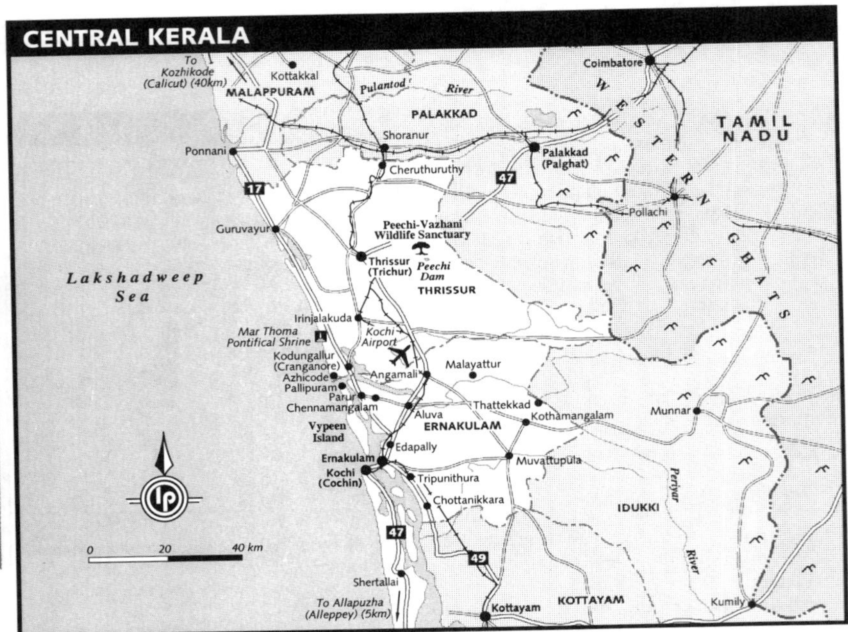

ruler, he possessed a strong sense of a just society. Under him, the feudal period of Cochin transformed to a more equitable central administration.

In 1791, after considering a possible alliance with the sultan of Mysore – Tipu Sultan – to outdo the British, Dharma Raja concluded a settlement with the English East India Company. Following Dharma Raja's death the state of Cochin was thrown into turmoil. Gross mismanagement supervised by the British led to virtual bankruptcy. Affairs of the state finally stabilised under the administration of Colonel Munro in 1812 who began a series of significant reforms that continued with subsequent leaders.

As with the neighbouring states of Malabar in the north and Travancore in the south, Cochin was a stronghold for the Indian National Congress with a committee operating in Thrissur as early as 1919. Following Independence, the two states of Cochin and Travancore merged to form a new state of Travancore-Cochin. This lasted until 1956 when they merged with northern Malabar to become the new state of Kerala.

KOCHI (Cochin)

☎ 0484 • pop 602,000

With its wealth of historical associations and its beautiful setting on a cluster of islands and narrow peninsulas, the fascinating city of Kochi perfectly reflects the eclecticism of Kerala. Here, you can see the oldest church in India, winding streets crammed with 500-year-old Portuguese houses, cantilevered Chinese fishing nets, a Jewish community with ancient roots, a 16th century synagogue, and a palace built by the Portuguese and given to the raja of Cochin. The palace, which was later renovated by the Dutch, contains some of the country's most beautiful murals. Another must-see is a performance of the world-famous Kathakali drama.

The older parts of Fort Cochin and Mattancherry are an unlikely blend of medieval Portugal, Holland and an English country village grafted onto the tropical Malabar Coast – a radical contrast to the bright lights, bustle and big hotels of mainland Ernakulam.

Kochi is one of India's largest ports and a major naval base. The misty silhouettes of huge merchant ships can be seen anchored off the point of Fort Cochin, waiting for a berth in the docks of Willingdon Island, an artificial island created with material dredged up when the harbour was deepened. All day, ferries scuttle back and forth between the various parts of Kochi. Dolphins can often be seen in the harbour.

Orientation

Kochi consists of mainland Ernakulam; the islands of Willingdon, Bolgatty and Gundu in the harbour; Fort Cochin and Mattancherry on the southern peninsula; and Vypeen Island, north of Fort Cochin. All these areas (except Gundu) are linked by public ferry; bridges also link Ernakulam to Willingdon Island and the Fort Cochin/Mattancherry peninsula. Most hotels and restaurants are in Ernakulam, where you'll also find the main train stations and bus stand. Two of the top hotels are on Willingdon Island where the old airport (not in use for the public) is also located. The new Nedumbassery airport (international and domestic) is 30km north east of Kochi.

Almost all the historical sites are in the tranquil setting of Fort Cochin.

Information

Tourist Offices The KTDC Reception Centre (☎ 353234), on Ernakulam's Shanmugham Rd and open from 8 am to 7 pm daily, organises accommodation at the Bolgatty Palace Hotel and arranges conducted harbour cruises. The tiny, privately operated Tourist Desk (☎ 371761, email palicha@giamd01.vsnl.net.in) at Ernakulam's main ferry jetty is a mine of information and staff are extremely helpful. Open daily from 9 am to 7 pm, it offers free brochures and maps and can arrange tours and accommodation. There's also a DTPC (☎ 381743) on Park Ave, Ernakulam.

The Tourist Desk on Bastion St in Fort Cochin, next door to the Hotel Park Avenue, is open 8 am to 8 pm daily. It provides free maps and information and makes bookings for backwater tours.

The helpful Government of India Tourist Office (☎ 668352), next to the Taj Malabar on Willingdon Island, offers a range of leaflets and maps. The airport tourist information counter is staffed for flight arrivals.

Money In Ernakulam, there's a State Bank of India opposite the KTDC Tourist Reception Centre and a very efficient Thomas Cook office in Mahatma Gandhi (MG) Rd. In Fort Cochin there is a State Bank of India near the Mattancherry Palace.

Thomas Cook has a moneychanging counter at both the departure and the arrival points of the Nedumbassery airport.

Post & Communications The general post office (GPO), including poste restante, is in Fort Cochin, but you can have mail sent to the post office on Hospital Rd in Ernakulam, as long as it's specifically addressed to there. STD/ISD booths are all over town.

KG Menon (☎ 361866) on Chittoor Rd, Ernakulam translate legal, personal and business documents for Rs 50 per page. The languages handled include Malayalam, Tamil, Hindi and English.

Internet Resources You can send and receive emails at Raiyaan Communication (☎ 351387, fax 380052, email raiyaan@giasmd01.vsnl.net.in) at Raiyaan Complex, Padma Junction, MG Rd. It charges Rs 25/10 (per 2500 characters) to send/receive emails, Internet browsing costs Rs 1 per minute. A similar service in Fort Cochin is available at Rendez Vous Cyber Cafe in Burgher St.

Bookshops Kochi is blessed with many fine bookshops. You'll find many along

Press Club Rd stocked with books in Malayalam while Cosmo Books or Current Books hold titles in English. Bhavi Books on Convent Rd, Ernakulam, is a good bookshop. Higginbothams, with a small selection, is on Chittoor Rd, at the junction with Hospital Rd. DC Books, with a huge collection of English-language classics, is out along Banerji Rd.

Idiom is probably the best bookshop in town. It has two branches, one is in Mattancherry (☎ 220428), opposite the synagogue, open daily until 6 pm. There is a more recent branch in Fort Cochin, near St Francis Church (☎ 224075), which is open daily until 9 pm. Both shops have an excellent selection on Indian art, culture, literature and religion; most of it is in English and French. The Fort Cochin branch also has an extensive range of books for children. Opposite Idiom in Mattancherry is another very good bookshop – Incy Bella, which stocks a good selection of reference books on India.

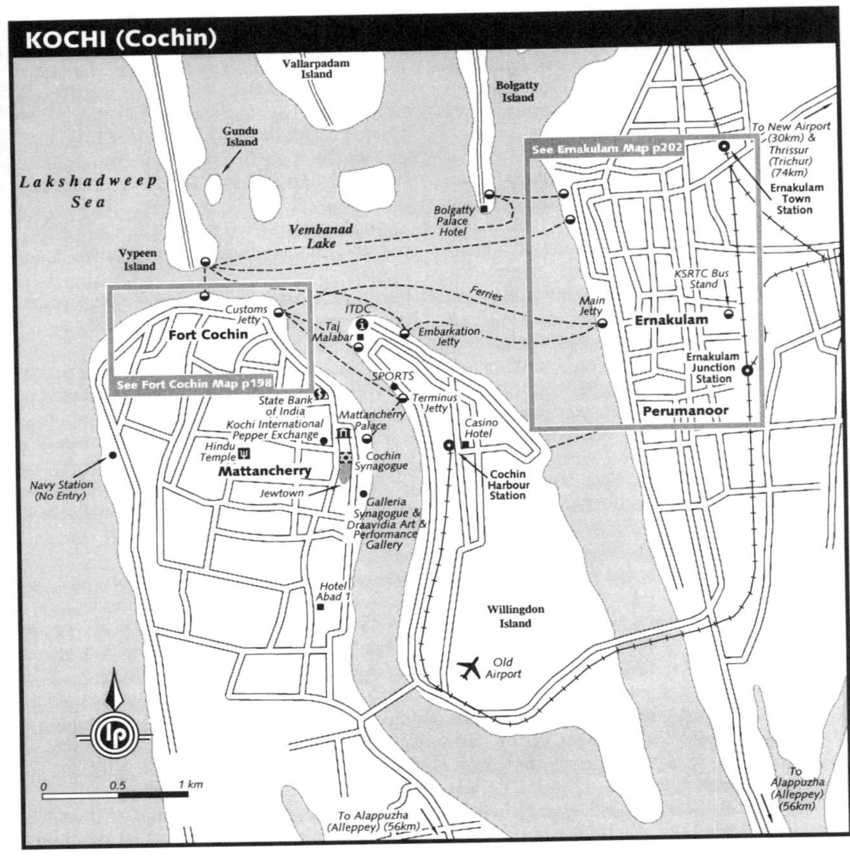

Medical Services The general hospital is appropriately in Hospital Rd. As elsewhere throughout Kerala, several places offer Ayurvedic treatment. Kerala Ayurveda Pharmacy (☎ 361202) has good reports of its massage as well as the helpful staff who dispense all types of medicines.

Emergency Ernakulam's Tourist Police are specially trained to deal with visitor queries. You'll find them near the KTDC Reception Centre (☎ 353234). They also maintain a presence at Fort Cochin, Mattancherry Palace, the airport and Ernakulam Junction train station.

Visa Extensions Apply at the office of the Commissioner of Police (☎ 360700), at the northern end of Shanmugham Rd, Ernakulam. Visa extensions can take up to 10 days to issue and you have to leave your passport at the office during that time.

Film & Photography A useful camera and film supplier is SP & Co on Convent Rd, Ernakulam. This is a good place for professional film and slide film and camera repairs.

Fort Cochin

St Francis Church Reputedly India's oldest European-built church was constructed in 1503 by Portuguese Franciscan friars who accompanied the expedition led by Pedro Alvarez Cabral.

The original structure was made out of wood, but the church was rebuilt in stone around the mid-16th century, the earliest Portuguese inscription found in the church is dated 1562. The Protestant Dutch captured Kochi in 1663 and restored the church in 1779. After the occupation of Kochi (Cochin) by the British in 1795, it became an Anglican church and it is presently being used by the Church of South India.

Vasco da Gama died in Cochin in 1524 and was buried here for 14 years before his remains were transferred to Lisbon. His tombstone can be seen inside the church. Rope-operated *punkahs* (fans) are one of the unusual features of this church.

Sunday services are held in English at 8 am and in Malayalam at 9.30 am, however the church is not open at other times.

Santa Cruz Basilica This Roman Catholic church was constructed in the late 1800s and consecrated early in the 20th century. The first church on this site was built by the Portuguese, in the 16th century. However it was destroyed by the British in 1795. The current church was raised to the status of a basilica in 1984 by Pope John Paul II. It's noted for its impressive interior murals.

Chinese Fishing Nets Strung out along the tip of Fort Cochin, these fixed, cantilevered fishing nets were introduced by traders from the court of Kublai Khan. You can also see them along the backwaters between Kochi and Kottayam, and between Alappuzha (Alleppey) and Kollam (Quilon).

Whilst the Chinese fishing nets have an aesthetic simplicity in their design, they are quite complex in their structure. The net is used like a big ladle which scoops the fish from the water. The whole thing works on the principle of weights and counterweights. The net is supported by a wooden frame and suspended from massive poles on a wooden platform. These poles can reach up to 30m in height. During high tide the net is lowered by ropes into the water with the help of large suspended rocks. Once in the water, these rocks help keep it below the surface. It takes a minimum of four men to raise the net. They walk along the platform, pulling hard on ropes that pass through a pulley system. Like the net, these ropes also have rocks attached. At a certain point the suspended rocks provide a counterweight that eases the net out of the water and onto the platform. It's then a race against time for the fisherman to grab the fish before the birds do.

Mattancherry

Mattancherry Palace Built by the Portuguese in 1555, Mattancherry Palace was presented to the raja of Cochin, Veera Kerala Varma (1537-61), as a gesture of goodwill

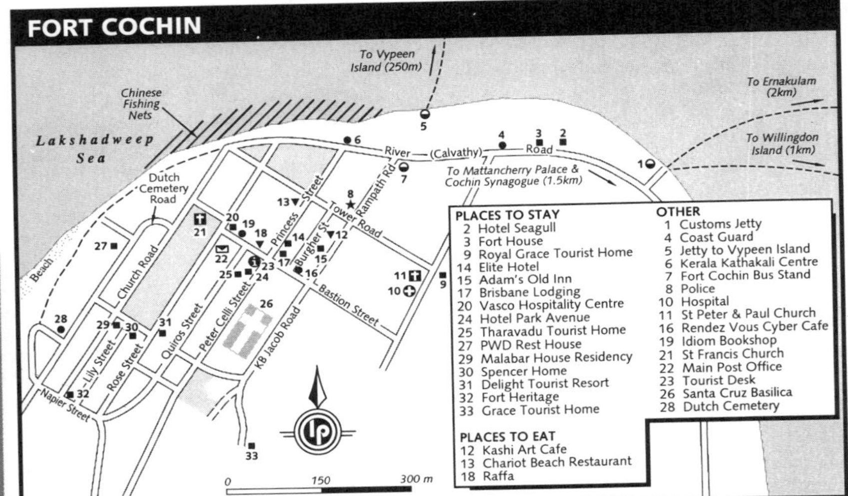

(and probably as a means of securing trading privileges).

The palace's alternative name, the 'Dutch Palace', resulted from substantial renovations by the Dutch after 1663. The two storey quadrangular building surrounds a courtyard containing a Hindu temple.

The central hall on the first floor was the coronation hall of the rajas. Their dresses, turbans and palanquins are now on display. More important are the astonishing murals, depicting scenes from the *Ramayana, Mahabharata* and Puranic legends connected with Shiva, Vishnu, Krishna, Kumara and Durga. These beautiful murals are one of the wonders of India. Downstairs, the ladies' bedchamber is worth seeing. It features a cheerful Krishna using his six hands and two feet to engage in foreplay with eight happy milkmaids.

The palace is open Saturday to Thursday from 10 am to 5 pm, entry is free but you may be asked to make a 'donation'. Photography is not permitted but there is a good booklet with colour reproductions of the murals on sale for Rs 35.

Cochin Synagogue Originally constructed in 1568, the synagogue was destroyed by cannon fire during a Portuguese raid in 1662 and was rebuilt two years later when the Dutch took over. It's an interesting little place, with hand painted willow pattern floor tiles brought from Canton in China in the mid-18th century by Ezekial Rahabi, who was also responsible for the erection of the building's clock tower.

A synagogue built at Kochangadi in 1344 has since disappeared, although a stone slab from this building, inscribed in Hebrew, can be found on the inner surface of the wall which surrounds the Mattancherry synagogue.

The area around the synagogue is known as **Jewtown** and is one of the centres of the Kochi spice trade. Scores of small firms huddle together in old, dilapidated buildings and the air is filled with the pungent aromas of ginger, cardamom, cumin, turmeric and cloves. Many Jewish names are visible on business premises and houses, and there are several interesting curio shops on the street leading up to the synagogue.

The synagogue is open Sunday to Friday, from 10 am to noon and from 3 to 5 pm. Entry is Rs 1. The synagogue's guardians are keen to talk about the building and the Jewish community.

Kochi International Pepper Exchange The harvesting and trade of pepper has always played a crucial role in the history of India. In Kochi the domestic pepper exchange has been a vital economic organ of the region for more than 50 years. In 1997, the Kochi International Pepper Exchange was established in an attempt to lure more foreign investment into the commodities market. Although it has been plagued with teething problems, the international exchange is an example of the extent to which the region is keen to embrace the principles and practices of a global economy.

The exchange is near the synagogue and visitors may observe the proceedings from 10 am to 1 pm and 2 to 4 pm Monday to Friday and Saturday from 10 am to 12.30 pm.

Ernakulam

Parishath Thampuram Museum This museum contains 19th century oil paintings, old coins, sculptures and Mughal paintings, but apart from some interesting temple models, it's nothing special. It is housed in an enormous, traditional Keralan building (previously Durbar Hall) on Durbar Hall Rd, and is open Tuesday to Sunday from 10 am to 12.30 pm and 2 to 4.30 pm, entry is free.

Ernakulathappan Temple Dedicated to Shiva this temple is associated with a fascinating legend regarding the disciple, Nagarshi. On killing a snake, Nagarshi was cursed to live with a serpent's head. His guru advised that liberation from the curse would only occur with devotion to Shiva. As luck would have it, Nagarshi discovered a lingam created by Arjuna (the *Mahabharata* hero). He set the lingam down near the sea, where it took hold permanently. Nagarshi understood this to mean that the curse was lifted. In honour of the event, he went to a local tank to bathe. But he disappeared within it. The area was subsequently named Rishinagakulam, the earlier name of Ernakulam. A temple was built on the site, and the legend is celebrated every January with colourful rituals and exciting cultural events. The bathing of the idol, on the eighth day, is particularly significant here.

Vypeen & Gundu Islands

Ferries shuttle across the narrow strait from Fort Cochin to Vypeen Island. The island boasts a lighthouse at Ochanthuruth (open from 3 to 5 pm daily), good beaches, and the early 16th century **Pallipuram Fort** (open Thursday). Known locally as Ayakkotta or Alikkotta, this fort was constructed by the Portuguese in 1503 and came under Dutch control in 1663. The raja of Travancore secured it by purchasing it from the Dutch in 1789. Now, under the jurisdiction of the Department of Archaeology it may be of historical interest to some. If the gate's locked you can crawl through the hole in the fence. To get there take the ferry to Vypeen Island (from Ernakulam, Fort Cochin or Bolgatty Island) and then a bus for the 25km journey along the length of the island to the fort. If approaching from Kodungallur (Cranganore) you can take a bus.

The smallest island in the harbour, Gundu, is close to Vypeen and belongs to the Taj Group of hotels, who plan to develop a five star hotel there. The coir (coconut fibre) factory on the island is not functioning so there is little to see, but you can visit the island by hiring a pricey private boat from Fort Cochin or Vypeen Island.

Organised Tours

The KTDC runs daily boat cruises around Kochi Harbour visiting Willingdon Island, Mattancherry Palace, the synagogue, Fort Cochin (including St Francis Church), the Chinese fishing nets and Bolgatty Island. The 3½ hour tour departs from the Sealord Boat Jetty, just north of the KTDC Tourist Reception Centre, at 9 am and 2 pm, (Rs 70). The sunset cruise from 5.30 to 7 pm costs Rs 35, but is frequently cancelled, so check early in the day to avoid disappointment.

Village backwater cruises in open country boats or covered kettuvallams are all the rage in Kochi. They visit coir making villages, coconut plantations and fish farms and give plenty of opportunity for birdwatching. It's a very relaxing way to experience traditional Kerala. Several trips, from two to six hours, are offered.

Indo World (☎ 370127), Heera House, MG Rd, offers a full day (six hour, Rs 800) cruise along canals and Vembanad Lake in a *kettuvallam* (traditional boat) which includes a traditional Keralan lunch served on a banana leaf.

KTDC (☎ 353234) cruises are similar to those available at Tourist Desk and depart from the Main Jetty at 8.30 am and 2.30 pm and cost Rs 300.

Salmon Tours (☎ 369669), Crystal Complex, Banerji Rd, has a four hour cruise (Rs 450) which also includes the opportunity to catch your lunch at a fish farm. This tour leaves at 9 am and returns at 2 pm.

Tourist Desk (☎ 371761) by the Main Jetty operates three hour village backwater cruises in traditional open canoes, which include bus transport (45 minutes each way) from the jetty car park to the starting point. The trips depart at 9 am and 2 pm and cost Rs 275 (direct bookings attract substantial discounts, with additional concessions for student card holders). If you're staying in Ernakulam, there's also a free hotel pick-up.

Special Events

The annual **Tourism Week**, from 26 December to 1 January, includes cultural performances, pop music, and an exciting snakeboat race. Any of the tourist offices will let you know the program.

Places to Stay

Ernakulam has accommodation in all price brackets. Fort Cochin has a handful of cheap places, a growing number of mid-range places and a couple of top-end places. Many travellers prefer Fort Cochin for its more romantic streetscapes and ambience. However, such popularity is giving rise to the fundamental dilemma of tourism – abuse of environmental heritage resulting from overdevelopment. Ernakulam may be frenetic in contrast to the more subdued Fort Cochin, but it's still possible to find quiet accommodation there. Local environmentalists are now urging travellers to stay in Ernakulam and enjoy Fort Cochin via regular ferry trips.

If you're looking for mid-range accommodation, it's worth checking the budget hotel listings which also have mid-priced rooms – they are the best choice in this price range.

As for accommodation on the islands, Bolgatty Island has one unique top-end place and Willingdon Island has a mid-range and two top-end places.

During December and January hotel space in all price brackets is severely limited, particularly during the ten day holiday period beginning 24 December. Where possible it's a good idea to book in advance.

Places to Stay – Budget

Fort Cochin The ***Royal Grace Tourist Home*** *(☎ 223584)* is a concrete budget hotel opposite St Peter & Paul Church. Large double rooms with bathroom cost from Rs 150 (downstairs) to Rs 250 (upstairs, brighter and breezy), or Rs 550 with air-con. Note that checkout is 10 am. Under the same management is the smaller, but similarly priced, ***Grace Tourist Home*** *(KB Jacob Rd)*, south of the Santa Cruz Basilica.

Tharavadu Tourist Home *(☎ 226897, Quiros St)* is an airy and spacious traditional house with good views of the surrounding streets from the rooftop area. Singles are Rs 135, or there's two top floor doubles for Rs 155 and Rs 205 which share a bathroom.

Elite Hotel *(☎ 225733, Princess St)* is a long-term favourite and has doubles with bathroom for Rs 150 to Rs 300. There's a popular but not especially good restaurant downstairs.

Brisbane Lodging *(☎ 225962, Princes St)*, a couple of doors away, has seven presentable rooms from Rs 150 to Rs 200.

PWD Rest House is nicely near the waterfront, but has just two double rooms for Rs 110 each. The enterprising housekeeper will organise village day trips using public transport, and personally guide you around.

Vasco Hospitality Centre (☎ *229877)*, near St Francis Church, has basic doubles for Rs 125, two rooms have private bathrooms.

Adam's Old Inn (☎ *229495)*, in quiet Burgher St, has comfortable singles for Rs 100 and doubles from Rs 150 to Rs 250, or Rs 350 with air-con.

Delight Tourist Resort (☎*/fax 228658, Rose St)* is opposite the old parade ground. More a friendly guesthouse than a resort, this large Dutch colonial home has seven double rooms from Rs 200 to Rs 600. All rooms have bathroom and mosquito netting on the windows. Lone women travellers give this place a strong recommendation.

Spencer Home (☎ *225409, Parade Rd)*, nearby is friendly and relaxing with clean and simple rooms from Rs 90 for a single and Rs 200 to Rs 300 for doubles. Note that checkout is noon.

Ernakulam There is no shortage of budget accommodation in Ernakulam.

YMCA International House (☎ *353479, fax 364641, Chittoor Rd)* is bright, clean and friendly. Rooms with bathroom in the economy block are Rs 125/150. Executive rooms are Rs 200/250 or Rs 350/450 with air-con. There is a well priced multicuisine restaurant downstairs.

Basoto Lodge (☎ *352140, Press Club Rd)* is small, simple, friendly and popular, so get there early. Singles with shared bathroom cost Rs 55, and doubles with private bathroom are Rs 120.

Hotel Seaking (☎ *355341, fax 372608)* is set back from busy MG Rd and is excellent value with singles/doubles for Rs 200/310, or Rs 495 with air-con. There is also a restaurant.

Hotel Hakoba (☎ *369839, Shanmugham Rd)*, conveniently located on the busy waterfront, is another good choice, although construction has spoilt the views. Doubles with bathroom start at Rs 194, or Rs 350 with air-con (prices include tax). There's a sad-looking restaurant, a noisy bar and even a (not very reliable) lift.

Maple Tourist Home (☎ *355156, fax 371712, Canon Shed Rd)*, near Main Jetty, is good value with doubles from Rs 230, or Rs 420 with air-con. The rooftop garden overlooks the jetty.

Bijus Tourist Home (☎ *381881, cnr Canon Shed and Market Rds)*, is a friendly place with rooms for Rs 165/350, and air-con doubles for Rs 475. It's good value and even has hot water. The management will help organise backwater/village tours as well as trips to martial arts displays and Kathakali performances.

Queen's Residency (☎ *365775, fax 352845)* is airy and aesthetic with rooms from Rs 175/220, or Rs 450 with air-con. Deluxe rooms are Rs 550 but all you get is an additional comfy chair.

Hotel KK International (☎ *366010)*, opposite Ernakulam Junction train station, is good value at Rs 160/290, or Rs 400 with air-con.

Geetha Lodge (☎ *352136, MG Rd)* has simple rooms for Rs 160/280.

Anantha Bhavan (☎ *382071)* nearby, has rooms from Rs 120/190 to Rs 180/280 and air-con doubles for Rs 650. Reports are that it only accepts Indian customers.

Hotel Luciya (☎ *381177)*, close to the KSRTC bus stand, is the best choice in this area. It has efficient and friendly staff and good value rooms at Rs 130/250, or Rs 285/435 with air-con. It has a restaurant and TV lounge.

Places to Stay – Mid-Range

Fort Cochin There are a number of mid-range places in Fort Cochin.

Hotel Seagull (☎ *228128, Calvathy Rd)* is right on the waterfront. Once one of the better places to stay, standards have slipped – visitors complain of noisy drunks. All rooms are doubles and cost Rs 350, or Rs 480 with air-con.

Hotel Park Avenue (☎ *222671, cnr Bastion and Peter Celli Sts)* is a compromise between Fort Cochin's development restrictions and hoteliers' greed. The height of the original two storey building was preserved but three storeys of hotel rooms were squeezed in, so most rooms are very tiny, some with no windows at all. Singles range

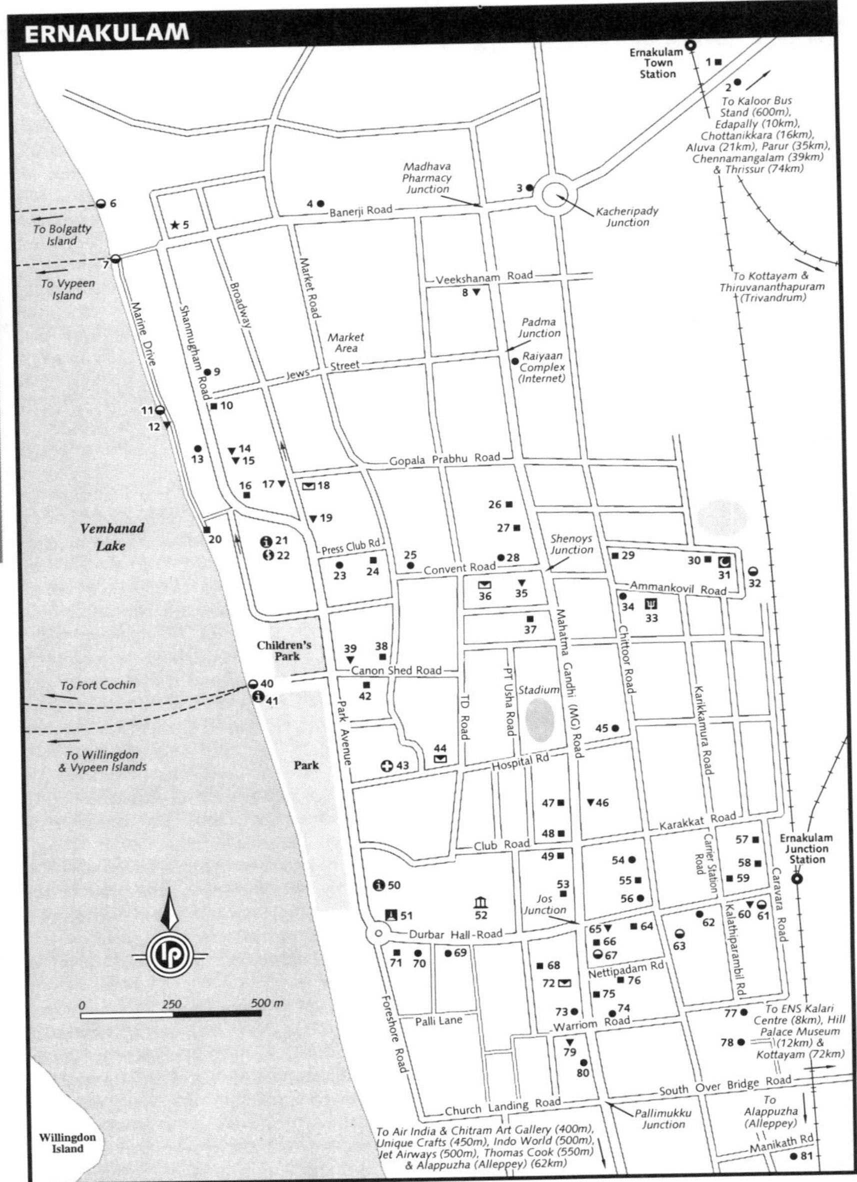
ERNAKULAM
Ernakulam Town Station
To Kaloor Bus Stand (600m), Edapally (10km), Chottanikkara (16km), Aluva (21km), Parur (35km), Chennamangalam (39km) & Thrissur (74km)
Madhava Pharmacy Junction
Kacheripady Junction
Banerji Road
To Bolgatty Island
To Vypeen Island
Veekshanam Road
To Kottayam & Thiruvananthapuram (Trivandrum)
Marine Drive
Shanmugham Road
Broadway
Market Road
Market Area
Padma Junction
Raiyaan Complex (Internet)
Jews Street
Gopala Prabhu Road
Vembanad Lake
Press Club Rd
Convent Road
Shenoys Junction
Ammankovil Road
Children's Park
Canon Shed Road
To Fort Cochin
To Willingdon & Vypeen Islands
Park Avenue
TD Road
PT Usha Road
Stadium
Mahatma Gandhi (MG) Road
Chittoor Road
Karikkamura Road
Park
Hospital Rd
Karakkat Road
Club Road
Carrier Station Road
Ernakulam Junction Station
Caravara Road
Jos Junction
Durbar Hall-Road
Kalathiparambil Rd
Nettipadam Rd
Foreshore Road
Palli Lane
Warriom Road
To ENS Kalari Centre (8km), Hill Palace Museum (12km) & Kottayam (72km)
South Over Bridge Road
Church Landing Road
Pallimukku Junction
To Alappuzha (Alleppey)
Manikath Rd
To Air India & Chitram Art Gallery (400m), Unique Crafts (450m), Indo World (500m), Jet Airways (500m), Thomas Cook (550m) & Alappuzha (Alleppey) (62km)
Willingdon Island
0
250
500 m

ERNAKULAM

PLACES TO STAY
1 Hotel Cochin Tower
10 Sealord Hotel
16 Hotel Hakoba
20 Taj Residency
24 Basoto Lodge
26 Hotel Abad Plaza
27 Hotel Seaking
29 YMCA International House
30 Hotel Luciya
37 Queen's Residency
38 Bijus Tourist Home
42 Maple Tourist Home
47 Grand Hotel
48 Woodlands Hotel
49 Geetha Lodge
53 Anantha Bhavan
55 The Hotel Sangeetha
57 The Metropolitan
58 Hotel KK International
59 Paulson Park Hotel
64 Hotel Joyland
66 Yuvarani Residency
68 Hotel Aiswarya
71 Bharat Hotel
75 Avenue Regent
76 Hotel Excellency

PLACES TO EAT
8 Frys Village
12 Ancient Mariner
14 Bimbi's; South Star
15 Arul Jyoti
17 Bharath Coffee House
19 Caravan Ice Cream
35 Chariot Restaurant
39 Indian Coffee House
46 Pandhal Restaurant
60 Jaffna Hotel
65 Bimbi's
79 Chinese Garden Restaurant

OTHER
2 Marikar Motors
3 Manuel Industries
4 DC Books
5 Commissioner of Police
6 High Court Jetty
7 Private Ferry to Vypeen Island
9 Sridhar Cinema
11 Sealord Jetty
13 GCDA Complex; Princy Tours
18 Post Office
21 KTDC Tourist Reception Centre; Tourist Police
22 State Bank of India
23 Cosmo Books; Current Books
25 SP & Co
28 Bhavi Books
31 Mosque
32 KSRTC Bus Terminal
33 Durga Temple
34 Magnetics
36 Ernakulam College Post Office; Ernakulam Public Library
40 Main Jetty
41 Tourist Desk
43 General Hospital
44 Main Post Office
45 Higginbothams
50 DTPC Tourist Information Centre
51 Ernakulathappan (Shiva) Temple
52 Parishath Thampuram Museum
54 Galleria Mareecheka
56 RG Mennoa Translators
61 South Bus Stand
62 Sound of Music
63 Ernakulam South Bus Stand
67 Bus to Fort Cochin
69 TDM Hall
70 Indian Airlines
72 Post Office
73 Kairaci
74 Ayurveda Pharmacy
77 See India Foundation
78 Art Kerala
80 Khadi Gramodyog Bhavan
81 Cochin Cultural Centre

from Rs 220 to Rs 550 and doubles are Rs 350 to Rs 900. The more expensive rooms have air-con.

Fort House *(☎ 226103, fax 222066, Calvathy Rd)* is good value at Rs 695 a double, which includes breakfast and all taxes. It has a good location and rooms are clean and comfortable.

Fort Heritage *(☎/fax 225333, Napier St)* has very spacious rooms in an old Dutch building. It has been in the same Syrian Christian family for a very long time and is furnished with antique rosewood furniture. It has a good restaurant including a *tandoori* (marinated North Indian-style) BBQ eating area with lawn service out in the back garden. Rooms are US$30/45 including breakfast. Air-con costs an extra US$10.

Ernakulam There are a number of mid-range places near Ernakulam Junction train station.

Paulson Park Hotel *(☎ 382170, fax 370072, Carrier Station Rd)* is an interesting design with all rooms facing an internal closed courtyard. It's good value with rooms for Rs 250/480, or Rs 480/650 with air-con. There's a choice of multicuisine or tandoori restaurants.

The Hotel Sangeetha *(☎ 368487, fax 354261,Chittoor Rd)* is a block west with a range of rooms from Rs 300/500 to Rs 680/790 with air-con. Prices include breakfast.

Hotel Joyland *(☎ 367764, fax 370645, Durbar Hall Rd)*, nearby, is well appointed and features a rooftop restaurant (Indian, Chinese and continental). Rooms are Rs 450/600, or Rs 520/800 with air-con.

Woodlands Hotel *(☎ 368900, fax 382080, MG Rd)*, a little north of Club Rd, is a long-time favourite. Rooms here are Rs 300/425, or Rs 475/650 with air-con. All rooms have TV and hot water, and there's a vegetarian restaurant and roof garden.

Hotel Aiswarya *(☎ 364454)*, near Jos Junction, is a pleasant new hotel with good-value clean rooms for Rs 260/360, or Rs 800 with air-con. All rooms have hot water and TV, plus complimentary tea or coffee in the morning.

Hotel Excellency *(☎ 374001, fax 374009, Nettipadam Rd)*, south of Jos Junction, has a three star rating and rooms from US$12/15, or US$25/30 with air-con. It has good facilities, a restaurant, and even throws in 'bed coffee'.

Bharat Hotel *(☎ 353501, fax 370502, Durbar Hall Rd)* is a huge place next to the Indian Airlines office. Rooms cost from Rs 550/650, or Rs 750/1000 with air-con. It has vegetarian and north Indian nonveg restaurants, a 24 hour coffee shop and a marriage hall on the roof. Checkout is noon.

Hotel Cochin Tower *(☎ 340910, fax 370645)* on busy Lissie Junction is close to Ernakulam Town train station. Comfortable rooms with satellite TV start at Rs 430/550, or Rs 600/760 with air-con. There are a couple of restaurants on the premises.

The Metropolitan *(☎ 369931, fax 382227)*, near Ernakulam Junction train station, is a glossy but quiet, centrally air-conditioned and friendly hotel with rooms for Rs 650/1150. There's a reasonable restaurant and a bar.

The ***Avenue Regent*** *(☎ 372660, fax 370129, MG Rd)* is a centrally air-conditioned four star hotel, south of Jos Junction. Rooms start from US$60. There's a restaurant, bar and round-the-clock coffee shop that sometimes has a buffet Indian dinner for Rs 200.

Yuvarani Residency *(☎ 370040, MG Rd)* is a glitzy new hotel set back from busy MG Rd just enough to shield the noise. Rooms are clean, bright and well priced at Rs 550/650 for non air-con and Rs 850/1050 for air-con. The Cheenavala Restaurant on the 1st floor is definitely worth a visit.

Hotel Abad 1 *(☎ 228212, fax 370729, Mattancherry)* has the same high standard and good value as its sister hotel in Ernakulam, with rooms from Rs 800 to Rs 1500. There's a coffee shop and a popular seafood restaurant.

Grand Hotel *(☎ 382061, fax 382066, MG Rd)* has spacious rooms (all air-con), but recent renovations have eroded the old world charm. Rooms cost Rs 900/1100. The hotel has two good restaurants offering a wide range of veg and nonveg meals.

Sealord Hotel *(☎ 382472, fax 370135, Shanmugham Rd)* has central air-con and is good value, though the rooms are showing signs of age. Singles/doubles are Rs 700/800, or Rs 900/1200 for deluxe rooms. There's two restaurants: one air-con with live music, the other on the rooftop with a bar.

Places to Stay – Top End

Fort Cochin The ***Malabar House Residency*** *(☎/fax 221199, Parade Rd)*, across the playing field from St Francis Church, has beautifully furnished, centrally air-conditioned rooms for US$120 and suites for US$150. But some of the rooms have short beds – for all that money you'd expect leg room. The restaurant has a good reputation for Indian and Italian cuisine and prices to match. It also has theme evenings with set menus and dance performances.

Ernakulam The modern ***Hotel Abad Plaza*** *(☎ 381122, fax 370729, MG Rd)* is an air-conditioned business hotel. Rooms start at Rs 1100/1450. It has restaurants, a coffee shop, a health club and a rooftop pool with great views over the city.

Taj Residency *(☎ 371471, fax 371481, Marine Drive)*, a more business-oriented sister to the Taj Malabar on Willingdon Island, is on the waterfront. It offers all mod cons (except a pool) and boasts the Harbour View Bar. Room prices start at US$80/90 and rooms with a sea view are US$100/115.

Bolgatty Island In a magnificent setting on the southern tip of this island there is a unique place to stay.

Nuts That Don't Deceive

There can be no escaping the coconut in Kerala. Aside from the disputed claim that the very word Kerala means land of the coconut, the fact remains that coconuts are a linchpin in the Keralan rural economy. In 1997, an estimated 7000 million nuts were 'produced'. This represents 60% of India's coconut production. Although spread throughout the state, yield per hectare is highest around Kozhikode.

Although referred to as a nut, the coconut does not belong to the nut family. Technically it is a seed. And it happens to be the largest seed in the world.

Apart from the actual nuts there exists a wide range of by-products which add considerable value to the industry. Uses of coconut products include:

wood – house building (especially rafters and posts), fuel and handicrafts.
leaves – thatching, fencing, brooms and handicrafts.
kernel – desiccated coconut and coconut cream.
copra – coconut oil and cake.
water – drinks, coconut milk and vinegar.
shell – fuel, charcoal, carbon and handicrafts.
husk – coir, used for making rope and matting.
sap – toddy (a potent form of liquor) and brown sugar.

Coconut growers refer to the product as 'nuts that don't deceive' and make a good living from them. A tree can produce 60 to 70 nuts per year. In Kerala, the maximum land holding for an individual or one family of two adults and two children is two hectares, this is ample for the 200 trees necessary to support the family.

The industry however is not without its problems. Leaf diseases, believed to be pollution related, afflict large areas. Harvesting the nuts is another problem; the men who shimmy up the trees demand Rs 5 per tree which, according to growers, makes the harvest unprofitable. The coconut pickers are ageing and their sons prefer 'softer jobs' so the future looks somewhat precarious. A plan to import Malaysian monkeys especially trained to pluck the nuts is being considered. Rumours are that opposition will be tough.

The impact of globalisation is also taking its toll. A free trade agreement between India and Sri Lanka will see the importation of Sri Lankan coconut product to India, which will have a profound impact on the economy of Kerala.

Bolgatty Palace Hotel *(☎ 355003, fax 354879)* was built in 1744 as a Dutch palace, then later became a British Residency. Extensively renovated, retaining much of its original splendour, it offers luxurious suites and cottages from Rs 1750. There's a pool, restaurant and bar and the attractive landscaping enhances the magical location. Even if it's beyond your budget, it's worth catching the boat to look around and maybe splurge on a drink. If you do wish to stay, telephone first or inquire at the Tourist Reception Centre, Shanmugham Rd, otherwise you'll waste a lot of time if the hotel is full. Ferries (Rs 0.40) leave the High Court Jetty in Ernakulam for Bolgatty Island every 20 minutes from 6 am to 10 pm, at other times private launches are available.

Willingdon Island The ***Taj Malabar*** *(☎ 666811)* is a five star hotel wonderfully situated at the tip of the island, overlooking the harbour. The hotel boasts the full range of facilities, including a pool and Ayurvedic massage. Rooms start at US$95/110 (singles/doubles). Those with a harbour view are a little more expensive and worth every extra cent with singles from US$115 to US$155 and doubles from US$130 to US$170. Deluxe suites are US$250 to US$350.

Casino Hotel *(☎ 668421)* also has an excellent range of facilities, including a pool. It's US$65/70, but its location near the train station and warehouses is no match for the Taj Malabar's.

Places to Eat

Fort Cochin The restaurant at the ***Ramathula Hotel***, near the junction of Irimpichi and New Rds, is better known by the chef's name, Kayika. Excellent chicken or mutton *biryanis* (Muslim rice dishes) are Rs 30. Be there between noon and 3 pm so you don't miss out.

Badhariya is a small non-veg restaurant where you can get curry and *paratha* (flat bread) for around Rs 15.

Behind the Chinese fishing nets, just west of the Kerala Kathakali Centre, are a couple of ***fishmongers*** and an even greater selection of fish fryers. The idea is you buy a fish (or prawns, scampi, lobster; Rs 50 to Rs 300 per kg), take it to one of the kitchens and they'll cook and serve it to you (about Rs 30 for a large fish). The main drawback is all the attention from the mangy kittens, bold crows and sticky flies. The advantage is that you should be able to determine the freshness of the catch first hand.

Kashi Art Cafe *(☎ 221769, Burgher St, email kashicafe@yahoo.com)* is the hip place in town. It opens at 8.30 am and serves a range of foods including home-baked chocolate cake and filter coffee (Rs 30 for two cups). Its goal is to support contemporary art and the cafe organises exhibitions, workshops and theatre performances. Interested artists can contact the cafe for possible networking and possible residencies.

The restaurant at the ***Elite Hotel*** *(Princess St)* is the old travellers' stand-by. It has a small range of fairly basic food including fish curries for around Rs 25.

Raffa, nearby, has budget Indian meals and ice cream but the limited choice of bland dishes is a sellout to tourists' bland tastes.

Chariot Beach Restaurant *(Princess St)* turns out uninspired Indian and western snacks and light meals, but it's a popular place to sit in the open, sip a cold drink and watch the world pass by.

The new top-end hotels all have good quality restaurants. In grand five star tradition, the biggest prices, smallest serves and longest waits are at ***Malabar House Residency*** which offers Indian and Italian dishes. The ***Fort House*** has already earned a good reputation for its preparation of seafood but two hours' notice is required.

Ernakulam Opposite the Main Jetty, ***Indian Coffee House*** *(cnr Canon Shed Rd and Park Ave)*, has quaintly uniformed waiters in cummerbunds offering good snacks and breakfasts. It's popular and always busy, although some women travellers report disturbing accounts of harassment.

Bimbi's *(Shanmugham Rd)* is a modern, self-serve restaurant near the Sealord Hotel. There is fast food (North and South Indian plus some western snacks) as well as sweets. An excellent *masala dosa* (stuffed pancake) costs Rs 12. There's another branch near Jos Junction.

South Star *(Shanmugham Rd)* is an air-con restaurant above Bimbi's. It is good value with mains for around Rs 50.

Lotus Cascades/Jaya Cafe *(MG Rd)*, in the Woodlands Hotel, turns out excellent vegetarian *thalis* (plate meals) for Rs 30.

Pandhal Restaurant *(MG Rd)* simulates a modern western chain restaurant. It turns out excellent North Indian food and OK pizzas (Rs 90), but the burgers should probably be avoided.

Chinese Garden Restaurant *(Warriom Rd)*, just off MG Rd, has good food and attentive service.

Frys Village (evenings only) on Veekshanam Rd just near Padma Junction is the place to go for authentic Keralan food.

Ancient Mariner *(Marine Drive)* is a mediocre floating restaurant.

Caravan Ice Cream, near the Tourist Reception Centre, is cool and dark with good ice cream and milkshakes (Rs 20). Try the cardamom or fig.

Arul Jyoti *(Shanmugham Rd)* is a straightforward 'meals' place with basic veg dishes for Rs 15. ***Bharath Coffee House*** *(Broadway)* offers similar fare.

Chariot Restaurant, with entrances on Convent and Narakathara Rds, has a similar menu as the Chariot Beach Restaurant in Fort Cochin.

Sealord Hotel *(Shanmugham Rd)* has two restaurants and two menus: Chinese and Indian/continental. The reasonably priced food is consistently good. The choice of venue is between air-con and live 'easy listening' rock, or the rooftop where conversation is accompanied by traffic noise wafting up on photochemical thermals.

Jaffna Hotel serves good inexpensive vegetarian meals from around Rs 15.

Cheenavala Restaurant in the new Yuvarani Residency on MG Rd has a wide and well priced selection of Indian, Chinese and western dishes, including a range of Keralan specialities. The boneless crab in chilli for Rs 70 is enticing.

The classy but reasonably priced ***Regency Restaurant*** *(MG Rd),* in the Hotel Abad Plaza, offers good Indian, Chinese and western food.

The Paulson Park Hotel, near the Ernakulam Junction train station, has the ***Moghul Hut*** tandoori restaurant in its central atrium.

Willingdon Island In the Taj Malabar, the ***Waterfront Cafe*** offers a lunchtime buffet for Rs 275. The Malabar's ***Chinese Jade Pavilion*** and the plush ***Rice Boats*** restaurants serve excellent seafood.

Casino Hotel has a buffet in its gloomy restaurant, or there's a brighter outdoor seafood restaurant by the pool which opens for dinner only.

Entertainment

Kathakali There are several places in Kochi where you can see Kathakali. For more information on this colourful traditional drama, see the Performing Arts section in the Facts about Kerala chapter.

Art Kerala *(☎ 366238)*, near the See India Foundation, Ernakulam, stages rooftop performances for Rs 90. Make-up begins at 6 pm and the show runs from 7 to 8 pm.

Cochin Cultural Centre *(☎ 367866, Souhardham, Manikath Rd)* is south of Ernakulam Junction train station. The performance (Rs 100) is held in a specially constructed air-con theatre designed to resemble a temple courtyard. Make-up begins at 5.30 pm and the performance runs from 6.30 to 8 pm.

Kerala Kathakali Centre *(no phone)* stages performances at the Cochin Aquatic Club on River (Calvathy) Rd, Fort Cochin, near the bus stand. Enthusiastic performances from young Kathakali artists nicely balance the more formal introduction to the art at the See India Foundation. Make-up begins at 5 pm, and the performance runs from 6.30 to 7.30 pm. The last ferry from Fort Cochin to Ernakulam departs after the performance at 9.30 pm. Admission is Rs 85.

See India Foundation *(☎ 369471, Devan Gurukalum, Kalathiparambil Rd)* is near the Ernakulam Junction Train Station. The show features an extraordinary presentation by PK Devan, who explains the drama's history and makes a plucky attempt to simplify the main elements of Hinduism for visitors. Make-up begins at 6 pm, and the performance runs from 6.45 to 8 pm, with time for questions afterwards. It costs Rs 120, though you may be offered a discounted ticket from hotel staff in Ernakulam.

If, after viewing one of these performances, you wish to experience more of this fascinating art, you can attend a traditional all-night performance. Once a month the ***Ernakulam Kathakali Club*** hosts all-night performances by major artists at the TDM Hall on Durbar Hall Rd, Ernakulam. Programs covering the story in English are distributed from tourist offices a week in advance. The cost (donation) is Rs 100.

Music The ***Draavidia Art & Performance Gallery*** in Mattancherry has evening (6 to 7 pm) performances of classical Indian music.

Cinema The ***Sridhar Cinema*** *(Shanmugham Rd)* screens films in Malayalam, Hindi, Tamil and English.

Spectator Sports

Martial Arts The ***Arjuna Kalari Centre*** *(☎ 365 440)* in Ernakulam is a good place to see students of kalarippayat, Kerala's traditional martial art, sparring at their school.

Shopping

Kochi has fine handicraft shops, antique emporiums, art galleries and clothing shops. Jewtown, in Mattancherry, is the place for antiques and reproductions. Some of the larger warehouses are a joy to explore, although one wonders how all these beautiful old carvings, obviously from churches, temples and grand houses, were obtained. Along with the tourists there's a steady stream of interior decorators from California and London vying for old teak columns and Chinese urns.

One of the more exciting developments in Kochi has been the encouragement of contemporary artists. In Fort Cochin, Kashi Art Cafe, Burgher St, exhibits and sells works by up-and-coming artists. In Mattancherry, you can see contemporary work at Galleria Synagogue and Draavidia Art & Performance Gallery.

On MG Rd, Ernakulam, are branches of the well known Kairali and Khadi Gramodyog Bhavan. Chitram Art Gallery, also on MG Rd (opposite Thomas Cook) and Galleria Mareecheka, Chittoor Rd, exhibit and sell works by well known and emerging artists. Also in MG Rd, near the intersection with Ravipuram Rd, the family-run Unique Crafts has a wide range of goods and helpful service.

If you fancy yourself with a sitar or set of tabla, head to Manuel Industries, Banerji Rd, Ernakulam. A sitar will set you back Rs 3500, while a set of tabla is Rs 1500. Cassettes and CDs of Indian and western music can be purchased at Magnetics and Sound of Music.

A new Enfield Bullet 350cc is yours for Rs 50,000 at Marikar Motors, on Lissie Junction. Second-hand motorcycles from its workshop can be had for much less.

Getting There & Away

Air The Indian Airlines office (☎ 370242) is on Durbar Hall Rd, next to the Bharat Tourist Home. Air India (☎ 351295, airport office ☎ 610010) is on MG Rd opposite Thomas Cook and Jet Airways (☎ 369423), a bit farther down MG Rd, also has services to and from Kochi. See the Flights from Kochi boxed text for flight details.

In mid-1999 the Nedumbassery airport (☎ 610115, fax 610012) opened in Kochi to provide a major international terminal for tourism and for the transportation of exports.

Domestic Flights to/from Kochi (Cochin)

destination	airline	frequency (to Kochi)	frequency (from Kochi)	fare (US$)
Agatti (in Lakshadweep)	IC	daily except Sun	daily except Sun	150
Bangalore	CD	daily	daily	70
Chennai	CD	Mon, Wed, Fri	Mon, Wed, Fri, Sun	105
Delhi	CD	daily	daily	300
Goa	CD	daily	daily	110
Mumbai	CD	daily	daily	150
	9W	daily	daily	150

Abbreviations: IC= Indian Airlines, CD = Alliance Air, 9W = Jet Airways

ALL PHOTOGRAPHS BY KAREN TRIST

ne hidden aspects of Kochi

p: The monsoon is a welcome relief from the heat. **Bottom left:** With the high level of literacy in erala, newspapers are widely read. **Bottom right:** The delicate light of the Santa Cruz Basilica.

EDDIE GERALD

LINDSAY BROWN

GREG ELMS

EDDIE GERALD

LINDSAY BROWN

Top left: A triple-headed Ganesh, the Hindu god of wisdom and prosperity. **Top right:** An Escher-influenced building in Ernakulam. **Left:** Elaborate lighting in the synagogue in Jewtown, Kochi. **Middle right:** Wooden masks on display in Kochi. **Bottom right:** Have your favourite scribbler fixed in Thrissur.

At the time of writing only services to the Middle East were operating, however more services to Europe and other countries were planned. The international and domestic terminals are walking distance apart. When fully operational the international terminal will process 1600 passengers per hour with the domestic terminal handling half that number.

Bus The KSRTC bus terminal (☎ 372033) is by the railway line in Ernakulam, between the train stations. Because Kochi is in the middle of Kerala, many buses passing through Ernakulam originate in other cities. Although it's still often possible to get a seat on these buses, you cannot reserve them, you simply have to join the scrum when the bus turns up. You can make reservations up to five days in advance for many of the buses which originate in Ernakulam. The timetable is in Malayalam and English, and the staff are usually very helpful.

There are private buses too, the Kaloor bus stand is north-east of Ernakulam Town train station and the Ernakulam South bus stand is right outside the entrance of Ernakulam Junction train station.

The fares and times listed are for super-express buses unless otherwise noted. Superfast services are usually a few rupees cheaper and stop more often. See the 'Buses form Ernakulam KSRTC Bus Stand' table for information on buses from Kochi.

Buses from Ernakulam KSRTC Bus Stand

destination	frequency (daily)	distance (km)	duration (hrs/min)	fare (Rs)
Alappuzha	37	57	1.30	25
Bangalore	3	565	15.00	192
Chennai	1	690	16.05	210
Coimbatore	4	198	5.00	75
Guruvayur	4	107	1.50	35
Kannur	8	317	7.30	105
Kanyakumari	2	302	8.45	95
Kasaragod	2	420	10.00	135
Kollam	37	159	3.30	55
Kottayam	35	76	1.30	30
Kozhikode	20	219	5.15	75
Kumily[1]	7	192	6.00	46
Madurai (via Kumily)	4	324	9.15	111
Munnar[2]	5	130	5.00	42
Palakkad	9	160	3.30	55
Sultan's Battery	2	326	8.30	112
Thiruvananthapuram (via Alappuzha)	37	224	5.00	80
Thiruvananthapuram (via Kottayam)	11	240	5.30	85
Thrissur	12	74	2.00	30

[1] Of the seven daily buses to Kumily, three are express buses.

[2] Private buses also run to Kothamangalam, from where several buses connect to Munnar.

In addition to the KSRTC state buses, private companies have daily superdeluxe video buses to Bangalore, Mumbai (Bombay) and Coimbatore. Check out Princy Tours (☎ 354712), in the GCDA Complex on Shanmugham Rd opposite the Sealord Hotel; Conti Travels (☎ 353080), at Jos Junction on MG Rd; and Silcon A/C Coach (☎ 394596) on Banerji Rd.

Train Ernakulam has two train stations, Ernakulam Junction and Ernakulam Town. The one you're most likely to use is Ernakulam Junction. However it's important to note that trains from Mangalore and Bangalore come to Ernakulam Town (not Junction). Note that none of the through trains on the main trunk routes go to the Cochin Harbour station on Willingdon Island.

Popular trains are detailed in the 'Major Trains from Ernakulam' table, below. At least five daily trains go north to Thrissur, Kozhikode and Kasaragod, stopping also at the smaller stations along the line. If you're heading to/from Udhagamandalam (Ooty), there are quite a few express trains which stop at Coimbatore (Rs 75/252, six hours, 198km). From Coimbatore you can take a connecting train to Ooty. See the table for more details.

Getting Around

To/From the Airport The new Nedumbassery airport is 30km from Kochi near Angamali. Taxis cost around Rs 275 one way. It's not a good idea to take an auto-rickshaw for this distance.

At the time of writing there were no airport buses, however some of the top-end hotels offered special coach services for Rs 100 to Rs 150 per person one way.

Public Transport There are no convenient buses between Fort Cochin and the Mattancherry Palace and synagogue, but it's a pleasant 30 minute walk through the busy warehouse area along Bazaar Rd. There are auto-rickshaws, and your negotiation skills will be tested – this is tourist territory.

In Ernakulam, auto-rickshaws are the most convenient mode of transport. The trip from the bus or train stations to the Tourist Reception Centre on Shanmugham Rd should cost about Rs 20 – a bit less on the meter. Flagfall is Rs 6, then Rs 3 per kilometre.

Local buses are good and cheap. If you have to get to Fort Cochin after the ferries stop running, catch a bus in Ernakulam on MG Rd, south of Durbar Hall Rd. The fare is Rs 3. Auto-rickshaws will demand at

Major Trains from Ernakulam

destination	train No & name	departure time[1]	distance (km)	duration (hrs/min)	fare (Rs) (2nd/1st)
Bangalore	6525 *KK-Bangalore*	8.15 pm EJ	637	13.00	187/650
Delhi	2625 *Kerala*	3.35 pm ET	2833	48.00	447/1933
Kozhikode	6307 *Cannanore*	4.50 pm EJ	190	4.15	53/258
Mangalore	6329 *Malabar*	11.00 pm ET	414	9.30	132/460
	6349 *Parsuram*	10.50 am ET		10.00	132/460
Thiruvananthapuram					
(via Alappuzha)	6305 *Guruvayur-Nagercoil*	11.27 pm ET	224	4.30	61/294
(via Kottayam)	6350 *Parsuram*	1.55 pm ET		5.00	61/294
	6335 *Nagercoil-Gandidham*	11.15 pm ET		5.45	61/294

[1] ET = Ernakulam Town, EJ = Ernakulam Junction.
All trains are express.

least Rs 80 once the ferries stop running after about 10 pm.

Taxis charge round-trip fares between the islands, even if you only want to go one way. Ernakulam to Willingdon Island could cost up to Rs 150 late at night.

Boat Ferries are the main form of transport between the various parts of Kochi. Nearly all the ferry stops are named, which helps to identify them on the timetable at Main Jetty in Ernakulam. The stop on the east side of Willingdon Island is Embarkation; the west one, opposite Mattancherry, is Terminus; and the main stop at Fort Cochin is Customs.

Getting onto a ferry at Ernakulam can sometimes involve scrambling across several ferries to get to the boat you want. Make sure you get onto the right ferry or you may find yourself heading for the wrong island – the skipper or deck hand will usually set you right.

Ferry fares are all Rs 2 or less. Ticket offices in Ernakulam open 10 minutes before each sailing.

Ernakulam-Fort Cochin/Mattancherry There are services to Fort Cochin every 45 minutes from around 6 am to 9.30 pm. It's a pleasant 20 minute walk from the Customs Jetty to Mattancherry. There are also seven ferries a day direct to/from Mattancherry.

Ernakulam-Willingdon/Vypeen Islands Ferries from Main Jetty to Vypeen Island (via Willingdon Island) run every 20 minutes from about 6 am to 10 pm. Ferries to Vypeen Island (sometimes via Bolgatty Island) leave from the High Court Jetty on Shanmugham Rd.

Ernakulam-Bolgatty Island Ferries for Bolgatty Island depart from the High Court Jetty every 20 minutes between 6 am and 10 pm. It's a five minute walk from the public jetty to Bolgatty Palace Hotel.

Fort Cochin-Willingdon Island Ferries operate between Customs Jetty and the Taj Malabar/Tourist Office Jetty about 30 times between 6.30 am and 9 pm from Monday to Saturday.

Fort Cochin-Vypeen Island Ferries cross this narrow gap virtually nonstop from 6 am until 10 pm. There is also a vehicular ferry every half hour or so.

Hire Boats Motorised boats of various sizes can be hired from the Sealord Jetty or from the small dock adjacent to the Main Jetty in Ernakulam. They're an excellent way of exploring Kochi harbour at your leisure and without the crowds; rates start at around Rs 300 an hour. Rowboats shuttle between Willingdon Island and Fort Cochin or Mattancherry on request for about Rs 40.

Car & Motorcycle A car will enable you to travel easily to the areas surrounding Kochi. It's best to hire one with a driver (around Rs 1000 per day). However if you wish to drive yourself ATS (☎ 304150), 4km east of Kochi near WYTOL Junction, has a Maruti 1000 for Rs 1000 per day, while a Maruti 600 is Rs 600 per day. You'll need to leave a licence or passport as security.

Motorcycle hire is generally not available and hiring bikes can also be difficult. However, you could make inquiries at the Tourist Desk in Ernakulam for the current situation.

ENS KALARI CENTRE

This centre, 8km east of Kochi at Nettoor, established in 1954, offers training and demonstrations in the ancient martial art of kalarippayat (see the boxed text 'Kalarippayat' in the Facts about Kerala chapter). Students from many countries come here to learn the art. The centre also has a massage facility and a library for research. Demonstrations of kalarippayat are staged daily from 6 to 7 pm. For further details write to call Mr ES Narayanan Embranthiri (☎ 0484-700810), Embram Madom, ENS Kalari, Nettoor, Ernakulam District, Kerala 682304.

The best way to get to the ENS Kalari Centre is by local bus from Ernakulam South stand or auto-rickshaw (about Rs 50 one way).

HILL PALACE MUSEUM

The Hill Palace Museum at Tripunithura, 12km south-east of Ernakulam, is en route to Kottayam. It houses the collections of the Cochin and Travancore royal families, including ancient manuscripts, sculptures and coins. It's open Tuesday to Sunday from 9 am to 12.30 pm and 2 to 4 pm; entry is Rs 1. Bus No 51 or 58 from MG Rd, Ernakulam will take you there.

CHOTTANIKKARA TEMPLE

Numerous stories attest to the early history of this 10th century temple, where tormented devotees found solace in the deity, Bhagavati. Today, it remains one of the most popular pilgrim sites in Kerala, devotees still flock here seeking liberation from torment. Sometimes they dance themselves into a frenzy in their battle between the demons and the deities.

The Goddess at Chottanikkara is revered here in three forms; she is Sarasvati (goddess of learning) in the morning, Bhagavati (fierce and destructive) at noon and Durga (divine mother) in the evening.

An annual nine day festival (February/March) involves a huge celebration where devotees, especially women, seek blessings for their marriage and families.

Buses come here regularly from Ernakulam, which is 16km north-west. Only Hindus may enter the temple.

MUSEUM OF KERALA HISTORY

The Museum of Kerala History at Edapally, 10km north-east of Ernakulam, en route to Aluva (Alwaye) and Thrissur, depicts the history of Kerala for the last two millennia. It's open Tuesday to Sunday from 10 am to noon and 2 to 4 pm; entry is Rs 2. Bus No 22 from MG Rd, Ernakulam runs to Edapally.

PARUR & CHENNAMANGALAM

About 35km north of Kochi is a busy little town a world away from touristy Kochi but with which it shares much history. Parur encapsulates the cultural and religious medley of this region, where international trade dominated for countless years. Just to the north of the central bus stop, beside the ochre-red former British Residency buildings, is the small though clearly signposted **Jew St**. There is one Jewish family remaining in Parur and they live on the premises of the disused synagogue. The dusty synagogue was built around the same time as its famous counterpart in Mattancherry, but the original pulpit and arch were shipped to Israel and many of the Belgian glass lamps are now cracked.

At the end of Jew St is a canal where a **market** is held midweek. Nearby is an *agraharam* (place of Brahmins), a small street of neat, close-packed houses which was settled by Tamil Brahmins brought here by the rajas of Cochin. Behind the large Roman Catholic church are the remains of the third church erected on this site. It was built in 1308 and partly demolished in 1964. The first church was built, so some believe, by the Brahmins converted by St Thomas the Apostle (Doubting Thomas) in the first century CE. Parur also boasts a Syrian Orthodox church, a Krishna temple and a temple to the mute goddess Mookambic.

Four kilometres from Parur, on the banks of the Periyar River not far from the historic port of Kodungallur, is the village of Chennamangalam. Here stands the oldest **synagogue** in Kerala – virtually in ruins, abandoned and locked, and slowly disintegrating under the ineffectual guardianship of the Archaeological Survey of India.

There is a **Jesuit church** and the ruins of a Jesuit college, the Vaippikotta Seminary, which was wrecked by Tipu Sultan in 1790. The Jesuits first arrived in Chennamangalam in 1577 and, soon after their arrival, the first book in Tamil (the written language used in this part of Kerala at that time) was printed here by John Gonsalves.

You can walk to the **Hindu temple** on the top of the hill overlooking the Periyar River. On the way you'll pass a 16th century **mosque** as well as Muslim and Jewish **burial grounds**.

Also in Chennamangalam is a 17th century **palace** built by the Dutch after they defeated the Portuguese at Cranganore, and presented to the Palayathachan – a dynasty of chief ministers to the royal family of Cochin. The palace is now in the hands of a trust which looks after the 60-odd Hindu temples in the immediate region.

Getting There & Away

To get to Parur, catch a bus from the KSRTC bus stand in Ernakulam. From Parur you can catch a bus, auto-rickshaw or taxi to Chennamangalam. Whereas Parur is compact and there are lots of locals to point you in the right direction, Chennamangalam is best visited with a guide. Indo World (☎ 370127, fax 380968) at 39/4155 Heera House, MG Rd, Ernakulam, can organise transport and a local retired history teacher to guide you.

MALAYATTUR

On the Periyar River, this town, believed to have been visited by St Thomas, is an important Christian centre. Many thousands of Christian pilgrims gather here, particularly on Palm Sunday. The nearby church, 2km walk uphill, was built around 900 CE.

KODUNGALLUR (Cranganore)

Kodungallur's colourful past represents a microcosm of Kerala's history. Evidence suggests that Kodungallur was the ancient port of Muziris referred to by Pliny the elder. It was from here, in the early centuries CE, that spices left for ports in the Middle East. This was the headquarters of the Chera dynasty. Christians believe that it was near here, at Malliankara, that St Thomas arrived in 52 CE. And for Muslims, Kodungallur was the landing place for Malik Bin Dinar, the missionary who introduced Islam to Kerala.

Malik Bin Dinar is credited with building the **Cheraman Mosque** here in 630 CE – reputedly the oldest in India. However the current structure is no more than 200 years old and renovations have rendered its aesthetic less appealing. It's 2km north of Kodungallur on National Highway 17 and male visitors with a particular interest may enter.

Two kilometres south east of the mosque the **Krishna** and **Mahadeva** temples (Hindus permitted only) are fine examples of Keralan architecture. **Kurumba Devi Temple**, dedicated to the goddess Bhagavati is famous and infamous for its Bharani Festival in March/April, when thousands of devotees parody erotic gestures on the outskirts of the temple. Such practices are shunned by many Malayalis and an earlier custom of animal sacrifice is now banned.

Regular buses (not ferries) run to Kodungallur from Ernakulam.

MAR THOMA PONTIFICAL SHRINE

This modern shrine honours St Thomas, credited with having introduced Christianity to India in 52 CE. The shrine is set in a semicircle, the small church in the centre flanked by statues of the saints. In front of the church there's a large statue depicting the moment when Thomas acknowledged the risen Christ (and henceforth ceased his doubting). Just behind a painting illustrates Thomas' arrival, being greeted by elephants, on the nearby shores of Malliankara. In 1953, relics believed to be bone from the right arm of St Thomas, were placed within the shrine. Each day at 3 pm a priest exposes the relics for viewing. St Thomas' arrival is celebrated annually with a huge festival on the Sunday following 21 November.

There's a small 'cool bar' selling drinks, hybrid rabbits and pious articles!

Getting There & Away

There are several ways to get to the shrine. From Ernakulam, catch a Kodungallur bus and alight just after Parur (it's well signposted). Or you can catch a ferry from Ernakulam to Vypeen Island and from there a bus to Munambam Jetty at the very north of the island just beyond the village of Pallipuram. Ferries leave the Munambam Jetty every 20 minutes except for a lunch break from midday to 1.45 pm. Take the ferry (Rs 0.75, 15 minutes) across the river to the Azhicode Jetty. From here turn right, following the river in a north easterly direction, past the government fish market, for about 10 minutes.

If you're coming from the north, (maybe Thrissur) take a bus to Kodungallur (1½ hours) and then take a bus, or private transport, the last 10km to the shrine.

THRISSUR (Trichur)

☎ 0487 • pop 77,700

Thrissur, meaning 'town with the name of Lord Shiva', is regarded as the cultural capital of Kerala. An important religious and cultural centre for centuries, Thrissur was occupied by the kingdoms of Kochi from the 16th to the 18th century. It briefly fell into the hands of the Zamorins of Kozhikode and then Hyder Ali in the late 18th century. Today Thrissur is still distinguished by its cultural importance with several government arts colleges. It features one of the largest temples in Kerala, the Vadakkunathan Kshetram and is the site for the renowned Pooram Festival.

Thrissur provides a good base for the visitor. From here you can visit Guruvayur with its Krishna temple and elephant stables and also experience much of Kerala's culture at nearby centres for the performing arts. (See the sections following for more information).

Orientation & Information

Thrissur radiates out from Vadakkunathan Kshetram. The encircling roads are named Round North, Round East, Round South and Round West.

The DTPC Tourist Information Centre (no phone) has a happy sweeper but don't waste your time seeking information.

The State Bank of India on Town Hall Rd cashes American Express and Thomas Cook travellers cheques but not cards. Canara Bank on Round South can handle cash advances on Visa cards.

The post office is on Round West. There are a few STD/ISD booths around town. As with much of Northern Kerala, fax and email are a hit and miss affair. The line is always 'getting ready'. Local faxes transmit, but not international ones. A good email place (when the line works) is IRS Computers & Communications (☎ 425560, fax 440037) on Round West. This is actually a computer training college and for Rs 1 per minute (plus a small fee for each additional person) you can surf the net and download email. It's open from 9 am to 8 pm on weekdays and 9 am to 6 pm on Saturday.

Things to See

Famed for its murals and artwork, the Hindu-only **Vadakkunathan Kshetram** is right in the centre of Thrissur. To the east and west, are the lesser known **Thiruampady** and **Paramekkavu temples**, which participate in the Pooram Festival (see following entry).

There are several significant churches including **Our Lady of Lourdes Metropolitan Cathedral**. Don't bother with the sad **zoo** and the amazingly dusty and decrepit **State Museum** in the zoo grounds. However, the **Archaeological Museum**, farther along Museum Rd, has temple models, stone reliefs, Gandharan pieces and reproductions of some of the Mattancherry murals. The museum is open from 10 am to 5 pm. The zoo and museums are closed on Monday.

Special Events

The annual April/May **Pooram Festival** is one of the biggest in India's south. First introduced by Sakthan Thampuram, the maharaja of the former state of Kochi, some 200 years ago, it has developed into an elaborate event. Elephants, 15 each from the nearby Thiruampady and Paramekkavu temples, are decorated with symbols of royalty, including gold and multicoloured umbrellas. They parade through the streets of the town, until they meet each other outside Thrissur's main temple, the Vadakkunathan Kshetram. Their riders, accompanied by musicians, then engage in an elaborate spectacle simulating a competition.

The **Festival of Women's Theatre** is conducted in Thrissur every January by the Sangeetha Nataka Academy (☎ 0492-622418). Some of India's leading actors participate in discussions, debates, workshops and performances.

Places to Stay

Ramanilayam Government Guest House *(☎ 332016, cnr Palace and Museum Rds)* is good value at Rs 45/50 for singles/doubles, or Rs 175/275 with air-con. Ring first as it's often full.

The KTDC ***Yatri Nivas*** *(☎ 332333, Stadium Rd)*, nearby, has rooms for Rs 100/150, or Rs 350/400 with air-con. There's a restaurant and bar.

Chandy's Tourist Home *(☎ 421167, Railway Station Rd)*, close to the bus and train stations has rooms for Rs 80 with common bathroom, or Rs 95/275 with private bathroom. There are several lodges nearby with similar standards and prices.

Jaya Lodge *(☎ 423258, Kuruppam Rd)*, around the corner, is unexciting but cheap with rooms for Rs 60/100, doubles with bathroom are Rs 110.

Paris View *(☎ 339566, cnr Round West and Round North)* has no real view, and Paris is a long way off, but it does offer comfortable, although small, double rooms

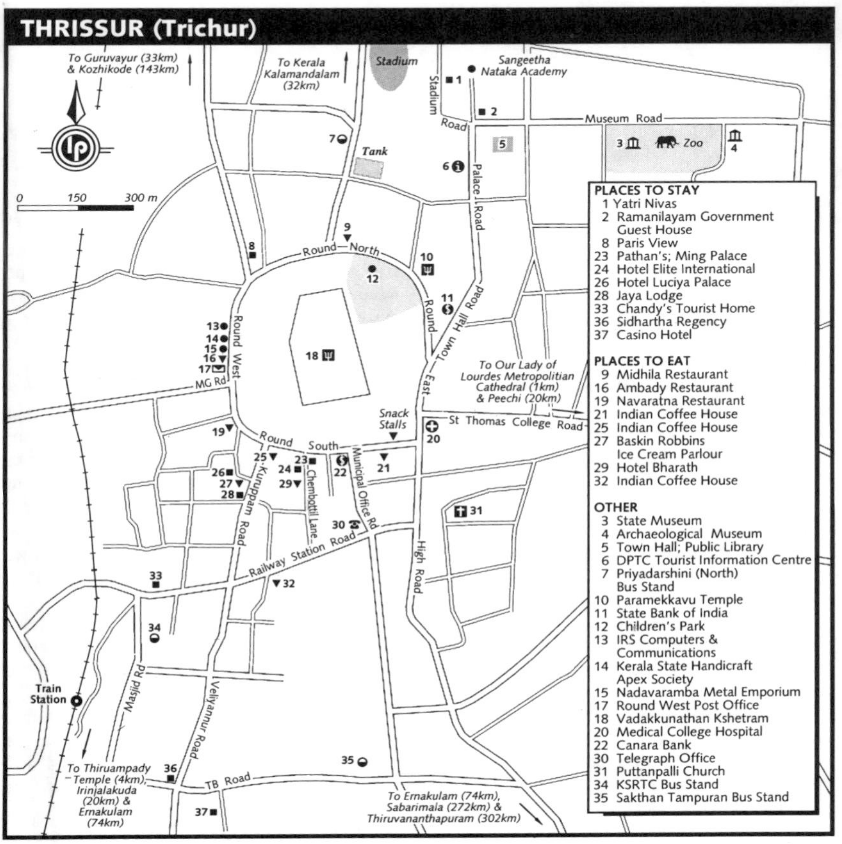

for Rs 160. There is a popular restaurant downstairs.

Pathan's *(☎ 425620, Chembottil Lane)*, just off Round South, has rooms for Rs 150/230, or very large doubles with balcony for Rs 280 with TV. The rooms are on the 5th floor so it's worth checking to see if the elevator is working.

Hotel Elite International *(☎ 421033, fax 442057)*, across the road, is a more comfortable option; rooms are Rs 210/260, or Rs 340 with TV. Air-con rooms are Rs 410/480. It has a bar and an air-con restaurant.

Hotel Luciya Palace *(☎ 424731, fax 427290, Marar Rd)*, just off Round South, is good value with clean, comfortable rooms with TV for Rs 350/475, or Rs 575/675 with air-con. At the time of writing the renovations were almost complete so the price may well jump. The hotel has an air-con restaurant, a bar and a delightful outdoor restaurant.

Sidhartha Regency *(☎ 424773, fax 425116, cnr TB and Veliyannur Rds)* is close to buses and the train station. It's welcoming and friendly, centrally air-conditioned and has pleasant rooms which even have a fridge. Prices start at Rs 600/750. There's also a good restaurant and a bar.

Casino Hotel *(☎ 424699, fax 220437, TB Rd)*, also close to the bus and train stations, is recently renovated. It's another pleasantly welcoming place and a popular hotel for wedding parties so you may have trouble getting a room. Singles/doubles are Rs 400/450, or Rs 600/750 with air-con.

Places to Eat

A cluster of ***snack stalls*** sets up near the corner of Round South and Round East each evening.

Indian Coffee Houses are on Round South; PO Rd, near Railway Station Rd; and upstairs in President Bazaar, on Kuruppam Rd.

Upstairs in ***Pathan's*** there's a good, basic vegetarian restaurant with an air-con section. A floor above Pathan's is the ***Ming Palace*** Chinese restaurant.

Hotel Bharath, farther down Chembottil Lane, is good, busy and vegetarian.

Paris View has good cheap veg and non-veg meals for breakfast, lunch and dinner. It's a popular place for Sunday morning breakfast and coffee.

Ambady Restaurant offers fast good, cheap vegetarian meals – thalis for Rs 15, with *chapati* (flat bread) *dosa* (pancake) and paratha for Rs 9.

Navaratna Restaurant *(Round South)* has excellent North Indian veg cuisine while ***Midhila Restaurant*** *(Round North)* has slightly upmarket South Indian vegetarian.

The mid-range and top-end hotels have decent restaurants which usually have air-con. The ***Luciya Palace*** has a popular outdoor restaurant where the beer is cold and the tandoor kababs are delightfully spicy and succulent.

Just around the corner from the Luciya Palace ***Baskin Robins*** sells its numerous flavoured ice creams from its upmarket outlet to its upmarket clientele.

Shopping

On a Sunday stroll around The Round you can purchase all sorts of things from the pavement vendors, including cheap watches, magazines, an amazing array of underpants and that back issue you always wanted of *The Hungarian Quarterly*.

Thrissur is a good place for bell metal and there are a number of shops crammed with lamps, household appliances and images of Ganesh, Nataraja and a host of other deities. Prices vary from a few rupees to many thousands. At Nadavaramba Metal Emporium (☎ 421679) on Round West, the proprietor knows his stuff and although prices are 'fixed', negotiation can result in generous discounts.

For typical Kerala handicrafts, you can try the Kerala State Handicraft Apex Society (☎ 420865) also on Round West just near the IRS computer college. There's a huge range from the unbelievably gaudy to genuine fine craft work. Here you can even purchase a working model of a Chinese fishing net. Prices are fixed and shipping can be arranged. It's open Monday to Saturday from 10 am to 1.30 pm and 3.30 to 7.30 pm.

Getting There & Away

Bus There are three bus stations in Thrissur – the KSRTC and Sakthan Tampuran in the south; with the Priyadarshini (also referred to as North) in the north.

Regular KSRTC buses go to Thiruvananthapuram (Trivandrum, Rs 85, 7½ hours), Ernakulam (Rs 25, 2 hours), Kozhikode (Rs 38, 3½ hours), Palakkad (Palghat, Rs 21, 1½ hours), Coimbatore, Periyar, Kottayam, Munnar and Ernakulam.

The large, private Sakthan Tampuran has buses bound for closer towns such as Kodungallur, Irinjalakuda and Guruvayur (Rs 8, one hour). The smaller, private Priyadarshini bus stand, has many buses bound for Shoranur and Palakkad (Rs 15, two hours), Pollachi and Coimbatore.

Train Trains to Ernakulam, 74km south, take about 1½ hours (Rs 28/149); trains to Kozhikode, 143km north, take about three hours (Rs 36/189). There are also several trains running to or through Palakkad (Rs 27/150) via Shoranur. The train station is about 1km south-west of the town centre.

Krishna's Temple

Guruvayur's vast Krishna Temple is one of the most important pilgrim centres in Kerala. One of its most famous devotees, the 16th century poet Narayana Bhattatiri, crippled with rheumatic pain sought solace in the temple deity Guruvayurappen, the infant Krishna. Within the temple he composed the *Narayaneeyam*. Inspired by the *Bhagavata Purana*, it is one of the most famous and highly acclaimed texts in Hindu literature. The poet recovered from his pain and the temple acquired a reputation as a place with special healing powers. Since then there have been numerous stories of devotees cured of physical or mental illness there. The temple operates an elaborate system for offerings, the most popular being *thulabharam*, where a devotee presents to the deity their own body weight in offerings of coconuts or bananas. The temple is also a popular venue for marriage as well as *Annaprasana*, when a child first receives solid food.

CENTRAL KERALA

GURUVAYUR

The **Sri Krishna Temple** at Guruvayur, 33km north-west of Thrissur, dates from the 16th century and is one of the most famous in Kerala (see the boxed text).

For entry, women must wear a sari and men must wear a *dhoti* (sarong) without a shirt. The wearing of *salwar kameez* (women's loose pants suit) is forbidden. Although non-Hindus may not enter, a walk around the outskirts gives a good idea of the temple's architecture and proportions. The large tank, with a statue of Krishna playing his flute, exudes a pleasant serenity.

The temple's elephants are kept at an old Zamorin palace, **Punnathur Kota**, about 5km from Guruvayur's bus stand. The bizarre sight of 43 elephants (or a few less if they've been called away to a temple festival) swaying and straining against their shackles amid piles of smouldering dung is unforgettable. You can wander around, avoiding the grass soccer balls, and watch the *mahouts* (keepers) bathe and feed their charges.

There are always a couple of elephants free to drag their chains around while collecting a feed of palm leaves or heading off for a bath. It's surprising how quickly they can move and fling those chains about. It's a sobering thought that four mahouts have been killed by elephants here in recent years. Never approach an elephant without permission and guidance from a mahout. Male elephants in *musth*, a time of heightened sexual desire, may be dangerous. You can tell when an elephant is in musth because the gland behind the eye secretes a visible discharge, but their erections are even more obvious! (see the 'Elephants in Kerala' boxed text in the Facts about Kerala chapter).

There are a few visiting rules. Smoking and alcohol are prohibited. Food can only be given to the elephants with permission from the keepers, however *annayoottu*, donations for elephant feed (Rs 400), are greatly appreciated. There are no guides so don't be enticed to pay for one – the mahouts will happily provide any information you require. The elephant yard is open from 9 am to 5 pm every day. Entry is free, though there's a Rs 25 camera fee. It's a Rs 20 auto-rickshaw ride from the Guruvayur bus stand.

KERALA KALAMANDALAM

This important academy of arts 32km north east of Thrissur at Cheruthuruthy (☎/fax 0492-622418) was founded in 1930 by the late poet Vallathol Narayana Menon and his associate Manakkulam Mukunda Raja. The present site was begun in 1973 and today the Kerala Kalamandalam is a campus of many aesthetic buildings in classical Keralan style (including a theatre that can accommodate an audience of 250) set in nine hectares of beautiful surrounds.

It's hard to overestimate the contribution that this organisation has made to the renaissance of traditional folk art in Kerala. Full time students undergo intensive training (often for six years) in Kathakali, Mohinyattam, Koodiyattam and Thullal. Courses are also available in percussion, voice and violin. All students are residential and they must rise at 4.30 am for physical exercise before beginning classes at 9 am. The centre has four performing groups comprising teachers and students which travel throughout India and sometimes abroad.

Visiting hours are from 9 am to noon and 3 to 5 pm. It's possible to stroll between the open air buildings and watch the classes in progress (special permission is required for video and photography). At the time of writing a gallery dedicated to traditional folk art was nearing completion.

Short courses (between 6 and 12 months) are available to foreigners for around Rs 950 per month plus accommodation nearby at Rs 1000 per month (food excluded). For information on courses as well as performances, contact The Secretary, Kerala Kalamandalam, Cheruthuruthy, GPO Thrissur, Kerala 679531.

To get to the Kalamandalam, you can catch a train from Thrissur to Shoranur, which is 1.5km from Cheruthuruthy. From there you can walk or take an auto-rickshaw. Numerous private buses make the journey from the Priyadarshini bus stand in Thrissur directly to Kalamandalam.

IRINJALAKUDA

☎ 0488

Irinjalakuda, 20km south of Thrissur, is an important site for temples, churches and cultural centres.

Koodal Manikyam Temple

This temple is dedicated to Bharata, the loyal and selfless hero and strong supporter of Rama. The deity at the temple is said to embody the joy and rapture experienced by Bharata, when he learned of the reunion of Rama and Sita. It's believed that this is the only temple in India dedicated to Bharata and devotees claim miraculous cures from disease and ill health. Several festivals are held here, but it is the annual Medom (April/May) that attracts thousands of devotees to colourful rituals and festivities.

St Thomas' Church

The original St Thomas' Church, a stone and wooden construction, was established in 1845 and dedicated to St George Foraine. It served Christian families who had been in the area for some time. The current impressive construction dates from 1917 and has 10,000 devotees. Each year, in early January an annual three day church festival honours St Thomas, St George and St Sebastian as well as the Epiphany of Christ. Processions visit each Christian home with an *umbur*, representing the arrow of St Sebastian, the patron saint of archers. The procession is greeted with fireworks. At the church, the *Pindi Peranul*, Epiphany procession, takes place whilst the church is illuminated in lights depicting Mary, the saints and other liturgical scenes.

Natana Kairali Research & Performing Centre

This is another important cultural centre in the Thrissur district. Under the directorship of G Venu, the centre offers training and discourse in a wide range of traditional arts including dance and some rare forms of puppetry. The centre hosts a 12 day annual festival beginning in the first week of January. Performances, usually in the evenings, are often preceded or followed by discussions (in Malayalam and English) on technique and meaning. Short appreciation courses (usually about one month) are available to foreigners. The centre has no accommodation but staff will help you find somewhere nearby to stay. The fee as well as the focus of the course should be discussed with the director. For details about courses, as well as performances it is advisable to telephone first or write to the Director (☎ 825559), Natana Kairali Research & Performing Centre for Traditional Arts, Ammannu Thakyar, Mathom, Irinjalakuda, Thrissur District.

Getting to this place is tricky, especially at night. The best way to navigate the dark labyrinthine laneways is by auto-rickshaw from Irinjalakuda. If you ask for the Natana Kairali locals will happily offer directions.

Getting There & Away

Regular buses leave the Sakthan Tampuran bus station in Thrissur for Irinjalakuda.

PEECHI-VAZHANI WILDLIFE SANCTUARY

☎ 0487

This large dam in the Western Ghats, 20km east of Thrissur, provides the area's drinking water while the attached sanctuary offers protection for animals. Visiting the sanctuary requires a permit from the Wildlife Warden's Office (☎ 782017), 4km to the west of the entrance. In theory the warden is on duty every day from 9 am to 5 pm and takes no lunch break. In practice he may be absent on other duties, so you can enjoy the company and humour of the other staff unauthorised to issue permits. The nearby information office is 'for namesake only'. At the dam site there's a littered picnic ground and a rather uninviting hotel for meals. About 150m down the steps closer to the dam, things improve. You can explore the beauty of the area on foot or by boat. A walk across the dam wall will cost you Rs 2 and boat hire costs Rs 150 for 30 minutes in a 12 seater. In theory the boatman comes daily from 10.30 am to 5 pm. In practice he just may not turn up.

The area has suffered serious environmental damage and supports little wildlife, except for land-dwelling birds such as jungle fowl and peacock. The best time to visit is between December and March.

There's accommodation here in the form of ***Peechi House*** *(☎ 78022)* – a bastion of decaying grandeur. Two rooms of this four bedroom mansion, once the province of government VIPs, are now let to travellers (the other two are in serious disrepair). The rooms are large and airy with basic furnishings and fittings. Each room is Rs 150 with meals at Rs 25.

KERALA FOREST RESEARCH INSTITUTE

This institute, established in 1975, undertakes research on a range of issues including medicinal plants, entomology, clonal propagation of plants, disease control and methods for reforestation. The library contains over 14,000 titles with 7000 research papers. Travellers are welcome to visit the library. Those with a particular interest in any of the research topics may organise to meet the appropriate staff by writing to the Director (☎ 0487-782037, fax 782249), Kerala Forest Research Institute, Peechi, Thrissur, 680653.

Northern Kerala

Unlike the crowded beach resorts and backwaters of the southern coast, Northern Kerala is an unusual travel destination. Don't expect to be harangued by tour operators and touts. There's very little visitor information available, maps are hard to come by and few people speak English. Yet this is a rewarding region to visit if you like to get away from the tourist traps.

Northern Kerala has not always been off the beaten track for foreigners. Once known as Malabar, this region attracted its fair share of traders, seafarers, vagabonds and other assorted opportunists that helped mould the history of the state. The most egregious of these was of course Vasco da Gama who dropped anchor at Calicut (now called Kozhikode) in 1498. Today the area remains relatively unexplored by domestic and foreign travellers. And it is mercifully untouched by the sort of developers whose trademark is to transform natural beauty into tacky theme parks. Developers are however hovering on the horizon and speculation is rife as to how long the region can resist their advances.

Considerable wealth flows into the area through expatriated income from Malayalis in the Middle East. This is reflected in the bustling bazaars, large buildings and opulent jewellery stores of Kozhikode, a good base from which to explore the northern districts.

Highlights

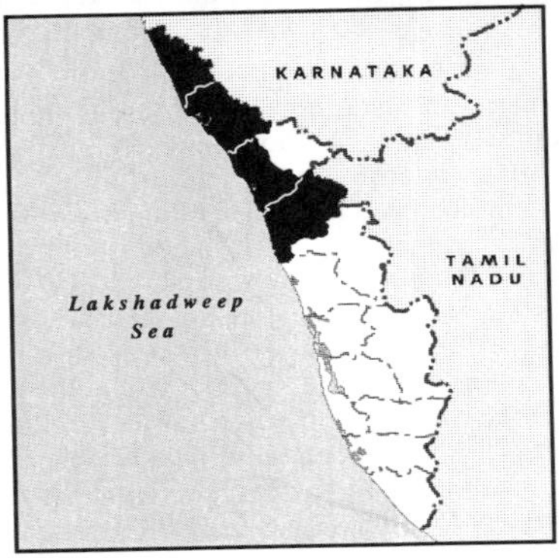

KARNATAKA
TAMIL NADU
Lakshadweep Sea

- Visit isolated beaches, far from the tourist crowds of Kovalam and Varkala
- Explore the enormous Bekal Fort
- Visit industrious cooperatives for a taste of the lives of Kerala's workers
- Watch the colourful spectacle of Teyyam ritual dance

HISTORY

From the 10th to 13th centuries the Malabar region came to prominence under the Zamorin rulers, many of whom were generous patrons of art, music and scholarship. By the end of the 15th century the rule of the Zamorins had spread to encompass nearly half of Kerala.

For hundreds of years Arab trading ships had plied the Malabar coastline but in the 1500s their successful trade was challenged by the Portuguese who were determined to acquire some of the lucrative bounty. Vasco da Gama's arrival at Kappad Beach near Kozhikode in 1498 heralded a new era for the region. Although at first welcoming the Portuguese, the Zamorins soon resented the newcomers, who began to meddle and exploit local rivalries. War soon broke out between the Portuguese and the Zamorins. Portuguese attacks in 1509 and 1510 were both repulsed, although Kozhikode was virtually destroyed in the latter assault. The Zamorins sought Dutch support against the Portuguese and in 1604 the first treaty between an Indian power and the Dutch was signed. However the Dutch influence waned as their attention was drawn to conflict in Europe.

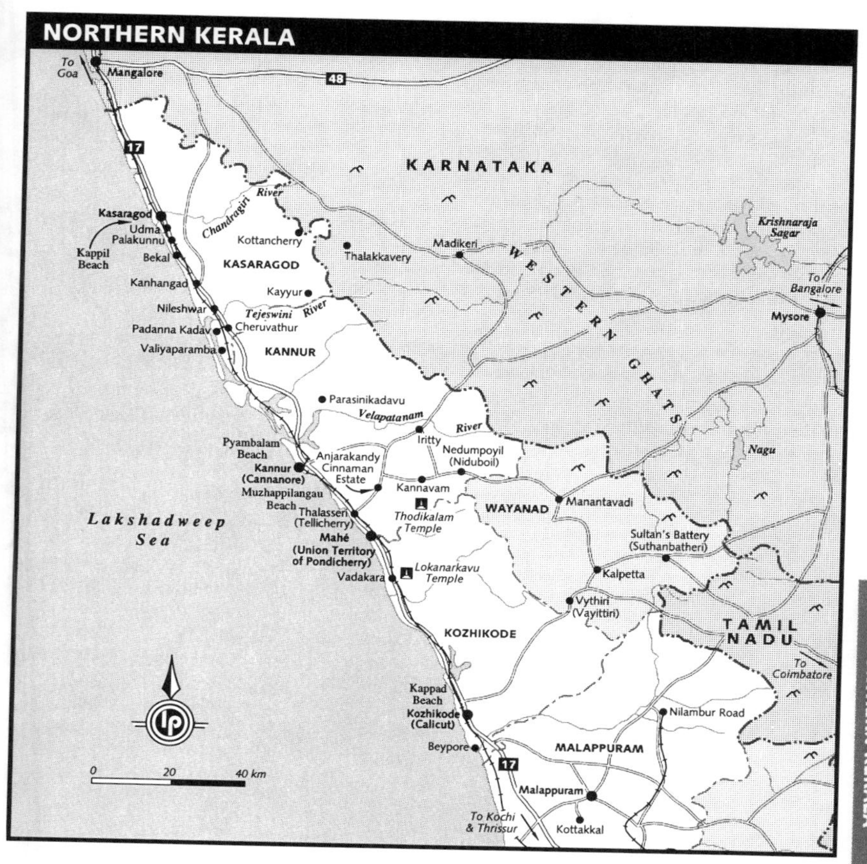

During the late 18th century, the Malabar region came under the control of the Mysorean rulers Hyder Ali and Tipu Sultan. They instituted new administrative practices in the areas of tax collection, landholding and transportation. Many of these reforms benefited the landless peasants who had previously been at the mercy of unscrupulous landlords; the landlords however were less than impressed.

The British gained control of the region in 1792, following protracted conflict with the sultans and deals negotiated with local chieftains. Seven years later, following a fierce battle at Srirangapatnam, Karnataka, which resulted in the death of the Tipu Sultan, British rule was consolidated. In 1800 Malabar became part of the Madras Presidency, which represented the southern area of India under British rule. The British made enormous changes to the economic structure (see the Kerala & the British section in the Facts about Kerala chapter) and to a great extent their administration supported the former landlords, which resulted in agitation and riots from agrarian workers.

By the late 19th century the emerging Indian National Congress, which aimed to oust the British, found an enthusiastic base in Malabar. The numbers swelled with the 1921 Malabar Rebellion, triggered by the suffocation of 61 prisoners in a closed and overcrowded railway carriage being transported from Tirur, 50km south of Kozhikode. Malabar residents supported the Gandhi-inspired civil disobedience movement. A 1939 split in the Indian National Congress party in Malabar resulted in the formation of the Communist Party of Malabar. This had a significant influence on the politics of the new state of Kerala that was formed in 1956, and comprised Malabar with the former southern states of Cochin and Travancore.

KOZHIKODE (Calicut)

☎ 0495 • pop 801,190

Kozhikode, on the Lakshadweep Sea, has been known throughout history as a signif-

Major Trains of Northern Kerala to/from Kozhikode

The following timetable gives departure and arrival information for trains heading north from Kozhikode to the major train stations of the northern region. Distance, departure time and fares are from Kozhikode station.

destination	train No	departure time	arrival time	distance (km)	frequency	fares (Rs) (2nd/1st)
Thalasseri	6334[1]	12.05 am	1.25 am	69	Wed only	20/140
	6336[2]	12.05 am	1.25 am		Thu only	20/140
	6338[3]	12.05 am	1.25 am		Fri only	20/140
	6636[4]	9.45 am	11.00 am		daily	20/140
	2617[5]	5.35 pm	7.10 pm		daily	20/140
Kannur	6334[1]	12.05 am	2.05 am	90	Wed only	30/161
	6336[2]	12.05 am	2.05 am		Thur only	30/161
	6338[3]	12.05 am	2.05 am		Fri only	30/161
	6636[4]	9.45 am	11.45 am		daily	30/161
	2617[5]	5.35 pm	8.00 pm		daily	30/161
Kanhangad	6636[4]	9.45 am	12.55 pm	155	daily	46/223
	2617[5]	5.35 pm	9.30 pm		daily	46/223
Kasaragod	6334[1]	12.05 am	3.40 am	175	Wed only	51/244
	6336[2]	12.05 am	3.40 am		Thur only	51/244
	6338[3]	12.05 am	3.40 am		Fri only	51/244
	6636[4]	9.45 am	1.20 pm		daily	51/244
	2617[5]	5.35 pm	10.15 pm		daily	51/244

Trains depart from Kasaragod for Kozhikode daily at 3.20 am and 10.20 am. Services to Kozhikode also run on Monday, Tuesday and Wednesday, departing at 2.15 pm (not stopping at Kanhangad).

1 *Trivandrum-Rajkot Exp*
2 *Nagarcoil-Gandidham*
3 *Kochi-Rajkot Exp*
4 *Kurla Netravathi Exp*
5 *Ern-Nizamudhin Mangala Exp*

icant port for trade and commerce. Its importance was further enhanced in the 10th century when it became the capital of the powerful Zamorin dynasty. Known also as Calicut, the quality cotton, calico is believed to have originated here.

Today Kozhikode retains its role as an important centre for timber and boat building. It's a thriving city with evidence of wealth and enterprise – the fruits of Malayali labour in the Middle East.

Information

Good tourist information in Kozhikode is seriously lacking. The tourist desk at the Hotel Malabar Mansion is now closed, however, a Kozhikode map is available from the hotel reception for Rs 5. The District Tourism Promotion Council (DTPC) and Joint Directorate of Tourism at Civil Station will shuttle you back and forth to each other – a complete waste of time and space. For a broader informative perspective, visit Current Books on Mavoor (Indira Gandhi) Rd.

Money can be changed at the State Bank of India. Head upstairs to the foreign exchange office and make sure you take a good book to read. The bank is open Monday to Friday from 10 am to 2 pm and Saturday from 10 am to noon. For faster options try PL Worldways, 3rd floor, Lakhotia Computer Centre, at the junction of Mavoor and Bank Rds or Lavanya Tours & Travels (☎ 753676) in MA Bazar, Bank Rd.

STD and ISD booths proliferate in town. Email however is more of a hit and miss affair. Try your luck at SR Enterprises in the Lakhotia Computer Centre, or Vaishaic Internet (☎ 383824) at Easthill Junction near the museum. Access at both places is around Rs 100 per hour.

Mananchira Square

There are subtle indicators in Kozhikode of its colourful past. The central Mananchira Square was the former courtyard of the Zamorins; Hindu temples, mosques and churches illustrate the region's long acquaintance with the major belief systems. Notable among them are the Tali Temple (non-Hindus prohibited), the **Church of South India** (CSI) and the Kuttichira Mosque. The **Tali Temple** contains two main shrines – one to Krishna and the other to Narashima. The temple is renowned for its intricate wooden carvings of animals in the eaves beneath the large overhanging wooden roof and for its large stone sculptures of many gods, including Bhagavati, Sarasvati, Rama and Hanuman which adorn some of the chambers. The **Kuttichira Mosque** is a fine 15th century mosque with roofs taking the Keralan pagoda style – unusual in a mosque. Inside an ornate ceiling is supported by massive wooden beams. Hidden behind numerous tailor shops, the mosque is in M Bavootyhaji Rd. Visitors are welcome to wander around the perimeter from 9 am to 4 pm, except on Friday (the Muslim day of prayer) when they are strictly prohibited.

The impressive new **Mananchira Library** reflects the significance Kozhikode has always placed on literature.

Planetarium

Near the new bus stand, the planetarium is open Tuesday to Sunday from 11 am to 7 pm. Entry is Rs 5.

Museums & Art Galleries

Five kilometres north of town, at East Hill, the archaeological displays at the **Pazhassirajah Museum** include copies of ancient mural paintings, bronzes, old coins and models of megalithic monuments – the earliest monuments of Kerala. If you're non-Hindu with a desire to see the interior of a Hindu temple, the temple models here provide a good example of what you're missing. Next door, the small **Krishna Menon Museum** has memorabilia, including clothes, speeches and photographs, of Krishna Menon, the former Defence Minister of India while the **Art Gallery** has paintings of Raja Ravi Varma and Raja Raja Varma.

All three places are open from Tuesday to Sunday, 10 am to 5 pm, except Wednesday when the Krishna Menon Museum and the Art Gallery open at noon. To get here you can catch a Kannur (Cannanore) bus to East

Hill which leave from the old bus stand every 20 minutes. From the East Hill bus stop it's a 100m walk to the museums.

Just 500m from the museums (you'll see the sign near the bus stop), is **Jay Bees Art Gallery** (☎ 383815), East Hill Rd, named after the artist and gallery owner Jayan Bilathikulam. With crayons and blades, he adopts an unusual 'scratch' method of painting to make his social commentaries, which are often critical of the state. He also produces oil paintings, leadlight, pottery and sculpture. The gallery is open daily and visitors can buy or place orders for works.

At the time of writing the **SK Pottekkad Art Gallery**, near the Pottekkad Memorial Park, was being completed. Built in honour of the renowned travel writer SK Pottekkad, it was intended as an exhibition gallery and a base for research and the development of travel writing.

Places to Stay – Budget

All of the following establishments have bathrooms attached.

Metro Tourist Home *(☎ 766029, cnr Mavoor and Bank Rds)* has doubles only for Rs 250 or Rs 500 with air-con and TV.

Hotel Sajina *(☎ 722975, Mavoor Rd)* has basic singles/doubles for Rs 100/140.

Two basic lodges share a courtyard with the Indian Coffee House on Mavoor Rd. ***NCK Tourist Home*** has basic rooms for Rs 165. Across the way the ***Delma Tourist Home*** charges Rs 170, but it's not really recommended for single women travellers.

The Lakshmi Bhavan Tourist Home *(☎ 722027, GH Rd)* is of similar standard and costs Rs 95/170.

Hotel Maharani *(☎ 722541, Taluk Rd)* is slightly off the beaten track, and quiet. Rooms are Rs 150/185, or Rs 470 for an air-con double. There's a bar and a garden.

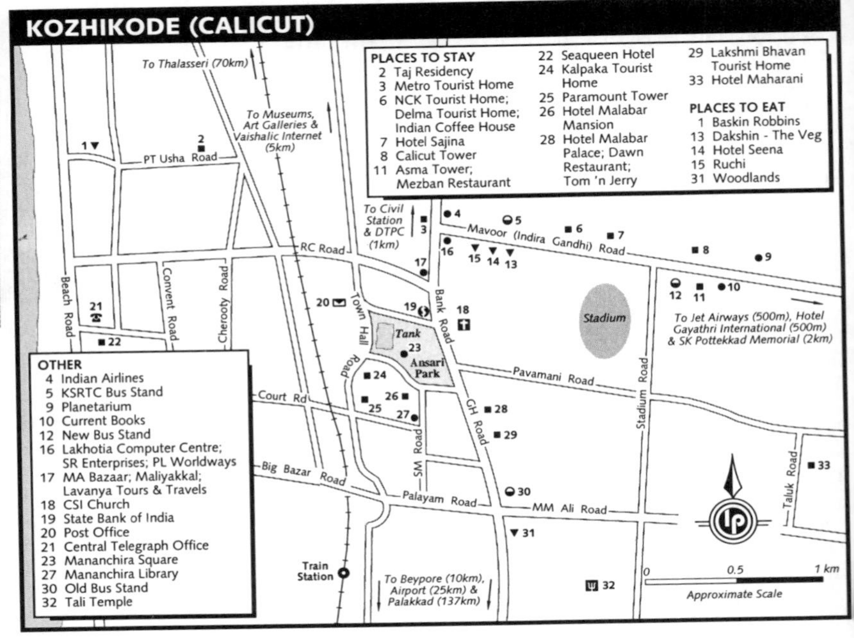

LINDSAY BROWN

CHRISTINE NIVEN

PETER DAVIS

TERESA CANNON

& middle: Chinese fishing nets use an ingenious arrangement of weights and pulleys. **Bottom left:** ling in the daily catch takes plenty of muscle and coir rope (**right**) made from coconut husks.

KAREN TRIST

LINDSAY BROWN

EDDIE GERALD

Top left: Hand-painted trucks are decorated with patterns as loud as their horns.
Top right and bottom: Mannequins and billboards display the season's hot new colours.

Hotel Gayathri International *(☎ 355367, Mavoor Rd)* is opposite, near the Jet Airways office. Only double rooms are available at the reduced rate of Rs 275, don't expect the air-con to work. The rooms are a little on the small side but the ceiling fan should help to move the air.

The KTDC ***Hotel Malabar Mansion*** *(☎ 722391, Mananchira Square)* is in the centre of town, near Ansari Park. Rooms are Rs 185/235, or Rs 370/420 with air-con. There's an air-con restaurant, beer parlour and snack bar.

Kalpaka Tourist Home *(☎/fax 720222, Town Hall Rd)* has singles/doubles for Rs 180/225, or air-con rooms for Rs 550. There is an OK restaurant.

Places to Stay – Mid-Range & Top End

Seaqueen Hotel *(☎ 366604, fax 365854, Beach Rd)* is by the waterfront, but Kozhikode's beach is nothing to get excited about. Rooms are Rs 385/520 or Rs 660/795 with air-con. The staff are friendly but the rooms are somewhat gloomy.

Paramount Tower *(Town Hall Rd)* has been extensively renovated and may well be open for business when you read this.

Calicut Tower *(☎ 723202, fax 720702, Mavoor Rd)* is reasonably priced at Rs 250/300 or Rs 420/500 with air-con, but the gloomy rooms are less than reasonable.

Asma Tower *(☎ 723560, Mavoor Rd)* is a new and friendly place with good service and bright rooms for Rs 250/300 or Rs 375/475 with air-con.

Hotel Malabar Palace *(☎ 721511, fax 721794, GH Rd)* with all the comfortable trappings of a three star hotel, has rooms for Rs 1150/1475.

Taj Residency *(☎/fax 766448, PT Usha Rd)* is a good business hotel with rooms starting at US$45/75.

Places to Eat

There's an ***Indian Coffee House*** hidden away just off Mavoor Rd. The glossy ***Woodlands*** vegetarian restaurant is easy to spot in the White Lines building on GH Rd.

Dakshin – The Veg has an extensive range with a fast food (pay before you eat) service downstairs and a more salubrious upstairs with table service. Its speciality ice creams include, 'The Angel in Four Light House' which combines strawberry, pistachio and vanilla ice cream with fruits, jellies and chocolate wafers. The nearby ***Ruchi*** in Mavoor Rd is also good with a wide vegetarian selection.

Hotel Seena is somewhat downmarket from Dakshin but the meals (veg) are good.

The restaurants in the ***Metro***, ***Kalpaka*** and ***Malabar Mansion*** hotels are reasonably priced, if not terribly exciting.

Mezban Restaurant at Asma Tower has an excellent range of dishes including a number of Keralan specialities.

The air-con ***Dawn Restaurant*** at the Malabar Palace is good and there's an ice cream parlour, ***Tom 'n Jerry***, in the garden outside the hotel. If you're a serious ice cream consumer, it's worth making the trek out to PT Usha Rd for some ***Baskin Robbins***.

The restaurant at the ***Seaqueen Hotel*** has good snacks and seafood and it also serves cold beer.

There are many supermarkets around town with bakeries attached. The offerings at these places are always fresh and the range is extensive. The ***Maliyakkal*** supermarket is in MA Bazaar.

Getting There & Away

Air The Indian Airlines office (☎ 766243) is in the Eroth Centre on Bank Rd, close to Mavoor Rd junction. Jet Airways (☎ 356052) is also on Mavoor Rd. See the table for flights out of Kozhikode.

Bus The KSRTC bus stand is on Mavoor Rd, close to the junction with Bank Rd. There's also the new bus stand, farther east along Mavoor Rd, for long-distance private buses, and the old bus stand, at the intersection of GH and MM Ali Rds, for local buses. Regular buses to Bangalore, Mangalore, Mysore, Udhagamandalam (Ooty), Madurai, Coimbatore, Pondicherry, Thiruvananthapuram (Trivandrum), Alappuzha (Alleppey), Kochi

Domestic Flights to/from Kozhikode (Calicut)

destination	airline	frequency (to Kozhikode)	frequency (from Kozhikode)	fare (US$)
Chennai (Madras)	IC	Wed, Fri, Sun	Tue, Thur, Sat	80
Coimbatore	IC	daily	daily	35
Goa	IC	Mon, Wed, Fri	Tue, Thur, Sun	
Mumbai (Bombay)	IC	daily	daily	140
	9W	daily	daily	140
	AI	Mon, Fri, Sat, Sun	Mon, Fri, Sat, Sun	

Abbreviations: IC = Indian Airlines, 9W = Jet Airways, AI = Air India

(Cochin) and Kottayam leave from both the KSRTC and new bus stands. The trip to Udhagamandalam has spectacular views.

Train The train station is south of Mananchira Square, about 2km from the new bus stand. It's 242km north to Mangalore (Rs 62/298 in 2nd/1st class, 4½ to 5½ hours), 190km south to Ernakulam (Rs 53/258, five hours) and 414km south to Thiruvananthapuram (Rs 95/471, 9½ to 11 hours).

Heading south-east, there are trains via Palakkad (Palghat, Rs 40/195) to Coimbatore (Rs 50/313) which then head north to Bangalore, Chennai (Madras) and Delhi. See also the table 'Major Trains of Nothern Kerala to/from Kozhikode', in this chapter.

Getting Around

There's plenty of auto-rickshaws in Kozhikode, and the drivers use their meters. It's Rs 10 from the train station to the KSRTC bus stand or most hotels. Prepaid taxis are available from the airport for Rs 250.

AROUND KOZHIKODE

Beypore

☎ 0495

Just 10km south of Kozhikode, Beypore is a small coastal area where Uru (country) **boats** are constructed out of local teak, ventak and jackfruit timbers. Not a single nail is used in these 700 tonne tubs. Nor will you see any power tools. If you'd like to see a blueprint you can't – the plans are inside the chief boat-builder's head. It can take 50 artisans more than a year to complete one ship. From Beypore they are towed to Dubai where diesel engines are fitted. They will then ply the Arabian Sea with cargo including goats and cattle.

Unfortunately lengthy delays in construction have led the Arabs to look elsewhere. A facility for building such craft has just been completed in Dubai (using imported Indian labour) and India may be seeing the last of the Beypore boat builders.

If you want to purchase a ship's anchor, this is the place. The street leading to the jetty has hundreds of them for sale, from tiny model anchors that will fit in your bag to serious looking things that may have suited the Titanic.

Also in Beypore is the **Tasara Creative Weaving Centre** (☎ 414233, fax 201861, email slo@giasbg01.vsnl.in). Established in the late 1970s Tasara provides a harmonious environment for artists to learn and develop skills with textiles. Works of art combine contemporary ideas with ancient methods. Genuine artists may apply for a residency that includes accommodation and food with costs dependent on duration of stay and materials used. Applications stating the purpose and expected duration of the proposed residency should be forwarded to the manager, Mr Vasudevan, Tasara Creative Weaving Centre, Beypore North,

Kozhikode, 673015. Visitors who wish to purchase articles should phone first for an appointment.

Buses to Feroke, the nearest town to Beypore, leave from Kozhikode old bus stand. From Feroke you can take a rickshaw (Rs 10) or walk the remaining 3km to Beypore.

Kottakkal

☎ 0493

Kottakkal, 48km south of Kozhikode, is home to the **Arya Vaidya Sala Hospital** (☎ 742216), renowned for almost 100 years for its Ayurvedic research and treatments. This hospital is only for those seriously interested in improving their health. Generally a minimum commitment of one month's stay is required. This costs Rs 50,000 which includes accommodation. Foreigners pay in foreign currency. You can organise treatment (currently there is a one year waiting list) by writing to the Chief Physician, Arya Vaidya Sala, Kottakkal, 676503.

Most north-bound buses from Kochi pass through Kottakkal, the bus station is just 1km from the hospital. Alternatively, the hospital can usually arrange transport from Kozhikode or a taxi may be hired from the airport.

Kappad Beach

☎ 0496

Sixteen kilometres north of Kozhikode, Kappad Beach marks the site of Vasco da Gama's landing. A nondescript cement pillar marks the incident, 1km from the beach. Nearby is the ambitiously named ***Kappad Beach Resort*** *(☎ 683760, fax 683706)* with rooms ranging from Rs 1300 for standard doubles to Rs 2600 for air-con doubles with full board. The resort offers Ayurvedic treatments as well as excursions to see Teyyam (ritual temple dance) and *kalarippayat* (martial arts) demonstrations. The resort can arrange transport for guests.

LOKANARKAVU TEMPLE

The Lokanarkavu Temple is 5km from Vadakara (Badagara), 20km south of Mahé. This serene temple complex has three temples; one to Durga – the main deity, one to Shiva and the other to Vishnu. All the temples are open to Hindus only. The Shiva temple contains vivid paintings, which are replicated in wooden carvings at the entrance. Visitors may view these carvings and wander around the complex. The temples are also noted for their 'rock-cut caves', which seem to exist more in mythology than in reality – let us know if you find them.

PETER DAVIS

Vasco da Gama brought the first European ship to India when he arrived at Kappad Beach

To get to the temple take the bus from Kozhikode old bus stand to Vadakara. From Vadakara you take a second bus for the remaining 5km. However the maze-like tracks make a rickshaw an easier option. You can also get there by train from Kozhikode (Rs 22/114).

MAHÉ

☎ 0497

Mahé, 60km north of Kozhikode, was a small French dependency handed over to India, as part of the Union Territory of Pondicherry, at Independence. Now administered through Delhi and not subject to Kerala's taxes, Mahé has changed hands often from French to British control. Except for **Alliance Française** (☎ 333029) and

St Therese's Church, there's little French influence left. The British influence is apparent at the **English factory**, established here in 1683 by the Surat Presidency to purchase pepper and cardamom. It was the first English factory on the Malabar Coast.

Mahé's main function now seems to be supplying truck drivers with cheap alcohol. Today mosques, temples and shops selling toilets and sinks are sandwiched between liquor stores – there are at least 75 outlets. In addition to the cheap booze (as little as one-third of the price for the same bottle in Kerala) there is some very cheap accommodation.

The **Malayala Kalagramam Centre for Arts & Ideas** (☎ 332961) is an important institution, primarily for locals, founded in 1993. Under the directorship of the well known and controversial artist MV Devan, it offers courses in dance, music, sculpture and painting – both contemporary and classical forms.

Foreigners are welcome to attend forums (some in English) on issues related to art, politics and philosophy. Poetry readings, dance performances and art exhibitions are other regular events.

The centre is keen to meet genuine artists interested in an exchange of ideas, and visitors may watch classes with permission from the director. The centre is closed on Thursday.

To get to the centre, in Kochi House, simply cross the bridge that leads into Mahé (from Kozhikode), turn immediately right and it's about 200m along the river.

Places to Stay & Eat

It's far more pleasant to stay at Thalasseri (Tellicherry), 8km north, though there are a few basic options in Mahé itself.

Government Tourist Home *(☎ 332222)*, near the river mouth, about 1km from the bridge, has singles/doubles for just Rs 12/20 with bathroom, but it's generally full. There is a very cheap 'meals' restaurant here as well.

Municipal Tourist Home *(☎ 332233, Church Rd)*, beside the courthouse, has singles/doubles/family rooms for Rs 12/22/30.

Hotel Arena *(☎ 33242, cnr Church and Cemetery Rds)* has doubles with bathroom for Rs 100, or Rs 325 with air-con. Its restaurant was closed at the time of writing but breakfast was being provided.

Aswathi Guest House is across Church Rd, east down Old Syndicate Bank Rd. Basic doubles with bathroom cost Rs 120.

Zara Resorts *(☎ 332503, Station Rd)*, 1km east of Church Rd, has standard doubles with TV for Rs 150, or Rs 275 with air-con. There's a restaurant and a bar.

Getting There & Away

Mahé is too small to warrant a bus stand, so buses stop at various places along Church Rd. There are a few buses each hour to Thalasseri, Mangalore and Kozhikode, fares are a few rupees. There is also a service between Mahé and Pondicherry in Tamil Nadu – make inquiries at the Government Tourist Home or the nearby Government Guest House (reserved for VIPs). A train line runs through Mahé, but trains do not stop here.

THALASSERI (Tellicherry)

☎ 0490

Thalasseri is not worth a special detour but if you are making your way along the coast it's a pleasant, unhurried place to stop for the night. The town's fishing fleet returns in the late afternoon, and the beach becomes an animated fish market as people haggle over the catch. You may even be lucky enough to catch an impromptu circus act in the street: Thalasseri is home to a touring circus school.

Near the waterfront, right behind the fire station, the British East India Company's 1708 **fort** is neglected but relatively intact, with a fine gateway flanked by two comical guards. There are at least two secret tunnels, one leading to the sea. The tunnels will be either 'closed', 'under repair' or 'inhabited by a cobra' but bring a torch (flashlight) and ask nicely at one of the government offices inside the fort and you may be offered a glimpse of a damp chamber. There's a disused **lighthouse** perched on one corner of the fort. Be careful of the broken glass and masonry that litters the area.

Between the fort and the sea are two churches and a school. The smaller **Church of South India** is disused and crumbling, its stained glass windows suffering from wayward cricket balls from St Joseph's schoolyard. The church's congregation is declining in this region. Its fascinating cemetery is overgrown and neglected, save for one grave which belongs to Edward Brennan 'A Sterling, upright Englishman and founder of Brennan College' who died in 1859 aged 75. Brennan College is a highly respected institution in Kerala to this day.

Logan's Rd runs from near the bus and train stations to the town's main square near the fort.

Places to Stay

You can reach all of the hotels (except Hotel Pranam) on foot by taking a right turn from the bus and train stations into Logan's Rd. An auto-rickshaw to any of them should cost around Rs 10. Most of the following places have rooms with bathroom attached.

Hotel Pranam *(☎ 220634)* has comfortable singles/doubles for Rs 86/165, or Rs 335 with air-con. There's an attached restaurant. From the train station turn left at Logan's Rd, then immediately right.

Brothers Tourist Home *(☎ 21558)*, at the bus and train station end of Logan's Rd, shares a courtyard with Shemy Hospital. It is cheap with rooms for Rs 50/85.

Impala Tourist Home *(☎ 220484)*, close by, is similar with rooms for Rs 45/65.

Minerva Tourist Home *(☎ 221731)*, a little farther along Logan's Rd, has basic rooms for Rs 50/80.

Chattanchal Tourist Home *(☎ 222967, Convent Rd)* is beyond the square, opposite the fire station. Doubles cost Rs 138 or Rs 345 with air-con.

Paris Presidency Hotel *(☎/fax 233666)*, close to the end of Logan's Rd, is welcoming and comfortable. It's good value at Rs 240/300, or Rs 390 for air-con doubles.

Paris Lodging House *(☎ 231666)*, adjacent and under the same management, is cheaper and also has good value rooms from Rs 70/115, Rs 288 for an air-con double.

The Residency *(☎ 232357)*, a few doors uphill from the easily seen Paris Presidency, has good rooms from Rs 86/129, or Rs 248/275 with air-con. Prices include tax.

Ayesha Manzil *(☎ 341590, Court Rd)* is an enormous heritage home overlooking the sea. The vast rooms, some with teak bookcases and king sized four-poster beds, are a little dark. Doubles are Rs 5000 (including meals).

Places to Eat

Parkview, near the railway crossing, is a simple nonveg eatery. Upstairs is the more comfortable though not much more expensive ***Kings Park*** which has a greater range and friendlier staff.

Hotel New Westend in the busy main square at the end of Logan's Rd has good nonveg food – the fish curry is excellent.

The ***New Surya Restaurant***, a couple of doors away, has great chilli chicken.

Kwality Sweets is one of a number of ice cream parlours and 'cool' shops around the square: they only sport the sign 'cool' or 'cool bar' after they open at 10 am.

The ***Paris Presidency Hotel*** has a good air-con restaurant.

Getting There & Away

Frequent trains and buses head north along the coast to Mangalore and south to Mahé, Kozhikode and Kochi. See also the table 'Major trains of Northern Kerala to/from Kozhikode', at the start of this chapter.

Getting Around

Many jeeps line the town streets. You can approach a driver and negotiate a price (usually around Rs 300 for half a day, but this may vary according to waiting time).

AROUND THALASSERI

Anjarakandy Cinnamon Estate

This estate 16km from Thalasseri is the largest of its type in Asia. Set in 150 hectares, it was established by the British East India Company in 1767. In those days it also cultivated pepper, nutmeg and cloves but it's the cinnamon that has survived. You can wander through here and see how the cinnamon bush is transformed into the popular spice while oil is extracted from the leaves and made into perfume.

About five daily buses from Thalasseri to Mysore pass the estate. Ask for Anjarakandy Cinnamon Estate or Brown's Plantation (Rs 4). From the main road it's a 1km walk to the gates of the estate.

Herman Gundert's House

Herman Gundert, the famous German Missionary from Basel settled at Illikunnu, near Thalasseri in 1889. He spent nearly 30 years in the expansive house on a hill and it is here that he wrote the first Malayalam journal and the first Malayalam-English dictionary. It's a pity that there is no information available or even a plaque in his honour. The house is worth seeing for its representation of classical Keralan architecture but it is now used as a retreat for school teachers and is not officially open to the public. If you have a particular interest the caretaker will show you through. It's 2km north of Thalasseri, off National Highway 17. Frequent buses (Rs 4) stop at Illikunnu but an auto-rickshaw will take you direct for around Rs 40.

Muzhappilangau Beach

If you're into calm beaches with picture postcard sunsets, this 4km stretch of golden sand, 7km north of Thalasseri, will suit. There is however one major drawback. The tourist authorities are promoting this as India's only drive-on beach, and they're actively encouraging private vehicles onto the compact sand. They even claim that it's environmentally sound! The cowboys with their jeeps and motorbikes no doubt agree. It's inevitable that the fishermen who continue a centuries old tradition on the beach will be among the first to lose out as a result.

Two hundred metres into the warm sea is the tiny uninhabited island known as **Dharmadam**. You can wade there in low tide or, if you're a very strong swimmer, head out in high tide. Once there you'll probably want to stay just to get away from the beach traffic. Currently the island is privately owned but the tourist authorities have a claim to develop it. The mind boggles. A speedway perhaps!

Thodikalam Temple

About 25km east of Thalasseri, the inner walls of this temple contain splendid murals. The 40 large panels, spread over 65 sq m, are believed to date from the 16th century and resemble those of the Mattancherry Palace in Kochi. Visitors are usually welcome but local tourist officials may advise you otherwise.

The best way to get there is to hire a jeep, which is easily obtained from the main street of Thalasseri (about Rs 300 return).

Nedumpoyil (Niduboil)

Near this small town, the delightful 30km **Pazhassy Raja Trekking Line** is a walking track that takes you through forest. The trail is known locally as the Pazhassy Raja Trekking Line and also the 29 mile trek, due to its proximity to the 28 mile sign post. It's popular with school groups, so it's well marked and even has handrails to help you along the steeper parts.

The track begins from the camp shed of the Kerala Forest Department which is clearly visible from the main road just past the 28 mile sign post. If you arrive before 8 am Mr Joseph (who lives directly opposite the camp shed) will be happy to guide you along the walk which takes around eight hours. The best time to come is in February/March when the winds and rains have subsided.

The ***Prakash Restaurant*** in the main street of Nedumpoyil is a good place to eat.

Nedumpoyil is 35km east of Thalasseri on the road to Manantavadi. Buses ply this route but if you intend doing the walk you are advised to organise private transport since there is no accommodation in the area. The best option is to hire a jeep easily obtained from the main street of Thalasseri (about Rs 300) return.

Aralam Wildlife Sanctuary

This 55 sq km sanctuary, 55km east of Kannur, is a refuge for sambar, sloth bears, elephants and mouse-deer. It is also rich in birdlife, reptiles and butterflies. However, infrastructure for visiting the park is inadequate, so at this stage it's best avoided. If you have an irresistible urge to visit, contact the Forest Range Office (no phone), Kannavam, the Assistant Wildlife Warden (no phone), Iritty or the Chief Conservator of Forests (☎ 0471-322217), Thiruvananthapuram.

KANNUR (Cannanore)

☎ 0497

Kannur's days of glory were under the Kolathiri rajas, and its importance as a spice-trading port was noted by Marco Polo. From the 15th century various colonial powers, including the Portuguese, Dutch and British, exerted their influence over this rich Malabar Coast region.

Most of Kannur's sites are a few kilometres out of town – see the following Around Kannur section.

There is a DTPC Information Centre at Taluk Office Campus (☎ 706336). It has no town map but it does have a pile of useless brochures.

Opposite is the State Bank of Travancore, which will cash American Express travellers cheques. For other brands and for cash advances on credit cards try the State Bank of India on Fort Rd.

The Portuguese built **St Angelo Fort** in 1505 on the promontory north-west of town. Under the British it became a major military base and today the Indian army occupies the cantonment area beside the fort. The fort is a Rs 10 rickshaw ride from town, but you will need to negotiate a waiting fee (about Rs 50 per hour) while you examine the grounds (entry is free). The solid laterite fortifications were modified by the British who also remodelled many of the buildings within the walls. There was some maintenance going on at the time of writing, but this appeared to be little more than patching with cement. A number of cannons have been set in cement and placed in very non-strategic positions but the constant sound of gunfire from the nearby army camp does lend a certain authenticity.

Places to Stay & Eat

Accommodation in Kannur is of a seriously low standard and you can expect to pay mid-range prices for far below mid-range standards.

Centaur Tourist Home *(☎ 68270)* is directly across from the train station entrance, about 200m down MA Rd. Basic singles/doubles are Rs 100/160. There are plenty of similar lodges in the vicinity which may be worth checking out if the following are full.

At the time of writing the KTDC ***Yatri Niwas*** *(☎ 500717)*, behind the train station, had been closed for nearly six months due to industrial disputes. Rumours are that it will remain closed for a 'very long time' but check it out – things do change.

Kamala International *(☎ 66910, fax 50189, SM Rd)* was having massive renovations at the time of writing.

Palm Grove Tourist Home *(☎ 503182, 151 Mill Rd)* has a sweeping landscaped entrance and an attractive lobby. It's a pity most of the rooms don't reflect the same qualities. They are small, grubby and musty, and at Rs 200/250 are way overpriced. If you want to splurge, the air-con deluxe for Rs 600 is the one exception. It's large, airy and almost conveys a sense of grandeur.

Adjacent to Palm Grove is ***Government Guest House*** *(☎ 706426)*. This lodge, reserved for government officials, is by far the best place in town. The rooms are vast and airy – especially those facing the sea. And at Rs 50 they're a bargain. If rooms are available, travellers are welcome. It's a good idea to ring the manager in advance. Meals can be arranged.

Costa Malabari *(☎ 821399)* is a beach resort in Thottada village, 10km south of Kannur. The location is very private and it's reasonably priced at Rs 500 for a double; or Rs 750 for full board including the catch of the day. To avoid disappointment, you can book through the Tourist Desk (☎ 0484-371761), KSRTC Boat Jetty, Ernakulam.

Parkins Chinese Restaurant, New Subway, Thadakkara, is the best eating place in town. The huge meals, Indianised Chinese, are usually enough for two.

Getting There & Away

Kannur is on the main north-south route for trains (see the table 'Major Trains of Northern Kerala to/from Kozhikode') and buses. You can go by bus or train from all points on the coast. There's a direct bus to Mysore.

AROUND KANNUR

Pyambalam Beach

Don't fall for the hype from the tourist officials this beach, just 3km north of Kannur, should definitely be missed. To get to it you have to walk past a foul smelling 'comfort station' (toilet block) and stacks of rubbish. If you make it to the water you shouldn't go any farther. This is not a safe swimming beach.

Cooperatives

There are 52 handweaving cooperatives in Kerala, employing an estimated 150,000 people. It's the 90 inch looms that make weaving in Kerala unique and the Kannur district plays a crucial role in the handweaving industry. At the **Kanhirode Weavers' Cooperative** (☎ 851259, fax 851865) 13km north east of Kannur, you can see the full weaving process. Established in 1952, this cooperative has 385 members who turn out high quality furnishing fabrics, saris and *dhotis* (sarongs) including some in fine silk. Around 70% of the goods are exported.

As with the cooperative sector throughout Kerala, the members are politically active and have struggled to secure good conditions and a minimal wage differential.

Visitors may buy direct for 20% less than showroom prices. A fine quality cotton dhoti costs Rs 120 and a silk sari is around Rs 2250. But phone the secretary first to arrange an appointment.

Kerala Beedi Workers Turn Over a New Leaf

Beedi workers (makers of the popular hand rolled cigarettes) represent a significant component of the Indian workforce (the third largest after agriculture according to some sources). The workers in this sector are among India's poorest employed people. The story in Kerala however is radically different. A trade union of beedi workers was established in Kannur back in 1934. Decades of political activity followed. Included in one log of claims was a demand that workers be allowed to read when they are not actually at their workstation! As a result of increased unionisation, private manufacturers (based mainly in Mangalore) shifted from large scale factories to decentralised home-based production. In 1967, when the communist government was successfully re-elected in Kerala, full support was given to the home-based beedi workers in the state. In response the giant Mangalore company Ganesh Beedi ceased production, immediately displacing 12,000 workers in Kerala. It was this situation that led to the birth of The Kerala Dinesh Beedi (KDB) Workers' Cooperative. Today KDB is the fourth largest beedi company in India. What is more important however is that in an increasingly competitive market, the members of KDB have sustained a high level of profitability as well as wages and conditions that far outstrip their counterparts in other states.

Like many nations, India is actually facing a decline in tobacco consumption. As well as this, competition for KDB is heightened by the entry of well known brands into the low end of the market. In response, the KDB members are pursuing an active policy of diversification. Packaged spices are their first breakaway from cigarette production but they also have an ambitious program to enter the realm of software production – something they believe to be far more socially useful than cigarettes.

For further reading on this fascinating area try the recently published *Democracy At Work in an Indian Industrial Cooperative* by Isaac, Franke and Raghavan. It's published by ILR Press, an imprint of Cornell University Press.

Four kilometres farther along the road towards Mysore you'll come across an inconspicuous cement dwelling with piles of dried leaves outside. This is one of the numerous workshops of the **Kerala Dinesh Beedi Cooperative** – makers of the popular Beedi cigarettes and a significant player in the Keralan economy (see the boxed text 'Kerala Beedi Workers Turn Over a New Leaf').

The leaves come from Orissa. Within what seems like a nanosecond, a worker will hand-cut a leaf, fill it with tobacco, roll it and pick up another leaf. Many smoke the product as they make more.

The cooperatives are on the Kannur-Mysore road and are easily reached by bus from Kannur for Rs 2.80. An auto-rickshaw costs around Rs 200.

For the weaving cooperative, ask to get off at Kudukkimotta.

Parasinikadavu

☎ 0497

The chief claim to fame of the small town of Parasinikadavu, 18km north-east of Kannur, is the beautiful **Parasinikadavu temple** on the banks of the Valapatanam River. A good place to see Teyyam dance (see the Performing Arts section in the Facts about Kerala chapter for more details), visitors are welcome if dressed appropriately. Performances usually start early at 4 am and continue until about 9 or 10 am. (Don't be persuaded by official tourist advice to arrive at 9 am – you may miss out.) The actual dates and times of the ritual vary so it is necessary to ask around at hotels, guest houses and restaurants to confirm details.

Two kilometres before the bus stand where you alight for the temple, the **snake park** offers a chance to see cobras and their lunch (live guinea pigs), turtles bathing with discarded ice cream cups, budgerigars, porcupines, owls, lion tailed macaques and langur. Fascinating though these creatures may be, they are cocooned for the perverse pleasure of the human gaze. This place is another reminder of the gulf that exists between the rhetoric and the reality of reverence for all living creatures.

The park is open 8.30 am to 5.30 pm. Entrance is Rs 2/5 for children/adults. Every hour there's a 10 minute talk about snakes and their poisons.

Places to Stay If you want to stay in the area there are a number of good, cheap lodges. Try the ***Parassini Tourist Home*** *(☎ 780545)* which has doubles for Rs 100 or ***Sree Muthappan Tourist Home*** *(☎ 780822)* with doubles for Rs 135.

Getting There & Away Buses leave the Kannur bus station for Parasinikadavu every five minutes and cost Rs 3.95. From the Parasinikadavu bus stand, it's a 2km walk downhill to the temple, or you can take one of the many jeeps for Rs 35 to Rs 40 one way. If you wish to see the Teyyam dance at 4 am you're better off staying overnight in Parasinikadavu; or if staying in Kannur, you can arrange a taxi-jeep from your hotel the night before for about Rs 200 one way.

BEKAL

☎ 0499

Bekal, also known as Bekel Fort, in the far north of the state, has long, palm-fringed beaches and a rocky headland topped by a huge fort.

Some patches of land in this region have been earmarked for resorts by private developers in conjunction with the Bekal Resort Development Corporation (a government body). There are plans to undertake sensitive development and leave the beach area relatively untouched, except for a car park and a cement promenade. One of the 'eco-friendly' proposals is to dam the Karicheri River in order to meet the projected needs of Bekal Fort.

Bekal Fort

The fort, built between 1645 and 1660, with north and south facing views from the battlements, is extensive and worth a visit, especially if you have not yet seen such structures. Much of the outer wall, which rises impressively from the shore, is intact. A tunnel leads from the inner section to the sea.

Northern Backwaters

The backwaters of northern Kerala remain relatively unexplored by travellers. However one favoured area for backwater tours is Valiyaparamba (also known as the nine islands) which derives its name from the largest of the islands, a narrow strip of land extending for 24km. The waters contain pristine stretches with many tranquil settings.

At various points you'll see clusters of old dried wood which are fishing traps. They lure the fish towards them to breed and enable fisherman to scoop out a regular catch. Mussel farming also occurs here; cordoned areas contain lengths of rope that dangle in the water, emulating a natural breeding area for mussels. The mussels are attracted to the rope and attach themselves to it. In three to six months they have matured and are easily harvested by raising the rope.

One place from which to begin a journey along these waters is Padanna Kadav. To get there travel north from Kannur for about 50km to the town of Cheruvathur. From here, go west for another 6km to reach the tiny fishing community of Padanna Kadav. A boat jetty is planned but at the time of writing it was still on the drawing board. To ensure a boat is available, contact the Thanal Facility Centre (☎ 0499-772900) at Bekal. Buses travel frequently from Kannur to Cheruvathur from where you'll need to catch an auto-rickshaw (Rs 25).

From these northern backwaters it's possible to boat into the connecting Tejeswini River. This region is historically significant because of the Kayyur Riot of 1941, which developed from a protest by freedom fighters against the imposition of taxes by landlords on farmers, condoned by the British. A policeman was killed and 60 of the protesters were arrested and tried for his murder. Four of the accused were sentenced to hang and are now remembered with an annual rally held on 29 March, the anniversary of the hangings.

***The Nalanda Resort** (☎ 0499-732662)*, in Keralan style architecture, was being developed at the time of writing. It's at Nileshwar, 21km south of Bekal Fort (two hours by boat from Padanna Kadav), on the waterway close to National Highway 17. A restaurant, bar and even a toddy making facility were planned. It was expected that prices would be around Rs 1500 for a double. Bookings are recommended as the owners are hoping the place will be popular with sailors from the naval base in Kannur.

For information on the backwaters trip between Kollam and Alappuzha, see the boxed text 'The Backwaters' in the Southern Kerala chapter.

PAUL BEINSSEN

The northern backwaters are a nice alternative to the more popular southern routes

Its early history is obscure but it is thought to have been constructed by the *Nayak* (local ruler), Shivappa, who ruled from Nagar, Karnataka. At various times it has fallen under the control of the Kolathiri rajas and the Vijayanagar empire. The British East India Company occupied it after the defeat of Tipu Sultan. Entry to the fort is Rs 2; Rs 25 to bring in a video camera (free on Friday). It's open daily from 9 am to 5.30 pm.

Hanuman Temple
Next door, almost seeking protection against the fort's outer wall, is the small temple dedicated to the Hindu monkey god, Hanuman. Representative of strength, the deity is known here as Anjaneya. It's believed the temple was built at the same time as the fort.

Thanal Facility Centre
Across the road from the fort entrance is the Thanal Facility Centre (☎ 772900). At the time of writing, it was planning to offer information and a reservation service for accommodation, restaurants and sites. The facilities include toilets, bathrooms, left luggage (Rs 5 for small bags, Rs 10 for larger ones), handicrafts store and a restaurant. A children's playground was also planned. The centre is open daily from 10 am to 6.30 pm.

Bekal Beach
Bekal Beach, at the southern end of the fort, is a good place to swim but beware of shifting sandbars. The best times to visit are January and February when it enjoys seasonal clean, fine sand and calm waters. At other times, especially during and after monsoons the beach can be awash with muddy water and strong rips can make swimming unsafe.

Bekal Hole Aqua Park
Bekal Hole Aqua Park is a small lake 1km north of the beach. Boating is available and it is also possible to take a backwater trip from here. The park is open daily from 10 am to 6 pm (closed during monsoon months). A paddle boat costs Rs 10 per person for 30 minutes.

Kappil Beach
Kappil Beach 6km north of the fort is secluded, unspoilt and a good spot for swimming. It also guarantees picture postcard sunsets. From either the bus or the train station in Palakunnu you'll have to walk the 2.5km to the beach or try to persuade an auto-rickshaw driver to take you along the precarious road.

Places to Stay & Eat
You can stay inside the Bekal Fort walls at the ***Tourist Bungalow***. There is one single for Rs 40 and one double for Rs 60, both with bathroom. To book, ring the District Collector (☎ 0499-430833), Kasaragod. Mineral water and soft drinks are available from the caretaker but for food you will have to go to the ***Thanal Facility Centre*** opposite or head to the villages north of the fort. You will need a torch (flashlight) if returning to the fort after dark, as there is a 1km walk from the gate to the bungalow – the howling is just foxes!

Eeyem Lodge *(☎ 736343)* is 3km north of the fort, at the village of Palakunnu, and has rooms with bath for Rs 50/60.

Hotel Sri Sistha, nearby, is a fairly basic restaurant but one of the few open during Ramadan. Meals and a good *masala dosa* can be had for under Rs 10.

The ***Fortland Tourist Home*** *(☎ 736600, Main Rd)* is 4km north of the fort at the village of Udma. Comfortable singles/doubles cost Rs 75/125, or Rs 350 with air-con. A dorm accommodating up to eight is Rs 400. The attached ***Sealord*** restaurant serves both veg and nonveg meals.

When visiting beaches in this region it is advisable to carry food and water as facilities are few and far between.

Getting There & Away
The train station for Bekal and surrounding beaches is called Kotikulum (the stop before Kasaragod) but it is in the village of Palakunnu, and despite its size, trains regularly stop here. Trains running south to Kozhikode (Rs 48/233) and Thiruvananthapuram (Rs 172/590) leave at 3.25, 4.35 and 10.25 am and 2.20 and 6 pm; running north to Mangalore and Mumbai (Bombay) they leave at 3.50 and 8.45 am and 1.30, 8 and 10.20 pm. Buses to/from Kasaragod (20km), the nearest town of any size, depart every 10 minutes. Ask for the Bekal Fort bus stop, not Bekal. Express buses won't stop at the fort. The town to town (TT) buses with fewer stops are quicker, but you might prefer the slower ones once you see the cowboy tactics

Walks Around Kottancherry

Kottancherry forest in the Western Ghats is a pleasant place for short walks. On the way up from Kasaragod you pass arecanut, rubber and cashew nut plantations – set up by southern Christians 50 years ago. Cashew *arak* is a very potent alcohol, and a popular cure for stomach problems. Apparently it's illegal, but authorities are kept at bay with the offer of a nip or two.

Official information on the walks varies considerably and at times is quite contradictory in regard to distances, times, routes and directions. Older locals have accurate information, but if you can't speak Malayalam, you obviously won't have access to such information. Don't be deterred by assumptions about your stamina, especially if you're a woman. If you're an experienced walker you'll manage the border walk and you'll easily cope with the slight gradients of the forest walks.

Take plenty of water. If you are joined by others 'who don't require water', take enough water for them too. If you're used to the local water, there's some at Base Camp. Wear sturdy shoes and take some insect repellent for the tiny leeches. Since there's no accommodation, you'll have to make it a day trip so start out early.

State Border Walk

This walk leads you along the border between Kerala and Karnataka, to a spectacular 360° view of the Western Ghats at a peak called many names, including Theyyam Kallu and Koombanmala. About 100m south of the Base Camp there are two paths to the top – one almost directly up, the other a more gentle incline. The direct route, almost due south for the entire 1km distance, begins on the border – a raised rock wall. The steep incline makes it a little slippery, but not impossible for fit walkers. Continue along this path until you reach a rock-face which is relatively easy to scale. From here follow the grassy and indistinct (but discernible) path over one hill and then to the top of the second hill – Theyyam Kallu. Again the flattened grass is slippery, but not impassable. The walk will take about 30 minutes each way – longer with stops to enjoy the views. Avoid the middle of the day when there's no respite from the sun and the haze impedes the views.

Forest Paths

From Base Camp there are many paths that can be explored. If you are an inexperienced walker, take a guide – try Thanal Facility Centre (☎ 0499-772900), or keep your walk short. The gradient is very slight, the walking very easy and you'll be in the shade of shola, syzygium and other beautiful forest plants.

Trekking to Thalakkavery, Karnataka

This seven day trek (return) leads across the hills to a temple at the source of the Cauvery River. The trek organiser has knowledge of the local tribal people. If you wish to organise a trek, write to Mr Karimbil Gopinath (☎ 0499-747379) Karimbil Estate, Konnakkad, Kasaragod District.

Getting There & Away

To get to Kottancherry from Kasaragod, you travel by road or train 20km south to Kanhangad (see the table 'Major Trains of Nothern Kerala to/from Kozhikode', at the start of this chapter), then 66km north-east to Konnakkad. There are two routes from Konnakkad to the grandly named 'Base Camp' at Karimbal – a 15km plantation route and a forest route. Don't take a jeep along the 'forest route'. It's blocked, you'll end up bush-bashing, and the impediments will finally prevent access to the top. Unless a way has been cleared since the time of writing, opt for the plantation route. Hire a jeep at Konnakkad (Rs 300 return) for the 40 minute journey to the Base Camp.

of the TT drivers. It's not too hard to find an auto-rickshaw or a bus at Bekal Fort to take you to/from Palakunnu (for the train station) and Udma (the nearest accommodation outside the fort).

KASARAGOD

☎ 0499

Kasaragod is about 20km north of Bekal and 47km south of Mangalore on the Chandragiri River. Its name may have derived from the Sanskrit words *Kaasaara* and *Kroda* – land of lakes, or *Kasara Kodu*, meaning wild buffalo horn.

Several nayaks have administered Kasaragod. These include Tipu Sultan and Hyder Ali, and also the British. Since the introduction of Islam to India, it's been an important centre for Muslims.

First impressions give little indication of the history and places of interest. However, the town is worth exploring. As you travel in Kasaragod, you'll no doubt see many Muslim men wearing *thalakarraa* (white caps with decorative sides). These caps, unique to the area, have been produced in the same families for generations.

As an important centre of Islam, Kasaragod has a number of mosques such as the beautiful **Malikdeenak**, which is believed to be the burial site of Malik Ibn Dinar.

Information

Travellers cheques can be cashed (slowly) at the State Bank of Travancore in Railway Station Rd. STD and ISD facilities are everywhere but at the time of writing, public email access was not available. There is a DTPC office in town but it has no phone, no sign and no information. For information, try Thanal Facility Centre (☎ 772900) at Bekal Fort.

There are a number of travel agents in town that can arrange flights, trains and organised tours. Moulavi Travel (☎ 430216, fax 430488), Railway Station Rd, is efficient, friendly and government approved.

Chandrigiri Fort

On a hillock, just 10km south of Kasaragod, is the small and picturesque, if dilapidated, Chandrigiri Fort. It offers spectacular views of the Chandrigiri River, but take care of concealed pits. A rickshaw should cost about Rs 60 return.

Yakshagana Bombeyata

Yakshagana is a folk art employing song, elaborate costume and movement to relate classic stories of the *Ramayana* and the *Mahabharata*. Originating around 400 years ago in Karnataka it remains popular in the rural and coastal regions of that state.

In Kasaragod, the art form has been developed to use puppets, and is known as Yakshagana Bombeyata. A performance involves song and commentary as well as manipulation of the puppets.

If you are interested in seeing a performance contact Ramesh (☎ 423927, after 8 pm) a founding director of the Sri Gopalakrishna Yakshagana Bombeyata Sangha, at his printery in Railway Station Rd, opposite the State Bank of Travancore. A show (with Malayalam or English commentary) can be arranged for groups of five or more if one weeks notice is given.

Yoga Courses

The government-approved **Yoga Institute** (☎ 780490) in Nileshwar runs yoga and meditation courses as well as offering dietary advice and massage treatment. Accommodation is also available here, for further information and bookings write to the President, Kavil Bhavan Physical Culture Institute, Nileshwar.

Places to Stay & Eat

Enay Tourist Home *(☎ 421164)* has basic single or double rooms with shower for Rs 100. Of a similar standard are the ***Ceeyel Tourist Home*** *(☎ 430177)* and the ***Aliya Lodge*** *(☎ 430666)* behind the post office.

Hotel City Tower *(☎ 430562)* at the bus stand end of MG Rd is a green and cream landmark. Rooms are Rs 175/295, or Rs 545 with air-con.

Hotel Apsara Regency *(☎ 430124)*, is opposite the KSRTC bus stand. However the back rooms are quiet. It offers comfortable singles/doubles for Rs 160/260 and Rs 360/400 with air-con and hot water. The attached ***Sri Nivas*** vegetarian restaurant is excellent and well priced. Take their advice – one meal is large enough for two.

Getting There & Away

Bus Kasaragod is a Rs 3 to Rs 5.50 bus ride from Bekal, depending on the bus and the route. Private buses for Bekal and Mangalore leave from the Municipal bus stand near the Hotel City Tower. More regular buses leave from the KSRTC bus stand 1.5km south of the Municipal stand. Buses to Kahangad will drop you off at Udma, Palakunnu or Bekal.

Train The train station is a couple of kilometres south of the town centre. Kasaragod is on the main north-south line. It only takes one to 1½ hours to get from Kasaragod to Mangalore by express train (Rs 21).

Trains depart for Ernakulam Town at 3.20 and 10.20 am; and for Thiruvananthapuram at 4.30 am, 2.15 and 5.55 pm.

See also the table 'Major Trains of Northern Kerala to/from Kozhikode', at the start of this chapter.

The Western Ghats

The Western Ghats are a series of mountains some 1500km long running from Mumbai (Bombay) to the southern tip of India and covering an area almost 160,000 sq km. They encompass parts of Maharashtra, Karnataka, Tamil Nadu and Kerala.

Named because of their position in the west of the subcontinent, the Western Ghats actually form Kerala's eastern border. The term *ghats* derives from the Sanskrit *ghatta* (to rub) and the Hindi *ghat* and generally refers to steps descending to water (where people usually bathe). Other definitions include a mountain range or pass. Certainly Kerala's ghats with their high peaks, wide passes and undulating hills falling to the coastal flats, fulfil these descriptions.

The ghats reach an average height of 900m with Anamudi, the highest mountain in India south of the Himalaya, at 2694m. The original forests of rosewood, ebony and teak have now mostly been replaced by rice, tea and coffee plantations, eucalyptus trees and huge dams. Conservationists are eager to preserve the remaining natural forests with their unique and rich biodiversity. (See the Flora & Fauna and Ecology & Environment sections in the Facts about Kerala chapter.)

Due to the mountain terrain, travelling along the ghats for any distance is generally not possible. Access to the ghats is via the east-west routes that traverse the passes between Kerala and Tamil Nadu. For travellers this means the ghats must be approached from either Thrissur (Trichur) or Kerala's main coastal towns. This chapter covers those areas of the ghats accessible from Kottayam, Ernakulam, Thrissur and Kozhikode (Calicut). Information on the ghats in the far north and south of the state is contained in the relevant chapters, see also the boxed text 'Walks Around Kasaragod' in the Northern Kerala chapter and Around Thiruvananthapuram in the Southern Kerala chapter.

Highlights

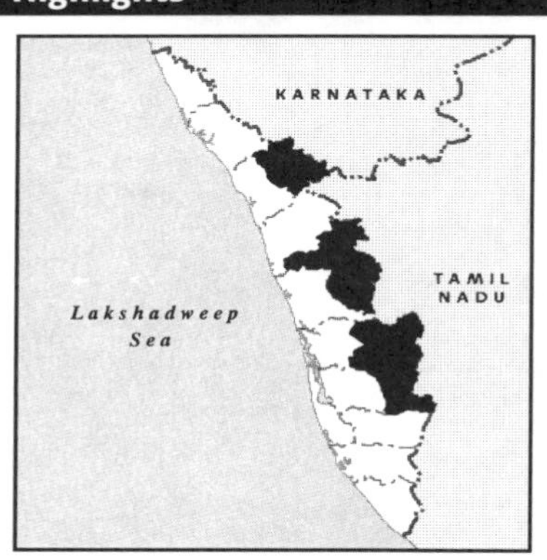

- Trek or cruise through the ever-popular Periyar Wildlife Sanctuary
- Tantalise your senses in Munnar's lush spice gardens
- Step back in time as you visit the ancient petroglyphs of the Edakkal Caves

The physical terrain may make the ghats somewhat impenetrable, but this is no match for the bureaucratic terrain. If you wish to avoid lengthy bureaucratic processes, or if you're short on time, visit the most accessible ghat sites – Periyar, Munnar and its surrounds, Pookote Lake and Edakkal Caves.

PERIYAR WILDLIFE SANCTUARY

☎ 0486

Periyar is South India's most popular wildlife sanctuary. It encompasses an area of 777 sq km and has a 26 sq km artificial lake surrounded by evergreen and deciduous forest, and grasslands – which was created by the British in 1895 to provide water to Madurai. It's home to bison, antelopes,

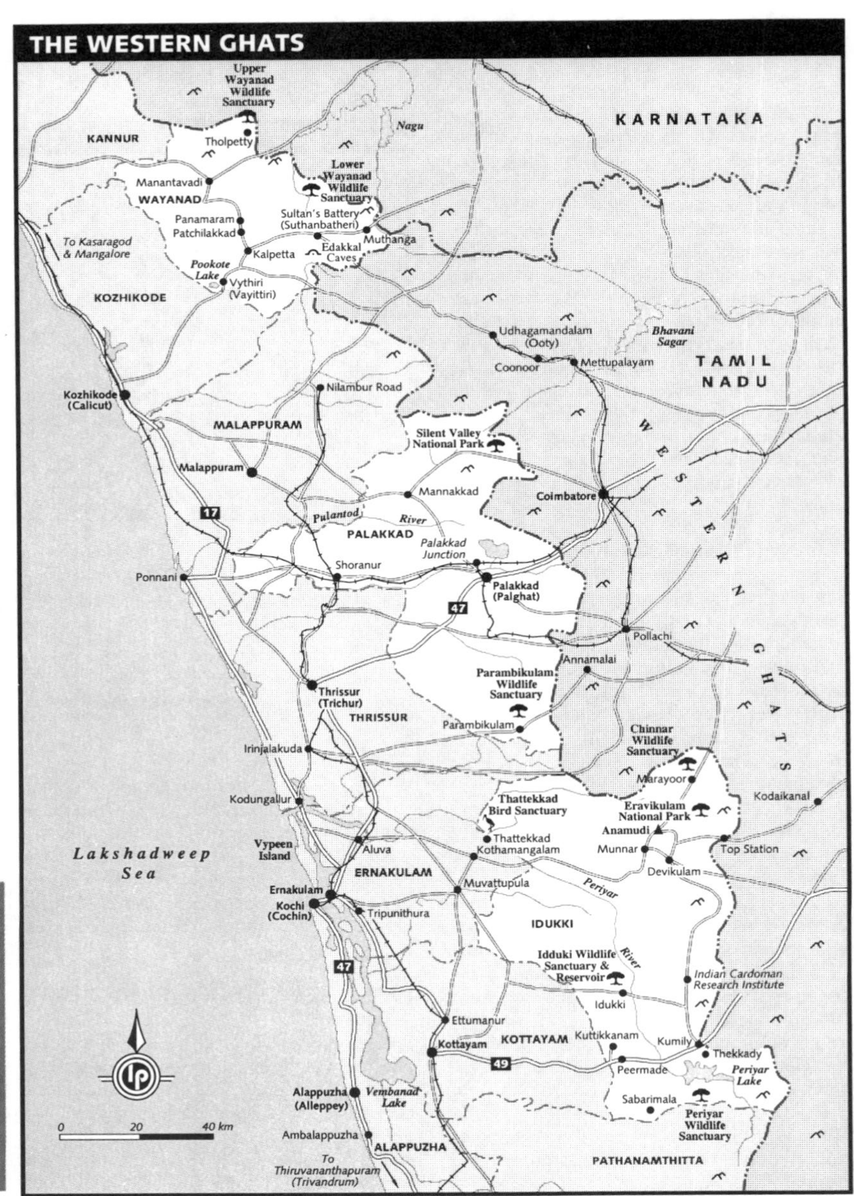

THE WESTERN GHATS

Periyar Wildlife Sanctuary is home to a small population of tigers.

sambar, wild boar, monkeys, langur, a variety of birds, some 750 elephants and an estimated 35 tigers. But if you hope to see tigers (or much wildlife at all), you're almost certain to be disappointed. If, on the other hand, you treat Periyar as a pleasant escape from the rigours of Indian travel, and an opportunity for a lake cruise and jungle walk, then you'll probably find a visit quite enjoyable. Bring clothing that's warm and waterproof.

Orientation & Information

Kumily, 4km from the sanctuary and the closest town, is a small touristy place with spice shops and Kashmiri emporiums, where the proprietors invent fantastic stories to lure you and your money. Thekkady is the centre inside the park with the KTDC hotels and the boat jetty. When people refer to the sanctuary, they tend to use Kumily, Thekkady and Periyar interchangeably, which can be confusing. The name 'Periyar' is used to refer to the whole park.

The Tourist Police office is halfway between the bus stations and the park entrance. There's a general hospital in town, the Kumily Central hospital, as well as an Ayurvedic hospital.

The Thekkady Wildlife Information Centre (☎ 22028) is near the boat jetty, but don't expect it to have maps or detailed brochures. And if you think you've come to terms with the DTPC, KTDC, ATDC, BRDC etc, now you're dealing with the IDTIO (Idukki District Tourist Information Office), with erratic hours, and the TTDC (Thekkady Tourism Development Council).

In Kumily, DC Books (☎ 322548) has helpful staff and a wide selection of books and cassettes, the Nature Shop (☎ 322763) markets WWF merchandise and quality publications, and the Eco Shop nearer the park has environmental literature and souvenirs. You can change money at Mukkadans Money Exchange at Thekkady Junction. This office also stocks useful items such as batteries, torches and all manner of electrical products.

Post & Communications The post office is near the park entrance. STD/ISD phone booths are abundant, however sending faxes is problematic; local and interstate faxes are theoretically possible, but generally impossible. International faxes are not possible. At the time of writing email was embryonic. Rissas Communications (☎ 322753) is painfully slow and even though rates are not high (Rs 2 per minute) your bill will be astronomical given the slow downloads. DC Books are planning an email facility.

Visiting the Sanctuary

Admission to the park enables multiple entries for three days and costs Rs 2/50 for Indians/foreigners.

Two-hour **boat trips** on the lake are the usual way of touring the sanctuary but your admission ticket to the park doesn't guarantee a place on the boat. Advance bookings are possible, but they are only accepted in the morning for afternoon tours. There's no communication between the entrance gate

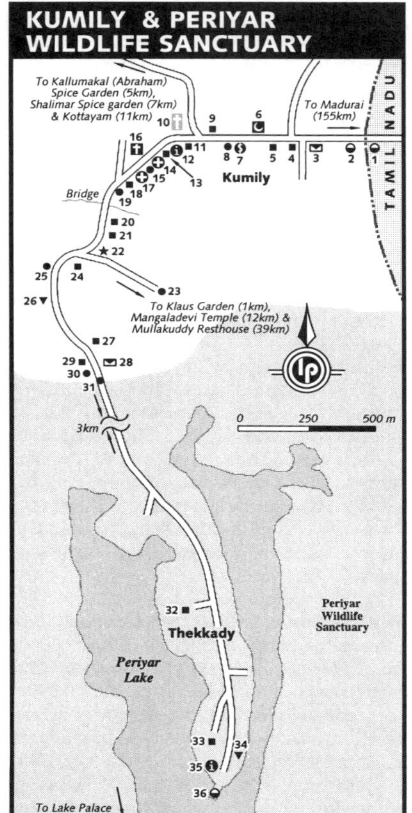

KUMILY & PERIYAR WILDLIFE SANCTUARY

PLACES TO STAY

4 Hotel Regent Tower
5 Muckumkal Tourist Home; Little Chef Restaurant
9 Lake Queen Tourist Home; Lakeland Restaurant
11 Rolex Tourist Home; Thekkady Tourist Development Council (TTDC)
13 Woodlands Tourist Bhavan
18 Michael's Inn
20 Spice Village
21 Taj Garden Retreat
24 Hotel Ambadi
27 Leela Pankaj Resorts
29 Ambika Tourist Home
32 Periyar House
33 Aranya Nivas

PLACES TO EAT

26 Coffee Inn
34 Snack Bar

OTHER

1 Tamil Nadu Bus Station
2 Bus Stand & Tourist Taxi Stand
3 Post Office
6 Mosque
7 Mukkadans Money Exchange
8 Rissas Communications
10 Lourdes Church
12 Idukki District Tourist Information Office (IDTIO)
14 Ayurvedic Hospital
15 DC Books
16 St George Orthodox Church
17 Kumily Central Hospital
19 Ninja Tailoring & Spices
22 Tourist Police
23 Wildlife Preservation Office
25 Nature Shop
28 Post Office
30 Eco Shop
31 Park Entry Post
35 Wildlife Information Centre
36 Boat Jetty

and the jetty (4km inside) so you may go to all the trouble to turn up for a boat, just to be turned away. It's best to be forewarned – many travellers are infuriated by this process. If you miss out on a boat, hang around and pursue other possibilities – a place may miraculously appear. All tickets for the Forest Department boats are obtained at the boat jetty. All tickets for the KTDC boats are available from Aranya Nivas Hotel.

Boat tickets cost Rs 25/50 on the lower/upper deck in the larger KTDC craft, or Rs 15 in the sad-looking Forest Department craft. There are five KTDC cruises a day at 7, 9.30 and 11.30 am and 2 and 4 pm and four Forest Department cruises (same times minus the early morning departure). The first and last departures offer the best wildlife-spotting prospects. It's a good idea to get a small group together (the smaller the better) and charter your own boat. They're available in a variety of sizes from Rs 500 per cruise for a 12-person boat. Tickets for video cameras cost Rs 25 from the Wildlife Information Centre. Don't forget to get one, they're strictly policed. And it's not much fun having survived the queues and hassles of getting a place on a boat to be turfed off at the last minute because you have a camera but no ticket for it.

Guided **jungle walks** depart from the Wildlife Information Centre daily at 7.30 am for about three hours and cost Rs 10 per person. Many visitors find these disappointing – there's no information and groups are often large and noisy. For walks further into the park guides can be arranged from the Wildlife Information Centre (☎ 22028). This activity isn't promoted because it's not official business – rather a sideline for the guides, so you must be insistent about it.

Serious **trekking**, with guides and guards can be arrnaged at the Nature Shop but it's better to do it in Thiruvananthapuram (Trivandrum), see Organised Tours following.

Another way to see wildlife is to spend a night in an ***observation tower*** or ***resthouse*** (see Places to Stay below). Elephant rides (Rs 30 for two people for 30 minutes) are for fun, not serious wildlife-viewing.

The best time to visit the sanctuary is from September to May and although the hot season (February to May) may be less comfortable it offers more opportunities for wildlife sightings because, with other water resources drying up, the animals are forced to the lakeside. Avoid weekends and public holidays because of noisy day-trippers.

Ayurvedic Medicine & Massage

Massage and other Ayurvedic treatments are available at many places around Kumily. If you are used to relaxation massage you may find the methods here somewhat disconcerting. The procedure is often mechanical and the ambience less than conducive to full relaxation. At some places masseurs talk to each other across flimsy divides, the towels are grubby and the traffic noise penetrates. Check out the facilities carefully before you book and consider bringing your own towel for a post massage wipe down. At the Ayurvedic hospital male and female masseurs offer an oily one hour 'relaxation' massage for Rs 350.

Organised Tours

A two day Periyar Wildlife Sanctuary tour leaves Thiruvananthapuram most Saturdays at 6.30 am and gets back on Sunday at 9 pm. It costs Rs 400 (transport only), and must be one of the silliest tours in India, since there's no time to see any wildlife – even if it were possible in the company of a busload of garrulous tourists.

Serious trekking including overnight camping in the sanctuary is possible. A three day (two night) 30km hike including camping gear, five guides, all meals and two armed forest officers is US$150 per person for a group of five (the maximum number allowed) or US$250 per person for two. The guides are former forest dwellers who made their living by stripping and selling cinnamon bark. With government (and World Bank) support they have been encouraged into more eco-friendly jobs. You can book these trips at the Nature Shop, but it's best to book in Thiruvananthapuram at Kerala Travels Interserve (☎ 0471-324158, fax 323154), Mangala Saudham, Vellayambalam.

Spice shops advertise tours to spice gardens, where you can see cinnamon, cardamom, pepper, cloves and many other spices in their pre-packed state. These tours are well worth it, especially if you have a knowledgeable guide. The average tour price is Rs 350 for 3½ hours (for independent visits to spice gardens see the Spice Gardens entry, later in this chapter).

The TTDC operates out of the Rolex Tourist Home and can organise tours to viewpoints and spice and tea plantations. Ninja Tailoring & Spices (☎ 22394) arranges a variety of tours including one to an organic spice garden.

Places to Stay

Because of the popularity of Periyar, accommodation can be hard to find in the peak season (21 December to 20 January), especially on weekends. To avoid disappointment you should make advance reservations. All three properties inside the park are operated by the KTDC and bookings for these can be made at any KTDC office or hotel. All budget accommodation is outside the sanctuary in Kumily, 4km from the lake. Prices quoted here are for the peak season unless otherwise stated. Discounts are available out of season.

Places to Stay – Budget

Muckumkal Tourist Home (☎ 322070) is close to the bus stand. Avoid the back rooms, which can be noisy if the hotel generator is switched on. Rooms with bathroom are Rs 80/160, air-con doubles are Rs 500. The Little Chef Restaurant is attached.

Hotel Regent Tower, nearby, is run by the same folk. Rooms cost Rs 120/220 which includes tax, and there's a restaurant, the Maharani.

Coffee Inn is more of a cafe than an accommodation place (see Places to Eat), but this popular place does have a couple of small rooms with shared bathroom available for Rs 150/175 including mosquito net.

Lake Queen Tourist Home *(☎ 322084)*, next to the Kottayam Rd junction, has 54 rooms from Rs 108/162 (including tax). The Catholic church runs it and all the profits go to charity. The Lakeland Restaurant is downstairs.

Rolex Tourist Home *(☎ 322081)*, along the road to the park, has clean singles/doubles with bathroom for Rs 100/250. For Rs 500 you can secure a small cottage in a plantation setting a few kilometres from town. There's also an information centre that organises tours and tickets.

Woodlands Tourist Bhavan *(☎ 322077)*, close by, is cheap but very basic and gloomy. Rooms are Rs 150/200 with attached bath. You might also find a cheap bed in one of the two large dorms.

Ambika Tourist Home *(☎ 322004)* has very small, basic singles with bucket shower for Rs 60. One double room has a shower and costs Rs 110.

Karthika Tourist Home *(☎ 322146)*, opposite the hospital, has rather grotty rooms with bath for Rs 150/200 and a canteen-style vegetarian restaurant.

Leela Pankaj Resorts *(☎ 22392)* has cute, clean cottages for Rs 500 and mosquito netting is provided. There is a restaurant featuring Indian, Chinese and continental cuisines.

Klaus Garden, a couple of kilometres out of Kumily, is a private home with small, seriously basic rooms and shared bathroom. There is no restaurant but guests can prepare their own food in the kitchen. Rooms are Rs 120/180. To get there turn off the Kumily-Thekkady Rd to the tank. From the tank it's a 100m uphill walk, past mounds of rubbish. At the top of the hill turn right and walk for another 100m.

Places to Stay – Mid-Range & Top End

Hotel Ambadi *(☎ 322193)*, in a beautiful setting, has dank and gloomy semidetached cottages, but many travellers find them OK. They're Rs 420 to Rs 690 and rooms are Rs 900.

Michael's Inn *(☎ 322355, fax 322356)* is clean, clinical and overdoses on sexism. Rooms are Rs 1200/1700 or Rs 2000/2500 with air-con. There's also a restaurant.

Taj Garden Retreat *(☎ 322401, fax 322106)* is a swish modern place not quite in keeping with its surrounds. Rooms are Rs 3000 for Indians, US$95/105 for foreigners.

Spice Village *(☎ 322314)*, part of the Casino Group, is a resort with attractive cottages in a pleasant spice garden with a swimming pool and restaurant. The tariff is US$95/105 or US$145 for deluxe bungalows. The hotel hosts early evening demonstrations on cooking and sari wrapping.

Inside the Sanctuary The KTDC has three hotels in the park. ***Periyar House*** *(☎ 322026, fax 322526)*, the cheapest of the three, is very popular. Rooms start at Rs 550/750, including breakfast and either lunch or dinner. You can hire bicycles, have a massage and change money here. If you're doing the 7.30 am jungle walk, tell the restaurant staff the night before and they will arrange an early, light breakfast.

Aranya Nivas *(☎ 322023, fax 322282)*, is less friendly than Periyar House but has very pleasant rooms for Rs 1200/2100 and air-con suites for Rs 1250/2300. There's also a bar, garden area, TV lounge, postal and banking facilities, a small handicrafts shop and excellent restaurant. Resident guests are entitled to a free morning and afternoon boat trip.

Lake Palace is well away from the noise of day-trippers. Guests should arrive at the Thekkady boat jetty by 4 pm (the final trip of the day) for transport to the hotel. The six suites in the palace, at one time the maharaja's game lodge, cost Rs 5110/7268, including meals and boating. It's a delightful place to stay and you can actually see animals from your room. With a guide, it's possible to walk to the Lake Palace from the boat jetty in about an hour. Bookings and reception are at Aranya Nivas *(☎ 322023, fax 322282)*.

Theoretically there are ***resthouses*** within the sanctuary at Manakavala (8km from Kumily), Mullakudy (39km) and Edappalayam (5km). No doubt they'll tell you at the Wildlife Information Centre that they're booked out or closed. The resthouses cost Rs 200/300 and have a keeper who will cook for you, although you must bring your own food.

The same goes for the ***observation towers*** for Rs 100, which can be booked at the Wildlife Preservation Office. They're basically enclosed platforms (one room) on posts. Although primitive (you must provide all your own food and bedding) observation towers give you the best chance of seeing animals.

But be forewarned, you can also waste a lot of time following up these options.

Places to Eat

Some of the mid-range and top-end hotels have excellent cuisine. For a special night out try the buffet lunch/dinner at ***Spice Village***. It caters for veg and nonveg western or Indian palates and is excellent value for Rs 300. Dining is in the atmospheric setting of the spice garden and traditional music is often performed.

The restaurant at the ***Aranya Nivas*** has excellent food and most nights there's a Rs 250 buffet.

The ***Taj Garden Retreat*** has a fine restaurant and the Indian food at ***Michael's Inn*** is very good, but give their breakfasts and coffee a miss.

Hotel Ambadi has a much better reputation for its multicuisine restaurant than for its rooms.

Coffee Inn is a popular outdoor cafe with an eclectic selection of music and good travellers' fare (including home-made brown bread).

You might also like to try out the ***Little Chef Restaurant*** at the Muckumkal Tourist Home, the ***Maharani*** at the Hotel Regent Tower or ***The Lakeland Restaurant*** downstairs at the Lake Queen Tourist Home. All these places serve good Indian food at reasonable prices.

There are a few cheap places along Kumily's main street and near the boat jetty in Thekkady, there's a ***snack bar*** offering basic food, snacks and drinks. The *bondas* (sweet dough balls) are particularly tasty.

Getting There & Away

Bus There are two bus stands in Kumily – the Tamil Nadu Bus Station, which operates the Tamil Nadu State Express Corporation (SETC) buses throughout the state of Tamil Nadu, and a second stand for local and state Kerala buses. Both are within a few metres of each other. At least 10 buses daily operate between Ernakulam and Kumily (six hours, Rs 50) and buses leave every half hour for the 110km trip to Kottayam (four hours, Rs 34).

At least two direct buses make the daily eight hour trip to Thiruvananthapuram (Rs 80). Another goes to Kovalam (nine hours), and another to Kodaikanal (6½ hours). Only private buses go to Munnar (Rs 36, 4½ hours). They all leave Kumily in the morning (from 6 to 9.45 am).

Getting Around

Although Kumily is 4km from the lake, you can either catch the semi-regular bus for Rs 2 (almost as rare as the tigers), take an auto-rickshaw (Rs 30 plus Rs 5 entrance for the vehicle), hire a bicycle (from Periyar House or Aranya Nivas for Rs 25 a day) or set off on foot; it's a pleasant, shady walk into the park. There are also taxis (jeeps) with drivers available. You'll find them at the tourist taxi stand near the post office. Costs are usually around Rs 850 per day.

AROUND PERIYAR

Mangaladevi Temple

The Mangaladevi Temple, 12km from Kumily, is a jumble of ruins that is generally closed to visitors. However, once a year (in April) it opens for one day for festival celebrations. Management of the temple area has been a source of dispute between the governments of Tamil Nadu and Kerala. It has also been alleged that politicians in both states have colluded to keep the temple closed so that many of the giant teak and sandalwood trees in the area can be secretly logged.

If you wish to visit the temple, you'll need special permission from the Chief Conservator of Forests (☎ 325385) Vazhuthacaud, Thiruvananthapuram. The only way to the temple is by jeep from Kumily. Count on a three to four hour round trip, depending on how long you wish to stay for the festival.

Spice Gardens

While spice shops dominate the streets of Kumily, spice gardens and plantations proliferate in its environs. You can visit coffee, tea or cardamom plantations and see the processing as well as the growing. Or you can visit a spice garden with its numerous plants, colours and aromas.

It's possible to drop in at some of these gardens without having to be part of an organised tour. But if you visit independently, make sure you leave a contribution of around Rs 50 to Rs 100 for the owner who takes time out to show you around.

Kallumakal (Abraham) Spice Garden

This spice garden is totally organic and is run by the Abraham family who have excellent knowledge of their plants. Because no pesticides are used here you'll get to see some extraordinary spiders doing what spiders are meant to do – killing bugs. You'll also see minute Asian honey bees and numerous spices and fruits including many varieties of banana. A comprehensive tour can take two hours – or even longer. Although there is no entry fee, it's usual to pay Rs 50 per person. Kallumakal is directly opposite Tropical Plantations. It has toilet facilities. Buses to Kottayam (Rs 1.50) pass the garden and an auto-rickshaw will cost around Rs 50 including waiting time.

Places to Stay & Eat About 7km from Kumily off the Kottayam Rd, ***Shalimar Spice Garden*** *(☎/fax 0486-322132)* is far from the intrusion of traffic horns and large tour groups; the tranquillity is immediately infectious. Every detail has been exquisitely designed by the Italian proprietor. Each cottage has a different design – one being in traditional Keralan style. At night, guests (max 24) are invited to sit before an open fire. The restaurant ***Mangiatutt*** (eat everything) has Indian and Italian (home made pasta) cuisine, and a range of quality wines. Food and service are superb. Prices vary from US$60/70 for rooms to $US80/90 for cottages, with discounts in the monsoon season. Ayurvedic packages are also available.

On the road to Munnar, about 20km from Kumily, ***Carmelia Haven*** *(☎ 0486-370252, fax 370268)* is set in spice and tea plantations with rooms from Rs 1250/1500 to Rs 3250/3500 in a treehouse. If you prefer an underground residence, you can stay in the cave for Rs 2500. All rooms (including the cave) are equipped with modern amenities and satellite TV, and there are activities such as trekking and fishing, but the claims of luxury are somewhat exaggerated.

Sabarimala

Over one million people visit Sabarimala during short pilgrimage seasons and authorities are becoming increasingly concerned about the resultant safety and environmental issues.

There are several ways to visit the shrine. The easiest is to catch a bus to Pamba which will bring you to within 12km of the shrine. From there it's a rugged trek amid swelling crowds and thick forest.

The temple is open in December/January, April, May/June and August/September. At these times, frequent buses go to Pamba from Kottayam, Thiruvananthapuram and Ernakulam. From Kumily, take a Kottayam bus and change for Pamba at Vandiperiyar.

If travelling from Kumily, you may prefer to hire a jeep to the beginning of the trek. Expect to pay around Rs 900 per day. You should take all your own provisions although accommodation is available in *choultries* (pilgrim accommodation).

The Tale of Two Temples

In the forests of south-east Kerala, the deity Ayyappan attracts hundreds of thousands of devotees, especially in December-January, the time of a 40 day pilgrimage.

Legends tell of Ayyappan having been born of the union of Shiva and Vishnu, during a time when Vishnu had transformed himself into a female being called Mohini. Known by many names (*Arya* – the noble, *Ayyannar* – the village deity), Ayyappan has grown in popularity and is now honoured as a deity who conquers evil and bestows special powers in his devotees.

For one month prior to the January festival, the streets of India are lined with pilgrims, dressed in black, all making their way to Sabarimala, home of Ayyappan's temple. On arrival they ascend the 18 golden steps. Each step represents a different sin and as the devotees ascend, they vow to abandon a sin, confident that the deity's blessings will ensure their success.

Hindus and non-Hindus alike may make the pilgrimage and enter the temple – as long as they are men. All women of menstruating age are prohibited. Ironically, conceived of the most feminine of forms (Vishnu as Mohini) and understood by some to be the expression of Shiva's feminine force, Ayyappan is out of bounds for women experiencing a vital and natural aspect of the feminine.

Just 50km west, the village of Chenganur (see the Southern Kerala chapter) is quieter and pilgrims are fewer. Here at the Mahadeva temple devotees celebrate the very phenomenon that Sabarimala prohibits. Dedicated to both Shiva and Parvati, it is the goddess who is significant at this temple. Celebrated in many forms – as Lakshmi, Sarasvati, Devi, Durga, Bhadrakali and Bhagavati – she is mostly honoured as Bhuvaneswari, the goddess and sovereign of the universe. Her image here reflects her compassion – a kindly face, with hands gesturing nourishment and the elimination of all fear.

Here there is the notion that Shakti (female energy) symbolised by the goddess is crucial to everything. Even the male deity can only function when energised by feminine power. Without this, he is impotent. This concept, particularly significant at Chenganur, is connected to another extraordinary notion – priests and devotees believe the goddess menstruates. During this time the inner sanctum is closed. After three days the image of the deity is taken in procession atop a huge elephant to the river for bathing. On her return she is greeted by the idol of Shiva also atop an elephant. They make a ceremonial return to their respective shrines. Attendance at this ritual is considered to be auspicious particularly for family health and wellbeing.

Kerala is a land of subtle mysteries and within this small southern area, the prohibition at one temple is a cause for ritual and celebration at the other.

Kuttikkanam

About 40km from Kumily, Kuttikkanam (5km west of Peermade) on the Kottayam Rd is the site of the former summer palaces of the maharaja and maharani of Travancore (today the region of Southern Kerala). Both palaces are now privately owned and closed to visitors but you'll see the maharaja's palace as you pass by from the road. The nearby ***Misty Mountain Plantation Resort*** (☎ *0486-332065, fax 0482-872954*) has doubles/cottages from Rs 500/650. It's a pleasant place where you can enjoy a quiet break, short easy walks through coffee and spice plantations, fishing, golf (nine hole course) and even catch a glimpse of the maharani's palace. The manager at Misty Mountain can also arrange trekking into the Periyar Sanctuary.

Indian Cardamom Research Institute

Just 52km from Kumily, on the road to Munnar, this institute (established 1978) undertakes research into herbs, spices and permaculture but the main areas of study are cardamom and vanilla. Here it's the small cardamom, rather then the large, that is the focus. The small cardamom is favoured for its greater oil content, pungency, finer flavour and higher price (reputedly three times the value of the larger variety).

Kerala produces 40 to 45% of India's total cardamom harvest – the remainder coming from Tamil Nadu and Karnataka. The cardamom plant may last from 15 to 25 years, usually producing pods after three years, although some plants may seed after just one year. In season (August to December), plants produce from 10 to 200 panicles which may contain from 100 to 300 pods. See The Cuisine of Kerala section in the Facts for the Visitor chapter for more information on cardamom.

For a viable crop, a farmer requires Rs 300 per kilo; at the time of writing the price was Rs 600. Travellers with a particular interest in spice research are welcome to call in. Dr BA Vadiraj (☎ 04868-37207, fax 37285), Kailasanadu PO, Myladumpara 685 553, Idukki District will happily show you around as long as you write or call at least two days ahead to make an appointment.

Idukki Wildlife Sanctuary

This 77 sq km sanctuary is on the banks of the Idukki Reservoir is about 120km to the north-east of Kottayam. It was established in 1976 and its vegetation comprises mainly deciduous forest and grassland at an altitude ranging from 900m to 1400m. Bisons, bears, wild boar, jackals, wild dogs, sambar etc are found in this area. The reservoir attracts large numbers of birds as well as migratory and resident elephants. Small tribal groups of Adivasis live in the higher areas. Visitors are restricted to boating on the reservoir, if you're interested in serious wildlife spotting you're better off going to Periyar.

The best and most comfortable time to visit is from November to March.

MUNNAR

☎ 0486

Set amid South India's most dramatic mountain scenery, the tiny town of Munnar (1524m) is the commercial centre of some of the world's highest tea-growing estates.

Little is known of the early history of the Munnar region. The area was heavily populated with wildlife including elephants and tigers from early times. It is also likely that various hill tribes would have made their home here. The Muduvan tribe (believed to have come from the area near Madurai) was still active in the region in the 1930s but today few Adivasi people here lead traditional lifestyles.

Before the name Munnar was ascribed in the early 20th century, the region was known as the High Range of Travancore and also the Kanan Devan Hills, after a local landlord. The first major land concession for agriculture was given to colonial pioneers, JD Munro and HG Turner in 1877. They experimented with many crops before settling for tea. The large tea estate, James Finlay & Co, was established in 1895. The giant TATA company came on the scene with a joint venture in 1964. By 1983 the TATA company had taken over most of the acreage and production of tea in the region. Today it is the largest producer of tea in the world.

The need to service the expanding tea estates led to the growth of the Munnar township. The name Munnar is Tamil, meaning three rivers.

The combination of craggy peaks, manicured tea plantations and crisp mountain air makes Munnar a delightful setting and an excellent base from which to explore the many points of interest in this area of the Western Ghats. Sport is also a high priority here – with plans to develop a high altitude sports stadium for professional training. The bustle and immediacy of the town's bazaar are interesting but if you've come for the beauty and tranquillity of the countryside, find accommodation a little farther afield.

Information

The DTPC Information Office, is inconveniently on Alwaye-Munnar (AM) Rd, 2km from the bus stand and town centre. It's open daily (in theory) from 10.30 am to 6.30 pm. It provides information on buses and a couple of sightseeing tours, and teases visitors with its last remaining tourist brochure. The small Munnar Tourist Information Centre (☎ 530249) provides information and also arranges tours. For more comprehensive information, head for the Tourist Information Service (☎ 530349), just opposite the Gandhi statue. Here you'll meet Joseph Iype, an enigmatic individual dedicated to promoting everything about Munnar. For a nominal price (Rs 50) he'll provide information on things to do as well as assistance in arranging accommodation, auto-rickshaws and tours.

The Wildlife Warden's Office, one of a myriad of forest and wildlife offices, is a little out of town up behind the PWD Guest House.

Several stores stock medical and grocery items and should you need to photocopy documents, you can try the delightfully named Photostat Operators' Association tucked away behind the shops in the bazaar.

If you need to purchase or confirm air tickets, book boats or buses, lease a house or secure a massage, head for the helpful Cross Country Tour Designers at the Mahalakshmi Lodge.

Money For changing money, there's the State Bank of India just west of the bazaar and the efficient and friendly State Bank of Travancore at the southern end of the bazaar.

Post & Communications The post office is just south of the bazaar. There are many STD/ISD booths but the few fax machines are STD only. At the time of writing, there were no email facilities within sight of Munnar.

Things to See & Do

While most sites of interest lie around the Munnar area, there are a couple of things to see and do within town. The stone **Christ church** (1910) is now administered by the Church of South India (CSI). Small and finely stained glass windows are almost encased within the solid stone walls, encapsulating the church's history. Except for the overgrown **cemetery** farther up the hill, brass plaques hung in memory of the tea planters are the sole historical records.

You can go **boating** on the Munnar waterway. Boats can be hired from the DTPC and cost Rs 150 for a motor boat (½ hour), Rs 20 to Rs 40 for a pedal boat (½ hour) and Rs 10 per person for a rowboat (one hour).

The **walks** out of Munnar in any direction offer spectacular views and frequently pass tea, coffee or cardamom plantations.

Organised Tours

If you'd hoped to stop into a tea processing factory, you can't. Visitors are no longer permitted. Cross Country Tour Designers (☎ 530329) has an office at Mahalakshmi Lodge from where helpful staff can organise local sightseeing trips.

Half day tour (9 am to 12.30 pm or 2 to 5.45 pm), Top Station, Mattupetty Dam and Kundalay Dam, Rs 175 (minimum 4 people).
Full day tour (9 am to 5.45 pm), Rajamalai Hills, Marayoor Sandalwood Forest and Chinnar Wildlife Sanctuary

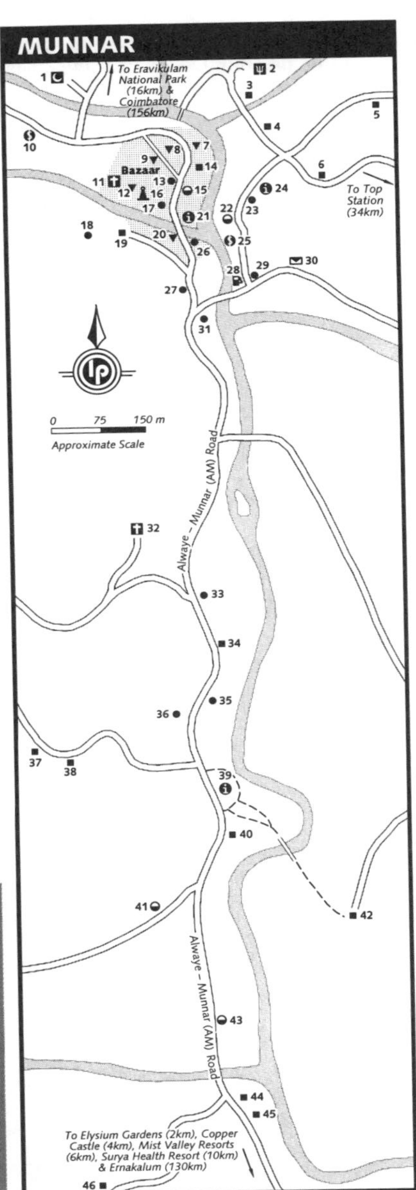

MUNNAR

PLACES TO STAY

3 Hotel Brothers
4 Edassery Eastend
5 Government Guest House
6 Isaac's Residency
14 Ambat Lodge; Krishna Lodge
19 PWD Guest House
34 Mahalakshmi Lodge; Cross Country Tour Designers
37 Poopada Tourist Home
38 Kannan Devan Hills Club
40 Sree Narayana (SN) Tourist Home
42 High Range Club
44 Hotel Hill View
45 Royal Retreat
46 Sinai Cottages

PLACES TO EAT

7 Hotel Hazrath; Produce Market
8 Rapsy Restaurant
9 Suganthi Tea Stall
12 Saravna Bhavan
20 St Anthony's Bakehouse

OTHER

1 Mosque
2 Temple (Hindu)
10 State Bank of India
11 Mount Carmel Church
13 Balaji Tarders
15 Private Bus Stand (Kumily buses)
16 Gandhi Statue
17 St Anthony Shrine
18 Wildlife Warden's Office
21 Tourist Information Service
22 Buses to Top Station
23 Munnar Wines & Foreign Liquor
24 Munnar Tourist Information Centre
25 State Bank of Travancore
26 Photostat Operators' Association
27 Happy Associates
28 Petrol Station
29 Susan Medicals
30 Post & Telegraph Office
31 Tata Tea Regional Office
32 Christ Church
33 Anglo-Tamil Government Primary School
35 Raja Cycles
36 Sports Ground
39 DTPC Information Office & Bike Hire
41 CTC & RMTC Buses to Tamil Nadu
43 KSRTC Bus Stand

Similar tours are available at similar prices from the Munnar Tourist Information Centre (☎ 530249). Be wary of tour companies that promote visits to the Indo-Swiss Project (a dairy research station) and to the Kundalay Golf Course. The Indo-Swiss project is out of bounds to everyone except those involved in relevant research. And, at the time of writing, the golf course was accessible only by 4WD vehicles. Also you may find that instead of a Rs 125 tour, you'll be talked into a Rs 300/600 tour in a rickshaw/jeep, when you can get to exactly the same places on a bus for Rs 11.

Places to Stay

Munnar is crying out for cheap, clean travellers' lodges. As it stands the few budget options that are OK are mostly close to the noisy bazaar. Most accommodation in and around Munnar is in the mid-range to top-end price bracket. Honeymooners come here, maybe oblivious to the conditions.

Places to Stay – Budget

The ***PWD Guest House*** is a dilapidated old bungalow with gloomy substandard rooms for Rs 50. Don't confuse this place with the Government Guest House.

The ***Sree Narayana (SN) Tourist Home*** *(☎ 530212, AM Rd)*, near the DTPC, is an average Indian lodge with doubles starting at Rs 330. Rooms with TV, shower and western toilet cost Rs 450.

Mahalakshmi Lodge *(☎ 530329)*, opposite the sports ground, has basic singles/doubles for Rs 80/160. It also has a helpful tourist advice office. Bucket hot water is available in the mornings only.

Ambat Lodge *(☎ 530661)*, in the bazaar, has cell-like rooms for Rs 65/130. Doubles have bathroom (bucket) attached, singles share a bathroom. This place suffers from noise from the bazaar and the rowdy staff who feel the need to make as much noise as possible at 6 am.

Krishna Lodge *(☎ 530669)*, next door, has larger rooms with bathroom for Rs 85/160.

Hotel Brothers *(☎ 530436)* is a small, friendly lodging place with doubles/triples for Rs 220/330. Two rooms have bathrooms, and there is a small restaurant (see Places to Eat).

Places to Stay – Mid-Range & Top End

The ***Government Guest House*** has spacious, clean doubles with shower and hot water for Rs 550.

Poopada Tourist Home *(☎ 530223)*, about 400m west of the DTPC has doubles with Indian bathroom for Rs 550. There's also a good, cheap restaurant.

Isaac's Residency *(☎ 530501, fax 530265)* has large rooms with cable TV and hot water for Rs 600/700. Deluxe rooms are Rs 900. However many rooms are becoming shabby and dismal, and if the nights get chilly, it's hard to wrestle another blanket from them. Credit cards are accepted and there's a mediocre restaurant and a noisy bar.

The ***Edassery Eastend*** *(☎ 530451, fax 530227)* has rooms in attractive plantation house buildings for Rs 650. Cottages cost Rs 1150 a double. There are two restaurants (see Places to Eat).

Elysium Gardens *(☎ 530510)* is 2km along Top Station Rd. There are great views but single/doubles at Rs 350/450 are ordinary. There is no restaurant but room service is available.

Hotel Hill View *(☎ 530567, fax 530241)*, about 2km from the town centre, is in a peaceful location and is OK at Rs 300/600. All the rooms have TV, telephone and hot water. There's also an OK multicuisine restaurant and tours and fishing can be arranged.

Royal Retreat *(☎ 530240, fax 530440)*, next to and somewhat overshadowed by Hotel Hill View, offers very nice rooms with all the extras from Rs 700 to Rs 1500, or Rs 1750 if you prefer a garden suite. There's a good multicuisine restaurant.

Sinai Cottages *(☎ 530560)* is one cottage with three double rooms, surrounded by tea plantations. Comfortable and clean singles/doubles with bathroom cost Rs 300/400 or the entire stone cottage can be claimed for Rs 11,000. There is hot water and plenty of peace and quiet. You'll need a torch (flashlight) to negotiate the path to and from the restaurants at the nearby Hotel Hill View and Royal Retreat.

Kannan Devan Hills Club *(☎ 530252)* evokes the era of the tea-planting Raj and provides lodgings for Indian nationals only in Muir Cottage for Rs 350 a double. There are games such as badminton and table tennis, as well as a spiffing little canteen.

High Range Club *(☎ 530253)* is even more Rajesque, resplendent with mounted heads of hunting spoils in the bar and billiards room. Full board ranges from Rs 1650 to Rs 2295 per double, or there are cottages for Rs 1950. There's golf, squash and tennis, but best of all you don't need to be a member to stay, so sit back, sip a gin and argue the toss about Kipling and Forster.

In the hills surrounding Munnar town are a number of hotels purporting to be resorts. The distance from town is compensated by the tranquillity. Four kilometres south of the town ***Copper Castle*** *(☎ 530633, fax 530438)* is perched precariously on a hillside, with spectacular mountain views. Double rooms range from Rs 1200 to Rs 2100 (there are no singles) and a family suite is Rs 3000. The rooms are large but after only a few months they were already showing serious signs of the grots.

A farther 2km south is ***Mist Valley Resorts*** *(☎ 530708, fax 318664)*. Set amid a coffee and cardamom estate, this place requires a real head for heights and a willingness to climb many steps. The 1km driveway is very steep and auto-rickshaws will only transport one person and their luggage at a time. The cottage type rooms are large and have a peculiar unfurnished mezzanine level that seems to serve no practical purpose. The views are stunning but the quality of plumbing and bedding is basic. Cottages range from Rs 1700 to Rs 2100. For residents with sturdy legs the staff will organise a 1½ hour 'trek' to the top of the hill.

Ten kilometres west of Munnar, off the Cochin Rd, ***Surya Health Resort*** *(☎ 563204, email surya@kerala.com)* is nestled into a hill. You enter almost at rooftop level and descend the steep steps to your room. The rooms are OK and, as with many hotels in these hills, views are stunning. Standard/deluxe doubles are Rs 600/750. There's no restaurant but room service is available and each room is fitted with a dining table and chairs. Various Ayurvedic treatments are available. A three day package of treatment and accommodation for singles/doubles is Rs 5000/8500.

Places to Eat

There are a couple of ***coffee stalls*** in the bazaar which open early and sell snacks, coffee and tea. At night an outdoor restaurant emerges adjacent to the Gandhi statue. Cheap veg and nonveg meals are served canteen style in an amiable atmosphere.

Saravna Bhavan is a relatively new veg restaurant along the laneway near the Gandhi statue. The food is good but the restaurant lacks the cleanliness and ambience of its namesakes in other towns.

Hotel Hazrath, near the produce market, does OK south Indian meals for Rs 12.

Rapsy Restaurant, in the arcade running from the centre of the bazaar, does an excellent chicken *biryani* (savoury rice) as well as a small selection of other dishes. It's a good place for breakfast. The service here is so fast that some meals literally fly through the air – sometimes landing in *dhotis*, and not to the amusement of the wearer.

Suganthi Tea Stall, almost opposite Rapsy in the arcade, is a popular and busy place with savoury and sweet snacks.

Edassery Eastend has two restaurants: upstairs, through the main entrance, is the upmarket one, and downstairs (entry at the back of the building) is the simpler, much cheaper one. Both are good quality (they use the same kitchen), but there is a smaller range and bigger serves downstairs. Service is thoughtful and award-winning for delays.

Hotel Brothers has a basic but authentic restaurant. Usually there is only one meal available – 'Keralan Dish' – which consists of fish curry and tapioca (Rs 15).

The mid-range and top-end hotels all have good restaurants, usually with the three cuisines ubiquitous to hotels in Kerala: Indian, Chinese and continental. It's better to stick with the Indian menu.

If you're looking for take-away snacks for walking, try St Anthony's bakehouse in the bazaar area.

Shopping

Munnar is not exactly a shopping paradise. If you're looking for quality crafts or clothing you're better off searching in bigger towns such as Thrissur or Ernakulam. But you can have a good time wandering

Going for Gold

Without gold, there is no life. This is the conviction of many a Malayali.

Gold symbolises permanence, light, wealth and truth; it is a symbol for life. And in Kerala, gold is significant throughout life, particularly at birth, marriage and death.

One of the first gifts to a child is gold – at least 50g to 100g, from the father's parents. To maintain good health, a child may be fed gold in its first year. This is administered in the form of a special paste made from wyamb root and gold dust. At marriage, gold assumes a vital role. It forms the jewellery worn by the bride and guests. It is the favoured gift. And it is usually the substance of the *tali* (thread tied around the bride's neck symbolising the union). For Hindus the tali may bear an *Om* sign; for Christians it usually bears the cross. At death, gold is often placed into the mouth of the dead person. A dead woman may have her tali placed in her mouth.

Buying gold is a family affair – one which involves time and deliberation – and maybe even conflict. Some family members place emphasis on aesthetics, for others investment is of primary importance. Government regulation, increased prices or reduced value has not affected the Malayali demand for gold.

Keralan jewellery has few stones or other embellishments. Generally it consists of gold only. Some of the more popular designs include:

Kasumala – from *kasu* meaning coin and *mala* meaning chain, this chain of gold coins usually depicts King George (the king prior to Independence) or the goddess Lakshmi. Christians usually take the king, Hindus may take either.
Mangamala – mango motif.
Nagapadam – golden snake.
Mullamottu – jasmine motif.
Palakka – based on the shape of a seed this design comprises green glass set in gold.

The above designs are popular as necklaces or bracelets and are all favourites for marriage. The *oddiyanam* (belt) and *vanki* (forearm adornments) are also prevalent. Earrings are particularly favoured especially the *jimka* bell style arrangement.

Since very little gold mining occurs in India, gold is imported in bars from Switzerland and London and converted into jewellery in Kerala, mainly in the Thrissur district which has a tradition of goldsmithing. Currently 2000 goldsmiths fashion the gold into traditional Keralan designs, as well as the more intricate Bengali styles.

In goldsmithing factories, men sit cross legged on the floor separating the tiny gold balls before placing them into the flame that will permit the shaping and fashioning. In small homes women undertake similar tasks. Traditions continue as they have for centuries. However some customs have changed. New designs are being developed from the old. And there is no longer a goldsmith's caste. As the locals say, 'now even Christians make jewellery'.

through the bazaar. Balaji Traders near the centre of the bazaar has a limited selection of brassware. And if you want something warm for a cool Munnar night you can get a decent bottle of port or brandy at Munnar Wines & Foreign Liquor.

Getting There & Away

The roads around Munnar are in poor condition and may be seriously affected by monsoons. Bus timings therefore may vary. The Tamil Nadu Bus Stand and KSRTC Bus Stand (for buses throughout Kerala) are situated to the south of the town, while the private bus stands are in the bazaar. Munnar is 130km east of Kochi (Cochin) and Ernakulam via Aluva (Alwaye) and 70km north of Kumily. It's best reached by direct (express) bus, other buses require too many changes. There are buses from Kochi (five daily, 4½ hours), Kottayam (four daily, five hours), Kumily (five daily, five hours), Thiruvananthapuram (four daily, nine hours), Coimbatore (two daily, six hours) or Madurai (one daily, six hours).

There are five KSRTC buses each day to Thiruvananthapuram. Two go via Kochi and Ernakulam (Rs 45, 8.40 and 11.40 am) and three via Kottayam (Rs 48, 10.30 am and 12.20 and 3.30 pm). In addition, there are private buses, which tend to stop more often and take longer.

To go to Kumily, 4km from Periyar, you will need to catch a private bus from the bus stand near the post office. There are only two direct buses a day (12.25 and 3 pm); other buses (1.20 and 2.45 pm) run to Poopara, from where you can catch a Kumily-bound bus. Some travellers advise that the midday buses from Ernakulam on school days are best avoided due to overcrowding.

Getting Around

Walking Munnar's easy to walk around but the distances from accommodation to the main part of town may lead you to seek other forms of transport.

Bicycle DTPC hires out bikes (Rs 10 for four hours), but they are quick to point out cheaper options. At Raja Cycles, it's only Rs 5 for the same time. A little farther south of Raja you can hire mountain bikes for Rs 5 per hour.

Auto-Rickshaws These are plentiful and will charge around Rs 10 from one end of town to the other. They are also happy to be hired for distances farther afield and reasonable rates can usually be negotiated.

Jeeps These line the main street of Munnar and can be hired for about Rs 400/600 for a half/full day.

AROUND MUNNAR

Most of the pleasure of a visit to Munnar is in exploring the outer areas. However before you set out, make sure you have accurate information. Visitors are continually disappointed when promised possibilities fail to materialise. But don't worry, there's much of interest to see and do and it's easily done by following any of the main routes out of the town. Two such routes (detailed below) with magnificent views are to:

Chinnar Wildlife Sanctuary Along this 58km route you can glimpse Anamudi, visit the Eravikulam National Park (16km), travel through a sandalwood forest near Marayoor (32km) and conclude with a short stop at the Chinnar Wildlife Sanctuary.

Top Station This easterly route takes you to Mudapetty Dam (10km) for boating and short horse rides, the Kundalay Dam (24km), and finally Top Station (34km).

Anamudi

Getting the lowdown on the highest peak in South India is no easy matter. Tourist and many forest authorities promote Anamudi as an excellent place for trekking. You may be advised that all you need is a permit from the WWO. However, due to the need to protect the Nilgiri tahr which inhabit the Anamudi region, such permits are rarely given. Don't be tempted by the private operators who may offer to take you up there. The tahr deserve their solitude. And you can see plenty of them at Rajamalai (see

Eravikulam National Park, following) where there are also stunning views.

Don't listen to the WWO at Munnar who'll advise you that trekking is possible through the DFO at Devikulam – the only trek you'll get to take by following this advice is a useless circular, bureaucratic one.

Eravikulam National Park

Stretching over 97 sq km in the tea-growing region of the Western Ghats, 16km northeast of Munnar, Eravikulam was proclaimed a national park in 1978 as a means to protect the threatened Nilgiri tahr. It contains shola forest, the tahr's favoured plant, although the predominant vegetation is grass. The main attraction is the resident population of extraordinarily tame Nilgiri tahr, often found just inside the entrance to the park proper. Indigenous to the area, the tahr, known locally as *varayadu* (rock goat), were in danger of extinction until the work of Clifford Rice, an American biologist reversed their decline. Of the 2000 remaining, there are an estimated 1000 in this park.

Having entered the park you can walk up Rajamalai (King Hill). The only permissible path is a 10km private road that leads to the TATA tea estate. To prevent further erosion, previous short cuts are now blocked and using them is prohibited. Despite the few vehicles that may pass you along the way, it's a pleasant, easy walk, affording stunning views. You'll pass a tiny shrine to the goddess Kali, almost concealed by the huge fig tree that shades it.

The Nilgiri tahr often greets visitors just inside the gates of the Eravikulam National Park.

Plastic is prohibited in the park so you must bring water in other containers. You can get here by bus to the park turn-off, 7km from Munnar (which is the nearest accommodation), then walk. But to get more time in the park it's much better to take a rickshaw from Munnar to the second checkpoint (16km for Rs 125 – more depending on how long you stay).

The park is open from 8 am to 5.30 pm and entrance is Rs 10/50 for Indians/foreigners, Rs 5 for two or three wheelers and Rs 100 for video cameras. The best time to visit is from November to March.

Marayoor

☎ 0486

The road to Marayoor from Eravikulam along the Munnar-Chinnar Rd, passes by tea estates sometimes dotted with Hindu shrines to Ganesh or other deities. At Marayoor, 32km from Munnar, you'll come to the **sandalwood forest**, reputed to be the only natural sandalwood forest in Kerala. Stories exist about sandalwood factories and possibilities for visits but they'll be denied when you arrive. Nevertheless, travelling through the forest is a pleasing experience. Under government control, it covers an area of 15,000 hectares. Twenty seven guards protect the valuable wood. Dead and diseased trees are collected for auction, fetching an average price of Rs 600,000 per tonne. The wood is used for the ever-popular carvings, while oils and particularly sandal paste are precious commodities in temples.

The ***Marayoor Tourist Home*** *(☎ 552231)* is a small lodge in town with OK double rooms with bucket hot water for Rs 125. The more upmarket ***Chandana Residency*** *(☎ 552222)* is in pleasant surrounds just 5km east of town with rooms from Rs 500. It has a good restaurant and bar, but no credit card facilities.

Chinnar Wildlife Sanctuary

Declared a sanctuary in 1984, the Chinnar Wildlife Sanctuary covers 90 sq km and is one of two Indian sanctuaries providing refuge for the endangered giant grizzled squirrel (Ratufa macroura). It's 20km from the sandalwood forest and 58km from Munnar, and is reputedly home to elephant, Hanuman monkey, gaur, common langur and deer. The rain shadow here results in comparatively little rainfall and a marked difference in vegetation consisting of dry scrub and deciduous forests with a little shola and grassland higher up. Just within the entrance there's a watchtower from where you can observe wild animals. They claim the time allowed on the tower is limited to 10 minutes and the noise of the forest staff directing people away would frighten off any animal which may choose to venture out. A 'small consideration' of Rs 10 per person may buy peace and time. The sanctuary is open from 6 am to 6 pm and the best months to visit are January and February. Entrance is Rs 5. Only day visits are permitted and the best time is late afternoon, although many visitors find the experience disappointing. Returning to Munnar at night is not advisable given the poor state of the road and, contrary to official advice, you can't stay in the Forest Resthouse, which is reserved for forestry personnel. Instead try the accommodation at Marayoor, 20km west.

Five buses a day leave Munnar for Chinnar (more frequent to Marayoor). Although the journey is only 58km the mountain roads make for a lengthy trip – allow at least three to four hours from Munnar. Given that late afternoon is the best time to visit, you may prefer to take a jeep from Munnar (Rs 400/600 per day). If you're staying in Marayoor, you can arrange for transport through your hotel. The sanctuary is also accessible from Udumalpet in Tamil Nadu.

Dams

On the Munnar-Top Station Rd, 10km from Munnar, the huge lake-like **Mudapetty Dam** is surrounded by the towering peaks of the Western Ghats. Administered by the DTPC, it's open every day from 9 am to 5.30 pm for boating and short horse rides. You can explore the waters for 15 minutes in a slow/fast speedboat for Rs 150/200. Boats take up to 20 people. Horse rides involve a 500m ride with the horse led by a man with a rope. Drinks and snacks are available.

Three kilometres beyond the Mudapetty Dam you'll see the entrance to the **Indo-Swiss Project** – a collaborative undertaking researching the dairy industry. Although milk is their concern, it's tea they'll try to flog off. Due to concerns about viruses, visitors are not permitted to visit the project (in spite of all the tourist hype to the contrary that you'll be offered before you set out from Munnar).

The scenic area of **Kundalay Dam**, 300m off the main road and 24km from Munnar, is a pleasant place to relax and picnic. There are no facilities here and it's clean and quiet. Four kilometres farther on there's a nine-hole **golf course**, but you'll need a jeep to negotiate the poor road.

Top Station

On Kerala's border with Tamil Nadu, 34km from Munnar, Top Station has spectacular views over the Ghats. There's precious little left of the **ropeway** which was used to transport tea – just some cement foundations. From here a path leads along the hilltop for about 100m from where you can get a better view of the panoramic surrounds. Like mountain areas anywhere, be prepared to find the view obscured by cloud.

Buses leave Munnar at 7.30, 9.30 and 11.15 am and make the steep 34km climb to Top Station in around an hour for Rs 11. Or catch one of the private buses going to Koviluo (the next stop after Top Station) at the bus stand near Happy Associates. At Koviluo the bus turns around and heads back to Munnar – giving you about one hour at Top Station. A jeep, which can be hired in Munnar for Rs 600 return, will enable you to stop en route. Auto-rickshaws also make the journey for about Rs 300 return. There are a couple of ***tea houses*** in the village near Top Station.

Devikulam Lake

Because this lake is on private TATA property, you must get permission from the

TONY WHEELER

LINDSAY BROWN

a pluckers hard at work in the green plantations of the Western Ghats.

SARA-JANE CLELAND

LINDSAY BROWN

PETER DAVIS

LINDSAY BROWN

The cooler climes of the Western Ghats. **Top:** A misty bus station in Kodaikanal, just over the Tamil Nadu border. **Middle left:** One of the many rivers flowing through the Western Ghats. **Bottom left:** The Nilgir tahr is protected by careful conservation. **Bottom right:** Coffee pickers negotiate a steep plantation.

TATA Regional Office in Munnar if you wish to visit it. If you turn up at the estate gate hoping to get in without a permit, you'll push the generous Indian hospitality too far and will be politely declined. Management is understandably tired of travellers, who, following tourist office advice, attempt to visit the lake without the required entry permit. If a permit is granted, present this at the estate gate just 3km off the main road from Devikulam town. From the gate it's a 7km journey up a steep winding road through tea plantations. The lake provides drinking water to nearby resorts and TATA management are keen to retain its pristine nature.

Local people believe this is a holy place – the site where Sita bathed. Now there's a small **temple** in her honour, Seliamman, nearby. There is also a Christ church and Shiva temple.

The road is rough, so you'll need to hire a jeep from Munnar or walk from Devikulam (20km return). Although the distance is short the jeep will take about one hour (one way) to negotiate the road.

Thattekkad Bird Sanctuary

This sanctuary is home to around 300 species of indigenous and migratory birds including Malabar grey hornbills, woodpeckers, rose and blue-winged parakeets, jungle fowl, herons, egrets, jungle mynas and rarer species such as the Ceylon frog-mouth and rose-billed roller. Established in 1983 by the renowned ornithologist, Salim Ali, the 25 sq km sanctuary provides a good location for important research. Entry fee is Rs 5.

Thattekkad, is 15km north-east of Kothamangalam, on the Ernakulam-Munnar road, roughly half way between the two towns. There is an inspection bungalow and a dormitory at Thattekkad. The ***Hornbill Bungalow*** has double rooms for Rs 300 and beds in the dormitory are Rs 50. Very good food is available for Rs 15 per meal.

To get there take a direct bus from Ernakulam to Kothamangalam or a more frequent bus to the larger town of Muvattupula, and change there for Kothamangalam – a further 8km. From Kothamangalam, you take the Thattekkad bus for the next 15km which will take about ½ hour. Then you and the bus will be ferried along the Periyar River to Thattekkad.

The best viewing time is from 5 to 6 am and the best visiting time is from October to March.

PALAKKAD (Palghat)

☎ 0491

In a natural depression in the Western Ghats and linking Kerala to the plains of Tamil Nadu, this small, dusty town is the centre of a large rice-growing region. Its former strategic importance is highlighted by the imposing **fort** built by Hyder Ali in 1766. All that remains of the neglected fort are the clumsily repaired bastions and a large wooden door, off its hinges, slowly disintegrating alongside worn stone carvings of fish and flowers. There is a functioning **jail** within the grounds, but that is about as interesting as it gets.

As it is near the border with Tamil Nadu, travellers moving between the states can use Palakkad as a base to visit Parambikulam Wildlife Sanctuary and Silent Valley National Park (see Around Palakkad).

The Tourist Information Office is in West Fort Rd, beside the fort and near the Fort Palace Hotel. It has minimal information but helpful staff will provide train times and help organise accommodation at Thunakadavu (for Parambikulam) or Mukkali (for Silent Valley).

Palakkad's banks are small branches not authorised to cash travellers cheques or cards. The Hotel Indraprastha will change money for guests only. There's a good bookshop within Hotel Indraprastha with travel guides, novels and a good selection of recipe books, primarily in English.

Places to Stay & Eat

Surya Tourist Home (*☎ 538338*) is just 300m south of the private bus stand. It's a little hard to find, look for the sign to ***Hotel Cauvery***, a popular veg/nonveg restaurant on the ground floor. Reception for the Surya is on the 3rd floor. Clean singles/doubles are Rs 175/275, Rs 225/295 with cable TV or Rs 500 with air-con.

Hotel Ambadi *(☎ 531244)*, across the road from the private bus stand, has doubles for Rs 250, Rs 450 with air-con. There is an attached multicuisine ***restaurant***.

Hotel Kairali *(☎ 534611)* is a good budget option near the KSRTC bus stand. Singles/doubles cost Rs 75/125, or Rs 350 for a double with air-con

Fort Palace Hotel *(☎/fax 534621, West Fort Rd)*, a Rs 5 rickshaw ride from the bus stands, is a good mid-range choice. Rooms are Rs 325/400, or Rs 450/550 with air-con. However, a ludicrous charge of Rs 85 for water and electricity will be added onto the bill along with the usual taxes.

Hotel Indraprastha *(☎ 534641, fax 534645, English Church Rd)* is the top hotel in town. Standard doubles are Rs 750, air-con rooms are Rs 900. There's an air-con ***restaurant*** (Indian and Chinese) and an excellent ***coffee shop*** at the entrance which is clean, comfortable and reasonably priced.

Getting There & Away

Bus Buses to Coimbatore in Tamil Nadu (Rs 14, 1½ hours, 51km) depart the KSRTC bus stand hourly. To Thrissur (Rs 21, 2 hours, 70km) buses depart every 20 minutes up to 9.45 pm. To Kozhikode (Rs 30, four hours, 130km) they leave about every 30 minutes.

To get to Annamalai for the Parambikulam Wildlife Sanctuary, catch one of the many regular buses to Pollachi in Tamil Nadu from the private bus stand. For Silent Valley catch one of the regular buses to Mannakkad, also from the private bus stand.

Train Palakkad Junction is 5km from town, with many trains heading east to Tamil Nadu and beyond, and west to Shoranur, the major junction with Kerala's north-south train, where connections can easily be made. There are several trains a day heading south to Ernakulam and Thiruvananthapuram, fewer heading north.

The *Kerala Express* departs Palakkad at 7.20 am for Ernakulam, Kollam (Quilon) and Thiruvananthapuram. In the other direction the *Kerala Express* departs from Palakkad at 7 pm for Coimbatore and Chennai (Madras). For northern destinations such as Kozhikode, Kannur (Cannanore) and Kasaragod, the *Trichy-Mangalore Express* departs at 1.30 pm.

Fares to Chennai (548km) are Rs 167/574 in 2nd/1st class, to Ernakulam (160km) Rs 47/224, Kozhikode (130km) Rs 40/205 and Mangalore (351 km) Rs 118/410.

AROUND PALAKKAD

Parambikulam Wildlife Sanctuary

The Parambikulam Wildlife Sanctuary, 135km from Palakkad (via Pollachi, Tamil Nadu), stretches around the Parambikulam, Thunakadavu and Peruvaripallam dams, and covers an area of 285 sq km adjacent to the Annamalai Wildlife Sanctuary in Tamil Nadu. It has an altitude of 450m to 1440m. Once profuse with teak forests, now, after heavy logging and unsuccessful reforestation, there's only eucalyptus plantations, grasses and marsh plants. In spite of this it seems the area is still home to many species including the greatest numbers of gaur, the odd tahr, wild boar, elephants, the Nilgiri as well as the common langur, lion-tailed and bonnet macaques, otters, bison, sloth bears, sambar, chital, crocodiles and a few tigers and panthers.

Three groups of Adivasis live within this sanctuary: the Kadas, the Muduvas and the Malai-Malsars. They cultivate crops and work as elephant keepers. The sanctuary is open all year, but is best avoided from June to August due to the monsoon.

Park headquarters are at Thunakadavu, where the Forestry Department has a ***Forest Resthouse*** and a treetop hut – book through the Forest Inspection Bungalow (☎ 0425-37233) at Thunakadavu. At Parambikulam, there's a ***PWD Resthouse*** and a ***Tamil Nadu Government Inspection Bungalow*** – book through the Junior Engineer, Tamil Nadu PWD, Parambikulam. There are also two ***watchtowers*** where you can stay overnight: one is at Anappadi (8km from Thunakadavu) and the other is at Zungam (5km from Thunakadavu).

The best access to the sanctuary is by bus from Pollachi, Tamil Nadu (40km from Coimbatore and 49km from Palakkad). There are four daily buses in either direction between Pollachi and Parambikulam (via Annamalai). The trip takes two hours. Boat cruises operate from Parambikulam and rowboats can be hired at Thunakadavu.

Silent Valley National Park

This national park of some 90 sq km became the subject of bitter dispute when its virgin forests (apparently the last tracts of tropical evergreen forests) were threatened with the development of a huge hydroelectric scheme. The dispute was settled in late 1984 with the establishment of the park and the preservation of the forests. The park now forms part of the Nilgiri Biosphere Reserve – an area set apart for complete preservation.

A rare remnant of primary evergreen forest, the vegetation provides habitat for a diverse range of wildlife, much of which is indigenous to the area. There are up to 100 species of butterflies and birds. Other wildlife includes the rare lion-tailed macaque, Nilgiri tahr, gaur, palm civets, Nilgiri martens, leopards, tigers, Nilgiri leaf monkeys, elephants and lion-tailed macaques.

The park is 80km from Palakkad in the Kundali Hills. The name derives from the eerie quietness resulting from the lack of cicadas. This is an important biosphere reserve and refuge of Adivasis and visitors are restricted to an area near the site of the proposed dam. Facilities are limited.

Accommodation is in the ***Forest Department Resthouse*** (☎ 0492-453225) at Mukkali, 22km from the park. It costs US$10 per person per day and there are local hotels in Mukkali for food. Regular buses run to Mannakkad from Palakkad (45km) from where it is easy to organise a lift to Mukkali.

WAYANAD (Muthanga) WILDLIFE SANCTUARY

Also known as Muthanga Wildlife Sanctuary, Wayanad, 105km north-east of Kozhikode, is a remote rainforest reserve connected to Bandipur National Park in Karnataka and Mudumalai Sanctuary in Tamil Nadu. It is part of the Nilgiri Biosphere and covers an area of almost 500 sq km divided into two regions by a wide area allocated to agriculture.

Wayanad means 'the land of swamps' and the plateau (650m to 900m) is swampy, particularly in the lower gullies. Grasses and bamboo proliferate in the swampland while there's moist deciduous forest with teak in the plateau. It is home to a range of fauna including elephants (seasonal), gaur, sambar, chital and barking deer. Many types of monkeys inhabit the region and there have been sightings of the slender loris.

Visiting the Sanctuary

Almost all the tourist literature gives the impression that Wayanad Sanctuary is an accessible place with vast areas open for trekking and other fascinating activities. The official advice varies greatly. The Chief Conservator of Forests in Thiruvananthapuram will advise that permits must be obtained from the Wildlife Warden's Office (WWO) in Sultan's Battery (Suthanbatheri). You will receive this advice consistently (at various tourist and forest offices) until you get to the WWO, Sultan's Battery to apply for a permit. There, the very thoughtful staff will advise that permits are issued by the District Forest Officer (DFO, ☎ 04968-540233) in Manantavadi (Mananthoody), some 50km north-west. Permits cannot be issued via phone or radio. You need to front up to have your application considered and approved. Before you take the journey back to apply for a permit, phone to ascertain the DFO's whereabouts. She may be at a conference or an auction sale or...

If you get the permit you may take it to one of four Assistant Wildlife Wardens at:

Sultan's Battery 3km along the road to Pulpally (also known as Garage Rd) at the northern end of town.

Kurichiat 5km farther along the Pulpally Rd from the Sultan's Battery Office.

Muthanga 18km east of Sultan's Battery, on the Mysore Rd.

Tholpetty towards Manantavadi.

The Tholpetty office deals with the northern section of the sanctuary, the remaining three deal with the southern sections. If you end up at Muthanga, you'll be advised that trekking is strictly prohibited and if you wish to enter the sanctuary you must hire a jeep. There are no jeeps in Muthanga, so you can look at some snakes in the **Snake Park**, accept the kind offers of the man who suggests you grab a mattress and bed down for the night or return to Sultan's Battery and try again.

At the time of writing the best procedure seemed to be to turn up at Muthanga with a jeep (easily hired in the main street of Sultan's Battery for Rs 6 per kilometre) at about 7.30 am, where you will be assigned a 'watcher' for the 20km trip around the outskirts of the sanctuary. The trip will take you through plantation forest which is logged and sent to Kozhikode for pulping. You may see boar, sambar, spotted deer and elephant. The skilful watcher will go to great lengths to locate wildlife. If you understand Malayalam, you'll receive much valuable and interesting information.

The sanctuary (outskirts) is open from 6 am to 6 pm. Entry to, or remaining in the park outside these hours is strictly prohibited. No trekking is permitted in the park. Entry to the outskirts costs Rs 25 per person, Rs 10 for vehicles and Rs 25 for a watcher. The best time to visit is from November to March. You may wonder why you bothered – the roads through the Western Ghats will give you better opportunities for seeing native flora. (For an alternative way of experiencing the forests of Wayanad, see Around Sultan's Battery later in this chapter.)

Places to Stay

Accommodation in a small ***dormitory*** is available at the edge of the forest buffer zone at Muthanga for a 'nominal' rent. For lodges and hotels, the nearest town is Sultan's Battery (see the following details). Alternatively, if you are detained in Manantavadi while you get permits you can stay at ***Hotel Riviera*** *(☎ 0493-540322)*. While this place doesn't quite exude the ambience of its name, the rooms are comfortable and the staff are friendly. Rooms are Rs 65/120, Rs 230 for a double deluxe and Rs 400 for air-con. Veg and nonveg ***restaurants*** are attached.

The bus station is 1km from this hotel on the road to Sultan's Battery.

Honouring Benevolence – the Festival of Onam

The festival of Onam is inspired by generosity, altruism and loyalty. It's based on the legend of Mahabali, a benevolent mythical king, who ruled in an ideal time when prosperity, equality and harmony reigned supreme. So perfect was this time, that the gods became jealous – threatened that human nature was becoming too close to godliness. Vishnu decided to terminate this development, and appeared to Mahabali as a dwarf – Vamana. He requested land, equal in size to three of his footsteps. Mahabali, being a magnanimous monarch, agreed. But Vishnu then assumed his full capacity – in the physical as well as the ethereal sense. With his first step he took the celestial world, with his second step he took the world of the demons. Realising that his third step would take the earth and result in the destruction of his people, Mahabali pleaded with Vishnu to take his third step over him and he surrendered his life. The people were spared. The gods were happy and Mahabali was granted a visit to his beloved people for one day each year.

The Onam festival commemorates the annual return of Mahabali. Some believe that he visits each family home. Elaborate celebrations mark the event.

The festival now has its critics who claim that its focus on affluence detracts from its essence. However for many it remains a time of reflection on goodwill, kindness and generosity.

SULTAN'S BATTERY

☎ 0493

Sultan's Battery, 97km east of Kozhikode, is on the road routes from Mysore and Udhagamandalam (Ooty) to Kozhikode.

Information

The nearest tourist office is the very helpful DTPC, adjacent to Civil Station in Kalpetta, 20km west.

The post office is on the 1st Floor, Jubilee Complex, Main Rd, 100m east of the mosque. STD/ISD and fax (local only) is available in Main St near the Prince Hotel. Of the many banks in Sultan's Battery, the only one that will change foreign currency is the State Bank of Travancore, almost opposite the post office.

Things to See

The town is named after Tipu Sultan but **Tipu's Fort** erected in the late 1700s, and destroyed by the British, is in ruins. It's alleged that Tipu's battery was actually a **Jain temple** in the town. The temple still stands, set back about 50m from the road, 1km west of the private bus stand on the Mysore Rd. It's sandwiched between the Vimal Jyothi Working Women's Hostel and the Adoration Convent. There is a small iron gate through which you can see a stone building. On first appearances it's apparently deserted, but the caretaker will eventually appear and unlock the gates to the chambers. You will need your own torch (flashlight) to see the stone carving in the ceilings. It's open from 8 am to noon and 2 to 6 pm.

Places to Stay

Along the main drag in Sultan's Battery, and within walking distance of the private bus stand, are several lodges including the ***Viyager Tourist Home*** and the friendly ***Hotel Jaya***, both with singles/doubles for Rs 45/65.

The Resort *(☎ 620510, fax 620583)* has rooms from Rs 250/325, or Rs 600 for air-con. All rooms have bathroom and TV and there's a decent restaurant, but some of the staff seem to frequent the bar a little too often. It's close to the private bus stand and about 1km from the KSRTC bus stand.

Dwaraka Tourist Home *(☎ 620358, High Lord Buildings)* has a seriously off-putting foyer. However, close your eyes as you ascend the first flight of grubby stairs and you cross to a new annexe that is reasonably comfortable. Doubles cost from Rs 125 to Rs 275, Rs 400 for air-con. Hot water is available. The attached ***Hotel Prince*** has mediocre food and a blaring TV, from which there's no escape.

Getting There & Away

There are regular KSRTC buses between Sultan's Battery and Kozhikode (Rs 30, 3½ hours) which are always crowded so it's worthwhile booking a seat. There are many buses running between Mysore or Ooty and Kozhikode, which stop at Sultan's Battery.

Getting Around

You can walk to most places within the town itself. There are buses and rickshaws to take you to places such as the WWO. However the roads around Sultan's Battery are in a poor state and most locals hire jeeps which line the main street. The rate varies but Rs 6 per kilometre is about right.

AROUND SULTAN'S BATTERY

Vythiri (Vayittiri)

If chasing forest officers for permits gets too much and you feel you're 'out of your tree' why not try living in a tree, 25m above ground. You can have this treehouse experience at ***Green Magic Nature Resort*** in Vythiri, 65km north-east of Kozhikode. This eco-friendly place is not for visitors used to regular creature comforts. It's for those who seek a genuine forest experience with minimal negative impact. Plastic is forbidden (including mineral water bottles) and appliances are powered by solar energy and gober gas (cow dung). The way up to the tree is via an ingenious cane elevator using a counter weight with water. To get to the treehouse you journey by jeep to a base camp and then walk for 40 minutes, carrying all your essentials. Accommodation for two people is US$150 including all meals. If you're not into heights you can try the ground level cottages for US$110 for two (all meals included). Guided walks through the Wayanad forest are also available. All bookings must be made through Tourindia (☎ 0471-330437, fax 331407) on MG Rd, Thiruvananthapuram.

Pookote Lake

This small and peaceful lake is nestled within the hills of the ghats. You can walk around its forested perimeter or row across its still waters, sections of which are covered in lotus. There's a children's park and a small ***restaurant*** serving *muntereneere*, a locally produced Ayurvedic drink consisting of grape juice, cardamom, cinnamon and sugar. Boat hire costs Rs 20/35 for 20 minutes for a pedal boat/rowboat. The lake is open daily from 9 am to 5.30 pm and entry is Rs 2/3. If you're seeking peace and quiet, weekends with crowds are best avoided.

Buses from Kozhikode take two hours and set down at the bus stop 500m from the lake. If you're coming from Sultan's Battery, catch the Kozhikode bus which sets down at Vythiri. From there you can hire a rickshaw (Rs 15) or walk the remaining 1km.

If you're tempted to stay in the area, the ***Hotel Dwarka*** *(☎ 621358, Mysore-Calicut Rd)* has luxury, well-positioned cottages that can accommodate eight people for Rs 1500.

Narayana Guru Kula Ashram

Right opposite the Pookote Lake is another of the ashrams dedicated to the ideas of Narayana Guru. For more information contact the Sree Narayana Dharma Sangham Trust (☎ 0471-602221, fax 550651) at Varkala or the Sree Narayana Association of North America Inc (☎ 516-775 4175) PO Box 260009, Bellerose, NY 11426-0009, USA.

Chain Tree

This large healthy ficus, covered in vines, shelters a tiny lingam shine. A chain hangs menacingly from the foliage to the shrine. This is a provocative memorial to the life of an Adivasi. The story goes that an English engineer secured the assistance of a local tribesman to find a path through the Western Ghats. Having found the path, the engineer killed the tribesman, and took the credit. But the soul of the dead man began to disturb local travellers, so a priest 'controlled' it by chaining it to the tree. The tree is directly opposite the Western Edible Oil Complex on the Mysore-Calicut Rd, 2.5km from Pookote Lake on the way to Kozhikode.

Edakkal Caves

Twelve kilometres south of Sultan's Battery, near Ambalavayal, the important archaeological site of Edakkal Caves features prehistoric petroglyphs. You can go the first 3km along the road to Kozhikode by bus, but it's much better to hire a jeep for the entire distance. The route is well signposted. The jeep will usually stop at the shrine to Our Lady, about 500m past the 1.4km sign to the caves. Here the signs stop and the 2km (not 1km) walk to the caves begins. Follow the path up almost due east for 50m to the **St George Malakara Catholic Church**, which is actually a shrine in front of a huge rock. Here the path turns left. Continue upwards. There's only one path which is steep at times but easy enough to negotiate. You'll pass through pepper and coffee plantations as well as some forest stands. About 1km on you'll see a toilet block on the left. Continue up the path to the ticket counter and rest area. From here it's a steep climb up to the caves via stone as well as iron steps. Iron railings also lend assistance.

When you arrive within the caves you'll be surrounded by huge rocks creating walls and a roof some 20m high. Drawings are sculptured into the walls. The images, somewhat Aztec-like, are formed by geometric lines. The guide (Malayalam and English) will help you distinguish male figures with feathered headdresses, female dancers, elephants, deer and flowers. The impressions remain distinct. Two scripts are represented – Pali and Brahmini. The latter apparently tells of the conquests of a man who killed numerous tigers and proclaims him Nandu (king). Some experts claim the sculptured images cannot be dated, the guide however suggests many are of the megalithic period dating from 10,000 BCE. The scripts he dates as 3rd century BCE. But dates and times seem insignificant within the womb-like imposing space of the cave.

The name, Edakkal, means between rocks and once within the cave the appropriateness of the name is evident. Three large rocks, set apart at the bottom, but meeting at the top, create the space that forms the cave. A very narrow but long vertical gap in the rocks enables views across the forest and ghats.

A visit to the cave is well worthwhile. However, although the distance is short, the uneven rocks and steep incline of the final section demand a level of fitness and surety of foot. Indian women saunter up in saris and sandals; westerners will no doubt find strong footwear and pants more comfortable. And take water.

The cave is open year round from 9.30 am to 4.30 pm. Early afternoon, when the sun casts a gentle light on the images, is a good time to visit. There is a Rs 2/3 entrance fee. Photography is strictly prohibited so unless you want photos of the scenery (stunning) leave yourself unencumbered by a camera.

Wayanad Heritage Museum

After your trip to the cave, you can survey your achievement from the steps of the Wayanad Heritage Museum on the Kozhikode Rd, 2km west past the Edakkal Cave turn off. It's well signposted. The museum has granite and cheenkallu sculptures of hero stones, Nandi and various deities collected from nearby areas and dating from the 14th to 16th centuries. Urvara, the goddess of fertility, stands large breasted with a wheat-like sheaf across her shoulder. The writer with the stylus takes a studious stance among the Grantha script. Tribal jewellery, hunting equipment, fish traps and agricultural tools are also in the collection. The exhibits are well maintained and displayed. The museum is open from 10 am to 1 pm and 2 to 6 pm, entry costs Rs 2/3.

Sculpture Workshop

At Kupamudi, 5km from the Wayanad Heritage Museum, on the return journey to Sultan's Battery, the artist Mr Raja, creates wooden sculptures. If you like wooden rearing horses and camels you may wish to call in, view the work and make some purchases. Prices vary, but it's about Rs 3,500 for a 60cm horse. This is apparently a bargain. According to local gossip, you'll pay three or more times this in the handicraft shops, where they sell the sculptures as antiques which once belonged to Tipu Sultan or some other notable personage.

Mr Raja's workshop is behind the small teahouse, called simply Hotel.

Patchilakkad Arecanut Factory

Kerala is India's second largest producer of arecanuts after Karnataka. Commonly known as betelnuts, arecanuts are chewed (often following a meal) for the stimulants they contain. Limited quantities are also used in Ayurvedic medicine. Declining yields and mooted government bans (due to the potential harm of its addictive properties) are impacting on farmers whose lives depend on this crop. Research is currently under way for alternative uses. Its alcaloids may make it effective in paint manufacturing.

At the Patchilakkad Arecanut Factory it's possible to see the arecanuts processed. Outside the factory, women sit on the grass and use small rounded knives to prize the nut from the husk. Inside, within the steam and smoke of the factory, the men sit, sort, boil and steam the nuts. Visitors are welcome.

The village of Patchilakkad is 4km south of Panamaram, which is 30km west of Sultan's Battery and halfway between Manantavadi and Kalpetta. Regular buses come here from Sultan's Battery, Kozhikode and Thalasseri (Tellicherry).

Lakshadweep

Between 300 and 400km off the coast of Kerala lie a group of islands that make up India's smallest Union Territory. Lakshadweep is an archipelago of coral atolls spread out along a roughly north-south axis, along a huge underwater ridge which is believed to be an extension of the Aravali mountain range in North India. To the west of the ridge the ocean floor drops some 4000m, while to the east, between the islands and the Indian mainland, the Lakshadweep Sea plummets to depths of over 2000m. Exposed to the might of the Arabian Sea, the 12 tiny atolls shelter 35 islands, 10 of which are inhabited. The total area enclosed within the reefs is around 300 sq km, but the total area of the islands themselves is only 32 sq km.

Until they were renamed in 1973, the islands were often considered as three groups, known as the Aminidivi, Laccadive and Minicoy islands. The northernmost group (the Aminidivi Islands) consists of Chetlat, Bitra, Kiltan, Kadmat and Amini. Just to the south of these, and almost due west of Kochi (Cochin) on the Indian coast, the Laccadive Islands comprise Agatti, Andrott, Kavaratti and Kalpeni. Much farther south, opposite Thiruvananthapuram (Trivandrum) on the mainland, is Minicoy, an island which has more in common with the Maldives to the south, than with the rest of the Lakshadweep archipelago. Other islands include Perumal Par, Sunhell, Cherian and Bangaram.

The islands were for many years closed to visitors, and tourists still require a special permit (see Permits & Restrictions later in this chapter). Foreigners can only visit the resort on Bangaram Island and the tourist facilities on Kadmat. Indian nationals are allowed to visit other islands, although only as part of an organised cruise.

The expense and restrictions of a visit to Lakshadweep will not appeal to everyone. For diving enthusiasts, however, the islands are a dream come true. A unique marine environment exists in the lagoons and along kilometres of coral reefs. Because of the limited number of visitors who make it to the islands, the dive sites are undisturbed and the coral undamaged. The Bangaram Island Resort, though expensive, has its own attractions. Away from telephones and TV, there's little to do except relax on an idyllic desert island, and stagger up the beach for a cold beer in the evening.

Highlights

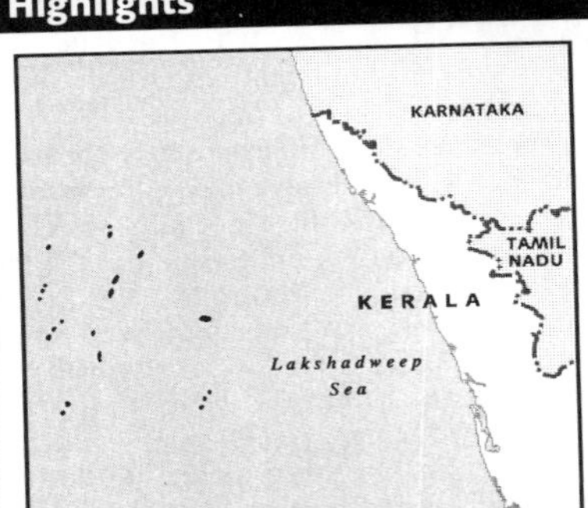

- Enjoy the pristine deserted beaches
- Learn to dive or snorkel in waters filled with dazzling sea life
- Stay in top-end accommodation on your own tropical island paradise

HISTORY

The early history of the islands is a matter of speculation. According to popular legend, the archipelago was discovered when the legendary ruler of Kerala, Cheraman Perumal, converted to Islam and set off for Mecca. His relatives sent a search party to bring him back, but the ships were wrecked

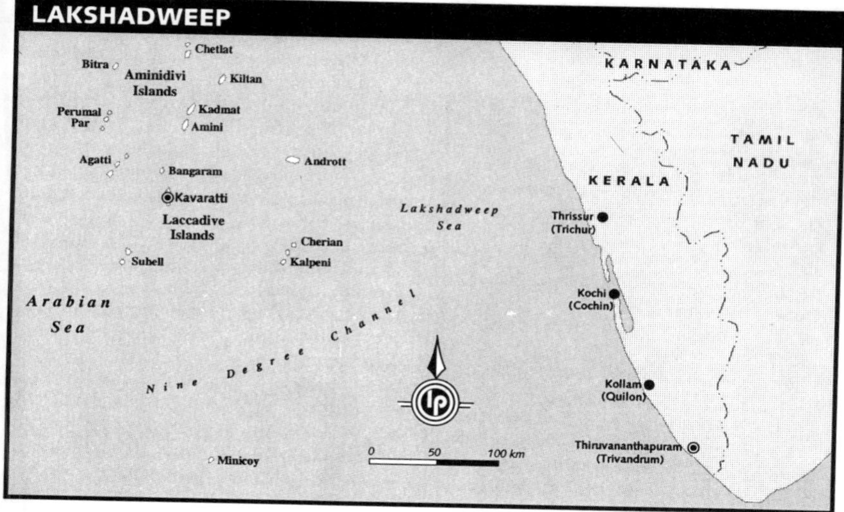

on Bangaram Island. Having made their repairs, the mariners sailed home to report what they had found, and were rewarded with the right to settle on the islands.

The earliest islands to be colonised in this manner were Amini, Andrott, Kalpeni and Kavaratti. These became known as the *Tarwad* islands (in reference to the traditional social system which prevails on the islands), and were controlled by the high caste families of the original settlers. The other islands were subsequently settled by the lower caste inhabitants who had travelled to Lakshadweep as servants of these ruling families.

Most historians now agree that the Cheraman Perumal legend has little foundation in fact, but there's no concrete evidence to suggest who the first settlers really were. Instead there are a number of tantalising clues.

The discovery of a Buddhist statue points to the islands having been settled as early as the 8th century, perhaps by mariners from Sri Lanka. On the other hand, the caste organisation, language and the matrilineal system of inheritance all suggest that the first inhabitants may have come from the Hindu mainland sometime around the 11th century. Finally, some have suggested that the islanders' Muslim faith points to initial settlement by Arab traders.

A compromise between these theories seems most probable. The islands of Lakshadweep lie on trade routes that have been in use for at least 2000 years. With their supply of fresh water and coconuts, the islands would have been well known to early mariners, and they may have had temporary residents from early times. Which particular group settled here first will never be known.

Around the 12th century the islands came under the control of the mainland ruler, the Ali Raja of Cannanore (now called Kannur). The Ali Raja held complete power over trade until the 16th century, when the Portuguese, tempted by the commercial value of the coir (coconut fibre) produced in the islands, demanded a huge annual levy. The sum required was so large that the Ali Raja soon defaulted, and in 1525 Portuguese troops occupied the islands. Over

Coral Bleaching

In 1998, the world's oceans experienced a temporary rise in sea temperature associated with global warming and the El Niño effect. For a period of about two weeks, surface water temperatures rose a few degrees, resulting in the loss of a symbiotic algae which lives within the coral polyps. The loss of this algae causes the coral to lose its colour ('coral bleaching'), and if the algae does not return, the coral polyps will die. Lakshadweep was one of the areas in the world worst affected by rising sea temperatures and coral bleaching has occurred, with varying degrees of severity, in shallow waters throughout the archipelago. Only hard corals have been affected – soft corals and sea fans are largely unharmed.

Many other coral reefs around the world have been affected by the changes in sea temperature. It seems to be a natural process, and one that has occurred in the past. In the Lakshadweep region, some corals recovered almost immediately as the symbiotic algae returned, while in other areas the old coral has died and it will take some years before it is completely recolonised by new coral growth. Marine biologists are watching this re-colonisation process with interest.

the following years the conquistadors exploited the inhabitants ruthlessly. One attempt by the islanders to get their revenge occurred in 1545, when they poisoned the entire garrison on Amini. The Portuguese retaliated swiftly, slaughtering several hundred islanders.

As Portuguese power waned, the islands came back under the control of the Ali Raja, who reasserted the old trade monopolies. The islanders were only permitted to sell their coir to the Ali Raja – at his prices – and had to put up with the atrocities committed by his agents. In 1783 the inhabitants of the northern (Aminidivi) islands decided that they'd had enough and sent a deputation to Hyder Ali asking him to take the islands into his kingdom, which he subsequently did. The Laccadive Islands continued under the rule of the Ali Raja, along with Minicoy.

Within a few years everything changed again. The British defeated Tipu Sultan (Hyder Ali's son) and took the northern islands. They blockaded the Bibi of Cannanore and forced her to pay a levy on the southern islands. The amount and payment of this tax caused constant disagreement throughout the 19th century until, in 1908, the islands were formally ceded to the British.

Although British rule over the islands was even-handed, there was no attempt to develop them in any way. It is said that when India achieved Independence in 1947 it was several months before the islanders knew anything about it. For the next 10 years this situation persisted, until, in 1956, the Indian government decided that the islands were so far behind the rest of the country in development that they should be centrally administered by the government in Delhi as a Union Territory. In 1973, the three sets of islands were renamed Lakshadweep.

The Islands Today Since 1956 huge progress has been made. Because of the classification of the indigenous population as Scheduled Tribes, the inhabitants of the islands have been given preferential treatment in education and in funding. There are now a number of schools in the islands, and many of the children progress to further education on the mainland. Perhaps the best indicator of the success in this area is in literacy rates. In 1951 only 15% of the population were literate, whereas by 1991 this was up to 79%. The literacy rate for women is particularly impressive – 71% compared with the Indian average of 39%.

All islands now have electricity, and almost all have medical facilities. Communications have been immeasurably improved with the building of all-weather docks on the leeward side of some of the islands, and with the establishment of regular flights from Kochi, and a helicopter service between the islands in the monsoon months.

There are, predictably, some problems – among them overcrowding. With good medical facilities and better food, the population of these tiny islands is burgeoning. At the beginning of the 20th century the total number of inhabitants of all islands was just 13,882. By 1981 the figure had leapt to 40,249, and in 1991 the islands were home to 51,681 people. Despite the appearance of peace and tranquillity in comparison with the mainland, the islands are one of the most densely crowded areas in India, with an average population density of 1615 people per square kilometre. Overcrowding in turn brings its own problems, high among them is the fresh water supply. The islands rely for their fresh water entirely on the monsoon rain, which filters through the sand to a thin layer of ground water only a metre or two below the surface, so it must be conserved carefully, and protected from contamination.

The main sources of livelihood for the islanders are the traditional trades of coir production (coconuts are the only crop of economic importance) and fishing. Apart

Island Culture

Lakshadweep culture has been formed by Indian and foreign influences, particularly those of Hindu and Arab traditions.

Status of Women

One of the most unusual features of island society, is the relative independence enjoyed by the women. This is largely due to the matrilineal system of inheritance, where property is passed down the female line. After marriage a woman continues to live in her own house, which her husband visits for the night. With her own property, the woman is not reliant on her husband, and therefore has more freedom than many Indian women. The tradition may have evolved from the necessities of island life, where the men were often away at sea for long periods.

Caste System

All of the islands have a caste system which is thought to have been brought by early settlers from the mainland. In the northern islands there are three main castes: *koyas* or landlords, *malmis* or sailors, and *melacheris* or labourers. In Minicoy the sailors are divided into two subcastes, and the groups are named differently, but the system still applies. Caste has been a source of considerable communal friction throughout the history of the islands.

Language

The islanders speak an ancient form of Malayalam – evidence which suggests that they descended from Keralan stock. Although this undoubtedly establishes an early connection, it's interesting to note that the islanders write their Malayalam in Arabic script.

Religion

The Lakshadweep islanders are all Muslims. A popular story tells of the advent of the faith on the islands. It is said that an Arab holy man named Ubaid-Allah was shipwrecked on Amini, and started preaching to the people. The inhabitants threatened the saint, who fled to Andrott where he converted the entire population by performing a miracle. Over the next few months he visited other islands and performed a succession of miracles until all the islanders embraced the faith. This story is regarded as a myth by many today. However the mosque on Andrott which houses the tomb of Ubaid-Allah is still revered as a holy place, and sailors passing by offer prayers to him.

from these there have been few other developments – a tuna canning factory in Minicoy and two small boatyards on other islands. Even the fishing industry which is judged to have considerable potential for expansion has not really been developed.

Climate

Rainfall is marginally higher on Minicoy than on the other islands (average annual rainfall is 150cm), but temperature is pretty much constant across the whole archipelago. November to March are settled, with average temperatures between 24°C and 34°C. During April and May the temperature starts to rise and can reach 40°C, the south-west monsoon arrives in June. The islands are affected by both the south-west and north-east monsoon, and consequently receive their annual rainfall from June to October. The northern islands, however, lie in the rain shadow of the Kerala coastline, and hence do not receive as much of the later rain as Minicoy does.

Flora & Fauna

The vegetation on the islands is dominated by coconut palms, of which there are two main varieties. A number of other plants grow naturally, or have been introduced for cultivation, including banana, chilli, cucumber, drumstick (an Indian vegetable rather like a squash, but shaped like a drumstick) and breadfruit. Attempts to grow rice have largely failed.

The fauna of the islands is, as might be expected, limited. Domestic animals such as cattle, goats and poultry are quite common. Cats are also found on the islands, and rats present a huge hazard to the coconut crop.

There are several types of sea birds, a few lizards and some coral snakes, but no land snakes. There are a variety of insects, including mosquitoes. See the boxed text 'Diving' for details of marine life.

Information

Tourist Offices The Society for the Promotion of Recreational Tourism & Sports

Coral Atolls

The most widely credited theory for the formation of coral atolls remains the one put forward by Charles Darwin in the 19th century. Observing that coral could grow only in shallow waters, Darwin suggested that rings of coral might have formed originally around islands that had gradually subsided into the sea. If the subsidence was very slow, he reasoned, the rate of growth of coral could keep pace with it. Thus while the island itself sank, the reef around the edge would grow upwards, forming a circular barrier around an inner lagoon.

Coral atolls are in a constant process of change. The living coral must remain healthy, not only to counteract the subsidence of the rocks below it, but also to counter the damage caused by the sea. By a process of erosion, fragments of dead coral are deposited in the waters of the lagoon. These are slowly swept onto the lee side of the lagoon and piled up into sandbanks, which, over time, become small islands. The final stage of the development of the island begins with its colonisation by sea birds. The birds' droppings form a rich layer in which seeds (also carried by the birds) eventually take root. Once plants are growing on the island, human habitation is only a step away.

The development of each of the Lakshadweep atolls is at a different stage. Almost all of the islands are still growing, although in many cases exposed shores are also subject to erosion. The 'newest' islands are little more than sandbanks, while others are covered with a thatch of palm trees, but as yet do not have groundwater supplies sufficient to support habitation. One of the 'oldest' islands, Andrott, now fills the whole area within the reef, leaving no lagoon at all.

in Lakshadweep (SPORTS) is the main Lakshadweep tourism organisation. Its office (☎ 0484-668387, fax 668155) is on IG Rd, Willingdon Island, Kochi, 682003.

The Lakshadweep Tourist Office in Delhi is useless for Bangaram bookings, but may be able to provide other information. Contact Mr Pukoya (☎ 011-338 6807, fax 378 2246), Liaison Office, UTF Lakshadweep, F306, Kusum Road Hostel, Kasturba Gandhi Marg, New Delhi, 110001.

Permits & Restrictions The reason for the restrictions on travel to the islands seems to be two-fold. Firstly the population of the islands are almost entirely classed by the government as Scheduled Tribes, and there is a concerted effort to protect not only their way of life, but also the unique environment of the islands (see Responsible Diving in the 'Diving' boxed text and Dos & Don'ts in the Facts about Kerala chapter).

Just as important is India's deep concern about the security of its coastline. Although the islands cover an area of only 32 sq km, they are of considerable importance to the nation, as they add 15,000 sq km to India's territorial waters and economic zone.

In practice, the only way to get to the islands is to book with one of the recognised travel organisations listed below. Allow plenty of time for the permit application to be processed (the Lacadives dive school recommend a month, minimum).

Foreigners are only permitted to visit Bangaram Island and Kadmat, whereas Indian nationals may also visit Kavaratti, Kalpeni and Minicoy. Both foreign and domestic tourists can travel on the cruise ship MV *Tipu Sultan*, which has accommodation on board.

Organised Tours

SPORTS (see Tourist Offices, earlier) offers a five day Coral Reef cruise (Indian tourists only) which leaves from Kochi and stops at Kavaratti, Kalpeni and Minicoy. A full day is spent getting to the islands (and back), and one day is allowed on each island, before passengers re-embark for an overnight cruise to the next island. The cruise costs Rs 6000 in tourist class, Rs 8000 in 1st class and Rs 10,000 in deluxe class.

An alternative (which foreign tourists are allowed to take) is a five day cruise to Kadmat and back, with the middle three days being spent in tourist cottages on the island. The cruise costs Rs 8000 in tourist class, Rs 9000 in 1st class, Rs 10,000 in executive class and Rs 10,500 in deluxe two-berth aircon. Another version of this, with three days on Kavaratti, is open to Indians only, and costs Rs 9000 in 1st class and Rs 9500 in deluxe two berth.

THE ISLANDS

The following is a brief rundown of the main (inhabited) islands in the group. Note that not all of them are open to visitors (see Permits & Restrictions earlier in this chapter).

Inhabited Islands: Area & Population

island	area (sq km)	population (1991)
Andrott	4.84	9119
Minicoy	4.37	8313
Kavaratti	3.63	8664
Kadmat	3.13	3983
Agatti	2.71	5667
Amini	2.59	6445
Kalpeni	2.28	4079
Kiltan	1.63	3075
Chetlat	1.04	2050
Bangaram[1]	0.58	61
Bitra	0.10	225

[1]Bangaram is 'inhabited' by tourist resort staff only.

Aminidivi Islands

The northern group of islands was traditionally known as the Aminidivi Islands. **Amini**, which is thought to have derived its name from the Arabic word meaning 'faithful', was one of the earliest islands to be settled, and is still the centre of administration for the group.

About 10km north of Amini is **Kadmat**, one of the five islands open to tourists (and one of only two islands open to foreigners);

Diving

SARAH JOLLY

Despite the alarming damage caused by rising sea temperatures (see the boxed text 'Coral Bleaching'), the extensive coral reefs of the Lakshadweep Islands are a paradise for sub-aqua enthusiasts. The shallow lagoons are perfect for novice divers and also provide the possibility of diving even in rough weather. Outside the reefs, there are dives of varying depths with crystal clear waters giving excellent visibility. Near Bangaram Island there are a couple of wrecks that provide interesting excursions, (the 200-year-old wreck of the *Princess Royal* is a regular dive site) and around both Bangaram and Kadmat there are specific areas which are known to harbour particularly rich marine life. Sharks, rays, hawksbill, green turtles and barracudas are among the larger inhabitants of the reefs, but there are innumerable others too, including butterfly, damsel, surgeon and parrot fish. In the lagoons, octopuses are plentiful.

There are only two dive centres in the islands. Bangaram Island Resort has a well run dive school for guests. Experienced divers have a range of options, and newcomers can also dive. A 'resort course' package for a beginner, consisting of a couple of lessons followed by a reef dive, is US$120, and an open-water certificate course is US$250. Experienced divers pay US$222 for a six-dive package, US$420 for 12 dives or US$600 for 18 dives. No dives are permitted below 35m. For details check with the Casino Hotels office in Kochi (see Places to Stay & Eat).

Lacadives, a dive school on Kadmat Island, has slightly better prices than Bangaram Island Resort. A week-long package with two dives a day, accommodation and food costs US$800. Transport to and from the island by plane or ship can be organised by Lacadives at an additional cost.

Bookings are via the company's office in Mumbai (formerly Bombay, ☎ 022-494 2723, fax 495 1644, email lacadives@hotmail.com) at E20, Everest Bldg, Tardeo, Mumbai, 400034. Visitors can opt to travel to or from the island by ship, on the MV *Tipu Sultan*. Lacadives' agent in the US is Natural Mystic Adventure Travels (☎ 212-683 3989, fax 683 2831, email info@naturalmystic.com), Suite 320, 300 East 34th St, New York, NY 10016.

Due to aircraft weight limits, most divers hire gear on the islands. Those going to Bangaram Island, however, can apply to the Casino Hotel office for increased baggage allowance.

When to Go

The best time to dive is between October and mid-May. Diving is still possible in the lagoons during the monsoon, and is also possible at times outside the reefs, but the weather can limit these opportunities severely.

Responsible Diving

- Avoid touching living marine organisms. Some can be damaged by even the gentlest contact. Never stand on coral, even if it looks solid and robust.
- Be conscious of your fins. Even without contact the surge of heavy fin strokes near the reef can cause damage.
- Practise and maintain proper buoyancy control. Major damage can be done by divers descending too fast and colliding with the reef.
- Resist the temptation to collect or buy coral or shells.
- Dispose of rubbish sensibly, including litter you find.
- Minimise your disturbance to marine animals.

it is the base for the Laccadives dive centre. The discovery of some gold coins on Kadmat from 1st and 2nd century Rome leads to the conclusion that the island was visited by traders well before it was finally settled.

Bitra is the smallest inhabited island in the territory, with an area of just 10.52 hectares. The northernmost inhabited island, **Chetlat**, is 65km north of Amini. To the south lies **Kiltan**, which is only about 3km long.

Laccadive Islands

The southern group of islands was known traditionally as the Laccadive Islands. Over 400km from Kochi is **Agatti**, the westernmost island of the group. Roughly 6km long and only 1km wide at its broadest point, Agatti has the only airstrip in the islands. Although all visitors arriving by plane must go through Agatti, the island is not open to tourists.

Bangaram, to the north of Agatti, is just visible on the horizon and is about two hours away by boat. **Andrott** is the nearest island to the mainland, and is also the largest of the group, being 5km long and 2km broad. According to tradition, the people of Andrott were the first islanders to embrace Islam, and the religious teachers of the island are still venerated.

Kalpeni, 87km south of Andrott, is another of the islands believed to have been colonised from early times. It was one of the islands worst affected by a great storm which struck in 1847 – out of a population of 1642 islanders, 246 people were drowned and a further 112 died of disease or starvation in the weeks that followed. Of the island's 100,000 palm trees, fewer than 1000 were left standing. **Kavaratti** is the headquarters of the whole Union Territory. The island is 6km long and about 1km wide. The people are renowned for their skill as woodcarvers and stonemasons.

Minicoy

Minicoy, 211km south of the Laccadives group, is supposed to have been visited by Marco Polo, who referred to it as the 'female island'. The island is more than 10km in length and has a large, deep lagoon. A small island at the northern tip of the main island was once used by the inhabitants for isolating smallpox patients.

Places to Stay & Eat

The ***Bangaram Island Resort*** is run by Casino Hotels, and is administered from its hotel in Kochi (*☎ 0484-666821, 668221, fax 668001, email casino@giasmd01.vsnl.net.in*).

The resort on the uninhabited island of Bangaram has been well designed to minimise the impact on the environment. There are only 30 rooms, allowing for a maximum of 60 guests. Double rooms with full board cost US$240 (plus 10% tax) during the high season between mid-December and May; single occupancy is US$230. Prices drop considerably during the low season. It's worth shopping around with travel agents in other countries, as some tour operators book through Casino Hotels and appear to be able to get a better deal as part of a larger package.

The resort has a good restaurant and a bar and activities include diving, snorkelling, deep-sea fishing and sailing. Casino Hotels will organise travel and permits for the islands.

Apart from the low row of thatched buildings that make up the accommodation, bar and restaurant, there's almost nothing else on the tiny island. If you go exploring among the palm trees, you'll probably stumble on the staff accommodation, and if you wander around to the far side of Bangaram (you can stroll around the entire island in under an hour) you may find some fishermen from Agatti, who occasionally stop off here. Apart from this the layout is remarkably simple. The low-lying island is covered almost entirely with a dense mass of palm trees and ringed with a thin ribbon of white sand.

Lacadives runs a dive centre based on Kadmat Island. Packages include accommodation and all meals. See the boxed text 'Diving'.

Getting There & Away

Air At the time of writing Indian Airlines operated six flights a week from Kochi to Agatti (US$300 return), and two flights a week from Goa to Agatti (US$310 return). The plane used for the Kochi flights is a tiny Islander aircraft, and passengers are restricted to 10kg of luggage. If you're staying on Bangaram Island, extra luggage can be left in the Casino Hotel on Willingdon Island, Kochi. The transfer from Agatti to Bangaram costs an extra US$30 by boat (1½ hours) or, in the event of rough seas, US$80 by helicopter.

Boat Timings for the departure of the MV *Tipu Sultan* can be picked up from the SPORTS office on Willingdon Island, Kochi. See the Organised Tours section for information on SPORTS boat cruises.

Language

India has a total of 18 official languages, which belong to the Indo-Aryan and Dravidian language famililies, as well as over 1600 minor languages and dialects. In many cases state boundaries have been drawn along linguistic lines. The diversity of languages in India is one of the reasons that English is still spoken over 40 years after the country gained independence, and is still the official language of the judiciary. Hindi has been promoted as the national language, and efforts have been made to gradually phase out English.

In Kerala, however, English is not widely spoken. You can get by with English if you stay in the most popular travel centres of Southern Kerala. The official state language is Malayalam, and making the effort to learn a few words and phrases will definitely endear you to the people of Kerala. If you plan to travel in the more remote parts of the state, you'll probably need to learn a little more of the language. It's particularly useful to be able to pronounce the names of places in Malayalam, so that you can at least ask for directions.

Often visitors find that as soon as they open their mouths in Kerala the person they are speaking to dashes out of the room. Don't mistake this for rudeness, more likely than not they will return again shortly with someone who can speak English.

The Lonely Planet *Hindi/Urdu phrasebook* is a handy reference if you want to increase your language skills.

MALAYALAM

Malayalam, the official language of Kerala, is spoken by around 30 million people. It forms part of the Dravidian language family, and includes many words borrowed from ancient Indian Sanskrit. Malayalam can be found in literary records dating back to the late 12th century. The *Ramacharitam*, a pattu poem, is one of the earliest written references.

Pronunciation

Vowels

The vowel system of Malayalam doesn't differ much from that of English. Vowels may be short or long. Long vowels are represented in this guide by a macron – a stroke above the letter. They're similar to the short vowels, but are held for a longer duration.

Short

a as in 'father'
e as in 'met'
i as in 'it'
o as in 'hot'
u as in 'put'

Long

ā as in 'far'
ē as the 'ai' in 'air'
ī as in 'marine'
ō as in 'shore'
ū as in 'flute'

ai as the word 'eye'
au as the 'ow' in 'how'

Consonants

Most consonants are fairly similar to those found in English. A few which could cause confusion include:

ch as in 'cheese'
g as in 'go'
k as in the 'c' in 'car'
ñ as in the 'ni' in 'onion'
s as in 'sit'
zh as in the 's' in 'pleasure'

The consonants **p**, **b**, **t**, **d**, **k** and **g** have both aspirated and unaspirated forms. In this guide, consonants pronounced with a puff of breath are distinguished with an 'h' following the consonant, as in 'kh'.

Basics

Hello.	*namaste*
Excuse me.	*ksamikkū*
Please.	*dayavayi*
Thank you.	*nandi*
Yes/No.	*ānātē/alla*
How are you?	*sukhamānō?*
Very well, thank you.	*sukham tanne*
Do you speak English?	*ninnal inglīṣa samsārikkumō?*
I don't understand.	*enikku ariyilla*
Where is the hotel?	*hottal eviteyanu?*
How far is ...?	*... etra duramanu?*
How do I get to ...?	*... aviṭe engina pokanam?*
left	*yerra totto*
right	*walla totta*
straight ahead	*narra*

How much?	*etra?*
This is expensive.	*vila kututhal anu*
Show me the menu.	*menu kānikkū*
The bill please.	*billu taru*
What's your name?	*nintae pay-r enthakunnu?*
My name is ...	*ente pēru ...*
What's the time?	*mani etrayēyi?*

big	*valiya/valuthu*
small	*cheriya/cheruthu*
hot	*chutulla*
cold	*thanuppulla*
today	*ennu*
day	*divasam*
night	*rātri*
week	*azhcha*
month	*māsam*
year	*varsam*
medicine	*marunnu*
ice	*ays*
fruit	*pazham*
vegetables	*pachakkaṛi*
rice	*ari*
egg	*mutta*
butter	*venna*
sugar	*panchasāra*
water	*vellam*
tea	*chāyya*
coffee	*kāppi*
milk	*pāl*

Numbers

1	*onnu*
2	*randu*
3	*mūnnu*
4	*nālu*
5	*añchu*
6	*āru*
7	*āzhu*
8	*yettu*
9	*ompathu*
10	*pathu*
100	*nūru*
1000	*āyiram*
2000	*randayiram*
100,000	*laksham*
1,000,000	*pathu laksham*
10,000,000	*koti*

HINDI

Yes.	*haan*
No.	*nahin*
OK.	*acha*
Hello/Goodbye.	*namaste*
Excuse me.	*khimaa kijiyeh*
Please.	*meharbani seh*
Thank you.	*shukriyaa*
You're welcome.	*koi baat nahin*
What's your name?	*aapka shubh naam kya hai?*
My name is ...	*meraa naam ... hai*
How are you?	*aap kaiseh hain?*
Very well, thanks.	*bahut acha shukriya*
Do you speak English?	*kya aap angrezi samajhte hain?*
I don't understand.	*meri samajh men nahin aaya*
What's the time?	*kitneh bajeh hain?*
How far is ...?	*... kitni dur hai?*
How do I get to ...?	*... kojane ke liye kaiseh jaana parega?*
Where is a hotel?	*hotal kahan hai?*
How much?	*kitne paise/hai?*

Please show me the menu.	*mujheh minu dikhaiyeh*
The bill please.	*bill de dijiyeh*

big	*bada*
small	*chhota*
today	*aaj*
day	*din*
night	*raat*
week	*haftah*
month	*mahina*
year	*saal*
medicine	*davaai*
ice	*baraf*
egg	*anda*
fruit	*phal*
vegetables	*sabzi*
meat	*mans*
sugar	*chini*
butter	*makkhan*
rice	*chaval*
water	*paani*
tea	*chai*
coffee	*kafi*
milk	*dudh*

Be careful with *acha*, the all-purpose word for 'OK'. It can also mean 'OK, I understand what you mean, but I can't help you'.

Numbers

The Indian numeric system is counted in tens, hundreds, thousands, hundred thousands, ten millions. A hundred thousand is a *lakh* and 10 million is a *crore*.

These two words are almost always used in place of their English equivalent. Thus you will see 10 lakh rather than one million and one crore rather than 10 million. Figures are generally written that way too – thus three hundred thousand appears as 3,00,000, and ten million five hundred thousand is written as 1,05,00,000 (one crore, five lakh). If you say something costs five crore or is worth 10 lakh, the denomination is always rupees.

There's no system for counting from 10 to 100 in Hindi – the numbers have to be learned individually.

1	*ek*
2	*do*
3	*tin*
4	*char*
5	*panch*
6	*chhe*
7	*saat*
8	*aath*
9	*nau*
10	*das*
11	*gyaranh*
12	*baranh*
13	*teranh*
14	*chodanh*
15	*pandrah*
16	*solah*
17	*satrah*
18	*aatharanh*
19	*unnis*
20	*bis*
21	*ikkis*
22	*bais*
23	*teis*
24	*chobis*
25	*pachis*
26	*chhabis*
27	*sattais*
28	*athais*
29	*unnattis*
30	*tis*
35	*paintis*
40	*chalis*
45	*paintalis*
50	*panchas*
55	*pachpan*
60	*saath*
65	*painsath*
70	*sattar*
75	*pachhattar*
80	*assi*
85	*pachasi*
90	*nabbe*
95	*pachanabbe*
100	*so*
200	*do so*
300	*tin so*
1000	*ek hazaar*
2000	*do hazaar*
100,000	*ek lakh*
10,000,000	*ek crore*

Glossary

For a guide to the names of common foods in Kerala see The Cuisine of Kerala section in the Facts for the Visitor chapter. For detailed explanations of the most popular gods, see the Religion section in the Facts about Kerala chapter.

aappam – breakfast pancake made from rice flour.
aarattu – see *arat*.
acchan – father.
Adivasis – indigenous tribal people.
agarbathi– incense.
Agastya – legendary sage, highly revered in the south as he is credited with introducing Hinduism to the region as well as developing the *Tamil* language.
Agni – fire; a major deity (the fire god) in the *Vedas*; mediator between people and the gods.
agraharam – place of *Brahmins*.
ahimsa – discipline of nonviolence, most famously practised by Mahatma Gandhi.
AIR – All India Radio, the national broadcaster.
amma – mother.
anantha – sacred serpent on which *Padmanabha* reclines.
Anjaneya – local name for *Hanuman*, used in Northern Kerala.
Annaprasana – when a child first receives solid food.
annayoottu – donations for elephant feed.
apsaras – heavenly nymphs.
arak – alcohol usually made from rice; sometimes from nuts.
arat – bathing of the image of the deity.
arecanut – nuts chewed (often following a meal) for the stimulants they contain; also known as betel nut.
Arjuna – *Mahabharata* hero who had the *Bhagavad Gita* related to him by *Krishna*.
Artha Sastra – renowned Hindu text which outlines the goals and moral codes for human existence.
Arvanas – former term for lower-caste people.
Aryan – *Sanskrit* word for 'noble'; refers to those who migrated from Persia and settled in North India.
ashram – spiritual community or retreat.
ashtamangalyam – eight items of 'good fortune' presented to a groom on his wedding day.
ATDC – Alleppey Tourism Development Co-op.
Attakatha – 17th century form of literature which forms the narrative for *Kathakali*.
auto-rickshaw – small, noisy, three-wheeled, motorised contraption for transporting passengers short distances; found throughout Kerala and the rest of India, cheaper than taxis.
avatar – incarnation of a deity, usually *Vishnu*.
Ayurveda – India's ancient form of medicine; uses a combination of herbs and massage to treat a range of ailments; particularly widespread in Kerala.
Ayyappan – One of the most popular deities in Kerala drawing vast crowds to the temple at Sabarimala; Ayyappan is believed to have been born of the union of *Shiva* and *Mohini*.

banyan – Indian fig tree.
basti – Jain temple.
bazaar – market area.
BCE – Before Common Era; used as an alternative to BC (before Christ).
beedi – see *bidi*.
betel – see *arecanut*.
Bhadrakali – see *Bhagavati*.
Bhagavad Gita – Song of the Divine One; *Krishna's* lessons to *Arjuna*, the main thrust of which was to emphasise the philosophy of *bhakti* (faith); part of the *Mahabharata*.
Bhagavati – manifestation of the fierce goddess *Kali*, widely worshipped throughout Kerala; also known as Bhadrakali.
bhakti – intense, personal devotion to god; the bhakti movement in South India rebelled against priests and the reliance on *Sanskrit*.

bhang – dried leaves and buds of the marijuana plant.
Bharat – Hindi for India.
Bharata Natyam – Tamil Nadu's own form of classical dance.
Bharatiya Janata Party (BJP) – Indian People's Party; right-wing nationalist party founded in 1980 that promotes self-reliance and Hindu revivalism; won ruling majority power in the 1998 national parliamentary elections.
Bhashakautaliyam – 12th century exposition in prose of the Hindu *Artha Sastra.*
bhavan – basic restaurant.
bidi – small, hand-rolled cigarette; really just a rolled-up leaf.
bindi – forehead mark worn by women according to marital status.
biryani – Muslim rice dish with either meat or vegetables.
BJP – see *Bharatiya Janata Party.*
Bodhisattva – one who has almost reached *nirvana*, but who renounces it in order to help others attain it.
Brahma – the creator; with *Vishnu* and *Shiva*, forms the Hindu triad, the representation of *Brahman.*
Brahman – godhead; the absolute.
Brahmanism – early form of Hinduism which evolved from Vedism; named after the *Brahmin* priests and the god *Brahma.*
Brahmin – member of the priest caste, the highest Hindu caste; in Kerala known as *Namboodri.*
BRDC – Bekal Resort Development Corporation.
Buddha – Awakened One; originator of Buddhism who lived in the 5th century BCE; regarded by Hindus as the ninth reincarnation of *Vishnu.*
burkha – one-piece garment used by Muslim women to cover them from head to toe.

cantonment – administrative and military area of a Raj-era town.
Carnatic music – South India's own form of classical music; places a heavier emphasis on song compared with its northern counterpart.
caste – one's hereditary station in life; classification or discrimination due to caste is now illegal in Kerala.
CE – Common Era; used as an alternative to AD (anno Domini).
chaitya – Buddhist temple; also prayer room or assembly hall.
chakara – coastal mud flats.
chakra – focus of one's spiritual power; disc-like weapon of *Vishnu.*
Chandra – the moon, or the moon as a god.
Chandragupta – important ruler of India in the 3rd century BCE.
chapati – flat, round bread.
chappals – sandals.
charas – resin of the marijuana plant; also referred to as hashish or hash.
charpoi – Indian rope bed.
chedi – see *dagoba.*
chela – pupil or follower, as George Harrison was to Ravi Shankar.
Cheras – early rulers in the Kerala region; there were two waves of Chera rule, the first wave occurred in the late centuries BCE and early CE; the second one occurred around the end of the first millennium CE.
Cheria Perunnal – see *Ramadan.*
chhatri – small, domed Mughal kiosk (literally umbrella).
chilappatikaram – the 'Epic of the Anklets'; 7th century *Tamil* text.
Chingam – Keralan month around August/September.
chinkara – gazelle.
chital – spotted deer.
Chola – prominent ancient South Indian dynasty.
choli – sari blouse.
chorunu – temple ceremony where a child is fed its first solid food.
choultry – pilgrim accommodation.
chowkidar – night watchman.
chundan vallam – low slung long boat otherwise known as a snakeboat.
Cochin – former name of Kochi, see also *Travancore.*
coir – by-product of the coconut husk, used mainly to make ropes and mats.
Congress (I) – Congress Party of India. Ruling party at the centre for much of the post-Independence period, founded in 1885; stands for democracy and secularism and, since 1991, economic liberalisation.

copra – dried kernel of the coconut.
CPI – Communist Party of India.
CPI (M) – Communist Party of India (Marxist).
crore – 10 million; see also *lakh*.

dagoba – Buddhist religious monument composed of a solid hemisphere topped by a spire, containing relics of the Buddha; also known as a pagoda, stupa or chedi.
Dalit – preferred term for India's casteless class; see also *Untouchable*.
dargah – shrine or burial place of a Muslim saint.
Darika – demon son of Duramati.
darshan – offering or audience with someone; viewing of a deity.
Devi – *Shiva*'s wife; she has a variety of forms.
Dhanu – *Malayalam* month around December/January.
dharma – Hindu-Buddhist moral code of behaviour.
dhoti – cloth (similar to a sarong) worn by men around the waist which falls to the ankles; sometimes it is drawn up between the legs.
Diwan – custodian, also an early term for chief minister.
dosa – large pancake.
dowry – money and goods given by a bride's parents to their son-in-law's family. Officially illegal but widely practised.
Dravidian – member of one of the original inhabitants of India; the Dravidian languages include *Tamil*, *Malayalam*, Telugu and Kannada.
DTPC – District Tourism Promotion Council.
dupatta – scarf worn with a *salwar kameez*.
durbar – royal court; also used to describe a government.
Durga – the Inaccessible; a form of *Shiva*'s wife *Devi*; major goddess of the *Shakti* cult.
dvarapala – doorkeeper; sculpture beside the doorways to Hindu or Buddhist shrines, also known as dwarpal.
dwarpal – see *dvarapala*.

Emergency – period in the 1970s when Indira Gandhi's national government assumed absolute power.
EMS Namboodiripad – first chief minister of Kerala and influential politician, leader and writer.
Eve-teasing – sexual harassment of women.
Ezhavas – toddy tapper subcaste.

fakir – Muslim who has taken a vow of poverty, but also applied to Hindu ascetics.

Gajendra Moksha – the depiction of the liberation of the elephant chief.
Ganesh – popular god, elephant-headed; son of *Shiva* and *Parvati*; worshipped as the remover of obstacles (among other aspects).
garbhagraha – receptacle for the symbol or image of the deity (in Hindu temples).
gaur – Indian bison.
ghat – range of hills, or road up hills; steps or landing on a river.
gopis – milkmaids with whom *Krishna* cavorted in the forests of Vrindavan
gopuram – soaring pyramidal gateway tower of a Dravidian temple.
Gosharee Puram – former name for the area of Kochi, including the islands.
Grandha – the written script of the *Brahmins*, from which *Malayalam* script is derived.
guru – teacher or holy person; in *Sanskrit* literally 'goe' (darkness) and 'roe' (to dispel).
Gurukkal – masters of *kalarippayat*.

haj – pilgrimage to Mecca.
Hanuman – the Hindu monkey god; leader of the monkey army in the *Ramayana*, and devoted servant of Rama.
Hari – another name for *Vishnu*.
Hari-Hara – The union of the two deities *Vishnu* and *Shiva*, often represented in sculpture.
Harijan – name given by Gandhi to India's *Untouchables*; this term is, however, no longer acceptable; see also *Dalit* and *Untouchable*.
hashish – see *charas*.
hero stones – monuments to heroes usually erected at the site of their courageous deed.
hijra – eunuch.
hotel – place to eat, and sometimes a place to stay as well.

howdah – seat for carrying people on an elephant's back.

Idavam – *Malayalam* month around May/June.
IDTIO – Idukki District Tourist Information Office
ikat – fabric tie-dyeing technique; practised in Andhra Pradesh.
illam – women's section of the *Namboodri* household.
IMFL – Indian Made Foreign Liquor.
inam – *Tamil* for baksheesh.
Indo-Saracenic – style of colonial architecture that integrated western designs with Muslim, Hindu and Jain influences.

jaggery – palm sugar.
Jama Masjid – Friday Mosque; the main mosque in each town.
Janmis – former high caste landlords of Kerala.
jatakam koda – exchange of horoscopes.
jatha – procession; this was the term given to the political marches in support of British withdrawal and the end of caste system held in Kerala during the Gandhian period.
jati – see *varna*.
jimka – bell style earrings.
jyoti lingam – the most important *Shiva* shrines in India, of which there are 12.

kabaddi – known as hu-tu-tu in South India; a game of tag.
Kadas – tribal group living in the Parambikulam Wildlife Sanctuary.
Kalabhras – regime thought to have ruled Kerala from the 6th to 8th centuries CE.
kalari – special arena for *kalarippayat*.
kalarippayat – The traditional martial art of Kerala, believed to be the forerunner of all eastern martial arts and integral to the technical development of other performing arts in Kerala, including *Kathakali*.
Kali – manifestation of *Parvati* in her ferocious form.
kalyanamandapam – marriage hall.
kameez – woman's tunic or shirt, see also *salwar kameez*.
Kammalas – artisan caste.
Kanchipuram – Tamil Nadu temple town famous for its handloomed silks.
Kanni – Keralan month around September/October.
karan – *Tamil* for *wallah*.
karanavar – oldest male member of the former *Marumakkathayam* matrilineal family and manager of the household.
Kari – the demoness character in the *Kathakali* drama.
karma – principle of retributive justice for past deeds in subsequent rebirths.
Karkatakam – *Malayalam* month around July/August.
Kartikkaya – see *Subramanya*.
Kathakali – One of the most popular forms of traditional performance in Kerala, based on stories from the *Mahabharata* and the *Ramayana*.
Kattalan – male counterpart of the demoness *Shurpanakha*.
Katti – the demons and villains of the *Kathakali* drama, such as *Ravana*, who are distinguished by a knife shape on the forehead.
Katyayani – another name of the goddess *Durga*.
Kauravas – kinsfolk of the *Pandavas*, the battle with whom forms the narrative of the epic *Mahabharata*.
kavadi – arches carried during Thaipooram festival.
kera – coconut.
kesabhara kiritam – the crown headgear worn by the royal and divine creatures of the *Kathakali* drama.
kettiam – building.
kettuvallam – traditional barge once used for transporting rice and other commodities along the backwaters, now converted into upmarket houseboats for tourists.
khadi – homespun cloth; Gandhi encouraged people to spin khadi rather than buy English cloth.
khan – Muslim honorific title.
kirtana – song of praise.
Knaithomman – Thomas Cana, a Syrian merchant who spread Christianity in Kerala in the 4th century CE.
kolam – traditionally a rice-paste design

drawn over the threshold of a home or temple to bring good fortune and ward off bad luck; also known as rangoli.
kootampalam – large hall at a temple used for festivals and prayer.
Koothu – *Sanskrit* drama performed by an individual; when performed by several artists, it is known as *Kootiattam*.
Kootiattam – *Sanskrit* drama performed by several artists at a temple.
Koran – see *Qur'an*.
Kozhikode – see *Travancore*.
Krishna – one of the nine incarnations of *Vishnu*.
Krishnanattam – dance of *Krishna*.
KSRTC – Kerala State Road Transport Corporation.
KTDC – Kerala Tourism Development Corporation.
Kulasekharas – former ruling high caste.
kumbh – pitcher or water pot.
Kumbham – Malayalam month around February/March.
Kummattikali – local version of the Patayani dance, performed in Palakkad (Palghat) and Thrissur (Trichur) districts.
kurta – shirt (men).

lakh – 100,000; see also *crore*.
Lakshmi – goddess of wealth; sprang forth from the ocean holding a lotus; also referred to as Padma (lotus) and Laxmi.
lathi – large bamboo stick; what Indian police hit you with if you get in the way of a lathi charge.
Laxmi – see *Lakshmi*.
lingam – phallic symbol; symbol of *Shiva*.
Lok Sabha – House of The People; Indian lower house in national parliament.
lungi – like a sarong; usually coloured or checked.

Madras Presidency – name of the district in South India administered from Madras (Chennai) during the British Raj.
Mahabharata – Great Vedic epic of the Bharata Dynasty; an epic poem, containing about 10,000 verses, describing the battle between the *Pandavas* and the *Kauravas*.
maharaja – king.
maharani – female ruler.
mahatma – great soul.
mahout – elephant keeper.
maidan – open grassed area in a city.
Makaram – *Malayalam* month around January/February.
makhnas – elephant without tusks.
Malabar – name of the Northern Kerala region during the British Raj.
malai – mountains.
Malai-Malsars – tribal group living in the Parambikulam Wildlife Sanctuary.
Malayala Manorama – publishing house in Kerala that produces one of India's largest circulating newspapers (in *Malayalam*) as well as the popular language Manorama Yearbook.
Malayalam – official language and script of Kerala.
Malayali – person from Kerala.
mandala – circle; symbol used in Hindu and Buddhist art to symbolise the universe.
mandapam – hall, pillared pavilion in front of a temple.
Manipravalam – Sanskritised form of *Malayalam* and the form used for the poetic text of the Kathakali.
mantra – sacred word or phrase used by Buddhists and Hindus to aid concentration; metrical psalms of praise found in the *Vedas*.
Mappilas – Muslims of Kerala.
Marumakkathayam – former matrilineal system unique to Kerala.
masala dosa – curried vegetables wrapped in a pancake.
masjid – mosque; see also *Jama Masjid*.
matha – mother.
Matsya – incarnation of *Vishnu*.
Medam – *Malayalam* month around April/May.
Meenam – *Malayalam* month around March/April.
mihrab – prayer niche inside a mosque within the centre of the wall facing Mecca.
Minukku – the servant class represented in the *Kathakali* drama.
Mithunam – *Malayalam* month around June/July.
Mohini – female form of *Vishnu*.

Mohinyattam – dance of the enchantress.
moksha – liberation, especially in reference to the cycle of re-birth.
monsoon – rainy season.
mudra – hand positions; refers to hand positions used in the *Kathakali* drama, and to the hand gestures of Buddhist iconography.
Muduvas – tribal group living in the Parambikulam Wildlife Sanctuary.
mukhabhinaya – the facial gestures of the *Kathakali* drama.
Mukkuvans – fisherfolk caste.
mullah – Muslim scholar, teacher or religious leader.
mund – village (eg Ootacamund).
mundu – sarong-like garment.
Murugan – see *Subramanya.*
musth – condition of heightened sexual activity in elephants – especially males.

naan – bread baked in a tandoori oven.
nadi – river.
nadi astrologers – astrologers who give advice according to ancient palm leaf manuscripts.
naga – serpent; naga stones depicting the spiritually potent cobra are found in temples in Kerala.
Nagaraja – the male form of the snake deity.
Nair – former warrior caste.
nalukettu – traditional Keralan home, built to resemble a temple.
namakaranam – naming ceremony for new born child.
namaskara mandapam – in temples, the hall of prostration.
Namboodris – *Brahmins* of Kerala.
Nandi – *Shiva*'s bull vehicle.
Nataraja – *Shiva* as Lord of the Dance.
neryathu – cloth worn over the shoulder by women.
nirvana – the ultimate aim of Buddhists, final release from the cycle of suffering existence.
NRI – non-resident Indian; of great economic importance for modern India.

oddiyanam – belt.
Om – sacred invocation representing the absolute essence of the divine principle.

paan – spices and condiments chewed with *arecanut.*
pacca – the royal and divine beings of the *Ramayana*, such as *Vishnu* and *Rama*, as they appear in the *Kathakali* drama.
padayatra – foot march.
padma – lotus; see also *Lakshmi.*
Padmanabha – manifestation of *Vishnu*, the deity who reclines on the serpent *anantha*, and who preserves and restores order; also known as Padmanabhaswamy.
palanquin – traditional box-like enclosure carried on poles on four men's shoulders; the occupant sits inside on a seat; no longer in use; may be seen in museums.
Pali – derived from *Sanskrit*; the original language in which the Buddhist scriptures were recorded; scholars still refer to the original Pali texts.
panchaloha – traditional form of metal craft using a combination of five (pancha) metals: silver, gold, copper, tin and iron.
Panchatantra – series of traditional Hindu stories about the natural world, human behaviour and survival.
Pandavas – protagonists in the epic *Mahabharata.*
paratha – dry-fried flat bread.
Parvati – goddess; wife of *Shiva*, also referred to as *Devi*, the divine mother.
Patayani – temple dance honouring *Bhagavati.*
pavakathakali – type of glove puppetry.
Perumal – ruler of the Second Chera empire.
perunnal – procession, usually of religious nature.
pooram – one of the major festivals in Kerala.
prasad – food offering.
puja – respect; offering or prayers.
punkah – cloth fan, swung by pulling a cord.
Puranas – ancient Hindu scriptures which contain legends about beneficent gods.
puri – deep-fried puffed bread.
puttu – popular breakfast dish made from rice flour dough and shredded coconut and steamed in a tube.
PWD – Public Works Department.

qibla – wall or courtyard facing Mecca, located within a mosque.

Qur'an – the holy book of Islam, also spelt Koran.

raga – any of several conventional patterns of melody and rhythm that form the basis for freely interpreted compositions; also known as raag.
raj/Raj – rule or sovereignty; specifically, the British colonial regime in India.
raja – king.
Rajasekhara – Pandyan king who found the abandoned *Ayyappan*, named him Manikanda and raised him as his son.
Rama – seventh incarnation of *Vishnu*. His life story is the central theme of the *Ramayana*.
Ramacharitam – classic 12th century poem, comprising over 1800 verses.
Ramadan – the most important annual festival on the Islamic calendar; during this month-long period devout Muslims eat only after sundown and many make the *haj*; also known as Ramazan, or locally as Cheria Perunnal.
Ramayana – the story of *Rama* and *Sita* and their conflict with *Ravana*. One of India's best-known legends, it is retold in various forms throughout almost all South-East Asia.
Ramazan – see *Ramadan*.
rangoli – see *kolam*.
rasa – literally flavour; the unique quality with which a skilled classical dancer imbues a performance.
rathas – chariots; temples in the style of chariots.
Ravana – the demon king of Lanka (modern-day Sri Lanka), who abducted *Sita*, wife of *Rama*.
rishi – originally a sage to whom the hymns of the *Vedas* were revealed; these days any poet, philosopher or sage.

Sakti – see *shakti*.
salai – Jain or Buddhist educational institution.
salwar kameez – traditional loose trousers and tunic shirt worn by women.
sambar – deer.
sangam – community, often used to refer to a monastery. Also the name given to the community of scholars who developed a body of literature in the early centuries CE; these texts are a valuable aid to scholars of early *Tamil* kingdoms.
Sanskrit – the ancient language of India dating from the first millennium BCE.
Sarasvati – goddess of speech and learning and consort of *Brahma*; also known as Saraswati.
Sarpayakshi – the female form of the snake deity.
sati – from the *Sanskrit*, sati means 'virtuous woman'; it is the once legal, and sometimes still practised, Hindu custom of a widow burning herself to death on her husband's funeral pyre.
Savarnas – former upper caste people.
Scheduled Castes – official term for *Untouchables* or *Dalits*.
SETC – Tamil Nadu state bus service.
shahada – declaration of faith by Muslims: 'There is no god but Allah and Mohammed is his prophet'.
Shaivaite – follower of *Shiva*.
Shaivism – the worship of *Shiva*.
Shakti – female energy manifest in various forms within the Hindu pantheon; can be benign or destructive.
Shiva – the Destroyer; also the Creator, in which form he is worshipped as a *lingam*.
shola – forest.
Shurpanakha – *Ravana's* demoness sister.
Sita – wife of *Rama*; she was abducted by the demon king of Lanka, *Ravana*.
Sree Narayana Guru – intellectual and activist (1855-1928) who preached 'one caste, one religion, one god for humanity'.
srikovil – inner sanctum of a temple.
Subramanya – second son of *Shiva* and *Parvati*; god of war; also known as Murugan and *Kartikkaya*.
sudda mandalam – long barrel-shaped drum used in the *Kathakali* drama
Sudra – term used to refer to low Hindu caste.
Surya – the sun; a major deity in the *Vedas*.
sutra – string; a list of rules expressed in verse; many exist, the most famous being the Kama Sutra.
swami – title given to initiated monks; means 'lord of the self'; a title of respect.

sweeper – servant who performs the most menial of tasks.

tabla – pair of drums.
tachan – builder of house boats.
tahr – goat-like animal, indigenous to the Western Ghats.
tala – basic rhythm or meter of a musical composition.
tali – thread tied around the neck of the bride in wedding ceremonies.
Tamil – people, language and script of Tamil Nadu.
tank – reservoir.
Tarawad – household units of the *Marumakkathayam*.
tarwad – traditional social system of the Lakshadweep islands.
tati – beard; the colour of the tati distinguishes various characters, known as Tatis, in the *Kathakali* drama.
Teppu – type of character in the *Kathakali* drama.
Teyyam – temple ritual dance of Northern Kerala.
thalakarraa – white caps with decorative sides.
thali – meal (usually lunch) consisting of rice and tasty side dishes; predominantly vegetarian and traditionally served on a banana leaf.
thulabharam – where a devotee presents to the deity their own body weight in offerings of coconuts or bananas.
Thulam – month around October/November in the *Malayalam* calendar.
Thullal – satirical narrative developed by the poet Kunchan Nambiar in the 18th century.
tika – mark devout Hindus put on their foreheads with *tika* powder.
Toda – tribal people of the Nilgiri Hills.
toddy – fermented palm juice.
Tolpava Koothu – shadow puppet play.
Travancore – kingdom of Southern Kerala which developed after the Second Chera empire disintegrated in the 10th century; Cochin (Central Kerala) and Kozhikode (Northern Kerala) developed at the same time.
TTDC – Thekkady Tourism Development Council.

Untouchable – former term for the lowest caste or 'casteless' for whom the most menial tasks were reserved. The name derived from the belief that higher castes risked defilement if they touched a lower caste person. Formerly known as *Harijan*, now *Dalit* or *Scheduled Castes*.
Upanishads – Esoteric doctrine; ancient texts forming part of the *Vedas* (although of a later date), they delve into weighty matters such as the nature of the universe and the soul.
utsavam – religious festival or celebration.

vanki – forearm adornments.
varna – the former system where society was divided into groups with *Brahmins* on top and *Sudras* at the bottom. Within one's varna one was further defined according to one's vocational calling, or *jati*. This defined one's caste.
vastu shastra – India's answer to the Chinese art of divine design, feng shui.
Vattezhuthu – the first script of Kerala.
Vedas – the Hindu sacred books; a collection of hymns composed in pre-classical *Sanskrit* during the 2nd millennium BCE.
vedi vashipadu – devotions to the gods in the form of explosions.
veena – fretted stringed musical instrument used in classical music performances in South India.
vel – spear; weapon of *Subramanya*.
vidyarambham – ceremony where a child is introduced to the alphabet and writing.
viitu – house.
vimana – principal part of a Hindu temple; in South India it's stepped as opposed to curvilinear.
Vindya Range – the symbolic division between North and South India.
Virchikam – *Malayalam* month around November/December.
Vishnu – the Preserver and Restorer, who so far has nine *avatars*: including *Rama, Krishna* and *Buddha*. The third in the Hindu trinity of gods along with *Brahma* and *Shiva*.

wallah – man (Hindi). A useful, multipurpose suffix, eg dhobi-wallah (clothes washer), rickshaw-wallah (rickshaw driver), etc; often used in Northern India; rarely in Southern India.

yakshagana – traditional form of folk theatre.
Yakshagana Bombeyata – puppet performance using both rod and string puppets.
yakshi – maiden.
yantra – geometric plan thought to create energy.
yatra – pilgrimage.
yoni – vagina; fertility symbol.

zamindar – landowner.
Zamorins – rulers of the Malabar region between the 10th and 13th centuries.

Phrasebooks

Lonely Planet phrasebooks are packed with essential words and phrases to help travellers communicate with the locals. With colour tabs for quick reference, an extensive vocabulary and use of script, these handy pocket-sized language guides cover day-to-day travel situations.

- handy pocket-sized books
- easy to understand Pronunciation chapter
- clear & comprehensive Grammar chapter
- romanisation alongside script to allow ease of pronunciation
- script throughout so users can point to phrases for every situation
- full of cultural information and tips for the traveller

'...vital for a real DIY spirit and attitude in language learning'
– *Backpacker*

'the phrasebooks have good cultural backgrounders and offer solid advice for challenging situations in remote locations'
– *San Francisco Examiner*

Arabic (Egyptian) • Arabic (Moroccan) • Australian *(Australian English, Aboriginal and Torres Strait languages)* • Baltic States *(Estonian, Latvian, Lithuanian)* • Bengali • Brazilian • British • Burmese • Cantonese • Central Asia • Central Europe *(Czech, French, German, Hungarian, Italian, Slovak)* • Eastern Europe *(Bulgarian, Czech, Hungarian, Polish, Romanian, Slovak)* • Ethiopian (Amharic) • Fijian • French • German • Greek • Hebrew phrasebook • Hill Tribes • Hindi/Urdu • Indonesian • Italian • Japanese • Korean • Lao • Latin American Spanish • Malay • Mandarin • Mediterranean Europe *(Albanian, Croatian, Greek, Italian, Macedonian, Maltese, Serbian, Slovene)* • Mongolian • Nepali • Pidgin • Pilipino (Tagalog) • Quechua • Russian • Scandinavian Europe *(Danish, Finnish, Icelandic, Norwegian, Swedish)* • South-East Asia *(Burmese, Indonesian, Khmer, Lao, Malay, Tagalog Pilipino, Thai, Vietnamese)* • South Pacific Languages • Spanish (Castilian) *(also includes Catalan, Galician and Basque)* • Sri Lanka • Swahili • Thai • Tibetan • Turkish • Ukrainian • USA *(US English, Vernacular, Native American languages, Hawaiian)* • Vietnamese • Western Europe *(Basque, Catalan, Dutch, French, German, Greek, Irish)*

LONELY PLANET

Mail Order

Lonely Planet products are distributed worldwide. They are also available by mail order from Lonely Planet, so if you have difficulty finding a title please write to us. North and South American residents should write to 150 Linden St, Oakland, CA 94607, USA; European and African residents should write to 10a Spring Place, London NW5 3BH, UK; and residents of other countries to PO Box 617, Hawthorn, Victoria 3122, Australia.

ISLANDS OF THE INDIAN OCEAN Madagascar & Comoros • Maldives • Mauritius, Réunion & Seychelles

MIDDLE EAST & CENTRAL ASIA Arab Gulf States • Central Asia • Central Asia phrasebook • Hebrew phrasebook • Iran • Israel & the Palestinian Territories • Israel & the Palestinian Territories travel atlas • Istanbul • Istanbul to Cairo • Jerusalem • Jordan & Syria • Jordan, Syria & Lebanon travel atlas • Lebanon • Middle East on a shoestring • Syria • Turkey • Turkish phrasebook • Turkey travel atlas • Yemen
Travel Literature: The Gates of Damascus • Kingdom of the Film Stars: Journey into Jordan

NORTH AMERICA Alaska • Backpacking in Alaska • Baja California • California & Nevada • Canada • Chicago • Chicago city map • Deep South • Florida • Hawaii • Honolulu • Las Vegas • Los Angeles • Miami • New England • New Orleans • New York City • New York city map • New York, New Jersey & Pennsylvania • Pacific Northwest USA • Puerto Rico • Rocky Mountain States • San Francisco • San Francisco city map • Seattle • Southwest USA • Texas • USA • USA phrasebook • Vancouver • Washington, DC & the Capital Region • Washington DC city map
Travel Literature: Drive Thru America

NORTH-EAST ASIA Beijing • Cantonese phrasebook • China • Hong Kong • Hong Kong city map • Hong Kong, Macau & Guangzhou • Japan • Japanese phrasebook • Japanese audio pack • Korea • Korean phrasebook • Kyoto • Mandarin phrasebook • Mongolia • Mongolian phrasebook • North-East Asia on a shoestring • Seoul • South-West China • Taiwan • Tibet • Tibetan phrasebook • Tokyo
Travel Literature: Lost Japan

SOUTH AMERICA Argentina, Uruguay & Paraguay • Bolivia • Brazil • Brazilian phrasebook • Buenos Aires • Chile & Easter Island • Chile & Easter Island travel atlas • Colombia • Ecuador & the Galapagos Islands • Latin American Spanish phrasebook • Peru • Quechua phrasebook • Rio de Janeiro • Rio de Janeiro city map • South America on a shoestring • Trekking in the Patagonian Andes • Venezuela
Travel Literature: Full Circle: A South American Journey

SOUTH-EAST ASIA Bali & Lombok • Bangkok • Bangkok city map • Burmese phrasebook • Cambodia • Hanoi • Healthy Travel Asia & India • Hill Tribes phrasebook • Ho Chi Minh City • Indonesia • Indonesia's Eastern Islands • Indonesian phrasebook • Indonesian audio pack • Jakarta • Java • Laos • Lao phrasebook • Laos travel atlas • Malay phrasebook • Malaysia, Singapore & Brunei • Myanmar (Burma) • Philippines • Pilipino (Tagalog) phrasebook • Singapore • South-East Asia on a shoestring • South-East Asia phrasebook • Thailand • Thailand's Islands & Beaches • Thailand travel atlas • Thai phrasebook • Thai audio pack • Vietnam • Vietnamese phrasebook • Vietnam travel atlas

ALSO AVAILABLE: Antarctica • The Arctic • Brief Encounters: Stories of Love, Sex & Travel • Chasing Rickshaws • Lonely Planet Unpacked • Not the Only Planet: Travel Stories from Science Fiction • Sacred India • Travel with Children • Traveller's Tales

Lonely Planet Travel Atlases

Lonely Planet has long been famous for the number and quality of its guidebook maps. Now we've gone one step further and produced a handy companion series: Lonely Planet travel atlases – maps of a country produced in book form.

Unlike other maps, which look good but lead travellers astray, our travel atlases have been researched on the road by Lonely Planet's experienced team of writers. All details are carefully checked to ensure the atlas corresponds with the equivalent Lonely Planet guidebook.

- full-colour throughout
- maps researched and checked by Lonely Planet authors
- place names correspond with Lonely Planet guidebooks
- no confusing spelling differences
- legend and travelling information in English, French, German, Japanese and Spanish
- size: 230 x 160 mm

Available now: Chile & Easter Island • Egypt • India & Bangladesh • Israel & the Palestinian Territories • Jordan, Syria & Lebanon • Kenya • Laos • Portugal • South Africa, Lesotho & Swaziland • Thailand • Turkey • Vietnam • Zimbabwe, Botswana & Namibia

---

Lonely Planet TV Series & Videos

Lonely Planet travel guides have been brought to life on television screens around the world. Like our guides, the programs are based on the joy of independent travel, and look honestly at some of the most exciting, picturesque and frustrating places in the world. Each show is presented by one of three travellers from Australia, England or the USA and combines an innovative mixture of video, Super-8 film, atmospheric soundscapes and original music.

Videos of each episode – containing additional footage not shown on television – are available from good book and video shops, but the availability of individual videos varies with regional screening schedules.

Video destinations include: Alaska • American Rockies • Argentina • Australia – The South-East • Baja California & the Copper Canyon • Brazil • Central Asia • Chile & Easter Island • Corsica, Sicily & Sardinia – The Mediterranean Islands • East Africa (Tanzania & Zanzibar) • Cuba • Ecuador & the Galapagos Islands • Ethiopia • Greenland & Iceland • Hungary & Romania • Indonesia • Israel & the Sinai Desert • Jamaica • Japan • La Ruta Maya • The Middle East (Syria, Jordan & Lebanon • Morocco • New York • Northern Spain • North India • Outback Australia • Pacific Islands (Fiji, Solomon Islands & Vanuatu) • Pakistan • Peru • The Philippines • South Africa & Lesotho • South India • South West China • South West USA • Trekking in Uganda • Turkey • Vietnam • West Africa • Zimbabwe, Botswana & Namibia

The Lonely Planet TV series is produced by: Pilot Productions
The Old Studio
18 Middle Row
London W10 5AT, UK

Index

Text

Bold indicates maps.

Bold indicates maps.

Boxed Text

MAP LEGEND

BOUNDARIES

International
Provincial
Regional

HYDROGRAPHY

Coastline
River, Creek
Lake
Intermittent Lake
Salt Lake
Canal
Spring, Rapids
Waterfalls
Swamp

ROUTES & TRANSPORT

Freeway
Highway
Major Road
Minor Road
City Freeway
City Highway
City Road
City Street, Lane
Tunnel
Train Route & Station
Metro & Station
Cable Car or Chairlift
Walking Track
Walking Tour
Described Trek
Ferry Route

AREA FEATURES

Building
Park, Gardens
Cemetery
Market
Beach, Desert
Urban Area

MAP SYMBOLS

CAPITAL National Capital
CAPITAL Provincial Capital
City City
Town Town
Village Village
Point of Interest
Place to Stay
Camping Ground
Caravan Park
Hut or Chalet
Place to Eat
Pub or Bar
Airport
Ancient or City Wall
Archaeological Site
Bank
Bird Sanctuary
Cave
Church
Cliff or Escarpment
Embassy
Hindu Temple
Hospital
Lighthouse
Monument
Mosque
Mountain or Hill
Museum
National Park
Palace
Pass
Police Station
Post Office
Synagogue
Telephone
Temple
Tomb
Tourist Information
Transport
Zoo

Note: not all symbols displayed above appear in this book

LONELY PLANET OFFICES

Australia
PO Box 617, Hawthorn, Victoria 3122
☎ 03-9819 1877 fax 9819 6459
email: talk2us@lonelyplanet.com.au

USA
150 Linden St, Oakland, CA 94607
☎ 510-893 8555 TOLL FREE: 800 275 8555
fax 893 8572
email: info@lonelyplanet.com

UK
10a Spring Place, London NW5 3BH
☎ 020-7428 4800 fax 7428 4828
email: go@lonelyplanet.co.uk

France
1 rue du Dahomey, 75011 Paris
☎ 01 55 25 33 00 fax 01 55 25 33 01
email: bip@lonelyplanet.fr
www.lonelyplanet.fr

World Wide Web: www.lonelyplanet.com *or* AOL keyword: lp
Lonely Planet Images: lpi@lonelyplanet.com.au